*A Publication of the Cambridge Group
for the History of Population and Social Structure*

Household and family in past time

Household and family in past time

Comparative studies in the size and structure of the domestic group over the last three centuries in England, France, Serbia, Japan and colonial North America, with further materials from Western Europe

edited, with an analytic introduction on the history of the family, by
PETER LASLETT
with the assistance of
RICHARD WALL
both of the Cambridge Group for the History of Population and Social Structure

Cambridge University Press

Cambridge
London   New York   Melbourne

Published by the Syndics of the Cambridge University Press
The Pitt Building, Trumpington Street, Cambridge CB2 1RP
Bentley House, 200 Euston Road, London NW1 2DB
32 East 57th Street, New York, NY 10022, USA
296 Beaconsfield Parade, Middle Park, Melbourne 3206, Australia

Library of Congress catalogue card number: 77–190420

ISBN 0 521 08473 3 hard covers
ISBN 0 521 09901 3 paperback

First published 1972
First paperback edition 1974
Reprinted 1977

First printed in Great Britain at the University Press, Cambridge
Reprinted in Great Britain by
Redwood Burn Limited, Trowbridge & Esher

This volume is dedicated to the memory of JAMES THORNTON
who died in 1969, Director of the London Branch of the Calouste
Gulbenkian Foundation of Lisbon. The studies at Cambridge which
gave rise to these published results for England were first supported
by the Foundation when Mr Thornton was its Director. The
international interchange at which many of the papers were read in
September 1969 also took place under the Foundation's patronage.
Mr Thornton showed a remarkable understanding of a new branch
of learning in the process of coming into being.

Contents

Contributors

Anderson, Michael	Lecturer in Sociology, University of Edinburgh
Armstrong, W. A.	Senior Lecturer in History, University of Kent, Canterbury
Biraben, Jean-Noël	Chargé de Missions, Institut National D'Études Démographiques, Paris
Blayo, Yves	Chargé de Recherches, Institut National D'Études Démographiques, Paris
Burch, Thomas K.	Associate Director, Demographic Division, the Population Council, New York
Clarke, Marilyn	Research Assistant, Cambridge Group for the History of Population and Social Structure
Demos, John	Associate Professor of History, Brandeis University, Waltham, Massachusetts, U.S.A.
Dupâquier, Jacques	Directeur D'Études, École Pratique des Hautes Études, VIᵉ Section, Paris
Goody, Jack	Professor-elect to the William Wyse Chair in Social Anthropology and Fellow of St John's College, University of Cambridge
Greven, Philip J. Jr	Professor of History, Rutgers College, New Brunswick, New Jersey, U.S.A.
Halpern, Joel, M.	Professor of Anthropology, University of Massachusetts, Amherst, U.S.A.
Hammel, E. A.	Professor of Anthropology, University of California, Berkeley, U.S.A.
Hayami, Akira	Professor of Economic History, Keio University, Tokyo, Japan
Hélin, Étienne	Professor of History, University of Liège, Belgium
Jadin, Louis	Research Assistant, École Pratique des Hautes Études, VIᵉ Section, Paris
Klapisch, Christiane	Maître Assistant, École Pratique des Hautes Études, VIᵉ Section, Paris
Laslett, Peter	Reader in Politics and the History of Social Structure and Fellow of Trinity College, University of Cambridge
Nakane, Chie	Professor of Anthropology, Institute of Oriental Culture, University of Tokyo, Japan

Pryor, Edward T. Jr   Chairman and Associate Professor, Department of Sociology, University of Western Ontario, London, Ontario, Canada

Smith, Robert J.   Professor of Anthropology and Asian Studies, Vice-Chairman, Department of Anthropology, Cornell University, Ithaca, New York

Uchida, Nobuko   Research Assistant, Faculty of Economics, Keio University, Tokyo, Japan

Wall, Richard   Research Officer, Cambridge Group for the History of Population and Social Structure

van der Woude, A. M. Senior Lecturer, Department of Rural History, Agricultural University, Wageningen, The Netherlands

Preface to the first impression

The appearance of a large, expensive, collective book on the history of household and family needs neither apology nor defence. This is a new, or a newly defined, area of study and its importance to human behaviour in the present as well as the past is manifest. The burgeoning subject stands in evident need of a body of comparative data and of an assemblage of techniques for their analysis. All twenty-two of the following chapters are intended to meet these requirements, whilst the first of them, the Introduction, also proposes a model of classifying and comparing forms of household and family over time and between countries. Deliberate aim has been taken at the object of opening out a new field of enquiry. But there has been no attempt at codification.

It is doubtless both inevitable and desirable that a work of this kind published at this time should be controversial. The issues which will arise may go very deep. A question might even be raised as to whether the form of the family has in fact played as important a role in human development as the social sciences have assigned to it. It is possible to wonder whether our ancestors did always care about the form of the families in which they lived, whether they were large or small, and even whether they contained kin or servants or strangers.

To go as far as this is not necessarily to deny that the form of the family has a determining influence on the outlook of individuals and the structure of society. Yet this determining influence may have been in fact of restricted significance. This would be because so little real variation in familial organization can actually be found in human history that examples of societies changing their character in accordance with changes in the family are very unlikely ever to be met with.*

Though a theoretical possibility, this is not the position expounded in the Introduction, which directs critical attention rather towards the assumption that in the past the household was universally large and complicated, and that historical progress has always been from big and complex to small and simple. Further, the usefulness of mean household size as a significant feature is called into question, since it is finally elusive in definition and unreliable as an indicator of household composition. What is here named the stem-family hypothesis is also run over with some scepticism, together with the supposition that the nuclear family is inevitably associated with the rise of individualism and with industrialization. These arguments will presumably themselves be disputed, and there are in fact already signs that the traditional positions associated with

---

* It is perhaps necessary to warn the reader here that the resident familial group alone is in question, not the kinship network, nor any 'familial' relationships between distinct households. The position described above is presumably that implied by Levy (1965).

[ix]

Le Play and established family sociology will be defended with spirit. It is possible indeed that this whole volume will be regarded as a polemic against the notion that the family group was ever large or complicated in the five cultural areas whose recent history is touched on here, or perhaps anywhere at any time.

It is my belief, however, that no open-minded reader of the Introduction or of any of the articles in this book could come away with such a stereotype in his head. There are repeated references to the existence of large households and of complex ones, with their possible significance for historical development. There is even (in the final section of the Introduction) a suggested criterion for deciding when complex family structure could be said to have dominated a particular culture. It is true that only Japan of the cultures examined is there admitted to have had the possibility of being dominated by a complex family tradition, with the nuclear family in a minority position even there, clearly predominant elsewhere, and virtually unchallenged in the Anglo-Saxon countries. But to make these claims is still not to declare at large against big and complex households, and it is fervently to be hoped that the determined controversialist will not pass this fact over.

There are two reasons why the point is of peculiar importance to me as author and editor, and I should like to set them out briefly here. The first is concerned with the industrialization of the West, and particularly with that of England, the first country to be industrialized. Assuming that nuclear family organization predisposes a society towards industrialization, the demonstration that in England such a form of the family was already predominant for centuries before industrialization constitutes a powerful argument as to why that country modernized herself earlier than any other. This argument creates a strong temptation to assume that England and the European West was uniquely disposed towards small and nuclear households, and it is therefore essential that this temptation should be guarded against. Such may be the reason why a certain *animus* against 'the myth of the extended family' manifested itself at the international conference on the comparative history of household and family held in September 1969 by the Cambridge Group for the History of Population and Social Structure.

The reader is left to make his own judgment on how far that conference did establish the temporal priority of the nuclear family in England, and how far England's early industrialization can be connected with these facts. The present volume originates with the papers presented on that occasion. What I have called the null hypothesis* (see below p. 73) in the history of the family, which is that the present state of evidence forces us to assume that its organization was always and invariably nuclear unless the contrary can be proven, was certainly an outcome of these interchanges.

The second point which I should like here to underline concerns the domestic

---

* In the Introduction the null hypothesis is propounded in respect of England and the history of the English family. But it must be taken to apply to all societies at all periods. In some cases, no doubt, the null hypothesis will be easily rejected. But it is always worth setting up.

cycle. Repeated insistence is rightly laid in this volume on the fact that only a few households in a community need to be complex at any one time for it to be true that a large number of others may have been complex at an earlier time, or may be due to become complex at a later one. Now this must not be allowed to obscure the fact that from the point of view of the experience of the persons in that community at the date in question, the nuclear family household constituted the ordinary, expected, normal framework of domestic existence.

Nevertheless since this book first appeared in 1972 the work of Dr Rudolf Andorka of Budapest and of Dr Lutz Berkner of the University of California and his associates has come to show that the extremes of familial organization, from the simplest to the most complex, may once have existed within the confines of the European Continent itself. More than this, Eastern and Western Europeans may have differed from each other in several further complementary but crucial ways; in the age gap between man and wife, in the period of childbearing in women, in respect of numbers of persons circulating from household to household as servants and so bringing about exogamy.

Notwithstanding, nothing is yet known to me which would finally sanction the assumption that the size and character of the family necessarily represents a value, a norm of belief and of attitude fundamental to human society. Even in Eastern Europe the form of household group does not appear to be a cultural value in itself alone. It seems rather to be a circumstance incidental to the practice of agriculture, to the customs of land distribution and redistribution, to the laws and traditions of land inheritance, and of succession in the patriline. My conviction remains, that the form of the domestic group cannot yet be demonstrated to be capable of doing all the work which social scientists have seemed to expect it to do.

Little room is left here for acknowledgments. Since so many obligations have been incurred in the course of producing this book, even beginning to list them would be out of the question. Our greatest debt is owed to the Cambridge University Press, and to Patricia Skinner in particular, and we must cite the name of the Social Science Research Council in London, which maintains the work of the Cambridge Group: the Gulbenkian Foundation is acknowledged on a previous page. Our debt to the co-operativeness and to the patience of our contributors must be evident to the reader, and we hope that these contributors will forgive us if we single out one name amongst them to cite, that of Gene Hammel who has been helpful in every direction and at every stage. To Marilyn Clarke we owe a great deal besides the index to the book.

A final word as to the division of editorial responsibility between us. The selection, compression and translation (where necessary) of individual pieces was undertaken by Peter Laslett assisted by Janet Laslett, but there his editorial duties came to an end. All the detailed and fatiguing tasks have been undertaken by Richard Wall, who has also inserted the cross-references in the footnotes.

July 1972 PETER LASLETT

Preface to the second impression

Since 1972 scholars have been scouring eastern and western Europe for signs of the complex household of the past, a reaction in part to the challenge posed by our null hypothesis that the nuclear family should be considered dominant unless the contrary could be proven. The result is that we now know a good deal more about the role of the household in countries which were unrepresented at the 1969 conference which gave rise to the papers contained in this volume. The debate continues too on the importance to be attached to the complex household when 'snapshot', once-only listings of inhabitants reveal that of all households only two or three per cent were 'multiple': two distinct nuclei sharing the same living space. To us it seems difficult to see why a short period in an extended family in one's youth must necessarily be treasured for life, or indeed why the peasant-landowner, the complexities of his household still under examination as far as England is concerned, has to provide the ideal for society. But these are difficult propositions to refute with the only witnesses centuries dead and their experience whether of three days', three weeks' or three years' duration buried with them, though microsimulation of household structures following a sixteenth-century English model scarcely suggests that the inhabitants were keen to live in such units. Beyond recall too are the living-in servants who could say whether they saw themselves or were seen by others as such intimate members of the household as their master's children. The possibility is that there will be greater variation in familial attitudes towards such household 'extras' as widowed relative, servant and lodger, whether co-existing in one room, two, or in completely distinct apartments, than in the 'physical' structure of the household, the number with and without certain types of member, which is all that listings can ordinarily reveal. The quantitive approach seems to fail us here but not entirely; for the merging of census and reconstitution-type studies will enable us to identify, for instance, who among the widowed and the orphaned continued to live alone when there were kin present in the village with whom they might have sought shelter.

Finally, it must be stressed that the present impression differs from the first only in the correction of typographical errors and the modification of references to the 'current' research of 1972.　　　　　RICHARD WALL

Cambridge Group for the History of
Population and Social Structure
April 1974

1. Introduction: the history of the family

Peter Laslett

I. THE HISTORY OF THE FAMILY

The family cannot be said to be neglected as a subject of study. More effort in fact is probably going towards the examination and analysis of this fundamental institution than in any other field of enquiry into human behaviour. The only comprehensive bibliography, a large volume of computer printout as it has to be, lists over 12,000 titles published in this century up to 1964, though over half appeared within the ten preceding years, and less than a twentieth before 1929.[1] Perhaps the number of studies devoted to the family will have doubled again before the present book appears, but it is not to be expected that many will have been added to the 250 or so which in 1964 the compilers assigned to the heading of *history*.

This lack of recent interest in the past condition and development of the human family seems to be due to a number of circumstances. The obvious, if perhaps not the effective cause, is scarcity of evidence and the difficulties of dealing with that which is known to exist. Prominent among these difficulties are the intricacies of defining the subject, and of deciding what are in fact the varying senses in which 'family' can be said to have had a history, or a series of histories. This volume, as will be spelt out at length in due course, is given over to the comparative history of the family in a particular sense, the family as a group of persons living together, a household, what we shall call a coresident domestic group.

I must insist as strongly as possible at this early point in the text, that this book is not concerned with the family as a network of kinship. As is made plain at several points in this introductory chapter, the evidence for the study of kin relations outside coresident domestic groups in past time does not yet exist for England, nor in any complete form for any other country known to me. The statements made here apply only to relationships *within* familial groups, not to relationships *between* them.

---

[1] Aldous and Hill, *International bibliography of marriage and the family* (1967). Works in Japanese seem to form a disproportionate part of those classed as in any way historical. It seems possible that authors of works on historical themes may have been less disposed to make that fact clear in their titles than others.

When we come to the knotty problems of detailed and precise definition, terminology and classification (see Section II below) we shall insist again on the uncertainties created by the paucity of usable materials on our chosen subject. Nevertheless some knowledge has always been available of the history of the family in all its senses. The reasons why it has failed to attract much attention in our generation from historians and social scientists generally are themselves of some interest to the study of the domestic group.

1　UNPOPULARITY OF THE SUBJECT

There is in the first place the relative indifference of social scientists to the time dimension, and of historians to the subject matter of the social sciences. Sociologists of the family have evidently been satisfied with contemporary materials and have tested their hypotheses about familial attitudes, the institution of marriage, and even the size and structure of the domestic group itself, with no more than occasional reference to the past. They have. set the American family alongside the family on the Malabar Coast, or in the Israeli Kibbutz, or amongst the Tikopia or the Beduin, without attempting to discover what the American family was like a century or two centuries ago. It seems that by the 1950s familial structure in no less than 565 cultures had been recorded, a sample believed to be representative of the whole range of variation in the world.[2]

In making such extensive contemporaneous comparisons, it does not seem to have been supposed that the human family had no discussable or discoverable past, but that this past was not available for comparative purposes. People have been inclined, therefore, to look upon some of the familial systems now extant amongst the more 'undeveloped' or 'primitive' cultures, as being representative of the past, and probably of the very remote past. 'It is legitimate to assume', says one of the standard authorities, 'that in the prehistoric period the familial structure resembled more or less that of contemporary primitive peoples. This is not merely an inference; it is supported by survivals found among many peoples, particularly among those of northern Europe at the dawn of their history.'[3] To this tendency, which goes back a long way in anthropological studies, has to be added the uncritical acceptance of standard or popular histori-

---

[2] See Nimkoff and Middleton, *Types of family* (1960), referring to Murdock, *World ethnographic sample* (1957). Comparisons in some detail over ten or a dozen cultures will be found in such works as Nimkoff, *Comparative family systems* (1965) or Bell and Vogel, *A modern introduction to the family* (1960). The practice of comparing familial structures between cultures goes a long way back, to Le Play and even to Montesquieu.

[3] Burgess and Locke, *The family* (1953): 15, reproduced unaltered from the first edition (1945): 18. This statement implies knowledge not only of the familial structure of the pre-Christian Scandinavians or Germans, but also of its particulars at the much remoter periods from which parts of that structure had 'survived'. It seems impossible that knowledge of either type can ever be anything but inferential, and the assumption about survival which appears whenever large scale or complex household structure is found, especially in advanced areas, is a major obstacle to the understanding of familial history.

cal impressions. It is almost as if something in the way of a folk memory of the former condition of the family is being consulted.

It has been shown elsewhere how firm popular conviction can be on such subjects and how misleading.[4] The social scientists, however, might well explain their uncritical attitude by claiming that it was for the historians to subject these impressions to examination, perhaps along with the demographers. Only very recently, however, have historians begun to acquaint themselves with demography, and only very recently has what can only be called the chasm which has divided historians for so long from social scientists generally begun to pass away.

The existence of this impasse has meant that such historical work as has been done on the domestic group in the past, and in particular on its actual size in Western Europe from the Middle Ages, has been little noticed by historians and has apparently never communicated itself to familial sociologists. Solid foundations for this particular study were laid almost twenty years ago by a historian of the traditional type.[5] Since then it has been gratuitous to assume for example, if such was the assumption being made either by historians or by familial sociologists, that mean household size in the Europe from which American settlers came in the seventeenth or eighteenth centuries was markedly greater than it was in the United States in the 1930s.

The unpopularity of familial history has led to the neglect of those opportunities which did present themselves in the available evidence. It also seems to have ensured that what had already become known to specialists would be overlooked. It is no criticism of the authors of Chapters 20 and 22 of this book to state that a discussion of the size and structure of the household in the Massachusetts census of 1769 or in the first United States Federal Census of 1790, could have appeared at any time in this century, and that a comparison of the census documents for Rhode Island in 1875 with those belonging to a subsequent occasion could have been undertaken at any point during the great outpouring of work on the family which has marked the last few decades. The same is true of the studies of Jean-Noel Biraben on Montplaisant in 1644 and 1836, and of Yves

---

[4] For example, the widespread conviction that most girls in England married in their teens in earlier times, for which the evidence, if requested, remarkably often turns out to be one literary context, Shakespeare's *Romeo and Juliet*. This splendid story seems to have spelt out just what most people, even well informed people, wish to believe. See Laslett, *The World we have lost* (1965 i, 1971): Ch. IV; see also Ch. x for a brief discussion of the purchase over the minds of people in our day of the idea that large familial groups ought to have been characteristic of the past. Occasionally literary evidence has been used to criticise the traditional accounts of familial development used by social scientists, as in Furstenberg, *Industrialization and the American family* (1966).

[5] See the three large volumes of Mols, *Démographie historique des villes d'Europe* (1955) referring to work on household size going back many years and by no means confined to towns. Many of these sources are referred to by Hélin in Chapter 13. Since his main object was to determine a multiplier (see below Section III), Mols confined himself for the most part to traditional historical questions, and showed little curiosity about familial structure or kin linkages; he gives no distribution of households by size from his enormous mass of materials, and does not discuss servants.

Blayo on Grisy-Suisnes in 1836 and 1851 in Chapters 8 and 9. Comparisons, then, between the size and structure of the domestic group in the present and in the past, and between cultural areas in the present and at given points in the past, which together go to make up the substance of the present volume, have in principle been open to the historian and the social scientist for many years.

But the social sciences themselves over these very years have been marked by a further characteristic which helps to explain the unpopularity of the history of the family. The very term *history* itself represents an earlier phase in their development which probably had to be rejected if properly empirical and adequately comparative research was to get under way.

Rejection of evolutionary theories

The movement which led to the recovery and tabulation of all the known forms of the domestic group began as a reaction against historical, or rather historicist, anthropology and sociology. Up to that time the grand evolutionary theories of such men as Bachofen, Maine, Morgan and McLennan had held the field, theories which stated that there was a necessary succession of familial form to familial form as phases in the development of the whole human race. These earlier thinkers, deeply impressed with the Darwinian theory of the descent of man from the animals, and assuming a time scale which we know now to have been woefully abbreviated, had to face the problem of explaining how civilised, monogamous man evolved from his Simian predecessors. They felt they had to account for the emergence from the 'primeval horde' of the familial group which they themselves experienced and admired. They showed a strong disposition to moralise as well, and this seems to have been less successfully overcome by those who have come after than the evolutionary bias. The family was regarded as fundamental to society not only as its final structural unit, but as the receptacle of its values.

Not everyone amongst these nineteenth-century scholars looked upon the monogamous family of contemporary Western Europe as the highest form of all. The theory of two of those who took a very different view still survives in a sense in our own day. This is the account which Engels and Marx adapted from Morgan, and which insisted that private property and the exploitatory family came simultaneously into being at the appointed stage of universal human evolution. The family cannot have been fundamental to society, because it was dependent upon productive relations.[6] But with this and other less important exceptions, the whole body of evolutionary, historicist thinking about the family succumbed in the middle years of the present century before the attacks of the anthropological field worker, the empirical, comparative social scientist.

[6] Engels, *Origin of the family, private property and the state* (1884, 1940), confessedly taken by him from Marx's papers. The enormous possible effect of theories of this kind in the hands of those who attain political power is to be seen in the policy towards the family both of the Russian Soviets and of the Chinese Communists in the early years of their régimes, aiming at abolition of the family along with other bourgeois property institutions.

Much of value has, of course, been taken into the social sciences from these earlier thinkers, but there can be no doubt of their systems being consciously cast aside. Indeed there are those who would say that when nineteenth-century evolutionism was rejected, the only comprehensive theory of familial development ever proposed disappeared without anything being put in its place. After the achievements in the actual observation of sexual and familial behaviour of the world's peoples by such men as Edward Westermarck and above all of Bronislaw Malinowski, little room was left for anything but functional comparison between contemporary 'savages', or members of less 'developed' societies, and industrial man. It is therefore understandable that the question of historical change in the family should seldom have been posed to themselves by those concerned with the family, even in the case of Western Europe and the United States in recent centuries. This especially if it could be tacitly assumed that slightly less advanced societies of the contemporary world represented previous states of the more advanced.

Belief in the large and complex household

The effect was to obscure the necessity for empirical research into the history of the family in all its aspects, but more particularly into the size and structure of domestic groups. Furthermore, a very general supposition that in the past the domestic group was universally and necessarily larger and more complex than it is today in industrial cultures was apparently left undisturbed.

This assumption seems, if anything, to have been strengthened by the innumerable exercises in contemporaneous comparison between pre-industrial and post-industrial. The reason presumably was that the process of modernisation always meant the simplification of social relationships based on kinship, the decline of the tribe and the clan, of the complicated rules which have governed marriage choices in many societies, the decay of familial authority and the progressive reduction of everything towards the rational, uncomplicated, small scale Western industrial model of familial life.

Such a triumph of individualism – a widely used phrase – seemed necessarily to have made the large scale complex household a thing of the past. It did not follow of course that families and households of this kind were therefore dominant in pre-industrial times. But in the prevailing state of opinion just described such a loose inference was evidently quite easy to make. This is apparently the intention of the following further passages from the standard authority already quoted.

The three chief historical stages in the evolution of the family are: the large patriarchal family characteristic of ancient society; the small patriarchal family which had its origins in the medieval period; and the modern democratic family which to a great extent is a product of the economic and social trends accompanying and following the industrial revolution.

The large patriarchal family was present in China, India and Japan. At present the majority of the human race probably lives in countries which still regard the approved type of family organisation as that in which the patriarch exercises more or less absolute control over his wife, his unmarried daughters and his sons and their wives and children. In the following case of a Hindu family the widow has succeeded her husband in the dominant position in the family which is composed of three sons and their wives and children and two unmarried daughters. 'My family is not very big. All members cooperate and work for each other. All cook and eat in the same place...'

The small patriarchal family. In medieval society, particularly in the towns, the development of the skills required by the crafts made the large patriarchal family an inefficient instrument. It was superseded by the small patriarchal family, composed of husband, wife and children, with generally the presence of one or two grandparents, one or more unmarried brothers or sisters of the parents, or other relatives.

The modern democratic family. The industrial revolution paved the way for the breakdown of the small patriarchal family and the emergence of the democratic type of family. In the United States, pioneer conditions, the rise of the public school, and the extension of democratic principles accelerated its development.[7]

No actual figures are given in these statements, although the concern is with size, and no references to sources which might contain them. It is not always quite clear whether the family as a coresident group only is being discussed, or whether relatives living elsewhere are also intended. Issues of authority are intermingled with issues of structure. Since none of the evidence surveyed in the studies we are publishing here goes back as far as the period of ancient society, we must suppose that the examples which we do discuss from traditional society are to be compared with the account of what the authors of the textbook we have quoted call the 'small patriarchal family'. Closer attention to their text suggests that the model they have in mind here is in fact the stem-family as portrayed by Le Play, which will have to concern us in the third section of this introductory chapter.

In addition to the indifference to figures there is a similar failure to appreciate the importance of the developmental cycle in domestic groups, and the importance of demographic issues. For the 'small patriarchal family' is apparently supposed to have contained grandparents at all points in time, which must imply an extended life expectation improbable in earlier epochs, and no accepted custom as to the point in the career of a family when the group divides. There are hints however that what is being described is not so much what actually existed universally in past time, but what was present then in people's minds as an approved type, a model to be imitated. Nevertheless we shall find that none of the statements made is likely to survive the critical analysis contained in this book, without fundamental modification.

[7] Burgess and Locke (1945): 18–21. In the second edition (1953) the Hindu example, from 'the private files of the authors', is omitted. In the full text this family group is said to contain servants, and even a priest; there is a 'big shop' in which the youngest brother works, so the family is not entirely agricultural. No claim is made that this single contemporary Indian family does represent a form of the domestic group in which all or a great part of the whole human race lived during the dominance of 'ancient society', but some such implication seems to be clearly intended.

Other statements of this persisting outlook both amongst sociologists and historians affected by their theories, if less incautious ones, are referred to by our contributors. The familial sociology of E. W. Hofstee as described in Chapter 12 implies that the 'modern, dynamic pattern of culture' developed unevenly out of a universal extended family situation whose 'remnants' can still be observed in the complex households of the surviving Dutch peasantry. Van der Woude makes short work of this position when he confronts it with the small size and simple composition of the domestic group in Holland and other Dutch provinces in the seventeenth century, though he refers to the 'rise of individualism' in explaining why families in that area were so surprisingly 'modern'. The same could be said of Hayami's account of the astonishing decline of mean household size in his selected Japanese county in Chapter 18. It is to be hoped that this book will help towards the abandonment of the rise of individualism as the universal explainer of familial change. The uncritical assumption of 'survival' must disappear altogether.[8]

There is nothing in the Marxian sociological system which would raise the expectation that in earlier times, both in the feudal and early bourgeois eras, the familial group would have been big and complex. Nevertheless the socialist outlook seems also to have contributed something to the belief in the large household of the past. This may have been due to the association of the mono-gamous family with exploitation both of women and of servants, whose simul-taneous presence might be supposed to have led to big households. Max Weber himself implies in his magisterial way that the rise of capitalist organisation was associated with 'the household community shrinking'.[9] But there is a much less scholarly, even a propagandist source for the disposition to assume that in one particular area of Europe now under socialist government the large household had originally been the repository of community solidarity of a socialist character, which the good nationalist had to vindicate against the advance of bourgeois capitalism. This was the area of Serbia, now part of Yugoslavia, where the *zadruga* was known to have been present.

The interest taken in the zadruga by scholars of all kinds during the present century may well have furthered the belief in the great household as universally associated with the life of the peasantry, if not of the townsfolk, in earlier times. This issue can safely be left with Eugene Hammel and Joel Halpern in Chapters 14 and 16.[10] Much greater in its effects in this direction, in my view, is the

[8] For English references to Hofstee's work, see Hofstee and Kooy, *Traditional household and neighbourhood group* (1956). The prevalence of such a high proportion of multigenerational extended families amongst the remaining Dutch peasantry in the 1950s discussed there seems due to the longer life they lived more than to any survival from the past. But recent work in the Netherlands goes to show that there was great variability in such matters from region to region.

[9] Weber, *General economic history* (1923, 1961): 111.

[10] See also Hammel, *Household structure in fourteenth-century Macedonia* (typescript), which has a short survey of the place of the zadruga in nationalist thinking and in the attitude to-wards modernisation in the Balkans. It was alternatively exalted and condemned.

endurance of a respect for that other nineteenth-century familial–historical theory which survived the critique of empirical social science, even if in an attenuated form. This is Frédéric Le Play's stem-family hypothesis to which we have referred.

The purchase over the minds of scholars of all kinds, of the general assumptions about the large and complex family of the past seems to me to be a singular phenomenon, not adequately explained by the considerations put forward here. As the evidence is surveyed, it becomes difficult not to suppose that there has been an obstinately held wish to believe in what William Goode has trenchantly described as the 'Classical family of Western nostalgia'.[11] This belief, or misbelief, certainly seems to display a notable capacity to overlook contrary facts and to resist attempts at revision.

It seems to have survived, for example, the great body of materials about family size and structure across the contemporary globe gathered by Professor Goode himself and by others[12] in an attempt to reformulate set notions about the association between industrialisation and family size and structure. It has persisted in spite of the fact that anthropologists have long been aware that by no means all, in fact only a bare majority, of the world's family systems could be called 'extended'. In Murdock's sample referred to earlier, '301, or 54.8 %, are characterised by the extended family system, and 248, or 45.2 %, by the independent family system'.[13] Even where the family system was held by Murdock and by the many anthropologists who have observed familial structure in contemporary societies to be extended, simple households were known to be common, sometimes very common. Indeed it is a capital question as to how many households have to be of a particular type, and as to where they must be placed in the social structure, before that familial type can justifiably be described as the predominant system. We shall have to return to this issue in the final section of the Introduction, where the proportion of persons who actually spend their formative years in families of particular types, or are socialised into them as the social scientists might say, will be taken to be the crucial variable.

But this does not complete the list of circumstances which might have been expected to disturb the belief in the large scale family as being characteristic of earlier societies, earlier in the developmental and in the temporal sense. There has been a full scale controversy over Murdock's own claim that 'the nuclear family is a universal human grouping'.[14] There has been widespread discussion

---

[11] See Goode, *The theory and measurement of family change* (1968): 321. This article contains a valuable sceptical survey of all the misbeliefs about the family in the contemporary world, and not simply those concerned with its size and structure. In his *World revolution and family patterns* (1963), Goode presented a very wide range of evidence on these topics.

[12] E.g. Petersen, *Demographic conditions and extended family households: Egyptian data* (1968).

[13] Nimkoff and Middleton (1960): 216.

[14] Murdock, *Social structure* (1949): 2. Murdock goes on to quote Lowie, *Primitive society* (1920), 'the one fact which stands out beyond all others is that everywhere the husband, wife and immature child constitute a unit apart from the remainder of the community', and names Malinowski, *Kinship* (1930) and Boas in further support. The persistence of the con-

of Marion Levy's bold assertion, made on demographic and other grounds, that most of humanity must always have lived in small families. By 1970, in fact, demographers generally had come to recognise that the nuclear family predominates numerically almost everywhere, even in underdeveloped parts of the world.[15] There are now many studies which call into question any necessary connection between industrialisation (however defined, which is part of the issue) and the small, simple, nuclear family of the contemporary world. It is true that these studies are rarely historical, and that they stress the fact that complex familial forms can survive industrialisation rather more than the fact that the nuclear family was there before industrialisation happened. Nevertheless, even in respect of the size and composition of domestic groups in Western society, quite apart from the figures published in successive census documents, there has been some discussion in the census reports themselves of household size, and of problems of housing which often raise issues of structure.[16] There was an *Analysis of the family* in an official publication of the United States Bureau of the Census as long ago as 1909, with figures for size and some structural information for America from 1790 to 1900,[17] and social scientists have sometimes referred to such sources.

But even where facts and figures have been available, it is notable how little analytic effort has gone into them. Numerical statements about the actual dimension and composition of any community of households – village, region or country – are rare, and efforts to recover evidence from before the census have been few.[18] In only one direction can the indifference we have been discussing be

trary view until quite recently is well brought out by his citation from Linton, proclaiming in *The study of man* (1936) that the nuclear family plays an 'insignificant role in the lives of many societies'. It must be remembered however that Murdock is not claiming that the nuclear family (simple family household) is the universal form of the coresident domestic group, as we call it here. His position is that within all such groups, whether simple, extended or multiple (i.e. joint or composite, to use alternative terms) the conjugal family unit of spouses and children retains an independent identity.

[15] See Levy, *Aspects of the analysis of family structure* (1965), Bogue, *Principles of demography* (1969), Kono, *The determinants and consequences of population trends* (typescript).

[16] For the family and industrialisation, see Greenfield, *Industrialization and the family* (1961), Castillo, Weisblat and Villareal, *The concepts of nuclear and extended family* (1968), etc., and for the censuses, references in Chapter 4. British census reports sometimes give foreign figures.

[17] United States Bureau of the Census, *A century of population growth* (1909): Ch. viii, the source used by Parten and Reeves, *Size and composition of American families* (1937). Nimkoff and Ogburn, *Technology and the changing family* (1955) are said by Goode to use census data to suggest that 'perhaps the family never has been large in size'. See Goode (1968): 321.

[18] Though see the work of Mols (1955) and that of Russell and others cited below. Social science textbooks are the least satisfactory in this respect; apart from Burgess and Locke (1953, 1945), see for example, Kirkpatrick, *The family as process and institution* (1955, 1963). Even Ogburn and Nimkoff, *A handbook of sociology* (1940, 1960) retain a chapter on the family sketching its historical development, never mentioning a mean or distribution by size, though it reads as if the family in earlier times must have been large. In this and most such accounts, it is the omission of all reference to household members other than kin, that is mostly the servants, which is so distortive as a description of earlier forms of the domestic group, especially in Europe.

said to have been partially incomplete, and then rather amongst the historians than amongst the social scientists. This is in respect to familial attitudes, the succession of ideas which men have had about what the family should be and how individuals should comport themselves within it. Even here of course the number of works is small as compared with those on other aspects of the family, and we shall not find that these studies have done anything to correct the misapprehension about size and structure. Quite the contrary. Nevertheless familial attitudes are as important to the history of the domestic group as they are to the remainder of this unwieldy field of enquiry, and we must give some attention to them.

2   THE HISTORY OF FAMILIAL ATTITUDES

The effect of family structure on attitudes, on sentiment, responses, on the set of the personality, is the major reason why it has attracted so much attention from the social scientists. Obviously there is little to be gained from recovering the facts about the size and composition of the domestic group unless their influence on behaviour can be gauged. But it is one thing to get to know what familial attitudes were in the past, and quite another to argue from them back to what the size and structure of the domestic group must have been.

Sources and literature

Lest it should be supposed that inferences of this kind are unimportant or uncommon, two examples are given in what follows. Both are drawn from discussions of the family and household amongst English speakers in pre-industrial times.

The seventeenth century patriarchal family had many of the characteristics of the patriarchal household. It included, not only wife and children, but often younger brothers, sisters, nephews and nieces: male superiority and primogeniture were unquestioned. More striking was the presence of a very large number of servants, whose subjection to the head of the household was absolute.

This is to be found in the introduction to a favourite source for the history of the family as conventionally conceived, a polemical work written by a man of the past to persuade his contemporaries on a particular social and political issue.[19]

The family familiar to the early colonists was a patrilineal group of extended kinship gathered into a single household. By modern standards it was large. Besides children it included a wide range of other dependents; nieces, and nephews, cousins, and, except for families at the lowest rung of society, servants in filial discipline. In the

---

[19] Laslett, *Patriarcha and other works of Sir Robert Filmer* (1949): 24. This passage was written in entire ignorance of what any set of domestic groups in seventeenth-century England actually consisted in. Filmer was the patriarchal writer who was attacked by John Locke, the philosopher, in his famous *Two Treatises of Government* (1690).

Elizabethan family the conjugal unit was only the nucleus of a broad kinship community whose outer edges merged almost imperceptibly into the society at large...By the middle of the eighteenth century [this passage comes a little later] the classic lineaments of the American family as modern sociologists describe them – the 'isolation of the conjugal unit', the 'maximum dispersion of the lines of descent', partible inheritances and multilineal growth – had appeared. In the reduced, nuclear family, thrown back upon itself, relationships tended toward ascription, marriage toward a contract between equals. Above all the development of the child was affected.

This comes from a survey of sources necessarily confined to statements in literary and legal contexts about familial attitudes because, as the author himself cogently complained, no other source had been made available to the historian intent on informing himself about the family so as to write adequately about the development of education. His argument was that American education was different from European because in transit across the ocean the family unit was stripped to its nuclear core.[20]

Comparison of these statements with the chapters in this volume devoted to the English and the Western European family (4–13) on the one hand and those on the American family on the other (20–22) will show how misleading they are at the crucial point: dimension of household and its composition, more particularly as to extended or joint households, those very groups of extended kinship gathered together in one domestic group.[21] Nevertheless the presence of servants was an important reality, as indeed was the existence of patriarchal authority, and when we turn to fully descriptive works on the history of familial attitudes it is remarkable how large and rich an impression can be gained. By familial attitudes here is meant more than feelings of affection and dislike towards members of the household and the kin, expressions and demonstrations of authority and submission, convictions as to what was right and wrong in the constitution of a family and its practices. Such customs as rites of passage – practices to mark birth, sometimes maturity, marriage and death – formal acts such as will-making, property agreements between kin, and marriage settlements, have all to be included. This means the use of legal and institutional records as sources, but the most informative and the most consulted are the literary productions of our ancestors, their letters, diaries, descriptions, sermons, polemics, journalism, plays, novels and the rest.

These sources are so informative and have turned out to survive in such quantity that their study might in the end have led to a revision of distortions of

---

[20] Bailyn, *Education in the forming of American society* (1960): 15–16. Bailyn is himself highly critical of the familial history which he found himself having to use, and it has to be said that he was influenced by the passage previously quoted, especially in the statements about the large extended family of Elizabethan England. In spite of the assertion about the loss of extension in the domestic group consequent upon colonisation, he may be quite correct in his claim that the eighteenth-century colonial American family was in a critical situation.

[21] See also Section III of this Introduction, and especially the tables at the end. It will be noticed that the American colonial family group may well have been marginally less complex than the English, perhaps indeed the simplest in form yet known to sociological history.

the kind we have just quoted, as indeed is implied by Richard Wall in Chapter 5.[22] Nevertheless, as has already been shown, literature, especially high literature, is so convincing, even when it is misleading to the reader of our day, that this revision seems unlikely to have happened without a more empirical, numerical attitude having intervened. In any case one 'literary' source cannot easily be used to show that another is inaccurate or unrepresentative. It may be that the persuasive and illuminating qualities of such writings are responsible for the impression given by works based upon them that they do in fact constitute the complete history of family and household. Their authors find themselves repeatedly protesting that the particular instance they are citing – court-case, letter, poem, speech or scene – is not necessarily typical, yet even the titles which they give to their books suggest otherwise. The reader might be forgiven for supposing that *A social history of the American family* would contain more than an account of attitudes as just defined, or *The puritan family*, or even *L'enfant et la vie familiale sous l'ancien régime*.[23]

Perhaps the most conspicuous, and unfortunate, effect of reliance on such sources is the support it seems to give to the very habit of attaching the name of a nation, or of a religious outlook, or of a social class, to a particular form of the family – the American family, the Puritan family, the bourgeois family and so on. This tendency is related to an even deeper seated expectation that change in matters of this kind will necessarily be related to change in other spheres, again usually in religion and in politics. But it exists for other reasons too and it will come under criticism in this book, especially in so far as it presupposes that the form of the family will be uniform over a national area.

Nevertheless in underlining the shortcomings of the history of familial attitudes, we must not be taken to exaggerate the value of the predominantly numerical studies presented here, nor to imply that literary and legal sources are necessarily incapable of distinguishing between differing parts of a country

[22] Though his materials are themselves observational so that it is not quite clear that they ought to be classified as literary. The same applies to such work as that done by Gregory King, which Wall discusses and which, if it had been properly scrutinised in 1949, would by itself have shown how misleading was Sir Robert Filmer's implied description of English households. That works of this kind are by no means confined to England is obvious from Vauban, *Projet d'une dixme royale* (1707) and such works as Manerio, *Tractatus de numeratione personarum* (1697).

[23] The original title of *Centuries of childhood* by Ariès (1960, 1962), a very valuable book which does in fact contain some numerical evidence. Two notable books have been written as *The puritan family*, one by Schücking (1929, 1969), which is subtitled *A social study from literary sources*, and the other by Morgan (1944, 1966), which uses materials from American colonial courts, sermons, and so on but which is applicable almost unaltered to pre-industrial England. The first title was used by Calhoun (1917–18, 1960) for the only book devoted to that topic over the whole of American history. Even when an abstract title is used, such as *The spiritualization of the household* by Hill for the chapter on the family in *Society and puritanism in pre-revolutionary England* (1964) the impression given is that structure as well as ideology and ideological change are being discussed. No work to correspond with Calhoun exists for England: for a partial bibliography of relevant works, see Laslett, *The World we have lost*, 2nd edn (1971).

or different periods. Almost every discussion of the changes in familial size and structure over time by our contributors refers to a decline in size, a simplification of composition. In fact almost the only example known to me in the history of pre-industrial Europe, or Western Europe, of a period and place in which domestic groups are thought to have grown larger and more complex over time is in certain areas of Southern France and probably the Southern Alpine and Northern Italian areas in the fourteenth and fifteenth centuries. The evidence for this movement comes entirely under the heading of the history of familial attitudes, though it consists of solemn agreements between parties to property transactions rather than of imaginative literature.[24]

Evidence for familial communities in late medieval Europe

The historians of French institutions do not seem to have escaped the urge to believe that households in the past must have been large and complex. When the record of a meeting of the French Estates General (a kind of national representative assembly) in 1484 was printed in 1835, a very conspicuous example of extended familial society came to light. A delegate from Normandy talked of customs whereby married sons and daughters resided with their parents, the whole group living in common and including up to four conjoined families with grandchildren, in-laws, and so on. He went on to describe a household of ten married couples comprising 70 people. This has been quoted by a succession of scholars, including Marc Bloch, with the implication that fifteenth-century French families may frequently have been big. It is not always mentioned that the original speech implied that these arrangements came about because of the weight of taxation and its method of assessment, hinting that such households may therefore have been fictitious, and were in any case strange, perhaps even 'unnatural'.[25] No other such instances are cited from that area at that time.

But there can apparently be no doubt of the considerable body of evidence, legal, quasi-legal and literary, for the growth in the fourteenth and fifteenth centuries of the practice of formally setting up familial communities in the area

[24] To this example of growth in size and complexity might be added that of Estonia between the late seventeenth and early nineteenth centuries. See Palli, *Size of household in the parish of Karuse, Esthonia* (typescript) and perhaps (in respect of complexity) that of industrialising England itself – see below.
[25] Bernier, *Journal des Etats Généraux de France* (1835): 583–5, cited by Clamagéran, *Histoire de l'impôt en France* (1857–76) II: 75; Esmonin, *La taille en Normandie* (1913): 281–3 (interpreting it as a taxation community resembling contemporary familial communities in Southern France); Bloch, *Les caractères originaux de l'histoire rurale française* (1931): 170; Le Roy Ladurie, *Les paysans de Languedoc* (1966) I: 167 (a parallel to 'the new, powerful and final revelation of the extended family' then to be seen in Languedoc), see ibid. I: 166. The original Latin speech said that people lived together 'at least in appearance' (saltem specie tenus), and added rather obscurely 'Mira res! Hoc ab illis extorsit amor nummi, quod natura vix aliquis concessit ut plures simul uxores communibus bonis, eademque autoritate conviverent.'

of Southern France where the *langue d'oc* was spoken. Wills, dowry documents and above all declarations of property transactions before notaries, a very common form of surviving record, all testify to the practice of *affrairement*, associating individuals in fraternal or fraternal-type groups. Whole lineages were bound together to live communally, and it would appear that large units were brought into being, perhaps surviving for several generations. Though the model was of brothers sharing their patrimony and their households, forming what is known as a *frérèche*, sisters' husbands and sisters themselves, other relatives and even strangers, could become incorporated into the *communauté familiale*. A recent writer has seen hints of homosexual association in these arrangements.[26]

The familial community was urban as well as rural, and affected craftsmen as well as cultivators. Descriptions of its arrangements and references to them are not confined to records surviving from this French region, nor to this particular period, but can be found in Italy and Spain at earlier and later times, and even as far away as Poland. But the current opinion seems to be that it was in archaic France (*la France archaïque*) in the southern, hilly districts, that this practice became very widespread in the later Middle Ages as a reaction to depopulation – the Black Death is seen as a causal influence – and to economic recession. Allusions become so frequent and the arrangements laid down so suggestive of the grand, authoritarian household that its establishment and persistence have been heralded as an epoch in ethnological history. Though it may have survived locally in some areas as late as the seventeenth or even the eighteenth century, and so help to explain the complication of family structure which Biraben in Chapter 8 suggests may well have existed at Montplaisant in 1644, it is thought to have declined quickly as prosperity increased and population grew in the sixteenth century. No claim has ever been made that it affected more than a minority of the population.[27]

[26] Le Roy Ladurie (1966) I: 166. My knowledge of this subject, which is rather remote from English scholarship and does not seem to have been anywhere discussed in our language, is derived almost entirely from this source and from the works which are there cited. These are the *thèse, Le régime des biens entre époux dans la région de Montpellier du debut du XIII siècle à la fin du XVI siècle* (1957) and subsequent articles of Jean Hilaire. Prof. Hilaire drew my attention to a short work which summarises the rather intricate issues, Gaudemet, *Les communautés familiales* (1963).

[27] Le Roy Ladurie (1966) I: 166: 'La restauration d'une famille élargie, patriarcale ou fraternelle, dans le Languedoc cévenol de l'extrême fin du Moyen Age est un grand fait d'histoire ethnologique.' The disclaimer about this institution ever involving a majority of the inhabitants of a whole village or region is made in a personal letter of September 1970. He makes persuasive use of the evidence of Chapter 10 as well as of Chapter 8 of this volume in support of the complexity of households in Southern European areas between the fifteenth and seventeenth centuries, and adds to them that from a listing of a village in the Montpellier area in 1691, published by Noël as *La population de la paroisse de Laguiole d'après un recensement de 1691* (1967). Tuscany in the fifteenth century has some stem families (see fn. 36 and Chapter 10), but scarcely bears out the case; and the two seventeenth-century French villages would be of greater use to Ladurie if they could be brought under the criteria for giving numerical expression to degrees of complication in household structure

This is not the opportunity for reviewing the documentary foundations for such a challenging thesis in any detail. We may notice that in Chapters 18 and 19 large scale Japanese households are stated to have persisted in certain villages because of their situation in mountainous, underdeveloped regions, and that Le Play uses the same argument. We may remark once again that in all these cases the view adopted is that large composite households were either a survival from a remote past, or a restoration of what anciently was. But we shall have to stop at this point, registering the interesting possibility that households grew in size and in complication of structure in Southern France and neighbouring regions at the time in question, but going for the present no further than registering. Until listings susceptible to numerical treatment become available for late medieval Languedoc there seems to be no grounds for assuming with confidence that the change necessarily occurred. Nor can it at present be supposed that the available evidence implies the continuous existence of this familial form until a later century.[28] It seems to be unjustifiable to infer a change in social structure, an ethnological epoch, from attitudinal evidence alone, however impressive and plentiful it may be. One or two pieces of numerical evidence coming from a scattering of dates, which is no doubt all that could be expected to be forthcoming, might still leave room for doubt about such a development in familial history. But it would do something to free the hypothesis from the uncertainties which must attach to legal and literary evidence which has no confirmation outside itself.

Propositions which are based exclusively on this material may be highly suggestive of general trends over wide areas, but they can give no reliable indication of how many communities were affected, nor what proportion of persons within them, nor for how many years. They cannot demonstrate the situation within any complete set of persons – a province, a city, a village, or indeed an

set out in Section II below. It does not seem that the listing of the 1691 village (Laguiole) is susceptible to this treatment, and the publication in 1971 of the full transcript of that for Montplaisant underlines the palaeographical and interpretative difficulties to which Biraben refers. From the transcript in its printed form it is not absolutely clear whether the list-maker was recording housefuls (inhabitants of each house in his village); households; or, at least from time to time, the extended family connections of his parishioners as they were known to him, without at all inferring that these connected individuals made up coresident domestic groups. If these obscurities could be cleared up Montplaisant and Laguiole would together provide a convincing indication of a tradition of complex households in these areas at that time, for each has a markedly high proportion of extended and joint households. Indeed the cameos for the households of Montplaisant appended to Biraben's chapter present a community with household structure more intricate than any yet known to us for Europe, Western, Middle or Eastern, more in fact than the one Japanese community we were able to analyse from a listing in time for this volume of studies.

[28] The belief that large scale households existed as a minority phenomenon, a somewhat different proposition, in certain towns and regions in France until the eighteenth century was expressed as late as 1968 by the distinguished social structural historian Pierre Goubert; see Goubert, *La famille française au XVIIIe siècle* (1969). Unfortunately no references are given in that context and I have been unable to discover the precise places Goubert had in mind.

individual household – at any one time, and this is in sharp contrast with what is shown up by community listings of the census type. Not only is the number of people or units at issue always unknown, but the population at risk as well. This is quite apart from the general disadvantages of all evidence of this kind, even that of wills and of declarations before notaries. It is inevitably biassed towards the propertied and the literate; therefore it could yield the true situation only if the distribution of property and of literacy were known, which it never is. Even legal or quasi-legal documents may not record what was, or had been, or was to be, but only what ought to have been. The possibility of convenient fiction, or of plain lying, is difficult to exclude. The disadvantages of evidence derived from what we have called familial attitudes must be borne in mind as we approach the subject of the stem family and its effects on the expectations which have been brought to the subject of familial history.

3   THE STEM FAMILY

We have insisted that those who have pronounced upon the family and its history have been tempted to look upon it both as the final unit of society, and as the citadel of its values, collective and individual. They have tended to believe that the integrity of a society, especially that of a nation, depended upon the stability, the simplicity, the immemorial integrity of the family (its time honoured virtue – all these phrases recur), and especially on the authority of the family head, the loyalty and obedience of his subjects. They have not often made a great deal of the actual shape or constitution of the domestic group, though they usually seem to assume a structure for it, a large scale structure. All this is particularly true of the French engineer, administrator and social reformist, Frédéric Le Play (1806–82), who was and perhaps still is, the strongest single influence on the historical study of the family.

Le Play and his followers, many of them also highly placed administrators and technicians, had as their avowed object the healing of social decay. Or perhaps more often, its prevention in the face of the rapid social change being brought about in the Europe of their day by the individualist legislation of post-Revolution governments, and by the spread of industry. Le Play himself laid great stress on the familial form, and held a theory of its change over time.

The domestic group, he considered, was of three types. The first, the patriarchal type, was stable in structure and faithful to the family line and to tradition; it kept all sons within the household after marriage. The second, the famous stem family, *la famille souche*, was also stable in structure and faithful to the family line, but to traditional values it added a novelty; the parents married off and kept within the group only one of their children whom they nominated successor. The others, being given their shares of the inheritance, went away to found their own households if they wished, but some stayed behind of their own free will even after succession had occurred, remaining themselves unmarried.

The third type, the unstable type, showed little attachment to the family line and was inclined to novelty; it came into being at marriage, grew as births took place and shrank with successive departures of the children, coming to an end with the death of the parents and the dividing up of the inheritance.[29] 'Under the new manufacturing régime in the West, *la famille instable* is predominant amongst working class populations: it is associated with their pauperization.' Le Play believed that the stem family took the place of the patriarchal family as society changed, but with no ill effects on the race or nation. The unstable family succeeded the stem family when bad customs and laws undermined patriarchal authority and led to property division at each succession. This did bring about instability, decay and the decline of the nation especially. The final sanctions of the familial code were the ten commandments.

Le Play and the history of the domestic group

Le Play never seems to have literally claimed that large scale, multiple households were once the universal order in the peasant world. But in the course of his voluminous writings he names a number of areas where the stem family could be confidently supposed to have been the predominant form for several hundred or even thousands of years, and one of them was the South of France. The very title of the book in which he made this last pronouncement, *L'organisation de la famille selon le vrai modèle signalé par l'histoire de toutes les races et tous les temps*,[30] and the general judgement in favour of 'the true model', which was indeed the stem family, inevitably tended to join with this expression of preference a historical presumption that the stem family had been the normal arrangement, or at least very much respected as the proper type.

Such, at any rate, appears to have been the sense in which subsequent social scientists have taken up his doctrine and our concern here is with this rather than with what Le Play actually stated, or even what he intended. Neither he, nor they, attempted any definition of what a *predominant* institution should be,

---

[29] Le Play, *Les ouvriers Européens* (1855, 1877–9) ɪ: 457, a free rendering, with additions, of the definitions given in a glossary: for the succession of familial form to familial form with the growth of wealth and industry, see ibid. p. 384. The citation comes from another, and an illuminating, discussion of familial forms, *La réforme Sociale*, 1864, 3rd edn 1901, vol. 1, book ɪɪɪ. On Le Play generally see Brooke, *Le Play* (1970) and Zimmermann and Frampton, *Family and Society* (1936): 361–586 contains a translation of Le Play (1877–9) ɪ.

[30] Le Play (1871): xxɪ. The full passage runs: 'Je ne fonde pas la description de la famille souche sur des généralités. Suivant la méthode dont l'efficacité est maintenant reconnue, je décris... une famille que j'ai longtemps étudié en 1856 et dont le type domine encore parmi nos populations du midi.' On p. 36 he announces that the stem family was 'l'institution par excellence des peuples sedentaires' and names Holstein, Hanover, Westphalia, South Bavaria, Salzburg, Carinthia, Tyrol, North Italy and Spain as sites. He says elsewhere, Le Play (1877–9) ɪ: 381, that in these vast areas where the simple races dwelt each family was composed of several conjugal units (plusieurs ménages). The citation of a particular family should be noticed, for Le Play had absolute confidence in the typical instance. His instructions as to method, printed in 1862, recommend the many researchers who collaborated with him and whose work makes up much of his books, to choose for study in depth a particular family not above nor below the average for the area in economic or in moral substance.

how many people should experience it and for how long; how many need never have personal contact with it. No doubt it was to be expected that Le Play's own evidence for the historical presumptions which seem to have been read into him should have been incidental and superficial.[31] But it is rather more surprising that his successors did not seem to go much further in collecting evidence from the past, since they were busy instituting that tradition of community surveys which has since become so important to empirical social science. Their concern, however, was rather with family finances than with kin relationships, although they showed a pronounced preference for the large family, and seem all to have supposed that decline in the size of the coresidential domestic group was a sign of general social disintegration.

This places these investigators firmly in the tradition already discussed, and it is understandable that Le Play assumed the stem family to be more fertile than others in view of the fact that a decline of the population of France was one of his great fears. When all resident relatives were included, a stem family household would frequently consist, he tells us, in fifteen members. Ideally, however, it would be even larger: 'dans les conditions moyennes observées chez les bonnes races, une famille-souche comprend 18 personnes'.[32] He was well aware, of course, that the fifty-seven typical households whose exhaustive examination forms the basis of his work and which stretched from the Donetz Basin in Russia to Spain, had a very much smaller average: one of them was a solitary outworker. But it was not the difficulty of showing that the stem family was in existence in his day, or had been common previously, which gave rise to criticisms of his system after his death, rather the serious doubts as to what the *famille souche* actually was, and whether it corresponded to any observable familial type.

This definitional uncertainty still persists, and since it has tended to obscure the history of the domestic group some of its details must be considered. Le Play himself certainly thought of *la famille souche* both as a domestic group and as a patriline, that is a succession of male heads of household directly descended from each other. As a domestic group it seems definitely to have consisted in an extended family of two married couples with their children, the head of the second being the child of the first, an arrangement to which we shall give the title *multiple family household, disposed downwards* (type 5b, see Section II, p. 31). The resident heir chosen by the household head was usually a son, perhaps as often the youngest as the oldest, though for want of sons the carefully

---

[31] E.g. the hamlet of Pinon cited in Le Play (1877–9) v: 189, which apparently serves as an authority both for household size and for endogamy, though it consisted of only 32 people and 4 family households. Even when he is introducing one of his household studies by describing the ecology of the family concerned, he rarely gives the population of the village to which it belongs, or any other information of this numerical character.

[32] Le Play (1877–9) I: 189, and 1901, I, 508, cf. Brooke (1970): 81. Brooke casts some doubt on whether all the research which is claimed to have been done on the fifty-seven families was actually carried out.

chosen husband of a daughter, a nephew or even a more distant male relative might be introduced: a successor's widow could also head a household. Inevitably such a group would have been large, for servants belonged to it as well as the senior couple, the junior couple, often brothers and sisters of the successor, and perhaps his children too. In fact household head and married successor could expect to be having children at the same time, over some period of years. What is more Le Play seems to have supposed that patriarchal and stem family households would have been constantly of the same large size, because it was one of the undesirable features of the unstable, nuclear family that it varied in size over time. Like the textbook writers of our own generation, he shows little awareness of the developmental cycle which must affect composition of the domestic group persisting over time and also its size, in the absence of compensatory arrangements. Neither demographic insight, which would have brought home to him the improbability of grandparents and grandchild usually being alive at the same time for long periods, nor an awareness of sampling arithmetic, which would have put him on his guard against typical examples, seem to have been part of the outlook of Le Play or of his followers.[33]

As a patriline, or as patriline permitting female succession occasionally, Le Play's stem family closely resembles the Japanese Ie, 家, discussed in Chapters 17, 18 and 19. A succession of direct descendants is identified with a house, a piece of land, or even a particular handicraft, and each in turn holds it inalienably and in trust for the family name and for all members of the line. The continuity of property attached to a patriline, especially land, is of the first importance, if only because it enabled the stem family to dispense welfare. Every eligible relative could presumably look to the trunk (stem, *souche*, *Stamme*) for assistance, and especially the children for a start in life. But only one of the head's sons could expect to succeed, and other offspring would have to find a living elsewhere if they wished to have their own families. It would seem that the successor might have to buy out his brothers from the family inheritance, and find dowries for his sisters, but his overriding obligation was to maintain the name, the place, the line. The stem family patriline, then, was the stem family

---

[33] This truncated account of the stem family household is based for the most part on Le Play (1877–9) III: 132–44, describing the *Hof* as Le Play observed it in Luneburg in the 1820s. In his classic work *English villagers of the 13th century* (1941, 1970): 445, Homans cites this passage in connection with peasant households in open field areas, and this seems to have raised the expectation that such a structure would turn out to be standard in England. But Homans is comparing only; he implies that on enclosed land familial arrangements were different. He does maintain, however, that the stem family household must have been large in England and quotes Demolins (Le Play's successor and critic) for the retirement arrangements which he suggests affected household composition, since they brought the parents of the head into the group. In view of the varying definitions of the stem family household or arrangement, it should be stressed that Le Play himself declares, ibid. p. 136, that the heir resided in his parental home with his wife and children, along with brothers and sisters as yet unmarried. It has to be said that Le Play does occasionally recognise that family group structure changed over time, but he does not seem to have been aware of the implications of this fact for his descriptions or prescriptions.

household perpetuated, which is presumably why Le Play does not seem to have wished to distinguish the two.

The period of persistence over time could be considerable, for he cites a family· having a holding bearing its name for some 850 years.[34] The Japanese houses described in this volume sometimes did endure for many generations, but no claim so ambitious is made for them, certainly no supposition that at all points in time each such family composed a multiple household. Some of the features of Le Play's account look imaginary, therefore, but certain features of it, or certain analogues to it, can undoubtedly be found in the familial record of Europe, unexplored as that archive mostly still is.

We have glanced at the circumstantial evidence, and the pieces of numerical evidence also, which provide such glimpses of the stem family tradition in Southern France. At the other end of Western Europe, in an Esthonian village in the late seventeenth and eighteenth centuries, indications of something similar have recently been recovered,[35] and from the Czech–Austrian border at about the same time a much more substantial body of data has now appeared which points in this direction. It includes an outstanding list of inhabitants for the year 1763 covering the lordship, *Herrschaft*, of Heidenreichstein which reveals the existence of marked extended family characteristics. Since this is the most conspicuous and best documented example so far to be recovered of a past European peasant community exhibiting stem family features we may dwell upon it for a little while.

The traits of Le Play's *famille souche* which are present include the inalien-ability of the land belonging to a house (in both its senses of a dwelling and of a patriline), the buying out of siblings by the chosen successor, and extensive provisions for retirement. Perhaps the most interesting resemblance to the familial form at issue is that domestic groups in Heidenreichstein do seem to have remained constant in size over the length of the family cycle, which is a feature not confirmed for any of the other communities cited in this volume, even those in Serbia and Japan. Although even in this Austrian locality not more than a quarter of the peasant households were extended in any way at the date on which the census was taken, it can be inferred that many more of them must have been so structured at an earlier date or were likely to be so at a later one. Nevertheless, few if any of the domestic groups seem to have approached the size and complication which Le Play portrays in his descriptions. It is only when the data of this one listing is analysed with a model of the life cycle of the

---

[34] 'Le *Bramerhof* à Hermannsburg est, depuis l'an 1000, possédé par la famille des *Bramer*', Le Play (1877–9) III: 140.

[35] In a paper *The size of household in the parish of Karuse, Esthonia*, communicated from Tallinn in November 1970, H. Palli states that it was quite common for adult sons with their wives and children to live with their fathers and their families. Often they lived together after the death of the father. No numerical evidence for this is given for the village concerned (Karuse in 1686, 1726 and 1816), but in conversation Professor Palli stated that they could be provided, and the figures he records do contain an occasional household of a Le Play dimension.

peasantry in mind that the possibility of the stem family being the dominant institution in the home life of these Austrian villagers comes into view.

It is notable that an extensive body of evidence on familial attitudes seems also to have survived from this region, which cannot as yet be parallelled from English or other Western European sources, not even by that concerning the *communauté familiale*. Although we have claimed that the existence of the complex household as an important institution should not be inferred from the evidence of familial attitudes alone, it seems that where such a situation existed, it could give rise to a great deal of literary and legal material. None of the facts we have cited makes it likely that the situation in Heidenreichstein can have been typical of any extensive region of Western Europe, and it will be seen from the contributions to this volume how strongly much of the available evidence makes against Le Play's hypothesis as a general proposition for pre-industrial Europe as a whole. There are other features of this particular locality which may mark it as exceptional, but the knowledge of its existence and the possibility of similar discoveries certainly enlivens the whole issue of domestic group structure in Europe in relation to industrialisation.[36]

Redefinition of the stem family

Many an appealing overtone in our own sentiments about home, holding and community is set echoing by the descriptions which Le Play offers to us. The school he founded worked in many parts of Europe in search of *la famille souche*, although within a dozen years of his death one of them announced that it was an illusion.[37] But it is never easy to demonstrate the absence of an institution from a particular area at any time, especially in the past, and even more so when it can be redefined so as to take account of evidence inconsistent with it. If it is shown that married successors were almost entirely wanting in peasant households, as for example in England since the sixteenth century as analysed in Chapter 4 below, then it can be replied that the stem family does not necessitate their presence. The chosen heir might live nearby, inside or outside what we

---

[36] The peculiarities of Heidenreichstein which may distinguish it from other areas are the rule about the inalienability of land from a holding; the high expectation of life, which seems to have enabled fathers to survive the latish marriage of their heirs in some numbers; the extensive retirement rules, together with evidence for particular peasants of the fact of retirement; the rules of military conscription. These last seem to have invited the peasant paterfamilias to nominate a successor, who would be exempt, thus underwriting a stem family feature whilst removing many men who might otherwise have headed nuclear families. The whole of the description in the text is owed to an impressive article in the *American Historical Review* by Lutz Berkner (*The stem family and the developmental cycle of the peasant household* (1972)), and I am indebted to him for the opportunity to discuss it in unpublished form. This study has been used by Prof. David Herlihy in a further analysis of Florence and surroundings in 1427 (cf. Chapter 10) to substantiate a form of the stem family there, using a very different and loose definition of the institution. The results of trying to analyse some English communities on Berkner's lines are presented below, pp. 150–1.

[37] See Brooke (1970): 176, quoting Demolins' preface to Butel, *Une vallée Pyrenéene* (1894), a book which I have not been able to consult.

shall call the houseful, and when he moved in his parent or parents would move out. Or he might simply postpone marriage until he succeeded, though this would imply that heirs married later than other offspring, perhaps not until the father died, and family reconstitution studies show that such was very unlikely to have been the case in peasant English families three centuries ago. Even this is not insurmountable, for those attached to the stem family hypothesis can maintain that to demonstrate its rarity is not to dispose of its importance. It may have been an ideal to which many or all aspired, but few achieved.

It certainly does not seem to have been difficult for the familial sociologist to discover in our own day what he is disposed to call survivals of the stem family institution, defined in one of the modes which have been suggested. We have already referred to the peasant families of the Netherlands, studied in the 1950s, but much more influential has been the evocative description of family and community in Ireland, published in 1940. This work does not employ Le Play's term, and provides no numerical evidence on the actual prevalence of multiple family households and their dwellings, with retirement rooms at the west end for the declining generation. Nevertheless it proceeds as if the succession to the Irish family farm was still going on as it had always gone on, by the chosen heir bringing his wife into the family house.[38]

This appears to me to be a telling illustration of the way in which the stem family criterion has determined the course of familial sociology. Its prevalence can be judged from the fact that Thomas Burch finds it necessary to provide separate calculations for stem families in the intriguing model of family sizes he presents in Chapter 2. So instinctive has this way of thinking about the development of family and household become that when the investigators of English familial structure wished to name a category to describe a pattern of residence repeatedly found in the 1950s, especially in working class areas, they resorted to the expression stem family all over again. This represented a further and even more radical shifting of ground in its definition. For the daughter, not the son, brings her working class spouse into the family circle; usually and preferably she sets up house within walking distance of mum and all that mum has to offer to a young mother.[39]

This is not coresidence; it occurs within a matriline, not a patriline; in no

---

[38] Arensberg and Kimball, *Family and community in Ireland* (1940, 1961). The chapter on marriage (VII) makes it quite clear that they assume that all brides of successors were ordinarily brought into the farm household. It seems possible to me that the situation regarded by Arensberg and Kimball as an immemorial survival could at least partially be explained as a recent accommodation of farm family composition to changed conditions and, especially, longer life, just as in the Dutch case. Berkner also finds retirement rooms (Stübli) in the houses of Heidenreichstein.

[39] Mogey, *Family and neighbourhood* (1956): 54, citing the work of Young and Willmott subsequently published as *Family and kinship in East London* (1957); *Family and class in a London suburb* (1960), etc. These studies also seem to assume that the pattern of kin and family solidarity which they show up were inheritances from the pre-industrial past rather than the product of existing conditions.

sense does it represent the provision of succession to a *house* in the genealogical sense; since those who engage in the practice are predominantly of lower social status, it cannot be said to provide a model which others are likely to imitate. The character of Le Play's stem family is therefore almost entirely lost, yet in using the title the object seems to have been to give this newly recognised pattern some historical roots, whilst acknowledging that the 'classical description' of the stem family had been woefully altered over time. To say this is not, of course, to deny the psychological importance of the propinquity of kin in familial development, in our own day or at any previous period; it is only to protest against the distortions which may arise from insisting on referring such permanent interchange to the supposed classical model of the stem family, its persistence or revival.

It may be agreed that some of the modifications which have been suggested in order to preserve the notion of the stem family weaken it so severely that it ceases to be of much use for the purposes of analysis. Indeed, once it is conceded that the successor need not reside inside the household, with or without a spouse, it is difficult to see how the stem family can be called a modification of the co-resident domestic group. If it is to exist at all, it must be in the form of a set of expectations from a family line, familial attitudes all over again, rather than in a set of particular shapes of the domestic groups.[40] If such shapes are to be recognised, moreover, precise, even very precise, measurements, definitions, and forms of classification must be worked out and adhered to. To these we now turn our attention.

II. DEFINITIONS, METHODS AND SCHEME OF ANALYSIS

This section of the Introduction is given over to the task of laying down suggested definitions and ways of exploiting the data provided by lists of inhabitants. It will propose a scheme of classification, as well as a method for the pictorial or ideographic representation of domestic groups. Much of the prose may seem to be an unnecessary elaboration of trivial issues; all such discussions do in social scientific enquiry, especially when the field is still novel.

1 DEFINITION OF THE DOMESTIC GROUP

The particular subject of this book was stated at the outset to be the comparative history of the domestic group. A preliminary definition of the family in this sense in contrast to the other senses which are possible is to be found in every-

---

[40] In this sense, where the emphasis is entirely on lineal descent and the inheritance of titles, status or possessions, the 'stem family' is a very widespread social institution, for it exists in all forms of aristocracies. Even if it could be shown to follow from this that most aristocratic households were organised on stem family lines, it would not follow that there was a general tendency in that direction in all traditional societies with aristocracies. Perhaps rather the reverse.

day experience. The domestic group is the family which the suburban worker leaves when he catches his bus in the morning, and returns to in the evening; it was the family which the English husbandman or petty farmer of our pre-industrial past sat with at table and organised for work in the fields. It consists and consisted of those who share the same physical space for the purposes of eating, sleeping, taking rest and leisure, growing up, child-rearing and pro-creating (those of them belonging to the class of person whom society permits to procreate). In earlier times, and nowadays in undeveloped societies, this same space was also where the domestic group worked at those tasks which could not be done in the open air, and these were not a few, even in agriculture. In the households of craftsmen, the industrial producers and service workers of that era, and in those engaged in commerce, everything went forward within this living space; such households made up fully a third of all domestic groups in pre-industrial England. Since the insistence is on residence, the full term to be defined is the *coresident domestic group*, and our interest is in changes in the structure and size of that group over time.

Even when spelt out in this way, the definition of the domestic groups is by no means sharp and unambiguous in all societies, as Jack Goody shows so plainly in Chapter 3. Apart from the problem of the actual boundaries of the household even in social situations which can now be observed, the great diffi-culty of the study of the domestic group in the past is that we ourselves cannot literally go back in time and examine any one such group or any number of them with the criterion of residence, or of shared activities, or of consumption, or of production, or of authority in mind.

All we have is some knowledge of the law and custom of our chosen areas and a few documents left behind by a handful of the myriads of communities which have consisted of such domestic groups. These documents consist of lists of inhabitants, and the task is to exploit them in such a way that the exactest possible comparisons can be made. For this purpose it is essential to lay it down who is to be included in the coresident domestic group and who excluded from it.

I must insist that in doing this no theory of domestic group organisation is being advanced, simply the rules which have to be observed if surviving docu-mentary evidence is to be made usable for comparative domestic group analysis. If faced with the challenge to answer the question what exactly is meant here by the terms family and household the only appropriate response would be an appeal to the past persons who created that evidence. The lists they left behind them consist of series of names of individuals in blocks, with clear indications of where one block ended and the next began; unless they made out exactly such lists their evidence has not been admitted. It requires no great perspicuity to see that these blocks of names must have been families, or households, and we know that the men of the past called them by these titles..Nevertheless we have to assume that in order to qualify for such descriptions the shape of these blocks was very far from being arbitrary, and in fact was determined by three main considerations. Persons would only appear together within those blocks if they had the three following characteristics in common; they slept habitually under the same roof (a locational criterion); they shared a number of activities (a functional criterion); they were related to each other by blood or by marriage (a kinship criterion).[41]

Location, shared activity and kinship

In this volume the first two criteria are taken to be universal. Everyone recorded as belonging with a block of persons in a list is supposed to have been living together with the others, and is assumed to have cooperated in many directions with them, to have had a relationship of support or dependence with some or all of them, perhaps relationships of both kinds. But not all such persons are taken to have shared the third characteristic, that of kinship, because some individuals, always a minority but not an unimportant minority, are known to have shared in the activities of the domestic group in which they lived though not related by marriage or blood to any other member. These were the servants, the visitors, boarders and lodgers, who appear along with other members of the family or household within the blocks of names which we are discussing.

It will be noticed that in adopting these criteria for the analysis of our evidence, we are assuming that they were also applied by those who originally drew up the lists of inhabitants from which we work. These were, and still are, a highly miscellaneous set of people, ranging from the priests, the estate officials, the town clerks, the village headmen or constables, and the plain busybodies, who made out such documents in earlier times and in very widely separate parts of the world, to the skilled census officials of the modern nations. We are assuming also that the writers of the studies published here have also used this same set of principles of interpretation.

It will be obvious that these assumptions can scarcely be regarded as secure. There must have been some inconsistency in outlook and practice at various points in an evidential chain which involves so many people of such different kinds in so many places and at such different periods. It is my considered view, however, that unless we proceed in this way we cannot make use of this, our only numerical evidence on the comparative history of the household and family in past time, and that the insecurity of our assumptions does not go so far as to invalidate our general conclusions, even if it makes the details somewhat problematical. Let us return to the task of describing the precise membership of the coresident domestic group when it is looked upon in this way.

[41] Prof. Hammel suggested these criteria, while warning me of their limitations for these purposes.

Members of the household

In the first place come the man, his wife and their socially recognised children. In the second place come all other resident relatives, as we shall call them in general, that is all those connected by blood or by marriage and living with the family. In the third place come all servants, those individuals who are now rare in modern society, but who were so common at all times up to those of our parents. They were commoner in England than in most other countries for they made up something like an eighth of the whole population in pre-industrial times. In Iceland in 1729 they amounted to no less than 17 %.[42]

Servants, like other members of the group, were subject to the jurisdiction of the head of the household, and this jurisdiction is usually defined by the legal system of the country or culture concerned. Common subjection to domestic authority is a widespread, if not universal, feature of all coresident domestic groups, so strongly marked in Western Europe, and no doubt elsewhere, that it made servants as much members of the master's 'family' (that is his household in our usage) as his wife, his children and his resident relatives, if any. All classes of persons in the service position came under this principle, even those who bore particular vocational descriptions such as 'apprentice', 'journeyman', or in England in the early Victorian census documents, 'trade assistant'.[43] It is possible that more servant labour was spent on agricultural, industrial, productive tasks during the years under consideration in this volume, than was spent on housekeeping. Work of this kind is still called 'economic' though its original meaning of 'to do with the household' has been transcended. Males were as common as females amongst servants until the beginning of the last century in England.[44]

But though we can be reasonably clear of membership of the domestic group up to this point, there were, and are, certain occasional or even semi-permanent residents in the household in an ambiguous position. These are the visitors, guests of the family, the lodgers and the boarders. It is not easy to decide whether our suburban paterfamilias would think of such persons as members of his family, if only temporary, and even more uncertain what would have been the attitude of the master of the household in earlier times, gentleman, yeoman, husbandman, craftsman or labourer. There can be no doubt of their being his responsibility and under his authority in certain matters, though in England he was in fact forbidden by law from harbouring them. We have tried to accommo-

[42] Based on figures given in Hansen, *Tabulation of the Icelandic Population Census of 1729* (Mimeograph).

[43] For the jurisdiction of the household head as a defining principle, see the English Census of 1851, quoted by Wall on p. 160 below. London shop-assistants were still living-in on a considerable scale in the early twentieth century, as were Japanese factory workers. On the trade assistants, see Alan Armstrong in Chapter 6, and on apprentices, etc. the works referred to in Chapter 4, especially those of David Glass.

[44] See Chapter 4. The tables at the end of this Introduction suggest that this was true of France, Serbia (especially), and Japan too.

date individuals in this uncertain familial position by counting them as part of the domestic group when it is looked upon from certain viewpoints, but not when the family itself, or even the household, is in question.

Once more the consideration has had to be the state of the evidence, which in its crudest exploitable form, and this is unfortunately the most usual, seems not to take separate account of visitors, lodgers and boarders, or lodging and boarding households. As we shall see, the position of these persons is undoubtedly unsatisfactory when an attempt is being made to define the domestic group for purposes of comparison over time.

Association short of membership

In spite of this difficulty, the list of those included in the family when it is defined as the coresident domestic group makes it reasonably clear who is excluded. Children who have left home are not included; nor are kin and affines who live close by, even if they collaborate so closely in the productive work of the family that for economic purposes they form part of it, and may frequently or usually take their meals at the family table. Such classes of person conform to the second and third of our criteria, but are excluded because they do not conform to the first. They are regarded as associated with the household, some of them very closely, but the association falls short of membership.

By this principle, which covers whole families collaborating for work as well as those simply sharing the labour of particular individuals, retired members of a former generation are not members of the domestic group, even if supported by it and still working with it, provided always that they would not be regarded by the family, or by an enquirer, as resident in the family home. The old farmer and his wife in the west room of a farmhouse being run by a married son in rural Ireland, that special domestic space reserved for the fairies and for the spirits of the dead as well as for this particular purpose, are members of the domestic group because they still live in it. But a retired couple occupying a cottage in the yard, or 'doing for themselves' in rooms set aside for them in the farmhouse, are not members. This is because it is supposed here that an observer, someone making out a list of the inhabitants of a community for example, would not be disposed to call them part of the household. He would, however, we assume, and this is an assumption important to our general position, be quite prepared to look on them as present along with members of the household in what we shall name the houseful.

Here again we reach ambiguities, because when faced with the borderline cases just described, some list-takers might be inclined to write down the people in question as within the household itself, rather than only the houseful.

Official national census-taking soon led to the working out of criteria making it possible to decide consistently on household membership, using such items as the physical boundaries of the dwelling, the extent of the group recognising the authority of a particular household head, and so on, as well as habitual places of eating and sleeping.[45] But this volume is particularly concerned to extend our knowledge backwards beyond the restricted period covered by national censuses, and there is no way of telling quite how such criteria were used by the men who drew up the lists of inhabitants on which such knowledge has to rely.

2   TERMINOLOGY AND SCHEME OF ANALYSIS

Although we have to assume that the men of the past thought as we do when they gave boundaries to the domestic group, we must not suppose that they made any careful distinction of terms. In England the word *family* was the ordinary term for what we should call, and call here *household*, but the word household was itself sometimes used and even the expression 'family and household'. The most interesting and fertile of all early observers of these units, the English political arithmetician Gregory King (1648–1712), seems to have written the word 'house' sometimes when he would otherwise have written family, and we would have written household. Some of his successors in the eighteenth century followed the same practice. Although this occasional usage complicates the task of those who study the English evidence, as will be seen from Richard Wall's discussion of the term in Chapter 5, it is suggestive nevertheless. For the ancient English word 'house' means both a physical structure and a line of people related to each other. It does, in this second sense, approach the Japanese usage, but the Tōyama Ie, 家, traced by Chie Nakane from 1818 to 1955 is a much better defined entity over time than the House of Percy or the House of Usher.

Types of family household

The terminology and classification recommended for the exploitation of lists of inhabitants should now begin to be clear. It must be strongly stressed that in this vocabulary the word *family* does not denote a complete coresident domestic group, though it may appear as an abbreviated title. The word *household* particularly indicates the fact of shared location, kinship and activity. Hence all solitaries have to be taken to be households, for they are living with themselves, and this is the case when they have servants with them, since servants are taken as household members. In fact because servants always modify the membership of households, we allot all domestic groups to one of two classes, those with

[45]   The definition which seems to correspond most closely to the one assumed here to be in the heads of persons making out lists of inhabitants in pre-census times is that quoted by Etienne Hélin in Chapter 13 from the Belgian Census of 1947 which reads in French: 'Ménage: unité simple ou collective, constituée soit par une personne vivant seule, soit par la réunion de deux ou plusieurs personnes qui, unies ou non par des liens de famille, résident habituellement dans une même habitation et y ont une vie commune.' Nevertheless it must not be assumed that once national censuses are available, problems of deciding who was and who was not a member of a family or household are no longer troublesome. Definitions change so often from census to census in the same country, and census-takers in the past were sometimes so inefficient, that all statements about differences between the sizes of household at succeeding census dates have to be made with caution; see Chapter 4 and the articles on which it is based. The Population Division of the United Nations defines the household much more laconically as 'a socio-economic unit of coresidents'. See Kono (typescript).

and those without servants. Nevertheless servants can hardly be said to affect the final structure of households, and when it comes to the more significant types of domestic groups, the form of description is by the title of the composition of the family in question, followed by the word household. Hence the descriptions 'simple family household', 'extended family household', 'multiple family household'. These terms require a little discussion.

The expression *simple family* is used to cover what is variously described as the *nuclear family*, the *elementary family* or (not very logically, since spouses are not physiologically connected), the *biological family*. It consists of a married couple, or a married couple with offspring, or of a widowed person with offspring. The concept is of the conjugal link as the structural principle, and conjugal linkage is nearly always patent in the lists of persons which we are using. For a simple family to appear then, it is necessary for at least two individuals connected by that link or arising from that link to be coresident: *conjugal family unit* (CFU) is a preciser term employed to describe all possible groups so structured.

No solitary can form a conjugal family unit and for such a group to subsist it is necessary for at least two immediate partners (spouses and/or offspring) to be present. More remotely connected persons, whose existence implies more than one conjugal link, do not constitute a conjugal family unit if they reside together with no one else except servants. Nor do brothers and sisters. Hence a widow with a child forms a conjugal family unit, but a widow with a grandchild does not, nor does an aunt with a nephew. Whenever a conjugal family unit is found on its own, it is always taken to be a household, just as solitaries are, and such a coresident domestic group is called a *simple family household*. The first mentioned person in the household of this and all other types is always taken to be head, and simple family households are classified along with the rest as with or without servants. It will be shown that simple family households with or without servants are the commonest form of coresident domestic group in practically all the communities referred to in this study, and that the most frequent of such simple family households is the one which consists in its entirety of man, wife and children, the 'nuclear family' in fact.

An *extended family household* in our nomenclature consists in a conjugal family unit with the addition of one or more relatives other than offspring, the whole group living together on its own or with servants. It is thus identical with the simple family household except for the additional item or items. If the resident relative is of a generation earlier than that of the conjugal family unit, say, a married head's father or a spouse's mother, or a widowed head's aunt, then the extension is said to be upwards. The headship of the household is irrelevant here. The resident relative may be head, or the child of the resident relative may be in that position.*

Similarly the presence of a grandchild (without either parent) or a nephew or niece creates downward extension, and that of a brother, sister or cousin of the

* This definition has been altered in this edition, since it was in error in the first printing.

head or of his spouse, implies sideways or lateral extension. Some groups are extended vertically and laterally, and it should be noted that the presence of any kin or affine of the conjugal family unit creates extension however distant the relationship, though the relatives of a servant do not do so. It is particularly important that the whole phrase 'extended family household' be used for this category of domestic group, because the words 'extended family' by themselves have a highly significant but quite separate further meaning, which covers all relatives in habitual contact with a person, irrespective of whether they live with him.

Multiple family households comprise all forms of domestic group which include two or more conjugal family units connected by kinship or by marriage. Such units can be simple or extended, and can be disposed vertically and laterally. The disposition of a secondary unit, that is of a constituent unit which does not contain the head of the whole household, is said to be UP if its conjugal link involves a generation earlier than that of the head, as for example when his father and mother live with him. Such a secondary unit can include offspring of the head's parents other than the head himself, that is his resident unmarried brothers or sisters, and the presence of such persons keeps this secondary unit in being if one or other of the head's parents dies. A secondary unit is disposed DOWN if, for example, a head's married son lives with him along with his wife and perhaps offspring, with similar implications about siblings and widowhood. Though more than one secondary conjugal family unit rarely occurs in the data used in this volume within a multiple family household, these principles are intended to apply to any number. Unless there is specific contrary indication, servants are regarded as attached to the simple, extended or multiple family household as a whole, and not to any individual or to any conjugal family unit within it.

If conjugal family units within households of the multiple kind are all disposed laterally, as when married brothers and/or sisters live together, the overall arrangement is the one often referred to as the 'fraternal joint family' by social anthropologists. The expression 'joint family' is also widely used, however, to refer to all the forms of multiple family household defined here. In our classificatory system laterally conjoined conjugal family units can be of two types; those with and those without a parent of the coresident married siblings.

If a parent is present, and it has to be a widowed parent since both would create a further unit of their own, then the arrangement is the lateral equivalent of the vertical dispositions just described. If no parent or other member of an earlier generation is present, and the siblings are connected entirely through the filial linkage of each to a conjugal unit no longer represented in the household, then the arrangement is given the title *frérèche*, adopted from the French.

We have already seen how in fourteenth-century France, frérèches could be founded by *affrairement*, and the evidence from Corsica in 1770 presented by Jacques Dupâquier in Chapter 11, with that from the area of Florence in Italy in 1527 presented by Christiane Klapisch in Chapter 10, suggests that the frérèche may have been a distinguishing feature of the familial structure of southerly Europe for many centuries. Dupâquier goes so far as to claim that it was a Corsican custom for quite young children bereft of both parents to continue to live together under the care of the neighbouring households, forming a frérèche of a simpler kind. He insists that this arrangement, which reads very strangely to an Englishman, continued until the age of marriage, and that this form of Corsican frérèche was not regarded by its members as a permanent familial institution.

Classificatory table

It can be seen that the analysis of the structure of coresident domestic groups can get very complex, especially when it comes to differing forms of multiple family household. The various types which we have found it necessary to distinguish and define in order to arrive at a scheme making it possible to use lists of inhabitants and to compare the familial structure of different communities at different times are set out in the following table. Perhaps they may make the tediously repetitive phraseology which we have used so far a little easier to follow.

Table 1.1 *Structure of households: categories and classes*

Category	Class
1 Solitaries	(a) Widowed
	(b) Single, or of unknown marital status
2 No family	(a) Coresident siblings
	(b) Coresident relatives of other kinds
	(c) Persons not evidently related
3 Simple family households	(a) Married couples alone
	(b) Married couples with child(ren)
	(c) Widowers with child(ren)
	(d) Widows with child(ren)
4 Extended family households	(a) Extended upwards
	(b) Extended downwards
	(c) Extended laterally
	(d) Combinations of 4a – 4c
5 Multiple family households	(a) Secondary unit(s) UP
	(b) Secondary unit(s) DOWN
	(c) Units all on one level
	(d) *Frérèches*
	(e) Other multiple families
6 Indeterminate	
'Stem families'	$\begin{cases} 5b \\ 5b + 5a \\ 5b + 5a + 4a \end{cases}$
Frérèches, alternative definitions	$\begin{cases} 5d \\ 5d + 5c \\ 5d + 5c + 4c \\ 5d + 5c + 4c + 2a \end{cases}$

In using this table for the actual classification and comparison of domestic groups, each category is divided into the class of those with servants and of those without servants.[46] The extra lines in Table 1.1 devoted to stem families and to frérèches are intended to enable all possible forms of these two types of domestic group to be recovered from the data. The various definitions of the frérèches should be obvious, but it may be useful to dwell a little on the possibilities presented for the stem family. This will give us the opportunity of showing how the scheme provides for change over time, or rather of how a domestic group might appear in the various categories of the table as that group passed through the developmental cycle.[47]

Problems presented by the developmental cycle

In any one list of inhabitants a stem family may appear as belonging to any one of the categories specified at the foot of Table 1.1. and to find the potential number of such groups in the community it may be thought necessary to add the households in these three classes together. When such a group appears under 5a, it is presumably supposed that the married successor is already head of the household with the conjugal family unit of his predecessor in the secondary position UP. The category 5b covers the case where the intended heir is himself still in the secondary position DOWN. It should be noticed that a group of type 5b turns into one of type 5a at such time as its head hands over to his successor, provided that the retiring couple continues to reside. If, of course, one of the parents had died during the period when the married heir was waiting to succeed, and there were no other child of those parents present to maintain the conjugal family unit of the surviving spouse of the older generation, then the household would change from multiple to extended, and be classed 4a. Only after the final disappearance of the surviving parent, and the departure of any siblings of the new head who still resided, would such a household become simple in its structure and almost certainly belong to class 3b. It would remain there until the next married· successor was introduced into the group, and its character as a stem family once more manifested itself. The developmental cycle could then be said to be complete.

It is impossible, in reality, to follow any particular domestic group throughout its developmental cycle from the evidence of only one listing of inhabitants of the community to which it belonged. The example of the stem family, intricate as it is, serves to demonstrate how difficult it is to establish from material of this kind the presence in any community of such a continuing institution. Something can be learnt of course from comparing groups which appear to have been at different stages of development at the time when the list was written out, and if the list is long such information may be appreciable. But it will be of very

---

[46] See Table 1.15 at the end of this chapter for an illustration.
[47] The classic exposition of this process is found in Goody, *The developmental cycle in domestic groups* (1958 i, 1966).

limited use except in those cases, so rare in our own country, where ages are given, and the help available from ancillary documents such as parish registers is unlikely to go very far. The establishment of the case for the existence of the stem family system at Heidenreichstein is an excellent example of what can be done when such documentation is exceptionally good, and the single available listing contains ages.

But in most cases only somewhat insecure inference is possible as to the point in the cycle reached by any particular domestic group at the time of the listing, with some implications about its probable past and possible future. It should be clear that in order to demonstrate conclusively the presence of any form of family household as an ongoing feature of the structure of a community, a country or a cultural area, many observations would be required over an extended period. To carry out the task which Murdock undertook for the contemporary world by assigning forms of the family to particular cultures in the past it would be necessary for an observer to possess a whole series of successive accounts of large numbers of households, the same households or patrilines, over many years.

It may be that this challenging undertaking would be helped by an even more complex terminology and classificatory system than those we have adopted.[48] But however intricate such a system became, it could not, I think, go much further than we have tried to do in allowing for the vaguenesses and inconsistencies of lists of inhabitants. The fact is that the evidence itself is poorly adapted for the recovery of the process of development and change in domestic groups.

There are occasions, even in Europe, when repeated listings of inhabitants took place, and when the documents survived to be used by the researcher.[49] In such an event the successive pictures of familial and community structure can

---

[48] The system of classification of coresident domestic groups developed for the purposes of this volume owes much to the only previous proposal of the kind, the one suggested in 1967 by Louis Henry. See Henry, *Manuel de démographie historique* (1967 i): Ch. II, *Exploitation des listes nominatives*, especially the section headed *Les ménages*: 44–6. Henry also looks on the conjugal bond as the structural principle, but he calls the conjugal family unit by the French name *noyau*, meaning kernel. This is an attractive usage which we shall occasionally have recourse to here, but Henry's method of classification is not by familial units, but by their heads. Thus the crucial distinction between simple or extended households on the one hand, and multiple or joint households on the other hand, depends on whether or not the whole domestic group contains more than one family head, *chef de famille*. The difference would be of little importance but for the fact that Henry classifies a widowed person coming first in the list of names for a household, that is the *household* head, as constituting a *family* head, whether or not there are accompanying children, and therefore as creating a multiple household where in our system there would simply be an upwardly extended one. Widowed persons coming later in a household are taken by Henry as dependent, and so not as constituting heads of families. This difference must be borne in mind when reading the contributions printed here from the Continent of Europe, where Henry's system has been in use.

[49] See references in Chapter 4, p. 128, footnote. Since this was written it has become clear that many such series of successive listings exist in the form of *libri status animarum* for the villages of Italy, at least in Tuscany.

be strung together so as to reveal process and change, and in the case of Japan it would seem that this is almost the standard situation for the Tokugawa era. But a collection of such individual listings is a collection of still photographs, and they cannot be used as if they were movie strips. The very drawback to the scheme we have adopted serves to bring out a general limitation on our analytic enterprise. We find ourselves for the most part forced to discuss a process as if it were in fact a state.

3   DOMESTIC GROUPS AND LIVING SPACES

We have dwelt until now with the internal, familial relationships of persons within the domestic group, rather than with its boundaries and external relationships, and we still have to consider groups with no familial structure and persons within domestic groups who have no familial connection with other persons. Non-familial groups, that is to say dwellers in institutions for the most part, appear along with households in lists of inhabitants, sometimes, unfortunately, not distinguished from them by the list-makers. Decisions have to be made about these issues before we can proceed to define mean household size itself with any approach to exactness. The simplest form of that ratio, numbers of persons in a list divided by numbers of blocks of persons, makes only rough comparison possible.

It seems best to leave the details of the different possible measures of mean household size until Chapter 4, where we have the English data before us, and to content ourselves here with principles as to the relationship of domestic groups to the spaces which they occupy, for it is this relationship which is at issue. We may approach it by glancing at the first two categories of Table 1.1, groups marked *No family* and *Solitaries*.

The household and its dwelling; inmates, lodgers and lodging

Solitaries have already been declared not to constitute conjugal family units, though they are assumed to be households. This is not because of the familial structure of their domestic groups, for they possess no structure, but because of a judgement made on a rather different criterion, that is their dwellings. Since the list-maker indicated that a person living on his own formed no part of any other group, he is taken to have implied that the demarcated space occupied by that person had no other inhabitant except possibly servants. We have found it useful to reserve the word *dwelling* for this living space, and to give it a quasi-technical meaning, certainly a restrictive one, denoting the bounded area reserved to one household. Such a *dwelling* would usually have filled out the total volume contained within the four walls of a free-standing house, even in the case of a solitary, at least in England and in the English countryside; the indications are that this was true of other areas as well. But such a dwelling could have been an apartment within a house or other building containing other apartments, or also used for different purposes.

At this point, questions such as the following arise. If a solitary, or any other householder, should take in a lodger or lodgers, are such lodgers to be regarded as members of his household? If not, and the very word *lodger* seems to imply that no other connection at most than the sharing of a dwelling should be inferred, then what assumption is to be made about the structure and status of a domestic group composed of landlords and lodgers? How is the relationship between households sharing a building to be defined?

The inference about what is being shared in the case of lodgers perhaps might have had to be different if the word *boarder* or *visitor* or the obsolete English description 'sojourner' had appeared instead of lodger. But the variations of meaning between these expressions is exceedingly difficult to gauge from lists of inhabitants, even if other evidence is present to fill out the picture. We have found from experience that most of the complications about the exact structure of the domestic group, at least in Europe, arise from the occasional presence of persons in this variegated class of those casually rather than permanently connected with households. This seems to have been recognised at the very outset of the study by Gregory King, who used the word *inmates* for all these persons, as we shall do. Many of the persons living in domestic groups in the second category of Table 1.1, those lacking familial structure, must have been related to each other in a similar way, though brothers and sisters living together, and more distant relatives too, may have formed more stable domestic groups than those consisting entirely of persons who can be regarded as 'inmates' in respect of each other. It is evident that a concept is needed to cover the relationship between such people, and between them and the conjugal family unit or household with which they were connected. It is evident too that such a concept must be of a neutral, or even of a suspensive character.

For although the use of a word such as lodger may indicate that the connection is not of the kind which we recognise as obtaining within a conjugal family unit or within a household, it does not seem justifiable to assume that such a connection can always and necessarily be excluded. It might turn out, if we got to know more, that some lodgers were in fact relatives paying rent; or some boarders, relatives paying board and lodging; or some visitors, much more permanent than is usually conveyed by the word.

There are scattered hints in the English evidence that very close relatives, even sons or daughters living at home after marriage, or aged parents resident with their children, could sometimes be regarded as inmates.[50] This might be said to call into question the very possibility of extended or multiple households in

---

[50] See Richard Wall in Chapter 5, p. 166, referring to Corfe Castle in 1790, etc. In the national Census of 1851 the household of John Allton, a labourer at Chilvers Coton in Warwickshire, consists of himself, his wife, 'Richard Coton, son-in-law, married, lodger, Millicent Coton [i.e. John Allton's daughter], married, lodger', another daughter 'Harriet Evans, married, lodger' and two grandchildren. In the same Census, at Ardleigh in Essex, 'Richard Mellor, father, lodger, receiving parish relief' is recorded in the household of his son, John Mellor.

our country, for it is exactly these persons whose presence in the domestic group is taken here to create such households in virtue of their *familial*, never their *economic* connection with the household head.

Although such examples seem to be rare, and the uncertainties they create must not be exaggerated, it is obviously desirable that our terminology and classificatory system should not obliterate them. This is also true of the indefiniteness which sometimes seems to mark the relations between households occupying dwellings located in the same building. Such contiguity might possibly conceal the existence of complex familial relationships interconnecting these households which is not apparent from the descriptions given, nor inferable from the sharing of surnames and so on.

The houseful and its premises; multiple occupation

The neutral or suspensive term which we have adopted to allow for such possibilities is the word *houseful*. A houseful means all persons inhabiting the same set of premises, and *premises* is another word we have found useful to endow with a restrictive usage for our purposes. Premises in our system denotes the accommodation provided by a building, or in certain cases of a number of conjoined or contiguous buildings, say in the case of Western Europe a farmhouse with a yard surrounded with outhouses which can be made suitable for occupation by people, or in the case of Africa, the complex of hutments described by Jack Goody in Chapter 3. A dwelling, as we have seen, is the arena occupied by a household, premises the arena occupied by a houseful, and a houseful (with the possible extensions just noticed) is the crew of a single building.

Let us consider the situation of a number of households within the same set of premises a little more closely. Where such groups can be assumed to be distinct from each other, then no question can arise of a degree of complication in the domestic groups present greater than is to be found within any one of them. But since there is a sense in which all persons resident in one place, in the same building, satisfy the first and really crucial criterion we are employing for the analysis of the domestic group, that of common location, it seems imperative that the possibility of some relationship between them should never be entirely excluded. Such a relationship could subsist between such groups in the same building in respect of any bond of kinship connecting any of their individual members.

In the industrialising town of Preston in 1851, for example, Michael Anderson finds that a fifth of all households sharing premises were related to each other, and perhaps a half in the surrounding countryside (in Chapter 7, p. 218 below), but it is very difficult to trace such linkages in pre-census data. Some lists of inhabitants do, like the Census of 1851, mark houseful divisions as well as household divisions, but none specify the kin relationships within housefuls. Unfortunately the present techniques of historical demography cannot be used to determine any but a very few such relationships existing in any community.

Hence, although the shape of housefuls – when and where distinct from households – is so rarely indicated there is always a possibility that these larger units themselves constituted some sort of extended family associations.

It so happens that one of the lists analysed in this volume is set out in housefuls, in such a way as makes it just possible by the use of kinship terminology and so on to infer, though with considerable uncertainty, what the household divisions were within such housefuls as had more than one household within them. This is the outstandingly important listing of the Orthodox Christian inhabitants of the city of Belgrade in 1733–4, whose housefuls are anatomised at length in Chapter 15 by Laslett and Clarke. Comparing this analysis with the columns for Belgrade in the twelve tables at the end of this chapter, where in some cases presumed household divisions and not the houseful divisions are used, should make the distinction between the two types of domestic group quite plain. Further comparison with the data considered by Etienne Hélin in Chapter 13 brings out the importance of the term houseful being left open ended in the way which is recommended.

In the cité at Liège in 1801, Hélin tells us, there were 200 houses containing five *ménages* and more. Now these seem almost certainly to have been blocks of flats, or apartment houses, where no relationships of a familial kind should be supposed to exist between any two ménages in the same house. But it is conceivable that one or other of these crews of buildings did in fact form a multiple household of five conjugal family units, or arranged in some other way. At Belgrade, on the other hand, the words of the document and Serbian kinship terminology go to show that 39 of the larger collections of persons living in each *Dom*, or house, were indeed multiple family households, or *zadrugas* as they have come to be called for this society. They have been taken to be such here, but we cannot exclude the possibility that other groups marshalled under the dom headings were also zadrugas, though not described in such a way as to enable us to recognise them.

Both at Liège and at Belgrade, therefore, there is a chance that the structure of the household was more complex than the documents make apparent, a very low probability for Liège but not so low for Belgrade, and affecting in each the really large and intricate domestic groups, the interesting ones in fact. Hence the usefulness of the suspensive term houseful for these places. These facts should serve to show once more how little the historical observer can tell about relationships between household units, and this is particularly so in questions of accommodation. We do not know whether members of the households found adjacent to each other in these two cities had chosen to be neighbours in the same premises for reasons of kinship, or whether they were in company only by chance. We know little in general about the effects of buildings on the structure of domestic groups.

Dwelling and *premises* seem to have had less effect on household formation, in England at least, than might be expected. Our ancestors appear to have blocked up doorways, divided rooms, added slipes and attic storeys to their cottages, and to have torn them all down again just as occasion demanded.[51] If it was the pressure on them of the culture pattern which impelled them to act in this way rather than to form multiple family households, or which induced them to postpone marriage so as to create family groups requiring separate living spaces only when these were available, then they were acting in accordance with a quite distinctive norm of behaviour.

It contrasts sharply with the norms observed by their Serbian or Japanese contemporaries, even though Joel Halpern in Chapter 16 goes far to modify the belief that all Serbs ordinarily lived in large scale zadrugas, and even though Chie Nakane in Chapter 19 is so sceptical about the joint household being part of the traditional Japanese familial system, or of what she calls the 'sociological ideology' of that country. Niggling and baffling as issues of definition and of terminology may seem when first encountered, they are crucial if such general social structural differences are to be established with clarity, or their extent estimated with accuracy.

The application of the concepts we are describing to the placing of inmates is quite straightforward. Inmates are thought of as being members of the same houseful as the one in which the household to which they are connected is to be found, and as having no other relationship with their landlords, or hosts. Similarly households and members of households found in the same building are also thought of as connected only by common membership (too strong a word, perhaps) of the same houseful, and this is true whatever the structure of the individual households. Although the idea of the houseful is suggested when multiple occupation is in question, that is when plural dwellings are physically distinct from the whole set of premises, it must be recognised that the houseful can still be said to exist when there is only one household and so only one dwelling. If this one household had an inmate, we should regard the dwelling it occupied as distinct from the premises. This is because an inmate is taken to share the premises, being a member of the houseful, but not necessarily the dwelling of the household concerned, since he is not a member of the household of his landlord or host. Physical space is treated in fact in a similar way to group membership, though not all differences of membership involve questions of physical space. Servants and resident relatives other than children are outside the conjugal family unit, but because (unlike inmates) they are within the household, they share the dwelling.

Inmates and shared premises can be handled in this way so as to provide the suspended judgement, the degree of inconclusiveness, of open endedness, which

[51] A slipe was the space added by building an extension in such a way that the sloping roof could be extended to cover it. The process of subdivision and recombining of family premises within buildings can be particularly closely observed in listings for the village of Puddletown in Dorset, where the exact disposition of dwellings is recorded in 1724 and again in 1769. Compare Wall, below, Chapter 5, pp. 198–199 for the possibility that shortage of accommodation did prevent the creation of households in England in the later eighteenth century.

has been shown to be necessary. But this is bound to cause some incoherence in a system which could not be entirely complete or consistent under any circumstances because of the nature of the data. Indeed it leaves inmates themselves in an equivocal position, not inappropriately perhaps, and this especially when they are found in a building of multiple occupation. Here they share the premises not only with their landlords, or hosts, but also with all other members of the houseful, and their attachment to a particular household is not specified. Conjugal family units dwelling as inmates are not here regarded as properly speaking households at all, as will be seen, nor their heads as household heads on a level with others.[52] This may seem strange, but it leads in our experience to no confusion.

Mean household size

The slight complications which can arise in connection with this apparently straightforward ratio are due to inmates and institutions. If numbers of persons in a list are divided by blocks of persons, then the result, which is called ratio 1 in Chapter 4 (see below, p. 133), only measures MHS under given circumstances. This is where there are no people living in institutions in the community, and no inmates. If such persons are present but not so described or not allowed for, then ratio 1 is too high and misrepresents the pattern of coresidence to some extent. Stricter analysis requires that ratio 4 be worked out if possible, that is total of persons less those in institutions and individual inmates, since neither class can be said to live in households. Where the data do not permit this then ratio 5, which disregards all inmates including inmate households, as well as institutions, may be used, or at least ratio 2, which is net of institutions only. Nevertheless only in exceptional circumstances does it turn out that these differing ratios make much difference to the figure for the mean size of the domestic group.[53] This is shown to be the case for the large English sample analysed in Chapter 4 (see below, p. 133) and with the exception of Belgrade would be true I believe of all the other sets of data discussed in this volume.

Nevertheless, in view of these facts about the reckoning of mean household size, it seems best to assume that where institutions and inmates are not mentioned by the writer of any study of this subject he must be taken to mean ratio 1, crude mean size of domestic group. It should be noticed that this largest and least informative measure does not correspond to mean size of houseful. This measure is only available where blocks of persons, that is households, are ranged

[52] Lodging craftsmen in England, or at least in London, were not regarded as 'inhabitants', and not allowed apprentices. See George, *London life in the 18th century* (1925, 1965), especially Ch. 5, which contains much of interest and importance on the sharing of premises and the equivocal position of inmates. Conjugal family units in the position of inmates are called *groups* in our terminology.

[53] These happen to occur in the case of Belgrade, where ratio 1 is 7.14 (see Chapter 15) and ratio 5 is 5.46 (see Table 1.6 at the end of this chapter; this definition of household is also used in Tables 1.7, 1.9 and 1.10, but an approximation to ratio 4 elsewhere). All the ratios are numbered and defined in Table 4.2, see p. 133 below.

into larger groups representing all the dwellers in a set of premises, as in the case of Belgrade, or Liège or the 1851 Census. If these larger groups alone are marked in the list, then it does not constitute a representation of households and so should in strictness not be used for the analysis of the size and structure of the domestic group.

We are still not at the end of the ratios which are sometimes useful in reckoning mean household size for investigatory purposes. There is mean experienced household size, or M(E)HS, which was introduced into the discussion by Joel Halpern; this looks at the household from the point of view of the individual rather than of the domestic group. It is an attempt at a single measure of all the answers which would be given if every member of a community were asked, what size of household do you live in?[54] Yet a further measure is mean size of household if groups of size 1 and 2 are excluded together with servants, on the grounds that persons in both of these classes can scarcely enter into any reckoning to do with extension and multiplicity in the domestic group. This figure can be used when size of household is being correlated with degree of complication in households (see below, p. 54).

But although it is desirable that these points be taken into consideration in respect of mean household size in their appropriate places, it would be wrong to allow them to obscure what seems to me to be the essentially straightforward character of comparing household structure over time and place. At Belgrade in 1733–4, it is true, it seems that every possible combination of unlikely events in fact occurred. Some of the family groups lodging there had servants of their own: there were extended lodging groups, and even multiple lodging groups; the housefuls were sometimes marvellously complex, sometimes perplexing in their simplicity, as when they consisted simply in a bunch of 'strangers'. But domestic groups we have surveyed were usually very much less complicated, at least in the English past, where they have so far been studied more than elsewhere. It seems to me that no model of the domestic group useful for comparative purposes could ever have been worked out from the simplicities of English listings alone, and the usefulness of Belgrade is above all in that it does provide guidance for working out a set of principles which will be reasonably systematic and take care of exceptional occurrences. In England and elsewhere in Northern and Western Europe the standard situation was one where each domestic group consisted of a simple family living in its own house, so that the conjugal family unit was identical with household and with houseful, and where dwelling was coterminous with premises. It must not be forgotten that in spite of the important differences which comparison reveals, the burden of the present volume is that this standard situation seems to have obtained to a remarkable extent everywhere else.

[54] See below, p. 54 and Chapter 16, p. 409. The ratio is reckoned by multiplying by the size category the total numbers living in each size category of household, adding these results together and dividing by the total population.

4 AN IDEOGRAPHIC NOTATION FOR DOMESTIC GROUPS

To describe, therefore, what is normally found in England and in English history as the standard situation for international and inter-temporal comparison is to be partial. But comparison has to begin somewhere, and the circumstances which led to this particular point of departure will shortly be described. The patient reader, if he has been willing to make his way through this long series of tedious descriptions, now has before him the whole set of categories and classes, conventions and nomenclature, which has been found necessary in order to make a start in the analysis of the structure of coresident domestic groups from historical documents taking the form of lists of inhabitants, with occasional prompting from evidence of other kinds.

Fig. 1.1 Ideographs representing domestic group structures

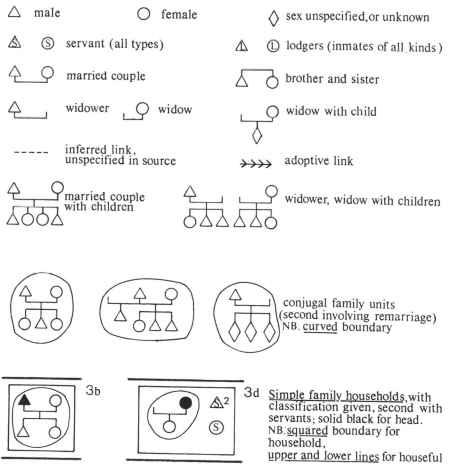

 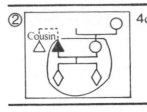

4a 4d Extended family households

① Extension upwards.

② Extension upwards and laterally.

③ Extension downwards with servant and lodgers.

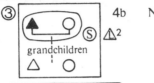

3 4b

grandchildren

NB. Where source names relative(s) etc, and linkage cannot be fully specified, word describing relevant person(s) is reproduced and inferred linkage indicated.

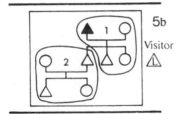

5b

Visitor

Multiple family household

secondary unit DOWN, units numbered (secondaries all after 1), with lodger (inmate) specified in source as visitor.

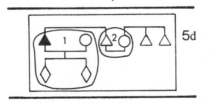

5d

Frérèche

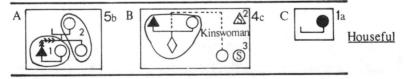

A 5b B 4c C 1a

Kinswoman

Houseful

A. Multiple family household, secondary unit UP, with adoptive link.

B. Laterally extended family household, with 2 male and 3 female servants. Note that resident kinswoman not specified as to which spouse she is related to is shown as attached to conjugal link.   C. Solitary widow.

Advantages of pictorial representation

The attempt has been to convey the system in its essentials, though not in detail, by prose explanation only. The reader must have been aware, however, that the use of diagrams might have made what was meant much clearer. Indeed whilst preparing the contributions to this book for publication the editor found himself forced to adopt a method of drawing pictures of the membership and structure of domestic groups as well as a classificatory model for relating and contrasting them one with another. Whenever any point of obscurity arises in the discussion of such organisations, the impulse to make them into pictures has become almost irresistible. The series of figures attached to Chapters 8 and 19, Biraben on Montplaisant and Nakane on Nishinomiya Hama-issai-chō, are examples of sets of diagrams recording in this pictorial form the relevant features of the composition of all domestic groups at those two places as they have been recovered from the lists of inhabitants which survive for them.[55]

These diagrams, it must be noticed, do more than simply record who was present within each block of names, with some of the detail provided for each person. They also present the decisions which have been made about how that evidence has been interpreted. They can be used, that is, not only to draw up any of the various types of analysis which have been carried out by contributors to this volume, but also to get back to the original data and, if the researcher feels disposed, to make different decisions about household composition. The use of ideographs in this way has also been found to make for greater precision of definition and greater conceptual insight in constructing the model of analysis. It is hoped that directly the reader glances at any of these cameos it will be immediately apparent to him what is being represented, and that he will perceive the structure much more quickly and decisively than is possible from any piece of writing. He should be able to do this whatever his linguistic background.

The ideographic system adopted was devised by Eugene Hammel as an extension of that already in use by social anthropologists, with certain additions and modifications made by the editor, particularly in respect of the drawing of boundaries round the various units. A full description of its resources and uses is being separately published by these two authors. Only enough is set out here to confirm what should, I trust, be intuitively clear in the diagrams, and to give examples of the pictures for the more important domestic group structures.

It will be noticed that the more complicated, and to the Western European, more unusual family structures are not represented in the pictures, those based on polygyny for example. Some plain language elements have also been retained where portrayal of the relationship in question would have required the insertion, perhaps as deleted, perhaps as dotted figures, of individuals not actually recorded in the list of inhabitants. The insistence has been on the delineation of

---

[55] On the use of the ideographic system to record the data presented by Chie Nakane, see note on p. 543 below.

those persons and only those persons whom the list-maker himself sets down. Nevertheless, no provision is made in the illustrations for ages (simply inserted in digits above the individual) and none appear in the ideographs appended to Chapter 19, though available for Nishinomiya. In the forthcoming fuller account of the whole system of classification and representation by Hammel and Laslett, provisional title *Comparing household structure over time and between cultures*, alternative ways of putting down a greater range of linkages and family forms will be provided. Conventions will be suggested which will make all plain language unnecessary, which is important if the cameos are to be used for record and for universal, international use, and one of them will allow of dotted figures. There is no intention of laying down the suggested code as authoritative, and it is expected that the whole system, ideographical and classificatory, will remain fluid for some time. But a standardised code of this kind is clearly necessary for comparative purposes, and it is hoped that one will soon be adopted.

Spurious incisiveness

In making this further and pictorial attempt at clarity and definiteness, it is to be hoped that no atmosphere of what might be called spurious incisiveness has been created. Perhaps it would be well to insist once more that only a series of recommendations of interpretive method have been made here, and no attempt at an inclusive theory of domestic group organisation.

The reader will be expected to make use of what he wishes, and to reject, modify or elaborate, as it suits him. The contributors to this volume were not aware of what the system would be when their contributions were composed, and no attempt has been made to impose its principles upon their analyses, though some revision of vocabulary has been carried out editorially, so as to avoid needless inconsistency.[56] The difficulty in the way of developing and modifying the system for general international comparisons over time and place may well turn out to be its origin in Western Europe and in England. Its definiteness perhaps arises because of the relatively simple and clear cut arrangements which are now believed to have been characteristic of Western Europe and of England particularly for the last ten generations, and it may be for many more than that. The desire to see the English family in contrast with the family in other areas outside the small region originally occupied by all the English speaking peoples led to the assembling of the studies now appearing together in this volume.

We must now turn our attention to the first substantive results of the numerical comparison of the size and structure of the domestic group at various periods in our chosen cultural regions.

[56] A special note has been made at the appropriate point in the text where it is thought that words such as household and family have been used in ways differing from those described above. These differences must be taken into account before comparisons are made between information in separate parts of the volume. This issue arises most often in the chapters relating to the United States and their colonial predecessors, especially in that of Philip Greven.

III. NUMERICAL COMPARISONS BETWEEN FIVE AREAS

It will be a long time before the historical study of the family is in a position to take any wide range of the world's peoples into account, or to rival in any way the recordings and comparisons which have been made for familial forms all over the globe as they exist in the late twentieth century. The past of only those societies with written records can ever be taken into the analysis, and even amongst them quite stringent conditions must be satisfied. The most important is that at points appreciably distant from the present there should have existed individuals with the motive and the capacity to record at least the name, sex, marital status, and position within the household of members of complete communities and, if only occasionally, age, calling, and so on.[57] Next comes the condition that such recordings should have survived to our day, to be discovered and worked on by the historical sociologist.

There are no doubt advantages to a position in which only a handful of international and intercultural comparisons can yet be made; at least we are spared the confusion of having too many instances and too much contradiction. With so little to go on in a gigantic field, we are perpetually aware of the danger of reading the whole for the part. It is nevertheless quite possible that the five cultural areas which have been selected for this first comparative exercise may be sadly unrepresentative. England, France and parts of Western Europe, Serbia, Japan and the United States are all important societies in terms of population – though Serbia least so – and politically and culturally they carry together considerable weight. But it must not be forgotten that almost no mention is made in this volume of the world's two largest societies, India and China, that Africa is represented by the examples chosen to illustrate one study only, and that the spread of cultural variation is extremely restricted. The famous *mir*, the Russian village community, is not even mentioned. The reasons why these particular areas were chosen can be stated quite simply.

The relatively small average size and uncomplicated structure of the domestic group in England in the past had become evident at Cambridge by the late 1960s. What was wanted was a comparative framework in which to judge this discovery, if discovery it can be called. It was essential to know if England's near neighbours shared the same familial characteristics. Hence the importance of comparing it with the situation during the history of France, a country with plentiful and well worked demographic records. It was further desirable to find an instance within close cultural distance of an area where households were known to have been large and complex in the past, which accounts for the choice

[57] It is sometimes possible, given enough general knowledge of a society and sufficient ingenuity, to reconstruct such listings from male names and descriptions only, and E. A. Hammel provides an outstanding example of such an achievement in Chapter 14. It seems dubious however if this could have been done unless other and more complete historical and ethnographic documents had also survived, if only from later periods.

of Serbia and the zadruga, also exceptionally well documented. It was obviously advantageous also to include a society of an entirely non-European character, especially if its familial characteristics were very different from the English and if its records were good. Japan met those requirements quite admirably. The choice of the United States needs no justification. A word or two of explanation may be needed, however, as to why it was England that was the starting point and why England may become the touchstone for future comparisons.

1 INVESTIGATION OF THE HISTORY OF THE DOMESTIC GROUP IN ENGLAND

Since 1964 every discoverable English list of inhabitants which gives evidence of being complete has been copied and analysed at Cambridge.[58] The original impetus came both from an interest in the history of population, and also from a desire to find out how the liberal political theory which emerged in seventeenth-century England was related both with the political theory which it replaced and with the actual structure of the society which gave it birth. Almost the first familial/historical questions asked, therefore, were about the outlook of that same political writer, Sir Robert Filmer, whose attitudes have been shown to be somewhat misleading as a guide to what literally existed amongst English domestic groups in his society in his lifetime. But there had been a number of previous attempts to recover at least some of the facts of the case, for as we have said, the study of the mean dimensions, if not of the composition, of the household in European history was already a recognised scholarly pursuit by 1955 (see above, p. 3).

The purpose of these earlier researches, however, seems to have been rather narrow and specific; in England they were mostly confined to the medieval period. They were directed towards the establishment of a multiplier, a figure which would make it possible to proceed from a knowledge of the number of households to the total population. This ratio, it was hoped, would enable demographic historians to use a whole class of records, mostly rental and fiscal documents, in order to estimate population sizes, and so the amount and direction of population change. The actual structure of the families and households, of the community in general, was relevant for the most part only in so far as it affected accurate determination of the multiplier, and no recording revealing household composition was available for the English Middle Ages, that is to say no complete and detailed listing of inhabitants.

We therefore find J. C. Russell, the historian of medieval English population, using a famous document of 1517 concerning the enclosure of land to show that

---

[58] For the file of listings of inhabitants instituted by the Cambridge Group for the History of Population and Social Structure in 1964, see Chapter 4 and Laslett, *The World we have lost*, 2nd edn (1971): *General Note*, with its references.

'an average of 3.5 to a house would not be far wrong'. This was in the year 1948, and the figure he gave was for what we should call a houseful. But when he repeated the statement in 1958 he insisted that what was meant was the conjugal family unit, 'the man-wife-children group'. A mean size of 3.5 for the domestic group, however defined, was scarcely compatible with any traditional sentiment in favour of the large and complex peasant household. Russell's persistent advocacy of this small multiplier, not for England only but for all medieval European society, has come under criticism for other reasons, historical and documentary. Nevertheless in 1962 he was still proclaiming that 'an average of 3.5 is what might be expected of a society in which the elderly and unmarried live for the most part separately in cottages'.[59]

Demonstration of small size and simple composition

This last statement shows how the issues we have had to survey here, issues of location and kinship, household and dwelling, houseful and premises, even stem family proclivities, were implied even when only a multiplier was in question. In declaring in favour of 4.5 or 5.0 for the area and period he knew, H. E. Hallam found himself invoking the retirement habits of the peasantry and the prevalence of situations where the father had handed over the land although still residing in the family house. It seems impossible, however, for the outsider to go back and disentangle conjugal family unit from household and from houseful in this material.

But it is certain that the figure of 4.68 which Hallam gives for mean household size (presumably crude mean size of domestic group, ratio 1) in South Lincolnshire in the later thirteenth century is based on the best empirical evidence yet available for medieval England. It cannot qualify for our collection of complete listings of inhabitants because it includes serfs, *nativi*, only, omitting freemen and their households; and because mothers are missing from household members. Although he found Russell's multiplier of 3.5 unacceptably small for these three manors of the Priory of Spalding in 1268–9, Hallam does not differ much in his account of residential patterns. Russell's statement about the elderly and unmarried living alone was 'not entirely true', though borne out in

[59] See Russell, *British medieval population* (1948): especially 24; *Late ancient and medieval population* (1958); especially 52; *Demographic limitations of the Spalding serf lists* (1962): especially 143. Krause, *The medieval household: large or small?* (1956), and Hallam have contributed to the study and revised Russell's conclusions, see Hallam's three valuable articles *Some 13th century censuses* (1957); *Population density in medieval Fenland* (1961); and especially his *Further observations on the Spalding serf lists* (1963) which seems to have disposed of the 'small multiplier' and of the controversy. Though no evidence from the few entirely complete listings of inhabitants then known but belonging to the later period of traditional English society was brought into this interchange, they have been discussed, for example in Marshall, *The rural population of Bedfordshire* (1934). In 1965 the present writer read to the international conference of economic historians at Munich a paper on the multiplier based on a number of complete listings dating between 1599 and 1705, and favouring a figure of 4.5. See Laslett, *Remarks on the multiplier* (1965 ii). This paper is now replaced by Chapter 4 below.

general, however sharply it made against traditional assumptions about the peasantry.[60]

For this record we are told, shows that 'the nuclear household was overwhelmingly predominant; any historian who attempts to establish the existence of great households of brethren and cousins must stumble against the evidence of the Spalding censuses'.[61] At this point the discussion shakes itself free of the multiplier, which in any case now no longer engages the attention of historians of population as much as it did. Hallam does not suppose that his figure of 4.5–5 applies outside his area and period, and he is prepared to grant that 3.5 may be true elsewhere, or generally. We may note that he invokes prosperity and rise in numbers to explain what might seem a large figure, whilst a page or two back we found others maintaining that big and complex households were due to depression and decline in population. It has already been laid down that it would be necessary to have observational evidence of a very different order from Russell's or Hallam's if it were to be shown that any form of the household were characteristic of a society over time, and this is so with simple, nuclear arrangements as well as with complicated ones. Accordingly and in obedience to the rule that only complete listings can be admitted as data, no suggestion is made in Chapter 4 below that the rough figure of 4.75 as a constant for English household size between the seventeenth and twentieth centuries might cover the Middle Ages as well.

Still only the evidence provided by what we have called the history of familial attitudes, as interpreted by some scholars, has so far been brought against such an argument. These indications include, as far as I know, nothing as interesting and persuasive as the documents of *affrairement* which we have noticed in such abundance in late medieval Languedoc. Some reason for supposing that extended and multiple households may have been more common in England than any known numerical evidence suggests does exist in the form of provisions made in wills and other documents. These clauses enabled ageing household heads, or their widowed spouses, to go on living within the dwelling, or anyway on the premises as part of the houseful. Apart from this, the striking thing about the surviving data for periods earlier than that for which we have acceptable numerical evidence from England, is how much they resemble that evidence when it does become available. This is particularly so with what Hallam found in thirteenth-century Lincolnshire.[62]

---

[60] Hallam (1963): 339; he gives the specific figure of 4.68 in Hallam (1957): 340, and the more general one of 4.5–5.0 in Hallam (1961): 80. Although he succeeds in showing that his sample of serfs was not unrepresentative, the omission of freemen and above all of the households of landowners, presumably not to be expected on monastic estates, implies that a general MHS for the area might have to be larger than 4.68.

[61] This in spite of the fact that impartible inheritance which George Homans (1941, 1970) had claimed led to large scale households – stem family households – was very frequent in the area, Hallam (1957): 353.

[62] Provisions for retirement form an important part of George Homans' case (1941, 1970) that in areas of impartible inheritance some form of the stem family was the norm, and a resem-

International exchange in 1969

When research on the size and structure of the domestic group at the Cambridge Group for the History of Population and Social Structure reached the stage which is represented by the conclusions in chapter 4 of this volume, it was decided that the time had arrived for international comparison. We wanted to judge whether what might be called English familial individualism had been an exceptional or quite an ordinary thing. This was particularly important in view of the peculiar position of English social and economic development in relation to the process of industrialisation. England had been the first of the world's societies to undergo that remarkable and momentous change, and it seemed quite possible that her pioneering role might have had something to do with the simple structure and small size of English households before ever industrialisation began.

If it turned out that in most societies where empirical, numerical evidence had become available that the family was frequently of the 'English' form, then the relationship with modernisation would look different. Accordingly an early version of what is now Chapter 4 was sent to a number of scholars who had worked in our five chosen areas, and nearly all the studies published here are those which were presented to the conference to which we invited them in Cambridge in September 1969.

Although the predominance of the simple family household in England seemed so clear, its tendency towards constant size and structure over time was not fully recognised when this international interchange was first planned. Nor was it known that the onset of industrialisation actually led in our country to a clear movement in the direction of more complex domestic groups. Not all of those invited could attend, and in the case of Etienne Hélin and Robert Smith (Chapters 13 and 17) essays written for different purposes were adapted for this one. The system of classification and the model of discussion presented in this introduction, as has been said, were only made possible by the outcome of this interchange, and much work has gone on in Cambridge to take account of its results between the time of the meeting and the commitment of its proceedings to the press (September 1969 to September 1971). This work includes the comparative tables on which we are about to comment, as well as consideration of such things as affrairement. These studies, therefore developed out of the Cambridge

blance is seen with what Arensberg and Kimball (1940, 1961) described in Ireland (see above, p. 22). Mrs H. M. Spufford finds that Tudor wills also imply more extended family arrangements than the few contemporary listings seem to provide for. It seems that we do not know enough yet to reconcile these inconsistencies, if such they really are, and ignorance about the familial arrangements of medieval men, especially humble men, seems deep enough. Some comparison with the figures of familial structure printed by Hallam in 1957 for his thirteenth century settlements is possible with the tables of Chapter 4 below. Proportions of solitaries, multigenerational households, households headed by widows and so on seems very similar.

meeting, and cannot be called a report upon it. More literal accounts have appeared elsewhere.[63]

Such is the reason why England became the point of origin for comparisons of this kind. The remainder of this introduction is given over to a commentary on the series of twelve tables presented at its conclusion, which give some sort of numerical expression of the resemblances and differences in family and household which appear when one individual community from each of the five areas is compared with what is termed the English standard and with the four others.[64] This standard is simply that of the one hundred English communities analysed in Chapter 4, and so subject, of course, to all the severe limitations as a sample which we there insist upon. The whole exercise, it must be stressed, was undertaken on an English model, and the reader must judge for himself how far this abbreviated numerical comparison does create a framework for the data which have been assembled for that single country. He must decide also whether the issue which recurs throughout the volume, as to how far familial history explains why industrialisation came earlier to some areas than to others, is illuminated by the figures.

The English village of Ealing in 1599 has been included so as to give an opportunity of comparing like with like as well as a village with a so-called standard. It is the earliest English age listing, and one of those present in our sample of one hundred. The Serbian community, the Christian Orthodox area of Belgrade in 1733/4, and the Japanese one, Nishinomiya Hama-issai-chō in 1713, appear in other studies presented here (see Chapters 15, 17 and 19). It will be seen that Nishinomiya was an urban district, rather than a rural community, and it must always be borne in mind that Japanese listings show a lack of children and especially below one year old, for reasons explained by Hayami in Chapter 18. But neither the French village, Longuenesse in the Pas-de-Calais in 1778, nor the colonial American township, Bristol, Rhode Island, in 1689, is discussed by our contributors. Longuenesse seems to have little to distinguish it from other Northern French villages under the *ancien régime*; in fact it is in some ways more

---

[63] See Burguière, *Le colloque de démographie historique de Cambridge* (1969), and Laslett, *Comparative history of household and family* (1970 ii). In both these accounts the tendency to stress at the meeting the rarity of households having any structure other than nuclear is somewhat over-emphasised, and a rather exaggerated impression of 'the myth of the extended family' is given. We had had no opportunity at Cambridge up to that time to study numerical evidence from the colonial United States, in particular the listing from Bristol, Rhode Island in 1689 (see below). The erroneous suggestion made during the interchange, that the colonial familial group must have been multiple in order to account for its inordinate mean size, therefore went uncorrected in these reports.

[64] This was the only comparative exercise open to us, because no study of anything approaching a national sample on the lines of Chapter 4 existed for any of the areas other than England. Hayami's Japanese material came closest, but it is particularly intended to show what one province was like over time, rather than the whole country. We had only one community for which we held an eligible listing of inhabitants for Serbia, Japan and the colonial United States, and in the case of France, only two or three. The Italian sources (see above fn. 49) and those for Heidenreichstein, have become known subsequently.

'English' than Ealing.[65] The listing of Bristol is of decidedly lower quality than the rest. Nevertheless it was the only community to hand, and the figures it yields seem to me sufficient to indicate the striking resemblances and the marked differences between the domestic group in traditional England and in her daughter society across the Atlantic.[66]

2 RESULTS OF NUMERICAL COMPARISON

The sample of one hundred communities, the English standard, provides no information on ages, and so cannot appear in Tables 1.5 and 1.9; the American colonial community, Bristol in 1689, is in a rather similar position. Other gaps in the English standard data affect their completeness for the purposes of Table 1.15 and for most of those of Table 1.11; this is also true of Bristol in respect of Table 1.4. Nevertheless, the overriding object of the whole series is to discover how far these five communities conform to the English standard. Statistical tests have been applied to the tables wherever appropriate, and the crucial question asked has been the following. Does the community in question differ in this particular respect from the English norm to such a degree that it is permissible to call the difference significant, in the statistician's sense?[67] The reader will be aware that with such small samples of uncertain quality quite random variation may give rise to apparently striking differences.

The features of the social structure which have been chosen for analysis in this group of tables are a selection of those which we have found likely to explain variations in size and structure of household over time and space, and come from a series which appears at greater length in the detailed examination of Belgrade in 1733–4 contained in the tables of Chapter 15. In our commentary points of departure from the English standard will be noticed, and some comparative reference will be made to studies presented later in this volume, as well as to other communities within Great Britain and without. Household structure, as portrayed in Table 1.15, the final table, will be the dependent variable, as the statisticians say, the final goal that is, of the whole analytic and comparative exercise.

[65] See Laslett (1965 i, 1969) for Longuenesse and its companion, Hallines.

[66] Bristol was analysed by Mr J. R. Hardy at Cambridge, and comparison with the few other similar materials held there shows that it does not seem to have been in any obvious way unusual.

[67] This question has concerned us rather than that of whether the communities differ between themselves, though that query has sometimes been posed. The level of significance attained is usually .01, and when less than this the fact is mentioned. Preference has been given to non-parametric tests, in view of the uncertainty about the shape of the distribution of the variables, and especially to the Kolmogorov-Smirnov one sample test for goodness of fit to a specified theoretical distribution, this distribution always being that of the English sample (see Siegel, *Non-parametric statistics* (1956): 46). Spearman's rank-order correlation test has been applied to the relationships between the dependent variable, household structure, and other variables, and some of the testing has been done in accordance with a technique developed but not yet published by Mr Michael Prentice of the Cambridge Group for the History of Population and Social Structure.

Sex, marital status, age and age gap between spouses: Tables 1.4 and 1.5

Belgrade appears to have differed most from the English standard in respect of proportions of the sexes and especially of proportions married. The figures show that Ealing and Longuenesse mostly conform to the English standard on the points at issue (though at Ealing males differed significantly) and that all three communities outside Western Europe had a clearly distinct pattern. Not much can be made of the sex ratios, for the English standard itself is somewhat puzzling (see below, p. 146), and variations in the number of widowed persons (noticeable at Nishinomiya) are difficult to interpret, if only because of the convention that spouseless persons are all regarded as widowed. A conspicuous feature of Table 1.4 and 1.5 is the excess of married persons in Belgrade, especially at the earlier ages; it amounts to 10 % overall and no less than 30 % for women.

More were married at Belgrade at almost every age than in the other settlements for which we have the information, and all were married earlier. A third of the males were husbands by the age of twenty-five, and as many as three-quarters of the women were wives in their teens, but none was married in either category in the other three settlements. Over 90 % of the women were married by twenty-five as against a .quarter in Nishinomiya. Even in the early thirties the population of Belgrade still had the highest proportion of males married, though Nishinomiya had equalled that for women and by those ages two-thirds of both the sexes were married at Ealing.[68]

But it cannot be shown that these peculiarities in the marriage pattern of Belgrade, and to a lesser extent at Nishinomiya, are associated with the difference in the prevalence of extended and multiple households recorded in Table 1.15. None of the correlations between proportions married, in either sex or by any age, and proportions in these two types of household turns out to be significant.

Another striking feature of Table 1.5 comes in the last column, recording the age gap between spouses. There is a sharp difference here between the two West European communities and the two others. At Ealing and Longuenesse the average difference is a third or a quarter of that at Belgrade or Nishinomiya, and at both these West European villages a noticeable proportion of wives were older than their husbands although their menfolk were themselves older than husbands in the Serbian and Japanese places. This difference in ages of spouses may turn out to be a distinctive feature of West European social structure, and more extensive data might reveal a significant correlation between age gap between spouses and complexity of household composition, not detectable here.[69] It is not

[68] See Chapter 15 for a fuller presentation of the figures for Belgrade concerning proportion married, and also Laslett, *Age at menarche in Europe since the early 18th century* (1971), a study of age at sexual maturation in women based on proportions married and with children by certain ages, as revealed by the listing.

[69] Family reconstitution of English communities shows that the age gap between spouses is rarely much bigger than that at Ealing or Longuenesse. At Colyton in the later seventeenth

surprising, perhaps, that such a relationship should occur, but it is evident from the position in fifteenth century Tuscany as portrayed in Chapter 10, that it does not follow from a large difference in age between spouses that considerable numbers of households will be multiple, even if the girls got married very early.

Mean household size and distribution of households by size: Tables 1.6 and 1.7

The relationship between mean household size and other features of the social structure, including the internal structure of the domestic group, is not as straightforward as is often supposed, which should already be apparent. This is aptly illustrated in the figures of Table 1.6, where comparison between the English standard and the other communities turns out to be a little disconcerting.

The mean size of Japanese households is there shown to be of the same order as the English and French. There are substantial differences between the columns, however, especially between the American colonial community and the others, but no simple division between Western European and the rest. Statistical testing of the distributions shows that in fact neither Ealing, Longuenesse nor Nishinomiya are distinguishable from the English standard in household size itself, whereas Belgrade and Bristol are significantly bigger. When experienced household size is investigated, with the larger figures which are involved because individuals rather than households are at issue, it appears that the communities can be grouped in the following way: Ealing and Nishinomiya are still indistinguishable from the English standard, whilst all the others are higher.[70]

The same interesting tendency comes out when differences in distribution of households by size in Table 1.7 are examined between individual communities rather than between the English standard and the rest. Ealing is shown not to be significantly different either from Longuenesse or from Nishinomiya, but Longuenesse does so differ from Nishinomiya and from Belgrade and Bristol, which also differ from each other. If the examination is extended to the distribution of experienced sizes of household, each place is found to differ significantly from every other, but the pattern remains. Longuenesse occupies an intermediate position between the American and Serbian, which are larger, and the Japanese and English, which are smaller. When it is stated that Ealing and Nishinomiya can be grouped together in this way, the claim is that the differences between them are less in their location on the scale of dimension, than in other directions. The remaining statistics of Table 1.6 show what these directions are: Ealing

century, wives were actually older on average than their husbands: see Wrigley, *Family limitation in pre-industrial England* (1966 ii). The figures are unstable for this feature of social structure however and further data from Japan yield smaller age gaps between spouses.

[70] For experienced household size, see p. 40 above. In judging the results the difficulty of choosing an appropriate ratio for Belgrade should be taken into account. The ratios in Tables 1.6 and 1.7 exclude all inmates and inmate households (see notes to tables and Chapter 15), but even when inmates are taken into account (as for example in the figures for Table 1.14) MHS at Belgrade is 4.97, still larger than Nishinomiya. It is not clear what the effect of including inmates would be on the remainder of the measures discussed, so that Belgrade cannot figure largely in the general argument.

and the English standard, have a greater range of household sizes than Nishino-miya and the Japanese, and this is reflected in their larger variance. The indications are that variability in household size, however measured, is appreciably less in Japan than in the other areas, and even Bristol has a more restricted range than Ealing or, indeed than many English villages with much smaller MHS.[71]

These shades of distinction may seem rather nice, but they are of signal interest when we look at Table 1.15 once more and recognise that Ealing and Nishino-miya are at the upper and lower ends of the scale adopted there for complexity in household structure. The paradox is even stronger than this. Bristol which has by far the largest households, also has the fewest showing any sign of extension, and none at all that is multiple. It would appear that knowledge of the number of households and their sizes would not be a reliable guide to their structure in these communities, and such measures as mean household size of very little use for the purpose.

Once again, a great deal more data and investigation would be needed to demonstrate that this rather surprising negative conclusion could be made general. It must obviously have some limits, for very small households cannot be extended or multiple. Servants, who are members of households, cannot by definition create complexity in household structure. Accordingly we have tested the correlation between degree of complication and mean household size first excluding households of sizes 1 and 2, and then excluding these households and all servants. No significant result emerged. It seems clear that dimension of domestic group will not help us in deciding such questions as to whether institutions like the stem family existed in the communities concerned.

Our final comment on these figures for size of household is rather surprising too. It is surely against our expectation to discover from the last line of Table 1.4 that the median answer to the question 'What size of household do you live in?' posed to any inhabitant of the communities in question would be six persons. Excepting only for the inhabitants of Bristol, Rhode Island, where the answer would be eight.

Heads of households and their children: Tables 1.8, 1.9 and 1.10

One way of judging a familial system, and from the point of view of personal experience and of the process of socialisation an important way, is to see how successful it is in providing a married couple at the head of each household. From the figures of Table 1.8 it can be seen that there are clear differences in this respect between our five selected areas, but it would be difficult to interpret them in such a way as to draw a sharp contrast between English, English speaking or West European families and others, between areas where simple family living was almost universal and those where it was modified by extension and multi-

---

[71] A sample of 3,600 households from twelve American states in 1790 kindly supplied to me by Prof. J. Potter has MHS 5.65 (variance 7.23) M(E)HS 6.92 (variance 7.14), showing that Bristol in 1689 was very similar to the whole society a century later in these respects.

plicity. Ealing and Longuenesse turn out to have about as many households complete in this sense as the English standard, but Nishinomiya has noticeably fewer, though the significance of this difference is not very marked (significant at .10). At Belgrade and Bristol, on the other hand, the numbers of married couples heading households is decidedly greater, and the effect at Bristol is a very conspicuous one.[72]

The American children, then, could apparently be the most confident of both a father and a mother in the household, and this must itself be one of the reasons why the average size was so formidable (compare Chapter 4, table 17). When it comes to the correlation of the features of Table 1.8 with household composition, only one effect is significant (at .05), and that is proportion of widowers heading households, and this effect may be due only to uncertainties in the Japanese listing. Table 1.9 is present in the series in order to make it possible to compare headship rates, as they are called, that is proportion of persons of each sex and in various age groups heading households, with corresponding rates in the contemporary world. It is becoming usual[73] to reckon such rates as a guide to the extent to which the domestic group has been 'nuclearised', that is, has lost extension and multiplicity. It transpires, however, that none of the details of this table can be shown to be significantly correlated with Table 1.15 and it would seem that in these data at any rate statistics of this kind are not very useful indicators. It is not without interest, however, to observe that women do seem to head households more frequently in the two West European places, and that there are faint signs in Serbia and Japan of a higher proportion of very young males in this position. Amongst these few young men – there were eleven altogether in the two cases – were some in a classic stem family situation, having succeeded during the lifetime of their predecessors, or of their predecessors' relicts, who were still residing in the household.

The particulars about children in Table 1.10 are interesting, and the differences are well marked, but they are too various to be easily interpreted. Children were numerous and widespread in these traditional communities, as might be expected, and very much so in America. Bristol differs highly significantly from the English standard for this reason, and it is remarkable that Belgrade does so too, but for the opposite reason: children were fewer there, and not so well distributed; there was a particular shortage of larger groups of children. The possible reasons for this are discussed in Chapter 15. The numbers of children in Nishinomiya seem to be quite high in spite of the paucity of babies in Japanese listings: this may however be due to the fact that all unmarried offspring are classed as children and in Japan many stayed at home after the age of twenty. There is no significant correlation that we can see between children and a complexity of household structure in these data. It could be claimed, however, that they make

---

[72] Berkner finds 96% in Heidenreichstein, which seems to mark that society as being very different indeed from any other so far examined in this particular.

[73] See Kono (typescript).

against any belief that composite households are a spur to fertility and a keeper of children in the parental home.

Kin, servants and composition of household: Tables 1.11, 1.12 and 1.13

The figures of these tables clearly divide English and colonial American society from the others, even from the French. These two had far fewer resident kin than the others, a narrower range of types in those who were present, fewer households with kin; they had more servants and more households with servants, sometimes many more. These effects stand out without statistical investigation.[74]

It is true that kin are hardest to identify in the materials, especially those in English, and that types of kin are difficult to distinguish outside Serbia and Japan. This means that the kin figures are the least reliable, and we cannot be very confident that there were in fact only 4 out of the 421 persons living at Bristol in 1689 who were related to the head of household in any way other than as offspring or spouses, or only 11 out of 427 at Ealing.[75] It means also that nothing can be said with any conviction at this preliminary stage about differences in the patterns of kin relationships. We cannot be at all confident, for example, that it was true in England in traditional times, as it seems to have been true in the nineteenth century, that grandchildren, especially grandchildren by daughters, residing without their parents, were a distinguishing feature of the familial system. We cannot pronounce for any of our areas as to whether those married couples who lived with parents after marriage would more often be found in the wife's or in the husband's families.

These are points of some importance to anthropologists as well as to familial sociologists, but like the others we have mentioned here must be left for more extensive research on better data. All that can now be added about kin is that they turn out to be even fewer than expected everywhere outside Nishinomiya, and even there it must not be forgotten that many were adopted, and could not exist as 'kin' anywhere else. It can be no surprise that proportion of kin in the population and proportion of households with kin are highly significantly related to proportion of extended and multiple households.

Servants, on the other hand, appear to have been more widespread in the communities we are examining than seemed likely even to researchers who began with traditional English society, where servants were indeed extremely common. Only one other country is so far known to have had a higher proportion of

---

[74] A model for non-parametric testing many of them would have to be rather more intricate than for those variables which have been checked in this way. In general the testing of means and proportions has not been attempted.

[75] The difficult issues about the numbers and types of kin in the 100 communities providing the English standard are discussed below in Chapter 4, p. 149. There is a possibility that some of the individuals making up the unidentified part of the 'mean household' (see Table 1.13, category 6) may have been kin. It will be seen, however, that even if all of this class were kinsfolk, their numbers would not have approached those at Belgrade and Nishinomiya, though they would be more than those at Longuenesse.

persons described as servants,[76] but the choice of Ealing as our English community may exaggerate the effect in our series of tables. The enormous number of servants in that village perhaps even dulls the effect of Table 1.13, which otherwise delineates the English family household for what it was in pre-industrial times; man, wife, children and servants, with practically nobody else, and the American family household just like this, only even more so, and much bigger, because of the children. However, even in Serbia and Japan, servants had their parts to play, for apparently those relatives who were there introduced into the household could not or would not do all that servants did.

For servants were in a sense alternatives to kin, and we find that there is a significant correlation (at .05) between the proportion of them in the population and the proportion of households with them on the one hand, and complexity of household structure on the other, though it is in the negative direction. The more servants there were in these communities, it would appear, the less likely were households to be extended or multiple. Now all this would be nullified if it could be shown that servants, especially servants in England, were in fact kin in disguise, disguised because the list-makers did not give them both their descriptions, 'servant *and* (nephew, niece, sister, cousin, etc.)'. This in itself would imply that the kin relationship was less important than the economic, but in the absence of complete information about the kin connections of all the members of these communities, the problem itself remains.

It is unlikely that the requisite information will ever be really complete for any body of data, and all we can do here is to record for the English case the result of comparing surnames of servants with the surnames of their masters and their neighbours.

Table 1.2 *Servants sharing surnames* (21 English communities)

Proportion sharing names with:			
Another community member		Head of employing household	
0–19 %	1	0 or less than 1 %	16
20–39 %	6	1–3 %	4
40–59 %	12	More than 3 %	1
60–100 %	2	More than 4 %	0
	21		21

Taken from our sample of 100, see Chapter 4: the issues discussed in the text are taken up there again. The theoretical maximum of servants sharing surnames with their employers is a little above 25 %, and it is very unlikely that as much as 100 % could be reached for the sharing of surnames with other community members. The figures certainly understate in both columns, and we know from literary and other sources that some servants were kin, even siblings, of employers; see below, Anderson, Chapter 7, for example.

[76] Iceland in the early eighteenth century, though I do not know enough about the definition of servant there to be quite certain that their familial role was strictly comparable. Once more the difficulty in respect of household units may make the Belgrade figures a little misleading; see Chapter 15.

These rough figures imply that servants were very unlikely to be agnates of their masters in traditional England, that is related to them through their fathers or the male line generally, but not at all unlikely to be agnates of other members of the community. It suggests that boys and girls found jobs as servants through the kinship network, either in their own communities, or in neighbouring communities, and even in the cities and the capital where that network extended. But it was felt inappropriate nevertheless that they should serve masters who were agnatic relatives.

We do not know, and perhaps never will know, whether the same would hold of uterine relatives, that is relatives through mothers and the female line. The probability is that slightly more English servants were related through these paths to their masters. Whatever may have been the case in other countries, it seems reasonable to suppose that servants were rarely kin in pre-industrial England. Apparently our ancestors were usually unwilling to submit their relatives to economic servitude, but quite prepared to see them, and their own children, working for their neighbours. In the relations of children to servants we may finally find more important and revealing social structural differences than in searching exclusively for signs of extended and multiple family living.

Generational depth and structure of household: Tables 1.14 and 1.15

Nevertheless the most interesting comparisons from the point of view of established criticism, and the sharpest challenges to our expectations, come from the details of generational depth and household composition. We may start with the most intriguing of them all, which is the contrast in Table 1.14 between the Japanese community and the others in the matter of generational depth.

That all the other figures of this table should be out of line with traditional analysis of the relations between the generations is impressive enough – only one household in sixteen with a generational depth of more than two in traditional England, only one in twelve in a village in northern France in 1778, only one in ten in Belgrade in the 1730s, only two of the seventy-two households in the single American colonial community we can examine. The growing awareness of demographic limits to social structural possibilities, especially in past time, makes it easier to accept the fact that over 93 % of all the households under review consist of one or two generations, excepting only in Japan. But the boundary to values for generational depth given the demographic conditions likely to prevail for the communities we are examining and assuming the pattern of residence decision usual in our day in England, is certainly higher than that recorded for the communities represented in Table 1.14, again excepting Nishinomiya. Indeed if all married couples, or widowed persons, with married children lived with one or other of those children – or had one of those children living with them – then we should expect something between about 22 and 27 % of all households, or perhaps even more, to have a generational depth of three or above.[77]

It is, therefore, both highly significant and very interesting that the villagers of Nishinomiya should have managed to maintain 30 % of their households as three-generational, and that with adoption this value should rise as high as 38 %. This is three times as many as in Belgrade and five times as many as in the English standard. This contrast is so startling that we are fortunate to be able to use the figures for generational depth presented by Hayami in Chapter 18, which show that in his Japanese county the proportion of households of three or more generations remained consistent at a level around 30 %, though his sub-regions vary between 22 % and 44 %.[78]

This implies, it would seem, that demographic limitations were not always the reasons why households containing several generations were so much less frequent in our other communities. These low proportions must have been the result of choices made in accordance with cultural traditions. The frequency with which widowed persons are known to have lived away from their descendants, as well as the facts presented in Table 1.15, certainly bear this out, but it cannot be pretended that the situation in Nishinomiya (and Japan) is yet understood.

There can be no surprise that only the households there, with and without adoption, differed significantly in this respect from the English standard. It is a little strange that those of Belgrade, with the next highest level of complication, were scarcely more often multi-generational than those of Longuenesse. But it is shown in Chapter 16 that in 1863 at least, Serbian communities could have a proportion of multi-generational households of 25 %. The figures of category 3 of Table 1.14, proportion of three-generational households, are significantly correlated with those of Table 1.15, but not the figures of any other generational category.

The obvious message of the evidence presented in Table 1.15 has already been stressed. The nuclear family predominates. In all the communities we are comparing, households of any form more complex than the simple family household were in a minority, and in a tiny minority in Ealing and Bristol; in fact the classic nuclear family of man, wife and children formed the household, with or without servants, in more than half of the Western European cases, and in a

---

[77] Compare Wrigley, *Population and History* (1969): 131–5. The highly simplified model which he tests there looks not inappropriate in its demographic assumptions to the communities we are discussing. Wrigley asserts that a proportion of 15 % of all households being multi-generational must mean on this model that it was usual for widowed parents to live with their married children, and this 15 % is a convenient minimum for the purposes of making a judgement about our communities, although their customs in the relevant respects were clearly slightly different from those assumed by Wrigley.

[78] Hayami, p. 504 below. In interpreting the Japanese figures the shortfall of very young children should be remembered. Van der Woude shows, however, that in Holland, with a much less complex household structure than Belgrade or Nishinomiya, the proportion of households of three generations or more could be as much as 15 %: see Chapter 12.

third of the others. This effect can be seen for a slightly larger number of areas and communities in Table 1.3 below, where the fact that multiple families seem to have been quite negligible in England is vividly apparent. The unimportance of all forms of complex household in Ealing and Bristol can also be observed by comparing the details of Table 1.15 with those of Table 1.14.

This being so at Ealing and at Bristol, it makes little sense to ask of their listings how far it is possible that any of the households recorded were at the time, or any previous time, of such complex familial forms as the stem family or the frérèche. A glance back at Table 1.1 on p. 31 shows that such possibilities are allowed for in a series of categories each permitting a more generous definition of the familial form at issue. There are three possibilities for the stem family (1: category 5b, 2: categories 5b and 5a, 3: 5b+5a+4a) and four for the frérèche (1: 5d, 2: 5d+5c, 3: 5d+5c+4a, 4: 5d+5c+4a+2a). It transpires that one household could have been a stem family at Ealing, and two at Longuenesse: none, on these definitions, could have been a frérèche at either place.

The figures at Belgrade are much more substantial, and 3.3, 8.1, or at highest 14.1 % could have been stem families there, and 3.3, 5.1 or at highest 8.1 % frérèches. At Nishinomiya the levels are of an order higher still. There could have been 12.9, 17.4 or even 32.5 % of stem families and 4.5, 5.3, 20.5 or even 22.8 % frérèches. These crude indicators must be handled gingerly because, except for the lowest in each instance, they record allowable (or just allowable) possibilities for familial forms that might have existed; no more than this. But even with this proviso it is obvious that the Serbian and Japanese communities were quite different in these respects from the English, the American colonial and the French communities. It is also obvious, even in the case of Nishinomiya, that it would not be very straightforward to try to make out a case for either of the two complex familial forms being the dominant institution.[79]

Judgements of this kind are going to be very difficult and cannot be expected to be convincing with the present data. It seems best to set out here (in Table 1.3) almost the whole body of knowledge which we so far possess (in March 1972) on the extent of complexity in household structure in the past, inside and outside our chosen areas. Many of the figures are highly approximate.

We cannot dwell at length on the implications of this set of crude figures for our general subject, nor prolong the commentary on our series of comparative tables much longer. Table 1.3 also contains the first numerical indications we have yet found for the modest growth in the degree of extended family living which occurred in England between traditional and industrial times. It will be seen that no parallel increase is apparent in the proportion of multiple households, and all the evidence we have confirms that such households were never more than a residual element in English communities urban or rural, 'industrial' or 'pre-

[79] Analysis of the Japanese village at Yokouchi (data supplied by Hayami) shows that the proportion of stem families and frérèches could be much higher (over 40% of stem family households in 1671 and in 1823), in spite of a steady fall in MHS. After two years (in April

Table 1.3 *Proportions of extended and multiple family households and mean household size*[a]

Country	Community	County/region	Date	No. of house-holds	MHS	Ext-ended (%)	Mult-iple (%)	Total (%)
International sample:								
Colonial America	Bristol	Rhode Island	1689	72	5.85	3	0	3
England	Ealing	Middlesex	1599	85	4.75	6	2	8
France	Longuenesse	Pas-de-Calais	1778	66	5.05	14	3	17
Germany	Löffingen[b]	Württemberg	1687	121	5.77	[5]	[5]	[10]
Italy	Colorno	Parma	1782	*66*	*4.16*	*9*	*11*	*20*
Japan	Nishinomiya[c]		1713	132	4.95	27	21	48
				(87)		(25)	(14)	(39)
Japan	Yokouchi	Suwa County	1676	27	7.0	0	52	52
Japan	Yokouchi	Suwa County	1746	76	5.5	21	28	49
Japan	Yokouchi	Suwa County	1823	98	5.1	28	28	56
Japan	Yokouchi	Suwa County	1846	107	4.4	14	24	39
Poland	Lesnica	Silesia	1720	311	5.4	5	0	5
Scotland	Aross-in-Mull	Western Isles	1779	211	5.25	11	3	14
Serbia	Belgrade		1733–4	273	4.95	15	14	29
English sample:								
	Ardleigh	Essex	1796	210	5.48	10	2	12
	Ardleigh	Essex	1851	366	4.48	14	0	14
	Bilston	Staffordshire	1695	192	5.19	11	1	12
	Bilston	Staffordshire	1851	*329*	*5.14*	*15*	*5*	*20*
	Bilston	Staffordshire	1861	*264*	*4.30*	*12*	*1*	*13*
	Chilvers Coton	Warwickshire	1686	177	4.41	8	1	9
	Chilvers Coton	Warwickshire	1851	*570*	*4.95*	*13*	*3*	*16*
	Clayworth	Notts.	1676	98	4.09	9	0	9
	Clayworth	Notts.	1688	91	4.49	7	1	8
	Clayworth	Notts.	1851	128	4.21	17	4	21
	Colyton	Devon	1851	*342*	*4.94*	*16*	*2*	*18*
	Colyton	Devon	1861	*449*	*4.48*	*14*	*3*	*17*
	Corfe Castle	Dorset	1790	272	4.84	8	1	9
	Corfe Castle	Dorset	1851	513	4.72	14	1	15
	Corfe Castle	Dorset	1861	297	*4.31*	*14*	*1*	15
	Ealing	Middlesex	1599	85	4.75	6	2	8
	Ealing	Middlesex	1851	*248*	*4.86*	*12*	*1*	*13*
	Ealing	Middlesex	1861	*209*	*4.50*	*19*	*2*	*21*
	Puddletown[d]	Dorset	1724–5	154	3.97	8	1	9
	Puddletown	Dorset	1851	264	4.91	11	1	12
	Puddletown	Dorset	1861	257	4.77	14	1	15
	Puddletown	Dorset	1871	271	4.89	18	2	20
	Puddletown	Dorset	1881	248	4.46	16	1	17

[a] From the files of the Cambridge Group, materials being analysed.
[b] Figures approximate.
[c] Alternative figures, leaving out adoptions.
[d] Not quite complete.

Figures in italics in this table are taken from samples.

1974) the preliminary figures in Table 1.3 still portray the situation fairly well. But in Transdanubian Hungary, Tuscany, Latvia, and Brittany, during the eighteenth century, settlements with high proportions of multiple households have been analysed. The Hungarian and Latvian proportions are the highest in Europe in pre-industrial times.

industrial'. Ardleigh was an entirely agricultural community between 1796 and 1851, Chilvers Coton and Bilston mixed mining and farming villages in 1684 and 1695 and mining towns in 1851, whilst Puddletown was a large village in a region little affected by industrial growth and social change in the nineteenth century.[80] The relation between size and structure of the household in this table is obviously arbitrary, and investigation shows that for this English sample, as for the figures of our five chosen communities, no significant connection can be found.

The same exercise on the figures in Table 1.3 relating to the international sample demonstrates, however, that a highly significant relationship between household size and household composition does finally appear when households of sizes 1 and 2 are excluded, together with servants, and when Bristol is omitted. Here, then, is the last result of a comparative exercise between our English data and those other examples we have assembled for the purpose. Perhaps the reader will conclude that there is some systematic difference between the English household and the rest, that the discovery of the unchallenged predominance of the simple family household in pre-industrial England was a significant one.

We must tread warily here, for we have not been comparing other countries or nations with the English, only individual communities elsewhere with an English standard and an English village. Longuenesse may not be easy to separate in a systematic way from the English standard, though we have seen that there would probably be no difficulty at all in doing so with settlements in the southern region of France. To assume, indeed, that the whole of France formed a distinctive national area from the point of view of familial structure would be absolutely unjustifiable. The same goes for taking Colorno for Italy, Lesnica for Poland, Löffingen for Germany, or even Belgrade for Serbia, Nishinomiya for Japan. Even the fascinating piece of evidence from the Scottish Isles in 1779, the only really telling contrast we have so far found within Britain as a whole,[81] should assuredly not be held by itself to show that all Scotland, or the whole of the clan-organised region, differed from eighteenth-century England in its familial composition. For the variation in the structure of the household *within* each national area could still be greater than that *between* them. England could be exceptional in this as well, in its national homogeneity.

But if we assume for the sake of exposition that the tables we have surveyed not only suggest but could be held to demonstrate that the simple family household represents the whole recoverable past of the whole of England, we are still left with the question of why men have tended for so long to believe otherwise. This brings us to our final problem, the relationship between familial ideology and familial experience.

[80] The possibility that differences in definition and in enumeration practice at successive census counts caused part of the changes found in these communities cannot be entirely excluded.

[81] Data published by Cregeen as *Inhabitants of the Argyll estate 1779* (1963), from the estate records of the Dukes of Argyll, unfortunately capable of only very inexact analysis, though including ages. No other data are forthcoming from the celtic areas of the British Isles as yet.

IV. FAMILIAL IDEOLOGY AND FAMILIAL EXPERIENCE

There must be few behavioural institutions of which it can be said that ideology and experience are entirely congruent. No one would question that the English society of our day is correctly described as monogamous, because monogamous behaviour is nearly universal amongst a people whose belief in monogamy as a value is very widespread, and whose conduct is consistent with monogamy as the norm. It could be called the marital institution under which the English live, for no other distinct practice-with-belief exists alongside it as an alternative. Yet divorce is now quite frequent, scepticism about single spouse unions often encountered, and sexual intercourse outside marriage a commonplace. Indeed we know that children have been begotten illegitimately in appreciable numbers in England during the whole period for which figures can be recovered.[82] This is a fact which we find notable presumably since here, too, we tend to project backwards into the past an ideal situation in which correct behaviour was unwavering *because* belief was unquestioned: ideology and behaviour were supposedly entirely congruent.

Departure from the monogamous ideal of behaviour, amongst English people nowadays, and perhaps amongst their ancestors, has been particularly conspicuous within the élite, and rejection of the beliefs associated with monogamy especially common with the intellectuals, the makers of opinions and of norms. Monogamy as an institution, then, has been underwritten by a general correspondence of ideology and experience, but is consistent with an appreciable degree of disharmony between the two. We do not find ourselves enquiring how much they could diverge before a practice ceased to be *the* institution, and became one amongst others, *an* institution. We do not easily contemplate a situation where plural institutions, or highly variable behaviour, exist in one society at one time in such matters as sexual behaviour and marriage.

Yet if we turn to the question of how far any of the forms of the coresident domestic group, which have been surveyed in the preceding sections, could be called *the* institution, or *an* institution, of the societies where examples of them are found, this issue becomes inescapable. Glancing again at England as it is today, it seems safe enough to claim that the nuclear family, the simple family household, is *the* familial institution, and that again because experience of it, belief in it, willingness to obey its norms, are in fact all congruent with each other. The nuclear family, of course, complements the English institution of monogamy in a particular way. But it has, and has had for hundreds of years as far as we can yet see, a markedly better claim to universality in behaviour and experience than monogamous marriage with exclusively marital sexual intercourse. Yet the nuclear family never seems to have possessed the normative force, certainly not the ideological potential of monogamy, in England or indeed in Western culture.

[82] See Laslett, *The World we have lost*, 2nd edn (1971): 142, and a forthcoming survey of illegitimacy in English history by Laslett and Oosterveen.

The hiatus, therefore, between familial experience and familial ideology is of a somewhat different character than that which divides the two in the matter of monogamy. The intellectuals and opinion makers who deal in the ideology of our world, have a tendency to deplore the circumstance that the complex family household is not sufficiently established as a norm in our society. Extended and even multiple households exist amongst us, but not in anything like enough numbers to ensure that the widowed and the elderly unmarried have a family to live in, or our children the emotional advantage of the presence of the extended kin in the households where they grow up. We have cited this as one reason why the social analysers and the social reformers have wanted to believe that such norms and such behaviour were realities in the pre-industrial past. But the truly outstanding contradictions between familial ideology and familial experience have still to be mentioned, and they arise under quite other circumstances.

We are all well aware that societies have existed, and do now persist in which familial ideology, or at any rate familial ideals and norms, and familial experience differ very much more obviously and in a very direct fashion. This must be so in all polygamous societies for example. The limits which demography places on plurality of wives or husbands are somewhat less drastic than is often supposed. If the age gap between spouses is big enough there can be a sufficient surplus of one sex over another at the relevant ages for many individuals to have more than one spouse, and most persons still to get married. Yet in polygynous societies, which are not uncommon in the world, it is true by and large that it is impossible for ideology to correspond with experience for all but an inconsiderable minority; there simply are not enough women to go round if the society is to reproduce itself. Under such circumstances, which obtain for example amongst the nations where Mohammedanism is established, much stress is laid on the élite having the experience which the multitude would like to have and which ideology commends or commands; they provide the approved model, surrogate experience for the mass. Monasticism illuminates this social process, for monks and nuns also form a tiny minority undergoing approved ideal experiences for and on behalf of, as a model to, the vast majority.

Here again the behaviour or propaganda of an élite is shown to be no reliable indicator of the experience of a whole population, even though they may be related in an interesting way with widely shared aspirations, however unrealistic. There are conceivable situations in fact which in a familial ideology can be a salient feature in a society, yet not even an élite undergo the experience which it enjoins. The question arises when this limit is reached, as to whether the practice can usefully be called an institution of any kind. Examples of such a situation may be that of the Mormons today, and an approach to it might be the position as to plural wives in the nations of the Middle East in our generation.

A recognition such as this, we may notice, could be used to make short work of the paradox which concerned us at the outset. If no-one, or only an insignificant minority, need have had the experience of extended family living for there to be a useful sense in which the extended family was an institution in the past of English society, then the historian or the social scientist is perfectly at liberty to suppose that the extended family was *an* institution if not *the* familial institution in that era. There will be no difficulty, as we have seen, in establishing a strong probability that some people did in fact live in extended families, and sufficient evidence as to familial attitudes could almost certainly be cited from any period to make out a plausible case for the extended family having existed ideologically. This case, and the whole position, would be strengthened if it could be assumed that the handful of people who did have the required familial experience belonged to the élite of the society.

Such an argument only has to be sketched in order to make it an urgent matter to establish forthwith some criterion for what is to count as *the* institution or *an* institution in the sense in which those terms are being used, which is as degrees of correspondence between ideology and experience. Now this is clearly a formidable problem and no-one would expect a final solution to it in the course of an abbreviated essay of the present type. Since some proposal must be made however, this is what is suggested.

A form of the coresident domestic group can be said to be *the* familial institution of a society in permanency over time if a sufficient number of persons being born into that society are being continuously socialised within domestic groups of the structure nominated. Only this will ensure that such a familial form is a fact of their experience in the particular sense which is necessary if that familial form is to be present as an established norm of behaviour. Under these circumstances alone will the whole society be dominated by individuals who, when they have to make decisions as to where they will live after marriage, or whether to permit or encourage their own relatives to reside with them, or their children to join their spouses to the family group, will tend to make those decisions in such a way as to reproduce the familial form in question.

If in addition to this spontaneous tendency in their behaviour, this predominant body of persons in the community should look upon this particular domestic group structure as a value, a value which is, or ought to be, shared by every member of the community, then the claim of that form of the family to be *the* institution for that society is strengthened. But it does not follow from the presence of this set of attitudes itself, this ideological situation alone, that any given proportion of the population in question is or has been actually living within domestic groups of the required character. Familial experience necessarily entails a familial ideology, of varying content, quality and degree of importance to the people who have had that experience. But a familial ideology does not necessarily entail familial experience amongst those who believe in it, expound it or regard it as an ideal.

The twelve tables (1.4–1.15) we are commenting on do not allow of the application of this criterion to our present data in any direct way. Indeed it was insisted earlier (p. 33) that not one listing of inhabitants, but many listings distributed over a number of years, allowing for many successive domestic cycles, would be necessary before any criterion could be conclusively used to prove a proposition in historical sociology relating to the form of the domestic group. But if we permit ourselves to assume that the children alive in Ealing in 1599, at Longuenesse in 1778, at Belgrade in 1733 and at Nishinomiya in 1713 were typical of succeeding generations of children in those communities over the whole period of traditional time, then this is the result.

All unmarried offspring resident in the household of their origin are taken to be children, it will be remembered, and of these 7 out of 147, or less than 5 %, were resident in Ealing in households of a structure more complex than a nuclear family. Only three of them were in a multiple household. This compares with 11.5 % in Longuenesse (2.5 % in multiple households), 21 % in Belgrade (16 %), and 53 % in Nishinomiya (27 %). Though we shall not attempt to specify what proportion of children must be socialised into domestic groups of a particular description, in order to give rise to an institution properly described as the dominant familial form, established over time, it is transparent that at Ealing the only possibility is the simple family household, the nuclear family.

This must surely have been true for all of the English communities cited here or in Chapter 4, and true whatever the familial attitudes and ideals. It must have been true however much ordinary English folk looked to their betters, to the élite, to the land-owning gentry and nobility, or even to the bourgeoisie, for vicarious experience of living in forms of the family not part of their own personal life histories. Members of the traditional English ruling class may perhaps have lived more frequently in complex households than others,[83] and it is probably correct to suppose that there was considerable vicarious sharing of their experience by the masses. But we have found no indication as yet that living in complex households was at all important in the privileged way of life which the populace envied, and would have imitated if they could have. In fact it is very difficult to discover an ideological strain in the literature of the time relating to the size and shape of the familial network within the domestic group, or any discussion of the family in ideal, mimetic terms.[84]

---

[83] It is admitted in Chapter 4 that research into household structure among the English élite is yet to be undertaken. Table 4.16 (below p. 154) shows that the gentry and clergy seem to have had more kin resident in their households than others.

[84] There are references to the excellence of the nuclear family and to the desirability of its independence. But the impression left (and here once more we meet with the elusiveness of literary evidence) is that the duty of taking in relatives made solitary by the break-up of their families is more common. I have seen almost no recommendation of the multiple family household as a value, though there was and still is a great deal of sentimentalism about the size of the aristocratic establishment. This attaches itself however to the troops of servants and to the practice of hospitality rather than to the number of resident kin, and these are very different things.

As far as our present discussion goes the inescapable conclusion would seem to be that both in Ealing and in all English communities so far recovered from the past, familial experience was in fact pretty well congruent with familial ideology, such ideology as there was, and that the operative term in both was the nuclear family, the simple family household. Longuenesse in 1778 can be classed in the same way, though superiority of the simple family household was apparently not so pronounced there as in Ealing, nor in France, especially perhaps Southern France, as in England.

Nevertheless, this is only the beginning of the analysis of the extent of experience of living in domestic groups of various types, given the evidence of lists of inhabitants providing ages as well as kin relationships. It is possible to show from analysis of the life cycle of individuals and the developmental cycle of households, that surprisingly high proportions of persons appearing in a list of inhabitants can have had some experience of the extended or even of the multiple household, even though the nuclear family is in a commanding position numerically. This demonstration belongs to that exercise in the analytic modelling of the behaviour of the family group over time which represents the next stage to the preliminary work published in this volume.[85] The outcome does not at present seem at all likely to upset the statements we have made about the household in England compared with other areas. But investigation of listings like those of Belgrade and Nishinomiya on these lines might make somewhat easier the task of deciding how far any particular form of the domestic group was *the* familial institution either in Serbia or in Japan.

The criterion we are using, as has been said, is a developmental one, belonging entirely with a social science of the properly historical kind. It requires a decision on the probability of a set of persons growing up within a community spontaneously reproducing a familial pattern which was part of their experience in their most impressionable years. If too few of them can be shown to have had the experience to ensure its reproduction as a dominant pattern, then it is claimed that the familial form should not be regarded as the institution of that society, over time. If the number is altogether too small, of the trifling order of those found in complex households in Ealing for example, then the following must be the principle. The reproduction of a familial form in one or two households in one generation which is similar to or identical with that which existed in a household or two in a former generation must be regarded as accidental, a matter of chance. For the possible types of the domestic group are few, certainly in comparison with the number of possible instances, which are infinite over time, even in a small village, since the situation of any one household at any point in

[85] E. A. Hammel made these first calculations at the University of California, Berkeley, and he is engaged in a large scale undertaking in the computer simulation of the processes at issue in which the Cambridge Group for the History of Population and Social Structure will collaborate. The assumptions made about age at marriage, life expectation and so on in order to read the result cited above are not all realistic for the communities in our tables, and least so for England.

its history has to be accepted as a legitimate example.[86] The probability of coincidence is therefore high, and the danger of mistaking a set of coincidences for an ongoing institution must be guarded against.

An intermediate position between the two considered in the last paragraph would produce a plural situation in which there was a dominant familial institution and a recessive one; such Mendelian terms might have their uses, but must not be pressed too far. Or there might be no arrangement which could be termed *the* familial institution and several which could be called *an* institution of the society concerned; often one where more than an inconsiderable minority of persons were living outside the aegis of any institutionalised familial form, and conceivably a condition of a community where most people were in that situation. In the case where one form of the domestic group qualified as an institution, the issue of its claim to dominance would certainly be affected by the position in the hierarchy of status which was occupied by the households so composed, and the degree to which they served as a model to others, their way of living as an ideal. But I have deliberately avoided making any specific proposals about the extent to which these things would have to be prevalent in order to establish degrees of institutionality, or of predominance, just as I have avoided any numerical propositions about the numbers of children who would have to be being socialised into any familial form in order to ensure that that form will be *the* ongoing institution of that society, or *an* institution within it.

It may be that an unwillingness to venture at such an early stage on decisions of this kind makes it impossible for us as yet to determine whether any form of the domestic group could be said to be *the* institution in a society whose familial organisation was typified by what we know of the households of Nishinomiya in 1713, though we can pronounce with fair confidence on what one might count as *an* institution within it. But the case of Belgrade seems to be fairly clear. A national society or cultural area whose households were generally organised on these lines, in these proportions, must be said to exhibit the nuclear family household as *the* familial institution, with such forms of the domestic group as the stem family and the frérèche having very strong claims to the status of *an* institution alongside the dominant simple family household.

A sharp distinction is being here drawn between Belgrade on the one hand, and Nishinomiya on the other, and thus between Nishinomiya and all the

---

[86] This applies even on those exceedingly rare occasions when enough is known to be sure that the situation in the household existing on the day of the count is entirely evanescent, as when a multiple household is created for one night only by a married son bringing his wife and children to stay with his parents. A possible alternative to that considered in the text is that a tendency to reproduce a particular form of the household can be inherited in a line of descent, just as a tendency to produce illegitimate children seems in some degree to be. But even if demonstrated for a certain number of families in a community, it would go little way towards establishing that familial form as an institution of the community as a whole, let alone *the* institution.

communities within our purview.[87] We can begin to justify this by pointing to Table 1.11. Over half of the households at Nishinomiya contained kin (some of them adoptive), just as over half of the children there were apparently being brought up in complex households, a figure which would be substantially greater if we took into account the numbers who had had some experience of such households.[88] The correspondingly adjusted figure for the children of Belgrade is one-third, and that for households with kin there about the same; these are minority figures, whereas the figures at Nishinomiya are majority figures. Moreover, there are three further arguments which might be deployed to show that only of Nishinomiya, and so perhaps of Tokugawa Japan generally, could it as yet be supposed with something like confidence that the complex household was the ongoing, historically perdurable, self-reproducing familial institution, existing alongside the simple family household but with a clear claim to dominance.

The first such argument is that identification with the patriline, the Ie, 家, the house and its inheritance, which has been repeatedly referred to. The second is the practice of adoption, which can plausibly be supposed to have had as its chief object the perpetuation of that patriline by the provision of the required succession.[89] Adoption could be described as interference with the dictates of demography for the purpose of altering the shape the domestic group would otherwise take over time. The third argument seems to me the most significant. It is the evident success of the household system at Nishinomiya and apparently traditional Japanese society in general, in ensuring that so many households should have a generational depth of more than two. This is a numerical argument to some degree; we have seen how much higher the proportions of such households were there than anywhere else that we know of. It is also demographic, since there were even more resident grandparents than the little we yet know of demographic expectation would seem to imply. But it is a general argument as well. The Japanese system seems deliberately to have provided for something like the gathering under one roof of the extended kin group which has been so widely and so unjustifiably regarded as typical of all the traditional households of the past, wherever they may be found.

[87] The possible exceptions are Montplaisant, to which many references have been made and Laguiole in 1691, and also conceivably Colorno in 1782, as well as Heidenreichstein.

[88] As for totals of persons, 11 % of the inhabitants of Ealing other than servants and individual inmates lived in complex households of one kind or another (20 in extended households, 12 in multiple): 18 % at Longuenesse (41 and 11): 37 % at Belgrade (205 and 191): 59 % at Nishinomiya (184 and 65; without adoption, 46 %; 186 and 125). Experience of complexity was apparently more widespread amongst adults than children, especially at Ealing and Longuenesse: evidently the influences making for coresidence of kin affected members of complete nuclear families less than other persons, even those with spouses but no children. Although the emphasis here is on complex family experience in relation to children, something must be allowed for its effects on adults too.

[89] But it had other objects too, for those adopted into households at Nishinomiya were by no means all in a likely position to succeed. Compensatory arrangements like this are being analysed in the project referred to in fn. 85.

The question of precisely which form of the complex household should be pronounced as typical for Nishinomiya cannot now concern us, and, as we have stated, there can be no question of final determination. But even if such definite judgements were open to us and could now be made, it remains the case that the simple family household would be recognised as very much more secure in its dominance as *the* institution in England and in Western European society generally than the complex household was at Nishinomiya and perhaps in Japan. In that Japanese settlement, it must not be forgotten, 43 % of all households were of the simple family type in 1713, and 48 % if no adoption had taken place.

A quarter of all the households were of the classic, independent nuclear family kind which has been thought of as characterising industrial society: father, mother, offspring and no-one else, except sometimes servants. Over half of all the households – and nearly 60 % without adoption – were innocent of any degree of extension, and nearly one-tenth lacked familial structure of any kind. It is true, as we have seen, that 59 % of all individuals were living in households exhibiting some complexity of structure, a proportion which falls to 46 % if adoption is excluded. It is also true that many of the nuclear families could justly be supposed to have been extended or multiple at earlier stages of the developmental cycle, or likely to become so at later stages. Nevertheless it seems to me that it is only when we invoke the considerations with which this section began, and which allow for a considerable departure between familial ideology and familial experience, that we can contemplate such a considerable minority under the régime of the nuclear family and still regard another familial form as the dominant institution.

Even this judgement implies that we know a lot about the familial ideology which occupied the minds of Japanese individuals ten generations ago. In particular we are required to be confident that the form of the household itself was the salient feature of their attitude, the operative reason why they compensated against heirlessness due to demographic misfortune, and brought, or kept, members of former generations within the familial circle. It could be that their predominant, almost exclusive ideological concern was with the family as a patriline, with the perpetuation of its name, its plot, its property, its craft, and not with its structure as a coresident domestic group at any point in time.[90] The instructive comparison here in European territory is with the hamlets of Heidenreichstein.

There is evidently sufficient information about familial policy and belief in that area of Austria at the time to imply that ideology did correspond to an appreciable extent with experience. What is known of that ideology, however,

[90] Professor Hayami has informed me that no single character, and no combination of characters existed amongst Japanese villagers of Tokugawa times to express the concept of complex households. It would seem that, as has sometimes been the case with European familial structure, these terms have had to be invented by subsequent scholars: it is notorious that zadruga was not the word used by Serbian peasants themselves for large scale households.

seems to attach itself far more strongly to the indivisibility of property and to the continuance of a family line than it does to the actual structure of households.[91] None of the data we have been able to collect for this volume can be shown to demonstrate the ideological primacy of the form of the household in the minds of any body of men in the past. Not, that is, before it became of such overriding ideological importance for Frédéric Le Play, and for his successors down to our contemporary familial sociologists.

There is one argument to which scholars in this tradition have sometimes committed themselves, and which is very widespread in the journalistic treatments of the family in our time, but which can, I think, be conclusively disposed of from the available evidence and the present discussion. This is the argument of psychic loss. The proposition seems to be[92] that the emotional development of the contemporary child brought up in an isolated, independent, nuclear family is in some way impoverished, as compared with that of his predecessors in earlier generations, and especially his predecessors in pre-industrial times. This is because the child of our day has only the presence of his parents and one or two siblings in the home during the crucial epoch of personality formation, and never in addition the presence of a member of a generation earlier than that of his father, nor that of kinsfolk of other kinds. We now know that such an argument is wholly untrue of English familial history as so far recovered, and that it might lack support even in areas which look more promising for it, in traditional Serbia for example. It is no very persuasive argument even for a place like Nishinomiya: an entirely universal experience of the required kind does not seem to be implied by the facts we possess for that community.

There is a further disposition to amend a case of this kind by appealing to the neighbourhood in which the family of babyhood was situated. If the missing kinsfolk were not actually in the home, they were all living in the same small community: grandfather, cousin and maiden aunt were present to the growing child in that sense. It might even be further suggested that in such a pre-industrial community the peasant family, parents and child, could find emotional experience of the required kind vicariously, because they could identify themselves with the working model of large family living which was to be contemplated in the manor house across the fields.

This further position seems to me entirely unconvincing. Whatever the loss of a model to imitate may mean, it cannot mean the loss of psychic experience for a child in its first months and years of life. The assumption about neighbourhood is not at all secure. If relatives had in fact been so intimately bound up in

---

[91] See Berkner (1972). I have not acquainted myself with the extensive literature he cites on Austrian familial attitudes, property rules and so on and cannot offer a first hand opinion. Berkner gives no figures for children within complex households, but it would not seem that they could have been high enough to imply that the stem family was the one, dominant familial institution over time.

[92] Expounded, to refer to one amongst what must be a massive array of books, by Sennett, see *Families against the city* (1970).

the family circle in pre-industrial England, then they would surely be found more often to have actually lived within it, more often that is than we found them to have done in the lists of inhabitants we have surveyed. Even their presence in the village is rather less certain than might appear, and the ease and frequency of kin contact found in the residential suburbs of the late twentieth century cannot necessarily be assumed for the villages and townships of an earlier England.[93]

We may bring this compressed, but too lengthy introduction to our volume to a close by returning for a moment to the persisting expectation that the further one goes back in familial history, the more likely it must be that families would be found to be large in size and complex in structure. Even if the negative demonstration put forward here were to be confirmed and become generally accepted, there might still remain a conviction that the task of the historical sociologist was to discover somewhere behind the evidence which in a country like England makes so overwhelmingly for the nuclear family as a dominant form, indications of an earlier, inner reality, surviving and persisting, which did incorporate the complex family, the extended household so familiar in the literature of social science.

Such a suggestion focuses our attention on that residual category of households which we can now observe in some English communities over the past three centuries which are not covered by the predominating, established institution of the nuclear family. It is reasonable to expect that there always will be persons living outside the institutionalised familial system, because no institution is so swift and efficient in its action that all members of a community are assigned forthwith to an appropriate place in its integrated structure. There are, moreover, demographic eventualities which are peculiarly difficult for each recognisable form of the domestic group to provide for.[94] The majority of these individuals outside the established system are found in groups lacking familial structure or in institutions, in English familial history, but some of them are found in extended and multiple households. The way in which unexpected demographic events arose which might defeat the familial system in the short term, though they could no doubt be accommodated in the long term, can be illustrated from

93 See Laslett (1965 i, 1971): especially 117, 292, 309. The one person removed from the English household at industrialisation was the father, for all of the working hours he now has to spend at the office or at the factory. This is an architectonic difference in the familial experience of everyone in industrial as contrasted with pre-industrial England (and it is true no doubt of other countries and cultures as well), yet is seldom given the stress reserved for the supposed absence of less intimate relatives from the household. Research on the extent to which neighbouring households were related to each other through kin is now in progress at the Cambridge Group.

94 Examples of conjunctures which an exclusively nuclear family system could not be expected to cover are the provision of spouses and so a CFU for elderly people after widowhood, which could only be done by successive remarriages after successive widowhoods, with consequent upheaval in the lives of the subjects and much moving about. The situations which are likely to be too much for an exclusively extended or multiple family institution are even easier to see. This is the reason why adoption is so interesting, and can be interpreted as a deliberate intervention with demography in favour of a familial form, as perhaps in the Japanese case.

a note made against a nuclear family in a list of inhabitants from Binfield in Berkshire in 1801, consisting of a married couple and two baby sons. 'The wife dead, and he and his family went to his mother's'. For a little while anyway Binfield had an extra extended or multiple family household. The proposition under critical examination is that in meeting these emergencies in this way our ancestors were in fact showing forth the operation of another, more complex and more interesting familial form than was an established fact for nearly all of their contemporaries.

The interplay of familial ideology and familial experience would at the margin allow for this possibility. Nevertheless, to my mind it lacks all reality. To claim that the few and scattered examples of multiple family households we find in English evidence in fact represent the survival of a familial form once widespread but overtaken by events, is to claim that what I should wish to call the null hypothesis in the English familial historical case can in fact be refuted. The null hypothesis states, as has already been hinted, that all such departures from the simple household form of the coresident domestic group in England must be regarded as the fortuitous outcomes of demographic eventualities and economic conveniences, and of particularly strong personal attachments as well. Even if we could collect enough usable English instances ever to attempt to refute this null hypothesis as thus proposed, it would seem impossible to specify the mechanism whereby such a tradition could survive over time, could in fact be supported by a verifiable proposition in a properly historical sociology.

The wish to believe in the large and extended household as the ordinary institution of an earlier England and an earlier Europe, or as a standard feature of an earlier non-industrial world, is indeed a matter of ideology. The ideology in question, it is suggested, is not to any extent a system of norms and ideals present in the minds of the men and women of the past who actually made the decisions giving their domestic group structures their characteristic forms. It has existed rather in the heads of the social scientists themselves. It came into being, and has been nurtured by a wish to be able to believe in a doctrine of familial history which until now has scarcely begun to be investigated in the surviving records of behaviour. Hence the imperative importance to the study of the family of a properly historical sociology. This cannot be the only area of social analysis where such a discipline is now a commanding necessity.

Tables to introduction

The figures in the first column of these tables are usually those of what is termed the English standard, that is those referring to the sample of 100 communities dated between 1574 and 1821, analysed in detail in Chapter 4 and listed in full on pages 130 and 131. This is not so in the first columns of tables 1.5, 1.9, 1.12, and 1.15 because the sample in question does not contain the necessary information. The figures themselves are proportions, adding up to 1,000 in the case of the English standard and to 100 in the case of the five communities, where 99 or 101 occasionally appear as a result of rounding; in tables 1.6 and 1.11, however, the figures are the actual values, and such values also appear in tables 1.13 and 1.15. The numbers at issue (N ...) usually are given at the foot of columns of figures expressing proportions.

The general practice in citing particulars from any census or census type document is to specify the total population, if not to be given in the body of the table, and the date. This practice is followed here, except in the headings of tables 1.13 and 1.15 where these details have had to be omitted to save space. It should be particularly noted that because of the issue of inmates (see pp. 34–40) the N values do not always correspond to the total population, and this is conspicuously so in the case of the figures for Belgrade in 1733/4.

Table 1.4 *Population by sex and marital status*

Marital status	English standard 100 communities, 1574–1821			English Ealing, Middlesex, 1599			French Longuenesse, Pas-de-Calais, 1778		
	Male	Female	Both	Male	Female	Both	Male	Female	Both
Single	617	592	604	72	61	67	64	63	63
Married	348	321	334	26	31	28	32	28	30
Widowed	35	87	62	2	8	5	2	8	5
Unknown	0	0	0	0	0	0	2	1	1
Totals	1,000	1,000	1,000	100	100	100	100	99	100
N	—	—	—	229	198	427	157	176	333
Sex ratio	—	910	—	—	115.0	—	—	89.0	—

Marital status	Serbian Belgrade, 1733–4			Japanese Nishinomiya, Hama-issai-chō, 1713			American colonial Bristol, Rhode Island, 1689		
	Male	Female	Both	Male	Female	Both	Male	Female	Both
Single	45	39	42	56	48	52	—	—	68
Married	36	43	39	31	35	32	—	—	32
Widowed	1	9	5	5	13	9	—	—	1
Unknown	18	9	13	9	3	7	—	—	0
Totals	100	100	99	101	99	100	—	—	101
N	732	624	1,356	347	304	653[a]	—	—	421
Sex ratio	—	117.0	—	—	114.0	—	—	—	—

[a] 2 persons of unknown sex.

Table 1.5 Marital status by age and sex

	Male										Female									
Marital status	15–19	20–24	25–29	30–34	35–39	40–44	45–49	50–59	60–69	70+	15–19	20–24	25–29	30–34	35–39	40–44	45–49	50–59	60–69	70+
English Ealing, 1599 Pop. 427																				
Single	100	100	77	38	62	29	50	12	20	0	100	84	57	36	14	0	12	0	12	0
Married	0	0	23	62	37	71	50	80	66	0	0	15	43	64	64	62	38	86	75	50
Widowed	0	0	0	0	0	0	0	8	14	0	0	0	0	0	21	38	50	14	13	50
Total	100	100	100	100	99	100	100	100	100	100	100	99	100	100	99	100	100	100	100	100
French Longuenesse, 1778 Pop. 333																				
Single	100	100	90	89	31	25	26	22	0	33	100	100	73	64	36	10	0	20	0	33
Married	0	0	10	11	69	75	73	56	75	33	0	0	18	29	64	85	100	60	75	33
Widowed	0	0	0	0	0	0	0	22	25	33	0	0	9	7	0	5	0	20	25	33
Total	100	100	100	100	100	100	99	100	100	99	100	100	100	100	100	100	100	100	100	99
Serbian Belgrade, 1733–4 Pop. 1,357																				
Single	100	67	32	15	17	3	7	7	5	10	23	3	2	4	0	5	0	0	0	14
Married	0	33	68	85	83	93	93	90	83	70	77	92	95	87	73	81	60	25	8	14
Widowed	0	0	0	0	0	3	0	3	11	20	0	5	3	9	27	14	40	75	92	71
Total	100	100	100	101	100	99	100	100	99	100	100	100	100	100	100	100	100	100	100	99
Japanese Nishinomiya Hama-issai-chō, 1713 Pop. 653																				
Single	100	100	86	71	21	0	0	0	0	0	100	72	17	13	0	0	0	0	0	0
Married	0	0	14	18	74	95	91	97	85	46	0	28	83	87	92	76	83	50	31	0
Widowed	0	0	0	12	5	5	9	3	15	54	0	0	0	0	8	24	17	50	69	100
Total	100	100	100	101	100	100	100	100	100	100	100	100	100	100	100	100	100	100	100	100

Age gap between spouses

Population	Mean	Median	Proportion of wives older than husbands
English Ealing, 1599	3.50	3.25	21 % (n = 62)
French Longuenesse, 1778	2.35	1.50	27 % (n = 43)
Serbian Belgrade, 1733–4	10.82	10.18	0.5 % (n = 192)
Japanese Nishinomiya Hama-issai-chō, 1713	10.36	9.10	1.9 % (n = 105)

Table 1.6 *Mean and median size of household with variances, etc.*[a]

	English standard, 100 communities, 1574–1821	English, Ealing, Middlesex, 1599, Pop. 427	French, Longuenesse, Pas-de-Calais, 1778, Pop. 333	Serbian, Belgrade, 1733–4, Pop. 1,357	Japanese, Nishinomiya, Hama-issai-chō, 1713, Pop. 653	American colonial, Bristol, Rhode Island, 1689, Pop. 421
Population	—	404	333	972	653	421
Households	—	85	66	178	132	72
Mean household size (MHS)	4.75	4.75	5.05	5.46[d]	4.95	5.85
Range of household sizes	1–50	1–21	1–15	1–16	1–12	1–15
Variance (for distribution of households by size)[b]	6.40	9.90	6.87	7.97	5.97[e]	8.02
Median	4	4	4	5	5	6
Mean experienced household size (M(E)HS)[c]	6.10	6.81	6.39	6.91	6.14	7.20
Median experienced household size	6	6	6	6	6	8

[a] All MHS ratios approximately correspond to uncorrected maximal mean household size (ratio 3 of Table 4.2 below) except in the case of Belgrade where it corresponds to ratio 5 in that table. This ratio excludes both individual inmates and inmate households.

[b] Values above 12 in these distributions are all taken as equalling 14.5 for the English standard, 15 for the communities being compared with it.

[c] Above p. 40.

[d] Mean size of houseful 7.14, see Chapter 15.

[e] Suwa County (Chapter 18) variance: 1681–1870 4.92; 1701–50 3.39.

Table 1.7 Distribution of households by size

Size	English standard 100 communities, 1574–1821		English Ealing, Middlesex, 1599 Pop. 427		French Longuenesse, Pas-de-Calais, 1778 Pop. 333		Serbian Belgrade, 1733–4 Pop. 1,357		Japanese Nishinomiya, Hama-issai-chō, 1713 Pop. 653		American colonial Bristol, Rhode Island, 1689 Pop. 421	
	House-holds	Persons	House-holds	Persons	House-holds	Persons	House-holds	Persons	House-holds	Persons	House-holds	Persons
1	56	12	9	2	0	0	3	1	7	1	4	1
2	142	60	14	6	17	6	6	2	9	4	8	3
3	165	104	18	11	18	11	16	9	14	9	7	4
4	158	133	14	12	12	10	18	14	15	12	15	10
5	147	155	13	14	17	17	14	13	17	18	13	11
6	118	149	7	9	11	13	14	16	12	15	18	18
7	80	118	11	15	9	13	9	11	11	16	7	8
8	54	91	2	4	6	10	7	10	5	7	10	13
9	31	59	5	11	6	11	3	5	4	8	8	13
10	19	40	1	2	2	3	3	6	2	5	4	7
11	11	25	3	8	1	3	2	3	1	2	3	5
12	7	18	0	0	0	0	0	0	2	4	1	3
13[a]	13	34	1	5	2	4	3	10	0	0	1	4
Total	1,000	1,000	99	100	100	101	100	100	99	101	99	100
N	1,000		85	404	66	333	178[a]	972	132	653	72	421

[a] Inmates and inmate households excluded – see note to Table 1.6.

Table 1.8 *Marital status of heads of households*

Marital status	English standard 100 communities, 1574–1821	English Ealing, Middlesex, 1599 Pop. 427	French Longuenesse, Pas-de-Calais, 1778 Pop. 333	Serbian Belgrade, 1733–4 Pop. 1,357	Japanese Nishinomiya, Hama-issai-chō, 1713 Pop. 653	American colonial Bristol, Rhode Island, 1689 Pop. 421
Married couple	704	71	71	83	64	93
Widower	37	3	6	3	9	1
Widow	167	17	12	11	9	1
Single male	22	0	8	1	17[b]	4
Single female	13	0	1	0	1[b]	0
Unspecified male	52	8	2	3	0	0
Unspecified female	25	1	0	—	0	0
Total	1,000	100	100	101	100	99
N	—	85	66	273[a]	132	72

[a] Host and inmate households separated, see Chapter 15. [b] Figures dubious.

Table 1.9 *Headship rates*

Age group	English Ealing, Middlesex, 1599 Pop. 427				French Longuenesse, Pas-de-Calais, 1778 Pop. 333				Serbian Belgrade, 1733–4[a] Pop. 1,357				Japanese Nishinomiya, Hama-issai-chō, 1713 Pop. 653			
	Male		Female		Male		Female		Male		Female		Male		Female	
	Nos.	% head	Nos.	% head	Nos.	% head	Nos.	% head	Nos.	% head	Nos.	% head	Nos.	% head	Nos.	% head
15–24	1–48	2	0–48	0	0–19	0	0–23	0	9–131	7	0–115	0	3–84	4	1–53	2
25–34	20–38	52	1–25	4	1–19	5	0–25	0	36–141	26	3–128	2	7–42	17	0–48	0
35–44	13–22	59	6–22	27	19–26	73	2–31	4	38–65	58	4–48	8	30–50	60	1–33	3
45–54	19–21	90	7–28	25	20–23	87	1–12	8	26–43	61	2–25	8	40–46	87	6–32	19
55–64	15–17	88	1–8	12	8–11	73	1–7	14	16–23	70	3–17	18	21–27	78	5–21	24
65+	2–4	50	1–3	33	7–9	78	5–14	36	8–16	50	1–9	11	17–22	77	1–21	5
Totals	70–148	47	16–134	12	55–107	5	9–112	8	133–413	31	13–342	4	118–271	43	14–208	5

[a] Figures uncertain: 31 male, 1 female heads with no age given. Inmate households omitted.

Table 1.10 *Distribution of children in groups*

	English standard 100 communities 1574-1821		English Ealing, Middlesex, 1599 Pop. 427		French Longuenesse, Pas-de-Calais, 1778 Pop. 333		Serbian Belgrade[a] 1733-4 Pop. 1,357		Japanese Nishinomiya, Hama-issai-chō, 1713 Pop. 653		American colonial Bristol, Rhode Island, 1689 Pop. 421	
Proportion of households with children	74.6%		71.8%		77.3%		76.5%		81.9%		87.0%	
Mean size of groups of children	2.73		2.40		3.05		2.37		2.68		3.64	
Group size	House-holds	Children	House-holds	Children	House-holds	Children	House-holds	Children	House-holds	Children	House-holds	Children
1	287	105	36	15	20	6	29	12	29	11	16	4
2	244	180	18	15	23	15	30	25	27	20	18	10
3	198	218	28	35	22	21	23	29	18	21	19	16
4	123	181	6	11	14	18	10	17	10	15	14	15
5	78	144	10	20	12	19	7	14	9	17	13	18
6	41	91	2	4	8	15	0	0	3	6	10	16
7+	29	80	0	0	2	5	1	2	4	10	10	20
Total	1,000	999	100	100	101	99	100	99	100	100	100	99
N	—	—	61	147	51	156	136	323	108	290	62	222

[a] Inmate households and other inmates excluded, see note to Table 1.6.

Table 1.11 Resident kin, other than spouses and children: numbers, types and proportions[a]

Type of kin Head's [and/or wife's]	English standard 100 communities, 1574–1821	English Ealing, Middlesex, 1599 Pop. 427	French Longuenesse, Pas-de-Calais, 1778 Pop. 333	Serbian Belgrade, 1733–4 Pop. 1,357	Japanese Nishinomiya, Hama-issai-chō, 1713 Pop. 653	American colonial Bristol, Rhode Island, 1689 Pop. 421
Father	—	1	0	2	5	0
Mother	—	1	3	35	31	0
Sister	—	4	6	21	18	0
Brother	—	0	3	34	24	0
Nephew	—	3	1	13	5	0
Niece	—	1	0	12	6	0
Son-in-law	—	0	2	7	5	0
Daughter-in-law	—	1	2	9	4	0
Grandchild	—	0	2	5	36	4
Other kin	—	0	3	28	19	0
Total	—	11	22	166	153	4
% in population	3.4%	2.6%	6.6%	12.3%	23.4%	1.0%
% households with kin	10.1%	13.0%	19.7%	27.0%	53.0%	3.0%

[a] Except for a few in Belgrade and Nishinomiya, all resident kin are related to head of household. For detailed analysis of types of kin in Belgrade including those related to members of the household other than head, see Chapter 15. Here the Belgrade household is defined as for Table 1.6, see note there.

Table 1.12 Servants: numbers, proportions and distribution by age and sex

Age	English Ealing, Middlesex, 1599, Pop. 427, 85 households		French Longuenesse, Pas-de-Calais, 1778, Pop. 333, 66 households		Serbian Belgrade, 1733–4, Pop. 1,357, 178 households[a]		Japanese Nishinomiya, Hama-issai-chō, 1713, Pop. 653, 132 households		American colonial Bristol, Rhode Island, 1689, Pop. 421, 72 households
	Male	Female	Male	Female	Male	Female	Male	Female	Both sexes
0–9	0	2	0	0	0	11	0	0	—
10–19	41	22	23	24	31	63	43	80	—
20–39	31	59	36	47	26	5	52	20	—
30+	28	17	41	29	16	21	5	0	—
Unknown	0	0	0	0	28	0	0	0	—
Total	100	100	100	100	101	100	100	100	—
N	68	41	25	17	121	19	21	5	—
Sex ratio (English standard 107)	166		145		637		420		56
Proportion in population (English standard 13.4%)	25.5%		12.6%		10.3%		4.0%		13.3%
Proportion of households with servants (English standard 28.5%)	34.2%		19.7%		29.6%		13.6%		30.1%

[a] Inmates and Inmate households excluded: see note to Table 1.6.

Table 1.13 Composition of household[a]

	English standard 100 communities,		English Ealing		French Longuenesse		Serbian Belgrade		Japanese Nishinomiya, Hama-issai-chō		American colonial Bristol	
	Value	Index	Value	Index	Value	Index	Value	Index	Value	Index	Value	Index
1 Mean number of persons per household in position of head or spouse of head	1.63	34	1.71	36	1.72	34	1.83	37	1.63	33	1.94	33
2 Mean number of children per household, excluding resident kin (nephews, nieces, cousins, grandchildren etc)	2.03	43	1.64	34	2.36	47	1.57	32	1.96	40	3.07	52
3 Mean number of resident kin per household	0.16	3	0.13	3	0.33	6	0.61	12	1.16	23	0.06	2
4 Mean number of servants per household	0.63	13	1.27	27	0.64	13	0.51	10	0.20	4	0.78	13
5 Mean number of individual inmates per household	0.07	2	0	—	0	—	0.01	—	0	—	0	—
6 Mean number of unidentified persons per household	0.23[b]	5	0	—	0	—	0.37	8	0	—	0	—
Total	4.75[b]	100	4.75	100	5.05	100	4.90	99	4.95	100	5.85	100

[a] All MHS ratios approximate to ratio 3 (see Table 4.2 below).
[b] English standard MHS, see Chapter 4. Actual figure for this ratio for 100 parishes is 4.77, so that unidentified persons probably amount to about 0.246.

Table 1.14 Households by generational depth

	English standard 100 communities	English Ealing N	English Ealing Proportion	French Longuenesse N	French Longuenesse Proportion	Serbian Belgrade N	Serbian Belgrade Proportion	Japanese Nishinomiya Hama-issai-chō N	Japanese Nishinomiya Hama-issai-chō Proportion	American colonial Bristol N	American colonial Bristol Proportion
1 Containing members of generation of head of household only	238	23	28	11	17	63	23	16 (16)[b]	12 (18)[b]	10	14
2 Containing:											
(i) Offspring etc. of head	704	59	69	47	76	} 180	66	66 (45)[b]	50 (52)[b]	60	83
(ii) Parents etc. of head		0		3				0		0	
3 Containing:											
(i) Offspring etc. of head and grandchildren etc. of head	58	0	2	2	8	} 25	9	50 (26)[b]	38 (30)[b]	1	3
(ii) Grandchildren only		0		0				0		1	
(iii) Offspring etc. of head and parents etc. of head		2		2				0		0	
(iv) Any other 3-generational combination		0		1				0		0	
4 Any 4-generational combinations	—	0	0	0	0	1	—	0	0	0	0
5 Unknown	0	1	1	0	0	4	1	0	0	0	0
Totals	1000	85	100	66	101	273[a]	99	132 (87)[b]	100 (100)[b]	72	100

[a] Host and inmate households separated: see Chapter 15. [b] Excluding households with adopted members.

Table 1.15 *Households by structure*

	English Ealing Servants With	out	%	French Longuenesse Servants With	out	%	Serbian Belgrade Servants With	out	%	Japanese Nishinomiya Hama-issai-chō Servants With	out	%	American colonial Bristol Servants With	out	%
1 Solitaries			12			1			2			7 (10)[b]			7
1a Widowed	1	3		0	0		0	2		0	1		0	0	
1b Single of unknown marital status	1	5		1	0		2	2		0	8		1	4	
2 No family			2			5			2			2 (2)[b]			0
2a Coresident siblings	0	0		1	2		0	0		0	3		0	0	
2b Coresident relatives of other kinds	0	0		1	0		0	0		0	0		0	0	
2c Persons not evidently related	1	1		1	0		0	5		0	0		0	0	
3 Simple family households			78			76			67			43 (48)[b]			90
3a Married couples alone	6	4		1	7		7	37		0	3		1	4	
3b Married couples with child(ren)	14	31		4	28		25	92		6	33		19	40	
3c Widowers with child(ren)	1	1		1	1		1	3		0	5		0	0	
3d Widows with child(ren)	0	9		2	6		1	18		1	9		0	1	
4 Extended family households			6			14			15			27 (25)[b]			3
4a Extended upwards	1	0		1	4		3	15		1	19		0	0	
4b Extended downwards	1	1		0	0		1	5		0	5		2	0	
4c Extended laterally	2	0		1	2		4	12		1	7		0	0	
4d Combinations of (a)–(c)	0	1		0	1		0	0		0	2		0	0	
5 Multiple family households			2			3			14			21 (14)[b]			0
5a Secondary units up	0	0		0	0		2	7		3	3		0	0	
5b Secondary units down	1	0		0	2		5	8		4	13		0	0	
5c Units all on one level	0	0		0	0		0	5		0	1		0	0	
5d 'Frérèches'	0	0		0	0		2	7		0	3		0	0	
5e Other multiple family households	0	0		0	0		0	3		0	1		0	0	
Totals	85		100	66		100	273[a]		100	132		100 (99)[b]	72		100

[a] Host and inmate households separated: see Chapter 15. [b] Presumed structure if no adoption had taken place.

Appendix to introduction

Suggested rules for interpreting English documents

It has been made clear that the interpretive and analytic system described in the Introduction was developed originally from documents from England alone, and has only recently been applied to those coming from elsewhere, with consequent elaboration and refinement. Although it may seem a little repetitive, I have thought it best to include here a copy of the rules which have been in use at Cambridge for the treatment of census-type documents, both in the hope that they may be of some use to future workers on these and perhaps other materials in Britain and in other countries, and in fuller explanation of what has been stated in the foregoing sections of this chapter. They should draw attention once more to the uncertainties of the task in hand, for it will be evident that they are often somewhat arbitrary. A list of definitions is first laid down, then a series of interpretive principles. It should be noted that the word *compiler* refers to the person who in the past made out the document being analysed, and the word *researcher* to the present-day enquirer. In reading these rules it should always be remembered that only a tiny proportion of all English listings specify ages, and that ancillary information is rarely available.

LIST OF DEFINITIONS
For use in tables of analysis of census-type documents

1 *Household*

A *household* consists of all those who appear in the list grouped together, or in any way clearly separated from groups of others before and after. Occasionally the compiler has made what appear to be subdivisions, to indicate more than one household sharing the same set of premises. In such cases the term *houseful* designates the larger group. A household is also to be described as the inhabitants of a *dwelling*, and the houseful as the inhabitants of a set of *premises*.

The *head of the household* is the person whose name appears first within the household division.

N.B. It should be noticed that the compiler will ordinarily have referred to the group here defined as a *household* by the term *family* which in earlier times covered what we call household. The term *family* will not be used by the researcher in this wide sense as the title of a domestic group, where there is a possibility of ambiguity.

2 *Marital status*

A man and woman are defined as a *married couple* when:
  i   they are stated to be man and wife by the compiler
  ii   they are presumed* married
  iii external evidence, e.g. a marriage register, shows them to be married.

* See *Rules for Presumption.*

Widow and widower are defined as:
  i   those stated to be such by the compiler
  ii those presumed* widowed
  iii those for whom parish register or other external evidence of broken marriage exists.
  N.B. It will be seen that deserted spouses or divorced persons are held not to be distinguishable from widowed persons.

An individual is defined as *single* when:
  i   he is stated to be so by the compiler
  ii he is presumed* single.

An individual is defined as of *unspecified marital status* when there is not sufficient evidence to assign him to any of the above categories.

3   Child

An individual is defined as a *child* when:
  i   he is stated by the compiler to be a *child*, son, daughter, grandchild, nephew, niece, parish or pauper child, nurse child or bastard, unless he is himself married.
  Offspring are children who live in the households of their own parent(s) and/or step-parent(s) and/or grandparent(s) and are themselves unmarried.
  An *orphan* is a child one or both of whose biological parents are known or assumed to be dead.
  N.B. It will be seen that age does not enter into the definition of a child.

4   Servant

A *servant* is one who:
  i   is called a servant, apprentice, journeyman, servant in husbandry, clerk, cook butler, coachman, footboy, etc., maid, housekeeper, etc., by the compiler and lives in a household headed by another.
  ii is presumed* by reason of his position in the household to be a servant.

5   Kin

Resident kin are defined as anyone within the household when:
  i   stated to be kin by the compiler
  ii presumed* to be kin
  iii external evidence, e.g. family reconstitution, shows them to be kin.

6   Conjugal family and conjugal family unit

A *conjugal family* or *conjugal family unit* (CFU) consists of either a married couple with or without offspring, or the remaining partner of a marriage with offspring present.

7   Inmates

Inmates are persons so described, or called sojourners, boarders, lodgers, etc. They can be individual inmates, or members of groups of inmates, and such groups can consist of unrelated persons, or of simple, extended or multiple family groups, all with or without servants. These units are parallel in definition to types of household, but since they do not occupy dwellings should not in strictness be called households.

* See *Rules for Presumption.*

4-2

N.B. All persons appearing within blocks of names whose relationship with the others is not apparent and cannot be presumed, are regarded as sharing the houseful, but never the household, with other persons named in the block.

8   *Institutions*

Institution covers poorhouse, workhouse, almshouse, school, gaol, prison, hospital etc. Their inhabitants are assumed to be analogous to inmates, though a keeper's family is regarded as a household.

RULES FOR PRESUMPTION

The following rules must be strictly observed in order that the analysis of each list is consistent with that of every other.

1   *Presumptions about marital status*

a   Those may be *presumed married* who are of opposite sex, appear first and second in the household and have the same surname. This presumption is strengthened if those following the first two have the same surname and/or are described as children.

Those may also be *presumed married* who appear later in the household, i.e. not first and second, but who have the same surname and are followed in the household by those who have the same surname and/or are described as children.

b   An individual may be *presumed widowed* who is
  i   described as either mother or father of the head or other member of the household (a spouse not being present)
  ii   the head of a household containing either or both a married couple and children (so described) with the same surname or with no surname given.

It will be seen that deserted wives or husbands are regarded as widowed and even those living separately from their spouses, or with their spouses temporarily absent.

c   An individual may be *presumed single* who is
  i   described as a child, son, daughter, nephew, niece, sojourner, servant, apprentice, journeyman, bastard, unless there is evidence to the contrary.
  ii   living with what is described as his or her bastard child or bastard with the same surname (and not described as married)
  iii   living in a household in which the only relative is a sibling.

N.B. *No presumptions should be made about the marital status of solitaries except where the above rules apply.*

2   *Presumptions about offspring*

An individual may be *presumed offspring* who is listed immediately after a married couple, a presumed married couple, a widowed person or a presumed widowed person and has the same surname or is listed without a surname.

3   *Presumptions about kinship*

a   An individual may be *presumed a grandchild* who is described in the list as the offspring of parent(s) whose own (presumed) parent(s) head(s) the household.

b   An individual may be presumed a parent of the preceding generation who is described as widowed in a household headed by a man or woman of the same surname.

c   Members of a household with the same surname may be presumed kin.

This final statement is perhaps the most arbitrary of all, since many surnames in English, such as Smith, are very unreliable as indicators of kinship, and all are unreliable to some degree. What is more, almost no affinal relationships can be recovered by use of this principle, since the wife's surname is known so seldom. The situation in France, and even in Scotland is better than that in England in this respect, but this can scarcely be held to recommend the English practice as the basis for comparative exercises.

2. Some demographic determinants of average household size: An analytic approach[1]

Thomas K. Burch

Descriptions of non-nuclear family systems in terms of their characteristic rules of residence often seem to imply very large and complex households. For example, in a classic patriarchal family system, a household containing a father, his wife, two married sons, and their wives and children would number ten or more persons. Such large households are seldom encountered as modal or average, however. A recent compilation of census materials reported in the U.N. *Demographic Yearbook* showed no bona fide case of a national average household size larger than six.[2]

Several explanations have been offered for this discrepancy between the ideal and the actual. Lang[3] has stressed economic limitations on household size and composition, arguing that only the better-off segments of any society can realize the ideal, because only they have the required land, housing and other material goods.

Hsu[4] has stressed the social psychological difficulties of maintaining large, complex households, and argued that relatively few male or female heads will have the social and administrative skill to hold these households together in the face of centrifugal forces (e.g., mother-in-law or sister-in-law problems).

Others have stressed demographic limitations, pointing out in particular the role of high mortality in hindering realization of the ideal household form. Some quantitative data on this point were presented by Collver[5] in his study of the Indian family life-cycle. The idea is developed at length by Levy[6] in a theoretical essay in which he argues that actual family structures have been rather similar in

[1] This paper was first published in *Demography* (1970) and was prepared for presentation at the session on 'Demography of the Family', at the 1969 Population Association of America Meetings, Atlantic City, N.J., April, 1969. Support for this research was provided by Ford Foundation Grant no. 63-75 and National Science Foundation Grant no. CS-2294. Philip Kreitner provided invaluable computational assistance.
[2] Burch, *The size and structure of families* (1967): 353–5 esp. Tables 1, 2 and 3.
[3] Lang, *Chinese family and society* (1946).
[4] Hsu, *The myth of Chinese family size* (1943).
[5] Collver, *The family cycle in India and the United States* (1963).
[6] Levy, *Aspects of the analysis of family structure* (1965).

societies of all times and places, regardless of the structural ideals.[7] The central notion in this approach is that high mortality makes the joint survival of siblings or of three or more generations in direct line of descent for one sex (or other survival contingencies needed to elaborate complex household structures) relatively rare events.

Little systematic work has been done to investigate the relations of demographic variables to household size and structure.[8] An elaborate simulation approach is described in Orcutt, Greenberger, Korbel and Rivlin,[9] but so far as I know it has not been utilized to study the kinds of questions raised in this chapter. Recent work by Coale suggests a fruitful approach to the problem, however. In a brief technical note appended to Levy's essay, Coale presents a life table technique for showing the variation in average household size for different family systems, defined in terms of rules of residence, in a stationary population with high fertility and high mortality ($e_0 = 20$ years; crude birth and death rates $= 50$ per 1,000). He finds that for the family system involving maximum extension of households, average household size is 75 per cent larger than for the nuclear family system under the same demographic conditions.[10]

The purpose of this chapter is to extend Coale's model to stable populations as well as stationary, in order to show the variation in average household size by family system, for different levels and combinations of mortality and fertility, and for different average ages at marriage. In addition, the model will be used to shed some light on variations in the structure as well as the size of households, by examining the average number of adults per household as well as the average number of all persons (adults and children).

The chapter comprises three sections: (1) description of the Coale model and of the modifications needed to apply it to stable populations; (2) presentation of the main conclusions as to the effects of varying rules of residence, fertility, mortality and age at marriage on family composition, as these are given by the model; (3) a discussion of the adequacy of the model as a representation of real family systems, and of needed or possible modifications.

DESCRIPTION OF THE MODEL FOR STATIONARY AND STABLE POPULATIONS

Calculations made by Coale and in the present chapter involve several general assumptions which should be mentioned at this point. First, all calculations relate either to stationary or stable populations, in the full technical sense. The stationary population model assumes unchanging age-specific birth and death

---

[7] See below, Goody, Chapter 3, pp. 104–106, for details of the controversy surrounding this subject.

[8] But see S. P. Brown, *Analysis of a hypothetical stationary population by family units* (1951): 380–94.

[9] Orcutt, Greenberger, Korbel and Rivlin, *Microanalysis of socio-economic systems* (1961).

[10] Coale, *Estimates of average size of household* (1965): 64–7 esp. Table 1.

rates which yield an unchanging age structure and total population size, i.e. the growth rate is zero. A stable population model involves assumptions of unchanging fertility, mortality and age structure, but allows the growth rate to vary over a wide range.[11] Second, the treatment is in terms of female populations only; total household size (i.e. males and females) is taken as twice that for females, a rough approximation.[12] Third, all females are assumed to marry. Fourth, all marriages take place exactly at the average age at marriage, and all births take place at the average age of child-bearing. Fifth, once a woman becomes a household head, she does not relinquish that status despite advanced age.

The general approach is to calculate age-specific headship rates (proportions of females who are household heads by age group) as functions of the family system, mortality, age at marriage, mean age at child-bearing, and fertility. These headship rates are applied to the appropriate population age distribution (stationary or stable) to calculate the number of heads. The total population size divided by the number of heads gives average size of household.

Coale defines four different family systems in terms of residence rules. Each of these is described below, along with the computational procedure used in the stationary and stable cases.

(a) NUCLEAR FAMILY

Every woman marries at the average age at marriage ($\overline{N}$) and thereupon establishes her own household. In other words all women at or above the average age at marriage are household heads. For the stationary case, average household size ($\overline{H}$) is simply $T_0/T_{\bar{N}}$ where T is the ordinary life table function and $\overline{N}$ is the average age at marriage. For the stable case, $\overline{H}$ is P (total)/$P(\overline{N}$ and over), where P refers to age groups in the stable population. It will be noted that for this model, $\overline{H}$ is a function of age structure and of the average age at marriage.

(b) EXTENDED FAMILY WITH FOSTER MOTHERS

Every woman marries at the average age at marriage, but continues to live with her own mother or a foster mother the same age as her own mother (who is assigned her if her own mother dies before the daughter reaches the marriage age). The daughter does not establish her own household until her mother (or foster mother) has died. In both stationary and stable populations, the proportion *not* maintaining their own household at age $\overline{N}$ is 1.00, by definition. At age $\overline{N}+X$, the proportion not maintaining their own household is $l_{\bar{A}+\bar{N}+X}/l_{\bar{A}+\bar{N}}$, where l is the life table function, $\overline{A}$ is the average age at childbearing and $\overline{N}$ the average age at marriage. (In the present calculations $\overline{A}$ is constant at 30 years.

---

[11] For a brief explanation see Barclay, *Techniques of population analysis* (1958): 131–4.
[12] For estimates of household size based on male populations, see below, Goody, Chapter 3, p. 111, and Hammel, Chapter 14, pp. 361–362.

For a discussion of connected problems, see below). In other words, at the time of marriage every woman is living with her mother (or foster mother), who is $\bar{A}$ years older than she. The proportion remaining in the parental household five years later is the proportion whose mothers or foster mothers survive over that interval of age. The headship rates calculated in this fashion are then applied to the stationary or stable age distribution. It will be noted that in this case, the headship rates are functions of age at marriage, mean age at childbearing, and of mortality. Thus, $\bar{H}$ is a function of age structure, age at marriage, age at childbearing, and of mortality.

(c) EXTENDED FAMILY WITHOUT FOSTER MOTHERS

Every woman marries at the average age at marriage. If her own mother has died, she immediately sets up her own household; if her own mother is still living, she remains in her mother's household until her mother dies. No foster mothers are involved. In the stationary and stable cases, the proportion *not* maintaining their own household at the average age at marriage ($\bar{N}$) is $l_{\bar{A}+\bar{N}}/l_{\bar{A}}$, where $\bar{A}$ is the average age at childbearing. In general at age $\bar{N}+X$, the proportion not maintaining their own households is $l_{\bar{A}+\bar{N}+X}/l_{\bar{A}}$. In other words, the probability that a woman will not head her own household at any age from age $\bar{N}$ on is the probability that her own mother will survive to that age. In this, as in the previous case, the headship rates are functions of mean age at marriage and at childbearing and of mortality..

(d) STEM FAMILY

Every woman marries at the average age at marriage. If her mother is dead, she immediately sets up her own household. If her mother is alive, she or one of her sisters remains in the mother's household until the death of the mother. The remaining sisters set up new households immediately upon marriage. The proportion not maintaining their own households at age $\bar{N}$ is the product of three factors: (1) the proportion of mothers surviving to age $\bar{A}+\bar{N}$ (i.e. the mothers' age at the time of their daughters' marriages); (2) the proportion of families having at least one daughter surviving to age $\bar{N}$; (3) the reciprocal of the average number of daughters surviving to age $\bar{N}$ in families having at least one. Factor (1) is the same, age for age, as that computed in case (c) above.

Factor (2) is $1.0-\alpha$, where α is the proportion of families with no daughters surviving to $\bar{N}$. In the stationary case, α is $(1-l_{\bar{N}}/l_0)^{l_0/l_{\bar{A}}}$. The expression in parentheses gives the probability of dying by age $\bar{N}$. The exponent is the average number of daughters born per mother. α is thus the combined probability of all daughters dying before age $\bar{N}$. $1.0-\alpha$ is the probability that at least one will survive to that age. In the stable case, $l_0/l_{\bar{A}}$ is replaced by the gross reproduction rate (GRR), to give the number of daughters born per mother on average.

Factor (3) in the stationary case is $(l_{\bar{N}}/l_{\bar{A}})/(1-\alpha)$. $l_{\bar{N}}/l_{\bar{A}}$ gives the number of daughters reaching age $\bar{N}$ per family. Dividing this by $(1.0-\alpha)$ gives the average number reaching the age at marriage in families having at least one reaching that age.

Factor (3) in the stable case is GRR $(l_{\bar{N}}/l_0)/(1-\alpha)$. GRR $(l_{\bar{N}}/l_0)$ gives the average number of daughters surviving to marriage age in all families. This factor divided by $1.0-\alpha$ gives the average number surviving to marriage in families having at least one surviving daughter.

For the stable case, then, the proportion of women not maintaining their own households at any given age equals the proportion from case (c) above multiplied by the product of factors (2) and the reciprocal of (3), or

$$[(1-\alpha)^2 \times l_0]/\text{GRR} \times l_{\bar{N}},$$

which is constant over all ages for given ages at marriage and at child-bearing and levels of fertility and mortality. In case (d), average household size bears a very complex relation to demographic factors; it is a function of the mean age at marriage and at childbearing, the level of fertility and of mortality, and age composition of the population.

RESULTS

For each of the family systems described above, calculations have been made of the average number of persons per household and of the average number of adults per household for various levels of fertility, mortality and age at marriage. Fertility levels are GRRs of 1, 2, 3 and 4. Mortality levels are e_0s of 20, 40, 60 and 77.5. Age at marriage is taken as 15, 20 and 25. The stable populations used in the calculations are from the model West female series given by Coale and Demeny.[13] (Life table functions are also model West female, with l_{100} assumed to be zero, and l_x for 85, 90, and 95 obtained by linear interpolation.)

Average age at childbearing has been kept constant at 30 years throughout. This involves two difficulties that should be mentioned. First, the stable population models used assume average age at childbearing to be 29, not 30, so that there is a small bias in the calculations. Second, although the average age at childbearing does not vary widely in actual fact, still the models would be more realistic were $\bar{A}$ varied over at least a small range. In particular, there is some inconsistency in combining very high fertility with a late average age at marriage, without assuming also a higher average age at childbearing. In this first approach to the problem, it seemed reasonable to accept these inconsistencies rather than to get involved in considerably more complicated computation. In any case, the errors involved would not seem to affect our major conclusions.

Table 2.1 gives the average size of household for each family system for different combinations of fertility and mortality. In the nuclear family, it is clear

[13] Coale and Demeny, *Regional model life tables and stable populations* (1966).

Table 2.1 *Average household size in stable population under different family systems, by mortality and fertility level*[a]
(age at marriage = 20 years)

Mortality and fertility levels	Nuclear	Extended, foster mothers		Stem
		Allowed	Not allowed	
$e_0 = 20$				
GRR =				
1.0	2.4	3.2	2.8	2.6
2.0	3.0	4.6	3.8	3.3
3.0	3.6	6.0	4.7	4.1
4.0	4.2	7.6	5.6	4.8
$e_0 = 40$				
GRR =				
1.0	2.6	4.0	3.6	3.2
2.0	3.4	6.5	5.4	4.3
3.0	4.2	9.4	7.2	5.2
4.0	5.0	12.4	9.2	6.0
$e_0 = 60$				
GRR =				
1.0	2.7	4.8	4.4	4.1
2.0	3.6	8.7	7.5	5.1
3.0	4.5	13.2	10.9	5.8
4.0	5.4	18.2	14.4	6.6
$e_0 = 77.5$				
GRR =				
1.0	2.7	5.6	5.4	5.4
2.0	3.7	11.2	10.7	5.5
3.0	4.6	18.4	17.2	6.2
4.0	5.6	26.9	24.9	7.0

[a] Figures are average number of females per household in the female stable population multiplied by 2.

that household size remains within moderate bounds under any of the demographic conditions given. To a lesser extent this is true also of the stem family. In both cases, $\overline{H}$ is well under ten, and pretty much in line with values observed in actual populations – for large populations, these seldom if ever exceed 7. In extended family systems (cases (b) and (c)), however, household size becomes extremely large when fertility and life expectancy are both high. About one-third of the values in Table 2.1 exceed 10. Such values have been observed, so far as I know, only for certain regions of tropical African nations, although these cases involve problems relating to census definitions of *household*.[14]

On the empirical level, the calculations tend to support two generalisations regarding demographic aspects of family structure. First, populations with high fertility, relatively low mortality and moderate household size (e.g. 5 or under) are operating under an actual family system that involves considerable departure

[14] See below, Goody, Chapter 3, pp. 106–110.

Table 2.2   *Average household size under stem and extended family systems relative to size under nuclear system, by mortality and fertility level*
(Nuclear system = 100)

Mortality and fertility levels	Nuclear	Extended, foster mothers		Stem
		Allowed	Not allowed	
$e_0 = 20$				
GRR =				
1.0	100	131	116	105
2.0	100	151	124	111
3.0	100	167	130	113
4.0	100	181	135	114
$e_0 = 40$				
GRR =				
1.0	100	156	138	122
2.0	100	193	158	128
3.0	100	224	173	125
4.0	100	249	184	120
$e_0 = 60$				
GRR =				
1.0	100	181	166	153
3.0	100	240	208	140
2.0	100	290	239	128
4.0	100	334	264	122
$e_0 = 77.5$				
GRR =				
1.0	100	208	203	200
2.0	100	305	292	150
3.0	100	396	373	133
4.0	100	480	445	125

from an extended family ideal. Were the extended family pattern being adhered to consistently, the average household size would be much larger than observed. Second, in populations with high fertility and extended family ideals, the decline in mortality creates powerful pressures at the household level for departures from or modifications of the extended family system or for the control of fertility. By powerful pressures, we mean the doubling or even tripling of average household size as mortality declines from very high to very low levels.[15] The theoretical effect of extended family systems on household size, however, even when mortality is high, is not negligible, as is brought out in Table 2.2. With a GRR of 3 and an e_0 of 40, for instance, household size in case (c) is 73 per cent greater than in the nuclear system; in case (b), household size is more than twice as large as in the nuclear system.

It is also apparent from Table 2.2 that the impact of an extended family system tends to increase separately with fertility and with life expectancy, and is

[15] These findings are in general accord with Levy's original hypothesis. See esp. Levy (1965): 56.

Table 2.3   *Relative size of households for different fertility levels,*
for each mortality level and family system
(GRR of $1.0 = 100$ for each e_0 level)

Mortality and fertility levels	Nuclear	Extended, foster mothers		Stem
		Allowed	Not allowed	
		$e_0 = 20$		
GRR =				
1.0	100	100	100	100
2.0	124	143	133	130
3.0	148	189	166	159
4.0	172	266	199	186
		$e_0 = 40$		
GRR =				
1.0	100	100	100	100
2.0	131	162	151	137
3.0	162	233	203	165
4.0	192	307	257	189
		$e_0 = 60$		
GRR =				
1.0	100	100	100	100
2.0	135	179	169	124
3.0	169	272	245	142
4.0	203	376	325	162
		$e_0 = 77.5$		
GRR =				
1.0	100	100	100	100
2.0	137	201	197	102
3.0	174	330	318	115
4.0	210	484	458	130

greatest when very high fertility and low mortality are combined. The reasons for this are clear. High fertility yields a large proportion of children in the population, none of whom become household heads, and thus inflates average household size. Low mortality increases the probability that a married adult will remain in her parental home, and similarly increases household size.

Under a stem family system, the relations are more complicated and somewhat different. Household size increases uniformly with fertility and life expectancy, as is apparent in Table 2.1. But the size of the stem family household *relative* to that in the nuclear system (see Table 2.2) tends to decline with higher fertility when life expectancy is relatively high. This is due to the fact that with a larger *number* of daughters surviving well into the adult years, the *proportion* remaining in the parental home declines.

Demographic interest attaches to the question of the relative influence of fertility and of mortality on household size under the different family systems. Some light can be shed on these problems by Tables 2.3 and 2.4, although the results there depend to some extent on the range of values chosen. In the nuclear

Table 2.4 *Relative size of households for different mortality levels,*
for each fertility level and family system
(e_0 of $20 = 100$ for each GRR level)

Fertility and mortality levels	Nuclear	Extended, foster mothers		Stem
		Allowed	Not allowed	
GRR = 1.0				
$e_0 =$				
20	100	100	100	100
40	106	126	126	123
60	110	151	157	159
77.5	109	173	192	208
GRR = 2.0				
$e_0 =$				
20	100	100	100	100
40	112	143	143	129
60	119	189	199	151
77.5	121	244	284	164
GRR = 3.0				
$e_0 =$				
20	100	100	100	100
40	116	155	154	127
60	125	218	231	142
77.5	128	304	367	150
GRR = 4.0				
$e_0 =$				
20	100	100	100	100
40	118	163	162	126
60	130	240	256	139
77.5	134	356	441	146

family system, it is clear that fertility is the more important factor affecting household size. This is because under the nuclear model, $\overline{H}$ is dependent only on age at marriage and age structure (but not on the survivorship of one's parents), and it is well established that fertility has a more powerful influence on age structure than does mortality.

In the extended family systems, the relative effects of fertility and mortality seem roughly similar, with a slight edge to fertility over the ranges included in Tables 2.3 and 2.4. In the stem family system (case (*d*)), once again the picture is mixed, but with mortality seeming to have a slightly greater influence, particularly at high levels of fertility.

Perhaps the most important general conclusion to emerge from these calculations is the strong independent effect of fertility on average household size, a point that has not been emphasized in previous discussions of the topic. The reason for this is clear analytically from the models. Fertility has a strong influence on the proportion of the total population who are children (say, under 15) most of whom are nonheads of households under any family system, and on the proportion

Table 2.5 *Average number of adults (persons 15 and over)*
per household, by family system and fertility and mortality level[a]
(age at marriage = 20 years)

Mortality and fertility levels	Nuclear	Extended, foster mothers		Stem
		Allowed	Not allowed	
$e_0 = 20$				
GRR =				
1.0	2.1	2.8	2.5	2.2
2.0	2.2	3.4	2.8	2.5
3.0	2.4	3.9	3.1	2.7
4.0	2.4	4.4	3.3	2.8
$e_0 = 40$				
GRR =				
1.0	2.2	3.4	3.0	2.6
2.0	2.3	4.5	3.7	3.0
3.0	2.4	5.4	4.2	3.0
4.0	2.5	6.3	4.7	3.0
$e_0 = 60$				
GRR =				
1.0	2.2	3.9	3.6	3.3
2.0	2.3	5.6	4.9	3.3
3.0	2.5	7.2	5.9	3.2
4.0	2.6	8.6	6.9	3.2
$e_0 = 77.5$				
GRR =				
1.0	2.2	4.5	4.4	4.4
2.0	2.3	7.2	6.8	3.5
3.0	2.5	9.8	9.2	3.3
4.0	2.6	12.5	11.5	3.2

[a] Figures are the average number of adult females per household in the female stable population multiplied by 2.

who are adults, and thus are candidates for household headship by virtue of their age. In brief, household size is strongly influenced by age structure.[16]

The fact that household size reflects the relative number of children in a population suggests computation of a different household measure, one that gives at least a rough index of the complexity of households. The index used here is simply the average number of adults per household, where an adult is taken as anyone 15 years or older. Table 2.5 shows how this measure varies with fertility and mortality for the four family systems.

It shows that in nuclear and stem family systems, households tend to remain relatively simple in composition, as well as relatively small, under almost any conditions of mortality and fertility. Only in a few instances for the stem family

[16] For a different view, see below, Goody, Chapter 3, pp. 115–117. Children also have an insignificant effect on household size in pre-industrial England although it has to be remembered that many older children were listed as servants in other households. See below, Laslett, Chapter 4, pp. 147–148.

and never for the nuclear family does the number of adults per household appreciably exceed 3. On average this means less than two married couples per household. In the extended family systems, by contrast, the large households are also extremely complex in the sense that they would contain (for certain levels of fertility and mortality) 5 or more adults and presumably 2 or more married couples.

Up until now, all calculations have assumed an average age at marriage of 20 years. What effect does variation of age at marriage have on household size? First of all, it should be noted that the interrelations mentioned above are largely independent of age at marriage. That is, roughly the same substantive conclusions would have emerged had Tables 2.1 through 2.5 assumed an average age at marriage of 15 or 25, instead of 20.

As for the direct effect of age at marriage on household size, within the limitations of the model, it would seem that later marriage yields larger households on average (assuming later marriage does not result in lower fertility). This is the case for almost all family systems, and all combinations of fertility and mortality. There are some exceptions for the stem family system when mortality and fertility both are low, but the differences are small, and the lack of sufficient refinements in the model would suggest that they should not be emphasized.

DISCUSSION

The above comments deal with the interrelations of household and demographic variables within the context of the model. How adequate are they as descriptions of these interrelations in the real world? To answer this question at least in part, it will be helpful to mention two kinds of limitations in the model as presented. The first are unrealistic assumptions that could be modified by changes in computational details. The second are limitations inherent in the basic approach used. The latter suggest the need for basically different analytic approaches to the problem.

In the first category, we can mention the following problems:

1. Whereas the model assumes universal marriage, in reality appreciable proportions of women never marry. The extent of non-marriage is thought to vary with family system, being slight in societies with extended family ideals, and relatively large in societies with nuclear or stem family systems. Since some proportion of permanent spinsters would remain in their parents' home, this non-marriage would tend to reduce the number of household heads and thus to increase average household size. The re-working of the models to build in appropriate assumptions regarding proportions married for each family system probably would have the net effect of reducing the size differences between extended and non-extended forms. If the assumptions regarding proportions married were introduced age for age, this would have the additional effect of relaxing the assumption that all marriage takes place at the average age at marriage.

2. In the above models, the proportion of women with their own households reaches 1.0 by age group 70–74 and remains at that level for age groups 75–79 and 80 and over. This assumption is unrealistic on two counts. First, the level of these headship rates is almost certainly too high. It is unlikely that empirical headship rates come close to 1.0 for any age-sex group under any family system. Second, the shape of the age-specific headship curve is incorrect. Empirical curves tend to reach a maximum in late adult years (in the 50s or 60s for males, a decade or so later for females) and then decline at the oldest ages. Some modifications of the model to take this into account would be feasible. Their net effect would be to increase the average size of household under all family systems.

3. The calculations presented above have been based on female stable populations. For most family systems, it probably would be more realistic, though more difficult practically, to compute household size using male stable population parameters. The effect of using male rather than female stable population is difficult to assess in advance. The later age at marriage would tend to increase household size. But the later average age at childbearing would tend to decrease the probability that a man's father would survive to any given age of the son, and to increase the number of heads in the son's generation, thus tending to decrease average household size.

Other shortcomings of our results would require a different approach. For instance, the models deal with stable conditions, and are not necessarily adequate as descriptions of changes in household size concomitant with demographic changes such as secular declines in mortality. For this purpose, it would be necessary to modify the calculations considerably so that they might be applied in the context of quasi-stable population models, or in the context of population projections.

A more basic shortcoming of the present approach is the limited detail of the household measures derived. It would be desirable to have more descriptive measures (such as number of married couples per household), distributions as well as averages, and descriptions of changes in size and composition over the family life cycle (e.g. by age of head of household). The generation of such detailed information would be best accomplished by a simulation of household formation and dissolution.

3. The evolution of the family

Jack Goody

Jack Goody

FAMILY, HOUSEHOLD AND DOMESTIC GROUP

Text books in the social sciences are full of statements about the general trend in human societies from patterns of extended kinship to conjugal families. On a more general level the change has been seen as one connected with the general move from kinship to territoriality, from status to contract, from mechanical to organic solidarity, from *gemeinschaft* to *gesellschaft*, from ascription to achievement. There is no need to lengthen the list of vague polarities.

With the general trend that this list implies few would disagree. But when we come to deal more specifically with the movements in family structure, difficulties arise. The main problem for the evolution of the family is to understand just what is evolving. The English term 'family' is a polysemic word used to describe a conjugal pair and their young ('starting a family'), the members of a household ('one of the family'), a range of bilateral kin ('relatives') or a patronymic group, usually associated with a title ('The Churchill family'). And there are wider semantic usages, extending to the human ('the family of man') and non-human ('the family of sweet peas') species.

Discussions of the evolution of the family and changes in household composition centre upon the emergence of the kind of family (referred to as elementary, nuclear or conjugal) that is supposed to be a concomitant of industrialisation, either as cause or effect. The implication here is that the 'nuclear family' has become more independent in economic, residential and other terms. Given that separate residence appears to be related to such independence, attention has been concentrated upon the mean size of households in order to obtain some measure of a change from the dominance of extended networks of 'kin' to smaller 'family' units.

An examination of the figures for England reveals however, as Laslett points out, that mean household size (MHS) has been relatively constant from the sixteenth century to the beginning of the present century.[1] Does this mean that special conditions obtained in Western Europe which assisted the emergence of industrial (i.e. non-familial) productive systems?

The hypothesis is tempting, especially as interesting suggestions have been

[1] See below, Laslett, Chapter 4, pp. 137–139.

made as to the possible relationships between delayed marriage and capital accumulation.[2] Certainly basic changes in kinship systems turn around the processes associated with industrialisation, urbanisation and 'modernisation'. But in my view the household is not a very sensitive indicator to such change. Indeed the whole problem has been clouded by analytic problems which have obscured the relationship of household composition to kinship structure in general, and more specifically to the elementary family.

The discussion concerning 'family' or 'household' size has got somewhat confused, largely because of miscommunication. Reacting against the myth of primitive promiscuity, Malinowski first established the existence of an elementary type of family among the Australian aborigines, and despite having worked among a society that emphasised social matriliny and rejected biological paternity, later insisted on the critical role of the family in social life. Using cross-cultural data, Murdock went on to argue that the elementary (or nuclear) family was universal, even as a residential unit. The theme was taken up by Talcott Parsons. Basing himself upon socialisation studies, cross-cultural research and the results of experiments in small groups, he claimed that the small family provided the most satisfactory framework for the bringing up of children; hence its universality.

Other writers, particularly comparative sociologists, have been critical of these ideas, partly because claims for the nuclear family often neglect theoretically important cases which, while they do not contradict the claim that some kind of small domestic unit is universal, do modify certain structural implications derived from the nuclear family model. More importantly, they have seen the core of the problem to lie not at the level of small family units but in the kind and degree of articulation of such units into larger kin-based structures. To put it another way, the opposition between 'family' and 'kinship' (or small and large family systems) is quite inadequate unless it recognises explicitly that all societies with more inclusive patterns of kinship also have, at the turning centre of their world, smaller domestic groups that are involved in the processes of production, reproduction, consumption and socialisation.

In this chapter I want to clarify some of the issues involved in discussing 'family change' and to place these in a broad comparative framework. Both clarification and comparison are essential, since the problems that are being discussed, implicitly or explicitly, concern the relationships of family composition to economic and other variables: these can be confirmed by two procedures, by examining the same society over time or by examining different societies at different stages of development. To do this we need a set of analytic constructs. But even the referent of the phrase 'elementary family' is not at all clear. When Malinowski and Murdock claim that the elementary family is universal,[3] the statement can be profitably discussed only when certain parameters are established. If co-residence is a defining characteristic of the 'family' in question,

[2] Hajnal, *European marriage patterns in perspective* (1965).
[3] Malinowski, *Kinship* (1930): 23; Murdock, *Social structure* (1949): 3.

then this contention holds neither for groups like the Nayar and Ashanti nor for Caribbean societies (at least in the behavioural sense – the normative position is less clear). Nevertheless it is clear that in the vast majority of societies, it is possible to isolate a significant unit that approximates to one of the various models of the elementary family.

Put in this way, the proposition is unlikely to arouse much objection. Put in a different way, with implications of extension[4] or of opposition between family and kinship,[5] and many a hackle will be raised. In sum, the situation has been thoroughly confused by the concepts we have failed to develop. For example, Levy's proposition concerning the gap between ideal (large) and actual (small) domestic groups is obscured by a failure clearly to distinguish family (as a demographic unit) from household (as a 'houseful')[6] and by the too radical distinction between family and kinship. Hence the validity of the point made by Fallers:[7] that Levy does not make sufficient allowance for the factor of fusion (e.g. in the case of the old, the orphaned, the adopted, the fostered and even the visitors) in the size of the domestic units. The point is a critical one in many situations of migration when the size of domestic groups may increase by the accretion of more distant kin than would normally be the case.[8]

But it is less clear that Faller's point 'conclusively disproves Levy's hypothesis that "the general outlines and nature of the *actual* family structure have been virtually identical in certain strategic respects (size, age, sex and generational composition) in all known societies in world history for well over fifty per cent of the members of these societies"'.[9] More than 'demographic reductionism' is involved in the central idea that small domestic units are universal, for the size of these units is related to the functions of childrearing, food production, cooking, etc. that Fallers asks us to examine.

Indeed the proposition is well supported by sociological theory,[10] by existing data, as well as by the models of Coale and Burch.[11] If this is so it follows that

---

[4] Malinowski (1930).

[5] Levy, *Aspects of the analysis of family structure* (1965). Levy's arguments are also discussed by Burch, above, Chapter 2, pp. 91–92 and Laslett, below, Chapter 4, p. 144 fn. 19.

[6] I.e. where one household makes up the whole houseful, though a houseful may contain several households. See above, Laslett, Chapter 1, pp. 34–39.

[7] Fallers, *The range of variation in actual family size* (1965).

[8] E. N. Goody has pointed out that in West Africa, the fostering of rural children by urban families may lead to the exploitation of more distant ties of kinship than in the purely rural situation.

[9] Levy (1965): 81.

[10] E.g. Parsons, *The incest taboo in relation to social structure* (1954).

[11] These models are discussed by Burch, see above, Chapter 2, pp. 92–95. See also Coale, *Estimates of average size of household* (1965) and Burch, *The size and structure of families* (1967). Burch tries to test Marion Levy's hypothesis concerning the essential similarity of actual family structures in all societies by examining United Nations' data on the type and size of households. See below, Table 3.2, which is a selective repetition of Burch's data (1967: 354–5), employing more recent material. Burch concludes that 'no bonafide case of national average size of greater than 6.5 persons was discovered' (1967: 358), though in this range the more industrialised nations tend to have smaller households than the developing

talk of the emergence of such a unit in recent centuries is virtually meaningless unless we can specify its context and its functions.

It seems more useful to approach the question from another direction. In discussing the way in which the developmental cycle influenced family and household,[12] we used the phrase 'domestic group' in order to circumvent some of the definitional problems and introduce an element of flexibility. This phrase is an overall term for three main kinds of unit, namely, the dwelling unit, the reproductive unit, the economic unit.[13] The economic unit is again a generic term which covers the persons jointly engaged in the process of production and consumption.[14] In agricultural societies (as well as in craft production) these units tend to be closely linked together; in industrial societies they are usually quite distinct.

THE HOUSEHOLD AS A DWELLING GROUP

It is frequently the first of these units, the dwelling group, that we refer to as a family ('living as one of the family'), though more usually we apply the almost equally ambiguous word 'household'.[15] Ambiguous because it carries both the meaning of consumption unit (Mrs Beaton's Household Management) as well as of dwelling group. In Western societies these ambiguities may present no great problem, at least if we think of an apartment house as a series of

countries. However, 'it became clear' he writes, '...that since children comprise a large portion of the average family of residence, variation in average size of private households as reported in the census data may have little to do with extended family structure, but reflect variations in the numbers of surviving children' (1967: 363). The ratio of 'nuclear family' to 'total family' in the household is always large (the Indian figure of 0.75 is the lowest) and it seems that these components tend to be inversely associated, that is, 'non-nuclear kin' tend to substitute for 'nuclear kin'. Numbers of this order would appear to be accounted for by institutions like kinship fostering, widowhood and proxy-parenthood.

12   Fortes, Introduction. In: Goody, *The developmental cycle in domestic groups* (1958).

13   For an attempt to clarify the words used in the analysis of domestic groups, see Castillo et al., *The concept of the nuclear and extended family* (1968).

14   In certain contexts each of these units has to be broken down a stage further for analytic purposes (e.g. into units of socialisation), but this necessary task cannot be undertaken here.

15   A failure to distinguish between the household as a dwelling group and unit of consumption and the family as a reproductive unit has been the subject of a considerable discussion of the West Indian domestic institutions. See especially Raymond T. Smith, *The negro family in British Guiana* (1956); M. G. Smith, *West Indian family structure* (1962); Adams, *An inquiry into the nature of the family* (1960); Mintz and Davenport, eds., *Working papers in Caribbean social organisation* (1961); Goody, *Illegitimacy, anomie and cultural penetration* (1961); Raymond T. Smith, *Culture and social structure in the Caribbean* (1963); Otterbein, *Caribbean family organisation* (1965); Goode, *Note on problems in theory and method* (1966); Bender, *A refinement of the concept of household* (1967). Much of this discussion is anticipated in Fortes' analysis of domestic groups among the Tallensi and the Ashanti of Ghana; in the former the units of consumption and reproduction are contained within larger dwelling units; among the latter, the reproductive and economic units are usually distinct from the dwelling group at any one time; the latter is more often based upon the sibling rather than the conjugal bond. See Fortes, *Web of kinship among the Tallensi* (1949 i) and *Kinship and marriage among the Ashanti* (1950). Adams' separation of the 'elementary family' into dyadic relationships is useful for a range of analytic problems.

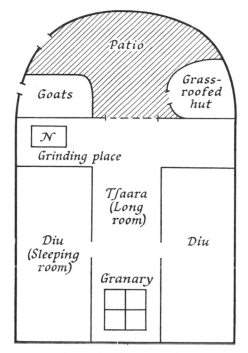

Fig. 3.1   A dwelling of the simplest type, occupied by an elementary family
(LoDagaba, northern Ghana)

Diagonal lines indicate unroofed walled area. Broken line indicates line of posts supporting roof.

After Goody, *The fission of domestic groups among the LoDagaba* (1958 ii): 81

separate 'households'. But in many other societies, the situation is much less clear cut. To bring out the nature of the problem involved, let me refer to the societies from a part of the world with which I am personally familiar. Figs. 3.1 and 3.2 are diagrams of LoDagaba compounds (houses) from northern Ghana. The dwelling group is a large one, an average of 16.3 ('Birifo', 1960 census; in 1948 it was 17.4). The production unit is often smaller in size; in the instance shown here there were three such groups, though in the largest of these, where the compound head farmed with the help of his sons, the young men planted certain crops on their own behalf, to sell for cash or to consume themselves. As far as consumption was concerned, the productive units were yet further divided; each wife was allotted her own share of grain out of the common granary and this she used to cook for her husband and her children.

When such a dwelling group divides, as the larger one later did on the death of the compound head, smaller dwelling units emerge, of the kind illustrated in Fig. 3.1. Two brothers (or a man and his growing son) decide to build a house of their own in the vicinity. With them will go the members of their respective units

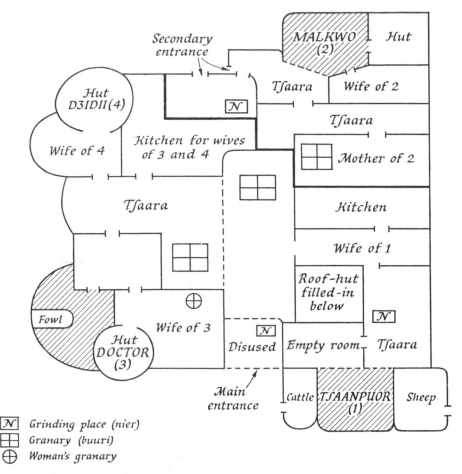

Fig. 3.2   A compound of the complex type (LoDagaba, northern Ghana)

Diagonal lines indicate unroofed walled area. Broken lines indicate line of posts supporting roof. Thick line indicates boundary of enclosed apartment with separate entrance. Quarters of the four adult married males are given in capitals.

After Goody (1958 ii): 82

of production. From the standpoint of the reproductive unit, nothing changes except the location. There is little change too for the productive unit since in most cases the migrating group will already have been working on its own, so both production and consumption are distinct by the time the 'household' (the dwelling group) splits up. Only residential unity is broken.

Though residential fission has great significance for the LoDagaba, the reason and the occasion vary among different sub-groups. Whereas in Birifu (LoWiili) the average compound size was 16.3, only a few miles away around Lawra

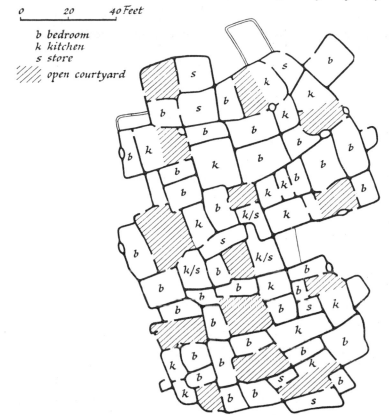

0   20   40 Feet

b *bedroom*
k *kitchen*
s *store*
///// *open courtyard*

Fig. 3.3   Plan of section of Seripe, Gonja, northern Ghana

After Wakely and Mumtaz, *Bui resettlement survey* (1965): 36

(among the LoSaala) the compounds number about 100 members.[16] Some hundred miles south, in Western Gonja, the 'compounds' are as large or even larger. Half a village may be under one roof, each sector being built up (quite literally) of small units very similar to the basic apartment among the LoDagaa. Fig. 3.3 shows one such unit at Seripe. According to the 1960 census Seripe has six 'houses' and a population of 356.

My point here is that for these groups an extensive comparison of family or household size (meaning the number of occupants of a dwelling) is not very meaningful from the standpoint of the structure of the domestic groups that occupy them;[17] 'household size' is relatively unimportant from the domestic standpoint, since the basic reproductive and economic units remain much the

---

[16] Bohannan, *Tiv farm and settlement* (1954): 4, records a similar variation in compound size among the Tiv of northern Nigeria; in the south the largest contained 80 persons, while the average was 17.

[17] There are differences, but these are not associated with the variables we are considering.

same in each case. It is true that the occupants of one of these sections may form a sort of kinship group, as indeed is almost bound to happen in communities where spatial mobility is low. But there is more to it than this, for each 'compound' (or ward) had a large central granary which supported the elders, and the occupants themselves speak of 'eating together'. In 1965 we lived in the town of Bole for several months and had a room in just such a section. We never saw a communal meal actually taking place. Reading our earlier notes provides a salutary reminder of the care with which one has to evaluate documentary material and informants' statements alike; what one first accepts as literal fact often turns out to be ambiguous metaphor.

But whether or not the section eat together is not all that important. In fact they operate in much the same way as a group of related kin living in adjacent but separate households; they helped each other in some of the basic productive tasks such as clearing land; they buried each other's dead and assisted with marriages; in other words they did much the same kind of thing as neighbours in many a village in Europe, where 'kith and kin' may join together in communal tasks. Despite the existence of these larger cooperating groups, the 'family' (in the shape of the units of reproduction, production and consumption) was not greatly different in size from that found in Western Europe today. Larger groups consisted of clusters of such basic units; whether these larger groups of kin (or non-kin) were all under one roof is of little importance from most points of view. An 'extended family' (in this sense) may consist of domestic groups either linked together in a large compound (household) or living nearby in the same locality; in the latter case it is morphologically a unit of rather the same kind of 'extended family' as exists among any small scale community with a relatively stationary population.[18]

If we accept this argument, then we have to be very careful about contrasting a so-called zadruga type of unit, which consists of, say, a fortress of 100 persons, with 'an extended family' that comprises a small farm, a conjugal family and a few attached relatives. As in the LoDagaba case the former is likely to be a multicelled version of the latter, the cells coming together for protection, for administrative convenience, or simply because that was the way the house had been built in the first place; permanent stone dwellings structure family composition in much more radical ways than mud huts and bamboo shelters, for the latter constantly change their shape according to the number and nature of those who live there.[19]

[18] The dangers of concentrating an analysis of kinship and the family upon the household have been discussed by Solien, *Household and family in the Caribbean* (1960). See also Raymond T. Smith (1963): 33. 'The concentration of attention upon the household as a functioning unit of child-care and economic organisation has tended to divert attention from the networks of relationship linking households to each other.'

[19] In studying the household comparatively, it is worth reminding ourselves that the sheltering functions of a dwelling are of considerably less importance in tropical regions than they are in cooler climates. Shelter is not a basic problem in the tropical or semi-tropical environment, partly because of climate and partly because the land and materials for the construction

THE UNITS OF PRODUCTION, REPRODUCTION AND CONSUMPTION

Certainly there are basic differences in the range of a man's kin and in their role that are effected by long-term evolutionary changes. But except in rather exceptional cases, the average size of the basic units of reproduction, production and consumption vary within fairly narrow limits from society to society, whatever the economy. One could substantiate this in terms of units of reproduction, by pointing to the fact that in polygynous systems most men have only one wife for most of the time; or that numbers of live births have usually tended to go down as the prospects of survival go up; in any case there is a physiological limit to the number of children a woman can produce. All this keeps the numbers of offspring of a mating pair within certain limits. These limits also apply to consumption groups, which usually centre upon an adult woman. But I want to make the same point with regard to another kind of group, the basic unit of production in agricultural societies, 'the farm family'.

Concentrating upon units of production rather than consumption means taking men rather than women as the focus of one's analysis, a procedure which tends in many cases to produce larger 'households'.[20] While the selection of this focus clearly presents difficulties when we are dealing with industrial societies, in which the units of production and consumption are inevitably distinct, the alternatives seem to me less realistic and less theoretically significant for agricultural communities. It is true that large groups of varying size often assemble to carry out certain major agricultural tasks, such as the clearing of new land, farming for affines, harvesting crops. But the usufructory rights over land and its produce are normally vested in a small group of persons who jointly carry out the day-to-day tasks of supplying and running a household in the economic sense.

How large is this 'farm family'? Figures are not easy to come by; the most reliable data are generally given in reports of small intensive surveys, and even here essential information on the size and organisation of the basic unit of

of a dwelling are more freely available. This fact has implications not only for the comparative study of family structure but also for the planning of development. In Africa, recently, architects and engineers of the European tradition have been responsible for spending millions of pounds of public money in the construction of standardised permanent dwellings in rural areas affected by dams and similar schemes, using large quantities of imported goods. Given the availability of land and materials, there would have been an enormous saving had individuals been encouraged to build improved dwellings of the traditional type, which would have given greater flexibility in accommodating population movements as well as the usual growth and decline of domestic groups. The standardisation of units has led to an overall lowering of standards of living in larger polygynous households. In the resettlement areas along the Volta lake in Ghana I have come across a man's wives having to share the same sleeping quarters in a manner unheard of in traditional society. Almost everywhere in West Africa the process of urbanisation involves living under more crowded and insanitary conditions than obtain in the country, even though water may come from a tap and light from an electric lamp.

[20] For an estimate of mean household size based on the male population, see below, Hammel, Chapter 14, pp. 361–362.

Table 3.1 *A comparison of units of agricultural production ('farm families') derived from intensive studies*

Continent	People	Productive system	Mean size of 'house-hold'^a	Units in sample	Acreage per head	Source
Africa: West	LoWiili (1950)	Traditional, savannah	11.1	50	0.9	Goody (1958 ii): 65
	LoDagaba (1950)	Traditional, savannah	7.0	50	1.8	Goody (1958 ii): 65
	Tallensi (1933)	Traditional, savannah	7.86	81	—	Fortes (1949 i): 64
	Hausa: Zaria (1950)	Savannah	6.7	90	—	M. G. Smith (1955): 177
	Katsina (1967)	Savannah (plough)	11.9	30	—	Anthony and Johnston (1968): 48a
	Katsina (1967)	Savannah (no plough)	6.4	30	—	
	Yoruba: Abeokuta and Ijebu	Cocoa	6.5	—	—	Galletti, Baldwin and Dina (1956): 133
	Ibadan	Cocoa	8.8	—	—	"
	Oyo	Cocoa	9.7	—	—	"
	Ondo	Cocoa	9.8	—	—	"
	Akan: Oda	Cocoa	4.41	—	—	Tetteh (1967): 214
	Ibo: Uboma	Traditional, forest	5.97	—	—	Upton (1966): 104
	Fulani: Wodaabe	Pastoral	5.1	39	—	Stenning (1959): 160
Africa: East	Sukuma	Traditional, savannah	7.11	—	—	Allan (1967)
	Mambwe	Traditional, savannah	5.18	—	—	"
	Lala	Traditional, savannah	4.81 and	—	—	"
	Lala	Traditional, savannah	4.22	—	—	"
	Lamba	Traditional, savannah	5.52	23	—	"
	Buganda: Kamira (1965) old	—	5.9	83	—	Robertson (1967)
	Budada (1965) new	—	4.45	43	—	Robertson (1967)
	Bunyoro: Buchunga (June 1961)	Savannah, with cash crops	3.75	102	—	Low (1961) App. 2
Asia: China	Yunnan^b (Spring 1938)	—	5.4	—	—	Fei and Chang (1948): 64
	(Autumn 1939)	—	4.9	—	—	Fei and Chang (1948): 64

					Reference
Asia: Tibet	dKang-mdzes village				
	Taxpayers	3.40	410	—	1.00	Carrasco (1959): 67–9
	Servants	2.80	38	—	0.2	"
	Subjects of monasteries	2.77	44	—	0.5	"
	'Side-dwellers'	1.88	56	—	0.9	"
Asia: India	North, Rampur^c (1953)				
	Jat	8.3	78	—	—	Lewis (1958): 118, 137
	Brahman	7.33	15	—	—	"
	Camar	5.1	21	—	—	"
	Bhangi	5.2	10	—	—	"
	Kumhar	5.57	7	—	—	"
	Mysore (1954)				
	Wangala	4.98	192	—	—	Epstein (1962): 21–4
	Dalena	4.62	153	—	1.04	Epstein (1962): 196–7
	Uttar Pradesh (1954–7)				
	Meerut and Musaffarnagar	7.6	—	—	1.4	Indian Agriculture (1967)
	Punjab (1954–7)				
	Amritsar and Ferozepur	8.1	—	—	2.2	"
	West Bengal (1954–7)				
	Hooghly and Parganas	6.4	—	—	0.5	"
	Madras (1954–7)				
	Coimbatore and Salem	5.4	—	—	1.4	"
	Maharashtra (1955–7)				
	Ahmednagar	7.0	—	—	3.0	"
	Nasik	6.5	—	—	2.8	"
	Akota and Amraoti	5.9	—	—	3.7	"
	Andhra Pradesh (1957–60)				
	West Godavari	5.5	—	—	1.5	"
	Orissa (1957–60)				
	Sambalpur	5.1	—	—	1.0	"
	Bihar (1959–60)				
	Monghyr North Zone	5.5	—	—	0.8	"
	Monghyr Central Zone	7.8	—	—	0.6	"
	Monghyr South Zone	7.1	—	—	1.5	"
	Haryana (1961–3)				
	Karnal, Rohtak, Jind	8.4	—	—	0.3	"

Table 3.1 *continued*

Continent	People	Productive system	Mean size of 'household'[a]	Units in sample	Acreage per head	Source
Asia: Ceylon	Pul Eliya[c] (1871)	Padi	3.57	14	—	Leach (1961): 332
	Pul Eliya (1954)	Padi	3.74	39	—	Leach (1961): 332
Asia: Sarawak	Land Dayak[d] (1950)	Padi	8.00	16	—	Geddes (1954): 36
America: West Indies	Dominica (1966) Belaire	—	5.6[e]	74	—	Spens (1970): 328

[a] Average size of unit of agricultural production.
[b] The figures are qualified by the remark, 'excluding the single adults'. I am not sure whether these figures apply to the whole community, including the landless labourers.
[c] I have assumed that the figures for families are also those for farm families.
[d] The Land Dayak figures are all from one longhouse; the ethnography suggests that there may well be some selection of longhouse occupants in favour of larger families.
[e] This figure refers to occupants of houses; excluding solitary persons, it rises to 6.1. Some individuals in large households have separate holdings and some households are divided economically; hence the number for the unit of production could be somewhat lower.

production is often lacking. The figures that I have managed to collect together are given in Table 3.1. These figures on farm families, work units or garden families, as they are variously called, display only limited differences in widely separated parts of the world. The range of average size is roughly the same in Africa and Eurasia. In Asia, the Jat of North India have farm units of 8.3 strong;[21] in another Indian area, Haryana, the figure is 8.4; the numbers for the Land Dyak of Sarawak, who are padi cultivators, are roughly the same.[22] In Africa, the figure for the Tallensi of Northern Ghana is 7.86; and that for the LoWiili 11.1.[23] If we turn to the other end of the scale, we find the lower castes in the Jat village of Rampur having a household strength of 5.3, nearly the same as Fei and Chang give for a village in the Yunnan province of China in spring, 1938 (5.4);[24] in Ceylon, the productive unit in Pul Eliya numbers 3.74;[25] in Tibet the units are smaller still. These lower figures are again very close to the size of the farm family in a number of East African peoples, where the lowest figure (3.75) occurs among the Bunyoro.[26]

The same thing is true if we look at the figures marshalled by demographers and discussed by Burch (1967). The most recent statistical information issued by the United Nations (1967) shows relatively little differences in 'household' size, that is, in the size of units of consumption (Table 3.2). In India the MHS is 5.2; in Africa the figures range from 3.5 to 5.2; only in rural South America do we reach numbers of six persons in a household. These small figures are recorded despite the widespread tendency to identify dwelling with units of production and consumption. While demographic factors are directly relevant to the size of the units of reproduction, they are clearly not the only ones tending to keep other domestic units so restricted in size; we have to introduce further variables such as the system of marriage, adoption, production, and inheritance; a 'stem family' is in effect defined by the mode of transmission. It is in spite of, not because of, variations in fertility and mortality that such groups remain relatively limited in size.[27] The reasons why they do so, interesting as they are, cannot be enlarged upon here.

The figures from intensive studies are more reliable and less averaging than the aggregate figures for nations that are differentiated by strata, ethnicity and

---

[21] Lewis, *Village life in Northern India* (1958).
[22] 8.00. Geddes. *The Land Dyaks of Sarawak* (1954).
[23] This is the highest figure I have for traditional agriculture, though the farming unit of the Tiv (northern Nigeria) appears to be much larger. Bohannan (1954) treats the compound as the labour unit for certain purposes; the average size is much like that of the LoDagaba, namely, 17. But he goes on to say that, 'a large compound breaks up into smaller groups in performing many agricultural tasks... full siblings tend to work together... When full brothers become older, with adult sons of their own, they are likely to farm separately.' See Bohannan (1954): 23–5. Since this developmental process is very much like that of the LoWiili, the unit of production will presumably be roughly the same.
[24] Fei and Chang, *Earthbound China* (1948).
[25] Or 4.56 if we work on the basis of 32 'families'; the boundaries vary. Leach, *Pul Eliya* (1961).
[26] Low, *Mutala survey of Buchanga* (1961).
[27] Burch, see above, Chapter 2, pp. 97–100, takes a different view.

Table 3.2   *Mean household size from census material[a]*

Country and year T Total U Urban R Rural			Mean size of household[b]	No. of households
Africa				
Congo (Brazzaville) 1958	U		4.0	13,428
Ethiopia 1961	U		3.5	123,755
Mauritius 1962	T		4.9	138,368
	U		5.2	46,227
	R		4.8	92,141
Morocco 1960	T		4.8	2,409,750
	U		4.3	787,450
	R		5.1	1,622,300
St Helena 1956	T		4.7	998
Tanzania 1958	R		3.9	20,349
United Arab Republic 1960	U		4.8	1,992,491
Elsewhere				
Canada	1961	T	3.9	4,554,493
		U	3.7	3,280,468
		R	4.2	1,274,025
Dominica 1960		T	4.2	14,218
Jamaica	1960	T	4.0	401,743
		U	2.7	142,298
		R	4.8	259,445
India	1960	T	5.2	83,523,895
		U	5.2	—
		R	5.2	—
Israel	1963	T	3.8	594,800
		U	3.9	—
		R	3.4	—
U.K.	1961	T	3.0	14,640,897
		U	3.0	—
		R	3.1	—

[a] Selected from United Nations Statistical Office, Department of Economic and Social Affairs, *Statistical Year Book* (1967).
[b] The highest figures in Asia are Kuwait (1961), 6.1 (n = 52,851); in Europe, San Marino (1965), rural, 4.8 (n = 678); in South America, rural figures reach 6.0.

by region. In Ghana, for example, there can be only a limited value in averaging material on northern (patrilineal) and southern (matrilineal) peoples, especially since, in the matrilineal groups, members of the reproductive unit, the productive unit and even the unit of consumption often live in separate dwellings.[28] Another factor to be reckoned with in interpreting these figures is the difficulty of defining a 'household' in such societies. While large compounds form a household in the residential sense, they break up into smaller for the major socio-economic tasks of reproduction, production and consumption. But even the polygynous family

[28]   Fortes (1949 i); (1950).

divides into its constituent elements for reproduction and consumption; for some purposes this element consists of the core mother–child unit. In many parts of Ghana it is a common sight to see a young girl taking an evening meal from the compound where her mother lives to her father's house; later that night the meal may be followed by the cook. Which is the household? Any polygynous society will present yet further problems if the criterion is 'one hearth', 'one cooking group'. In order to avoid these difficulties I shall concentrate upon the figures presented in Table 3.1. Here we see that the continental distribution shows no great difference in the *range* of average size. Difference in continent also means a difference in agricultural economy. Many African societies still practice shifting agriculture with the hoe; many Asian societies farm more intensively, using more advanced techniques (irrigation and the plough) and more productive crops (e.g. rice); while in Western Europe, the economic situation was yet more developed even before the onset of the industrial and agricultural changes of the eighteenth century. Yet this long-term, evolutionary type of change in the economy has no direct counterpart in unidirectional changes in the size of the farm family, that is in the unit of production and consumption. Indeed, from the standpoint of size, we find smaller average households in agricultural societies in Africa and in Asia than we do in England. Laslett notes that 'mean household size remained fairly constant at 4.75 or a little under, from the earliest point for which we have found figures [sixteenth century] until as late as 1901. There is no sign of the large extended coresidential family group of the traditional peasant world giving way to the small, nuclear, conjugal household of modern industrial society.'[29] The same words could be used about household size in most parts of the traditional peasant world of Asia and Africa, if we are referring to the size of the basic units of production. This similarity exists despite the effects of (i) polygyny, (ii) what Hajnal calls the 'European marriage pattern', with its late marriage age and its high proportion of people who never marry at all, (iii) the possibly associated differences in birth and death rates.[30]

But while the overall *range* of the mean size of the farm family is roughly the same, the tentative figures we have assembled do display some differences. The farm family in Africa tends to be slightly larger than in Asia; and that in West Africa larger than in East. Such differences in size can clearly be related to differences in the generation structure, or in the number of children, of adult women (wives or sisters), of adult men (husbands or brothers), of attached personnel, i.e. those in servile statuses (slave, servant, client) or of more distant kin. The demographic factors making for an increase or decrease in the number of children cannot be considered here; obviously the greater expectancy of life that characterises 'advanced societies' makes for a potential increase in the size of the farm family, while the commitment to monogamy makes for a decrease.

[29] See below, Laslett, Chapter 4, p. 126.
[30] Hajnal (1965): 131.

LHF

Setting on one side these very important factors, I want to concentrate upon adult males and their relationship to the productive processes.

One major factor determining the size of farm families is the point in the developmental cycle of domestic groups where a split occurs in the units of production and consumption. In his discussion of the Tallensi material, Fortes notes that, 'economic needs and structural cleavages are chiefly responsible for fission in the joint family...'[31] In an agricultural society the economic factors have mainly to do with rights in the means of production, namely land, and especially in plough farming and livestock. When the land is split, the group that farms it inevitably divides; and the opposite process also occurs. The land is likely to split, to be reallocated, at the death of the holder, where more than one member of the inheriting group survives. Alternatively, where members of the sibling group continue to farm together after their father's death (and in polygynous societies this is especially likely to occur with full brothers), then the farm unit will be correspondingly larger. Such a practice accounts for the relatively large size of the farming group among the LoWiili of Northern Ghana (11.1); earlier fission of the group accounts for the smaller size of the farming unit among the LoDagaba and the Tallensi of the same region.[32] In a previous publication I have tried to relate this difference between the LoWiili and the LoDagaba to differences in the system of inheritance. Among the LoWiili 83 % of men farmed with another adult kinsman; in two-thirds of the cases this male was a brother. Among the LoDagaba the proportion was less. The 'unit of production' consisted of 11.1 members among the LoWiili and 7.0 among the LoDagaba; in the former case the average farm was 0.9 acres per person, in the latter 1.8. Neither of these differences had any direct bearing on the size of the compound, that is of the household in the sense of houseful.[33]

Hence while the basic work groups generally remain small, their size varies with the timing of family fission. The rhythm of the domestic cycle differs from society to society. In some cases sons set up their own economic and residential units before the father dies; in others they separate at his death, and in others they continue to farm together until their own children reach adulthood. The structure of the farm family thus depends on a variety of factors, such as the nature of inheritance, the type of economy (mixed economies may require more hands), etc. But the important point to notice is that, excluding servants, the variations in size all fall within the group of close siblings or affines, so that the range is not great. Looking at the problem of 'family evolution' in terms of the three types of unit mentioned above, we can conclude that the domestic 'family' never was extended to any degree; so that the changes in size wrought by the

[31] I should finish the rest of the quotation which is at least equally relevant: 'and religious and jural sanctions for the reintegration of an expanded family'. Fortes (1949 i): 77. Many formal models of the family processes direct their attention almost exclusively to the dominant process of fission, forgetting the subordinate process of fusion.

[32] Fortes (1949 i); Goody (1958 ii).

[33] Compare Laslett, above, Chapter 1. pp. 34–39.

industrial revolution, urbanisation, modernisation, etc. though significant, are small. The extended family did not break up with the industrial revolution; it was already segmented for most social purposes, including the basic ones of reproduction, production and consumption. On the average households and housefuls became somewhat smaller.

I have concentrated here on the comparison of the size rather than of the composition of critical domestic groups and in doing so have perhaps placed too great an emphasis on the similarity in the structure of industrial and pre-industrial societies in order to dispose of the myth of the extended 'family' as some sort of undifferentiated commune. The main changes that have occurred do not centre upon the emergence of the 'elementary family' out of 'extended kin groups', for small domestic groups are virtually universal. They concern the disappearance of many functions of the wider ties of kinship, especially those centring on kin groups such as clans, lineages and kindreds. The ties may continue (as in the case of a Scottish clan) but the functions radically alter with the proliferation of other institutional structures that take over many of their jobs. It is the process whereby kinship relations shrink, largely but not entirely, to the compass of a man's family of birth and family of marriage, a change which has been so well discussed in Goode's comparative study.[34] Changes of this kind cannot be derived from the study of the household alone, since they have to do with the relationships between members of separate households, and especially adjacent ones. Specific steps have to be taken to obtain the information required to document changes in the morphology or function of such a network and it is rarely possible to do this from the usual type of census based upon domestic groups. While numerical statements about these changes can be made, the problem of doing so is far from easy.

If one employs 'family' for domestic units of this kind and uses 'kin' (or 'relatives') to describe wider ties, then it is clear that the term 'extended family' is almost invariably misleading unless one is thinking of a certain frequency of, say, three-generational or fraternal households in the total population. The variations in size among domestic groups are inevitably small, but the fact that they are so should not obscure the importance of 'extended family' ties in another sense, especially when these more distant kin form the basis of local groupings. In this respect there is certainly a major difference between more and less industrialised societies, though at what point the change occurs is difficult to ascertain; the kind of information to answer this question cannot be derived from census data as presently collected. To put it another way, the fact that the 'family' or 'household' is always small does not say anything about the importance attached to kinship ties in a more general sense. Indeed even the kind of 'stem family' sometimes found among Scandinavian farmers or among Irish countrymen, where the parents have retired to a special house on the farm might well get classified as distinct 'households' if the main focus of attention

[34] Goode, *World revolution and family patterns* (1963).

was separate hearths, or even separate houses. But such households are maintained out of the same productive estate and hence constitute one 'farm family'. It is a realisation of this fact that makes many anthropologists suspicious of the distinction between 'family' and 'kinship' and hence of conclusions that turn on this distinction.[35]

Their doubts bear directly on a controversial issue in discussions of the demography of medieval Europe. There is disagreement as to whether one should use 3.5 or 5.00 as a multiplier when attempting to calculate population figures from lists of landholders in Domesday Book and in manorial extents.[36] The argument revolves around the nature of the relationship between 'household' and 'holding'. Do these lists refer to the nuclear family (as Russell suggests) or might the tenement contain (as Homans claims) a number of dwellings housing the holder's wife and children, parents, unmarried brothers and sisters, servants, and his subtenants and co-parceners. If we accept the latter possibility, then a count of the occupants of distinct dwellings (and this is even more true of the 'hearth')[37] can tell us only a limited amount about the social organisation of a village; to increase our understanding we need to know the relationships, preferably over time, of the householders and occupants of neighbouring dwellings and neighbouring villages. The last requirement is desirable where landed property is transmitted to women and hence may act as an important factor in the determination of the residence of their husbands. Agreement about the size of the multiplier (or the household) is important for calculating the size of medieval populations; it is of less significance in the analysis of village structure. Certain arguments on both sides appear to give too much weight to the consumption and residential units; the question of 'nuclear' or 'extended' kin groups, much less that of 'individualism' or 'communalism' (with the various implications for the industrialisation of Western Europe), does not turn on the difference between a mean size of household of 3.5 ('small') or 5 ('large').

There is however one aspect of the figures given in Table 3.1 I have not touched upon. While the range in the size of the farm family is roughly comparable in Africa and Asia, there is a trend towards larger units in Africa, particularly in the West. This difference seems to reflect long-term changes. When we compare the systems of inheritance and succession in these two major continental areas of the Old World, we find that Eurasia is characterised by lineal modes of transmitting relatively exclusive rights while Africa is much more mixed. Certain areas of East and Southern Africa are marked by a lineal form of inheritance

---

[35] E.g. Fallers, *The range of variation in family size* (1965); Schueider, *Kinship and biology* (1965).

[36] For a discussion of these issues see Homans, *English villagers of the thirteenth century* (1941); Russell, *Late ancient and medieval population* (1958) and *British medieval population* (1948); Hallam, *Some thirteenth century censuses* (1957); Titow, *The thirteenth century population increase* (1961); Krause, *The medieval household* (1956); Russell, *Recent advances in medieval demography* (1965).

[37] On the difficulties of this concept, see Russell (1965): 90.

whereby property is divided among a man's children according to their maternal origin. The system, where each matri-segment gets an equal (*per stirpes*) share, has been called by Gluckman 'the house-property complex'.[38] But in West Africa, where the units of production are larger, lateral inheritance prevails (especially in matrilineal systems).[39] When brothers stand in expectation of inheriting goods or movables from one another, it seems reasonable to suggest that they will farm together for a longer period than when their property goes direct to their sons. In other words, the lineal inheritance of productive resources means, all else being equal, the earlier fission of the unit of production, since brothers are unlikely to farm together unless they also inherit from each other. From this standpoint, primogeniture is simply an aggravated form of lineal transmission.[40]

In Eurasia the transmission of property to offspring is also marked by a feature which is rarely if ever found in non-Muslim Africa, namely the passing down of male property to both sons and daughters, either by the dowry or *causa mortis*. I have argued elsewhere that 'downward' or lineal transmission is a means of preserving socio-economic differences and is related to advanced agriculture, where status depends to a greater extent upon the holding of land and property. In African societies, on the other hand, agriculture is generally shifting, extensive, and rights to land can be acquired through membership of a kin group as well as by inheritance from close kin. The system, in other words, is more corporate and less particularistic than in Eurasia; inheritance is therefore more likely to be lateral. The Eurasian system is one in which, since women are bearers of (male) property, marriage involves the conjunction of two property holders and the establishment of some kind of conjugal fund, which again tends to differentiate brother from brother. The effect of these differences on the structure of the unit of production (especially important when women control land) is to lead to earlier fission between parents and children as well as between members of the sibling group.

The figures in Table 3.1 raise a further question. Why is there a greater tendency to lineal inheritance and smaller productive units in East Africa? The answer is far from clear but it is possibly related to the greater importance of cattle and other livestock on that side of the continent. Cattle create a possible focus for differentiation and hence may tend to a pressure on downwards transmission, on providing for one's lineal descendants before one's collaterals. Where parcels of property are of roughly equal value, the direction in which they move is of little importance. Their distribution becomes of critical importance where the parcels are of different value.

There is a final problem which arises from differences within rather than

---

[38] Gluckman, *Kinship and marriage among the Lozi and Zulu* (1950).
[39] I have discussed this point in more detail in *Sideways or downwards* (1970) and in *Inheritance and women's labour in Africa* (1972).
[40] Gavelkind was equally lineal, but more sons participated.

between societies. In looking at the size of units of production, it is clear that the richer (or more progressive) farmers live and work in larger groups than the average for that community. This difference emerges in all the African studies done by the Stanford group (Table 3.3) and it is equally the case in India and Tibet that the economically higher castes have larger 'farm families' than the lower ones. At first sight this fact might appear to contradict the hypothesis that the more advanced the agricultural or industrial economy, the smaller the mean size of households (within small limits and an unsteady trend). However, in differentiated societies larger households (consisting of kin plus non-kin) generally occur among the richer individuals, whether peasants or nobility.[41] Even where the dwelling and reproductive units are actually smaller, the network of relationships between kin may be stronger. As Goode notes, 'even in the modern Western world, upper-strata families maintain a far larger extension of kin and far greater control over their own young than do lower-strata families.'[42] In Northern Nigeria plough farmers have larger 'farm families' than hoe farmers.

CONCLUSION

A consideration of the problems arising out of the comparative analysis of the 'family' and 'household' suggests that, especially in pre-industrial societies, particular importance should be given to the study of the unit of production, the farm family. Figures on the size of this group in some African and Asian societies (see Table 3.1) show that although the range of variation is relatively small, there were some important differences.

First, unless factors of house construction interfere (e.g. where a shortage of housing forces young couples to live with in-laws, against the trend of current norms and individual preference), there is inevitably an internal variation in the *size of individual households* in both senses of the word, dwelling groups and units of consumption. Demographic factors apart, a major factor in the variation is the stage in the developmental cycle of domestic groups; most societies will have nuclear, extended (lineally) and expanded (laterally) families in different proportions; the terms characterise domestic groups, which rarely have one unchanging form.

Secondly, variation in the *mean size of household* often exists among the sub-groups of a 'society', defined either by territory (e.g. the Yoruba) or by status (e.g. Rampur, North India).[43] In stratified societies the upper status groups tend to have larger domestic units (as well as more land and capital).

[41] In particular see the studies of pre-industrial England, Laslett, Chapter 4, pp 153–154; Anderson's analysis of rural Lancashire in 1851, below, Chapter 7, pp. 220–221; and the study by Klapisch of fifteenth-century Tuscany, below, Chapter 10, pp. 275–277. Even in twentieth-century America kin are more prevalent in the wealthier households, see Pryor, Chapter 22, pp. 577–578.

[42] Goode (1963): 372.

[43] On the absence of 'joint families' among Untouchables, see Epstein, *Economic development and social change in south India* (1962): 176.

Table 3.3 *Mean size of farming unit, comparing 'progressive' farmers and their neighbours*[a]

People	Mean size of unit			N	Average acreage			Source
	Progressive farmers[b]	Neighbours[b]	Subsample[b]		Progressive farmers	Neighbours	Sub-sample	
Gusii (Kenya)	10.0 (2.6)	9.1 (2.9)	9.1 (2.6)	120	11.9	7.0	8.2	Field Survey, No. 2: 58a, 59b
Teso (Uganda)	10.8 (5.5)	8.3 (3.8)	8.9 (4.2)	60	34.3	12.7	18.1	Field Survey, No. 3: 63a, 64b
Geita district (Tanzania)	—	—	7.06 (2.9)	60	—	—	20.5	Field Survey, No. 4: 52a, 53a
Mazabuka district (Tonga, Zambia)	16.3 (4.9)	8.0 (3.0)	n.d.	60	56	21	n.d.	Field Survey, No. 5: 55a, 57a
Northern Katsina (Nigeria)	Plough 11.9 (6.7)	No plough 6.4 (4.1)	—	60	Plough 20.2	No plough 6.7	—	Field Survey, No. 6: 48a, 48c
Bawku (Ghana)	—	—	9.4 (5.2)	60	—	—	10.7	Field Survey, No. 7: 43a, 45a
Akim Abuakwa (Ghana)	—	—	8.5 (3.2)	60	—	—	Cocoa groves: acreage 45.2	Field Survey, No. 8: 51a, 52a

Note: 'Progressive farmers' were those farmers considered to be so by the local departments of agriculture.

[a] Based on Stanford Food Research Institute, Field study of agricultural research, *Reports*.
[b] The number of adults per farming group is given in parentheses.

Thirdly, there is much variation between societies, even when we hold continent and economy constant; these variations depend upon factors such as mating pattern, phasing of family dispersal, system of inheritance, type of economy and nature of migration.[44]

Fourthly, there appears to be a trend towards larger productive units in certain parts of Africa, which is related to the greater stress on lateral modes of inheritance and ultimately to the simpler system of agricultural production.

I have tried to establish that it is not only for England that we need to abandon the myth of the 'extended family' – as the term is often understood. In one form or another this myth has haunted historical and comparative studies since the time of Maine and Fustel de Coulanges, whether the work has been undertaken by historians, sociologists or anthropologists. Whatever the shape of the kin groups of earlier societies, none were undifferentiated communes of the kind beloved by nineteenth century theorists, Marxist and non-Marxist alike. Units of production were everywhere relatively small, kin-based units; differences in size and context are important in the comparative study of the family, but they should never obscure the basic similarities in the way that domestic groups are organized throughout the whole range of human societies.[45]

[44] Though we often think of urban migration mainly in terms of men (hence the suggested link with the increased proportion of female-headed household), the movement of women is more pronounced than that of men under certain conditions. By and large this is true of Europe in the past as well as the present; in Zurich between the fourteenth and seventeenth centuries, the proportion of women, especially of single women, was high (i.e. 2,974 to 2,185 in 1637), Hajnal (1965): 117.

[45] See in particular Hammel's study of the evolution of the zadruga, below, Chapter 14, pp. 335–340, 370–373.

4. Mean household size in England since the sixteenth century

Peter Laslett

Our interest in this chapter is directed towards one particular subject, the size of the domestic group in England, or England and Wales, from the late sixteenth to the late twentieth century.[1] This is the period of time which separates the era of industrialisation, now perhaps of high industrialisation, from the era of traditional society. Accordingly we begin by discussing mean household size itself, since this ratio has been of considerable significance for social scientists, in spite of the marked limitations in its usefulness which have now begun to be manifest. For the demographer, and especially the historical demographer, it has been employed as a multiplier for calculating total populations from known numbers of domestic groups, generally named and assumed to be households. The anthropologists and sociologists have tended to treat it as a preliminary indicator of household structure. Where mean household size is large they have presumed that the presence in the society of the extended family was probable, and when small that the domestic groups consisted exclusively or for the most part of the simple, nuclear or primary family household of man, wife and children.

It is tempting to extend the demographic argument and to proceed from household size, or more often from changes in mean household size over time, to demographic experience. Smaller mean size is then usually taken to indicate

[1] This chapter is a revised and extended form of an article originally written for two purposes. One was for circulation to those invited to participate in the meeting at Cambridge on the comparative history of household and family which took place in September 1969, and whose papers form the body of the present volume. The other was to present some of the results of the work on the family and household using lists of inhabitants which had been going on at the Cambridge Group for the History of Population and Social Structure for some years. These results are to be published in *Population Studies* under the title *Size and structure of the household in England over three centuries* and the present essay is the first of two, appearing in *Population Studies* (1969): 199–223. The second article, which will be concerned with sub-periods and regions as well as with variables associated with changes in household size, is still in preparation.

Parts of the original text have been used in Chapter 1, and so are omitted here. One or two tables and graphs have been added from a note subsequently published in *Population Studies* (1970): 449–54 with the title *The decline of the size of the domestic group in England*. As much as possible has been retained of these sources here, including some statements which subsequent research makes a little naif. But errors have been corrected, and new matter added.

low or reduced fertility because of fewer children or higher mortality, and larger mean size to imply more children and hence higher fertility, or lower mortality: or both.[2]

Fundamental change, even transformation in the whole or part of a society, may be associated by sociologists and anthropologists with pronounced alterations in mean household size. Structural contrasts between region and region (say between town and countryside) may be supposed to exist when mean household size differs markedly from one to the other. It is recognised that changes in fertility and mortality have to be allowed for when arguing in this way, and that much more information, specifically about relationships within the domestic group, would have to be available to make such an inference secure. But structural evidence is frequently absent from both past and present data, and it is understandable that mean household size should have been so heavily stressed. The association of the nuclear family, and therefore the small household, with industrial society and industrial society alone has been very strong, as is shown in Chapter 1.

The evidence from one hundred communities in pre-industrial England studied here seems to call into question assumptions like these. It was shown in Chapter 1 that mean household size in a community does not appear to be correlated at all highly with the degree of complication of the households in that community. In fact unless servants are dropped from the population, and households of sizes 1 and 2 disregarded, no correlation appeared to exist in the evidence analysed there, and the same is true of such materials as have yet been worked on from the English files. We shall try to prove in this chapter how questionable it would be to assert that the transformation of English society by industrialisation was accompanied by any decrease in the size of the average household until very late on in that process. The facts presented will show that mean household size remained fairly constant at 4.75 or a little under, from the earliest point for which we have found figures, until as late as 1901. There is no sign of the large, extended coresidential family group of the traditional peasant world giving way to the small, nuclear, conjugal household of modern industrial society. In England in fact, as was suggested elsewhere, now almost a decade ago,[3] the large joint or extended family seems never to have existed as a common form of the domestic group at any point in time covered by known numerical records.

Nevertheless the collection and analysis of the most informative sample we could find of detailed evidence on the size and structure of the household in pre-industrial England has brought to light a number of unsuspected facts and cir-

[2] See above, Burch, Chapter 2, pp. 97–100 and Goody, Chapter 3, pp. 115–117, also below pp. 147–148.

[3] See Laslett and Harrison, *Clayworth and Cogenhoe* (1963); Laslett, *The World we have lost* (1965 i), and *New light on the history of the English family* (1966 ii). The present studies are intended to register the body of evidence on which the suggestions made in these contexts were based. Glass confirms them for London in *London inhabitants within the walls* (1966). I should like to acknowledge the encouragement and help I have received from Professor Glass both in the research here reported and in the preparation of these essays.

cumstances. The relationships between parents, children, servants and kin within the English household, and the interplay of its size and structure with economic and demographic development, make up an intricate adaptive mechanism which we are only now beginning to understand. A start will have to be made here with the data. They are very imperfect, as must be expected, and the facts are complicated, difficult to marshal and to describe. They were, of course, determined to a large extent by the miscellaneous body of persons living in our country between the years 1574 and 1821 who went to the trouble of counting and describing the inhabitants of the hundred communities whose figures have been recovered and analysed. A certain amount of description of their actions has survived, but nothing like a written definition of the family or household.[4] In every case, however, they arranged the names of persons in blocks, which are almost always unambiguously recognisable as households, and in every case they left a clear indication of where one block ended and the next block began. We say in every case, because only these documents which show what seem to be unambiguous divisions between each household have been admitted to the sample. All others have been left aside, along with any showing signs of omission.[5] In the divisions which they made in their lists of persons, these original compilers in fact defined the domestic group for our purposes, as was demonstrated in Chapter 1.

The phrase 'pre-industrial' is even more difficult to specify than household, and we shall likewise have to leave it to be defined by the evidence. It is assumed that all the communities whose figures have been used were pre-industrial in their social structure at the time when their inhabitants were listed. This does not

[4] King discussed these issues more extensively than any other inhabitant of pre-industrial England: see his famous *Natural and politicall observations* (1696), anatomising the demographic and general social structure of England for the year 1688. He was responsible, directly or indirectly, for a number of 'censuses' of English communities in the 1690s. Two of them, Lichfield in 1695 (Table 4.1, no. 19) and Harefield in 1699 (no. 35, actually taken or supervised by him), are present in our collection. He comes near to defining the crucial terms but never quite does so, and in any case we do not know how far he can be taken as representative: see Glass, *Gregory King and the population of England and Wales at the end of the 17th century* (1965 i) and *Gregory King's estimate of the population of England and Wales 1695* (1965 ii). Parson Sampson of Clayworth was one of those who recorded the circumstances of his writing out his lists of inhabitants (nos. 11 and 15): see Laslett and Harrison (1963). Parson John Kelly drew up his list of inhabitants for Ardleigh in 1796 (no. 84): 'In consequence of the avowed intention of the French to make a descent upon this coast, such a list may be useful either to assemble us, in order to make a resistance, or in case of dispersion upon our return to discover and ascertain our respective claims and settlements.' Ardleigh Parish register, October 1796; information copied and supplied by Mr F. H. Erith.

[5] It is rarely possible, of course, to be certain when persons or classes of persons have been overlooked in a listing, unless the compiler confesses the fact. But we have learnt to be suspicious of those which record no servants, or which yield extreme values for such variables as the sex ratio. In a number of cases we have been able to check the information in a list with that contained in the relevant parish register. The sources, availability and characteristics of documents of this kind in England are described by Laslett in *Social structure from listings of inhabitants* (1966 i). The procedures set out there for analysing these data for social structural and demographic purposes have been somewhat modified since that date. For the definitions and presumptions used, see appendix to Chapter 1 above, pp. 86–89.

necessarily imply that the social system in England was in fact homogeneous in respect of household size and structure between the years 1574 and 1821, the dates of the first and last listing used. Such an inference would only be justified under two conditions. One is that our hundred parishes could be shown themselves to display such systematic homogeneity. The other is that they could be held to constitute a properly representative sample over the whole country and over the whole time period. We shall boldly proceed as if both these conditions had been satisfied. The variations in household size and structure shown by this collection of data are taken as variations within the definable boundaries of a particular social system, and this system is taken to have covered all of the country in all the years which preceded industrialisation. Nevertheless, it goes without saying that the hundred communities in question do not in fact constitute a sample of the required kind.

All that can properly be claimed for them is that they comprised the largest number for which usable evidence on the subjects in hand had been worked out at the time when this study began. It cannot even be said that these hundred communities are a representative sample of those which were held at Cambridge in 1967, because we now know that too few small places are present.[6] The numerous miniature communities found in the pre-industrial English countryside may not have been identical in familial structure with the larger ones: indeed there are signs that their MHS was larger. But only a modest proportion of the population lived in them, and however carefully we choose our sample it seems unlikely that the student of household and family structure in England will ever have evidence as good as that which might become available for other countries, for France for example, or Austria, or above all for Italy and Japan.[7] These circumstances require that the reader be given the best possible opportunity of assessing for himself the status of the evidence used here and the analytic work which has been carried out upon it.

In Table 4.1 he will find a complete list of the hundred English pre-industrial

---

[6] In 1967 we seem to have been unduly suspicious of settlements with few inhabitants, on the ground that such lists may be incomplete. It now appears that many of the small communities we rejected for the sample of 100 were as well enumerated as those we accepted. Comparison with 100 places from the 1801 Census shows that we took only 2 with less than 100 people (14 in 1801 containing 1.5 % of the population), and 19 below 200, less than 5 % of the population (39 in 1801 containing 9.2 % of the population). It may be for this reason that the relation between mean and median household size in our 100 communities differs from that found by Richard Wall; see below p. 137 and Chapter 5, pp. 191–192.

[7] An appreciable number of further English community listings has come to light since this study was begun (see footnote 9 below), but little to encourage us to think that the evidence will ever be very good. French materials on household size and structure in the past are reviewed in the footnotes to Laslett, *Le brassage de la population en France et en Angleterre* (1968). The remarkable series of repetitive censuses of Japanese villages dating from the beginning of the Tokugawa times (1600 onwards) to the later nineteenth century are described by Smith, Chapter 17, pp. 431–436, and Hayami, Chapter 18, pp. 474–475. For a notable series of Austrian recordings see Berkner (1972), and for Italy, Shifini, *Exploitation des listes nominatives de Fiesole* (1971).

communities whose data have been analysed and enter into the present discussion. This, in brief, is what has happened in the case of each of the communities named and for the body of data they comprise together.

First, a document has been recovered for every place, usually an ecclesiastical parish, but sometimes a different unit. This document contains what we believe to be reliable recordings of total population and of total number of households; it contains in addition, in about two-thirds of the cases, information (not always quite complete) on household structure. Secondly, a series of tables has been worked out by hand for each community, using in nearly all cases a photograph of the original document for the purpose. These tables record the crucial means and proportions, and the interpretive rules used for treating the data are those detailed above. Thirdly, a body of figures from these tables has been summed, averaged and correlated by computer, the correlations being tested for significance. The variables so analysed were selected from tables primarily for their importance to the structure of the domestic group but it was not possible to include the whole body of information, and analysis by age was left over as we shall see, along with other particulars. The computer analysis was carried out for means of means. That is to say each selected ratio or proportion was calculated for each community yielding the required information, and these variables were then summed and averaged: measures of skewness and kurtosis were computed for each such distribution. The computer repeated the process for the seven sub-collections into which the whole collection has been broken down. These sub-collections comprise three time periods (before 1650, 1651–1749, 1750–1821), and four regions (East, North and Central. South and West, London).[8]

Such were the three steps in the analysis originally planned, but further ones have subsequently been taken. In the fourth place overall ratios and proportions, as distinct from means of means, have been calculated for certain variables particularly significant for household size and structure. For example, in the case of mean household size itself, we have an overall mean (total population in households divided by total households less dwellers in institutions, that is ratio 3 in Table 4.2) as well as a mean of means (average of all such mean household sizes). In the case of the proportion of children in the population we have an overall proportion (population of communities where children can be distinguished from the rest divided into the total number of those children) as well as a mean of proportions (average of all proportions of children.) These calculations were done by hand for the kin and servant variables as well as for those relating to children, and repeated for periods and regions. Fifthly, what were judged to be the twenty most significant variables from the point of view of the history of the domestic group were submitted to the stepwise regression programme of the computer system in question. This was in an attempt to discover what were in fact the best indicators of household size for this collection

[8] Almost no use of the sub-samples by region and by period is made in the present study.

Table 4.1   *One hundred English parishes in date order 1574–1821,*
giving population, mean household size, county and region

No.	Date	Period	Parish	Pop.	MHS[a]	County	Region
1	1574	I	Poole	1,357	5.28	Dorset	SW
2	1599	I	Ealing	427	4.75	Middsx.	E
3	1622	I	Stafford	1,551	4.05	Staffs.	NC
4	1624	I	Cogenhoe	176	5.30	Northants.	SW
5	1645	I	Chester	3,700	5.62	Cheshire	NC
6	1662(?)	II	Abinghall	160	4.00	Glos.	SW
7	1662	II	Hewelsfield	213	5.33	Glos.	SW
8	1662(?)	II	Little Deane	526	4.22	Glos.	SW
9	1662	II	St. Brevills	394	5.70	Glos.	SW
10	1674	II	Stoke Edith	186	4.77	Herefs.	NC
11	1676	II	Clayworth	401	4.09	Notts.	NC
12	1676	II	Goodnestone	280	4.45	Kent.	E
13	1684	II	Chilvers Coton	780	4.43	Warwicks.	NC
14	1685	II	St Bees (Whitehaven)	1,078	4.05	Cumbs.	NC
15	1688	II	Clayworth	412	4.43	Notts.	NC
16	1695	II	Bilston	1,006	5.19	Staffs.	NC
17	1695	II	Kirby Kendal (Strickland Gate)	743	4.58	Westmnd	NC
18	1695	II	Kirkby Lonsdale	552	5.16	Westmnd	NC
19	1695	II	Lichfield	2,861	4.55	Staffs.	NC
20	1695	II	London, All Hallows Staining	857	5.60	(London)	L
21	1695	II	London, St Andrews Wardrobe	505	4.75	(London)	L
22	1695	II	London, St Bartholomew the Great	1,574	5.68	(London)	L
23	1695	II	London, St Benet Paul's Wharf	557	4.68	(London)	L
24	1695	II	London, St Ethelburga	645	4.88	(London)	L
25	1695	II	London, St Lawrence Pountney	423	5.70	(London)	L
26	1695	II	London, St Mary Le Bow	669	6.25	(London)	L
27	1695	II	London, St Mary Woolchurch	483	7.00	(London)	L
28	1695	II	London, St Mildred Poultry	556	7.22	(London)	L
29	1695	II	Southampton, St John's	211	3.76	Hants.	SW
30	1696	II	Southampton, St Lawrence	290	4.68	Hants.	SW
31	1696	II	Southampton, St Mary's	176	4.19	Hants.	SW
32	1696	II	Southampton, Holy Rhood	763	3.83	Hants.	SW
33	1697	II	Southampton, All Saints Witht. Barr.	376	3.69	Hants.	SW
34	1698	II	Ringmore	188	3.91	Devon	SW
35	1699	II	Harefield	558	4.80	Middsx.	E
36	1700	II	Hillmarton	397	4.09	Wilts.	SW
37	1701	II	Stoke-on-Trent	1,627	4.36	Staffs.	NC
38	1705	II	Ash	1,172	4.67	Kent	E
39	1705	II	Eastry	464	4.21	Kent	E
40	1705	II	Ickham	263	5.06	Kent	E
41	1705	II	Littlebourne	272	4.00	Kent	E
42	1705	II	Monkton	207	5.58	Kent	E
43	1705	II	Preston	263	4.38	Kent	E
44	1705	II	St Nicholas at Wade	245	4.22	Kent	E
45	1705	II	Shepherdswell	160	5.00	Kent	E
46	1705	II	Woodnesborough	430	4.73	Kent	E
47	1740	II	Chichester	3,711	4.73	Sussex	SW
48	1744	II	Stanton St Bernard	249	4.22	Wilts.	SW

[a] Where information is available, corresponds to ratio 3 in Table 4.2,
otherwise to ratio 2 or ratio 1.

Table 4.1 *continued*

No.	Date	Period	Parish	Pop.	MHS	County	Region
49	1747	II	Wymondham	3,213	4.68	Norfolk	E
50	1749	II	Cambridge, St Benets	386	4.10	Cambs.	E
51	1752	III	Forthampton & Swinley	288	5.33	Glos.	SW
52	1760	III	West Wycombe	1,141	4.40	Bucks.	SW
53	1762	III	Leverton	262	4.76	Lincs.	E
54	1765	III	Maryport	1,167	5.25	Cumbs.	NC
55	1768	III	Baconsthorpe	200	4.88	Norfolk	E
56	1768	III	Bodham	194	3.70	Norfolk	E
57	1775	III	Beaminster	1,949	4.54	Dorset	SW
58	1777	III	Carleton Rode	726	5.20	Norfolk	E
59	1778	III	Wembworthy	222	5.41	Devon	SW
60	1781	III	Landbeach	215	4.39	Cambs.	E
61	1787	III	Bampton	678	4.48	Westmnd	NC
62	1787	III	Barton	237	4.64	Westmnd	NC
63	1787	III	Bolton	292	4.56	Westmnd	NC
64	1787	III	Brougham	143	6.50	Westmnd	NC
65	1787	III	Cliburn	152	4.75	Westmnd	NC
66	1787	III	Clifton	196	4.08	Westmnd	NC
67	1787	III	Crosby Ravensworth	276	4.68	Westmnd	NC
68	1787	III	Great Strickland	187	4.68	Westmnd	NC
69	1787	III	Hartsop and Patterdale (Barton Parish)	317	4.95	Westmnd	NC
70	1787	III	Kings Meaburn	161	4.47	Westmnd	NC
71	1787	III	Lowther, Hackthorpe & Whale	163	4.41	Westmnd	NC
72	1787	III	Lowther, Constablewick	257	5.71	Westmnd	NC
73	1787	III	Martindale (Barton Parish)	158	4.27	Westmnd	NC
74	1787	III	Morland	233	4.09	Westmnd	NC
75	1787	III	Newby	212	4.32	Westmnd	NC
76	1787	III	Rosgill & Hedale	252	4.75	Westmnd	NC
77	1787	III	Shap Constablewick	346	4.37	Westmnd	NC
78	1787	III	Sockbridge (Barton Parish)	164	4.55	Westmnd	NC
79	1787	III	Little Strickland	98	3.63	Westmnd	NC
80	1787	III	Thornship, Talebert & Praed	125	5.21	Westmnd	NC
81	1787	III	Thrimby	54	5.40	Westmnd	NC
82	1790	III	Corfe Castle	1,239	4.84	Dorset	SW
83	1793	III	Bocking	2,943	4.58	Essex	E
84	1796	III	Ardleigh	1,145	5.48	Essex	E
85	1797	III	Harlow	1,543	5.36	Essex	E
86	1800	III	Melbury Osmond	334	5.14	Dorset	SW
87	1801	III	Binfield	800	4.86	Berks.	SW
88	1801	III	Exton	222	5.28	Hants.	SW
89	1801	III	Sturminster Newton	1,406	4.41	Dorset	SW
90	1801	III	Thorpe Next Norwich	419	5.18	Norfolk	E
91	1801	III	Hitchin	3,155	4.35	Herts.	E
92	1809	III	Wakes Colne	264	5.07	Essex	E
93	1811	III	Great Bircham	317	4.80	Norfolk	E
94	1811	III	Horndon on the Hill	378	5.03	Essex	E
95	1811	III	Littleover	353	5.43	Derbs.	NC
96	1811	III	Mickleover	580	5.09	Derbs.	NC
97	1811	III	Oxted	743	6.63	Surrey	SW
98	1821	III	Braintree	2,983[b]	4.56	Essex	E
99	1821	III	Marnhill	1,273	4.68	Dorset	SW
100	1821	III	Woodlands	396	4.90	Dorset	SW

[b] Studied in a 25% sample.

of communities.[9] Finally a number of further hand calculations were made on the data after the original publication of 1969, the most important being those concerning inmates and institutions presented in Table 4.2 below. In this chapter we are concerned for the most part with the analysis of the whole collection, since it is impossible, even in a volume of this size, to present all of the materials.

The details on age in six of the lists (2, 13, 19, 37, 82, 84) had to be passed over, along with such things as orphans, widowed persons and their familial situation, and much of the similar information about inmates, that is lodgers, boarders, visitors and such.[10] But inmates, as was shown in Chapter 1, are of some importance to the definition of what exactly is to be taken as the household in studies of this kind, along with dwellers in institutions. They give rise to most of the usually slight, but sometimes significant errors which often arise in calculating the appropriate ratio to express the size of the domestic group for comparative purposes. The MHS figures in Table 4.1 are themselves slightly misleading in this respect, for they do not always correspond to the definition recommended in Chapter 1 as the best for analysing the household (see note to that table). Accordingly the inmates and the institutionalised persons detectable in our 100 parishes have been investigated in a little detail with a view to the results presented in Table 4.2, where it will be seen that no less than five slightly different ratios for overall MHS are set out, quite apart from the mean of means. It will be appreciated that estimating the total numbers of persons in these categories by extrapolation from the few lists which actually record their presence is a tricky business, so that the ratios which involve them are subject to a degree of error difficult to specify.

A reassuring feature of this rather formidable array of figures is the quite narrow range of the values for mean household size itself. Ratio 4, the expression recommended in Chapter 1 as the best for the purpose, is clearly the smallest in the list at 4.470 and is divided from ratio 5, marginally the largest, by 0.380: MHS is actually quite sensitive to changes in the proportions of inmates and inmate households. But this difference is not much more than a third of a person, and about 8 % of 4.75, which we have adopted as our standard. Statistics 6, 7, 8

---

[9] Steps 1, 2 and 4 were carried out at the Cambridge Group for the History of Population and Social Structure, and the work has gone on over five years. Elspeth Burrows, Valerie Smith and Gabrielle Marchbanks undertook this laborious task, together with others working from time to time. I should like to record my gratitude to them for their devotion to this intractable material. Step 3 (the initial computer analysis by DATATEXT, though with one or two operations in another system) was carried out at Stanford, California, when the author was a fellow of the Center for Advanced Study in the Behavioral Sciences in 1968. I here gladly record the instruction and assistance of Mr David Peizer of the Center, as well as the actual programming which he did, and also the work undertaken there on the data by Mrs Joanne Fleischman. I owe a particular debt, too, to my contemporary at Stanford, Professor Douglas Price of the Department of Political Science at Harvard. After his return to his university, he freely undertook the regression analysis by DATATEXT (Step 5) at the Harvard Computer Center, although the work had no connection with his own.

[10] See above pp. 34–36, 39–40.

Table 4.2 *One hundred English communities, 1574–1821:*
Overall statistics, ratios and measures

Statistics		Ratios and measures		
1. Total population	68,407	1. Crude mean size of domestic group (total population over numbers of name blocks, institutions included)	$\frac{1}{6}$	4.841
2. Less { 595 known to be in institutions (n = 21)	67,812	2. Corrected mean size of domestic group (excludes known institutions)	$\frac{2}{6}$	4.798
3. Less { 430 estimated to be in institutions (n = 79)	67,382	3. Uncorrected maximal mean size of household (excludes known and estimated institutions, combines host and inmate households)	$\frac{3}{6}$	4.768
4. Less { 439 known to be and 590 estimated to be individual inmates (n = 15)	66,353	4. Corrected maximal mean size of household (excludes individual inmates, separates host and inmate households)	$\frac{4}{7}$	4.470
5. Less { 543 known to be and 719 estimated to be members of inmate households	65,091	5. Exclusive maximal mean size of household (excludes all inmates and inmate households)	$\frac{5}{8}$	4.850
6. Minimal total households (Nos. of name blocks of which some may be institutions or housefuls)	14,131	6. Mean of mean household sizes[a] Variance 0.673, standard deviation 0.453 99% confidence interval 4.65–4.99 Moment coefficient of skewness 1.020 Moment coefficient of kurtosis 1.761		4.821
7. Plus { 256 known and 456 estimated to be inmate households	14,843	7. Median of mean household sizes 4.73 Range 3.63–7.22 Interquartile range 4.39–5.19		
8. Less { 712 known and estimated inmate households	13,419			

[a] Approximate to ratio 3 above.

show why it is that all MHS values have to be called maximal: it follows from the fact that the denominators for these fractions are themselves minimal, since they may contain blocks of persons other than households, institutions that is to say, or housefuls. Nevertheless, it is not possible to work out from lists of inhabitants of the usual kind anything like a ratio for mean size of houseful, that is number of persons occupying a set of premises, whether or not those premises contain more than one household each with its own dwelling. This is because of the assumption which we make that blocks of persons in listings usually represent households and only exceptionally housefuls.[11] The table as a whole may well give the impression that the suggested standard for MHS is indeed a little high at 4.75,. and should be 4.66 or even 4.50. But the refinements necessary in order to get at a lower and perhaps more realistic figure are so pernickety and so seldom possible with data of this kind that it seems best to stick with 4.75. In this chapter, therefore, most calculations relate to the household as defined for ratio 3 in Table 4.2.

The presence of institutions and of inmates (mostly lodgers in these data, but including boarders, sojourners, visitors and so on) is the complication which gives these refinements their meaning. In the original study of 1969 these features of traditional English social structure were passed over as being almost trivial, but we have since found that they were more appreciable in number than we then realised. Institutions appear in only 21 of our 100 lists of inhabitants (which explains the reference n = 21 in Table 4.2). This at once raises the question of how often their failure to appear in the 79 others was due to their actual absence rather than to incomplete recording. Some help in deciding this comes from the fact that they seem to be confined for the most part to the larger settlements: they make up 2.4 % of the population of the 21 communities where they appear, and our tentative estimate of their proportion of the whole population is 1.7 %. Institutions become common as the nineteenth century approaches, and could sometimes by then account for a fifth of the population of a place. Nothing we know from their figures could be used to show that institutional living was at all usual in traditional English society.

Inmates seem to have been somewhat more frequent over the whole period, although it was an offence to harbour them in the household in England, and prosecutions are recorded for doing so in the seventeenth century. Only 15 of our 100 lists record their presence: here they made up no less than 9.7 % of the population and 18.1 % of domestic groups contained them. They were commonest in London, commoner in the towns than in the countryside, but apparently to be found in communities of all sizes. These high proportions fall to 7.5 % of the population and 14.7 % of the households when the 6 London parishes which record inmates are dropped from the 15, and our even more tentative estimate for the proportion in the whole body of data is 3.4 % of the population. This may be somewhat modest, and it seems certain that inmates exceeded resident kinsfolk appreciably in number, and may have been of the same order as servants.[12]

[11] See above, Chapter 1, pp. 34–40 for households and dwellings, housefuls and premises and for variant usages (together with lists which may in fact be ranged in housefuls). See also the references there to Richard Wall's discussion of these issues in Chapter 5.

[12] Compare Tables 4.12 and 4.13: the proper contrast is with the statistics for the 21 settlements with known institutions and the 15 with known inmates, not the estimates for the whole body of data, As will be seen, I have not attempted such estimates for other variables, and have only done so for institutions and inmates because they affect the actual measurement of household size. Lodgers are so few in the listings which give ages that it is impossible to say whether their presence is related to the domestic cycle in the interesting way which is described by Berkner (1972).

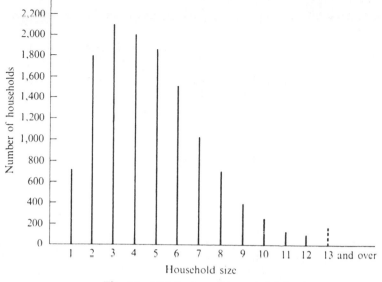

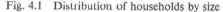

Fig. 4.1   Distribution of households by size

The final interval in this figure indicates the total of all households containing 13 persons or more. In all calculations of persons belonging to such households the mean size has been taken as 14.5. The distribution of households at this end of the scale was abbreviated in this way for computer analysis.

The ratios and measures at the lower end of Table 4.2 are for the distribution amongst communities of mean household sizes themselves, and it is interesting that the mean and median fall within the range of the rest. It is known that household size, and also apparently settlements by household size, are positively skewed in their distribution. This comes out in Figs. 4.1 and 4.2: the tail for individual household sizes in fact extends as far as 50 in these data, a size represented by one household, that of the Earl of Lonsdale in the village of Lowther in Westmorland in 1787, which consisted of the Earl himself, a bachelor, and 49 servants.

The impression left by the examination of similar distributions from other areas and from other periods is that the particular shape apparent in Fig. 4.1 may be characteristic of pre-industrial England, and the remainder of Northern and Western Europe may have been similar.[13] The contrast in this respect between England in our own time and in the era which concerns us in this chapter is made clear in Table 4.3. It must be insisted that a majority of all persons lived

[13] Iceland in 1703 had not a dissimilar distribution (see the population census of that year published in 1960), though with a larger proportion of bigger households. The chapters on Japan in this volume show that the upper tail of this distribution was briefer than in England, though MHS was larger. In colonial America, with even greater MHS, both upper and lower tails seem to have been shorter.

Table 4.3   *Households by size and persons in households of various sizes*

Sizes	100 Communities, 1574–1821		England and Wales, 1961 (10% sample)	
	Households	Persons	Households	Persons
1–3	36.3	17.5	65.4	46.4
4 and 5	30.5	30.5	28.2	39.7
6+	33.2	53.0	6.4	14.1
	100%	101%	100%	100%

in the larger households in traditional England, those above six persons in size, in spite of the fact that only a third of all households were in this category and that the overall MHS was less than five. The chronology of the change since pre-industrial times will concern us in due course, when we shall find that the turning point came much later than might be expected in England and Wales.

When we turn from the distribution of persons by household size in our hundred pre-industrial places to the distribution of communities by mean household size slight deviations from the normal curve are easily seen.

Fig. 4.2 plots percentages of the hundred communities which have mean household sizes belonging in the various intervals. The curve is rather erratic, as must be expected with such small numbers, but the straggling tail at the right end of the scale is conspicuous, giving rise to the slight positive skewness. In fact there are signs of a second, higher distribution, containing the communities with large mean household sizes, those above six.

These tendencies appear in an exaggerated form in the curves which have been drawn in on Fig. 4.2 for two of the time periods, the middle period (1650–1749) with 45 communities and the later period (1750–1821) with 50 communities. In spite of the confusion which these even smaller numbers introduce into the picture there is an evident hint of a general difference in the distribution of mean household sizes between the middle and later periods. In the middle period a high peak comes below the mean and the rest of the distribution tends to be concave. In the later period the higher peak comes above the mean and the curve is convex at higher values. The implication is that smaller households may well have been more common in the middle than in the later period, although we shall see that the overall mean household sizes for the two periods (ratio 3) – 4.696 for the middle and 4.776 for the later – are quite close to each other.

But it will be appreciated that the task of distinguishing differences due to the passage of time from differences due to locality in evidence of this kind is inevitably intricate and uncertain. Richard Wall returns to this problem in the chapter which follows, but the evidence he uses precludes him from discussing issues of household composition. It may in fact be the case that there were quite marked differences in the structure of the household over time brought about

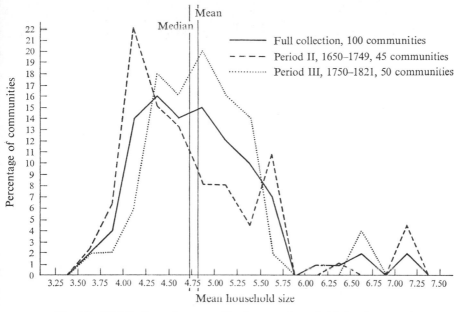

Fig. 4.2   Distribution of communities by mean household size, in percentages

inter alia by changes in the family, and so connected with demographic developments, but that the consequent differences in household size were surprisingly
slight. Even if it were to prove possible to make out a persuasive case for change
of this kind from our present data, it would have to be confined to development
between the middle and the later periods, since the number of communities for
which we have evidence for the first period – before 1650, five communities
only – is too small to be of much use.

There are two sets of facts and circumstances which must be set out before
any such exercise can be undertaken and the remainder of the present chapter
will be devoted to them. One is the evidence on mean household size in England
and Wales before 'industrialisation' and after it, figures which seem to imply
something approaching constancy in this ratio over time. The second is the
structural characteristics of our one hundred English pre-industrial communities
regarded as a static sample. These appear to be the first historical figures for the
size and structure of the household to become available for any collection of
communities in a country which has later become industrialised, since those
calculated by Hayami in Chapter 18 were subsequently obtained. Previous knowledge has been confined for the most part to individual settlements.

In Table 4.4 figures for mean household size are set out for England since the
sixteenth century. They begin with those recovered from listings, pre-census
figures, and continue with those published in the census reports for England and

Table 4.4   *Mean household size in England 1564–1921*
Mean household size in England and Wales 1801–1961[a]

Date(s)	Mean household size	Index Nos. (4.75 = 100)
1564–1649 ($n = 5$)	5.073	106.8
{ 1650–1749 ($n = 45$)	{ 4.696	{ 98.9
{ 1650–1749 ($n = 36$)[b]	{ 4.502[b]	{ 94.8
Kent 1705 ($n = 34$)	4.434	93.3
1740–1821 ($n = 50$)	4.776	100.5
Westmorland 1787 ($n = 24$)	4.611	97.1
{ 1564–1821 (ratio 3 in Table 4.2)	{ 4.768	{ 100.4
{ 1564–1821 (ratio 4 in Table 4.2)	{ 4.470	{ 94.1
1801	*4.60*	*96.8*
1811	*4.64*	*97.7*
1821	*4.72*	*99.4*
1831	*4.68*	*98.5*
1841	not available	
1851	*4.73*	*99.4*
1861	4.38	92.2
1871	4.40	92.6
1881	*4.54*	*95.6*
1891	*4.60*	*96.9*
1901	*4.49*	*94.5*
1911	*4.36*	*91.8*
1921	*4.14*	*87.2*
1931	3.72	78.3
1941	no census	
1951	3.19	67.2
1961	3.04	64.0

[a] Figures for MHS correspond more or less to ratio 3 of Table 4.2 up to the start of the Census in 1801, and then to ratio 4. Between 1801 and 1921, apart from the two occasions 1861 and 1871, the Census provides ratios for 'Family or separate occupier' only, i.e. presumably ratio 3, though perhaps ratio 2 or even 1. These figures have therefore been reduced to something like ratio 4 by the use of the function estimated by Laslett (1970(i), 450) and so are printed in italics. In no case does this calculated MHS differ from the Census figure by more than 0.11. After 1921 the Census gives ratios for 'Private family', which are net of lodgers and institutions, and the 1861 and 1871 Reports also supply figures which appear roughly to correspond with ratio 4.

[b] Omitting London parishes.

Wales, starting in 1801, the first British Census. Unfortunately, the relevant information seems not to have been included in the reports for the census year 1841. After each figure for mean household size in Table 4.4, an index figure is given, with base 4.75 as 100. Two regional figures have been included in the table, for Kent in 1705 and for Westmorland in 1787. These represent two collections of neighbouring communities for which we have evidence at Cambridge. Some, though not all of these listings, have been used in our collection of one hundred (see Table 4.1, nos. 38–46 and 61–81).

It would seem from this list of figures that mean household size did not change markedly between the pre-industrial social order in England, and that which succeeded it in the nineteenth century. The series as a whole seems to justify the standard of 4.75 for mean household size from the late sixteenth to the first decade of the twentieth century, if a little high as has been said – it was never apparently quite attained during the nineteenth century. Nevertheless I hope that it will not be looked upon as a universal multiplier, that is as a figure which could be used to proceed from numbers of households to totals of population for any community or small group of communities over this period of time. Table 4.1 shows how misleading this would be. It now seems best to abandon the quest for a single multiplier of this kind. In spite of the fact that English household size seems to have differed so little from period to period and region to region, individual settlements were evidently liable to vary quite widely one from another.

This tendency towards constancy in mean household size has come as a somewhat surprising discovery, especially for the period usually regarded as that of industrialisation or of social mobilisation, which lasted from the late eighteenth to the mid-nineteenth century in England. Though the comparative study of this subject is only just beginning, there is evidence which implies that household size in our country was somewhat more resistant to the economic, social structural and demographic changes which came in the nineteenth century than it was in other Western countries. Census records show that MHS had already fallen below 4.0 in France by 1880, and even in Sweden where industrialisation came still later. The ratio was higher in the United States and Canada than in England over the whole period after 1850, but by 1900 these three countries were closer to each other in this respect, apparently because MHS was slower to fall in England.[14] The indications are, therefore, that the movement of mean household size over time is strongly associated with demographic changes, for this is the period of the demographic transition in all the countries concerned. The domestic group grew smaller as fertility and mortality fell, whilst expectation of life rose. But it is quite obvious, even from these preliminary figures, that demographic causes were not the only ones in play, especially in England and Wales. This comes out when we look a little more closely at the exact point at which MHS began to fall in England, and when we plot the movement of MHS over time against the net reproduction rate.

[14] These figures have been assembled in the Population Division of the United Nations by Dr Shigemi Kono for the handbook on household structure and its tendencies over time, which is in preparation there. They appear in a preliminary form in a mimeograph dated August 1971 (ESA/P/WP/Rev. 1). The rank order of the countries of known MHS in 1880–1 was (1) Canada (5.4), (2) U.S.A. (5.0), (3) Belgium (4.6), (4) England and Wales (4.5), (5) Sweden (3.9), (6) France (3.7). In 1900–1 it was (1) Canada (5.1), (2) U.S.A. (4.8), (3) England and Wales (4.5), (4) Belgium (4.3), (5) Sweden (3.7), (6) France (3.6). All these figures are approximate, of course, and the exact basis of calculation (which of the ratios listed in Table 4.2) is not clear. See also Kono, *The determinants and consequences of population trends* (typescript).

Table 4.5   *Domestic group in England and Wales 1801–1961:*
Mean figures and fall in size

Census figures for 'family or separate occupier'		Laslett's figures for household	
Averages			
1801–1891	4.68	1801–1891	4.59
1801–1901	4.68	1801–1901	4.58
1801–1911	4.66	1801–1911	4.56
1801–1921	4.63		
Fall			
1891–1911	4.7%	1891–1961	34%
1891–1921	9.1%	1901–1961	32%
1911–1921	4.7%	1911–1961	30%
		1911–1921	5%
		1911–1931	14%

As for the point of decline, Table 4.5 presents a number of averages, and of percentage declines over various periods.[15]

The figures show then that the size of the domestic group in England and Wales began to fall sharply in 1891 and has not ceased to fall since that time. It is true to say that the whole period 1891–1961 elapsed before the decline reached the full one-third which seems to be the order of the fall we are examining. Nevertheless the level reached in 1911 was only very slightly lower than that of 1861, and the rate of fall was markedly greater after that date than before it; the descent in the fifty years 1911–61 was only 4 % less than in the seventy years 1891–1961. Some of the variation between count and count was undoubtedly due to changes in the definition of the domestic group used by the census takers; the rise to a peak in 1851 took place when 'occupier' replaced 'family', and the sharp fall in 1861 when lodgers were first officially counted as 'occupiers'. The changes which went on between the second and the fourth decades of the twentieth century are much more likely to have been wholly due to alterations in the actual composition of the domestic group, and they appear to me to represent its final and definitive transformation.

When the process is represented graphically in Fig. 4.3, this impression becomes clearer. The recovery of household size between 1871 and 1891 stands out in the curves, as does the precipitous descent after 1911, only checked in the final decade 1951–61 and then very slightly. The remarkable feature of this diagram, however, is the relationship between the behaviour of the net reproduc-

---

[15] Taken from Laslett (1970 i), along with Fig. 4.3 and the discussion of them. Nixon, *Size and structure of the household in England over three centuries: a comment* (1970), had pointed out that a numerical miscopy was responsible for the claim in Laslett (1969) that the fall in MHS in England began even later than it did, after 1911 rather than after 1891. The discussion reprinted here was in reply to Nixon's comment.

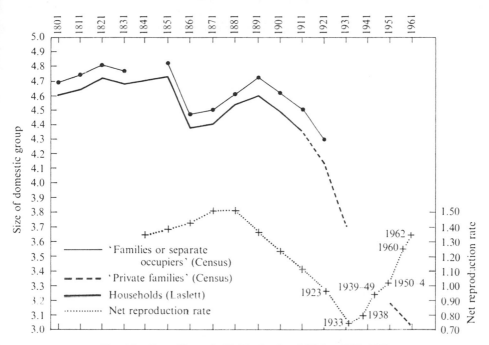

Fig. 4.3   Size of household, England and Wales, 1801–1961

tion rate after 1841 (when this index first becomes available[16]) and the behaviour of household size. For the first forty years the two are roughly parallel, and though they begin to converge after that, it is tempting to infer that much of the variation in the size of the domestic group was, as might be expected, due to demographic fluctuation with a twenty-year time lag. It should be stressed that this deduction is hardly secure in the present state of our knowledge about the function relating the two expressions, and what happened after the 1920s flatly contradicts it. Between the early 1930s and the early 1960s the net reproduction rate rose conspicuously in England and Wales whilst the size of the domestic group continued to shrink rapidly.

Not only does it appear that mean household size altered little over what is usually called the period of demographic transition associated with industrialisation. It seems that the distribution of households by size may also have stayed about the same until the early decades of the twentieth century. Figures for the

[16] See Wrigley, *Population and history* (1969): 195, Table 5.16, the source of the data. It must be added that Kono (typescript) finds a similar pattern for France, Canada, the U.S.A., and especially Japan, using gross rather than net reproduction rates. Secular fall in MHS is associated with a fall in that rate, until recent decades when the rate goes up whilst MHS continues to go down. There is a complication in the French case, for between 1930 and 1940 MHS seems actually to have increased sharply there, though I am not aware of how far this may be an artifact of definition of household.

Table 4.6   *Percentage distribution of households by size in England and Wales since the sixteenth century*

Group size	100 communities 1574–1821	York 1851	Census				
			1911	*1921*	*1931*	*1951*	*1961*
1	5.7	5.1	5.3	6.0	6.7	10.7	11.9
2	14.2	15.0	16.2	17.7	21.9	27.7	30.1
3	16.5	16.0	19.3	20.8	24.1	25.3	23.4
4	15.8	17.7	18.1	18.6	19.4	19.0	19.1
5	14.7	13.6	14.4	13.9	12.4	9.6	9.1
6	11.8	13.3	10.3	9.4	7.3	4.3	3.8
7	8.0	6.7	6.9	6.0	4.1	1.9	1.5
8	5.4	4.5	4.3	3.6	2.1	0.8	0.6
9	3.1	2.9	2.5	2.1	1.1	0.4	0.3
10 and over	4.9	5.2	2.5	1.9	0.9	0.3	0.2
	100%	100%	100%	100%	100%	100%	100%

distribution of households by size are hard to come by in the earlier British census reports, and those for 1851 in Table 4.6 have been taken from a recent enquiry by Dr W. A. Armstrong into the city of York, using the original enumerators' books of the 1841 and the 1851 Censuses.[17] Fig. 4.4 represents the figures of Table 4.6 in diagrammatic form.

The percentages of Table 4.6, and above all the lines in the accompanying diagram seem to me to illustrate graphically enough the general points we have been discussing about size of household in England, its constancy until the early decades of the twentieth century and its sudden and dramatic change. The crucial character of the years 1911–30 is particularly clearly seen. It was not until this English generation which came very late in the process of industrialisation in the oldest industrial society in the world, that the immemorial tendency of English people to live in households of a particular range of sizes began at last to change. By this time something like a century and a quarter separated them from the fully traditional, pre-industrial world of their great-great-grandparents. In these numerical respects, it is claimed, the English evidence is enough by itself to demonstrate that the household does not necessarily change in size during industrialisation, and that even demographic influences are limited in their immediate effects.[18]

[17] See Armstrong, *The interpretation of census enumerators' books* (1968): 70 and below, Chapter 6, pp. 205–206. A set of percentages of the kind contained in Table 4.6 below is printed there from Laslett, *Remarks on the multiplier* (1965 ii) where a figure of 4.50 rather than 4.75 was tentatively suggested for that elusive ratio. The series of percentages contained in the 1965 paper show no marked difference from those prepared for our 100 communities and set out in Table 4.6.

[18] Compare Goody, above, Chapter 3, pp. 115–117. Burch, above, Chapter 2, pp. 97–100 takes a different view.

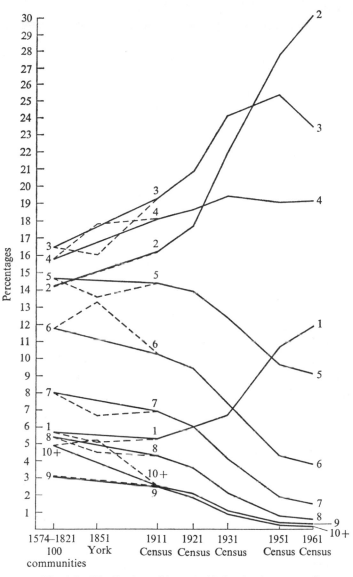

Fig. 4.4   Distribution of households by size (percentages)
The figures from 1 to 10 + on the drawing refer to numbers of persons per household

But questions of mean size and of distribution by size are to be sharply distinguished from questions of structure, and we have still to explore the composition of English households during the era before industrialisation began to transform English society. We may pause here for a moment to point out that the evidence cited here and the whole body of data now available to the Cambridge

Group for the History of Population and Social Structure on the family and household is fully consistent with the theoretical revision which is now in progress on the subject of the domestic group. This goes to show that the human family, if not necessarily the household, must always have been small and almost always nuclear. The boldest assertion of this position is that of Marion Levy:

The general outlines and nature of the actual family structures have been virtually identical in certain strategic respects [of which size of membership is the first, small size] in all known societies in world history for well over 50 % of the members of those societies.[19]

It does not necessarily follow from this that mean household size should vary only slightly over time. In order to attempt an explanation of this tendency apparent in the figures, it is essential that particulars of the household membership of persons other than man, wife and children should be added to the biological and demographic arguments put forward in favour of the universal predominance of the small family.

Our collection of one hundred lists of inhabitants of communities from pre-industrial England does provide us with such evidence. Unfortunately, as has been stated above, it is not available for all the places we have had to include in order to obtain a collection of adequate size to establish the bare facts of household size and its variance. It may be borne in mind as we read the particulars listed in Tables 4.7 to 4.17 that many of them are inaccessible in English materials for dates after 1871 and so cannot be used to make inferences about the reasons why mean household size over the whole country seems to have varied within such restricted limits over so long a period of time during and after, as well as before, industrialisation.[20]

---

[19] See Levy, *Aspects of the analysis of family structure* (1965): 41–2. Burch, *The size and structure of families* (1967) provides evidence bearing on Levy's contention. The standard adopted is that 50 % of persons in any society must ordinarily be expected to live in households of between three and six persons, with an insignificant percentage in single-member households and in institutions. Our 100 English pre-industrial communities conform, with 55 % of persons in households size 3 to 6, 1.2 % in one-member households and 1.7 % in institutions. The controversies surrounding Levy's work are also discussed by Goody, see above, Chapter 3, and Burch, see above, Chapter 2. Very full consideration of the small family hypothesis is given by Kono (typescript and see above), though in discussing the fall in household size now going on all over the world, leading to a universal convergence, he retains the word 'nuclearisation' as a general description. This seems unfortunate to me, not only because the small family case is that the family group has always been almost universally nuclear, but because it fails to allow for servants, for whose possible functions in maintaining household size, and overall constancy in household size, whilst they persist, see below pp. 156–157.

[20] Access to nominal information from English official census material is at present permitted only up to 1871. It should be added here that in order to create a viable model for the behaviour of the household in response to demographic and social structural variation (fertility, mortality, age at marriage, and time of leaving parental household, likelihood of the presence of servants, etc.) the data ought preferably to be analysed by individual household rather than by community, as they have to be for the most part in the present chapter. The conditions under which the data were recovered and processed (see above p. 129) were responsible for their ordering by community, with consequent lack of definition and susceptibility to misleading ecological inferences.

Table 4.7 *One hundred English communities, 1574–1821. Basic data statistics for whole collection. Set I: Population by sex and marital status*

	N	Overall	Means of means and proportions	Standard deviation (for means of means and proportions)
1. Sex ratio of the population	70	91.3	—	—
2. Proportion married in population	61	33.4%	33.4%	6.3%
3. Proportion widowed in population	61	6.2%	6.0%	2.2%
4. Proportion single in population	61	60.4%	60.5%	7.0%
5. Proportion of males married	61	34.8%	34.5%	7.1%
6. Proportion of males widowed	61	3.5%	—	—
7. Proportion of males single	61	61.7%	—	—
8. Proportion of females married	61	32.1%	32.7%	6.2%
9. Proportion of females widowed	61	8.7%	—	—
10. Proportion of females single	61	59.2%	—	—

Here we shall be content to record the demographic and social-structural details which have been worked out for the whole number of our one hundred pre-industrial communities. The differences between them and those shown by the sub-collections drawn from regions and from time periods, the surprisingly slight contrasts between rural and urban communities – always excepting central London – the full discussion of possible determinants of mean household size, must all be left on one side. But a comprehensive selection from the variables calculated as means of means of the one hundred communities and recorded in the computer output is included in the following series of tables numbered 4.7 to 4.17.[21] Much of the information contained in them was used in Chapter 1 for the purposes of establishing an English standard for comparative purposes, and it should now be apparent that the standard has palpable limitations. This can be gathered from the appearance under the letter N in each table of a column of figures indicating, as was done in the case of institutions and inmates, for how many communities the information in question is available in the material. Even for the elementary characteristics reviewed in Table 4.7, the first of the series, this number falls sharply from the full 100. This is not only because a few of our

[21] The number of variables in the output available for the whole collection and for each of the sub-collections is 165. In addition, 229 further variables are included for the whole collection, giving the average value for each of the items of data (e.g. the average number of widows per community), together with measures of dispersion and concentration. As must be expected, many of the results reveal very little, and some nothing; some just did not work out. A high proportion of the huge correlation table is also of problematic value to the analysis. Nevertheless, this enormous body of results illustrates vividly how much can be learned by the use of contemporary methods from seemingly uninformative lists of persons who lived in past communities.

Table 4.8   *One hundred English communities, 1574–1821. Basic data statistics for whole collection. Set II: Proportion of households of size 1 to 13 and over*

Variables Household sizes				N	Overall	Means of means and proportions	Standard deviation (for means of means and proportions)
1. Proportion of households size			1	98	5.7%	5.6%	4.7%
2.	,,	,,	2	98	14.2%	13.3%	5.8%
3.	,,	,,	3	98	16.5%	16.2%	5.3%
4.	,,	,,	4	98	15.8%	15.8%	4.6%
5.	,,	,,	5	98	14.7%	15.2%	4.5%
6.	,,	,,	6	98	11.8%	12.1%	3.6%
7.	,,	,,	7	98	8.0%	8.1%	3.5%
8.	,,	,,	8	98	5.4%	5.2%	2.9%
9.	,,	,,	9	98	3.1%	3.3%	2.6%
10.	,,	,,	10	98	1.9%	1.8%	1.7%
11.	,,	,,	11	98	1.1%	1.3%	1.5%
12.	.,	,,	12	98	0.7%	0.7%	1.3%
13.	,,	,,	13 and over	98	1.2%	1.3%	1.9%
14. Mean household size				100	4.768	4.821	0.673

chosen lists fail to specify sex and marital status altogether, but also because about one-third of them provide unacceptably incomplete data of this kind. In view of the importance of this basic information it will be seen that an overall mean has been worked out for all the items in this table and in Table 4.8.

The sex ratio of the population, 91.3 males to every 100 females, is perhaps a little low, although it has always been supposed that females predominated in England at that time. This may indicate some underregistration amongst the 70 communities concerned, but seems better interpreted in the reverse way. If in a decidedly male-dominated society females were so well recorded that the sex ratio is low, then it looks as if recording must have been fairly complete. The final column shows that there was, on the whole, little variation in these per-centages from community to community, and the general picture presented is one which can be confirmed from many directions, demographic and social structural. In pre-industrial England marriage came relatively late, and took place between people of about the same age. Therefore the proportion of single persons was high in both sexes.[22]

Table 4.8 sets out the proportions of households of various sizes which have already been discussed. It will be noticed from the first two tables that the figures for means of means are quite close to those for overall means, which confirms

[22] See the important article by Hajnal, *European marriage patterns in perspective* (1965).

Table 4.9   *One hundred English communities, 1574–1821.*
Basic data statistics for whole collection. Set III: Household heads

	N	Overall	Means of proportions	Standard deviation (for means of proportions)
Proportion households headed by				
Married couples	70	69.7%	70.4%	11.4%
Widowers	70	—	5.2%	3.3%
Widows	70	—	12.9%	6.4%
Single males	70	—	2.1%	2.6%
Single females	70	—	1.1%	1.9%
Unspecified males	70	—	5.0%	4.7%
Unspecified females	70	—	2.3%	3.1%

the fact of consistency from community to community, and adds confidence to means of means as a basis for the analysis.

When we turn to Table 4.9 we meet a situation which seems indicative of a high mortality rate amongst the older, responsible members of the community, since well over one-quarter of all households turn out to be headed by a single person rather than by a married couple. The proportion of the remainder headed by widows is notable, but it is not always clear from the list whether all 'widows' were in fact without living husbands. These figures may therefore imply a certain number of deserted wives, when those we have had to call 'unspecified' are added to them. Some of them may only have been on their own on the day of the count because their husbands were away on visits.

We shall find that variation in respect of proportions of single-headed households between communities does seem to have some positive effect, not perhaps as great as might be expected, on mean household size. It is fourth in order of variables positively and significantly related to mean household size in Table 4.17, the correlation table.

Children, however, who are perhaps universally supposed to have most influence in maintaining, increasing or decreasing the average size of households seem to be in a paradoxical position in Table 4.17, the proportion in the population being highly significantly *negatively* correlated with mean size of household. This little puzzle may be explained in part by remembering that servants were simply children who had changed households, from the parental home to the household of a master. The more servants, then, the fewer children, and the larger the MHS, for Table 4.17 also shows how strongly proportions of households with servants and of servants in the population were correlated with dimensions of domestic groups. It follows from this that if a decision had to be made about the size of what might be called the rising generation, the total of those at risk to succeed their married and widowed seniors in the society,

Table 4.10   *One hundred English communities, 1574–1821.*
Basic data statistics for whole collection. Set IV: Children: descriptions

	N	Overall	Means of means and proportions	Standard deviation (for means of means and proportions)
1. Proportion of children in the population	66	42.6%	41.5%	9.8%
2. Sex ratio of children	61	91.4	—	—
3. Proportion of households with children	66	74.6%	73.9%	7.4%
4. Grandchildren as proportion of all children	61	—	2.3%	2.7%
5. Proportion of children orphaned	16	—	20.7%	9.0%
6. Proportion of children called bastards	13	—	1.2%	1.4%
7. Mean size of groups of children (sibling group ≥ 1)	66	2.761	2.730	0.429

Table 4.11   *One hundred English communities, 1574–1821.*
Basic data statistics for whole collection. Set V: Groups of children

	N	Overall	Means of proportions	Standard deviation (for means of proportions)
Proportion of children in groups of 1	66	—	11.2%	5.4%
,, ,, 2	66	—	18.4%	7.9%
,, ,, 3	66	—	23.1%	8.7%
,, ,, 4	66	—	18.1%	6.5%
,, ,, 5	66	—	13.4%	6.6%
,, ,, 6	66	—	7.7%	5.7%
,, ,, 7 or over	66	—	7.2%	6.9%

children and servants would have to be added together. In this respect the particulars in Tables 4.10 and 4.11 have to be taken along with those of Table 4.13. In fact, together with the proportion and distribution of servants, we find that the figures relating to children show the most interesting variations and correlations.

If the tables setting out the figures for children are marked by quite large and varying numbers, the table devoted to kin (Table 4.12) may be thought to be remarkable both for the small numbers and for their constancy. Although there were over 16,000 children and over 7,500 servants, in the communities where they can be identified, the 46 places recording kin report only 946 in a population of

Table 4.12   *One hundred English communities, 1574–1821.*
Basic data statistics for whole collection. Set VI: Resident kin

	N	Overall	Means of means and proportions	Standard deviation (for means of means and proportions)
1. Proportion of resident kin in population	46	3.4%	3.7%	2.1%
2. Proportion of households with resident kin	46	10.1%	11.7%	5.4%
3. Ratio of husbands' resident kin to wives' resident kin	42	—	163.4	—

nearly 30,000, present in 626 out of 5,843 households. These figures and proportions seem to me to dispose of any supposition that the traditional English household usually, or even often, contained resident kin, and that the presence of these persons was one of the reasons why the mean household size could be expected to be large.

Indeed, a further glance forward at the correlation in Table 4.17 will show that proportion of kin in the population seems to have had no detectable relationship with mean household size. Since the primary object of the original exercise was to examine the behaviour of this latter variable, rather than the details of the internal kin relationships of the domestic group in England, we cannot now go on to use the materials we are analysing so as to break down the category 'resident kin' in accordance with the criteria laid down in Chapter 1 at all satisfactorily. It is known, however, that of the 946 persons so classified, 230 were parents or parents-in-law of household heads, 105 their brothers and sisters and at least 200 their grandchildren. Many or most of these grandchildren were present without their parents: the fact is that only 39 of the 5,843 households contained a married child living with spouse and married parents (29 with the husband's people, 10 with the wife's). If widowed parents were included this number would rise, but could not exceed 150. The remaining 20 or so resident kin were aunts, uncles, 'cousins' of various kinds, but mostly unspecified, and plain 'relatives'.[23]

[23] In reading the above discussion of resident kin and their paucity, it must be borne in mind that our fragmentary knowledge of the kinship and affinal relationships between members of the population of each or any of our hundred communities makes it impossible to suppose that all resident relatives have been counted in the analysis. This makes it necessary to warn the reader against drawing strong inferences about the kin structure of pre-industrial English households from the data being discussed. For example, since surnames have often been used to trace kin relations, the preponderance of husbands' to wives' resident kin recorded in Table 4.12 is undoubtedly too high. Even the implication that the share of resident kin in household size was small has to be judged in relation to the fact that the proportion of persons of unidentifiable kin status (see above, Chapter 1, Table 1.13, p. 83) in the population is greater than the proportion of persons known to be resident kin.

We are not in a position to examine how the presence of these kinsfolk who did reside was related to the developmental cycle of the household in our sample, because of that crippling lack of adequate age data which has been lamented several times in discussing the English materials. A determined attack on the six in the present sample which do contain that information, along with the one or two others which have been discovered since 1967, may make it possible to get some idea of how the domestic group did vary in composition in the process from formation at marriage to dissolution on the death of the crucial members. An attempt of this kind is in progress at Cambridge, though it does not seem very likely to produce any results which could be called reliable. It has already been shown in Chapter 1 how infrequent extended and multiple households seem to have been in England and in the colonial United States in comparison with other areas, and how difficult it might be to make a case for an institution like the stem family as an established, ongoing, feature of preindustrial English society. As for frérèches, no single instance of coresident married siblings has so far appeared.

Nevertheless it may be worth citing here a fact or two which have been turned up when applying to two good English listings of inhabitants which do give ages, both of them entirely rural, the kind of criterion used by Berkner in his illuminating discussion of the stem family characteristics of the peasant households of Heidenreichstein in Austria in 1763.[24]

If types of family in Ealing in 1599 (no. 2 in Table 4.1) and Ardleigh in 1796 (no. 84) are analysed by age of head, there appears to be some resemblance to the Heidenreichstein pattern. Such extended and multiple households as there are occur at the beginning and towards the end of the developmental cycle, as indeed must always be the case. But, except for extended households at the end of the cycle, the effect is much less, and when the persons whose presence creates complexity are examined the resemblance with Heidenreichstein fades. In all but two of the ten cases of young householders having members of a previous generation living with them, it is the widowed mother or mother-in-law, sometimes with a child: only these two households were in the clear-cut, classical stem family situation. The extension which appears to be more common at the

---

[24] See Berkner (1972), and above, Chapter 1, especially pp. 20–21. In his article Berkner comments on the failure of my original essay of 1969 either to analyse the English material individually rather than aggregatively, or to recover the developmental cycle from the study of ages. He apparently overlooks the statements made there and repeated here about analysis by whole communities rather than by individual households (above p. 144) and all that was said about the absence of age information, as well as the entire lack of the detail he has used so effectively for his villages. He also cites the small number of English listings dating before 1650, and of all the listings being, as he supposes, weighted against the peasantry, to support his suggestion that there may have been a transition from the stem family but that it took place before the beginnings of industrialization. It could have been due, he suggests. to the earlier decline and virtual disappearance of those classes, i.e. peasant landowners, of which such a family form is characteristic. This is possible, but my knowledge of the materials makes it seem to be unlikely, just as is the possibility that the hundred communities analysed here are underrepresentative of the English peasantry pure and undefiled.

end of the cycle at Ardleigh than it is in the Austrian villages, comes about entirely because of the presence of grandchildren residing with grandparents without their own parents, which has already been described as being probably characteristic of England. Comparison with age listings of English towns, for example Stoke-on-Trent in 1701 (no. 37) shows that these tendencies were certainly weaker there, but they existed nevertheless. In neither case would it seem that a persuasive argument could be made for these details representing the residual survival of some complex familial form like the stem family.[25]

It would be a different matter if all servants or inmates could be assumed to be resident kin, points which are argued at some length in Chapter 1. This brings us to Table 4.13 of our present series and we may begin by citing the conclusion of that earlier discussion which seemed to show that servants, though frequently related to other members of the *community* of which they were members, were seldom related to the *households* in which they served at least through their *fathers*.[26] The question of servants in traditional English society is as much in need of extended investigation as the question of resident kin, and we shall have to pass over Table 4.13 very briefly here. Let it simply be said that the substantial proportion of persons who turn out to be living in the households other than those into which they were born, looks to us like something of a sociological discovery.[27] Their presence and social functions go a long way towards accounting for the paradoxes about household size and demographic rates which have been repeatedly referred to here and will concern us later. It

[25] If the households of craftsmen, and all not likely to have owned land or rights to land, are left out in the analysis of Ealing and Ardleigh, the resemblance to Heidenreichstein becomes weaker rather than otherwise. Attempts to recover the pattern for the 'peasant' village of Cardington in 1782 failed completely, as they did in the case of William Wordsworth's own village of Grasmere listed by age in 1683 – and what could be more rural than that? (It is possible that this last result may have been due to poor evidence.) Berkner himself does refer to figures which were supplied to him from Cambridge showing that English households emphatically do not show constancy in size over the developmental cycle, but then neither do those of Belgrade or Nishinomiya (see above p. 20). In this respect, as in that of proportions of households headed by married couples (see above p. 55), it seems to be Berkner's communities which are exceptional. The results of the analysis of this English rural evidence for correlations between other variables of possible significance for the developmental cycle and the stem family form are even less satisfactory and almost entirely negative. It seems to have been husbandmen (that is, landholders not owning their land, for the most part) who were most likely to have resident relatives, but the proportions were lower than in the hundred communities (about 10% as against 17%, see Table 4.16). At Ardleigh, the tradesmen and craftsmen actually had more extended families than the yeomen, who correspond best to the Heidenreichstein peasantry. There was no discernible pattern in the English communities when the presence of servants was correlated with the age of the head of the household, or the age of the first-born son, or the number of children.

[26] See above, pp. 57–58. Anderson, however, sees a strong connection between kinship and servant status in nineteenth-century Preston, see Chapter 7, p. 228, and the lack of any information in our present data on relationships through mothers is a very serious matter.

[27] The proportions are similar to those found in certain agricultural areas of the eighteenth-century Netherlands, see below, van der Woude, Chapter 12, pp. 307–308. Compare the proportion of households with servants in parts of Tokugawa Japan, below, Hayami, Chapter 18, pp. 503–504; Nakane, Chapter 19, pp. 521–522.

Table 4.13   *One hundred English communities, 1574–1821.*
Basic data statistics for whole collection. Set VII: Servants

	N	Overall	Means of means and proportions	Standard deviation (for means of means and proportions)
1. Proportion of servants in the population	63	13.4%	14.6%	7.8%
2. Sex ratio of servants	62	—	106.6	—
3. Proportion of households with servants	66	28.5%	32.9%	17.8%

should be noted that males predominated among servants in traditional times; they were not simply domestics, in our sense of the word, the Victorian sense, and may have been rather different in their social role from those at issue in Table 4.18.

Table 4.14 is the last of that part of the series which deals in characteristics of the whole population, undifferentiated by social and economic status. Its message is even simpler and more telling than that of Table 4.12. Very few households can be identified containing more than two generations – parents and their children – in the society we are analysing. The figures are a little crude for our purposes and it would have been more meaningful if households of 1, 2 and 3 persons had been excluded. These could scarcely ever have contained persons from more than two generations. But it is a striking fact that only 230 persons who could be called grandparents have been found in the 61 communities in question, and merely three households containing great-grandchildren: there were only 86 husbands' mothers and only 24 wives' mothers.[28] As we have noted already, our ancestors do not seem to have had much truck with resident mothers-in-law, a feature of their lives which mark them out as being very different from the lives of the Chinese or the Japanese, for example.

Tables 4.15 and 4.16 are not wholly relevant to demographic discussion, but are nevertheless of considerable significance to the subject of mean household size because of the obvious tendency towards larger households at the upper levels of society. The set of categories showing social and economic status has grown out of the material; it is an adaptation from Gregory King and from other census-takers working in the era before the Census. It has only this to recommend it, apart from any authority it may derive from the symmetry of descent displayed in these tables. One of many drawbacks of this set of classes is

---

[28] For the frequency of this type of household in nineteenth-century and twentieth-century England, see below, Anderson, Chapter 7, pp. 221–224.

Table 4.14 *One hundred English communities, 1574–1821. Basic data statistics for whole collection. Set VIII: Multi-generational households*

	N	Overall (%)	Means of pro- portions (%)	Standard deviation (for means of pro- portions) (%)
1. Proportion of households of one generation	61	23.8	25.1	7.3
2. Proportion of households of two generations	61	70.4	69.2	6.6
3. Proportion of households of three generations	61	5.8	5.7	4.8
4. Proportion of households of four or more generations	61	—	0.0	0.1

that it creates a category out of 'clergy', a class of very varied economic standing, and too small at that. Still the gradation has worked quite well in the very crude social categorisation which is all that the historical sociologists working over such a long period can expect at present to be able to do.

Tables 4.15 and 4.16 clearly demonstrate hierarchy in the social structure. That it should be displayed in mean household size, and quite uniformly from top to bottom both by overall means and means of means, is what we have been led to expect from data of every kind on the social structure here considered. A little reflection shows that this hierarchy was likely to come out in the proportions of households with servants and with kin.[29] The steps in the hierarchy in those respects turn out to be quite regular. It is interesting that servants should be a feature of almost one-quarter of the households of a category as low as no. 5, tradesmen and craftsmen, in the centre of the social scale, and that some labourers should have had servants. The upturn which comes in the final category in all cases except that of size of groups of children is due to the fact that 'not stated' includes many households of widows, some of them substantial, often containing servants and more than the usual number of kin. But the regular descent order from gentry at the top, to clergy, yeomen, husbandmen, tradesmen, labourers and paupers is not found in recordings for groups of children.

Gentry had fewer children in their households than husbandmen, and almost as small a number as tradesmen and craftsmen. Only labourers and paupers had smaller groups of children than yeomen. The hierarchy is broken in this column

[29] A similar hierarchy can be observed in rural Lancashire in 1851, see below, Anderson, Chapter 7, pp. 220–221, and compare Klapisch in Chapter 10, pp. 275–277 (fifteenth-century Tuscany) and Pryor in Chapter 22, pp. 575–578 (nineteenth-century U.S.A.). See also Goody, Chapter 3, pp. 122–123.

Table 4.15   *One hundred English communities, 1574–1821. Basic data statistics for whole collection. Set IX: Size of household by social status*

	N	Overall	Means of means	Standard deviation (for means of means)
1. Gentlemen	26	6.63	7.54	3.92
2. Clergy	25	5.83	5.60	2.51
3. Yeomen	21	5.91	5.70	1.72
4. Husbandmen	35	5.09	5.39	1.05
5. Tradesmen and craftsmen	40	4.65	4.72	0.81
6. Labourers	33	4.51	4.34	0.99
7. Paupers	16	3.96	3.74	1.50
8. Others	39	3.72⎫	3.59	1.41
9. Not stated	19	4.29⎭		

Table 4.16   *One hundred English communities, 1574–1821. Basic data statistics for whole collection. Set X: Size of groups of children, proportion of households with servants, proportion of households with kin, by social status*

	Mean size of groups of children		Mean proportion of households with kin		Mean proportion of households with servants	
	N	Overall	N	(Means of proportions)	N	(Means of proportions)
Gentlemen	26	2.94	16	27.6	18	84.1
Clergy	12	3.53	12	25.0	16	81.2
Yeomen	17	2.76	9	17.0	14	71.9
Husbandmen	33	3.10	14	17.3	21	46.8
Tradesmen and craftsmen	42	2.90	18	12.3	25	23.3
Labourers	32	2.70	16	7.9	21	2.2
Paupers	13	2.34	6	7.7⎫		
Others ⎫ Not stated ⎭	37	2.31	18	15.0⎭	26	13.9

of Table 4.16 and where it persists the steps are shallower. This seems to be against expectation and a challenge to the interpreter.[30]

Gentry had a tendency to marry earlier than others.[31] They lived better, so that their babies might be expected to have survived more often. They were

[30] In fifteenth-century Tuscany it is clear that the wealthy supported noticeably more children than others, see below, Klapisch, Chapter 10, p. 274.

[31] See Laslett (1965 i, 1971): 86, and Chambers, *The vale of Trent* (1957): 52. Neither context can be said to demonstrate this principle beyond doubt, and Hollingsworth fails to confirm this finding for his secondary universe, which consisted largely of gentry, in his *Demography of the British peerage* (1964).

Table 4.17 *One hundred English communities, 1574–1821. Select variables correlated with mean household size (means of means and proportions)*

Coefficient when household size is correlated with:

1. Proportion of households with servants	+0.599**
2. Proportion of households of gentry	+0.528**
3. Proportion of servants in the population	+0.437**
4. Proportion of households headed by married couples	+0.296*
5. Mean size of groups of children	+0.239
6. Proportion of households with resident kin	−0.003
7. Proportion of households with children	−0.015
8. Proportion of resident kin in the population	−0.038
9. Proportion of households of three generations	−0.153
10. Proportion of children in the population	−0.335**

* Significant at the 0.05 level.   ** Significant at the 0.01 level.

under no economic pressure to send their children out to service. Therefore they might be expected to have more, not fewer, children at home. Presumably yeomen, the closest in status to gentry, to some extent shared their situation.

It would be unwise to base too much on the present evidence as to the size of groups of children in the households of gentry and yeomen. The number of communities in question is small, as the table shows. There may have been several influences at work: perhaps resident, housekeeping gentry were usually at a different stage in the life-cycle from other household heads. But an attractive explanation is that the gentlemen, and the yeomanry, limited their families for fear of downward social mobility.[32] The clergy do not seem to have done so, however. The Rev. Quiverful is already present in these tables.

The final list of results we can include in the present series is a brief extract from the enormous correlation table for the full one hundred communities, registering the relationship between mean household size and ten select variables.[33]

This set of correlations, I believe, serves to clarify and to confirm the suggestions of the present chapter in respect of household size and its aetiology. They cannot be said to explain why mean household size was high in some places and at some periods in pre-industrial England, and low at other places at other

[32] On family limitation and its presence in England at the relevant time, see the crucial article by Wrigley, *Family limitation in pre-industrial England* (1966 ii) and on the behaviour of the Genevan bourgeoisie (a whole social group presumably deliberately providing against the possibility of having too many children to support), cf. Henry, *Anciennes familles Genevoises* (1960). If the gentry consistently succeeded in interfering with their net reproduction rate in such a way as to prevent downward social mobility of their progeny, some of the suggestions made in Laslett (1965 i, 1971) about their social situation and dynamics will have to be revised. Hard evidence should be forthcoming when fertility by social status is available from family reconstitution exercises.

[33] These variables should be compared with a parallel series for Japan in the Tokugawa era, see below, Hayami, Chapter 18, pp. 491–496.

times in spite of the overall tendency towards constancy. This interesting problem must be reserved to a future occasion.[34] But the figures of the table leave no doubt that high social status led to large households in the traditional English social order, along with and because of the presence of large numbers of servants which high social status – and also large scale economic activity – made imperative.

The completeness of the households in question also had a bearing on mean household size, completeness in the sense of being headed by both members of a married couple and of the children born to them still being in the home. But the mere presence of children in most households had no such effect, and where the proportion of children in the population was high households tended to be small, as we have seen, because of the reciprocal relationship of children with servants. The presence, or absence of resident kinsfolk, on the other hand, was of no significance at all in determining mean household size, because their numbers were so low as compared with children and servants, and because they so very seldom went to compose a second conjugal family unit within a household. Even the proscribed inmates, strangers taken in for convenience and against regulation, must have bulked larger in the domestic groups and may have had a trace effect in bringing about variance in mean household size, whereas the kinsfolk had none. But inmates are not included in Table 4.17.

We may return in conclusion to the relative constancy which has been suggested in mean household size between the society so crudely anatomised in this little series of tables on the one hand, and the society which succeeded after 1821 on the other. Though these two societies shared this common characteristic, it does not necessarily follow that mean household size remained fairly stable in both for exactly the same reasons. I believe that a convincing case can be made out in favour of the household as the fundamental unit in pre-industrial European society for social, economic, even educational and political purposes. A reasonably regular distribution of household sizes in each community may well have been a consequence of this architectonic feature of the social structure, and an important means of maintaining this distribution must surely have been the servants. This exchange of persons in considerable numbers between households, it is suggested, is one reason why the traditional social structure of England and Wales, and perhaps of other Western countries, was slow to respond to the effect of demographic change in the period of demographic transition. Servants, in fact, may have dampened the operation of birth rates, marriage rates and death rates on mean household size.

It may be significant that the proportion of servants in the population seems actually to have increased between 1851 and 1871, during an important earlier phase of this transition. This was in spite of what must have been a sharp decrease

---

[34] This will be the second study referred to above on p. 125. The sub-collections for periods and areas to be discussed there do not all show the same correlations between the variables of Table 4.17 and mean household size.

Table 4.18 *England and Wales: proportion of servants in the population, with sex ratios*

One hundred communities, 1574–1821, 13.4%   Sex ratio 107

1831	4.8%	Sex ratio 19	1901	4.1%
1851	5.1%	Sex ratio 16	1911	3.7%
1861	5.5%	Sex ratio 14	1921	3.0%
1871	6.6%	Sex ratio 12	1931	1.8%
1881	4.7%	Sexes no longer given	1951	0.4%

The extraction of figures of servants from the census documents is no easy matter, and these are based on those published by J. W. Nixon (see Nixon (1970), and references) though with some differences. They must be regarded as very approximate indeed.

in the earlier decades of the nineteenth century, about which almost nothing is yet known. Moreover, their numbers fell only reluctantly until after 1911. These are the implications of the very tentative figures of our last table, Table 4.18.

The evident discontinuity between my pre-industrial figures and those of the census makes it likely that many persons, especially males, were counted as servants in the pre-industrial era who were not so regarded in the nineteenth century. This being so, the dampening effect at issue may have been larger than the data imply. There is a wisp or two of evidence to suggest that servants declined in numbers earlier in France than in England: indeed they may never have been as numerous in that country. This might help to explain why MHS fell there so rapidly as fertility declined, and it is worth remarking that when Hayami reports in Chapter 18 the conspicuous fall of MHS which took place in Suwa County along with demographic change, he also reports a virtual disappearance of servants.[35]

It is perhaps important to insist finally on the limitations of our data once again. I have tried to make it clear here and in Chapter 1 how 'household' has been defined for the pre-industrial period, but the definitions of the census-takers of the nineteenth century, in Britain and elsewhere, are bewildering in their variety. It is not always obvious, even in twentieth-century censuses, whether one- and two-member households have been distinguished, and there are often, in fact, inmate groups not counted here as households proper. Since the creation of such households in large numbers was obviously of great importance in the final decline of mean household size, this obscurity is significant. Too much must not be concluded from small differences in means. What is more, as was emphatically stated in Chapter 1, almost nothing emerges from the present discussion about relationships between households as a whole, or between individual members of different households. We simply do not know from data of this kind

[35] An alternative explanation of constancy in MHS between pre-industrial communities and nineteenth-century York is advanced by Armstrong, see below, Chapter 6, pp. 210–211. See also Anderson, Chapter 7, pp. 234–235.

how strong the kinship tie was between two brothers in eighteenth-century England, each cultivating his share of an inherited plot, though heading separate households. We do not know whether the mother-in-law might not in fact have played a commanding role in village society, in spite of the fact that she was so seldom a resident of the family of son or of daughter.

It is easy to be overimpressed with a uniformity never before noticed. But the fact itself remains, and the resolution of the issues raised by the relative constancy of mean household size in England over the years between the early seventeenth and the early twentieth centuries may take a considerable time to solve. There will be years of intricate analysis of scarce and difficult data, wearisome to assemble and exasperating in their irregularity.

5. Mean household size in England from printed sources

Richard Wall

PRELIMINARY

This study is concerned with the household in England from the time that Gregory King provided the first authoritative summary of English census material in 1695/6, until the publication of the first state Census in 1801.[1] Unlike many of the contributions to this volume no attempt has been made to analyse documents in which every individual of a particular settlement is listed according to the household in which he belongs. Instead, the publications and important manuscripts of the leading political arithmeticians (and under this head are comprised all those interested in the state of England's population), together with works by other prominent authors of the seventeenth and eighteenth centuries, have been examined with the object of eliciting the extent of their knowledge of the social structure of which they formed part. Their opinions and, perhaps even more important, their assumptions about household size are valuable in their own right. It is possible, however, to use some of the statistics that they provided not only to confirm their statements but, as in the latter part of this chapter, to account for the fact that the mean household size of one type of settlement differs considerably from that of another. Their evidence is, however, of even greater value, for whatever the views of later writers, it is now clear that eighteenth-century observers did not suppose that multiple family households, or extended family households, were present in any significant numbers. They are certainly impossible to discern in the statistics of household size that they provided.

HOUSEFUL, HOUSEHOLD AND FAMILY: THE PROBLEM OF DEFINITION[2]

Yet there is one great problem. Although we may know today exactly what we mean by the word household, the attempt to trace the history of such an institution in the past is fraught with considerable dangers, not least because of imperceptible changes in terminology which may have occurred over the centuries.

[1] I am grateful to Mr P. Laslett, and Dr R. S. Schofield for their comments on an earlier draft of this chapter and to Mr M. Prentice for statistical advice.
[2] See also above, Laslett, Chapter 1, pp. 23–28, 34–40, Chapter 4, pp. 132–134.

One of the more explicit definitions of what constituted a household occurs in the introduction to the Enumeration Returns of the State Census of 1851.

The first, most intimate, and perhaps most important community, is the family, not considered as the children of one parent, but as persons under one head; who is the occupier of the house, the householder, master, husband, or father; while the other members of the family are, the wife, children, servants, relatives, visitors, and persons constantly or accidentally in the house.[3]

The use of the word 'family' where we would prefer 'household' is important, but otherwise this definition seems straightforward enough. In practice, however, difficulties were encountered particularly when lodgers were present in any numbers. The overseers and schoolmasters who were responsible for carrying out the enumerations of 1801–31 were instructed that 'those who use the same kitchen and board together, are to be deemed members of the same family'.[4] Single persons, inhabiting or lodging, but not boarding in another's house were to be reckoned as a separate household. The note in the Enumeration Abstract for 1801 that the number of families in Middlesex had been exaggerated because some London parishes had returned *each* lodger as a separate family seems to be in line with this.[5] Yet an analysis of fourteen enumeration subdistricts in the 1851 Census showed that rarely had enumerators counted lodgers as separate families.[6] It would be unlikely if inaccuracies in the sixth state Census were to exceed those in the first. In this event, it may well be asked if anything useful can be learnt about household size from the 1801 returns.

One of the most discouraging things about the Census Returns of 1801 is that its very compiler, John Rickman, questioned the reliability of some of its data. The information relating to families he thought to be particularly suspect, not just because in many counties the term 'family' had been variously understood but because in others the question had been completely ignored.[7] In the latter event, the number of families was assumed to equal the number of inhabited houses, although as was recognised at the time, this understated the true number.[8] Rickman's phraseology implies widespread disagreement about the nature of the family but in this respect it may be misleading. For example, his statement might more properly be interpreted as referring only to a minority of places in various counties as opposed to whole counties in which the information about

[3] *Census of Great Britain 1851. Population Tables I* P.P. (1852–3) LXXXV: xxxiv. Compare the definitions of household current on the continent. See below, Blayo, Chapter 9, p. 255, Hélin, Chapter 13, p. 321.

[4] *Census of Great Britain 1831* (1833): ix.

[5] *Census of Great Britain 1801* (1801–2): 216. The italics are my own. Compare the definition of 'family' used in the Rhode Island Census of 1875, see below, Pryor, Chapter 22, pp. 572–573, and earlier American censuses may have conformed, see below, Greven, Chapter 20, p. 545.

[6] Details of this analysis are given in *Census of Great Britain 1851. Population Tables I* (1852–3): xl. Armstrong, see below, Chapter 6, pp. 212–214 discusses it in some detail.

[7] *Census of Great Britain 1801* (1801–2): 496.

[8] *Census of Great Britain 1801* (1801–2): 40.

families was defective. In support of this view it can be pointed out that the one county whose returns were specifically said to be unreliable in this respect was Cheshire, and even here the number of places in which houses and families were equal in number form no more than a quarter of the total. In addition, the possibility that some of these settlements were in fact genuine cases of one family per house cannot be ruled out.[9]

When we turn from the state Censuses to the statistical compilations of earlier writers, we enter realms of even greater uncertainty, because so many of them failed to give an adequate definition of the terms that they employed. Where suitable information is available it appears that populations were usually divided into the primary units of houses, meaning the number of persons residing within a distinct house,[10] or houseful and families, meaning parents plus resident children and other co-residents, or household. The definition of the latter, being more fluid, poses the greater difficulty and the inclusion in the household of non-resident children and the exclusion of servants is not unknown.[11] These cases, however, may safely be considered as exceptional although few enumerators are likely to have succeeded in emulating those responsible for the Nottingham census of 1779.[12] With a thoroughness worthy of a modern census, they included in their respective families persons on a temporary visit to another locality and children who were boarding in City schools and whose parents were resident in Nottingham. Militiamen, soldiers (but not their families), children boarded outside the City, and persons visiting Nottingham were not regarded as part of the resident population. Inmates of hospitals and other institutions were enumerated but the institution was not regarded as constituting a 'family'. This latter is a particularly valid point since institutions are a special sort of household and ought to be excluded from any analysis of household size. It is unfortunately impossible to do this because on many occasions the inmates of workhouses and hospitals were enumerated and the institutions themselves counted as 'families'.[13]

This failure to distinguish between a building such as a workhouse and the domestic group or family is only one aspect of a much more serious problem – the failure on the part of some writers to make the appropriate distinction between the houseful and the household. In a short space it is impossible to examine the views of every writer on this subject, but the attitude of two of the most influential political arithmeticians – Gregory King and Richard Price – cannot be ignored.

---

[9] See below, Table 5.6.   [10] Compare Laslett, above, Chapter 1, pp. 34–39.
[11] Young, *Annals of agriculture* (1784–1815) VI: 32–8; IV, 305–20.
[12] These details are from Lowe, *General view of the agriculture of Nottingham* (1798): 179–83.
[13] This was true occasionally even of the state censuses e.g. *Census of Great Britain 1801* (1801–2): 173. Compare the definition of 'family' used in the Rhode Island census of 1875, see below, Pryor, Chapter 22, pp. 572–573. For a brief discussion of the effect of institutions on MHS during the nineteenth century see, Laslett, *The decline of the size of the domestic group in England* (1970 i).

King's calculation of the population of England in the late seventeenth century is now well known and a high value is deservedly placed on other detailed material which he collected, including enumerations of the inhabitants in accordance with the Marriage Duty Act of 1694, which seems to have formed the basis of much of his work. Its value is lessened, however, by King's silence on the exact relationship between his calculations and the basic data,[14] and this confusion extends to his handling of the Marriage Duty returns, which are presented in the form of houses, population and persons per house.[15] The natural assumption is that the statistics (and hence the associated calculations) deal with inhabited houses rather than households and this was the view taken by Jones and Judges in their work on the City of London.[16] The strongest evidence in favour of this interpretation is that King rejects the return for the parish of St Katherine's Tower on the grounds that 'They [the Assessors] having reckond all the divided houses or those in which there is 2 or 3 families for so many distinct houses, but these divided houses are generally but one or 2 in a family being generally Pensioners.'[17] This certainly seems to suggest that the usual practice was to treat each house as a separate unit, but it is possible that King's real point was that small groups of lodgers should not be treated as separate entities. Although it cannot be claimed that King in any way anticipated the modern distinction between lodgers who do or do not board with the principal household, King's attempt to find a definition for the 'family' which would make sense when applied to the multi-occupied houses of late seventeenth-century London certainly has its parallel in the efforts of the compilers of the early state censuses to agree on an acceptable method of relating lodgers to households.

Although this is King's only reference to the problem, it is possible to use one of the surviving assessments, for example the return for the parish of St Benet Paul's Wharf to discover how the summary total of 'houses' was achieved.[18] The first point that must be made is that King did not attempt to improve on the divisions between the units made by the enumerator. Lodging households were therefore included with all other units in a single entity. Since this is exactly the procedure followed by the Cambridge Group for the History of Population and Social Structure in making certain calculations about household size, it is hardly surprising that recent analyses of household structure yield results almost identical with King's figures based on 'houses' and population.[19] The inclusion of lodgers on a large scale certainly removes one of the main distinctions between 'houseful' and 'household' size and it may go some way towards explaining

[14] Glass, *Gregory King's estimate of the population of England and Wales 1695* (1965 ii): 198–9.
[15] E.g. King, Burns Journal (Manuscript i): 90.
[16] See Glass, *London inhabitants within the walls* (1966): xxviii.
[17] Quoted in Glass, *Gregory King and the population of England and Wales at the end of the 17th century* (1965 i): 178.
[18] The returns are in the possession of the Corporation of London Record Office. Summary figures are in King (Manuscript i): 124–7.
[19] Cf. Glass (1965 i): 175, and Laslett, above Chapter 4, p. 130.

why so many writers of the seventeenth and eighteenth century found nothing exceptional in dividing populations into units described ambiguously as 'houses or families'. This expression also occurs in the work of Gregory King although the figures are exactly the same as those which are later said to relate to houses.[20] Yet the fact that elsewhere King attempted separate estimates of the average number of persons per house and per family[21] must mean that he knew that there was a distinction which could and ought to be made between the two. It is difficult to reconcile this statement with King's ambiguous terminology but if we re-examine the assessment for St Benet Paul's Wharf, it will be seen that the enumerator has distinguished each household within the Herald's Office, rather than grouping all the inhabitants together into one large unit. This suggests the possibility – and it must be stressed that at present it is only a possibility – that households were separately enumerated only when they were of equal status, that is when each unit either owned or rented from a non-resident landlord its section of the house. If, on the other hand, one household was superior to another in the sense that the latter was present only because some rooms had been let or sub-let by the former, then it would constitute a lodging household and be included as part of the main unit.

This hypothesis, if substantiated, clearly carries important implications for the comparative history of the household. In the first place, a comparison with nineteenth-century data is made extremely difficult since in the statistical sense there is no seventeenth-century equivalent of the people who lodged but did not board with other households. Far more important than this is the implication that there had been a decisive shift away from the notion of the household as an all embracing unit and towards an emphasis on the separateness of its constituent parts.[22] However, one important qualification has to be made. This is that some of the figures for 'household size' given by King are so small that it seems inconceivable that lodging households can have been included within the principal households. To some extent this is not unexpected, since it is thought that in country districts lodgers were rare. In Sevenoaks, for example, a listing definitely known to have been consulted by King, there are no examples of units containing more than one married couple.[23] On the other hand, it is most unlikely that lodgers were absent from such populous Middlesex settlements as Ratcliff and St George in-the-East, yet this is what the low figures for mean household size would suggest. Lodgers may simply have been omitted rather than counted as separate units and, unless the original assessment can be traced and

[20] Cf. references to the Essex hamlet of Brook St in King (Manuscript i): 92 and King, *Exercises in political arithmetic and various miscellaneous papers* (Manuscript ii).

[21] King (Manuscript i): 225.

[22] In this connection it is interesting that Blayo associates a tendency for households in nineteenth-century France to correspond with the conjugal family model with the growth of greater independence in each familial nucleus. See below, Blayo, Chapter 9, p. 264.

[23] King, *Computation of the numbers of people in England 1695* (Manuscript iii): 15–17.

examined, it is impossible to be sure one way or the other. It is equally difficult to establish with any degree of certainty the reason why the group of Devon parishes, of which Colyton was one, had a noticeably higher mean 'household' size than that of any other rural areas listed by King.[24] One possibility is that Devon was one of the few areas outside London where lodgers were present in considerable numbers. This seems less likely, however, than an alternative hypothesis that 'household' size appeared large because the enumerator had included in one unit all persons sharing a common roof, whereas elsewhere, as in later centuries, households even when they occupied only part of a house, were regarded as independent.

In the present state of our knowledge, further speculation would be pointless and since some of Gregory King's data do undoubtedly relate to household size, his figures have accordingly been included in some of the tabulations.[25] It has to be admitted that not all of his material is equally reliable in this respect but in exactly what ways and to what extent it is defective may never be known. A thorough examination of enumeration procedures in the seventeenth century certainly deserves the highest priority.

Richard Price, writing three-quarters of a century after King, is a less dominant figure not only because of the increase in the number of people interested in all questions relating to the state of England's population, but because his calculations were on a much more modest scale. Nevertheless Price's work on population, first published in 1779, with a sixth edition appearing in 1803, provides by far the most comprehensive contemporary survey of population trends in England in the latter part of the eighteenth century. It is therefore particularly important that his approach to the problem of household and houseful size should be understood. At first glance everything appears straightforward enough. Price was certainly aware of what earlier writers such as Davenant had said on the subject[26] and when he compiled his own tables he made provision for data relating to both persons per house and persons per family, concluding that there was no significant difference between the two.[27] Finally when William Morgan reissued Price's works in the early years of the nineteenth century he was able to declare that although the recently published state Census proved that there had been a considerable increase in the average number of persons per house in the previous thirty years, there had been little change in the mean size of the household.[28] These are two very important pronouncements and fortunately they can be confirmed by evidence on household and houseful size drawn from a wide

---

[24] King, (Manuscript i): 92,100. Cf. Hollingsworth, *Historical Demography* (1969): 191. Hollingsworth's argument appears to be that Colyton contained either many lodgers or, if under-registration of baptisms was prevalent, many children.

[25] See below, Tables 5.1–5.3.

[26] Price, *An essay on the population of England from the Revolution to the present time* (1780): 43–4.

[27] Price, *An account of progress from the Revolution and the present state of population* (1779): 294.

[28] Price, *Collected edition* (1803) II: 70–2.

variety of independent sources.[29] Nevertheless, Morgan's editorial note cannot be accepted as reliable evidence, for the simple reason that at the same time some of the information in the tables which had previously consisted of *houseful* sizes was now said by Morgan to relate to *household* sizes. The obvious assumption is that faced with the evidence of the 1801 Census, Morgan hurriedly corrected all the figures which appeared inconsistent with its findings. Indeed, John Howlett, one of the chief critics of Price's belief in England's declining population, had suggested twenty years earlier that the lower values in his opponent's tables related to persons per household rather than persons per house.[30] In Morgan's defence it should be said that the earlier editions of Price's works were not always clear on this point. In the first separate edition of 1780, the word 'houses' which had appeared as one of the column headings in the first edition was omitted and, for the fifth edition of 1792, replaced by the word 'families'.[31] However, the heading of a parallel column 'persons per house' was retained, suggesting some hesitancy if not confusion about the nature of the information contained in the tables, and in this case Morgan might have been attempting clarification rather than correction. The fact remains that the alteration undertaken so long after the date of first publication and apparently without reference to the original listings, was almost certainly mistaken. Some of the figures turn up in the works of other writers under the heading 'houses',[32] and even on one occasion under 'families',[33] but for others Price appears as the only source. The material is clearly suspect and the only course is to exclude it from all the tabulations relating to household and houseful size.

The difficulties experienced by Price and King with regard to the basic differences between 'house' and 'family' lead one to question the ability of people less skilled and less interested in the subject to distinguish between the two. Such people, ranging from gentlemen and clergy to the lowly parish constable, are important because however industrious the political arithmeticians were, they could supervise personally the collection of only a fraction of the data that they utilised in their tables.[34] Unfortunately, few left any record of the decisions they must have taken before they could separate one household from another. One notable exception is provided by the antiquarian Edward Rowe-Mores. In 1757 Mores drew up a list of the inhabitants of the small Kentish parish of Tunstall.[35] The list was arranged in the form of one houseful to a line but from an earlier summary[36] it is clear that he was able to identify sub-units

[29] See below, Table 5.8. For a full list of works consulted see below, Table 5.1, pp. 174–190 and bibliography, pp. 590–609.

[30] Howlett, *An examination of Dr Price's essay on the Population of England and Wales* (1781): 44, 48.

[31] Price (1780): 6–8 and *Collected edition* (1792), 298–301.

[32] Enfield, *Essay towards the history of Liverpool* (1774): 24

[33] Short, *Comparative history of the increase and decrease of mankind* (1767): 38.

[34] King (Manuscript i): 100 and Price, *Collected edition* (1816) VI: 43 fn.

[35] Mores' manuscript was printed by J. Nichols in 1780: see his *Bibliotheca Topographica Britannica* (1780–1800) I: 105.   [36] Nichols (1780–1800) I: 2.

within the houses, giving them the name 'family' even when they consisted of only one or two persons. The same procedure is found in Sinclair's *Statistical Account of Scotland* published towards the end of the eighteenth century.[37] This exactitude in matters of terminology is very unlike that of Gregory King and some suggestion that it was not an isolated phenomenon comes from a statement by the influential writer George Chalmers that 'house' and 'household', altho..gh synonymous terms in the time of Davenant, had since acquired distinct meanings.[38] Chalmers was of course referring to hearth tax returns rather than assessments under the 1694 Marriage Act, but despite this the point remains valid. There is ample evidence, however, to suggest that confusion between 'houses' and 'families' persisted into the eighteenth century.[39] The word 'tenement' indicating separate living accommodation within the house, which gradually became more popular, did not always help to ease the confusion because tenements were themselves sometimes equated with families and sometimes with houses.[40] As in the seventeenth century difficulty arose whenever more than one household shared the same house. For example, in an analysis of the parish of Harleston and Retenhall in 1789 the total number of families was found to be 240 but the 'true' number was held to be somewhat less because nine families were living in separate apartments in the same house.[41] All persons resident in a particular house could be regarded as holding some place, however insignificant, in one large household. In a listing of inhabitants of the parish of Corfe Castle drawn up in 1790, the population is divided, possibly in order of precedence, into four groups: housekeepers, children and grandchildren resident with their parents, lodgers and inmates, and servants and apprentices.[42] It is particularly interesting that married children with their families were included under the heading lodgers together with persons not related to the head of the household. Some suggestion that this was not exceptional comes from William Boys, writing in 1792. Referring to an enumeration of Sandwich in 1776, he classed as lodgers unmarried children resident in the parental home and above the age of thirty.[43] Therefore, in pre-Census times a somewhat broader definition of what constituted a household was current than was later adopted by the compilers of the state Censuses. The older notions of family, household and house persisted, however, into the nineteenth century, as the inconsistencies in some of the early volumes show.

[37] Sinclair, *Statistical account of Scotland* (1791–1799) v: 400.
[38] Chalmers, *An estimate of the Comparative Strength of Great Britain* (1782): 115.
[39] E.g. Rudder *A New History of Gloucestershire* (1779): 484; T. Brown, *General View of the Agriculture of Derby* (1794): 36.
[40] See Sir John Cullam's analysis of Hawstead, in Young (1784–1815) II: 332–8.
[41] Young, *General view of the agriculture of Norfolk* (1804): 111.
[42] Hutchins, *History and antiquities of the county of Dorset* (1796–1815) I: 290.
[43] Boys, *History of Sandwich* (1792): 393.

INFORMED ESTIMATES

These differences of opinion have to be taken into account when the various estimates of mean household size are examined. But in addition it is clear that the estimates also varied according to the context in which they were made. For example, they were high when writers were examining the causes of poverty amongst labourers, and reasonably accurate when the aim was to calculate the total population of the country. Obviously not all the estimates can be grouped so conveniently and the object of the enquiry always has to be borne in mind if the significance of the final figure is to be appreciated. Probably the best example is provided by Arthur Young's enquiry into the average amount of meat consumed by the correspondents of his periodical publication, *The Annals of Agriculture*.[44] These correspondents were gentlemen interested in farming matters rather than persons who actually tilled the soil and this is reflected in the replies received by Young, two of the correspondents asserting that the membership of their families consisted of fourteen and sixteen persons respectively.[45] What appears to be the most illuminating point is that passing tradesmen, labourers employed on a seasonal basis and harvesters, were for the duration of their stay counted as part of the 'family'. Young's question, however, was specifically directed to the question of board, and the 'family' was consequently defined with this in mind, so that it does not *necessarily* follow that this was a universal criterion by which the 'family' was delineated.

It is therefore to be expected that the most accurate data will be found in works dealing solely with the question of household size. Unfortunately this was a subject which in its own right aroused little interest in either the seventeenth or eighteenth centuries. This may appear as something of a paradox in view of the amount of information about household size, either actual or estimated,[46] which found itself in print before the close of the eighteenth century. A careful scrutiny of this material reveals, however, that it was always collected with some other object in view, a common motive being a desire to use mean household size as a multiplier for calculating the total population of the kingdom. The fact that even a small margin of error in the multiplier will effect a considerable alteration in the final figure means that accuracy was as important as if the household itself was being examined. Here, if anywhere, we may expect to learn what informed opinion thought about mean household size.

Significantly, most of the writers insisted upon a mean of four or five persons per household.[47] There are of course certain exceptions, of which the first calculation of this sort known to have appeared in print is one. John Graunt's estimate

---

[44] Details in Young (1784–1815) xxxii: 279–622.
[45] Young (1784–1815) xxxii: 517, 525.
[46] See below, Table 5.1, pp. 174–190 and bibliography, pp. 590–609.
[47] Not all sections of the community were expected to conform to this mean. See, for example, Gregory King's data on cottagers and paupers in Chalmers, *Estimate of the Comparative Strength of Great Britain* (1802): 414.

of an average of eight persons per family for London allowed for three servants
or lodgers as well as a man, wife and three children[48] although, as the assessments under the Marriage Act of 1694 were to show, only rarely did families
contain anything like these numbers of children, servants or lodgers. The estimates of Sir William Petty made a little later on in the century are also somewhat on the high side.[49] King's calculation of an average of between four and
five persons per 'house', depending on the size of the settlement, therefore provided a useful downward correction.[50] Later writers even when they made no direct
use of King's work, gave figures which tended to support his conclusion. For
instance, E. Hatton, writing in 1708, summarised the thoughts of both Graunt
and Petty and added his own estimate of 'five in a family including double
families (by which he meant houses occupied by two or more families) for I find
by observation that those who have reckoned more have put too many'.[51]

Of all the political arithmeticians of the seventeenth century only King was
definitely known to have based his estimates on a large number of actual enumerations[52] and in this respect the majority of later writers differ sharply from
their predecessors. There was still room for a difference of opinion, however, as
is shown by the respective conclusions of those two great opponents in the
eighteenth century population controversy, Richard Price and John Howlett,
the former favouring an average of 4.5 and the latter 5.4 persons per house.[53] The
difference seems too great to have arisen by chance but it must be remembered
that Howlett and Price were not in a position to select enumerations which would
lend support to their respective arguments since information about household
size was available for, comparatively speaking, only a minute proportion of
the country's parishes. If later political arithmeticians tended to support Howlett's view of a general increase in England's population since the time of the
Revolution of 1688, it was Price's figure of 4.5, applied sometimes to the household rather than the 'house', which seems to have been more widely used.[54] At
the same time there was a definite trend in favour of a more sophisticated use
of the 'multiplier'. A case in point is the survey of Sheffield and the surrounding
area which was based on the ratio of 4.25 for Sheffield itself and 4.5 persons per
house for the suburbs.[55]

[48] Graunt, *Natural and political observations upon the Bills of Mortality* (1662): 56.
[49] Petty, *Economic writings* (1899) II: 627–34.
[50] King (Manuscript i): 276–7.
[51] Hatton, *A new view of London* (1708): iii–v. But not all writers thought households were so
small. See for instance the introduction to Templeman's *A new survey of the Globe* (1729).
[52] Some of Petty's work on Ireland may have been based on the Poll Tax returns, see Petty
(1899): 141–2.
[53] Howlett (1781): 44, 146.
[54] Cf. Eden, *An estimate of the number of inhabitants in Great Britain and Ireland* (1800): 82;
and *The state of the poor* (1797) III: 847. For the application of a mean of 4.5 to the houseful
see Young (1784–1815) XXXI: 161–2.
[55] R. Brown and G. Rennie, *General view of the agriculture of the West Riding of Yorkshire*
(1799) Appendix: 718–19. A ratio of 5.0 persons per house was used when no allowance had
to be made for empty houses.

By the last two decades of the eighteenth century so much information about household size had become available that some writers even felt obliged to explain why certain enumerations revealed a higher than average mean household size.[56] In 1782, for instance, Thomas Nash pointed out that the town of Kidderminster had an average of five persons per house because of the number of apprentices in the employ of journeymen weavers.[57] A few years later John Aikin went even further by declaring that some mistake must have been made in the enumeration of the settlement of Saddleworth because the mean household size (5.74) was much larger than that found elsewhere in the industrial areas of Lancashire and Yorkshire.[58] For a more cautious viewpoint it is necessary to turn to the 1770s and a prominent Liverpool historian, W. Enfield. Since his statement about houseful and household size is probably the most lucid made by an English writer prior to 1801, it is worth quoting in full.[59]

Calculations formed on the number of houses or the proportion of inhabitants which die annually, are by no means absolutely to be depended upon. The number of houses in a town though exactly taken, which is not so easily done as might at first view be imagined, is no sufficient ground of computation, because towns which are nearly the same size, differ exceedingly in the averaged number of people in each house. In villages and small towns the number is from 4 to $4\frac{3}{4}$, and sometimes 5; in large towns and cities from $4\frac{1}{4}$ to 6; and if we take in Edinburgh, and other cities inhabited in the same manner, the difference will be much greater. The number of families is a more certain ground from which to infer the number of persons, as the average number in each family is generally between 4 and $4\frac{3}{4}$;[60] But this is not known without nearly the same trouble as a personal enumeration, and after all is attended with considerable uncertainty.

Three decades were to elapse before a state census was able to confirm the majority of these pronouncements.

As well as making available a vast amount of English demographic material, political arithmeticians became increasingly eager to bring to the attention of an English audience the researches of famous continental scholars. In this way the work of Moheau, Lazowski and Mirabeau all found its way into such a publication as Arthur Young's *Annals of Agriculture*.[61] Not that there was anything particularly new about this search for comparative material because Sir William Petty had compared his findings for London with those of Auzout for Paris many years before.[62] What was significant, however, was that the evidence, fragmentary as it was, appeared to provide further confirmation of a mean of between four

---

[56] For surprise at a particularly low MHS see Hutchinson, *A history of the county of Cumberland* (1794) II: 117.

[57] Nash, *Collections for the history of Worcestershire* (1781–1799) II, 39–41. No reason is advanced for journeymen rather than fully qualified master weavers employing large numbers of apprentices.

[58] Aikin, *A description of the country round Manchester* (1795): 557.

[59] Enfield (1774): 22–3.

[60] These figures may represent the family exclusive of lodgers, see Table 5.1 below.

[61] Young (1784–1815) XV: 537–47; XII: 74, 121–2.

[62] Petty (1899) II: 528.

and five persons per household. However, apart from one reference by Short to an enumeration of Tunis,[63] this information was drawn entirely from West European sources and Arthur Young was proceeding on a somewhat shaky ground when he attempted some calculations for Bengal on the basis of five persons per household.[64]

CHANGES OVER TIME

Young's important assumption was that mean household size would be the same regardless of creed or race. It is impossible to check whether this was a common belief in eighteenth century England since Young's is the only calculation of its kind so far discovered. On the other hand, a very popular notion was that household size remained constant over time. If there were fewer houses in a parish than in former times, then it was assumed that the population had decreased in proportion.[65] Another sign of this was that Gregory King's figures for household size were considered applicable to the late eighteenth century. At the same time certain qualifications have to be made. Arthur Young, for instance, stated that there had been a change – indeed an increase – in houseful size during the period 1690–1770.[66] However, he provided no hard evidence in support of his assertion. Secondly, several writers commented on a change in social relations which, if true, must have had a very important effect on the size of the household.[67] For example, the decline in the practice of keeping unmarried servants under the farmer's roof would considerably alter the distribution of persons between households, although if this resulted in people marrying earlier and having more children, the reduction in mean household size would be small. Only rarely, however, did political arithmeticians seek to trace the effect of such changes on the mean size of the household. Joseph Plymley, Archdeacon of Shropshire, and author of the *General view of the Agriculture of Shropshire* was exceptional when he suggested that the increase in houses, proportionately greater than the increase in either families or population, in the parish of Madeley between 1782 and 1793, was the result of the Lord of the Manor's policies of building houses for the old and the distressed and of granting 99-year building leases.[68] Of more general interest is Plymley's view that in rural areas houseful size varied with the paucity or plenty of cottages in proportion to farms. The argument is rather complicated but in essence Plymley appears to have distinguished between two types of village, in the first of which mean houseful size was generally high, in

[63] Short (1767): 61 quoting from *The modern universal history*. The MHS was 6.25.
[64] Young (1784–1815) XLV: 242–3, although it should be noted that in Japan the Tokugawa government chose five persons per household as a model for revenue collecting purposes in 1734, see below, Nakane, Chapter 19, p. 523.
[65] E.g. Rudder (1779): 785.
[66] Young, *Political Arithmetic* (1774): 90.
[67] By G. Robinson, in Young (1784–1815) XXI: 105–7. See also Call, *An abstract of baptisms and burials* (1800): 482.
[68] Plymley, *General view of the Agriculture of Shropshire* (1803): 343.

the second generally low. For instance, the villages in which mean houseful size was high were characterised by improved cultivation, the destruction of some houses, the merging of small farms in large and, since the latter were usually worked by *unmarried* servants, little or no increase in total population. Conversely, when mean houseful size was low the land was unimproved and the settlements thickly populated, as indicated by a low average rent per person. It is difficult to test either of these statements but there is some evidence that settlements with high mean household sizes lost population during the late eighteenth century (see below, pp. 200–201).

MISLEADING ESTIMATES

In order to substantiate these points a comprehensive review of all the available evidence is required. This cannot be attempted here, but a preliminary examination of the census material left by Plymley and his contemporaries shows that there is a definite relationship between changes in houseful size and household size, and between household size and population increase.[69] However, before proceeding with an analysis of this evidence it is apposite that some consideration be given to those people who through inexperience or misjudgement made estimates of mean household size which other evidence indicates as having been far in excess of the truth. Here, interest is focused less on the actual figure given for mean household size than on the reasons why such a high value was given. The most simple case arises from a desire to exaggerate the total population whether the area concerned is a single settlement or the whole country. Fortunately, this seldom seems to have occurred, but one example is to be found in the computation of between six and ten persons per family for those metropolitan parishes which in the reign of Queen Anne were thought to be in need of additional churches.[70]

A far more common fault was to distort the size of one of the constituent parts of the household. The difficulties which were likely to arise in the enumeration of lodging households have already been referred to and are an obvious source of error. Arthur Young, for example, suggested a national average of 9 families to 6 houses or 8 families to 5 houses, both estimates being far in excess of the truth.[71] Another of Young's mistakes was to exaggerate the average number of children, particularly in labourers' families, which he believed to be larger in this respect than those of the farmers.[72] This was a widely held view in the eighteenth century and it is not difficult to account for its popularity. In the first

---

[69] See below, Tables 5.8 and 5.11.
[70] House of Commons Journals XVI: 542, quoted by Middleton, *General View of the Agriculture of Middlesex* (1807): 588–9.
[71] Young, *A Six Months Tour through the North of England* (1770) IV: 565–7. See also Table 5.7, below.
[72] Young (1770): 396–8. For the mean size of groups of children in the families of labourers, husbandmen and yeomen, see above, Laslett, Chapter 4, pp. 153–155.

place large families are more noticeable than families with few children. To take one example, George Lipscomb, describing a journey into Cornwall in the late 1790s, noted in the 'miserable little village' of South Zeal, 'one woman standing at her door with eleven little ones ranged by her side, all without shoes and stockings, and exhibiting the plainest indications of extreme poverty'.[73] Lipscomb was only one of many writers to see an association between poverty and a family of young children. This can also be inferred from the fact that the agricultural societies, eager to award premiums to those labourers who had brought the greatest number of children up to the age of six years with least call on the parish, found very few who had never been in receipt of relief. [74]

It is easy to assume from all this that every labourer's family was as large and as burdened with children as the ones that so often arrested the attention and exercised the concern of eighteenth-century society. For example, studies of the amount of grain likely to be consumed by a labourer and his family were usually based on the assumption that the 'average' labouring family consisted of not less than five persons (that is a man, his wife and three children) and not more than eight.[75] The vast majority of families were in fact far smaller than this because of a number of factors, ranging from the custom of placing children in service to a heavy mortality, particularly among infants, which the people making these estimates completely overlooked. The statement of Adam Smith that in the Highlands of Scotland it was not uncommon for a mother who has borne twenty children to have only two alive,[76] stands almost alone in writings of the eighteenth century.

When we turn from these works, serious in tone and intent, to the books, essays and criticism which pass for the literature of the age, difficulties immediately arise. Wit and irony require so much writing for effect that it is difficult to be certain for example, whether Charles Lamb genuinely believed that families generally comprised so many as the eight or ten persons (exclusive of servants) that he found so unbearable.[77] Similarly, George Cruikshank's creation of the Victorian household of 47 persons – 25 children, parents, grandparents, 2 great-grandmothers, 3 aunts, 1 uncle, 3 cousins and 7 servants[78] – can rarely have

[73] Lipscomb, *A journey into Cornwall* (1799): 166.
[74] E.g. Young (1784–1815) xxi: 401. Van der Woude, see below, Chapter 12, p. 316, notes that families with large numbers of children stood the greatest chance of receiving relief, especially when the household head was a widow.
[75] Young (1784–1815) xxiii: 650; xxv: 487; xxix: 468, and in particular Davies, *The case of labourers in husbandry* (1795): 136–87.
[76] Smith, *Wealth of Nations* Book I P.C. viii, quoted in Jones, *Some population problems relating to Cumberland and Westmorland in the 18th century* (1959): 133. Smith implies that only two out of twenty children born would survive to adulthood and thus exaggerates what many of his contemporaries overlooked altogether. For a recent assessment of the level of mortality in pre-industrial populations see Wrigley, *Mortality in pre-industrial England* (1968).
[77] Peacock, *Selected English Essays* (1922): 203.
[78] Cruikshank, *Comic Almanack and Diary* (1851).

troubled the Census takers of 1851, and it seems inconceivable that Cruikshank can have regarded this household as anything but a figment of his imagination.

Whatever their real intentions were, however, both Lamb and Cruikshank gave the impression that families were large, containing many children and, in the case of the latter, many resident kin. Certain antiquarians also succeeded in giving this impression, as they travelled about the country making notes of whatever was exceptional, passing over all that they thought commonplace. T. D. Fosbroke, for example, accepted without comment the story (these tales were rarely available at first hand) of a Mrs Church who had died aged 100 in February 1797 at the Gloucestershire village of Staunton.[79] In Fosbroke's own words, 'She remembered the rejoicing at Queen Anne's succession, in 1702, and under the same roof lived the old lady, her daughter, and her granddaughter, and granddaughter's children – 4 generations in one house.'

MEAN HOUSEHOLD SIZE IN PRINTED SOURCES:
A STATISTICAL APPROACH

Only a little imagination is required to make the above account typical of what life was like in the small, closely knit villages of pre-industrial England. It is therefore particularly fortunate that it is possible to make use of the data provided by other eighteenth-century writers to counteract this impression. All the evidence that has so far come to light has been reproduced in Table 5.1.[80]

Since this information has been drawn from a wide variety of sources, it follows that any analysis of it is likely to proceed on different lines from that adopted by earlier writers who, even if they had envisaged such procedures, would have lacked sufficient data to carry them to fruition. In other words, it is possible not only to review pronouncements on the question of household size made during the course of the eighteenth century but also to attempt an entirely new type of analysis. At the same time it must always be borne in mind that its reliability depends on the care with which the various places were enumerated[81] and in particular on the extent to which the enumerator was able to make the appropriate distinction between houseful and household.[82]

[79] Details in Fosbroke, *Abstracts of records respecting the county of Gloucester* (1807) II: 182.
[80] A few listings of inhabitants first published or summarised later than 1800 have also been included, see below. Some of the sources are noticed in Law, *Local censuses in the 18th century* (1969): 87–100.
[81] Certain villages were so small that a house-to-house survey was probably unnecessary. Gross approximations, e.g. the population total rounded to the nearest ten and all instances of the use of household size as a multiplier have not been included.
[82] See above. 'Family' and 'tenement' (when it clearly implied a subdivision of a house) have been, assumed to be synonymous with the household. All other terminology has been rejected, for example, 'houses and families' (except in the case of Gregory King) and 'householders' (as wives of household heads were sometimes included).

Table 5.1 *Mean household size of 409 English settlements abstracted from printed sources and from the Census of Great Britain, 1801*

| County | Place[c] | Date[a] | Population | Households | MHS | Census of Great Britain 1801[e] | | | Source |
						Population	Households	MHS	
Beds.	Pertenhall	1799	167	44	3.79	190	44	4.31	Young, *Annals of Agriculture* (1784–1815) XXXIII: 126–8
Bucks.	Edgcott	1712	80	20	4.00	122	30	4.06	Willis, *History of Buckingham* (1755): 183
Bucks.	Hillesden	1712	200	38	5.26	183	34	5.38	Willis (1755): 196
Bucks.	Lillingstone Dayrell	1712	105	20	5.25	111	22	5.04[a]	Willis (1755): 217
Bucks.	Maids Moreton	1712	126	41	3.07	239	73	3.27	Willis (1755): 230
Bucks.	Radclive with Chackmore	1712	120	29	4.13	252	47	5.36[a]	Willis (1755): 256
Bucks.	Shalstone	1712	118	22	5.36	158	35	4.51	Willis (1755): 264
Bucks.	Thornborough	1712	369	82	4.50	458	115	3.98	Willis (1755): 291
Bucks.	Thornton	1712	50	12	4.16	85	14	6.07[a]	Willis (1755): 299
Bucks.	Tingewick	1712	430	107	4.01	642	139	4.61	Willis (1755): 315
Bucks.	Water Stratford	1712	105	24	4.37	143	23	6.21[a]	Willis (1755): 343
Bucks.	Wycombe	1774	2,461	500	4.92	4,248	962	4.41	Price, *Collected edition* (1803) II: 70–2
Cambs.	Little Wilbraham	1798	167	38	4.39	183	41	4.46	Young (1784–1815) XLIII: 54–9
Cheshire	Bramhall	1754	534	113	4.72	1,033	190	5.43	Watson, Collections for Cheshire (Manuscript): 129
Cheshire	Bredbury	1754	597	128	4.66	1,358	264	5.14	Watson (Manuscript): 129
Cheshire	Brinnington	1754	104	15	6.93	890	164	5.42	Watson (Manuscript): 129
Cheshire	Chester	1774	14,713	3,428	4.29	15,052	3,427	4.39	Price, *Collected edition* (1816) VI: 247
Cheshire	Chester St Michael	1772	618	151	4.09	725	152	4.76	Price (1803) II: 70–2
Cheshire	Disley	1754	576	135	4.26	995	198	5.02	Watson (Manuscript): 129
Cheshire	Dukinfield	1754	678	151	4.49	1,737	308	5.63[a]	Watson (Manuscript): 129
Cheshire	Etchells	1754	380	86	4.41	—			Watson (Manuscript): 129

County	Place	Year							Source
Cheshire	Hyde	1754	467	93	5.02	1,063	187	5.68[a]	Watson (Manuscript): 129
Cheshire	Marple	1754	548	129	4.24	2,031	347	5.85	Watson (Manuscript): 129
Cheshire	Norbury	1754	313	73	4.28	592	107	5.53	Watson (Manuscript): 129
Cheshire	Offerton	1754	169	39	4.33	351	61	5.75	Watson (Manuscript): 129
Cheshire	Romiley	1754	376	74	5.08	825	160	5.15	Watson (Manuscript): 129
Cheshire	Stockport (township)	1754	3,144	741	4.24	14,830	2,965	5.00	Watson (Manuscript): 129
Cheshire	Stockport (township)	1765	3,713	837	4.43	14,830	2,965	5.00	Watson (Manuscript): 164
Cheshire	Tattenhall	1774	781	176	4.43	746	162	4.60[a]	Percival, *Collected edition* (1807) IV: 58
Cheshire	Torkington	1754	161	31	5.19	218	35	6.22	Watson (Manuscript): 129
Cheshire	Waverton	1774	642	116	5.53	594	111	5.35[a]	Percival (1807) IV: 59
Cheshire	Werneth	1754	358	69	5.18	1,152	211	5.45	Watson (Manuscript): 129
Cumberland	Ainstable	1794	434	98	4.42	444	90	4.93	Eden, *The state of the poor* (1797) II: 46
Cumberland	Bewcastle	1790/4	1,029	234	4.39	917	186	4.93[a]	Hutchinson (1794) I: 77
Cumberland	Blackwell	1780	354	64	5.53	370	72	5.13[b]	Lonsdale, *Life of J. Heysham* (1870): 34
Cumberland	Blackwell	1796	378	73	5.17	370	72	5.13[b]	Hutchinson (1794) II: 675
Cumberland	Botcherby	1780	98	22	4.45	94	19	4.94[b]	Lonsdale (1870): 34
Cumberland	Botcherby	1796	78	19	4.10	94	19	4.94[b]	Hutchinson (1794): II: 675
Cumberland	Brampton	1790/4	1,951	458	4.25	2,125	480	4.42[a]	Hutchinson (1794) I: 130
Cumberland	Brisco	1780	192	34	5.64	224	44	5.09[a]	Lonsdale (1870): 34
Cumberland	Brisco	1796	191	35	5.45	224	44	5.09[a]	Hutchinson (1794) II: 675
Cumberland	Carleton	1780	133	30	4.43	185	36	5.13	Lonsdale (1870): 34
Cumberland	Carleton	1796	187	34	5.50	185	36	5.13	Hutchinson (1794) II: 675
Cumberland	Carlisle	1763	4,158	1,059	3.92	9,521	2,172	4.38	Hutchinson (1794) I: 667
Cumberland	Carlisle'	1780	6,299	1,605	3.92	9,521	2,172	4.38	Hutchinson (1794) II: 667
Cumberland	Carlisle'	1796	8,716	2,314	3.76	9,521	2,172	4.38	Hutchinson (1794) II: 675
Cumberland	Castle Carrock	1790/4	232	42	5.52	252	54	4.66	Hutchinson (1794) I: 179
Cumberland	Cockermouth	1784	2,652	663	4.00	2,865	690	4.15	Hutchinson (1794) I: 117
Cumberland	Cummersdale	1780	110	22	5.00	382	68	5.61	Lonsdale (1870): 34
Cumberland	Cummersdale	1796	222	36	6.16	382	68	5.61	Hutchinson (1794) II: 675
Cumberland	Cumrew	1790/4	146	34	4.29	181	36	5.02[a]	Hutchinson (1794) I: 181
Cumberland	Dalston	1790/4	1,900	377	5.03	2,120	432	4.90	Hutchinson (1794) II: 452
Cumberland	Harraby	1780	72	10	7.20	47	8	5.87[a]	Lonsdale (1870): 34
Cumberland	Harraby	1796	51	8	6.37	47	8	5.87[a]	Hutchinson (1794) II: 675

Table 5.1 *continued*

County	Place	Date	Population	Households	MHS	Census of Great Britain 1801			
						Population	Households	MHS	Source
Cumberland	Harrington	1795	1,412	307	4.59	1,357	438	3.09	Eden (1797) II: 78
Cumberland	Hesket	1795	1,150	330	3.48	1,285	238	5.39[a]	Eden (1797) II: 80
Cumberland	Kirkbride	1790/4	227	55	4.12	249	56	4.44	Hutchinson (1794) II: 483
Cumberland	Longtown	1749	1,541	309	4.98	1,335	300	4.45	*Census of Great Britain 1801* (1801–2): 56
Cumberland	Middle	1790/4	707	141	5.01	573	124	4.62[a]	Hutchinson (1794) II: 554
Cumberland	Morton Head & Newby	1780	124	27	4.59	—	—	—	Lonsdale (1870): 34
Cumberland	Morton Head & Newby	1796	145	31	4.67	—	—	—	Hutchinson (1794) II: 675
Cumberland	Moat	1790/4	309	53	5.83	291	48	6.06[a]	Hutchinson (1794) II: 554
Cumberland	Nether	1790/4	590	107	5.51	245	77	3.18	Hutchinson (1794) II: 554
Cumberland	Newtown	1780	92	19	4.84	—	—	—	Lonsdale (1870): 34
Cumberland	Newtown	1796	114	23	4.95	—	—	—	Hutchinson (1794) II: 675
Cumberland	Nichol Forest	1790/4	600	103	5.82	668	149	4.48	Hutchinson (1794) II: 554
Cumberland	Ponsonby	1792	154	23	6.69	78	13	6.00[a]	Hutchinson (1794) I: 593
Cumberland	Renwick	1790/4	188	44	4.27	201	38	5.28[a]	Hutchinson (1794) I: 212
Cumberland	Rockcliffe	1790/4	544	128	4.25	518	110	4.70[a]	Hutchinson (1794) II: 526
Cumberland	Skelton	1786	678	135	5.02	729	141	5.17[a]	Hutchinson (1794) I: 514
Cumberland	Skelton	1792	631	126	5.00	729	141	5.17[a]	Hutchinson (1794) I: 514
Cumberland	Upperby	1780	89	21	4.23	119	31	3.83	Lonsdale (1870): 34
Cumberland	Upperby	1796	93	22	4.22	119	31	3.83	Hutchinson (1794) II: 675
Cumberland	Warwick	1795	347	63	5.50	333	65	5.12[a]	Eden (1797) II: 92
Cumberland	Wasdale Head	1790/4	47	8	5.87	31	7	4.42[a]	Hutchinson (1794) I: 583
Cumberland	Whitehaven	1693	2,272	450	5.04	8,742	2,403	3.59	Hutchinson (1794) II: 49
Cumberland	Wreay	1780	114	18	6.33	118	23	5.13	Lonsdale (1870): 34
Cumberland	Wreay	1796	114	21	5.42	118	23	5.13	Hutchinson (1794) II: 675
Devon	Alvington West	1791	228	52	4.38	655	116	5.64	Polwhele, *History of Devonshire* (1797): 471
Devon	Clayhanger	1772	125	37	3.37	213	29	7.34[a]	Polwhele (1797): 374
Devon	Clyst St Mary	1791	107	18	5.94	97	23	4.21	Polwhele (1797): 204

County	Place	Date							Source
Devon	Colyton	1695/6	1,554	237	6.55	1,641	334	4.97	King, Burns Journal (Manuscript i): 100
Devon	Exeter St Mary Major	1695/6	1,820	255	7.13	2,135	552	3.86	King (Manuscript i): 100
Devon	Exeter St Stephens	1695/6	443	69	6.42	481	74	6.50	King (Manuscript i): 100
Devon	Kingsbridge	1795/6	686	122	5.62	1,117	226	4.94	King (Manuscript i): 100
Devon	Peter Tavy	1791	230	49	4.69	221	47	4.70	Polwhele (1797): 449
Devon	Ringmore	1698	188	48	3.91	309	60	5.15	King, Miscellaneous Papers (Manuscript iv): 146–7
Devon	St Thomas juxta Exeter	1695/6	1,705	309	5.51	2,189	501	4.36	King (Manuscript i): 100
Devon	Shillingford	1790s	60	11	5.45	71	13	5.46	Polwhele (1797): 111
Devon	Tiverton	1695	7,351	1,616	4.54	6,505	1,397	4.65	King (Manuscript i): 98
Devon	Widworthy	1695/6	255	51	5.00	245	45	5.44[a]	King (Manuscript i): 100
Dorset	Beaminster	1775	1,955	443	4.41	2,140	340	6.29	Hutchins, *History of Dorset* (1796–1815) i: 438
Dorset	Blandford Forum / Blandford St Mary / Bryanston, Langton	1773	2,110	442	4.77	2,789	499	5.58[a]	Hutchins, *History of Dorset* (1861–73) i: 242
Dorset	Corfe Castle	1790	1,239	256	4.84	1,344	294	4.57	Hutchins (1796–1815) i: 290
Dorset	Lytchett Matravers	1790/6	340	74	4.59	416	84	4.95	Hutchins (1796–1815) i: xc–xciii
Dorset	Symonsbury	1790/6	735	117	6.28	791	167	4.73	Hutchins (1796–1815) i: xc–xciii
Durham	Chilton	1780s	148	37	4.00	176	39	4.51[a]	Hutchinson, *History of Durham* (1785–94) iii: 327
Durham	Ferryhill	1780s	468	123	3.80	507	123	4.12	Hutchinson (1785–94) iii: 327
Durham	Hett	1780s	165	40	4.12	157	39	4.02	Hutchinson (1785–94) iii: 327
Durham	Merrington (township)	1780s	236	60	3.90	228	59	3.80	Hutchinson (1785–94) iii: 327
Durham	Witton-le-Wear	1780s	678	130	5.21	450	78	5.76	Hutchinson (1785–94) iii: 327
Essex	Bocking	1726	3,164	638	4.95	2,680	594	4.51	Young (1784–1815) xxxvi: 615–31
Essex	Bocking	1793	2,943	634	4.64	2,680	594	4.51	Young (1784–1815) xxxvi: 615–31
Essex	Brentwood	1696	638	139	4.58	1,007	182	5.53	King (Manuscript i): 92
Essex	Brook St	1696	164	37	4.43	—	—	—	King (Manuscript i): 92
Essex	Toppesfield	c. 1781	624	129	4.83	685	133	5.15	Howlett, *An examination of Dr. Price's essay on population* (1781): 50, 144–5

Table 5.1 *continued*

County	Place	Date	Population	Households	MHS	Census of Great Britain 1801			Source
						Population	Households	MHS	
Essex	Uplands	1696	368	84	4.38	—	—	—	King (Manuscript i): 92
Essex	Weald South (parish)	1696	1,170	260	4.50	1,888	349	5.40	King (Manuscript i): 99
Glos.	Ablington	1770/3	91	22	4.13	118	24	4.91	Rudder, *A new history of Gloucestershire* (1779): 285
Glos.	Abson & Wick	1712	230	50	4.60	571	112	5.09	Atkyns, *Ancient and present state of Gloucestershire* (1712)
Glos.	Allerton	1770/3	231	49	4.71	—	—	—	Rudder (1779): 528
Glos.	Arlington	1770/3	255	55	4.63	274	68	4.02	Rudder (1779): 285
Glos.	Barnsley	1770/3	217	54	4.01	271	65	4.16	Rudder (1779): 261
Glos.	Bibury (village)	1770/3	307	59	5.20	315	80	3.93	Rudder (1779): 285
Glos.	Chedworth	1770/3	787	181	4.34	848	199	4.26	Rudder (1779): 334
Glos.	Coates	1770/3	200	40	5.00	226	46	4.91	Rudder (1779): 393
Glos.	Coberley	1770/3	178	27	6.59	161	25	6.44[a]	Rudder (1779): 399
Glos.	Colesbourne	1770/3	254	48	5.29	231	52	4.40	Rudder (1779): 384
Glos.	Coln Rogers	1770/3	125	26	4.80	110	27	4.07	Rudder (1779): 387
Glos.	Coln St Aldwyn	1770/3	392	80	4.92	385	83	4.63	Rudder (1779): 385
Glos.	Coln St Denis	1770/3	112	26	4.30	163	34	4.79	Rudder (1779): 386
Glos.	Didmarton	1770/5	72	17	4.23	74	20	3.70[a]	Rudder (1779): 408
Glos.	Dowdeswell	1770/3	199	34	5.85	196	47	4.17	Rudder (1779): 415
Glos.	Eyford	1770/3	25	2	12.50	57	11	5.18[a]	Rudder (1779): 668
Glos.	Gloucester	1696	4,756	1,126	4.22	7,579	1,732	4.37[a]	Chalmers, *Estimate of the comparative strength of Great Britain* (1802): 446
Glos.	Gloucester	1743	6,521	1,610	4.05	7,579	1,732	4.37[a]	Furney, History of Gloucester and suburbs 1749 (Manuscript): 12
Glos.	Hazleton	1770/3	77	14	5.50	98	21	4.66[a]	Rudder (1779): 480

Glos.	Kempley	1770/3	257	45	5.71	218	45	4.84[a]	Rudder (1779): 509
Glos.	Kempsford	1770/3	493	106	4.65	656	120	5.46	Rudder (1779): 512
Glos.	Miserden	1762	460	112	4.10	469	118	3.97	Rudder (1779): 556
Glos.	Moreton Valence	1770/3	169	38	4.44	265	55	4.81	Rudder (1779): 559
Glos.	Nass	1770/3	35	6	5.83	—	—	—	Rudder (1779): 529
Glos.	Northleach	1770/3	683	149	4.58	814	150	5.42	Rudder (1779): 581
Glos.	Oxenhall	1770/3	202	46	4.39	313	63	4.96	Rudder (1779): 590
Glos.	Pebworth	1770/3	436	104	4.19	579	124	4.66	Rudder (1779): 600
Glos.	Pirton	1770/3	44	8	5.50	—	—	—	Rudder (1779): 528
Glos.	Quedgeley	1770/3	166	33	5.03	165	33	5.00	Rudder (1779): 614
Glos.	Quenington	1770/3	267	54	4.94	239	57	4.19[a]	Rudder (1779): 619
Glos.	Rendcomb	1770/3	139	23	6.04	147	35	4.20	Rudder (1779): 623
Glos.	Saul	1770/3	151	29	5.20	349	72	4.84[a]	Rudder (1779): 645
Glos.	Sevenhampton	1770/3	288	63	4.57	349	73	4.78[a]	Rudder (1779): 647
Glos.	Slaughter Lower	1770/3	194	39	4.97	198	45	4.40	Rudder (1779): 665
Glos.	Slaughter Upper	1770/3	178	84	2.18	253	57	4.43	Rudder (1779): 667
Glos.	Snowshill	1770/3	236	48	4.91	263	60	4.38	Rudder (1779): 671
Glos.	Southrop	1770/3	216	47	4.59	238	59	4.03	Rudder (1779): 681
Glos.	Stoke Gifford	1770/3	283	60	4.71	281	54	5.20	Rudder (1779): 700
Glos.	Stratton	1770/3	173	35	4.94	166	40	4.15	Rudder (1779): 710
Glos.	Stroud	1756	2,024	415	4.87	5,422	1,355	4.00	Rudder (1779): 716
Glos.	Swell Upper	1770/3	69	14	4.92	74	13	5.69	Rudder (1779): 724
Glos.	Tredington	1777	169	30	5.63	121	27	4.48	Rudder (1779): 777
Glos.	Turkdean	1770/3	113	25	4.52	143	30	4.76[a]	Rudder (1779): 778
Glos.	Westonbirt	1770/3	106	22	4.81	157	40	3.92	Rudder (1779): 810
Glos.	Winson	1770/3	127	24	5.29	145	34	4.26	Rudder (1779): 286
Glos.	Winstone	1770/3	160	30	5.33	143	34	4.20[a]	Rudder (1779): 834
Hants.	Awbridge	1794	163	36	4.52	—	—	—	Young (1784–1815) xxiv: 221–5
Hants.	Braishfield	1794	220	46	4.78	—	—	—	Young (1784–1815) xxiv: 221–5
Hants.	Medstead	1800	393	67	5.86	393	67	5.86	Robbins, Annual Hampshire repository (1799–1801) ii:]98–9
Hants.	Michelmersh	1794	230	43	5.34	—	—	—	Young (1784–1815) xxiv: 221–5
Hants.	Michelmersh (parish)	1794	613	125	4.91	664	136	4.88	Young (1784–1815) xxiv: 221–5

Table 5.1 *continued*

County	Place	Date	Popula-tion	House-holds	MHS	Census of Great Britain 1801 Popula-tion	House-holds	MHS	Source
Hants.	Selborne	1783	676	136	4.97	762	146	5.21	White, *Natural history of Selborne* (1947) Appx: 271
Herts.	Barnet	1695/6	850	176	4.82	1,258	293	4.29	King (Manuscript i): 90
Hunts.	Catworth Great	1798	349	78	4.47	386	83	4.65	Young (1784–1815) xLIV: 53
Hunts.	Holywell	1799	126	32	3.93	—	—	—	Young (1784–1815) xLIV: 184
Hunts.	Holywell (parish)	1799	507	128	3.96	623	136	4.58	Young (1784–1815) xLIV: 184
Hunts.	Needingworth	1799	381	96	3.96	—	—	—	Young (1784–1815) xLIV: 184
Kent	Boughton[g]	c. 1781	495	102	4.85	—	—	—	Howlett (1781): 50, 144–5
Kent	Meopham	1796	612	117	5.23	748	129	5.79	Eden (1797) II: 289
Kent	Riverhead	1695/6	371	80	4.63	750	130	5.76	King (Manuscript i): 90
Kent	Sandwich St Clement	1776	634	167	3.79	731	159	4.59	Boys, *History of Sandwich* (1792) II: 393
Kent	Sandwich St Clement	1786	691	146	4.73	731	159	4.59	Boys, *History of Sandwich* (1792) II: 393
Kent	Sevenoaks (town)	1695/6	891	206	4.32	1,403	412	3.40	King (Manuscript i): 90
Kent	Tunstall	1757	115	20	5.75	136	25	5.45	Nichols, *Bibliotheca Topographica Britannia* (1780–1800) I: 2
Kent	Weald	1695/6	311	80	3.88	487	99	4.91	King (Manuscript i): 90
Lancs.	Ashton-under-Lyne	1775	7,956	1,570	5.06	15,632	2,983	5.24	Percival (1807) IV: 56
Lancs.	Barton	1776	3,742	735	5.09	6,197	1,150	5.38	Aikin, *A description of the country round Manchester* (1795): 222–3
Lancs.	Barton	1780	3,958	740	5.34	6,197	1,150	5.38	Aikin (1795): 222–3
Lancs.	Barton	1785	4,341	785	5.52	6,197	1,150	5.38	Aikin (1795): 222–3
Lancs.	Barton	1790	5,085	922	5.51	6,197	1,150	5.38	Aikin (1795): 222–3
Lancs.	Barton	1793	5,646	1,004	5.62	6,197	1,150	5.38	Aikin (1795): 222–3
Lancs.	Bury (town)	1772	2,090	464	4.50	7,072	1,400	5.05	Percival (1807) IV: 9

Lancs.	Barton Clifton Pendleton Pendlebury Worsley	1778	9,117	1,685	5.41	16,119	2,896	5.56[a]	Price (1803) II: 70–2
Lancs.	Clifton Pendleton Pendlebury Worsley	1776	2,256	391	5.76	4,860	815	5.96[a]	Aikin (1795): 222–3
Lancs.	Clifton Pendleton Pendlebury	1780	2,170	390	5.56	4,860	815	5.96[a]	Aikin (1795): 222–3
Lancs.	Clifton Pendleton Pendlebury	1785	2,717	437	6.21	4,860	815	5.96[a]	Aikin (1795): 222–3
Lancs.	Clifton Pendleton Pendlebury	1790	3,118	542	5.75	4,860	815	5.96[a]	Aikin (1795): 222–3
Lancs.	Clifton Pendleton Pendlebury	1793	3,926	634	6.21	4,860	815	5.96[a]	Aikin (1795): 222–3
Lancs.	Lancaster (township)	1784	8,584	1,783	4.81	9,030	1,998	4.51	Clark, *Historical account of Lancaster* (1811)
Lancs.	Liverpool	1773	34,407	8,002	4.29	77,653	16,989	4.57	Enfield, *Essay towards the history of Liverpool* (1774): 24
Lancs.	Manchester (township)	1773	22,481	5,317	4.22	70,409	15,917	4.42	Percival (1807) IV: 2
Lancs.	Manchester (township)	1788	42,821	8,570	4.87	70,409	15,917	4.42	Percival (1807) IV: 63
Lancs.	Manchester (out parish)	1773	13,786	2,525	5.45	28,280	5,178	5.46[a]	Percival (1807) IV: 38
Lancs.	Radcliffe	c. 1793	2,032	409	4.96	2,497	495	5.04	Aikin (1795): 259
Lancs.	Salford	1773	4,765	1,099	4.35	13,611	2,943	4.62	Percival (1807): IV: 2
Lancs.	Worsley	1776	2,725	522	5.21	5,062	931	5.43	Aikin (1795): 222–3
Lancs.	Worsley	1780	3,020	560	5.38	5,062	931	5.43	Aikin (1795): 222–3
Lancs.	Worsley	1785	3,464	609	5.68	5,062	931	5.43	Aikin (1795): 222–3
Lancs.	Worsley	1790	4,227	742	5.89	5,062	931	5.43	Aikin (1795): 222–3
Lancs.	Worsley	1793	4,693	817	5.74	5,062	931	5.43	Aikin (1795): 222–3

Table 5.1 *continued*

County	Place	Date	Popula-tion	House-holds	MHS	Census of Great Britain 1801			Source
						Popula-tion	House-holds	MHS	
Leics.	Barkestone	1789	199	44	4.52	238	49	4.85	Nichols, *History of Leicester-shire* (1795–1815) II: 19
Leics.	Bottesford (village)	c. 1792	499	128	3.89	—	—	—	Nichols (1795–1815) II: 89
Leics.	Bottesford (parish)	c. 1792	772	188	4.10	804	195	4.12	Nichols (1795–1815) II: 89
Leics.	Branston	1790/2	206	47	4.38	209	47	4.44	Nichols (1795–1815) II: 108
Leics.	Broughton Nether (village)	1790/2	287	72	3.98	324	79	4.10	Nichols (1795–1815) II: 120
Leics.	Broughton Nether (village)	1795	298	82	3.62	324	79	4.10	Nichols (1795–1815) II: 20
Leics.	Buckminster	1790	170	38	4.47	262	56	4.67	Nichols (1795–1815) II: 123
Leics.	Clawson Long	1789	542	112	4.83	604	124	4.87	Nichols (1795–1815) II: 133
Leics.	Dalby Little	1781	123	22	5.59	162	28	5.78	Nichols (1795–1815) II: 160
Leics.	Easthorpe	1792	178	39	4.56	—	—	—	Nichols (1795–1815) II: 104
Leics.	Eastwell	1790	98	18	5.44	107	20	5.35	Nichols (1795–1815) II: 167
Leics.	Eaton	1790/2	208	41	5.07	247	46	5.36	Nichols (1795–1815) II: 173
Leics.	Frisby	1798	306	65	4.70	386	88	4.35	Nichols (1795–1815) III: 261, 556
Leics.	Garthorpe	1791	142	24	5.83	134	29	4.62	Nichols (1795–1815) II: 190
Leics.	Goadby Marwood	1791	188	33	5.69	181	39	4.64	Nichols (1795–1815) II: 196
Leics.	Harby	1790/2	322	60	5.36	343	72	4.76	Nichols (1795–1815) II: 212
Leics.	Harston	1790/3	124	31	4.00	136	35	3.88	Nichols (1795–1815) II: 215
Leics.	Heather	1695/6	134	33	4.06	314	64	4.90	King (Manuscript i): 90
Leics.	Hose	1790	256	48	5.33	264	57	4.63	Nichols (1795–1815) II: 220
Leics.	Knipton	1790/3	223	46	4.84	262	49	5.34	Nichols (1795–1815) II: 235
Leics.	Leicester	1785	12,784	2,726	4.68	16,953	3,668	4.34	Throsby, *History of Leicester* (1791): 409
Leics.	Normanton	1792	95	21	4.52	—	—	—	Nichols (1795–1815) II: 105
Leics.	Plungar	1790/3	145	25	5.80	157	34	4.61	Nichols (1795–1815) II: 296
Leics.	Redmile	1790/3	246	57	4.31	301	62	4.85	Nichols (1795–1815) II: 300
Leics.	Saltby	1790/3	196	41	4.78	185	40	4.62[a]	Nichols (1795–1815) II: 305
Leics.	Scalford	1790/3	339	75	4.52	333	75	4.44	Nichols (1795–1815) II: 315

County	Place	Date							Source
Leics.	Sewstern	1790	210	44	4.77	221	59	3.74	Nichols (1795–1815) ii: 123
Leics.	Sproxton	1790/3	243	53	4.58	250	57	4.56	Nichols (1795–1815) ii: 329
Leics.	Stapleford	1790/3	163	25	6.52	179	28	6.39^a	Nichols (1795–1815) ii: 337
Leics.	Stonesby	1793/4	153	36	4.25	181	41	4.41	Nichols (1795–1815) ii: 363
Leics.	Swepstone	1695/6	145	40	3.62	412	84	4.90^a	King (Manuscript i): 90
Leics.	Waltham	1793/5	403	91	4.42	440	105	4.19	Nichols (1795–1815) ii: 382
Leics.	Wyfordby	1793/5	54	11	4.90	—		—	Nichols (1795–1815) ii: 397
Lincs.	Riby	1800	144	28	5.14	158	31	5.09	Young (1784–1815) xxxvii: 589
Lincs.	Swinderby	1771	224	52	4.30	254	52	5.68^a	Price (1816) vi: 43
Lincs.	Woolsthorpe	c. 1742	333	71	4.69	372	75	4.96	Nichols (1795–1815) ii: 84
Lincs.	Woolsthorpe	c. 1792	284	64	4.43	372	75	4.96	Nichols (1795–1815) ii: 84
London	All Hallows Bread St	1696	512	85	6.02	430	102	4.21	King (Manuscript i): 124–7
London	St Andrew Wardrobe	1696	505	108	4.67	900	226	3.98	King (Manuscript i): 124–7
London	St Anne & St Agnes Aldersgate	1696	852	145	5.87	952	232	4.10	King (Manuscript i): 124–7
London	St Benet Gracechurch	1696	396	65	6.09	429	92	4.66	King (Manuscript i): 124–7
London	St Benet Paul's Wharf	1696	562	124	4.53	620	153	4.05	King (Manuscript i): 124–7
London	St Botolph Aldersgate	1696	4,966	1,241	4.00	5,382	1,360	3.95	King (Manuscript i): 58
London	St Botolph Billingsgate	1696	350	60	5.83	196	31	6.32^a	King (Manuscript i): 124–7
London	St Bride	1696	5,145	1,241	4.14	7,078	1,592	4.44	King (Manuscript i): 58
London	St Clement Eastcheap	1696	372	60	6.20	352	67	5.25	King (Manuscript i): 124–7
London	St Dunstan-in-the-West	1696	2,671	437	6.11	3,021	747	4.04	King (Manuscript i): 58
London	St Giles Cripplegate	1696	8,528	1,842	4.62	11,446	3,118	3.67	King (Manuscript i): 58
London	St Gregory by St Paul's	1696	1,661	282	5.89	1,634	344	4.75	King (Manuscript i): 124–7
London	St John Zachary	1696	475	83	5.72	507	137	3.70	King (Manuscript i): 124–7
London	St Margaret New Fish St	1696	461	73	6.31	365	78	4.67	King (Manuscript i): 124–7
London	St Michael Bassishaw	1696	846	149	5.67	747	146	5.11	King (Manuscript i): 124–7
London	St Peter Cornhill	1696	1,111	186	5.97	1,003	129	7.77	King (Manuscript i): 124–7
London	St Peter Paul's Wharf	1696	373	70	5.32	353	98	3.60	King (Manuscript i): 124–7
London	St Steven Coleman St	1696	2,713	429	6.32	3,225	755	4.27	King (Manuscript i): 124–7
Middlesex	Bethnal Green	1695	5,585	1,013	5.51	22,310	5,630.	3.90	King (Manuscript i): 150–1
Middlesex	Bromley St Leonard	1695	539	109	4.94	1,684	335	5.02	King (Manuscript i): 150–1
Middlesex	Clapton	1695	616	84	7.33	—		—	King, Computation of the numbers of people in England 1695 (Manuscript iii): 17
Middlesex	Dalston	1695	102	15	6.80	—		—	King (Manuscript iii): 17

Table 5.1 *continued*

County	Place	Date	Popula-tion	House-holds	MHS	Census of Great Britain 1801			Source
						Popula-tion	House-holds	MHS	
Middlesex	East Smithfield	1695	4,906	1,241	3.95	6,153	1,752	3.51	King (Manuscript i): 150–1
Middlesex	Hackney	1695	1,936	379	5.10	—	—	—	King (Manuscript iii): 17
Middlesex	Hackney St John (parish)	1695	2,896	535	5.41	12,730	2,420	5.25	King (Manuscript iii): 17
Middlesex	Harefield	1695	563	122	4.61	951	180	5.28	King, Exercises in political arithmetic (Manuscript ii) (Manuscript i): 90
Middlesex	Holy Trinity Minories	1695	538	131	4.10	644	142	4.53	King (Manuscript i): 150–1
Middlesex	Kingsland	1695	62	19	3.26	—	—	—	King (Manuscript iii): 17
Middlesex	Limehouse	1695	3,761	806	4.66	4,678	1,046	4.47	King (Manuscript i): 150–1
Middlesex	Mile End New Town	1695	1,600	313	5.11	5,253	1,484	3.53	King (Manuscript i): 150–1
Middlesex	Mile End Old Town	1695	1,688	361	4.67	9,848	2,137	4.60	King (Manuscript i): 150–1
Middlesex	Newington	1695	88	25	3.52	—	—	—	King (Manuscript iii): 17
Middlesex	Norton Folgate	1695	2,349	449	5.23	1,752	420	4.14	King (Manuscript i): 150–1
Middlesex	Old Artillery Ground	1695	1,635	162	10.09	1,428	347	4.11	King (Manuscript i): 150–1
Middlesex	Poplar and Blackwall	1695	2,255	575	3.92	4,493	1,107	4.05	King (Manuscript i): 150–1
Middlesex	Ratcliff	1695	4,792	1,294	3.70	5,666	1,513	3.74	King (Manuscript i): 150–1
Middlesex	St George-in-the-East	1695	9,310	2,450	3.80	21,170	5,771	3.66	King (Manuscript i): 150–1
Middlesex	St Katherine by the Tower	1695	2,614	743	3.51	2,652	637	4.16	King (Manuscript i): 150–1
Middlesex	Shacklewell	1695	92	13	7.07	—	—	—	King (Manuscript iii): 17
Middlesex	Shadwell St Paul	1695	7,891	1,443	5.46	8,828	2,647	3.33	King (Manuscript i): 150–1
Middlesex	Shoreditch St Leonard	1695	6,629	1,585	4.18	34,766	9,224	3.76	King (Manuscript i): 150–1
Middlesex	Spitalfields	1695	11,335	1,868	6.06	15,091	4,205	3.58	King (Manuscript i): 150–1
Middlesex	Stratford-le-Bow	1695	772	178	4.33	2,101	437	4.89	King (Manuscript i): 150–1
Middlesex	Tower Extra	1695	239	50	4.78	—	—	—	King (Manuscript i): 150–1
Middlesex	Tower Infra	1695	343	60	5.71	—	—	—	King (Manuscript i): 150–1
Middlesex	Wapping St John	1695	5,530	1,496	3.69	5,889	1,574	3.74	King (Manuscript i): 150–1
Middlesex	Whitechapel St Mary	1695	11,439	2,583	4.42	23,666	6,141	3.85	King (Manuscript i): 150–1
Norfolk	Dunham Little	1792	206	44	4.68	210	47	4.46	Young, *Agriculture of Norfolk* (1804): 101

County	Place	Year							Source
Norfolk	Eaton	1696	153	36	4.22	—	—	—	King (Manuscript i): 118
Norfolk	Eynsford Hundred	1695/6	5,880	1,437	4.09	8,175	1,452	5.63[a]	King (Manuscript i): 92
Norfolk	Foulden	1782	367	89	4.12	376	88	4.27	Young (1804): 109
Norfolk	Harleston & Redenhall	1789	1,344	240	5.60	1,459	287	5.08	Young (1804): 111
Norfolk	Hellesdon	1696	65	14	4.64	—	—	—	King (Manuscript i): 118
Norfolk	Hethel	1787	149	29	5.13	175	33	5.30	Young (1784–1815) viii: 187–90
Norfolk	Kenninghall	1736	700	132	5.30	1,052	202	5.20	Blomefield and Parkin, *Topographical history of Norfolk* (1805–10) i: 227
Norfolk	Ketteringham	1787	166	27	6.14	181	28	6.46[a]	Young (1784–1815) viii: 345–51
Norfolk	Lakenham	1696	223	81	2.75	428	89	4.80	King (Manuscript i): 118
Norfolk	Lopham North	1736	460	92	5.00	588	110	5.34	Blomefield and Parkin (1805–10) i: 241
Norfolk	Lopham South	1736	470	95	4.94	692	124	5.58	Blomefield and Parkin (1805–10) i: 241
Norfolk	Mileham	1788	314	63	4.98	323	71	4.54	Young (1784–1815) xi: 305–13
Norfolk	Norwich St Andrew	1696	916	194	4.72	1,858	236	7.87	King (Manuscript i): 118
Norfolk	Norwich St Augustine	1696	907	246	3.68	1,232	338	3.67	King (Manuscript i): 118
Norfolk	Norwich St Edmund	1696	319	60	5.31	446	137	3.25	King (Manuscript i): 118
Norfolk	Norwich St George at Colgate	1696	1,157	264	4.38	1,132	293	3.86	King (Manuscript i): 118
Norfolk	Norwich St George of Tombland	1696	723	149	4.85	750	186	4.03	King (Manuscript i): 118
Norfolk	Norwich St Giles	1696	812	180	4.51	1,076	270	3.98	King (Manuscript i): 118
Norfolk	Norwich St Lawrence	1696	674	173	3.89	899	248	3.62	King (Manuscript i): 118
Norfolk	Norwich St Margaret	1696	663	168	3.94	652	186	3.55	King (Manuscript i): 118
Norfolk	Norwich St Martin at Oak	1696	1,196	306	3.90	1,747	413	4.23	King (Manuscript i): 118
Norfolk	Norwich St Martin at Palace	1696	820	212	3.86	936	264	3.54	King (Manuscript i): 118
Norfolk	Norwich St Mary at Coslany	1696	948	224	4.23	1,018	303	3.35	King (Manuscript i): 118
Norfolk	Norwich St Michael at Plea	1696	480	128	3.75	446	80	5.57	King (Manuscript i): 118
Norfolk	Norwich St Michael at Coslany	1696	1,064	251	4.23	1,031	261	3.95	King (Manuscript i): 118

Table 5.1 *continued*

County	Place	Date	Population	Households	MHS	Census of Great Britain 1801			Source
						Population	Households	MHS	
Norfolk	Norwich, St Peter Hungate	1696	260	51	5.09	371	103	3.60	King (Manuscript i): 118
Norfolk	Norwich St Peter Mancroft	1696	1,933	400	4.83	2,120	493	4.30	King (Manuscript i): 118
Norfolk	Norwich St Peter per Mountgate	1696	1,381	376	3.67	1,350	311	4.34	King (Manuscript i): 118
Norfolk	Norwich St Saviour	1696	697	129	5.40	984	235	4.18	King (Manuscript i): 118
Norfolk	Norwich St Swithun	1696	496	117	4.23	503	138	3.64	King (Manuscript i): 118
Norfolk	Oxborough	1782	233	43	5.41	296	56	5.28	Young (1804): 149
Norfolk	Roydon	1736	240	60	4.00	430	91	4.72	Blomefield and Parkin (1803–10) I: 39
Norfolk	Shotesham	1782	708	136	5.20	791	139	4.69[a]	Young (1804): 165
Norfolk	Thorp & Hellesdon (hamlets)	1696	134	31	4.32	155	33	4.69[a]	King (Manuscript i): 118
Norfolk	Thorp	1696	69	17	4.05	—	—	—	King (Manuscript i): 118
Norfolk	Tottenhill	1783	170	39	4.35	220	44	5.00	Census of Great Britain 1801 (1801–2): 243
Norfolk	Wormegay	1783	165	35	4.71	224	51	4.39	Census of Great Britain 1801 (1801–2): 243
Norfolk	Wymondham	1747	3,213	686	4.68	3,567	749	4.76[a]	Young (1784–1815) xxxvi: 609–14
Northants	Stoke Doyle	1720s	70	18	3.88	115	25	4.60	Bridges, *History of Northamptonshire* II: 376
Notts.	Nottingham	1779	17,417	3,556	4.89	28,861	6,707	4.30	Price (1803) II: 70–2
Shrops.	Attingham Chilton Cronkhill Emstrey	1695/6	161	33	4.87	—	—	—	King (Manuscript i): 90
Shrops.	Madeley	1782	2,690	560	4.80	4,758	942	5.05	Plymley, *Agriculture of Shropshire* (1803): 343
Shrops.	Madeley	1793	3,677	851	4.31	4,758	942	5.05	Plymley (1803): 343
Shrops.	Shrewsbury Holy Cross	1695/6	935	222	4.21	1,200	288	4.16	King (Manuscript i): 90, 98

County	Place	Date							Source
Somerset	Frome	1785	6,342	1,348	4.70	8,748	1,853	4.71	Collinson, *History of Somerset* (1791) II: 186
Somerset	Taunton^b	1790	5,472	1,199	4.56	5,794	1,308	4.42	Toulmin, *History of Taunton* (1791): 189
Staffs.	Biddulph	1779	1,035	207	5.00	1,180	237	4.97^a	Price (1816) VI: 43
Staffs.	Blithbury	1797	115	24	4.79	—	—	—	Shaw, *History of Staffordshire* (1798–1801) I: 201
Staffs.	Featherstone	1695/6	65	14	4.64	48	8	6.00	King (Manuscript i): 90
Staffs.	Hill Ridware	1797	143	33	4.33	—	—	—	Shaw (1798–1801) I: 200
Staffs.	Lichfield^k	1695/6	3,038	655	4.63	4,712	1,033	4.56	King (Manuscript i): 90
Staffs.	Mavesyn Ridware	1797	73	13	5.61	—	—	—	Shaw (1798–1801) I: 188
Staffs.	Mavesyn Ridware (parish)	1797	464	95	4.88	486	79	6.15	Shaw (1798–1801) I: 187
Staffs.	Rack End	1797	133	25	5.32	—	—	—	Shaw (1798–1801) I: 200
Suffolk	Coney Weston	1790s	212	36	5.88	198	38	5.21	Young, *Agriculture of Suffolk* (1813): 39
Suffolk	Fornham St Genevieve	1785/6	108	16	6.75	116	23	5.04	Young (1784–1815) VI: 413
Suffolk	Fornham St Martin	1784	134	30	4.46	160	38	4.21	Young (1784–1815) II: 448–9
Suffolk	Hawstead	1783	415	70	5.92	392	75	5.22	Young (1784–1815) II: 332–8
Suffolk	Icklingham	1785	336	68	4.94	335	75	4.46	Young (1784–1815) IV: 51–3
Suffolk	Mellis	1790s	339	70	4.84	371	75	4.94	Young (1813): 306
Suffolk	Semer	1793	199	42	4.73	203	44	4.61	Young (1784–1815) XXIII: 49
Suffolk	Woodbridge	1781	2,600	591	4.39	3,020	656	4.60	Young (1784–1815) XII: 332–6
Suffolk	Yoxford	1794	826	167	4.94	851	175	4.86	Young (1785–1815) XXIII: 29–30
Surrey	Chobham	1781	940	214	4.39	1,176	229	5.13	Young (1784–1815) XXXVI: 583–6
Surrey	Epsom	1790/6	1,671	371	4.50	2,404	537	4.47	Eden (1797) III: 705–7
Surrey	Guildford	1738/9	2,574	536	4.80	2,634	579	4.66	Manning and Bray, *History of Surrey* (1804–14) I: 32
Sussex	Firle West	1793	421	77	5.46	494	87	5.67	Young (1784–1815) XXII: 324
Sussex	Glynde	1788/9	212	30	7.06	216	39	5.53	Young (1784–1815) XI: 141–3
Sussex	Glynde	1793	222	35	6.34	216	39	5.53	Young (1784–1815) XXII: 325
Sussex	Ringmer	1793	903	170	5.31	897	178	5.03	Young (1784–1815) XXII: 324
Sussex	Tarring Neville	1793	80	14	5.71	74	13	5.69	Young (1784–1815) XXII: 324
Warks.	Coleshill	1695/6	1,109	245	4.52	1,437	290	4.95	King (Manuscript i): 98
Warks.	Shustoke	1695/6	275	59	4.66	499	98	5.09	King (Manuscript i): 98
Westmorland	Kendal (township)	1784	6,775	1,623	4.17	6,892	1,671	4.12	Eden (1797) III: 750–1

Table 5.1 *continued*

188

County	Place	Date	Popula- tion	House- holds	MHS	Census of Great Britain 1801 Popula- tion	Census of Great Britain 1801 House- holds	Census of Great Britain 1801 MHS	Source
Westmorland	Kendal (township)	1793	7,154	1,701	4.20	6,892	1,671	4.12	Eden (1797) III: 750–1
Westmorland	Kirkland	1784	796	236	3.37	1,086	300	3.62	Eden (1797) III: 750–1
Westmorland	Kirkland	1793	935	237	3.94	1,086	300	3.62	Eden (1797) III: 750–1
Wilts.	Calne	1770s	3,467	776	4.46	3,767	852	4.62	Price (1803) II: 70–2
Worcs.	Ablench	1770s	80	16	5.00	89	17	5.24^a	Nash, *History of Worcester- shire* (1781–99) I: 454
Worcs.	Bewdley	1773	1,932	329	5.87	3,671	814	4.50	Nash (1781–99) II: 279
Worcs.	Bushley	1776	296	56	5.28	282	67	4.20	Nash (1781–99) I: 182
Worcs.	Castlemorton	1770s	506	111	4.55	659	151	4.36	Nash (1781–99) II: 109
Worcs.	Doverdale	1770s	58	7	8.28	60	6	10.00^a	Nash (1781–99) I: 293
Worcs.	Droitwich^j	1770s	1,156	249	4.64	1,371	381	3.60	Nash (1781–99) I: 307
Worcs.	Eastham (village)	1770s	343	79	4.34	385	77	5.00	Nash (1781–99) I: 363
Worcs.	Eckington	1776	472	101	4.67	550	121	4.54	Nash (1781–99) I: 368
Worcs.	Evesham All Saints	1777	1,052	253	4.15	1,197	300	3.99	Nash (1781–99) I: 411
Worcs.	Evesham St Lawrence	1777	796	190	4.18	968	205	4.72^a	Nash (1781–99) I: 411
Worcs.	Fladbury (village)	1770s	346	67	5.16	424	79	5.36	Nash (1781–99) I: 454
Worcs.	Hanley Child	1770s	166	37	4.48	158	32	4.94	Nash (1781–99) I: 366
Worcs.	Hanley William	1770s	105	22	4.77	138	23	6.00	Nash (1781–99) I: 365
Worcs.	Hill	1770s	53	11	4.81	—	—	—	Nash (1781–99) I: 454
Worcs.	Hill & Moor (hamlets)	1770s	239	40	5.97	235	56	4.20	Nash (1781–99) I: 454
Worcs.	Inkberrow	1761	947	214	4.42	1,335	289	4.61^a	Eden (1797) III: 803
Worcs.	Inkberrow	1770	889	215	4.13	1,335	289	4.61^a	Nash (1781–99) II: 6
Worcs.	Longdon	1770s	600	112	5.35	533	136	3.91	Nash (1781–99) II: 107
Worcs.	Mamble	1770s	268	51	5.25	338	58	5.84	Nash (1781–99) II: 157
Worcs.	Moor	1770s	186	29	6.41	—	—	—	Nash (1781–99) I: 454
Worcs.	Orleton	1770s	94	17	5.52	89	21	4.24	Nash (1781–99) I: 366
Worcs.	Overbury & Conderton	1777	348	80	4.35	425	99	4.29	Nash (1781–99) II: 235
Worcs.	Pershore	1756	1,434	339	4.23	1,910	454	4.20	Nash (1781–99) II: 250
Worcs.	Pershore	1777	1,655	377	4.38	1,910	454	4.20	Nash (1781–99) II: 250

County	Place	Year							Source
Worcs.	Piddle	1770s	121	22	5.50	144	35	4.12	Nash (1781–99) I: 454
Worcs.	Piddle North	1770s	121	22	5.50	103	26	3.96	Nash (1781–99) II: 188
Worcs.	Pirton	1781	194	38	5.10	191	37	5.16	Census of Great Britain 1801 (1801–2): 401
Worcs.	Shelsley Gt	1770s	393	88	4.48	263	61	4.31	Nash (1781–99) II: 352
Worcs.	Shrawley	1770s	457	89	5.13	504	120	4.20	Nash (1781–99) II: 354
Worcs.	Strensham	1770s	330	64	5.15	286	65	4.40	Nash (1781–99) II: 390
Worcs.	Stock & Bradley	1770s	124	28	4.42	181	41	4.42	Nash (1781–99) I: 454
Worcs.	Throckmorton	1770s	120	25	4.80	150	30	5.00	Nash (1781–99) I: 454
Worcs.	Wichenford	1730	287	53	5.41	357	62	5.75	Nash (1781–99) II: 459
Worcs.	Wribbenhall	1783	618	138	4.47	—	—	—	Nash (1781–99) II: 39–41
Yorks. E.R.	Hull[k]	1792	22,286	5,256	4.22	27,609	7,027	3.92	Eden (1797) III: 827
Yorks. W.R.	Armley	1776	1,715	359	4.77	2,695	551	4.89	Wales, Enquiry into the present state of population (1781): 41
Yorks. W.R.	Attercliffe	1736	1,075	245	4.38	2,281	476	4.79[a]	Hunter, Hallamshire (1869): 20
Yorks. W.R.	Attercliffe / Brightside-Birelow	1781	3,974	847	4.69	6,311	1,356	4.65[a]	Eden (1797) III: 869
Yorks. W.R.	Attercliffe / Brightside-Birelow	1786	4,722	972	4.85	6,311	1,356	4.65[a]	Eden (1797) III: 869
Yorks. W.R.	Beeston	1776	862	192	4.48	1,427	289	4.93[a]	Wales (1781): 41
Yorks. W.R.	Bramley	1776	1,378	311	4.43	2,562	508	5.04	Wales (1781): 41
Yorks. W.R.	Brightside-Birelow	1736	983	211	4.65	4,030	880	4.57	Hunter (1869): 20
Yorks. W.R.	Chapel Allerton	1778	894	109	8.20	1,054	243	4.33[a]	Young (1784–1815) XXVII: 309
Yorks. W.R.	Eccleshall / Nether Hallam / Upper Hallam	1736	2,352	503	4.67	8,130	1,625	5.00	Hunter (1869): 20
Yorks. W.R.	Farnley	1776	540	116	4.65	943	190	4.96	Wales (1781): 41
Yorks. W.R.	Headingley	1776	667	143	4.66	1,313	208	6.31[b]	Wales (1781): 41
Yorks. W.R.	Holbeck	1776	2,045	508	4.02	4,196	929	4.51	Wales (1781): 41
Yorks. W.R.	Hunslet	1776	3,367	806	4.17	5,799	1,258	4.60	Wales (1781): 41
Yorks. W.R.	Leeds (township)	1775	17,117	4,099	4.17	30,669	7,122	4.30[a]	Aikin (1795): 571
Yorks. W.R.	Manningham	1780	726	161	4.50	1,357	326	4.16	Cudworth, Manningham, Heaton and Allerton (1896): 76–8

Table 5.1 *continued*

County	Place	Date	Popula-tion	House-holds	MHS	Census of Great Britain 1801			Source
						Popula-tion	House-holds	MHS	
Yorks. W.R.	Potter Newton	1785	456	97	4.70	509	106	4.80[a]	Young (1784–1815) xxxvii: 309
Yorks. W.R.	Saddleworth	1790s	10,471	1,822	5.74	10,665	1,873	5.69	Aikin (1795): 557
Yorks. W.R.	Sheffield	1736	9,695	2,152	4.50	31,314	6,754	4.63	Hunter (1869): 20
Yorks. W.R.	Sheffield	1755	12,983	2,677	4.86	31,314	6,754	4.63	Eden (1797) III: 869
Yorks. W.R.	Skipton (township)	1794	2,096	464	4.51	2,305	517	4.45	Eden (1797) III: 875
Yorks. W.R.	Wortley	1776	894	196	4.56	1,995	386	5.16	Wales (1781): 41

[a] The number of inhabited houses equals the number of families in the population returns of 1801.

[b] The number of inhabited houses exceeds the number of families in the population returns of 1801.

[c] Where appropriate, spelling has been modernised. See Bartholomew, *Gazetteer of the British Isles* (1966) and *Census of Great Britain 1851, Population Tables* I (1852–3).

[d] Where the text did not specify the date of the enumeration an approximate date has been given based on the publication date of the work in which the figures first appeared.

[e] Unless the text suggested otherwise, the 1801 figures were based on the parish and township totals as given in the *Census of Great Britain 1851, Population Tables* I (1852–3). A special note has been made of all instances in which figures relating to a township were used when alternative figures were available for a parish of the same name. The totals for cities such as Chester and Nottingham do not include the sections of city parishes lying outside the walls.

[f] Botcherby, Brisco and Cummersdale are listed separately

[g] Boughton appearing as a component of several Kentish place names it proved impossible to identify the parish in the population returns of 1801.

[h] In 1790 small parts of the adjacent parishes of Bishops Hull and Wilton were included on the grounds that they were connected by buildings to the town of Taunton.

[i] The city of Lichfield includes the Close.

[j] The part of Dodderhill lying within the borough of Droitwich has not been included.

[k] Hull includes the adjacent parish of Sculcoates.

Mean household size 1693–1801

In Table 5.2, the 409 settlements for which information about mean household size was available are grouped by decade, and the overall mean, mean of means and median calculated. These three separate calculations are necessary because each reflects a different attribute of the material. For instance, the overall mean household size is calculated by dividing the total number of inhabitants in all the settlements by the total number of households. Thus a particularly large settlement contributes a large proportion to both sides of the calculation and therefore dominates the overall mean household size. On the other hand, the mean of means is calculated by summing the individual mean household sizes for all the settlements and dividing by the number of settlements concerned. Thus the mean of means is dominated by settlements with extreme mean household sizes. In calculating the median, however, each settlement is given equal treatment and hence in all calculations where settlements have not been grouped by size, it is the median which is probably the best average measure.[83] In this particular table no consistent trend is visible even in the median value, but this is hardly surprising in view of the unevenness of the distribution of the settlements between the decades. However, the rise in both the mean of means and median after the 1760s suggests that in the last quarter of the eighteenth century, households, on average, may have been larger than at any time during the previous century.[84]

Some confirmation of this is provided by Table 5.3, in which the settlements have been regrouped into two broad periods, with the additional information from the Population Returns of 1801, enabling a comparison to be made with the opening years of the nineteenth century. In order that the comparison might be more meaningful the settlements were also subdivided into regions – the City of London, an eastern region comprising all the counties east of a line from Lincoln to London, and a south and west region consisting of all counties from Surrey and Sussex westwards and south of a line from Gloucester to Northampton. The remaining counties were formed into a vast north and central region.

It can be argued that the figures show a remarkable consistency. In both the east and south and west regions the median value for household size seems to have risen during the second half of the eighteenth century only to fall again by 1801, although still remaining above its pre-1750 level.[85] The unreliability of the

[83] It will be noticed that the overall mean is usually lower than the median. One reason for this is that in the large centres of population mean household size was seldom high. The positions of the overall mean and median are, however, reversed in Laslett's study of mean household size, see above, Chapter 4, pp. 136–137 and clearly more work needs to be done on the relationship between mean household size and size of settlement (compare Table 5.5 below).

[84] This suggestion is insecure statistically, for the 95 % confidence limits of the decadal medians overlap.

[85] These results are insecure statistically since the 95% confidence limits of the medians in the various categories concerned overlap.

Table 5.2   *Household size by period*

Period	No. of settlements	Overall mean	Mean of means	Median
1691–1700	94	4.54	4.86	4.64
1701–1710	—	—	—	—
1711–1720	11	4.34	4.42	4.37
1721–1730	3	4.96	4.74	4.95
1731–1740	9	4.60	4.69	4.67
1741–1750	4	4.33	4.60	4.68
1751–1760	18	4.63	4.81	4.69
1761–1770	5	4.17	4.20	4.13
1771–1780	116	4.59	4.97	4.80
1781–1790	54	4.89	4.94	4.84
1791–1800	95	4.63	4.92	4.78

Table 5.3   *Household size by region*

Region	Period	No. of[a] settlements	Overall mean	Mean of means	Median
London	Pre-1750	18	4.86	5.51	5.85
	1751–1800	—	—	—	—
	1801	18	4.10	4.58	4.24
East	Pre-1750	65	4.50	4.65	4.51
	1751–1800	33	4.74	4.87	4.83
	1801	85	4.05	4.57	4.54
North and	Pre-1750	15	4.60	4.58	4.63
Central	1751–1800	185	4.67	4.89	4.77
	1801	186	4.66	4.87	4.88
South and	Pre-1750	23	4.63	4.79	4.54
West	1751–1800	70	4.71	5.09	4.86
	1801	80	4.59	4.87	4.70

[a] There is a discrepancy between the number of places identified in 1801 and the figures for the earlier periods because certain settlements were not separately listed in the *Census of Great Britain 1801* (1801–2).

1801 returns for London and the inclusion of the fast growing northern industrial areas explain the different patterns of the remaining areas. This interpretation, however, leaves certain questions unanswered. For example, the possibility cannot be ruled out that geographical bunching is responsible for apparent changes in household size. This could arise because within each period different settlements are being compared, settlements which could in theory at any rate, have had widely differing types of household at all stages of their history. In the south and west region, for example, the 1801 figure might be the result of averaging a group of settlements with a low mean household size (by chance originally enumerated before 1750) and some with a high mean household size (by chance originally enumerated after 1750). This may seem somewhat

Table 5.4 *Household size by region and county[a]*

Region	County[b]	No. of settlements	Period 1751–1800			Census of Great Britain 1801			Change since first enumeration		
			Overall mean	Mean of means	Median	Overall mean	Mean of means	Median	Overall mean	Mean of means	Median
South-East		14	4.84	5.28	5.27	4.96	5.24	5.33	+0.12	−0.04	+0.06
South-West		11	4.64	4.90	4.59	4.71	4.90	4.70	+0.07	0	+0.01
West Midlands		58	4.66	4.88	4.80	4.49	4.65	4.40	−0.17	−0.23	−0.40
	Gloucester	30	4.60	4.87	4.80	4.34	4.69	4.40	−0.26	−0.18	−0.40
	Worcester	25	4.77	4.92	4.80	4.30	4.51	4.31	−0.47	−0.41	−0.49
South Midlands		5	4.63	4.30	4.39	4.44	4.48	4.46	−0.19	+0.18	+0.07
East		19	4.79	5.01	4.84	4.72	4.79	4.86	−0.07	−0.22	+0.02
	Norfolk	8	5.06	4.87	4.84	4.84	4.79	4.77	−0.22	−0.08	−0.07
	Suffolk	9	4.74	5.20	4.94	4.70	4.79	4.86	−0.04	−0.41	−0.12
North Midlands		28	4.76	4.76	4.69	4.43	4.61	4.62	−0.33	−0.15	−0.07
	Leicester	25	4.65	4.76	4.68	4.58	4.60	4.61	−0.13	−0.16	−0.07
North-west		32	4.72	4.93	4.92	4.70	5.18	5.38	−0.02	+0.25	+0.46
	Cheshire	14	4.34	4.70	4.38	4.88	5.29	5.28	+0.54	+0.59	+0.90
	Lancashire	18	4.79	5.11	5.15	4.67	5.10	5.38	−0.12	−0.01	+0.23
Yorkshire		11	4.61	4.58	4.51	4.50	4.72	4.63	−0.11	+0.14	+0.12
North		26	4.10	4.63	4.32	4.26	4.42	4.38	+0.16	−0.21	+0.06
	Cumberland	18	4.07	4.87	4.80	4.35	4.55	4.57	+0.28	−0.32	−0.23

[a] Places not separately listed in the *Census of Great Britain 1801* (1801–2) together with those places in which in 1801 the number of families equalled or exceeded the number of houses, have been excluded.

[b] The county sub-totals form part of the preceding regional totals.

unlikely, but no difficulty need arise if the comparison is confined to those places which can be identified in each period.[86] Unfortunately, this involves the loss of places which were not separately listed in 1801 together with all enumerations belonging to the pre-1750 period. It was also decided that although the whole problem of regional variations really deserves separate treatment, some sub-division into smaller regions was essential if trends over a period of time were to be properly interpreted. Accordingly, the country was divided into ten regions (including London) based on the Registrar General's divisions which were first used for the Population Returns of 1851. These regions were further divided into counties whenever sufficient information was available.

Table 5.4 shows clearly that it was in the counties of Gloucester, Worcester, Norfolk, Suffolk and Cumberland that the decline in household size was most marked. In a second group of regions, the south-east, south-west and south midlands, there was a slight increase in household size. Only in the fast growing settlements of Cheshire and Lancashire was there any marked increase.[87] A general decline in household size during the last part of the eighteenth century would therefore seem to have been by no means universal. This second analysis does not, however, altogether eliminate another weakness, the contrasting behaviour of the median and the other measure of average size, the overall mean, which suggests that within each region mean household sizes of many settlements, particularly the larger ones, may have moved in the opposite direction to the general trend. Accordingly, further calculations were made of household size in settlements of varying sizes but on a national, as opposed to a regional, basis as there were too few places to justify any subdivision (Table 5.5).

Looking first at the settlements as originally enumerated, it appears that mean household size was highest when settlements were small. This difference between settlements of different size is not, however, statistically significant and an analysis of the same settlements as listed in the Census of Great Britain of 1801 fails to show a similar difference.[88]

Neither is there much consistency to be observed over time within each group. For example, although there was a marked decline in household size in settlements with a population of between one and three hundred, slightly larger settlements (300–1,000) showed a rise in mean household size while larger places again failed to follow any pattern.

[86] This, however, causes further difficulty. Hélin, below, Chapter 13, pp. 331–332, found that when the same community was counted on separate occasions, differences between the distribution of households were mostly insignificant due to random variation. On the other hand, when the populations came from different districts, the distributions were independent of each other.

[87] The differences between the three groups of settlements are too small for them to have any statistical significance. Indeed in each region the 95 % confidence limits of the median house-hold sizes in each period overlap.

[88] The difference between the mean household size of settlements with up to 399 inhabitants and the mean household size of settlements of 400 inhabitants and above is not significant at the 95 % level ($P > 0.25$).

Table 5.5   *Household size by size of settlement, 1751–1800 and 1801[a]*

Size of settlement	Period 1751–1800				Census of Great Britain 1801			
	No. of[b] settlements	Over-all mean	Mean of means	Median	No. of[b] settlements	Over-all mean	Mean of means	Median
1–99	8	4.84	4.95	5.19	5	4.87	5.05	5.46
100–199	47	4.78	5.00	4.97	40	4.57	4.66	4.62
200–299	30	4.79	4.91	4.74	32	4.55	4.63	4.58
300–399	20	4.79	4.82	4.88	22	4.81	4.85	4.80
400–499	10	4.59	4.67	4.54	8	4.81	4.89	4.94
500–999	24	4.69	4.79	4.69	23	4.89	4.90	4.96
1,000–1,999	12	4.74	4.77	4.62	14	4.34	4.47	4.38
2,000–2,999	11	4.60	4.62	4.64	10	4.86	4.95	4.97
3,000–3,999	9	4.74	4.78	4.46	3	4.50	4.59	4.60
4,000–4,999	5	4.92	5.08	5.52	4	4.75	4.75	4.78
5,000–9,999	10	4.51	4.63	4.63	21	4.77	4.89	5.05
10,000+	9	4.60	4.67	4.68	13	4.52	4.65	4.57

[a] Places not separately listed in the *Census of Great Britain 1801* (1801–2) together with those places in which in 1801 the number of families equalled or exceeded the number of houses and those places, part only of which had been enumerated, have been excluded.
[b] The numbers in each group differ as a result of the growth or decline in population of the various settlements in the intervening period.

Various suggestions can be advanced for the failure of any definite pattern to emerge. The first and most important point is that it would indeed be surprising if all settlements of a certain size in different parts of the country behaved in exactly the same way. This is particularly true of the larger places, which could include stable or declining market towns as well as the fast growing textile villages of the north-west. A more detailed analysis of the relationship between household size and population growth is called for, but consideration must first be given to certain weaknesses in the above data which may also affect the validity of the results. In the first place it should constantly be borne in mind that some irregularity in the figures is to be expected in view of the paucity of information on which some of the calculations have been based. Secondly, the inclusion of settlements on each occasion of their enumeration, especially when there are only a few places in a particular category, could conceivably distort both the distribution of settlements by size and all calculations relating to the household size of settlements comprised within that category. For example, the mean household size of the medium-sized settlements reflects in the main the larger than average households of industrialising Lancashire. Another more important weakness is caused by the old problem of the confusion between household and houseful size. At an early stage of the analysis, it was decided, in the light. of the warning given in the Census of Great Britain in 1801,[89] to

[89] See above, pp. 160–161.

Table 5.6   *Household size by size of settlement, 1751–1800 and 1801; those settlements only where the number of inhabited houses equals the number of families in 1801*

	Period 1751–1800				Census of Great Britain 1801			
Size of settlement	No. of settle-ments	Over-all mean	Mean of means	Median	No. of settle-ments	Over-all mean	Mean of means	Median
Under 100	8	5.87	6.86	6.12	9	5.23	5.66	5.24
100–499	23	4.99	5.10	5.02	20	5.08	5.25	5.06
500–999	12	4.87	5.01	4.74	9	5.00	5.00	4.93
1,000+	5	4.18	4.25	4.25	10	4.46	4.88	4.77
Agglomerations[a]	11	5.37	5.34	5.45	11	5.46	5.49	5.58

[a] Included in this category are places part only of which had been enumerated as well as units covering more than one settlement.

exclude for comparative purposes all places where the number of inhabited houses in 1801 was said to equal or exceed the number of families. The latter situation is manifestly impossible and exclusion of places of this nature needs no justification, but the first class of settlement cannot be dismissed so easily.

'HOUSEHOLD' AND 'HOUSEFUL'

Looking in Table 5.6 at the change between the time of first enumeration and 1801, a substantial increase in mean 'household' size is to be observed in all categories of settlement except the smallest.[90] This trend, which is more definite than those suggested by the previous analysis, together with the fact that the figures are on the whole far higher than was found in other places in 1801, tends to support the view that in many instances the persons who enumerated those settlements in 1801 failed to make the correct distinction between houseful and household. However, a more disturbing picture emerges when the overall means of the original enumerations are compared with the figures in Table 5.5. It immediately emerges that, with one exception, the mean household size of these settlements was considerably higher than that found in other places of similar size.[91] Two conclusions are possible. The first is that there was some special feature of the communities that made it impossible on both occasions to make the appropriate distinction between houses and households. This is perhaps less likely than the alternative hypothesis that these were genuine instances of one family per house. In the absence of the enumeration schedules it is impossible to decide the matter with any certainty, but the probability must be that some

[90] The difference is insecure statistically since the 95 % confidence limits of the medians overlap.
[91] Since in each size group the 95 % confidence limits of the medians overlap, this result is also statistically insecure.

Table 5.7   *Household and houseful size by region 1751–1801*[a]

Region	Period	No. of settle- ments		Overall mean	Mean of means	Median
East	1751–1800	17	household	4.71	4.99	4.83
			houseful	5.66	6.40	6.09
East	1801	17	household	4.71	4.78	4.60
			houseful	5.77	6.49	6.10
North and Central	1751–1800	20	household	4.70	4.77	4.73
			houseful	6.08	5.48	5.26
North and Central	1801	20	household	4.53	4.79	4.83
			houseful	6.21	5.75	5.40
South and West	1751–1800	8	household	4.65	5.03	4.50
			houseful	5.13	6.71	5.63
South and West	1801	8	household	4.87	5.20	5.28
			houseful	5.60	6.98	6.34

[a] Settlements enumerated on more than one occasion have been counted once at the later date. Places in which in 1801 the number of families equalled or exceeded the number of houses have been excluded.

settlements with genuinely large households have been mistakenly excluded and that the figures in Table 5.5 relating in particular to places with fewer than 100 people ought to be revised upwards. The effect, however, would be to accentuate and not to change the general pattern of the relationship between household and settlement size both in itself and as regards the variation between the time of the original enumeration and 1801. It is more difficult to gauge the effect on the regional analysis of Table 5.4 but settlements, when distributed amongst the various counties, are sufficiently few in number to render unnecessary anything more than minor modifications to the figures.

Also of great interest are places in which there was a sharp difference between mean household and mean houseful size. The evidence for these settlements is presented in Tables 5.7 and 5.8.

Although details were available for only forty-five places, there is no reason to consider the settlements as completely unrepresentative, at least in so far as household size is concerned (cf. Table 5.2). This does not mean that the difference between mean houseful and mean household size – about 10 % in the north and central region, 20 % in the south and 25 % in the east – is necessarily typical of those regions, let alone that there were in any one area many settlements with mean household sizes approximating to this average. The differences between overall mean, mean of means and median again imply the contrasting patterns of different communities. A more thorough analysis, however, is hindered by the small number of settlements for which the information is available.[92]

[92] The small number of settlements in each category means that the above results may lack statistical significance.

Table 5.8   *Change·in mean household size by change in mean houseful size, 1751–1801*

Change in mean houseful size	Change in mean household size[a]									
	In-crease 1.00+	In-crease 0.50–0.99	In-crease 0.10–0.49	In-crease 0.01–0.09	No change	De-crease 0.01–0.09	De-crease 0.10–0.49	De-crease 0.50–0.99	De-crease 1.00+	Total
Increase 1.00+	2	3	1	—	—	—	2	—	—	8
Increase 0.50–0.99	—	3	4	1	—	—	2	1	—	11
Increase 0.10–0.49	—	1	3	2	—	—	4	1	—	11
Increase 0.01–0.09	—	—	1	—	—	—	—	—	—	1
No change	—	—	—	—	—	—	—	—	—	—
Decrease 0.01–0.09	—	—	—	—	—	—	—	—	—	—
Decrease 0.10–0.49	—	—	2	—	—	1	2	—	—	5
Decrease 0.50–0.99	—	—	—	—	—	1	—	1	—	2
Decrease 1.00+	—	—	—	—	—	—	3	—	4	7
Total	2	7	11	3	0	2	13	3	4	45

[a] Settlements enumerated on more than one occasion have been counted once at the later date. Places in which in 1801 the number of families equalled or exceeded the number of houses have been excluded.

The relationship between household and houseful size is basically a simple one. Houses being composed of one or more households, any increase in the number of household members must be followed by an increase in houseful size, and this is exactly what occurred in two of the three regions. The relationship is, however, complicated by the presence of inmates, for example lodgers, in various houses and obscured by the difficulty experienced by the enumerator in making an appropriate division between these smaller units and the household proper. The importance of these factors emerges when a comparison is made of the variation in household and houseful size in each settlement (Table 5.8).

It is immediately apparent that while the settlements in which house*hold* size increased between the time of original enumeration and 1801 were balanced by those in which it decreased, places in which during the same period there was a rise in house*ful* size occurred over twice as frequently as places in which there was a fall.[93] In several instances, therefore, a decrease in house*hold* size must be associated with an increase in house*ful* size, although the majority of the latter were restricted to cases involving only a moderate reduction in household size.[94] The relationship between the changes in household and houseful size demands the closest attention. Looking first at those settlements which increased in house*ful* size, the distribution of changes in house*hold* size was

[93] The binomial test showed that the latter result was statistically significant ($Z \simeq 2\cdot5$).
[94] This result was not statistically significant according to the binomial test because of the small number of settlements involved ($Z < 2$).

found to be fairly even $(Z < 2)$. However, almost all the settlements which increased in house*hold* size also experienced an increase in house*ful* size.[95] In other words, it was almost certain that mean house*ful* size would increase if mean house*hold* size increased, while a higher mean house*ful* size did not necessarily imply an increase in mean house*hold* size. In the absence of detailed information on the economic background of the relevant settlements, interpretation is both difficult and dangerous. One possibility is that in certain settlements an acute housing shortage was overcome not by young adults delaying marriage and therefore remaining longer as servants, or as dependents in their parents' household, but by an increase in the number of households sharing a dwelling with at least one other household. Yet a shortage of housing is also one of the signs of rapid population growth, and the final section of this analysis is therefore devoted to the influence of this factor on variations in household size.

MEAN HOUSEHOLD SIZE AND POPULATION GROWTH[96]

Table 5.9 shows the mean household size of 181 settlements at the time of original enumeration. Comparable figures for 1801 (Table 5.10) show that during the course of the late eighteenth century there had been a downward movement in mean household size. The most marked reduction is to be observed in the frequency of settlements with a very high mean household size. At the same time the number of settlements in which there were fewer than four persons to a household almost doubled. Indeed the only exceptions to this general pattern are to be found among settlements with mean household sizes ranging from 4.50 to 5.49. Nevertheless it is impossible to prove that the changes were statistically significant.[97]

The tables, however, reveal not only the distribution of mean household sizes at different periods but the relationship between this distribution and the extent to which the population had changed since the date of the original enumeration. The object, here, was to see whether any group of settlements with a mean household size of a particular value were more or less subject than others to an increase in population. Similarly, it was thought that it would be interesting to look at the problem from the opposite angle, to attempt to establish, for example, whether there was any tendency for places which experienced the largest increase in population to have in 1801 households significantly larger than or smaller than the average. It should not be forgotten, however, that the period concerned is one in which many settlements were experiencing a growth and sometimes a substantial

[95] The binomial test showed that it was extremely unlikely that this second result could have arisen by chance $(Z > 3)$.
[96] In Japan during the Tokugawa era, the relationship between these two seems to have been somewhat different, see below, Hayami, Chapter 18, pp. 506–507. Greven, however, Chapter 20, p. 555, sees rapid population growth as one of the factors behind a rise in mean household size in Hampshire, Massachusetts in the latter half of the eighteenth century.
[97] This conclusion is based on the Kolmogorov-Smirnov two tailed two sample test $(P > 0.10)$.

Table 5.9   *Mean household size 1751–1800 by population growth 1751–1801[a]*

Percentage change in population	Mean household size						
	Under 4	4.00–4.49	4.50–4.99	5.00–5.49	5.50–5.99	Above 6	Total
Increase 100 % +	—	7	5	2	—	1	15
Increase 50–99 %	—	7	7	1	1	1	17
Increase 10–49 %	4	23	23	14	5	—	69
Increase 1–9 %	3	11	16	5	5	3	43
No change	—	—	1	—	1	—	2
Decrease 1–9 %	1	3	7	4	10	1	26
Decrease 10–49 %	—	1	1	4	2	—	8
Decrease 50–99 %	—	—	—	—	1	—	1
Total	8	52	60	30	25	6	181

[a] Settlements enumerated on more than one occasion have been counted once at the later date. Places in which in 1801 the number of families equalled or exceeded the number of houses have been excluded.

Table 5.10   *Mean household size 1801 by population growth 1751–1801[a]*

Percentage change in population	Mean household size						
	Under 4	4.00–4.49	4.50–4.99	5.00–5.49	5.50–5.99	Above 6	Total
Increase 100 % +	—	1	4	7	3	—	15
Increase 50–99 %	—	4	7	4	2	—	17
Increase 10–49 %	7	21	16	19	4	2	69
Increase 1–9 %	3	15	16	5	2	2	43
No change	—	1	—	—	1	—	2
Decrease 1–9 %	2	9	6	7	2	—	26
Decrease 10–49 %	2	5	—	—	1	—	8
Decrease 50–99 %	1	—	—	—	—	—	1
Total	15	56	49	42	15	4	181

[a] Settlements enumerated on more than one occasion have been counted once at the later date. Places in which in 1801 the number of families equalled or exceeded the number of houses have been excluded.

growth in population. In the case of 32 settlements (17 % of the total) the increase in inhabitants from the time of first enumeration exceeded 50 %. This compares with the 35 places (19 %) in which some decrease was recorded. If not exactly rare, places which come within these categories were somewhat exceptional. It is therefore particularly interesting that settlements in these two groups appear to have had originally (Table 5.9) a more consistent mean household size than the larger number of places which experienced a moderate increase in population. Thus of the 35 settlements which were to suffer a decline in population 14 had more than 5.5 persons per household. A Kolmogorov-Smirnov one tailed two sample test of the differences in M.H.S. between settlements which lost and those which were increasing moderately in population was significant at the 1 % level (0.001 < P < 0.01). On the other hand, the future centres of fast growth show remarkably low values for mean household size. In this case, however, a Kolmogorov-Smirnov two tailed two sample test of the differences in mean household size between settlements which were increasing strongly in population and those which were increasing only moderately in population yielded a result that was not statistically significant (P > 0.10). In 1801 (Table 5.10), the settlements which had experienced the most dramatic increase in population tended to have the largest mean household sizes, while villages which had lost inhabitants during the intervening period were over-represented amongst settlements with under 4.5 persons per household.[98]

Some transfer of people from one type of settlement to the other may be implied, but it is impossible to be sure about this because the factors which caused the variations in household size are unknown. With rather more certainty it can be stated that settlements with a considerable number of large households seem to have been unable to expand at the same rate as settlements composed mainly of smaller households. However, it seems difficult to see why a lack of regular employment or an overstraining of a village's resources, two likely causes of declining population, should particularly affect settlements with a preponderance of large households, unless it can be assumed that a shortage of cottages for newly married couples was the critical factor behind the high mean size. It is hoped further information will become available as a result of a detailed analysis of parish register evidence but a shortage of both time and space preclude such an examination here. Meanwhile, in order to examine in yet greater detail the relationship between population change and household size, a further table (5.11) was devised in which, for each settlement, the growth or decline in population since the time of original enumeration was related to the alteration in mean household size.

Settlements in which mean household size fell (53 % of all settlements) were less numerous than might have been expected on the basis of the figures discussed earlier. The apparent discrepancy arises from the fact that settlements in which there was an increase in household size were significantly outnumbered only in the group of places in which the variation in household size was greatest. More revealing, however, is the rarity with which there was a rise in household size at the same time as there was a decline in overall population (only 5 cases in 35).[99] The fact that net outward migration[100] was not associated with an increase in

---

[98] Neither of these results was statistically significant according to the Kolmogorov-Smirnov two tailed two sample test (in the former 0.05 < P < 0.10; in the latter P > 0.10).
[99] The binomial test showed that the result was highly significant (Z > 15).
[100] It is recognised that variations in fertility and mortality also determine population trends but this does not affect the argument.

Table 5.11   *Change in mean household size by population growth 1751–1801[a]*

Percentage change in population	Mean household size									
	In-crease 1.00+	In-crease 0.50– 0.99	In-crease 0.10– 0.49	In-crease 0.01– 0.09	No change	De-crease 0.01– 0.09	De-crease 0.10– 0.49	De-crease 0.50– 0.99	De-crease 1.00+	Total
Increase 100% +	3	3	5	1	—	—	1	1	1	15
Increase 50–99 %	1	4	6	—	—	—	2	3	1	17
Increase 10–49 %	3	14	17	5	1	5	16	4	4	69
Increase 1–9 %	2	4	7	2	—	6	10	6	6	43
No change	—	—	—	—	1	—	1	—	—	2
Decrease 1–9 %	—	—	2	2	—	4	6	4	8	26
Decrease 10–49 %	—	1	—	—	—	—	1	3	3	8
Decrease 50–99 %	—	—	—	—	—	—	—	—	1	1
Total	9	26	37	10	2	15	37	21	24	181

[a] Settlements enumerated on more than one occasion have been counted at the later date. Places in which in 1801 the number of families equalled or exceeded the number of houses have been excluded.

the size of the remaining households seems to imply that the migrants were drawn from a large number of households rather than from a few units in particular. An alternative explanation, which cannot at present be ruled out, is that the reduction in population eased the employment and housing situation for the remaining residents, thus promoting the subdivision of some of the larger households. The other results of the analysis are no less interesting. Since settlements which experienced a decline in population (35) occurred less frequently than those in which there was a fall in mean household size (97), it is inevitable that there must be some settlements in which population rose at the same time as household size fell. Of these 66 places, however, 37 experienced only modest growth and a moderate decrease in household size.[101]

The important point in this is that given an increase in mean household size it would be possible to predict an overall increase in population whereas it would be impossible to infer from a growth in population that there had been a similar increase in mean household size. Indeed, a little reflection will show that mean household size cannot in justice be expected to vary with every fluctuation in the overall numbers of inhabitants. For example, the movement of gentlemen and their families into and out of small parishes and the growth of artisan communities in industrial areas will each influence the mean household size of the settlement concerned to such an extent as to obliterate the evidence of any change due to a variation in the number of residents.

[101] According to the binomial test this result was significant at 0.001 ($Z \simeq 3$).

CONCLUSION

The purpose of this study has been to assess the relative effect on mean household size of such factors as location, size of settlement and population growth and decline. The statistical tests would suggest that the crucial relationship was between mean household size and population change, but it cannot be assumed from this that all the other factors were insignificant, since many of the categories into which the settlements have been divided are so small that it would be unlikely if many of the results were significant in the statistical sense. One thing, however, is clear; much is to be learnt about the history of the household from a study of the 'literary' evidence. Although a nationwide picture of the relationship between household size and population growth may be slow to emerge, at least one contemporary observer, in attempting to trace the effect of the removal of houses on the overall population of the parish of Shrewsbury Holy Cross, has left evidence which could be used as part of a detailed study of migration, fertility and changes in mean houseful size.[102] This is the direction in which future research may be expected to move but clearly much work has to be done before the factors affecting the mean size of the household can be fully appreciated.

[102] Details in Price (1803) II: 397–8.

6. A note on the household structure of mid-nineteenth-century York in comparative perspective

W. A. Armstrong

In this chapter I intend to compare the household structure of mid-nineteenth-century York[1] with that of the pre-industrial settlements described by Mr Laslett.[2] Certain similarities are immediately apparent, for example, in the overall mean household size and in the proportion of the population in households of various sizes.[3]

It is possible, however, to draw attention to some further close similarities and important differences in household structure,[4] although in the event such an elaboration and any generalisations based upon it may turn out to be somewhat premature, for the following reasons:

1. The York statistics require slight revision. When the sample of 781 households was drawn from the census enumerators' books a few years ago a rather different convention was used for the demarcation of households from that recently and persuasively recommended by Dr Anderson.[5] A preliminary check

---

[1] Some results have already been published, see Armstrong, *The interpretation of census enumerators' books* (1968).

[2] See above, Laslett, Chapter 4, pp. 125–158.

[3] See below, Tables 6.1 and 6.2. For the proportion of households of sizes 1 to 13 and over, see above, Laslett, Chapter 4, pp. 142–143.

[4] Most of the York results quoted here, like the statistics quoted in Armstrong (1968), are based on an analysis of 781 households – a 1 in 10 sample. Wherever available, (e.g. Tables 6.6 and 6.8), I have used printed census data for the whole population in preference.

[5] By far the greater proportion of households are unambiguous cases, and would be treated identically under either convention. Each household begins with a 'head' (so described), and is concluded by a long line; another 'head' begins the next household, and so on. But in some urban areas the practice of enumerators in distributing schedules varied, as did the way in which they interpreted the instruction to rule short and long lines in the enumeration books between different occupiers and distinct dwellings. See *Census of Great Britain, 1851. Population Tables I* P.P. (1852–3) LXXXV: cxlii. For York I used the longer line to distinguish households, and it will be appreciated that in a few cases, a household so defined could include more than one person designated as 'head'. I should strongly recommend future researchers to follow Dr Anderson's advice. He argues that with one or two specified exceptions, the household (co-residing group is his preferred terminology), should comprise all the names following one designated head, and that the introduction of a new head should mark the cut-off point where a new household begins. See M. Anderson, *Standard tabulation prodecures* (1972 ii).

Table 6.1   *Mean household size*

| 100 pre-industrial communities | 4.77 |
| York, 1851 ($n = 781$) | 4.70 |

Table 6.2   *Proportion of total population in households of various sizes (%)*

	1–3	4–5	6 and over
100 pre-industrial communities	17.5	30.5	53.0
York, 1851 (n = 3,670)	17.6	29.5	52.9

shows that some 34 out of 781 households will require attention (truncation), which will entail a fairly substantial reduction in my original count of lodgers, and slightly affect mean size and distribution of households. On the other hand, other York statistics to be quoted in this paper (pertaining to children, relatives and servants), will be unaffected by such a revision.

2. Mr Laslett's present figures are in the main the outcome of a gigantic averaging process which may conceal significant regional and temporal variations.

3. It is not obvious how far York's social structure and demography can be assumed to be representative of English towns in general in the middle of the nineteenth century. It was decidedly not a modern industrial city since true factory or large-scale production was unknown there, and steam engines a rarity outside the recently arrived railway yards and workshops of the 1840s. 'We have no manufactures, we have no complicated machinery in operation, we have no weavers, no dyers, no shipbuilders, no mines', commented a newspaper correspondent in 1827, and throughout the century York remained primarily a market centre for agricultural produce and a place where goods and services were sold. Except for railways the community remained steadfastly 'pre-industrial' in 1851. This may mean that York was more typical of urban England in general than any manufacturing town could have been at that time, bearing in mind the notable regional concentration of advanced industry, and Clapham's contention that in 1851, the voyage to the 'industry state' was not yet half over.[6] Nevertheless, York was by no means stagnant. Once England's second city, it was still twenty-ninth in size in 1851 – bigger than Cardiff, Exeter, Halifax, Huddersfield, Ipswich, Southampton and Swansea. Further, its population had risen from 16,846 to 36,303, that is by 115 % between 1801 and 1851. This reflects a rather faster rate of growth than the national figure and was distinctly greater than the growth achieved by Bath, Chester, Exeter, Norwich, Nottingham, Reading, Shrewsbury,

[6] Clapham, *Economic history of modern Britain* (1950) I: 42, II: 22. The most useful discussions of York's nineteenth-century economy are Duckham, *The economic development of York* (1956), and Sigsworth, *Modern York* (1961). The newspaper quotation is from the *York Herald*, 25 May 1827.

Table 6.3   *Size of households by social status*

				York 1851			
				Individual classes		Combined classes (I & II: IV & V)	
	Pre-industrial communities[a]						
	N	Overall mean		N	Overall mean	N	Overall mean
Gentlemen	26	6.63	Class I	59	6.02	} 166	5.31
Clergy	25	5.83	Class II	107	4.93		
Yeomen	21	5.91	Class III	386	4.66	386	4.66
Husbandmen	35	5.09	Class IV	103	4.15	} 201	4.48
Tradesmen and craftsmen	40	4.65	Class V	98	4.80		
Labourers	33	4.51					
Paupers	16	3.96					

[a] See above, Laslett, Chapter 4, p. 154.

Wakefield, Warrington and Yarmouth, in the same period.[7] York had therefore been the scene of extended urbanisation, and in the 1840s exhibited many of the apparently inescapable symptoms of this in terms of public health problems, fairly high death rates, etc.

With these reservations in mind, two further tables (6.3 and 6.4) may be brought forward to show that there were several other respects in which York's social structure closely resembled that of Laslett's pre-industrial communities – or, put otherwise, to show that other pre-industrial characteristics were still evident in a growing mid-nineteenth-century town of York's type.

First, there is a strong suggestion that household size and social status were positively related in both societies, even though the respective schemes of stratification have nothing in common other than that they both attempt an ordered hierarchy,[8] and the class V result for York appears to be out of line.

Mr Laslett attributes this feature partly to in-service (domestics *and* trade assistants), which at once tended to augment higher class households while depleting the lower of their adolescent children.[9] Certainly the superior household size of classes I and II in York owed a great deal to this factor, since on the average each such householder employed 1.15 domestics. I feel less sure about

[7] These approximate calculations are based on data published in Mitchell and Deane, *Abstract of British historical statistics* (1962): 24–6.

[8] The rationale behind the application of a slightly modified Registrar-General's scheme of social stratification to 1851 data is discussed in Armstrong, *The use of information about occupation* (1972). Mr Laslett's hierarchy is described as having grown out of the material, being an adaptation from Gregory King and other census takers working in pre-Census times. See above, Laslett, Chapter 4, pp. 152–153.

[9] Laslett, *The World we have lost* (1965 i): 64–5, 70 and *Remarks on the multiplier* (1965 ii).

Table 6.4   *Distribution of households by marital status of heads* (%)

	70 pre-industrial communities (means of proportions)[a]	York 1851 (n = 781)
Married couples	70.4	73.0
Widowers	5.2	4.9
Widows	12.9	13.8
Single males	2.1	3.4
Single females	1.1	4.9
Unspecified males	5.0	—
Unspecified females	2.3	—

[a] See above, Laslett, Chapter 4, p. 147.

the reciprocal effect on classes III, IV and V, since the overwhelming majority of York's domestics were drawn from outside the city.[10]

Secondly, the distribution of marital status of household heads is closely similar, except that Laslett was unable to place 7.3% of his household heads. Notice however, that the 2.3% described as 'unspecified females' could not, however distributed, have raised the proportion of single female heads in the pre-industrial communities to the level prevailing in York.

Table 6.5 brings out a still more remarkable parallel, and suggests that despite the views of some of the men of the time, in reality society's experience of what was 'usual' or 'ordinary' in the distribution of family size (meaning, in this context, children), perhaps did not change very much over the years. On the other hand it should be emphasised that many different combinations of fertility and child mortality could give rise to the same pattern; it does not follow that the levels prevailing in York in the 1840s were also typical levels of pre-industrial society.

Table 6.5   *Proportion of children in groups of various sizes* (%)

Group size	66 pre-industrial communities (means of proportions)[a]	York, 1851 (n = 517)
1	11.2	11.7
2	18.4	19.8
3	23.1	22.1
4	18.1	18.6
5	13.4	11.6
6	7.7	7.4
7 and over	7.2	9.4

[a] See above, Laslett, Chapter 4, p. 148

[10] Of all domestic servants in York municipal borough in 1851, 67.5% were born in the three Ridings excluding York itself. Armstrong, *The social structure of York, 1841–51* (1967).

Table 6.6   *Sex ratios*

	Males per 100 females
70 pre-industrial communities[a]	91.3
York, 1851 (Census: printed volumes)	87.8
England and Wales, 1851	95.6

[a] See above, Laslett, Chapter 4, p. 145.

Table 6.7   *Proportions married, widowed and single* (%)

	Married %	Widowed %	Single %
(i) Males			
61 pre-industrial communities[a]	34.8	3.5	61.7
England and Wales, 1851	33.7	3.8	62.5
(ii) Females			
61 pre-industrial communities	32.1	8.7	59.2
England and Wales, 1851	33.0	7.2	59.8

[a] See above, Laslett, Chapter 4, p. 145

Table 6.8   *Proportions married, widowed and single* (*per 1,000 aged 20 and over*)

		Married %	Widowed %	Single %
York Registration	Males	61.0	6·8	32.2
district, 1851	Females	53.4	13.3	33.4
England and	Males	62.6	7.1	30.2
Wales, 1851	Females	58.7	13.0	28.3

So far we have stressed some of the main similarities between Laslett's pre-industrial communities and York in 1851. We shall now turn to some clear differences, the first of which is demographic. York's surplus of females was larger than that in Laslett's communities and even greater than in England and Wales as a whole in 1851 (Table 6.6).[11]

Further, while the distribution of marital status in England and Wales in 1851 and in Laslett's communities was very similar (Table 6.7), York clearly had more single adult females than did the country as a whole in 1851 (Table 6.8). It is therefore likely that York had more single females than did the pre-industrial communities, although the comparison is indirect (see also Table 6.4).

[11] London had a similarly large surplus of females, attributed by the census authorities to the presence of large numbers of female domestics and of women preparing articles of dress. *Census of Great Britain, 1851. Population Tables II* P.P. (1852–3) LXXXVIII: xxvi. However, neither London nor York were extreme cases when the proportion of *married* females aged 20 and over is considered (as in Table 6.8). Their respective proportions stood at 53.3% and 53.4%, as against 48.9% for Exeter, 44.9% for Cheltenham, and 42.7% for Bath.

Table 6.9   *Statistics of children*

	66 pre-industrial communities[a]	York 1851
(i) Proportion in population	42.6%	37.4% (n = 3,670)
(ii) Proportion of households with children	74.6%	66.2% (n = 781)

[a] See above, Laslett, Chapter 4, p. 148.

This difference is probably responsible for the further finding that children were a somewhat lower proportion of the population than in pre-industrial England, and that slightly fewer York households contained children (Table 6.9).

It will be appreciated that this feature would work in the direction of lowering mean household size in York, as would the fact that fewer York households had resident servants than is found with Mr Laslett's communities – 19.7% as against 28.5%. It must be pointed out that Laslett's figures include trade assistants, apprentices etc., and that the York figures relate to domestics only. To have included trade assistants with the York servants would have closed the gap to some extent, but not fully, since many households with such assistants also had domestic servants. Thus, although York was well-endowed with servants by comparison with other urban communities in 1851 (see Table 6.12 below), there are grounds for thinking that the proportion was rather lower than in the pre-industrial communities.

Counter-balancing tendencies seem evident when we go on to consider kinship co-residence and the incidence of lodging. The proportion of resident kin in the population, and proportion of households with kin, is seen to be about twice as great in York, as in the pre-industrial communities. This is also reflected in a higher proportion of three-generational households (Tables 6.10 and 6.11).

The proportion of households with lodgers was clearly far higher in York. For reasons mentioned above, my evidence on this point is open to question, and an initial computation that 21.3% of households contained lodgers will have to be reduced as a consequence of redrawing some household boundaries. Even so, the figure in question will not fall below about 15%, while Laslett insists that outside London, there were very few lodgers indeed in pre-industrial England.[12]

Summarising this elementary analysis of 'components', it would appear that

[12] See Laslett, *Size and structure of the household in England over three centuries* (1969). This conclusion has now been revised (see above, Laslett, Chapter 4, p. 134). Only nine listings of inhabitants in pre-industrial England (exclusive of London) record the presence of lodgers but in these settlements the proportion of households with lodgers is as high as 14.7%, a figure in line with the above findings for mid-nineteenth-century York. For the number of lodgers in certain other nineteenth-century communities, see below, Anderson, Chapter 7, p. 220.

Table 6.10 *Resident kin*

	46 pre-industrial communities[a]	York 1851
Proportion of resident kin in population (%)	3.4	6·4 (n = 3,670)
Proportion of households with resident kin (%)	10.1	21·6 (n = 781)

[a] See above, Laslett, Chapter 4, p. 149.

Table 6.11 *Multi-generational households*

	61 pre-industrial communities[a]	York 1851 (n = 781)
Proportion of households containing 1 generation (%)	23.7	32.9
Proportion of households containing 2 generations (%)	70.4	58.5
Proportion of households containing 3 generations (%)	5.8	8.6

[a] See above, Laslett, Chapter 4, p. 153.

two features of York society making for a rather higher household size than that characteristic of pre-industrial England (presence of more kin and lodgers), were being cancelled out approximately by two opposed features – rather fewer servants, and a higher proportion of households headed by single females, widows, etc. which were less likely to contain children. Put otherwise – if such a crude distinction is permissible – two 'social structural' variables were higher, one social structural and one 'demographic' variable were lower, the net effect of which was to leave mean household size in York at much the same level as in pre-industrial England.[13]

Can one generalise from these findings, especially bearing in mind the initial reservation regarding the typicality of York? It is not possible to delve further here into whether or not the demographic difference which I have alluded to was peculiar to York, but a certain amount of comparative material on the social structural aspects (lodging, kin co-residence and in-service), is now to hand. A document recently drawn up by Professor K. M. Drake and Mrs C. G. Pearce shows that in Ashford in 1851 (mean household size 4.85), the proportion of households with kin was 21.0, with lodgers 17.5, with servants (domestic only), 16.9 %.[14] Ashford and York, apart from absolute size, clearly had much

[13] The overall constancy in mean household size is viewed in a wider context by Laslett, above, Chapter 4, pp. 139–143, 156–157. See also Anderson, Chapter 7, pp. 234–235.
[14] These are among the first results to emerge from this important study, and I am grateful for permission to quote.

in common from an economic point of view, since both were primarily market towns with developing railway interests as their sole concession to modernity. Also, Dr R. J. Smith has studied Nottingham, which was much more obviously industrialised and heavily dependent on hosiery and lacemaking, although it should be noted that in 1851, little steam power was used and the typical unit of production was small. Here, with average household size standing at 4.47, the proportions of households with kin, lodgers and servants were 17.3 %, 21.8 % and 11.7 % respectively.[15] When these figures are compared with Mr Laslett's, the main differences are again along the same lines as those indicated for York – fewer households containing servants, more containing lodgers and kin.[16]

Beyond these cases, a rough idea of household structure in other mid-nine-teenth-century communities may be gained from the published Census Report of 1851 and in particular from the detailed analysis of family structure in fourteen sub-districts.[17] A major problem, however, is that some bachelors, spinsters and widowed persons were classed in the relevant tables as heads of families and their status as lodgers ignored.[18] To circumvent this difficulty I have tried to set upper and lower limits to the number of households, based on two assumptions:

A. That *all* the 'sole'[19] married couples, widowed persons, bachelors and spinsters were really separate households, and would be so treated by a present-day researcher, working on Anderson's principles (see above, p. 205).

B. That *none* of these people would be so treated; that they would all be classed as lodgers and would not count as households in a modern analysis.[20]

The data for fourteen sub-districts may now be used to calculate the proportion of households with servants, trade assistants and kin, with upper and lower limits to the divisor. Thus for Witley in Surrey, summing the relevant columns shows that 436 census families contained servants. Using as the divisor the *total* number of families (3,112 on assumption A), the proportion with servants is 14.0. On assumption B, i.e. omitting 625 'sole' married couples, widowed persons and bachelors and spinsters, the proportion is 19.0 %. The whole of Table 6.12 is drawn up on this principle.

[15] R. J. Smith, *Social structure of Nottingham* (1968). I have used here only the results from this study previously quoted in Armstrong (1968). Dr Smith used the 'York' conventions for the demarcation of households described in footnote 5 above, so that the incidence of lodging may be slightly overstated. The standard economic and social history of this town is Church, *Economic and social change in a Midland town* (1966).

[16] For the proportion of households with lodgers in Preston and rural Lancashire in 1851, see below, Anderson, Chapter 7, p. 220. But see footnote 12, above.

[17] *Census of Great Britain, 1851. Population Tables I* (1852–3): XL, c–ci.

[18] In the original schedules, lodgers even when married, were rarely counted as separate families, see above, Wall, Chapter 5, p. 160.

[19] I.e. no other co-resident member of the family (defined as parents, children, relatives, visitors, servants and trade assistants).

[20] On balance assumption B is almost certainly the more realistic: see footnote 18, above.

Table 6.12 *Proportion of households with (i) servants (ii) trade assistants (iii) relatives, in 14 sub-districts, 1851 (%)*

Registration sub-district	Servants		Trade assistants		Relatives	
	(A)	(B)	(A)	(B)	(A)	(B)
Hambleton, Witley, Surrey	14.0	19.0	1.8	2.4	15.0	20.3
Godstone, Godstone, Surrey	14.9	19.9	1.3	1.7	16.0	21.4
Skirlaugh, Skirlaugh, Yorks	25.3	31.1	3.8	4.7	25.1	30.8
Newcastle on Tyne, All Saints	8.5	12.2	0.4	0.6	13.1	18.7
Carlisle, St Mary	9.7	13.7	1.2	1.7	17.2	24.1
Leeds, North Leeds	4.8	7.5	0.5	0.8	13.7	21.3
Birmingham, St Martin	8.7	14.6	1.1	1.9	12.0	20.1
Hull, St Mary	8.1	12.8	1.8	2.8	12.5	19.8
Shrewsbury, St Chad	19.8	29.6	3.5	5.2	13.6	20.3
Marylebone, Rectory	15.5	25.1	3.3	5.4	10.5	17.1
Bristol Castle Precincts	19.9	31.3	3.4	5.4	14.1	22.2
Hanover Square, Mayfair	44.4	63.2	5.0	7.0	12.4	17.6
Manchester, Deansgate	6.6	11.1	0.9	1.6	11.2	18.9
Liverpool, Howard Street	4.9	8.2	0.5	0.8	9.9	16.7
All 14 communities	10.9	17.0	1.5	2.3	12.6	19.7

Clearly, the 'margins of error' are quite large, and it is obvious that individual sub-districts will not necessarily typify the towns in which they are situated. Even so, I believe that a number of interesting inferences can be drawn from Table 6.12 which support the views already tentatively advanced as a result of comparing York, Ashford and Nottingham with Mr Laslett's pre-industrial communities. These are as follows:

1. In-service was on the whole a good deal less evident than in Laslett's communities. Even on the least favourable assumption to the case (B), the proportion of households with servants averages only 17.0%, as against Laslett's 28.5%. This conclusion still stands even if the maximum figure for households with trade assistants is *added* (2.3%), which is in any case unrealistic as a certain proportion of households would have had both.

2. The pattern of variation is also interesting, and may point to the direction of change. In Table 6.12 the communities with an above-average proportion of servant-keeping households included (apart from Mayfair and Marylebone), three rural sub-districts, and the select quarters of two ancient cities, Shrewsbury and Bristol. By contrast, the lowest proportions of servant-keeping households were the Leeds, Liverpool and Manchester sub-districts. Together with Newcastle All Saints, these three also had the lowest proportion of households with trade assistants, probably reflecting a high proportion of purely wage-earning households.

3. With the exception of Skirlaugh (by far the smallest of the communities),

8

the proportion of households with kin is not so varied as one might have imagined. Overall, the proportion lay between 12.6 and 19.7 (probably very much nearer the second figure), and it would therefore appear that the incidence of kin co-residence had been significantly raised across the whole of English society, bearing in mind Laslett's tentative pre-industrial proportion of 10.1 %.

For reasons already explained, Table 6.12 tells us nothing of lodging, but the figures quoted for York, Nottingham and Ashford strongly suggest that the proportion of householders with lodgers was sharply up in all expanding urban situations. This would certainly accord with commonly held presumptions that rapid population growth and migration into towns must have put severe pressure on housing. Concluding a useful review of the different sources on this point Professor Flinn has recently said that 'there is probably just sufficient evidence to say that the increasing share of the national income going to rent indicated a steadily mounting pressure of urban population on the supply of housing'.[21]

The findings discussed in this chapter suggest that the constancy of mean household size concealed a series of shifts in household composition by 1851, of the greatest interest to social historians. These features demand more detailed analysis before satisfactory explanations can be assembled.[22] I have said little or nothing about possible changes in the mean size of the *nuclear* families and sibling groups at the core of each household, but by contrast these may have been quite slight in most communities: present evidence seems to indicate that the still-mysterious changes in fertility and mortality accounting for population increase resulted in a multiplication of family units of approximately 'traditional' average size. The following table,[23] drawn from the various studies quoted in this chapter, appears to support the possibility that the size of family units might even have fallen slightly:

Table 6.13   *Mean size of nuclear family*

	Average size of nuclear families	Average number of children
Laslett's pre-industrial communities	3.8	2.1
York, 1851	3.5	1.8
Ashford, 1851	3.6	1.9
Nottingham, 1851	3.5	1.8

[21] Flinn, Introduction to Chadwick, *Report on the sanitary condition of the labouring population* (1965): 3–7.

[22] Dr Anderson's close analysis of the household structure of Preston in this volume, see below, Chapter 7, pp. 215–235, points the way, for example by posing the question, who were the kin?

[23] Dr Anderson's Preston figures do not accord with this generalisation, however, the mean family size being 4.2 and average number of children 2.5. In his chapter he attributes the high mean for children partly to age-composition factors, and partly to the fact that Preston provided special opportunities to remain in the parental home right up to the point of marriage. See below, Anderson, Chapter 7, pp. 232–233.

7. Household structure and the industrial revolution; mid-nineteenth-century Preston in comparative perspective

Michael Anderson

AIMS OF THE SURVEY

The Lancashire cotton towns in the middle of the nineteenth century were in many ways a half-way house between a predominantly rural pre-industrial England, and the predominantly urban–industrial/commercial post-capitalist England of the present day. Communities like Preston, the town I shall most be concerned with here, had between a quarter and a third of their adult male population directly involved in factory industry. Because of the extensive use of child labour, however, a considerably higher proportion of the population were at one time or another of their lives employed in the dominant cotton textile industry. The domestic handloom sector still survived, but it was of ever-shrinking size. Of those not employed in industry hardly any had agricultural occupations. The prosperity of the mass of the population of almost 70,000 was firmly linked to the cotton textile industry.

These communities were, then, firmly a part of the urban–industrial order, oases in the midst of a predominantly rural nation. In them were to be found all the problems which beset capitalist societies – cyclical unemployment, over-crowding, large families struggling on low wages, factory working wives and mothers, and large inmigrant populations. But this was still an early stage in the transition to the more integrated advanced industrial society we know today. The problems had emerged with full force but the social changes which were to ameliorate or remove them had not yet appeared. Thus bureaucratically organised social security provision for the old, the sick, the unemployed, the pregnant mother and the large family was minimal and only given at great social and psychological cost to the recipient. Bureaucratically organised community social welfare services were almost non-existent. Average family size was still high, and mortality was as high or higher than ever. Wages were low, primary poverty widespread, housing appalling and relatively expensive.

Obviously, these communities have particular interest to the social historian and the sociologist. By investigating their family and household structure we can perhaps get clues which will help us resolve the many paradoxes which appear when we compare pre-industrial England with the present day. Here I want to concentrate particularly on two of these. Firstly, why, contrary to all that one might be led to expect by the predictions of the cruder, and even of many of the more sophisticated, proponents of the thesis of convergence of family structures with industrialisation towards a conjugal type, has there apparently been a massive *increase* over the past two centuries in co-residence of married couples and their parents, and precisely how and when did it come about? Secondly, what light can a study of a nineteenth-century Lancashire industrial town shed on the problem of the marked stability of mean household size in England and Wales over four centuries, to which Mr Laslett has drawn our attention?[1]

What I propose to do in this Chapter, therefore, is to present some (necessarily selective) data on various aspects of household and family structure in Preston in 1851, and to contrast it, on the one hand, with some of the figures which Mr Laslett has at various times made public from his investigations on pre-industrial England, and, on the other, with recent data on British family structure, notably from the 1966 sample census and from Rosser and Harris's study of Swansea.[2] Where the data are available, I have also included for contrast figures for 1851 from Dr Armstrong's survey of York,[3] a predominantly non-industrial Victorian town, and from my own data on the Lancashire agricultural villages where many of the migrants to Preston had been born.

The data in the sample census are not always presented in as detailed a form as one would like. Some of the census household types have had therefore to be allocated in a somewhat arbitrary manner to the classifications used in this chapter. Since most of the groupings treated in this manner contain comparatively few cases, the overall bias must, however, be small. The Swansea data are from a sample of *individuals* from the electoral register. This means that the more persons aged 20.5 and over that there were in any household, the greater its chance of inclusion in the sample. Thus, the figures for household composition presented by Rosser and Harris show the proportion of adults living in any given type of household, and not the proportion of households of any given type.

In making the estimates for Swansea I have had, therefore, to guess at the mean number of adults in each type of household (which is an index of its chances of inclusion in the sample), taking into account the facts that some parents and married children were widowed, that some married children were too young to appear on the electoral register, but that some unmarried co-residing children were on the register. I have assumed that households containing only

[1] See above, Laslett, Chapter 4, pp. 137–141.
[2] General Register Office, *Sample census 1966* (1968). Rosser and Harris, *The family and social change* (1965.)
[3] Armstrong, *The interpretation of census enumerators' books* (1968). See also above, Armstrong Chapter 6, pp. 205–214.

married couples, and those containing parent(s) and unmarried child(ren), had on average about twice the chance of a single person household of inclusion in the sample. That households with siblings only and those in the 'other' category had three times the chance, and that those with parent(s) and married child(ren) had four. For the purposes of Table 7.5 (generation depth), I have arbitrarily assumed that three quarters of married children co-residing with parents had at least one child, and I have allocated the 'other' category one quarter each to one- and three-generation households and one half to two-generation households.

Many of the interpretations in what follows are necessarily rather speculative. We still do not have nearly enough studies of the family structure of nineteenth-century factory towns to be able to make firm generalisations about the impact of the various facets of urban–industrial life. Nor do we yet have, at least to my knowledge, any very clear idea of household structure in that vast preponderance of Victorian rural England where the agriculture was based on large farms employing outdoor day labourers rather than on the not unprosperous (particularly in Lancashire), almost peasant-type, subsistence family farming of the regions studied by Professor Williams[4] and myself. In these regions, in contrast to most of the rest of England, what employed labour there was, was mainly indoor farm servants, marriage was late and many never married, and children remained at home into their twenties in the expectation of an inheritance of the farm or of a portion of the family estate.[5]

SOURCES AND METHODS

There is no space here for a detailed discussion of the data sources, of the samples, of the methods used, nor of the criteria by which households and family groups were distinguished. Detailed discussions of these topics are already or will shortly be available elsewhere.[6]

The Preston data are from a 10 % sample of houses taken from the enumerators' books of the 1851 Census. The rural sample is not representative of any finite population. It was drawn with the object of comparing the family structure of that sector of the Preston population who had migrated to Preston from rural areas[7] with the family types which were found in the villages from which

[4] Williams, *A West Country village* (1963).

[5] M. Anderson, *Family structure in nineteenth century Lancashire* (1971) Chapter 7.

[6] For the enumerators' books as a source, Armstrong, *Social structure from early census returns* (1966); Tillott, *Inaccuracies of census statistics* (1972). For the samples, M. Anderson (1971) Ch. 3. For more details on indices, techniques and issues in the study of family structure in the nineteenth century, M. Anderson, *Sources and techniques for the study of family structure* (1972 i). For detailed discussion of the household definitions, M. Anderson, *Standard tabulation procedures* (1972 ii).

[7] The sample is confined to villages where more than half the 1831 population had been employed in agriculture. The 1831 Census is the last which gives occupation data by villages. It is also useful because 1831 is the last Census before the main collapse of handloom weaving

they had come. A variable fraction stratified sample was therefore drawn so that the percentage of sample households taken from any one village was proportional to the percentage of all the migrants into Preston who had come from that village. Since, however, the family and household structure of these migrants turned out to be little different from that of the population as a whole, I shall here, for convenience, use the rural sample data for comparisons with the whole Preston population. Households are taken as 'census families'. Doubtful cases follow the rules outlined elsewhere.[8]

HOUSES AND HOUSEHOLDS

In all societies, one theoretically possible alternative to joining an existing household is, instead, to take over part of a house but to live as a separate domestic group. The factors which decide whether two families, related or otherwise, maintain two separate households in the same house, rather than joining together into one are but little understood.[9] In all, 10 % of houses in Preston were shared by two or more households, compared with 2 % in the rural sample. It seems likely from stated relationships where given, and from comparison of surnames, that up to 20 % of sharing households in Preston were related to each other, and perhaps a half of those in the rural sample were related in this way. In general, in both town and country, as might be expected, it was the poorer sections of the community who shared houses as separate households. The sharing of a house was but little dependent on family size, but most of those families who lived as lodgers or kin in the households of others had few or no children.[10]

HOUSEHOLD SIZE

Tables 7.1 and 7.2 show the distribution of household sizes for Preston and the rural sample, compared with figures for twentieth-century England and Wales, nineteenth-century York, and pre-industrial England.[11] The Preston and rural sample figures exclude visitors.

No very constructive comment is possible on these figures until the end of

which turned many weavers back to small farming and generally disrupted their social structure. These rural villages, then, had always been predominantly agricultural, and were thus much less touched by this catastrophe.

[8] Anderson (1972 ii). See also above, Armstrong, Chapter 6, p. 205.
[9] Cf. Rosser and Harris (1965): 148–50. One point which seems worth investigating, besides the simple difference in proportion of houses that are of a tenement type, is whether there are systematic variations related to differences in the internal layout of the dominant community housing type.
[10] For a detailed discussion, see Anderson (1971) Ch. 5. The question of relationship between separate households within the houseful is also discussed by Laslett, above, Chapter 1, pp. 36–37 and by Pryor, below, Chapter 22, p. 582.
[11] The figures for England and Wales and for Preston are from General Register Office (1968): 3, 57. The figures for York from Armstrong (1968): 70; for pre-industrial England from Laslett, see above, Chapter 4, p. 142.

Table 7.1 *Number of persons per household,*
%, for various communities

	Household size										Mean household size
	1	2	3	4	5	6	7	8	9	10+	
England and Wales, 1966	15	31	21	18	9	4	1	1	0	0	3.0
Preston, 1966	18	32	19	15	8	5	2	1	1	0	2.9
York, 1851[a]	5	15	16	18	14	13	7	5	3	5	4.8
Preston, 1851	1	10	16	17	14	12	10	8	5	8	5.4
Rural Sample, 1851	3	12	13	12	14	12	11	9	6	9	5.5
100 communities, 1564–1821	6	14	17	16	15	12	8	5	3	5	4.8

[a] These York figures use slightly different criteria for distinguishing households, which probably tend to deflate them slightly.

Table 7.2 *Number of persons per household, cumulative %,*
for various communities

	Household size equals or less than									
	1	2	3	4	5	6	7	8	9	10+
England and Wales, 1966	15	46	67	85	94	98	99	99	100	100
Preston, 1966	18	50	69	84	92	97	98	99	100	100
York, 1851[a]	5	20	36	54	67	81	87	92	95	100
Preston, 1851	1	11	27	44	58	70	80	88	92	100
Rural Sample, 1851	3	16	28	41	54	66	77	86	92	100
100 communities, 1564–1821	6	21	38	53	68	80	87	93	96	100

[a] See footnote to Table 7.1.

the chapter after household and family composition have been analysed in detail. Nevertheless the fact that the mean household sizes in Preston and in the rural sample were so high will obviously need further comment.

HOUSEHOLD COMPOSITION

Table 7.3 is the first of a series of tables on household composition.[12]
The most marked differences which seem to emerge here are:

[12] The figures for England and Wales are from General Register Office (1968): 1–2. Those for Swansea are derived from Rosser and Harris (1965): 148. The figures in the original are for household, not family composition, and contain a 4% 'other' category, which includes both co-residing non-kin and families with kin other than married children and their children, and siblings. The figures for York are from Armstrong (1968): 72 and Armstrong, above, Chapter 6, pp. 210–211. Those for pre-industrial England are from Laslett, above, Chapter 4, pp. 149. 152, except for the lodger figure which is from Armstrong (1968): 72.

Table 7.3   *Percentage of households with kin,*
lodgers and servants for various communities

	Percentage of households with		
	Kin	Lodgers	Servants[a]
England and Wales, 1966 (approx.)	10	—[b]	0
Swansea, 1960 (approx.)	10–13	< 3	< 3
York, 1851	22	21[c]	20
Preston, 1851	23	23	10
Rural, 1851	27	10	28
Laslett, 1564–1821	10	< 1[d]	29

[a] Servants include apprentices in Preston and the rural samples.
[b] Not available.
[c] Somewhat less as a different convention was used for the demarcation of households. See above, Armstrong, Chapter 6, pp. 205–206.
[d] See Laslett, *Size and structure of the household in England over three centuries* (1969). This conclusion has now been revised (see above, Laslett, Chapter 4, p. 134). Only nine listings of inhabitants in pre-industrial England (exclusive of London) record the presence of lodgers but in these settlements the proportion of households with lodgers is as high as 14.7%. Compare the proportion of households with lodgers in eighteenth-century Holland, see below, van der Woude, Chapter 12, pp. 315–316.

(a) When compared with pre-industrial England the larger proportion of households with kin in all three 1851 samples, to a level well above the modern figure, which, indeed, approximates to that for pre-industrial England. The Lancashire rural sample is probably not typical of England as a whole, though Professor Williams's Ashworthy figure (between 31% and 34%) is actually higher.[13] Both Ashworthy and North Lancashire had a predominance of family farms and few farm labourers, and as Table 7.4 suggests, it was above all on these family farms that kin, particularly married children co-residing with parents, were to be found.[14]

(b) The far larger number of households with lodgers in York and Preston, compared both with pre-industrial England and with Swansea. In Preston, lodgers made up 12% of the sample and over 20% of the 20–24 age group, 48% were never married, 69% of all households with lodgers had only one or two, and only 4% had six or more. The married couples in lodgings were largely young and with small families, and inmigrants were over-represented in their number.[15]

[13] Williams (1963): 218.
[14] For a fuller discussion and explanation, see Anderson (1971) Ch. 1 and 6. Note a similar decline by socio-economic group revealed for farm-families in Asia and Africa, by Goody, above, Chapter 3, pp. 122–123, for pre-industrial England by Laslett, above, Chapter 4, pp. 153–154, and for fifteenth-century Tuscany by Klapisch, below, Chapter 10, pp. 275–277. Compare also Pryor's analysis of twentieth-century America, below, Chapter 22, pp. 577–578.
[15] Details in Anderson (1971) Ch. 5. For a revised estimate of the numbers of households with lodgers in pre-industrial England, see note d of Table 7.3 above.

Table 7.4 *Percentage of households with kin, by occupation of head of household, selected occupations, male heads only, rural sample 1851*

	Percentage of households with			
	Parent(s) and married child(ren)	Other kin	Any kin	N =
Farmers, 100 acres and over	14	24	38	140
Farmers, 20–99 acres	9	23	32	114
Farmers, 0–19 acres	3	21	24	76
Agricultural labourers	4	18	21	171
Artisans	2	13	15	54

(c) Servants in Preston in 1851 already show signs of the ultimate decline to which this class was destined. Employment in the factories was, of course, not conditional on co-residence, and the opportunities it offered to the young made it difficult to recruit suitable children to service. Servants and apprentices made up 3 % of the population. Most of the domestic servants were inmigrants, and the main source of recruitment was purely agricultural villages where the children, lacking much previous contact with industry, seem to have found in service the easiest adaptation to urban life in a factory town,[16] and seem to have been particularly sought after by the middle class.[17]

In the rural sample servants made up 16 % of the sample population aged over fifteen. By contrast with the towns, the number of men more or less equalled the number of women, and the 225 farm servants who were aged over fifteen made up 43 % of the paid agricultural labour force in these age groups. Ninety-three per cent of both men and women servants had never been married. The vast majority of servants of both sexes were under twenty-five, but there were significant numbers of servants in all age groups.

FAMILY COMPOSITION

Table 7.5 looks at the generation depth of the families of the household heads.[18]

In all six populations, two-generation households are a majority. Preston has considerably more three-generation households than Mr Laslett's sample, and Swansea about the same. There are a very large number of three-generation households in the rural areas of Lancashire. Single-generation households are notably high in modern communities, and in York in 1851.

[16] Anderson (1971) Chapter 10.
[17] A number of advertisements in Lancashire newspapers of the early nineteenth century specify that all applicants must be from rural areas.
[18] For England and Wales, from General Register Office (1968): 1–2; for Swansea, from Rosser and Harris (1965): 155; for York from Armstrong, above, Chapter 6, p. 211; for pre-industrial England, Laslett, above, Chapter 4, pp. 152–153.

Table 7.5   *Generation depth of families of household heads*
Number of generations (%)

	1	2	3	4	All %	N =
England and Wales, 1966 (approx.)	43	52	4	0	99	1,533,954
Swansea, 1960 (approx.)	35	58	7	0	100	1,958
York, 1851	33	59	9	—	100	781
Preston, 1851	15	75	9	0	99	1,240
Rural, 1851	19	66	14	0	99	855
Laslett, 1564–1821	24	70	6	—	100	—

Table 7.6[19]   *Structure of the families of household heads*

Family type	England & Wales 1966 (approx.)	Swansea 1960 (approx.)	Preston 1851	Rural 1851	Laslett 1564–1821
No related person	17	10+	4	5	⎫
Married couple only	24	22+	10	12	⎬ 90
Parent(s) and unmarried child(ren) only	49	54+	63	56	⎭
Parent(s) and married child(ren) but no other kin	5	9+	9	6	⎫
Parent(s) and married child(ren) with other kin	0	⎫ < 5ᵃ	1	0	⎬ 10
Other combinations of kin	4	⎭	13	21	⎭
All %	99	100	100	100	100
N =	1,533,954	1,958	1,240	855	—

ᵃ Some of this group are here because they have co-residing non-kin, since the figures for Swansea are for household structure, not structure of the families of the household heads.

This table, however, conceals rather than reveals a number of sociologically highly significant trends, and attention is best turned to two rather different modes of demonstrating differences in family composition, which are shown in Tables 7.6 and 7.7.

The markedly lower proportions of households containing kin in both present-day Swansea and in England and Wales as a whole are obviously the most striking features of Table 7.6. At the same time the proportion living without any relative in their household is correspondingly higher. The different distribution of childless couples compared with couples with unmarried children mainly reflects the fall in family size and the older age distribution of the Swansea population.

[19] For comment on the Swansea figures see footnote 12 above. The pre-industrial figures are derived from Laslett, above, Chapter 4, p. 149.

Other highly significant differences appear in the remaining rows. Mr Laslett's communities have very few parent/married child households indeed.[20] By contrast, in Preston, 10 % of all families were of this type, and Rosser and Harris's modern figures are at about the Preston level, though the figures for England and Wales as a whole are lower. Foster also found a 10 % figure for Oldham in 1851.[21] The urban–industrial revolution, then, seems, contrary surely to all expectations ten years ago, to have been associated with a considerable increase in co-residence of parents and married children. However, Foster's finding[22] that the comparable 1851 figures for Northampton and South Shields, both industrial towns, were only 5 % and 4 % respectively suggests that the issue is not as simple as it might at first appear. Further discussion of this issue appears below.

The other main point to emerge from Table 7.6 is the way in which 'other kin' family types maintained or even increased their proportion into the urban industrial society, and only fell away in the past one hundred years. This issue too is best discussed below. Suffice to note here that Foster[23] found these 'other kin' in 12 % of Northampton families, 16 % of Oldham families, and 11 % of South Shields families. Certainly this family type was a widespread phenomenon. Just who these co-residing kin were is explored further in Table 7.7.

By far the most remarkable thing to modern eyes about both columns of this table is the immense number of 'parentless' children, 28 % of all kin in Preston, and 42 % in the rural sample. I have been unable to find any comparable tables for present-day communities, but a glance at the first column of Table 7.6 suggests that the figure is well under 5 %. By contrast the proportion for pre-industrial England may well have been higher still, and can certainly have been little lower.

Thus in Preston, while there were also still large numbers of this 'parentless' group so rare today, there was also a much larger number of the 'new', 'twentieth-century' group of one or two grandparents, one or two married children and their families, and married siblings and their families. We appear, therefore, to have in Preston something of a half-way stage in the transition, with both pre-industrial and modern types of kinship superimposed.

Before trying to analyse just who these various groups were, and why they were co-residing, attention is perhaps usefully turned to Tables 7.8 and 7.9. Aggregate tables on family structure, such as Tables 7.6 and 7.7, can be rather misleading in a comparative perspective, because, given the typical English pattern where co-residence of married children and parents is mainly confined to the first years of marriage, and to the old age (particularly the widowhood)

---

[20] See above, Laslett, Chapter 4, p. 149.
[21] Foster, *Capitalism and class consciousness in earlier 19th century Oldham* (1967): 314.
[22] Foster (1967): 314. Firth, *Family and kinship in industrial society* (1964): 74, found that only 16% of his Highgate sample (though 30% of the middle class, Crozier, *Kinship and occupational succession* (1965): 17) had co-residing kin, which suggests that in London, too, this family type was not as predominant as it was in Lancashire.
[23] Foster (1967): 314.

Table 7.7   *Relationship of kin to household head (% of all kin)*

	Preston, 1851		Rural, 1851	
Father or father-in-law	3.3[a]		3.2[b]	
Mother or mother-in-law	5.7[a]		4.0[b]	
Married/widowed son or son-in-law	11.1		6.9	
Married/widowed daughter or daughter-in-law	12.3		5.9	
Grandchild with parents	13.7		10.9	
'Stem' family members		46.1		30.9
Unmarried siblings (married head)	9.1		8.4	
Unmarried siblings (unmarried head)	5.0		8.6	
Unmarried members of family of orientation		14.1		17.0
Married or widowed siblings or siblings-in-law	5.1		4.0	
Nieces/nephews with parents	4.3		2.2	
Married siblings and family		9.4		6.2
Nieces/nephews without parents	15.0		11.9	
Grandchildren without parents	13.3		30.2	
'Parentless' children		28.3		42.1
Uncles, aunts and cousins	1.4	1.4	2.0	2.0
Others	0.8[c]	0.8	1.7[d]	1.7
All %	100.1	100.1	99.9	99.9
N =	513	513	404	404

[a] All widowed.
[b] All but one widowed.
[c] Son-in-law's father, son-in-law's brother, grandmother, great nephew.
[d] Five not specified (probably nieces/nephews, siblings-in-law, or cousins), great niece and her illegitimate child.

of the parents, such tables are highly sensitive to varying population age structures. Before proceeding further, then, it is instructive to look briefly at some tables where age or life-cycle stage are controlled.

Table 7.8 shows the co-residence patterns of the section of the community aged over 65.[24] The marked pattern of co-residence with children in Preston is particularly worthy of notice. Few old people there lived apart from a relative. Indeed, when the proportion of old people who could have had a child alive at all is estimated (and this figure is considerably below that for modern Britain and probably below the rural figure) it is obvious that well over 80 % of those old people who had a child alive were, in Preston in 1851, in fact living with one or other of their children.[25]

Table 7.9 shows the residence patterns of the young childless couples.[26]

[24] The figures for Britain are from Stehouwer, *Relations between generations* (1965): 146.
[25] For details of the estimate, see Anderson (1972 ii).
[26] For Swansea, see Rosser and Harris (1965): 167.

Table 7.8   *Household composition of the over 65s* (%)
(*Listing in priority order*)

	Married			Widowed, single and separated		
	Britain, 1962	Preston, 1851	Rural, 1851	Britain, 1962	Preston, 1851	Rural, 1851
Living with:						
Married child(ren)	6	16	13	27	41	26
Unmarried child(ren)	26	47	36	27	29	21
Spouse only	68	37	50	—	—	—
Other kin only	—	—	—	4	8	18
No related person	—	—	—	42	22	35
All %	100	100	99	100	100	100
N =	1,022	70	143	889	124	106

Table 7.9   *Residence patterns of childless couples
where the wife was aged under 45* (%)

	Swansea, 1960	Preston, 1851	Rural, 1851
% Living:			
In own household	57	58	80
Co-residing with parents	40	16	13
Other (including lodgers)	3	26	7
All %	100	100	100
N =	97	158	46

In Preston, as in Swansea, only just over half of all childless younger couples lived in households of their own and apart from their parents. In contrast to Swansea, however, where most of the rest lived with parents, over half of this group in Preston lived as lodgers in another household. (None in Preston co-resided in a household headed by a kinsman other than a parent.) Part of this difference may be due to the rather different criteria by which households are distinguished in the two studies, but there is no doubt that many of these lodger couples did, in fact, share a common table and would therefore have been classified by lodgers even by Rosser and Harris. Compared with Mr Laslett's figures, in contrast, even the 16 % who lived with parents are probably a very numerous body indeed.

Thus it seems likely that urban–industrial life of the cotton-town type markedly increased the proportion of wage earner families in which parents and married children co-resided. It also markedly increased the alternative form of residence for the young married couple, living as lodgers with another family. Compared with pre-industrial England, however, the proportion of unmarried siblings and 'parentless' children did not decline, and may even have increased somewhat. Twentieth-century urban life saw a marked reduction in this latter group but some considerable further increase in the co-residence of young married children and their parents, probably to some extent at the expense of the lodger group. But, in spite of this increase, more old people live alone today than in nineteenth-century Preston; possibly more do so than did in pre-industrial England.

THEORETICAL FRAMEWORK[27]

I have argued elsewhere[28] that if we are to understand variations and changes in patterns of kinship relationships, the only worthwhile approach is consciously and explicitly to investigate the manifold advantages and disadvantages that any actor can obtain from maintaining one relational pattern rather than another, and I have outlined what I see as the main considerations which must be taken into account in any such approach. Here I want to go further and suggest that, in the case of *co-residence*, a very special set of hypotheses, which consider only economic advantages and disadvantages, may be appropriate. In short, I am suggesting that any significant proportion of one group of actors in a society (say young married men) will generally only be found *co-residing* with another given class of kin (say widowed parents) if:

(a) the time-discounted, average life-span, economic advantages to most of them of doing so (bearing in mind that co-residence will normally imply some sharing of resources and support if necessary) outweigh or at least are not greatly exceeded by the economic disadvantages which they would suffer either directly from the kinsman, or from third parties, and

(b) if most of the other party also would receive net advantages calculated in the same way.

Conscious calculation of these advantages is seen in this approach as only occurring under rather special conditions;[29] generally norms develop to set a seal on conduct which is in line with these economic pressures. In highly stable and fairly prosperous societies (which the societies we are concerned with here were not), where the future is reasonably predictable, it can be shown, on the premises used, that norms would logically develop as a kind of insurance policy to secure at least for all who have relatives, some minimum standard of living provided by kin, except if assistance at this minimal level were seen as obtainable from some other outside agency.

There is no space to go further into this matter in this chapter. Here I am

[27] Compare Demos' assessment of some factors affecting household structure in colonial America, see below, Chapter 21, pp. 561–569.
[28] Anderson (1971) esp. Ch. 2.
[29] These problems, together with those raised by the next sentence, and such problems as the determinants of rates of time discounts, are discussed at some length in Anderson (1971) Ch. 2.

mainly concerned with the principle as a conceptual framework which may help us to understand changes and differences in patterns of co-residence. To this detailed problem I now return.

'PARENTLESS' CHILDREN

Firstly, then, who were these parentless children who seem to have been present in a sizeable proportion of households over most of rural and urban England?

Some of the odd grandchildren were undoubtedly illegitimate sons and daughters of co-residing daughters, or, indeed, of daughters who had left home to marry or for other reasons.[30] It is now impossible except by reconstitution techniques to ascertain what this proportion might have been, but it does seem as if this was a fairly standard behaviour pattern. A second group were children who were orphans, children who had lost one parent (particularly the mother), and also children of mothers who had remarried. In all these cases it seems to have been normal for relatives to take over the children, assisted often by a small parish allowance in return.[31] Children in this class undoubtedly make up a not-inconsiderable proportion of the group as a whole. A third, and probably small, group are those who, though they had parents alive and living in the community, lived with aunts, uncles, or grandparents to relieve the overcrowding in their own households or, possibly, to provide aged grandparents with some company and help around the house or in a small shop. Several cases which look very like this cropped up during the work on enumerators' books, and the phenomenon of 'lending a child' is not unknown in modern working class communities.[32]

Certainly, for one reason or another, widows and single women were more than twice as likely to have such 'parentless' kin in their households as were the rest of the population. Most of these young men and women were already earning and would thus be already keeping themselves and, indeed, probably making some useful contribution towards the family finances (about 80 % were over ten years of age). Many more would soon be doing so in a society where child labour was the norm (and many of those who were sent out to work very young do indeed seem to have been being cared for by kin).[33] Many of the rest would have been the children of co-residing daughters who more than paid for their keep.

To this social welfare function, however, one must also add an important

---

[30] For the detailed references in support of this statement see Anderson (1971) Ch. 10.

[31] Anderson (1971) Ch. 10. In eighteenth-century Corsica, on the other hand, some households consisted entirely of orphaned children. There were no co-resident adults of any sort. See below, Dupâquier, Chapter 11, pp. 292, 294. Similar instances occurred in nineteenth-century Serbia, see below, Halpern, Chapter 16, p. 405.

[32] Cf. e.g. Willmott and Young, *Family and kinship in East London* (1957): 38.

[33] Cf. e.g. *First report of the Commissioners on the employment of children in factories*, P.P. (1833) xx, DI: 34, and see also Anderson (1971) Ch. 11.

economic function of kinship which both overlapped with the first and also made its own independent contribution to the figures. In the nineteenth century it was above all through the agency of kin that one got a job.[34] Where one had a kinsman who had his own business or farm he might frequently offer a job directly, particularly to the sons of siblings who had fallen on hard times, and this would frequently involve co-residence.[35] Some of these kin are described in the occupation columns of the schedules as servants, while many so-called servants were almost certainly kin.[36] Their status in the household was probably often little different from that of the non-relative who would otherwise have been given the place. The net cost, therefore, was minimal. Also the system meant that orphans and the children of destitute kin were provided for, and kin were probably easier to sanction, less likely to leave their jobs, and probably, therefore, more reliable.

In the towns, of course, most of the population were employees, but recruitment to jobs in the factories or in the labouring gangs was similarly influenced by kinship considerations. Asking for a job for kin was normal in the factory towns, and the employers used the kinship system to recruit labour from the country.[37] This process of drawing in kin from rural areas continued in London to the end of the nineteenth century at least.[38] Most of these kin were single, being especially siblings, and nieces and nephews. When they got to the town to the job their kinsman found for them, they had nowhere to live, so they normally lodged with him. This, then, is the second major source of 'parentless' kin. It is also, surely, the reason why inmigrant couples (except significantly those from other factory towns) had almost as many siblings, nieces and nephews, and cousins in their households as did the Preston-born,[39] and also, surely, the reason why it was above all the better-paid factory workers – overseers and spinners and the like – who had these relatives in their homes.[40] These were the men with the greatest influence over factory recruitment.

In sum, then, in industrialising England, men continued to be able, and indeed possibly became more able, to perform functions for their kin which were to these kin a considerable economic advantage. They could, moreover, do this at minimum cost to themselves except sometimes in the rather short run. The twentieth century, by contrast, reduced the control of kin over jobs, and reduced the scale of migration of young single persons. At the same time orphanage decreased and the Welfare State cushioned the poor from the worst ravages of crises. In consequence this class of kin largely disappeared from British homes.

[34] For a detailed discussion see Anderson (1971) Ch. 9.
[35] Anderson (1971) Ch. 9 and 10.
[36] Pre-industrial communities appear to differ in this respect, see above, Laslett, Chapter 1, pp. 57–58.
[37] Anderson (1971) Ch. 9 and 10.
[38] Perhaps the classic discussion of this kin-based migration and occupational recruitment service is in Booth, *Life and labour of people in London* (1892) III: 132–5.
[39] For details see Anderson (1971) Ch. 10.
[40] Anderson (1971) Ch. 9.

PARENTS AND MARRIED CHILDREN

To explain[41] the co-residence of parents and married children in larger proportions in Preston and Oldham both than in pre-industrial England and than in
other nineteenth-century towns so far studied, is a considerably more difficult
problem. By contrast with the situation among the better-off farmers in rural
Lancashire a fairly simple economic explanation based on economic co-opera-
tion in a family enterprise and the promise of future rewards from it is clearly
unsuitable;[42] by far the larger proportion of the population of Preston were
employees, and, anyway, there was there no clear association between socio-
economic group, and parent–married child co-residence.

Rather, as I have argued at greater length elsewhere,[43] my interpretation
requires that attention be turned to other aspects of urban social life. In most
working-class communities before the coming of the Welfare State, if someone
survived to old age (and many did not), then he could look forward to a life of
poverty. This was particularly true, perhaps, in the towns, where the cost of
living, and also rents, were higher. It seems probable then that old people,
particularly widows, would in general have been best off if they could co-reside
with married children. They would thus save on rent and participate in the
economies of scale of the common table. Young married couples, too, might
benefit from sharing, because they too would save on rent. But, and this is the
crucial point, nineteenth-century society and the society which preceded it, were,
in general, poor societies, societies where after one had done one's best for one's
own nuclear family, there was little left for anyone else, unless that someone else
could contribute to the family's resources in return. And, if one was young and
newly married, to take an old person into one's household or to join the household of that old person meant that this person could not but be given some of
these scarce resources now, and also in the future when one's family was larger
and poverty loomed at the door; the old persons would probably need some help
even if they were receiving a parish pittance. If one refused to take them in, the
Guardians would usually make sure they did not die of want; indeed their
standard of living would probably be little if at all lower. Usually, moreover,
this person could not give much of use in return. This, I would argue, explains
the reluctance of the population of most nineteenth-century towns, and
probably also of nineteenth-century and indeed pre-industrial rural areas, to
share with old people even when soon after marriage they could for a while
afford to do so. It is much more difficult to eject someone than never to take
them in.

In the cotton towns, however, the situation was different. Here, though poverty

---

[41] Very different reasons are advanced for the amount of co-residence in the French village of
Montplaisant in the seventeenth century, see below, Biraben, Chapter 8, p. 243, and rural
Tuscany of the fifteenth century, see below, Klapisch, Chapter 10, p. 275.

[42] Anderson (1971) Ch. 6.

[43] Anderson (1971) esp. Ch. 10–12.

was widespread, it was a little less biting than elsewhere, and it lasted for a shorter part of the life cycle.[44] The drain of a non-productive relative was thus, anyway, somewhat less severe. But, and this may have been the crucial issue, the relative could also substantially *increase the family income*, not usually by seeking employment in the labour market, but by caring for the children and home while the mother worked in the factory. In this way the mother could have child and home looked after better, and probably more cheaply, than by hiring someone to do so, and the income she brought in kept the relative and gave a considerable surplus to the family budget.

Thus in these communities the old person could be valuable, not a drain on family resources. Even if the wife did not work; the old person could frequently earn her keep by performing similar services for a neighbour who did. It is, then, perhaps not surprising that few old people lived alone.

By contrast, however, not all young married couples had parents alive, and many were inmigrants whose parents lived elsewhere. It was migrants in particular who lived in lodgings rather than with kin, though some actually brought their parents in to join them. Some others had many siblings still living at home, so here considerations of overcrowding appear to have inhibited their co-residing, though many lived nearby. It would thus seem that only a minority of young married couples, even in Preston, were physically able to co-reside.

One may then perhaps suggest more speculatively that in the later nineteenth- and early twentieth-centuries these advantages of co-residence continued in Lancashire and gradually spread elsewhere. The advantages to young married couples of co-residence if anything increased, as housing continued to be in short supply. At the same time the decline in family poverty meant that, proportionally, the cash disadvantages to them of taking in dependent kin declined. At the same time family size began to fall. More space thus became available at home, and fewer other married siblings were competing for the right to co-reside. More people had parents available too, because inmigrants came to be a smaller proportion of the total population, and some decline in adult mortality set in.

On the other hand, this very stabilisation of communities, together with the old age pension, changed the situation for the old. They could live near their children, not with them,[45] and more and more could afford to pay rent for a home of their own. Their children anyway were younger and most had left home for a while before widowhood struck.

Thus, while more and more couples came to co-reside for a few years after marriage, the proportion of old people who wished to co-reside probably began to fall. Some detailed investigations of household structure in the early twentieth century are necessary before we can understand the full situation here. The

[44] Cf. Foster (1967).
[45] For a similar observation on modern communities, cf. Willmott and Young, *Family and class in a London suburb* (1960): 43.

changes brought about by the introduction of the old age pension in 1908 may well have been particularly significant.[46]

What evidence is there in support of this interpretation? Firstly, it is possible to show that in Preston it was only those in more affluent states who took in kin who could not support themselves. In Preston, of all households whose family standard of living was estimated as being within 4s of the primary poverty line, only 2 % contained kin none of whom had a recorded means of support; of those with a standard of living of 20s and above, the figure was 11 %. By contrast, 9 % of the first group and 12 % of the second contained kin at least one of whom was self-supporting.[47]

There is also considerable contemporary comment by members of the working class that the possibility of assistance to kin was severely circumscribed by the costs which it incurred, unless such kin could either bring in some income through employment, or unless the poor law authorities were prepared to pay them some relief.[48] The Poor Law Commissioners of 1834 found a similar attitude to support of parents to be prevalent in many parts of rural England.[49] In addition, calculating reactions of this kind to assistance to kin in situations of extreme poverty have been pointed out by my own research on pre-famine rural Ireland,[50] by Banfield in Italy,[51] and by Sahlins as typical of primitive societies.[52]

Secondly, there is also supporting evidence for the special interpretation which has been offered for the cotton towns. Just such an explanation was offered for the low Lancashire poor rates by the special commissioner sent to enquire into the state of Stockport in 1842.[53] Households with children under ten where the wife worked were three times as likely to have had a co-residing grandmother.[54] Some married couples actually took unrelated old people into their households rent free and all found, to provide just such a service,[55] and others brought their

---

[46] A statement by a ninety-years-old pensioner to a *Nation* investigator following the introduction of the pension does indeed suggest a contemporary realisation by at least some of those affected, of the kinds of changes hypothesised here. He remarked: 'Often 'ave we thought as 'ow it would be a-best for us to go, and sometimes a-most 'ave prayed to be took; for we was only a burden to our children as ke'p us...But now we wants to go on livin 'for ever, 'cos we gives 'em the ten shillin' a week, and it pays 'em to 'ave us along with em...' See, Aronson, *Liberalism in the village* (1912), cited in Gilbert, *The evolution of National Insurance* (1966). I am grateful to Alan Armstrong for drawing my attention to this observation.

[47] Cf. Anderson (1971) esp. Ch. 11. The method of calculating the standard of living is set out in Anderson (1972 i).

[48] See Anderson (1971) Ch. 10 and 11.

[49] E.g. *Report from his Majesty's Commissioners for inquiring into the poor laws*, P.P. (1834) XXVII: esp. 54.

[50] Anderson (1971) Ch. 7.

[51] Banfield, *The moral basis of a backward society* (1958): esp. 121.

[52] Sahlins. *On the sociology of primitive exchange* (1965): esp. 165.

[53] *Inquiry into the state of the population of Stockport*, P.P. (1842) XXXV: 7, 77.

[54] Anderson (1971).

[55] Cf e.g., Waugh, *Factory folk during the cotton famine* (1881): 85, cited in Anderson (1971) Ch. 11.

Table 7.10   *Children in the population of various communities*

	England, 1564–1821	Rural, 1851	Preston, 1851	York, 1851
Children as % of population	43	47	49	37+
% of households with children	75	74+	81+	66+
Mean size of groups of children	2.8	3.0	2.9	2.7
Mean number of children per household *c.*	2.1	2.6	2.7	1.8+
% of children in groups of given size or less (cumulative):				
1	11	7	10	12
2	30	19	25	32
3	53	34	42	54
4	71	52	58	72
5	84	67	76	84
6	91	81	86	91
7 and over	100	100	100	100

parents in from the country.[56] Booth's data on poor relief for the elderly, compiled at the end of the century, show markedly fewer old people in receipt of relief in areas where married women habitually worked.[57]

Obviously, at this stage, such an interpretation remains speculative, but it does seem to offer considerable scope for future research. The problem is a complex one, and many factors are obviously involved, which we are only gradually coming to understand.

NUCLEAR FAMILY

I want to turn attention now to nuclear family membership in Preston and in rural Lancashire, looking first at the distribution of children in the population. These data are represented in Table 7.10.[58]

Not merely are there more kin per household in the Preston sample than in pre-industrial England, there are also more households with children. There are also more households with more than one nuclear family, with the consequence that although the mean size of each group of children is only marginally above the figure for pre-industrial England, the mean number of children per household is substantially higher. Rural Lancashire has marginally larger groups of children and many more households with more than one nuclear family, and so it, too,

[56] *Report on the state of the Irish poor in Great Britain*, P.P. (1836) XXXIV: 25, 69; *Select committee on the irremovable poor*, P.P. (1859) Session 2 VII: 116; *Report on the operation of the Poor Law Amendment Act*, P.P. (1837–8) XIX: 309, and sample data.

[57] Calculated from Booth, *The aged poor in England and Wales* (1894).

[58] The pre-industrial England data are from Laslett, see above, Tables 4.10 and 4.11, except for the mean number of children per household, which is estimated from figures given in that chapter. The figures for York are both estimates based on figures given in Armstrong (1968). See also above, Armstrong, Chapter 6, pp. 208, 210.

has a higher mean number of children per household than that shown by Mr Laslett's figures for pre-industrial England, though a figure similar to that for Preston. The York figures, by contrast, are below even those for pre-industrial England.

The immediately striking question is how it is that, in spite of its notoriously high infant and child mortality rates,[59] Preston managed to keep up such a high mean number of children per household.

Three factors seem to be responsible. Firstly, it did have a considerably earlier mean marriage age,[60] though this is inadequate as an explanation by itself. In spite of their earlier marriages, Preston mothers in the 35–44 age group had a mean of 3.4 children at home compared with 4.0 for mothers of this age in the rural sample. (By contrast, marriages in York may have been marginally later.)

Secondly, and more importantly, while 71 % of the married women in the rural sample fell into the age groups 25–54 (the groups with the largest numbers of children at home), 79 % of the married women in the Preston sample fell into these groups. (By contrast, it is possible that rather fewer married women in York were in these age groups.)

Thirdly, and probably the crucial factor, children remained at home much longer in Preston than they did in the rural areas of Lancashire, and, surely also, than they had in pre-industrial England. Though the mean number of children of mothers aged 35–44 was higher in the country, it was almost the same (3.4 compared with 3.3) for mothers in the 45–54 age group. This point is even clearer if attention is turned to Table 7.11.

In Preston it was possible for employed children to continue to live at home until they married. Most of those who did not do so were either orphans or inmigrants. Hardly any voluntarily left home to live in service and few, in spite of widespread contemporary comment, did so to live in lodgings.[61] By contrast, in the country, though the relationships with their parents of those who did remain at home were almost certainly closer,[62] only a bare majority were able to remain at home until they married. Most of the children of landless labourers and smaller farmers could not be employed and live at home. They had either to migrate to the towns or leave home to become a domestic or farm servant in the household of another family. (Similarly, in York, it looks as if many more must have gone into apprenticeship or service, or left the city.) In rural England as a whole, however, farm service was becoming very rare. I should predict therefore, that mean nuclear family size in these other areas will prove to have been markedly larger, though the proportions in service correspondingly smaller.

---

[59] Proctor, *Poor Law administration in Preston Union* (1966): 154 claims that Preston had the highest death rate in the kingdom.

[60] For details see Anderson (1971) Ch. 9.

[61] Cf. Anderson (1971) Ch. 9.

[62] Anderson (1971) Ch. 6 and 9. This should remind us that co-residence is only one, and not necessarily the most important, aspect of family relationships. There is also a discussion of this point in Anderson (1972 i).

Table 7.11   *Residence patterns of young persons aged 10–24,*
by age and community, 1851

	With parents		With other kin		In lodgings		In service		All (100%) N	
					% living					
Age (yrs)	P[a]	R[a]	P	R	P	R	P	R	P	R
Boys										
10–14	92	75	4	6	3	1	1	15	392	296
15–19	79	56	8	8	10	1	3	35	376	266
20–24	65	53	6	6	24	5	3	36	217	194
Girls										
10–14	86	86	10	4	11	1	1	3	349	217
15–19	67	62	9	6	21	1	3	31	387	268
20–24	62	46	6	10	29	5	3	39	261	143

[a] P = Preston, R = Rural sample.

HOUSEHOLD SIZE

Finally, I return to the mean household size figures. Table 7.12 presents these broken down by residential group. Nuclear family figures here are for the families of the household heads only. Children of lodgers and kin are classified under these headings. Visitors are excluded. The figures for York and for pre-industrial England are rough estimates derived from published writings.[63]

At least to my knowledge, no estimate can at present be made for England after 1851, and data on family and household structure in other types of town in 1851 and in more normal rural areas, are at present too scanty to enable us to make more than the most speculative comment on the overall question of change and stability in household size over the past century. The mean national figure for 1851 was 4.8, so Preston and the rural sample are both well above this, assuming that the criteria used are comparable, which they should be if the census authorities kept to the stated procedures.[64] Many of the larger towns for which published data can be obtained had figures well below the 4.8 mean, but some were considerably above, and the number of communities for which data are published is anyway limited; they may also not be typical. A further disadvantage is that no published data are available on any rural areas.[65]

[63] For York see Armstrong (1968) and above, Chapter 6, pp. 208–211. For pre-industrial England see above, Laslett, Chapter 4, pp. 134, 147–153.
[64] See Anderson (1972 ii) for details.
[65] In addition to the fourteen registration subdistricts for which data are presented in the 1851 Census published tables, figures are given for all subdistricts where the number of households exceeded the number of houses by over 10%. The accuracy of these data is not known. They are in *Census of Great Britain 1851. Population Tables I*, P.P. (1852–3) LXXXV: xcvii–xcviii, cii.

Table 7.12   *Mean household size, divided into component parts*

	Community			
	York, 1851	Preston, 1851	Rural, 1851	England, 1564–1821
Mean number per household of:				
Heads	1.0	1.0	1.0	1.0
Wives	0.7	0.7	0.8	0.7
Children	1.8	2.5	2.5	2.1
All nuclear family	3.5	4.2	4.3	3.8
Kin	0.3	0.4	0.5	0.2
Lodgers	0.5	0.6	0.2	0.0
Servants	0.3	0.2	0.6	0.6
All	4.7	5.4	5.5	4.7

I should like, however, on the basis of the earlier discussion, to speculate that the delayed fall in household size into the early twentieth century, in spite of the beginnings of the fall in completed family size, may be due not only to some parallel fall in child mortality, but also to a further rise in parent–married child co-residence, possibly to a level above its modern figure.[66] Such a possibility at least seems worth pursuing in future research on this topic.

[66] For an explanation of the constancy in mean household size between pre-industrial communities and mid-nineteenth-century York, see above, Armstrong, Chapter 6, pp. 210–211. See also Laslett, Chapter 4, pp. 139–143, 156–157.

8. A southern French village. The inhabitants of Montplaisant in 1644

Jean-Noël Biraben

HISTORICAL AND GEOGRAPHICAL FRAMEWORK

The parish of Montplaisant (see Fig. 8.1) which has become a civil commune without changing its boundaries, is situated in Périgord Noir, four kilometres south of the lesser Dordogne river, and two kilometres north of Belvès. Half of its area is on a plateau, and the other half in the valley of the Nauze, a little tributary which flows from the left into the Dordogne. On the plateau the soil is light and chalky, but in the valley it is a heavy fertile clay. Housing is scattered in hamlets of one or two households all over the territory of the commune. There is no large settlement in it, and apparently there never has been. In the valley, on the Nauze and its tributaries, there are many mills to be found. Before the Revolution not only did the parish belong to the castellany of Belvès but also formed an integral part of the community of Belvès. It was administered on the one hand by the aldermen, the mayor and his deputies and on the other by the Bailiff of the Archbishop of Bordeaux, who was the liege lord of the castellany.

THE POPULATION IN 1644

The document which has been used for this chapter is a *liber status animarum* (*état des âmes*) for the parish of Montplaisant drawn up in 1644 by Murat, the parish priest. It is inserted into the parish register, and consists of a list of inhabitants grouped together by locality and by household or by *feu*, as the French expression is.

Two other documents make it possible to check this list and refine certain points. They are:

(*a*) The parish register which begins in 1620, but is very irregularly kept. The records of baptisms and marriages show frequent and serious omissions between 1620 and 1644, and burials really do not begin until 1644, for there is only one burial registered before that date, in 1627.

(*b*) Another list of 206 persons drawn up in 1651, on the occasion of Easter confession, can be used as evidence for the presence or absence of individuals and families.

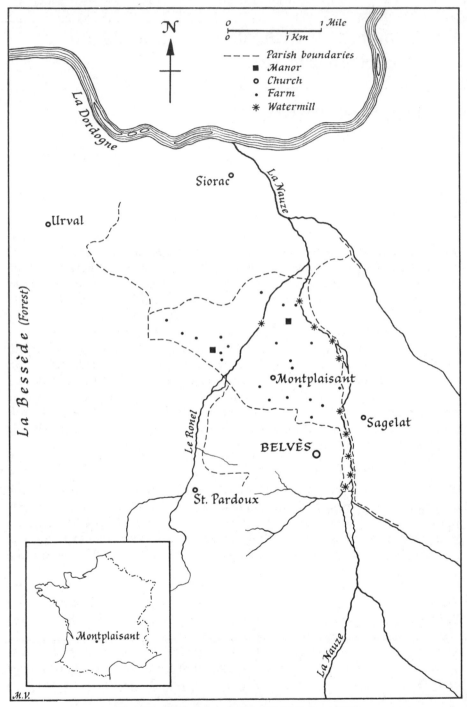

Fig. 8.1   Map of the parish of Montplaisant, 1644

Because of these documents we have been able to correct the list of 1644 to a very small extent and to recover a picture, which seems to us to be relatively accurate, of that rural population in the middle of the seventeenth century.

For example, the list of 1644 leaves eight names blank or incomplete and with the aid of the parish registers we have been able to restore four of them. Secondly, again thanks to the parish registers and to the list of 1651, we have been able to bring to light several omissions from the list. These are two children (both female) who were certainly present at the date of the census (Jeanne-Claude de Robert and Marque Miquel), although the second may have been temporarily absent, since her mother had taken a place for a few months as a wet nurse at Cadouin, several kilometres away. In addition, amongst the families referred to in the entries in the parish register but not mentioned in the census, several belonged to neighbouring parishes, others had disappeared because of deaths or because of migration before 1644, but five of them, of which one or both spouses made confession at Easter 1651, seem in fact to have belonged to the parish and to have been present at the time of the enumeration. These 5 families had in all 12 children born to them up to 1644, though we do not know how many of these children survived to that date, with the exception of one girl who was born on 1 October 1634, and who is to be found in the list of confessions of 1651. We have no knowledge of course of the unmarried relatives or of servants present in the households of these 5 families.

The parish registers enable us in addition to date the census during the later months of 1644, that is to say after the devastating storm of 29 July. The last entry in the parish register for the year 1644 can be ignored as it refers to the baptism of a child from a family in a neighbouring village. The preceding entry, a marriage of 7 August, is recognised by the list, which gives the newly married couple. The entry following that of 21 August is a death on 16 January 1645 and concerns one of the omissions we have just mentioned. The enumeration was carried out therefore by the priest Murat between 8 August 1644 and the end of the year. The addresses which he entered on the list permit us to infer that he went methodically round the parish, between the various farms, mills and other dwellings indicated on the map (Fig. 8.1).

Of the 62 heads of household entered, 35 lack any sort of social description. These seem to have been small cultivators, yeomen, *censiers* (who might cultivate a plot of land for which they had to pay a small rent to a lord), or tenants: two of them lived in a mill and were perhaps millers. Thirteen of the 62 were share-croppers, 6 (or perhaps 8) were millers, 3 were papermakers, 3 were nobles, and 1 is described as a valet. The 8 other valets were counted as part of the households in which they served.

The structure of the households is more interesting, though unfortunately ages are given for too small a number of persons, 46 out of 338, to make it possible to study this variable. We have said that there were 62 households recorded, though the number was perhaps 63, because it seems that the Rev.

Murat may have forgotten a division between two of them which seem to be arbitrarily united. There were in fact 68 of course, if we include the 5 households present but not mentioned, and 69 if we count the priest himself. The total of those recorded as living in Montplaisant is 338, 340 if we add the two little girls who were missed out, and 363 counting the 5 households with their 12 children together with the priest. That is to say there were 5.48 people to a household, and to a *feu*.

The household often consists of an extended family of the patriarchal type. The eldest person present, male or female, is always recorded at the top as head of the household (*chef de ménage*), and around him or her are grouped children and grandchildren.[1]

Singletons are rare. There are three households consisting of solitary men, one widow without children, and two spinsters. Of the latter one is noble and living with a valet and a chambermaid, the other solitary.

There are 11 households without children, of which 7 consist of married couples living alone, without kin, persons related by marriage, or servants.

There are only 20 households containing two generations, that is parents and children, the nuclear or biological family. Two of these have a widow as head of family.

Six other households include two generations, but together with kin, or affines, or servants.

Those including married children, that is to say sons and daughters-in-law, come to 19, of which 14 have grandchildren, and even in one case a great-grandson. But of these 19, 2 include also kin and affines: the mother-in-law of a son in one case, and 2 brothers and a sister of the father in the other. Four of the 19 have servants, and one includes the brother of a son-in-law, a valet, and 4 apprentices.

In total, of the 63 households recorded, 9 include collateral relatives, or persons connected in various ways.

Of the 338 inhabitants 23 had domestic employments and 14 of the 23 were of the masculine sex. Of the 23,

9 are described as valets (8 in 6 households, and 1 with his own household),

6 are chambermaids in 6 households,

5 are apprentices; 4 apprentice papermakers and 1 apprentice shoemaker in 2 households,

3 are shepherdesses in 3 households.

In all, 12 households with one or more servants, variously described.

The Rev Murat says nothing of his own household. It does not seem that he had a curate, but he may perhaps have had a maid and some relative in his presbytery.

[1] See the ideographs in Appendix I, below.

COMPARISON WITH THE NOMINAL LIST OF INHABITANTS FOR 1836[2]

The oldest of the nominal lists of inhabitants drawn up for the official census makes possible interesting comparisons with the list of 1644, in spite of the fact that it was not drawn up in exactly the same way. In particular addresses were not given in the later list. It dates from the year 1836, that is to say 192 years after 1644.

There are 81 households, including the priest's, and 367 inhabitants, that is 4.53 persons per household. Of the 81 heads of household 33 are described as agriculturalists or cultivators, and it seems that one male labourer and two female day-labourers should be added, and indeed many wives and children not heading households are given the title 'labouring', or 'day labouring'. Fourteen are share-croppers, 6 millers, 2 papermakers, and 1 oil manufacturer: these 9 occupy the mills. There are no longer any nobles, but there are 9 'proprietors' listed, and probably 10 if the mayor is added. Most of these seem to be in a relatively modest way: their wives are often described as cultivators.

But apart from these there is a large variety of artisans as compared with the 1 shoemaker of 1644, and this signifies a much higher standard of living for the population. There are two tailors, 1 clog maker, 1 barrel maker, 1 upholsterer, 1 cartwright, 1 blacksmith, 1 retailer (probably a grocer), 1 publican or tavern keeper and 1 teacher. In addition to these, there are many children of working age apart from the heads of households. A further teacher, a tile maker, a turner, a working papermaker, a clerk to his father who is the retailer, and a soldier.

Finally there is a servant with his own household as in 1644 and the priest, named Lavergne, lives with two servant girls and an old man of eighty, whom he keeps for charity.

There are 7 households of solitary persons. Three are unmarried people, 1 a cultivator of sixty-five years, and 2, the mayor of fifty-two and another of seventy, are well-to-do proprietors. One of the solitaries is an unmarried woman of fifty, and another a widow of seventy, both day workers, and a third is a widow of eighty-two described as a cultivator. Finally, one mill-owner lives with 3 apprentice millers.

Only 10 households include 1 or more grandparents, who are never themselves household heads, and there are 4 with collateral relatives. Two of these are sisters of the household head, both unmarried, another is a widow with three young children, and the fourth is an aunt.

Two great changes have taken place therefore in the two centuries. In the first place a considerable diversification in the number of crafts represented, and in the second, a marked decline in the patriarchal, extended family.

It can be added that in 1836 there are 27 'domestics' amongst the 367 inhabitants, of whom 26 live in 13 households. Of these 27, 16 are of the female

[2] See also the ideograph for the two censuses in Appendices I and II, below.

Table 8.1 *Distribution of households by size:* (%)

	Persons per household														
	1	2	3	4	5	6	7	8	9	10	11	12	13	14	Total
1644 No.	6	8	4	8	7	12	3	6	3	1	3	1	—	1	63
%	9.5	12.7	6.3	12.7	11.1	19.0	4.8	9.5	4.8	1.6	4.8	1.6	—	1.6	100
1836 No.	7	13	10	10	11	10	14	5	—	—	1	—	—	—	81
%	8.6	16.1	12.3	12.3	13.6	12.3	17.3	6.2	—	—	1.2	—	—	—	99.9

Table 8.2 *Distribution of households by type* (%)

	1644					1836				
Biological family[a]	None	Affines	Servants	Affines and servants	Total 1644	None	Affines	Servants	Affines and servants	Total 1836
One generation										
Celibates, widowed persons, and solitaries	9.5	—	1.6	—		9.9	—	2.5	—	
Two generations										
Households without children	11.1	3.2	3.2	—		12.3	—	1.2	1.2	
Households with children	30.2	4.8	4.8	1.6		46.9	1.2	11.1	—	
Three generations										
Households with kin and married children	4.8	—	1.6	—		1.2	—	—	—	
Households with grandparents	14.3	4.8	3.2	1.6		9.9	1.2	1.2	—	
Total	69.9	12.8	14.4	3.2	100.3	80.2	2.4	16.0	1.2	99.8

[a] As defined by Henry, *Manuel de démographie historique* (1967): 44. Blayo, Klapisch, Dupâquier and van der Woude, below, Chapters 9–12, also define nuclear families in the same way, which differs from that suggested by Laslett, above, Chapter 1, pp. 28–33.

sex (no doubt chambermaids or shepherdesses as in 1644) and 11 are males (of whom the 5 employed in the mills are probably apprentice papermakers or millers).

We can summarise types of household in the two censuses by comparing the percentages in Tables 8.1 and 8.2.

These show clearly how households containing three generations got fewer, falling from 19.1 % in 1644 to 11.1 % in 1836, and that in addition the households containing collateral relatives declined from 16 % to 3.6 %. Solitaries and households with servants on the whole changed little. But we may notice a certain tendency for domestics to be confined to households with children. It is possible to explain the larger households of the earlier period in terms of the prevalence of peasant unrest. By 1836 it was no longer necessary for extended families to provide physical protection for the members of the household.[3]

We may finally add that of the 64 different familial names appearing in the list of 1836, only 11 are to be found in the list of 1644. Thanks to the friendliness of the mayor of Montplaisant, we have established that 7 families in Montplaisant still in 1969 carry a name which is to be found in the list of 1644.

[3] Klapisch, see below, Chapter 10, p. 275 also found large households in the economically backward and war-devastated Tuscan countryside of the early fifteenth century. On the other hand, in Victorian England economic motives seem to have been the important factors behind the co-residence of parents and married children, see above, Anderson, Chapter 7, pp. 229–232.

Appendix I

Ideographs representing household structure: Montplaisant, 1644

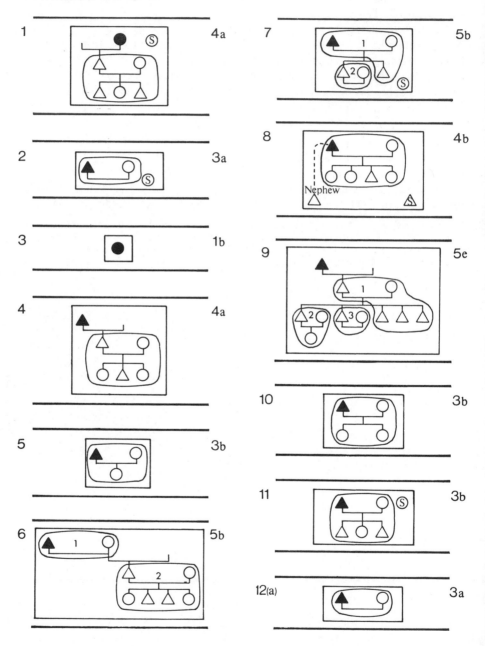

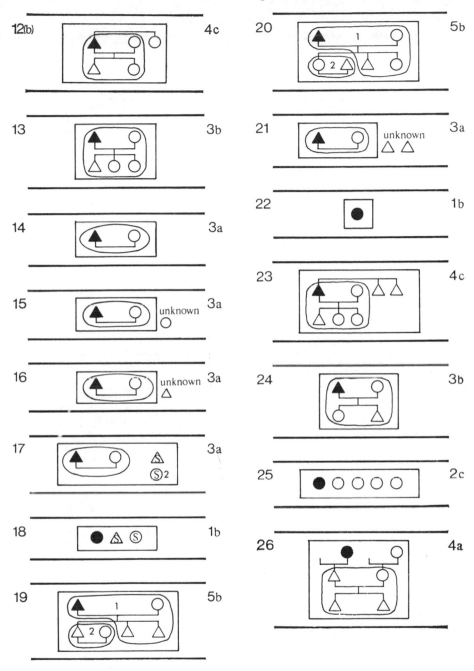

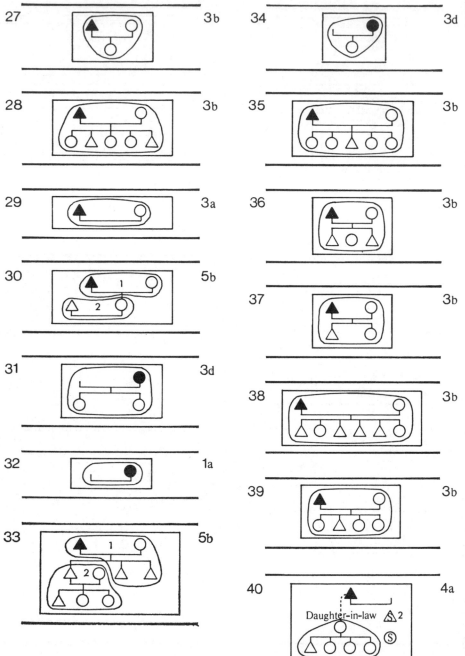

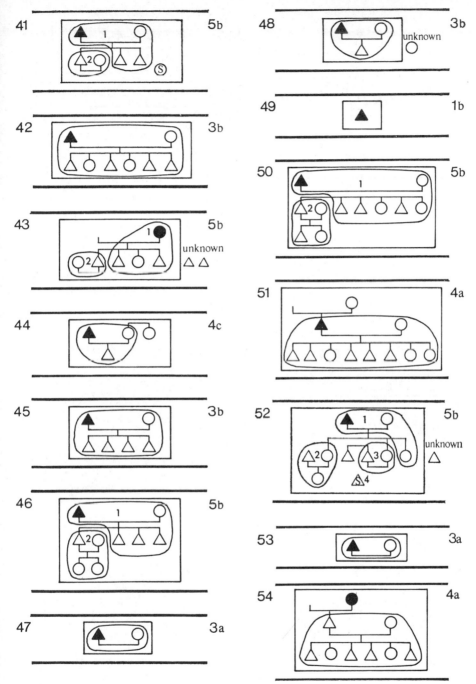

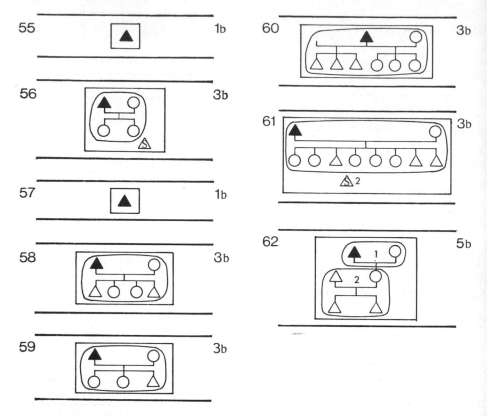

EDITORIAL NOTE

Monsieur Le Docteur Biraben originally supplied the details of the listing of Mont-plaisant in 1644 in tabular form. The document itself was subsequently published in *Annales de Démographie Historique*, Paris, 1970, as 'L'état des âmes de la paroisse de Montplaisant en 1644'. It was decided editorially to publish these data as ideographs following the system drawn up by Laslett in Chapter 1, above.

Appendix II

Ideographs representing household structure: Montplaisant, 1836

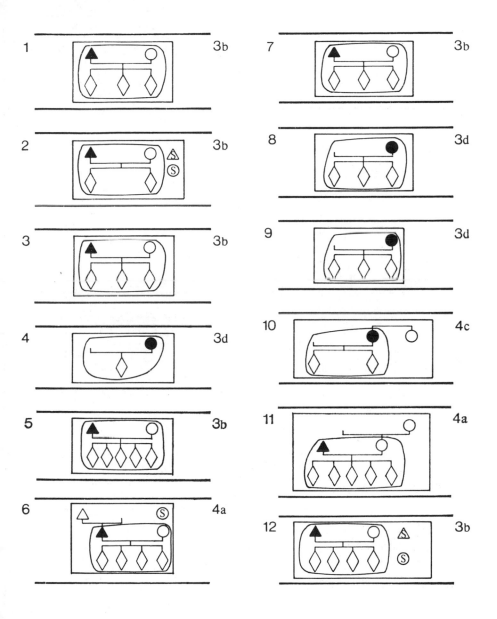

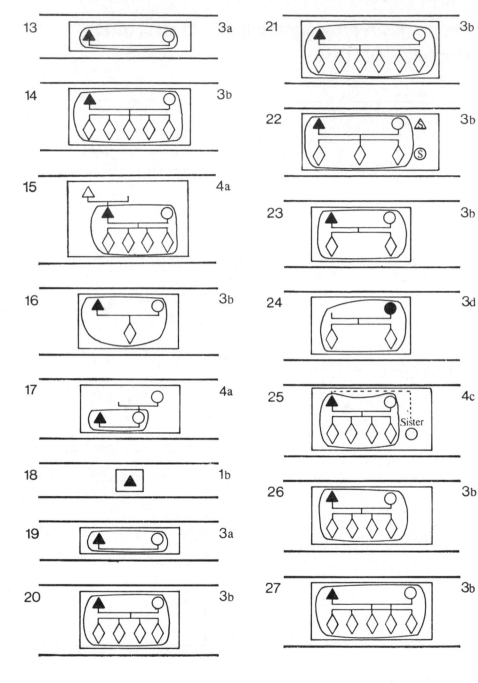

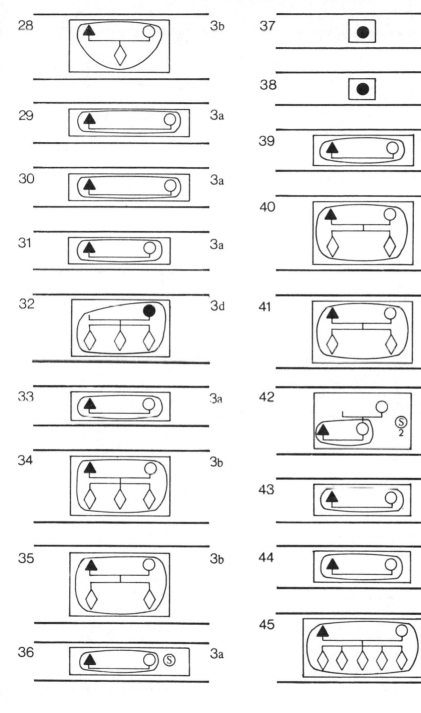

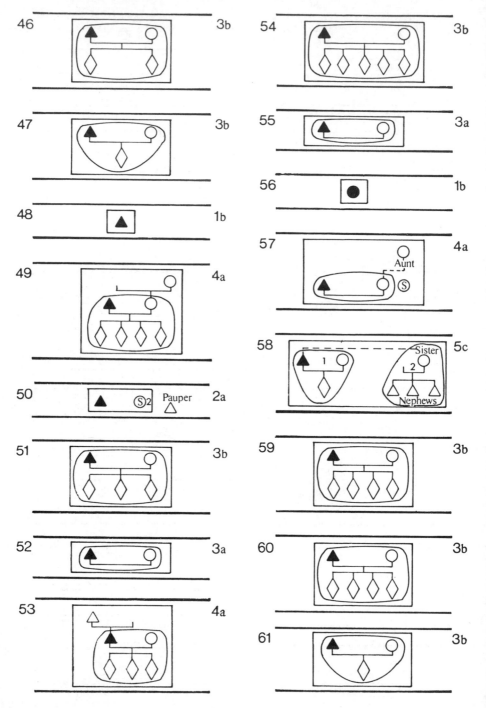

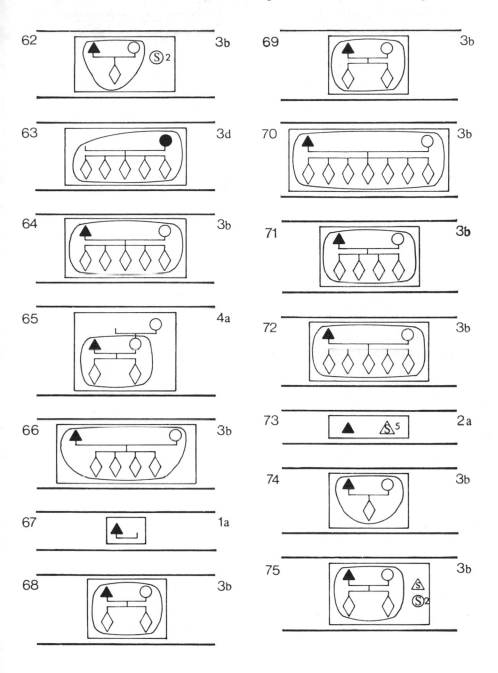

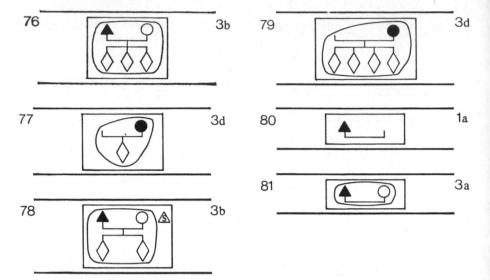

EDITORIAL NOTE:

NB (1) Children not distinguished from grandchildren.
　　(2) Spouses' parents not distinguished between husband's and wife's (father's allotted to men, mother's to women).

9. Size and structure of households in a northern French village between 1836 and 1861

Yves Blayo

The enumerators' books for the village of Grisy-Suisnes in the canton of Brie-Comte-Robert in the department of Seine-et-Marne survive for every census since 1836 in the departmental archives office at Melun. These lists were made up every five years and were set out by households. Comparison between them makes it possible to make a detailed examination of the composition of households.[1] The object of the present study is to set out some results obtained by making such comparisons, especially for the documents drawn up in the years 1836 and 1861.

Table 9.1 *Size of household at Grisy-Suisnes 1836–61*

	1836		1841		1846		1851		1856		1861	
	No.	%	No.	%	No.	%	No.	%	No.	%	No.	%
1 person	25	9.3	34	12.2	30	10.8	33	10.6	39	12.3	54	16.2
2 persons	55	20.5	61	21.9	65	23.4	93	29.8	83	26.3	102	30.5
3 persons	80	30.0	81	29.0	71	25.5	76	24.4	87	27.6	69	20.6
4 persons	52	19.4	53	19.0	58	20.9	52	16.7	57	18.0	47	14.1
5 persons	27	10.1	30	10.8	27	9.7	32	10.3	25	7.9	33	9.9
6 persons	17	6.3	12	4.3	11	3.9	12	3.8	13	4.1	10	3.0
7 persons	2	0.7	2	0.7	7	2.5	7	2.2	5	1.6	10	3.0
8 persons	5	1.9	4	1.4	3	1.1	4	1.3	4	1.3	5	1.5
9 persons	3	1.1	—	—	2	0.7	2	0.6	1	0.3	3	0.9
10 persons	—	—	2	0.7	1	0.4	1	0.3	1	0.3	1	0.3
11 persons	2	0.7	—	—	3	1.1	—	—	1	0.3	—	—
Total	268	100.0	279	100.0	278	100.0	312	100.0	316	100.0	334	100.0
$\bar{x}$	3.444		3.222		3.381		3.192		3.146		3.069	

---

[1] *Household*, i.e. *ménage*, defined by Henry, *Manuel de Démographie* (1967 i): 44, thus; 'The ménage for statistical purposes is a group of persons living together, either under the authority of the same head, or sharing the same premises.' This definition is compatible with nineteenth-century English usage, see above, Wall, Chapter 5, p. 160. Compare the definition of household in the Belgian National Census of 1947, below, Hélin, Chapter 13, p. 321. Laslett, above, Chapter 1, pp. 23–28, 34–40 discusses the problem of definition in some detail.

Table 9.2   *Mean number of children under fourteen per family by age of family head*

Age of head of family	1836 list	1861 list
Less than 20	—	—
20–24	0.67	0.20
25–29	0.80	0.77
30–34	1.09	1.66
35–39	1.45	1.61
40–44	1.07	1.58
45–49	1.07	1.41
50–54	0.34	0.45
55–59	0.35	0.16
60 and above	—	—
Total	0.71	0.73

SIZE OF HOUSEHOLD

As can be seen from Table 9.1 mean size of household changed in this quarter of a century from 3.4 to 3.1 persons. Though distribution of households by size retained in 1861 the same general shape that it had had in 1836, it was definitely displaced towards the left: the particular points to notice are that size 2 replaced size 3 as the mode and that the proportion of households of solitaries almost doubled. Overall the percentage of households of three persons and below changed from 30 % in 1836 to 47 % in 1861.

MEAN NUMBER OF CHILDREN TO A FAMILY

It has been decided to restrict the analysis to children less than fourteen years old. Their distribution is set out in Tables 9.2 and 9.3 as numbers of children to a family.[2]

The mean number of children under fourteen is the same in 1836 and 1861 if heads of families are taken as a whole. But if we take only those heads of families of the age group 30–34 and above, those in 1861 had on average more children under fourteen than those of 1836.[3]

It is clear that the slight fall in the size of households between 1836 and 1861 did not come about from a reduction of the size of the family. This is so, always

[2] Henry (1967 i): 41, gives the following definition: 'The family for statistical purposes is composed of the parental couple, or a surviving spouse, and surviving offspring if any.' Biraben, above, Chapter 8, p. 242 and Klapisch, Dupâquier and van der Woude, below, Chapters 10–12, pp. 267–318 also use this definition which differs slightly from that adopted by Laslett, above, Chapter 1, pp. 28–33.

[3] In 1836 the proportion of heads of families under thirty years of age was 11.7%. It was 8.8% in 1861.

Table 9.3 *Distribution of families with children under fourteen*

Number of children	1836 list		1861 list	
	No.	%	No.	%
0	160	54.9	218	62.4
1	76	26.0	57	16.3
2	42	14.4	39	11.2
3	10	3.4	24	6.9
4	3	1.0	7	2.0
5	1	0.3	3	0.9
6 and above			1	0.3
Total	292	100.0	349	100.0

supposing that children under fourteen were no more able to move independently of their parents in 1836 than they were in 1861.

The figures in Table 9.3 reveal the considerable increase in the proportion of families with no children under fourteen, and the decrease of families with 1 or 2 children in this age group.

COMPOSITION OF HOUSEHOLD IN 1836 AND 1861

The most important criterion for distinguishing different types of household is the number of heads of families within the household.[4] The 9 following categories are employed:

A. Households with one head of family
  1. Solitary widower or widow,
  2. Widower or widow with one or more unmarried children,
  3. Married couple with or without children,
  4. Others.
B. Households with several heads of families
  5. Married couple, or surviving spouse, with one or more ascendant kin married or widowed,
  6. Married couple, or surviving spouse, with one or more descendant kin married or widowed,
  7. Horizontally extended household: brothers or sisters married or unmarried living in the same household,
  8. Others.
C. Households without heads of families
  9. Households of unmarried persons with or without other persons.

[4] Cf. Henry (1967 i): 44–5. Laslett, see above, Chapter 1, pp. 28–33 employs a different classificatory system.

Table 9.4   *Households by category, 1836 and 1861*

	1836 households				1861 households			
	With-out ser-vants	With ser-vants	Total		With-out ser-vants	With ser-vants	Total	
Households with:			No.	%			No.	%
One family head:								
1. Solitary widows	20	1	21	7.9	51	1	52	15.6
2. Widows with children	21	4	25	9.4	17	1	18	5.4
3. Married couples	168	16	184	68.9	223	13	236	70.6
4. Others	5	0	5	1.9	10	0	10	3.0
Several family heads:								
5. Married couples with ascendant kin	14	2	16	5.9	10	1	11	3.3
6. Married couples with descendant kin	2	0	2	0.8	1	0	1	0.3
7. Horizontally extended households	3	0	3	1.1	1	0	1	0.3
8. Others	3	2	5	1.9	0	0	0	—
No head of family:								
9. Households of unmarried persons	5	1	6	2.2	4	1	5	1.5
Total	241	26	267	100.0	317	17	334	100.0

The distinction between types 5 and 6 is based on the fact that the head of household is entered first in the enumerators' books. Experience shows this distinction to be of little use at Grisy, because households of type 6 make up less than 1 % of all households at the two dates in question. An additional exploration of the membership of households has been made in Table 9.4 in order to locate and describe those which had servants.

Both in 1836 and in 1861, conjugal families made up about 70 % of all households. Between these two dates, the proportion of households with only one head of family rose from 88 % to 95 %. But the most important alteration was the doubling of the strength of solitary widows in this quarter of a century, which took place at the expense of widows with children and especially of vertically extended households, that is married couples with ascendant or descendant kin. It looks as if households with several heads of families disintegrated into households having a single nucleus, and this fragmentation brought with it a reduction in the mean size of household.

OCCUPATIONS OF MEN OF 18 AND OVER

Occupations for men of this age are given for 1836 and for 1861 in Tables 9.5 and 9.6. Important changes in occupational structure clearly occurred between

Table 9.5 *Occupations of men of eighteen and over, 1836*

Agriculture		Building and quarrying		Equipment and utensils		Textiles		Food		Professional, commercial, etc.	
Landowners	6	Clay-cutters	1	Farriers	3	Weavers	5	Butchers	1	Teachers	1
Cultivators	8	Stone-cutters	1	Cartwrights	1			Grocers	1	Deputies	1
Vine-growers	96	Masons	7	Harness-makers	2			Bakers	2	Priests	1
Labourers	71	Sawyers	1	Cobblers	3			Millers	1	Bailiffs	1
Day labourers	1	Carpenters	1	Sieve-makers	1					Constables	2
Carters	20			Coopers	1					Marketkeepers	1
Gardeners	14									Soldiers	3
Nurserymen	1									Surveyors	1
Shepherds, Herdsmen	11									Musicians	1
Keepers	2									Publicans	2
Servants	3									Pedlars	1
										Wood-sellers	1
										Roadmen	1
										Transport workers	5
										No occupation	3
Total	233		11		11		5		5		25
	80.4%		3.8%		3.8%		1.7%		1.7%		8.6%

Total with occupations 290 (100%)
Occupation not given 17
Grand total 307

Table 9.6 *Occupations of men of eighteen and over, 1861*

Agriculture		Building and quarrying		Equipment and utensils		Textiles		Food		Professional, commercial, etc.	
Landowners	8	Stone-cutters	1	Farriers	5	Weavers	2	Butchers	1	Teachers	1
Cultivators	17	Masons	8	Cartwrights	3			Grocers	2	Priests	1
Vine-growers	100	Squarewrights	1	Harness-makers	1			Bakers	2	Constables	2
Labourers	75	Sawyers	3	Cobblers	4			Egg dealers	1	Musicians	1
Drivers	23	Carpenters	2							Innkeepers	2
Gardeners	9	Locksmiths	2							Publicans	3
Nurserymen	11									Rag pickers	1
Rose-growers	3									Hay dealers	1
Shepherds	8									Personal servants	3
Keepers	4									Carters	9
Servants	5									Coachmen	4
										Roadmen	7
										Private means	7
										No occupation	4
Total	263		17		13		2		6		46
	75.8%		4.9%		3.7%		0.6%		1.7%		13.3%

Total with occupations 347 (100%)
Occupation not given 2
Grand total 349

Table 9.7 *Servants by age and sex, 1836 and 1861*

	1836		1861	
	Male	Female	Male	Female
Servants of fifteen and over	15	20	14	16
Population of fifteen and over	341	348	368	375
Proportion of servants	4.4%	5.7%	3.8%	4.3%
Total population	463	460	515	506
Proportion	3.2%	4.4%	2.7%	3.2%

these two dates. This is especially so in the column 'Professional, commercial, etc.' and to a rather less extent in the column 'Building and quarrying', both of which became more important, whilst agriculture and above all weaving lost ground. The development of the occupation of roadman will be particularly noticed amongst miscellaneous callings, and the growth in the number of carters is probably connected with this, whilst the presence of persons of private means and the appearance of a description 'personal servants' is also to be remarked. These people described as personal servants include a porter (*concierge*), a valet, and a butler, and they were employed in the two great houses (*châteaux*) in Grisy. The three servants counted in 1836 were men described as such. It would perhaps be correct to add to this list the various apprentices (*garçons*) – apprentice stone-cutter, apprentice gardener, etc. It is reasonable to think that they had domestic duties as well as those of apprenticeship. If 'personal servants' is taken in this larger sense, servants of eighteen years and above in 1836 come to 10, and there were 5 others between fifteen and seventeen. The figures for both sexes are given in Table 9.7.

The fall in the proportion of servants between 1836 and 1861 was accompanied by a decline in the number of households with servants. In 1861 2 households alone employed 12 servants. The type of servants changes between the 2 periods; there were 9 working servants amongst the 15 males in 1836, but only 2 in 1861. Lastly, the proportion of household staff in the population fell markedly in the twenty-five years, because of the fact that working servants almost disappeared, though on the other hand, the proportion of domestic servants in the strict sense increased.

CHANGES IN THE COMPOSITION OF HOUSEHOLDS

A comparison of the composition of households in 1836 and 1861, as recorded in Table 9.4, does not allow one to grasp the process of change which went on during the interval between these two dates. This development can only be understood by identifying each household at each census date. What happened within the space of one census interval? New households were formed by marriage, or came into the village by immigration, or were created by the break-up of multiple households.

Households present.at the first of the two censuses could disappear by emigration, or as a consequence of the death of all the members of the household, or by being merged with another household. They could also be transformed into households of other types, by marriage, re-marriage, death (of a spouse or of children), births (in the households of solitary widows), migration of individuals, or again by association with other households, or by breaking off from other households. They could also be present in the same category of household in the second of the two censuses.

Thus households in any of the nine categories present in 1836 could develop in seven or eight possible ways before the census of 1841. We can say that there were sixty-odd possibilities for the 9 categories together. If we wished to follow every one of these households through six successive censuses, the number of possible transformations would be of the order of 9×7^5, though this number would be liable to be reduced because of the existence of very improbable types of change and because of merging of categories of household.

But we can, if we wish, work from category of household and retain only three possible types of change during one interval of five years. These possibilities are as follows: staying in the same category, emigrating, and changing category. In the last case it is right that we should indicate the type into which the household was transformed. Moreover, for every census starting with the second, the former state of a household has to be indicated (staying in the same category, immigration, formation by marriage, etc....). Thus 45 tables could be drawn up for 9 categories of household and 6 censuses, though this number could also be reduced by merging certain categories of household.

As a first experiment we have reconstructed in this way the history of the development of the 184 conjugal households, with or without children, present at Grisy in 1836.[5] A conjugal household present in 1836 thus goes out of observation if it leaves the village, or if it changes its household category. In this latter case it enters into another cohort. The results presented in Table 9.8 accordingly have to be completed by drawing up tables of the same type for the other categories of household observed in 1836, and for all cohorts of households (by category) present from 1841 and on, from 1846 and on, from 1851 and on, and from 1856 and on. The 5 tables relating to the same category of household could be merged for certain calculations.

The results set out in Table 9.8, relating to conjugal households, present in the census of 1836, show that the 135 households which left the cohort did so in six distinct ways. Those which quitted the village number 29, and 106 changed category: of those which changed category, 89 % became solitary widows, or

[5] Compare the durability of households in Tokugawa Japan, see below, Hayami, Chapter 18, pp. 513–515; Smith, Chapter 17, pp. 438–440, 470–471. See also Hammel's account, below, Chapter 14, pp. 343–344, 348 of population turnover in sixteenth-century Serbia.

Table 9.8   *Cohort of conjugal households present in 1836*

			Manner of quitting the cohort				
			By change of category				
			Households with several heads of families				
Enumerators' book	Conjugal households still present on lists of date indicated	Death of spouse	With ascendant relatives	Hori- zontally extended	Others	By emigra- tion	Total
1836	184	16	1	—	—	15	32
1841	152	19	5	—	1	7	32
1846	120	19	2	—	1	5	27
1851	93	19	1	1	—	1	22
1856	71	21	—	—	—	1	22
1861	49						
		94	9	1	2	29	135

widows with children, and 8 % took into their households an ascendant relative, whilst 3 households merged with other households.

The data in Table 9.8 also allow us to calculate the probability of change of category for conjugal households present in 1836, together with the probability of these households emigrating as complete groups. In Table 9.9 the results of these probability calculations are set out.

As time goes by, the mean ages of heads of households and their wives get higher, so that the risk of changing of category grows with the risk of death of one or other of the spouses. It would be an advantage therefore to carry out a study of this kind, distinguishing categories of household heads by age.

The figures of Table 9.9 can be used to calculate the probability of any one household remaining in the village and retaining its category between any of the census dates. It is only necessary to subtract the probability of emigration during any one period from 1.000 to get the probability of remaining in the village, and if the same probability is wanted for any number of periods, these reciprocals can be multiplied. A household present in 1836 for example, had a probability of 0.914 of being present in 1841, a probability of 0.868 of being present in 1846, and 0.805 of being present in 1861. That is to say, a conjugal household in Grisy in 1836 had one chance in five of setting itself up somewhere else before 1861.

In the same way in the column k_i the result of multiplying reciprocals of the five figures shows that the probability of a conjugal household of 1836 being still in the same category at the end of twenty-five years was about 0.331. In other words, a conjugal household of 1836 had two chances in three of changing its category in twenty-five years.

Table 9.9   *Conjugal households present in 1836,*
probability of emigration and of change of category

Between lists of:	Probability of emigration e_i	Probability of change of category k_i
1836 and 1841	0.086	0.096
1841 and 1846	0.050	0.168
1846 and 1851	0.046	0.187
1851 and 1856	0.012	0.227
1856 and 1861	0.016	0.298

CONCLUSION

We could scarcely expect that the households of Grisy-Suisnes would have undergone profound change during the twenty-five years centred upon the middle of the nineteenth century, And, indeed, considering only mean size of household, change was not very important between 1836 and 1861. Nevertheless distribution of households by size was displaced *en bloc* towards the small sizes, without diminution of the mean number of children per family less than fourteen years old: on the contrary mean number of children of this age actually grew in families where the head was thirty or over. This was because the proportion of households containing several heads of families showed a marked fall (10 % to 4 %). The tendency of households to correspond more and more to the conjugal family model was no doubt an accompaniment of greater independence in each familial nucleus.[6] The other changes which have been observed, those in occupational structure for men of eighteen and above, seem also to display this tendency.

It has to be remembered, however, that the distribution of households by size varies greatly from one community to another for the same date. Grisy-Suisnes is marked by certain peculiar characteristics when it is compared to some other communities taken as controls, with the exception of the village of Echevronne. The distribution of household types was in 1836 already more modern at Grisy than it was at Guimaec for example, and this can be seen without a detailed analysis of the composition of households in the latter village. It is possible to suppose, then, that the households of Grisy in 1836 had already undergone the changes, and in particular a reduction in their mean size, which the households of the other villages, with the exception of Echevronne, did not experience until later. Consequently the reduction of the size of households and the modification of their composition between 1836 and 1861 could not be as important as it would have been if this evolution had not taken place earlier.

[6] Wall, see above, Chapter 5, p. 163, notes a new emphasis on the separateness of the constituent parts of the household in late eighteenth-century England.

Table 9.10 *Distribution of households by size in certain communities in 1836*

Size of household	Grisy-Suisnes (Seine-&-Marne)		Echevronne (Côte d'Or)		St Julien de Briola (Aude)		Gargas (Vaucluse)		Germond (Deux-Sèvres)		Videix (Haute-Vienne)		Guimaec (Finistère)	
	No.	%	No.	%	No.	%	No.	%	No.	%	No.	%	No.	%
1 person	25	9.3	11	9.0	2	2.3	16	7.3	4	2.5	12	7.0	35	8.9
2 persons	55	20.5	24	19.7	8	9.1	31	15.2	17	10.4	14	8.1	57	14.6
3 persons	80	30.0	32	26.2	12	13.6	38	18.5	30	18.4	23	13.4	36	9.2
4 persons	52	19.4	29	23.7	22	25.0	37	18.1	29	17.8	25	14.5	57	14.6
5 persons	27	10.1	19	15.6	20	22.8	28	13.7	30	18.4	26	15.1	49	12.5
6 persons	17	6.3	4	3.3	11	12.5	25	12.3	22	13.5	32	18.6	45	11.5
7 persons	2	0.7	3	2.5	3	3.4	13	6.4	13	8.0	13	7.6	45	11.5
8 persons	5	1.9	—	—	5	5.7	5	2.5	8	4.9	10	5.8	22	5.6
9 persons	3	1.1	—	—	1	1.1	7	3.4	7	4.3	8	4.6	16	4.1
10 persons	—	—	—	—	1	1.1	2	1.0	2	1.2	5	2.9	16	4.1
11 persons	2	0.7	—	—	2	2.3	1	0.5	1	0.6	1	0.6	10	2.6
12 persons	—	—	—	—	1	1.1	1	0.5	—	—	2	1.2	1	0.3
13 persons	—	—	—	—	—	—	—	—	—	—	—	—	2	0.5
14 persons	—	—	—	—	—	—	—	—	—	—	—	—	—	—
15 persons	—	—	—	—	—	—	—	—	—	—	1	0·6	—	—
Total	268	100.0	122	100.0	88	100.0	204	100.0	153	100.0	172	100.0	391	100.0
Population in 1836	923		411		422		867		774		874		1,943	
Mean size of household	3.44		3.37		4.80		4.25		4.75		5.08		4.97	

10. Household and family in Tuscany in 1427

Christiane Klapisch

THE QUALITY OF THE DATA

The task of representing at one and the same time both Italy and the Middle Ages in this volume is a formidable one. All that I feel able to do for the history of family and household structure is to set out some of the preliminary results of a study of a fiscal document with the title *catasto* dating from 1427 and relating to Tuscany. This study was undertaken to determine the value of the catasto as a demographic source and to find out whether modern methods of treatment and analysis could be applied to these data without bringing about too many distortions.

David Herlihy of the University of Wisconsin was the first to suggest analysing the whole of this huge document with the aid of computers, and it turns out to be a splendid source, although it has to be handled with care. It is a document of remarkable fullness and precision to come from the early part of the fifteenth century, but one which is full of pitfalls because its nature reflects the requirements of taxation.

As for its size, there are nearly 360 volumes and bundles, shelved in the archives of Florence and of Pisa. The Florentine government decided in May 1427 to carry out a complete census of persons and of goods in the whole of the territory belonging to the city, that is to say from the sea to the Appenine Ridge. This was not only a novelty in Tuscany and in Italy, it was perhaps a new departure in institutional and fiscal procedure in Western Europe as a whole, and its implications for historical sociology are clear. The population listed is something like 264,000 persons distributed among about 60,000 rural or urban households. The social coverage of the document is as remarkable as its geographical coverage. In theory everybody, even paupers and those exempt from tax,[1] had to remit a declaration describing and estimating his family and his goods.

This was the first time that Florence extended almost the same conditions of taxation over all the inhabitants of Tuscany, and the information gathered from each of the districts is quite consistent. The authorities contemplated a relatively

[1] On the catasto of 1427, see especially Karmin (1960); Sorbi (1962); Conti (1966); Casini (1964 and 1965).

short period of time for the return of declarations. Time in fact was short, since the government was anxious to carry on the struggle against Milan using the resources which this new tax would yield. Abandoning the old system of *estimo* and of *lira*,[2] it was decided to tax the real property and movables of everybody by weighting his assets with his family responsibilities. It was thus clearly a registration of real property or *cadastre* as well as a census. We propose to analyse this remarkable body of evidence schematically, making the best use we can of its accuracy, its systematic character, and of the fact that it all belongs to a short period of time.

As to its accuracy, it is vouched for by two circumstances, though account must be taken of the fiscal character of the document about which I shall say more in a moment. The first is that the evidence collected was subjected at the time to close checking. The taxation officials verified both the goods and the dependent 'mouths' (*bocche*) declared by each householder, taking advantage of previous taxation returns, comparing the values declared with those mentioned in deeds authenticated by a notary, carrying out enquiries on the spot with the help of established local people. In the second place there is the fact that several versions of the document exist. Apart from the original declarations which were written by the taxpayer himself, or dictated to a more capable person, we have the registers into which these declarations were copied, and in which the total tax liability was worked out, and finally summaries where the principal features of each family from the fiscal point of view were noted down.[3] The facts are sometimes slightly changed between these versions: some mistakes are corrected, and other emendations made which no doubt corrected evasions. These successive versions amplify and correct each other in respect of different details about individuals and families. We have accordingly placed our confidence in one particular version of each entry, to the extent to which it seemed to us worthy of being trusted, that is to say less liable than the others to be affected by evasion.

The last and by no means least advantage of this document is that it describes both people and their patrimonies at one and the same time. This allows us to place a family in its proper social and economic milieu without having to consult other sources.

The catasto of 1427 thus offers us what might be called a photographic copy of Tuscan society which is from many points of view unique. It is true that it would have been a great advantage to be able to put it in its proper perspective

---

[2] Cf. Fiumi (1957). The Florentine estimo like the lira functioned in the following fashion. A certain sum was assigned to each parish or commune, and this was then redistributed among the households according to their relative ability to pay. The figure assigned to each household was its assessment, and the tax would be declared and collected in terms of a certain portion or percentage of this (e.g. one shilling per pound or lira of assessment, or the like).

[3] The bundles of original declarations are called *portate*, the registers into which they were copied *campioni*, and the summaries of the tax rolls *sommari*: many of the studies based on the catasto make use of the sommari alone.

in social structural history. But such a perspective is at present almost entirely lacking, since the history of the family in Italy has still to be written or re-written.[4] The catasto of 1427 was succeeded, it is true, by several other censuses and descriptions of the same type up to the end of the fifteenth century. But it seems that evasion, especially evasion by omission, got worse from one catasto to the next, so that this class of document grows less reliable the more we progress into the fifteenth century. The picture we are painting may well have no sequel, at least of comparable quality.

Even the image which the catasto has preserved for us of Tuscan society in the year 1427 is somewhat affected by its fiscal character. The conclusions we have reached and the calculations we have made on many points of importance are bound to be tentative. All I wish to emphasise here are the ways in which the Tuscan household is likely to have been distorted both in its size and structure by appearing to us through the medium of the taxation office.

As was previously mentioned, this instrument of taxation of properties and patrimonies seems to have been a novelty not only in Tuscany and Italy but in Western Europe as a whole. Further, certain deductions were permitted to every patrimony subject to tax, such as the value of the house or houses kept entirely for the use of the family, and an allowance for each 'mouth' supported by the patrimony which had been declared. The total assets liable for tax, therefore, depended in each case on the number of individuals who benefited from those assets. The head of the household had, in consequence, an obligation to draw up a list of the members of his household in such a way as to indicate clearly the kin relationships of every person to himself. Finally, the law for the catasto set up a system of personal taxation to be paid by every adult male.[5] The head of the household had consequently to record the ages of members of his family as well as their sex so as to make possible calculation of tax on the 'heads' he was responsible for.

These fiscal provisions had the result of specifying the following for each patrimony: the name of the beneficiary or beneficiaries; total assets; house or houses where the family dwelt, or which were reserved by the family for its use; 'mouths' which had to be fed, males and females of all ages; finally the number of males who were subject to the personal levy.

Every individual was correspondingly described by sex, age, kin relationship to head of patrimony, matrimonial status, expressed or understood (often inde-

---

[4] To the older works, Tamassia (1910) and Besta (1933), have to be added numbers of special studies, of which most are referred to in Goldthwaite, *Private wealth in Renaissance Florence* (1968): 251–75. On the psychological atmosphere surrounding the concept of family see Lugli (1909).

[5] The definition of adult male subject to the head tax (*testatico*) varied between Florence itself, the other Tuscan towns, and the countryside. In Florence all men from eighteen to sixty years were included, and in other places those from fourteen to seventy. Boys who were to attain the lower limit of the age specified during the three years in which the catasto was in force, were included among the *teste*, and old men who would pass beyond the upper age limit were exempt.

terminate, especially for the men),[6] and finally by various details pertaining to tax liability. These details included sickness or infirmity, which exempted an adult male from being counted as a 'head';[7] illegitimacy which theoretically meant losing the deduction allowed for every 'mouth'; status of being a stranger to the family or of having no links of kinship or through marriage with the head of the family (servants and apprentices for example), which had the same effect as illegitimacy. Finally, the law obliged taxpayers to declare such modifications in their families as might change their tax assessment within a year or two after the submission of their declarations, so that assessable properties could be fixed for the years to come. Marriages, deaths or births had to be marked in this way on the official record against the name of the party concerned, as well as indications of young brides leaving home.[8]

The following sources of inaccuracy have to be reckoned with because of their tendency to distort returns and because of the way in which the tax worked.

NUMBER OF HOUSEHOLDS

The very poorest households and the most mobile would no doubt have been the most liable to escape the returning officers. Nevertheless there was a fair chance that practically all existent households would be counted, even many of the poorest, because the communities had less interest in concealing a proportion of the members than they had had under the old system of estimo. There was on the other hand an even greater danger that more households would be counted than really existed. The catasto in effect described patrimonies and the families which lived from them rather than households existing on the ground. Residence was an important element in defining the family for the catasto, though not as important as the patrimony. Some families, therefore, which were in fact distinct, might be grouped together in the catasto under the single heading of their common patrimony. But it was much more likely that numbers of households which merely consisted in the goods belonging to individuals who were in fact members of quite other and genuine households might appear as fictional households.

One indication of the fictitious character of certain households was the failure to declare a house of residence for tax exemption. In Florence 85 % of the

[6] Very few individuals are indeterminate as to sex: for example 23 of the 38,000 inhabitants of Florence. Age is more often left unspecified; in Florence there are 426 males and 755 females in this category, that is 2 % and 4 % of the male and female population. As for matrimonial status, it can often be inferred from the context, especially in the case of widowers. We have systematically counted as indeterminate, men of the age of eighteen and above, whose spouses or children are not mentioned in the document.

[7] Women, although they were not subject to the head tax, often set out their physical ailments in the hope of moving the taxation authorities to pity and so getting their tax abated.

[8] These events were considerably underregistered for several reasons, one of which was the desire to benefit from as great a deduction as possible on account of dependent 'mouths'.

citizens declared that they owned or rented their houses. Amongst the remaining 15 % there were a certain number of persons given shelter, that is free accommodation, but the rest were probably for the most part fictional households brought into being by the operation of the tax. The establishments ('ménages') of orphans under age, most often living in the houses of their tutors or with their mothers, must also be deducted from the number of real households. Mothers in these cases made their own returns of their wealth, and except when mothers were declared to be at the charge of their children and a house of residence was specifically mentioned, most of these households must be taken to be artifacts. Finally, the Arezzo sample has shown that a high proportion of women filing returns of their own, did not in fact constitute genuine households. These were most often to be found in the countryside, where 45 % of solitary women, declaring nothing more than a field or a vineyard which made up their dowry, were in fact part and parcel of the household of one of their children, or children-in-law. In the city of Arezzo itself, where such widows who were heads of household were much more numerous than in the countryside (8.4% as against 2.2 %), only 28 % of such women failed to declare a house of residence. In actual fact opportunities for renting accommodation in the city enabled many women to live alone.

COMPOSITION OF HOUSEHOLDS

The households in the catasto are much more likely to be biological families, or remnants of such families, than complete household establishments. They tend in fact to be specified without mention of those residents not recognised as family members: wage earners of various kinds, guests and those given shelter, widows, spouses or relatives who made separate returns of their own goods, their dowries, and so on. Households are also liable to have gained one or two members who judged it preferable for taxation reasons to unite their declarations to those of other household heads. It is quite difficult to establish a balance between these gains and losses. Losses are certainly more important than gains, but we do not know by precisely how much.

DISTRIBUTION BY AGE AND SEX

There are one or two sorts of evasion which might have affected this proportion: married daughters still appear on the declarations made by their fathers; males are 'feminised' or made younger to escape the head tax (testatico); old men are turned into centenarians to lend them dignity and authority. The sex ratio is also likely to be influenced by omissions of babies, for example, or of women overlooked or underregistered, and by additions arising from individuals counted more than once (widows, servants), not to speak of inaccuracies of an entirely spontaneous and innocent kind, such as excessive rounding of ages. An even greater source of error arose no doubt from the disappearance of a sizeable part of the population behind the walls of monastic establishments, whose members are either described by the catasto in a very summary way, or omitted altogether.

In my view the really serious danger to the study of the household and family comes about in the following ways. Firstly, from the number of servants, whose omission or partial registration everywhere reduces the size of the household. Secondly, from the existence of multiple households which might have been artifacts, or of smaller households which arose from fiscal division. Thirdly, from those households which did not exist in fact but which were merely declarations of patrimony. Until more precise research has been done, one can only presume that these different types of bias affected all social classes equally. Acting on this supposition and leaving out of account those households which are obviously suspect, we can compare the rest both in their financial standing, their professional status and their place of residence. Though we cannot give variations in the household over time, we can present an outline of its variations in the social structure.

Information of several kinds on the size and structure of the household has been drawn from a preliminary sample of a thousand families, that is about 4,000 persons, taken both from the city of Arezzo and from the surrounding countryside, and from a first computer analysis of the city of Florence where about 39,000 persons were registered.[9] This information also makes it possible to establish certain demographic features of the society which I shall discuss briefly.

DISTRIBUTION OF HOUSEHOLDS BY SEX AND MARITAL STATUS
OF HOUSEHOLD HEAD

The proportion of those married in lay society (the celibates in religious orders cannot be examined) shows that the majority of women were married by the age of eighteen. Apparently women from the upper classes were more often celibate than others, but since they went into the convent while they were still young, that is when their fathers found it impossible to marry them off, the proportion of the unmarried among lay women was very small even in these rich families. In Florence the average age at marriage was for men thirty-two or thirty-three, but male age at marriage was even higher among her rich. The difference in age between spouses, which had a mean as high as thirteen years for all married persons, reached almost fifteen years amongst the most affluent.[10]

---

[9] The results of this work are presented in Herlihy, *Vieillir à Florence au Quattrocento* (1969) and Klapisch, *Fiscalité et démographie en Toscane* (1969). A discussion of some of the topics dealt with in these articles and in the present one, but extending over a much longer period of time, is to be found in Litchfield, *Demographic characteristics of Florentine patrician families* (1969).

[10] This age gap between spouses should be compared with that found by Laslett and Clarke at Belgrade in 1733, see below, Chapter 15, p. 380.

Table 10.1 *Distribution of households by marital status of head* (%)

	Florence	Arezzo (Sample)	Arezzo countryside (Sample)
Married couples	58.3	57.8	74.6
Widowers	4.3	5.2	6.8
Widows	13.8	17.6	6.0
Unmarried males	3.9	0.2	0.4
Unmarried females	0.8	0.0	0.4
Unspecified males	18.0	13.8	7.6
Unspecified females	0.9	5.4	4.2
	100.0	100.0	100.0

These peculiar features of their matrimonial practices account to some extent for the extraordinary sex ratio amongst the richest families. According to the catasto, the sex ratio (males per 100 females) comes out at about 116 at Florence, 111 at Pistoia, 110 at Pisa and Arezzo for adults, excluding children and the aged. In the city of Florence the ratio climbs to 158 in the richest families. Even if one assumes a general underregistration of adult women, this reveals a deep disequilibrium within the ruling minority, which, since it was so heavily taxed, had every interest in making sure that none of its women was overlooked. A large number of their adult sons were kept celibate until very late, and eligible women were singularly scarce.

The matrimonial status of heads of households is a commentary upon this situation. In the city of Florence 58.3 % of households were headed by married couples, in Arezzo 57.8 %. But in the surrounding countryside this proportion rose to 75 %, as is shown in Table 10.1 above.

If only male heads of households are taken into account at Florence, the proportion of households headed by married couples rises to 68.9 %, which reveals the importance of widows among urban householders.[11] This influence can be discerned in the literature, the moral customs and the religious sensitivity of the time; could it likewise affect economic behaviour and the direction of familial patrimonies? Considerable numbers of households in the towns had female heads: 23 % in Arezzo and 15.6 % in Florence, as against 10.6 % in the Arezzo countryside. But the proportion of households headed by widows was much higher at lower social levels. The figure for Florence falls abruptly in the richest families, for only 2 % of households in the highest, and 5.5 % in the second highest category of wealth had women as heads, and nearly all were widows. Thus the influence of women in social and economic matters was greater among the poor than among the rich.

[11] Compare these figures and those in the table with some from the population of Bologna in 1384; married heads of household 74.3 %, widowed heads of household 20.3 %, unmarried or unspecified 5.4 %. Cf. Montanari (1966).

DISTRIBUTION OF HOUSEHOLDS BY AGE OF HEAD
AND NUMBER OF OFFSPRING

Age of head of household brings out regional variations which were no doubt due for the most part to local economic conditions. At Florence 43.6 % of households had a person of more than forty-five at the head, but at Arezzo 63.2 % of households belonged to this category, with 61.8 % in the surrounding countryside. It may be significant that Arezzo was a frontier city recently laid waste in military operations and much affected both by the epidemics of the preceding year and even more by her economic decline since her submission to Florence in the 1380s.[12] Even there, there was marked variation with wealth. Of some 2,000 families in the highest income group in Florence, only 38.6 % had heads of households older than forty-five.

The number of offspring in the biological family shows that the rich supported markedly more children than others.[13] We find that the highest proportion of brothers and sisters under fifteen years old, for every child aged one or below, comes in the three highest categories of wealth. The relationship index between children 0–4 years and married women between 15 and 44 is also much stronger in these three categories, as shown in Table 10.2.

It is clear therefore that families in the ruling class had their own demographic characteristics. Analysis of the size of households reveals a similar peculiarity at these social levels (Table 10.6).

Table 10.2   *Number of children by value of assets, in 1427*

Categories of wealth (florins)	Number of siblings < 15 years for every child < 1	Number of children 0–4 for 100 married women 15–44
0	1.90	101.3
1–25	1.80	108.6
26–50	1.56	119.5
51–100	1.85	117.8
101–200	1.83	110.7
201–400	1.91	106.3
401–800	2.37	124.0
801–1,600	2.26	144.3
1,601–3,200	3.75	160.7
3,201 and above	3.12	149.6
Mean	2.23	119.2

[12] Arezzo had 1,166 taxable households in 1423 (the catasto of 1427 numbers 1,207), but 848 persons died during the plague of 1425–6.
[13] On the other hand this does not seem to be true of pre-industrial England, see above, Laslett, Chapter 4, pp. 153–155.

Table 10.3   *Size of household in town and country*

	Persons per household	
	Town	Countryside
Florence	3.8	5.1
Arezzo[a]	3.5	4.4
Pistoia	3.6	4.6
Prato	3.7	5.0
San Gimignano	4.0	7.5
Volterra	4.2	
Pisa	4.4	

[a] A preliminary sample of 1,000 households, see above, p. 272.

DISTRIBUTION OF HOUSEHOLDS BY SIZE

The size of household seems to have been modest everywhere. Mean size of household in all the cities of Tuscany which we have studied, or which have been studied by others, comes out at a figure less than 4.5. In the countryside the mean is around 5.[14]

These are crude figures: they cover the whole population, and include fictitious as well as real households. If we eliminate all households without a house of residence from the figures for Florence, the mean size comes out at 4.4 but this would undoubtedly be going too far, especially since people declaring themselves to be living rent-free are also omitted. In assessing these figures it should be remembered that most of these cities were, in the year concerned, at the very bottom of the demographic curve as is evidenced by the extremely large proportion of small households of 1–3 persons. In Arezzo for example 59 % of households contained 1–3 persons, and only 25 % 4 or 5 persons. The countryside around, by contrast, although it had been laid waste by war and by the mercenaries of the king of Naples, sustained households on average much larger, notwithstanding its position at the lower end of the economic scale in the Tuscan countryside: it also had a higher proportion, 30 %, of households of size 4–5.[15] Even at Florence the proportion of households of 1–3 persons was substantial at 48 %, though there households of 4–5 persons also approached 30 %, as is clear from Table 10.4.

Computer analysis of Florentine households in relation to categories of wealth

[14] These differences between town and country seem to be common to many European populations, see below, van der Woude, Chapter 12, pp. 308–309, and Hélin, Chapter 13, pp. 332–333, and despite important differences in household composition, can even be observed in Serbia, see below, Halpern, Chapter 16, pp. 401–402.

[15] Biraben, see above, Chapter 8, p. 243, explains the large households in the French village of Montplaisant in the seventeenth century in terms of the prevalence of peasant unrest. In Victorian England, economic motives seem to have been the most important cause of the co-residence of parents and married children, see above, Anderson, Chapter 7, pp. 229–232.

Table 10.4   *Distribution of households by size* (%)

Persons per household	Florence	Arezzo (Sample)	Arezzo countryside (Sample)
1	20.5	18.8	9.0
2	12.9	22.0	14.2
3	14.7	18.2	18.6
4	12.7	15.0	14.4
5	16.1	9.8	14.2
6		7.6	11.0
7		1.6	7.2
8	20.7	0.4	3.0
9		0.4	3.0
10		(10+) 1.2	(10+) 5.4
11 and over	2.4	—	—
	100.0	100.0	100.0

Table 10.5   *Distribution of population by size of household* (%)

	Florence	Arezzo (Sample)	Arezzo countryside (Sample)
1–3	27.9	34.4	20.4
4–5	40.4	32.0	28.0
6 and over	31.7	33.6	51.6
	100.0	100.0	100.0

demonstrates the correlation between size of city households and taxable wealth. It appears that size of household grew quite regularly with prosperity and status.[16] In the six lowest of the ten categories of value which we have distinguished, mean size varied about 2.6, but it reached 6.3 amongst the richest taxpayers, and the 2,000 wealthiest families were all above the mean (Table 10.6).

If attention is directed towards occupations, the same disparity is found between the whole number of families and those which belonged to major crafts, to the professional aristocracy of trade, industry and banking (Table 10.7).

[16] A similar hierarchy can be observed in the social structure of pre-industrial England, see above, Laslett, Chapter, 4, pp. 152–155. In England, however, it is the proportion of households with kin and servants which explains the gradations whereas in Tuscany servants were only partially registered and the wealthy supported larger numbers of children as well as more kin. Some form of hierarchy in the social structure is a very common feature of differentiated societies, see Goody, Chapter 3, pp. 122–123; and the detailed studies of nineteenth-century rural Lancashire, Anderson, Chapter 7, pp. 220–221 and twentieth-century America, Pryor, Chapter 22, pp. 577–578.

Table 10.6   *Size of household by value of assets, Florence 1427*

Categories of wealth (florins)	Number of families	Size of household
0	3,081	2.8
1–25	440	2.5
26–50	455	2.4
51–100	657	2.6
101–200	1,000	2.6
201–400	1,148	2.8
401–800	1,109	3.3
801–1,600	893	4.1
1,601–3,200	581	5.4
3,201 and over	472	6.3
Mean		3.8

Table 10.7   *Numbers and mean size of households by social and occupational status,   Florence 1427*

Occupational status	Households	Persons	M.H.S.
Agriculture	24	96	4.0
Unskilled labourers and workers	1,750	6,604	3.7
Shopkeepers, craftsmen not in corporations	1,077	4,690	4.3
Minor crafts	841	3,892	4.6
Major crafts	483	2,690	5.5
Messeri (nobles and lawyers)	45	263	5.8
Services (administration, intellectuals, clergy)	588	2,550	4.3
Total population with occupation given	4,808	20,785	4.4
Whole population	9,846	38,594	3.8
% with occupation given	48.7%	53.6%	

SERVANTS AND SLAVES

The household as defined in this way by its dimension is a group of persons united by ties of kinship, yet cut off from some of its members, who were considered as belonging to the *famiglia* nevertheless. Included in our first calculations are domestic slaves whom we have added to the list of members of the household in spite of the fact that they are counted amongst the animals in the document itself. We have only discovered about three hundred in a population of 38,000 people in Florence, 58 out of 7,500 inhabitants of Pisa, and few or none at all in the other Tuscan towns in the interior. Only one citizen of Arezzo possessed a slave, a young one fourteen years of age, and no citizen of Cortona had a slave at all. Although domestic slavery had quite an important place in the fourteenth century in a city like Florence,[17] at this time it affected only a restricted part of the population and, except for two or three hundred affluent families, it seems to have had only a very slight influence on familial behaviour.

But although it is not difficult to get to know the exact number of slaves since they were considered as property and liable to tax, it is almost impossible to get at a satisfactory estimate of the number of servants. We have counted about 235 in Florence, none of whom managed to bring about a reduction in liability to tax although they were all included in the list of dependent 'mouths'. Nevertheless a number of declarations refer to wages of servants and their support, when setting out expenditures which might qualify for deductions. Did this first class of person actually live within the family and did the second live away from it? Unfortunately it is impossible to accept this explanation. Adding together all references to servants from every heading contained in the catasto, we still arrive at a very low percentage of households with servants: 3 % or more at Florence and Arezzo, 2 % at Pisa.[18] It is probable that these proportions represent only a part of the total, but we have no way of checking this. Most of the servants will be missing from the households where they actually lived: they are nevertheless recorded somewhere else in the catasto, in their own families, which for the most part will belong to the kind described above as fictional households. The unfortunate fact is that we do not know exactly the total number of servants within the city.

Without these strangers to the family, what are the predominant relations of kinship or affinity which remain?

SIMPLE AND MULTIPLE HOUSEHOLDS

In my view, a distinction ought first to be made between simple and multiple households, that is to say between those which consist of a single family nucleus, whether extended or not, and those which consist of several. In the system of analysis used here a multiple household consists of a primary family, which may be either one person only, for example a widow, or a conjugal family together with a secondary family of at least two persons. This may be a married couple with or without children, but a widowed person with a child suffices.[19]

[17] Compare Origo, *Eastern slaves in Tuscany* (1955).

[18] At Pisa only 35 households out of 1,750 claimed for the support of servants in their returns, and some of these individuals were subsequently included among the 'mouths' of the families concerned on the campione register, although without benefit of exemption. In the town of Arezzo 27 householders out of the total claimed for their servants either in the original declaration or in the official revision. The total number of servants, house servants, wet nurses and valets (*famigli*) amounted to 36 people, only 13 of whom were subsequently included on the list of 'mouths' in the campione. One merchant in Pisa declared 43 serving people, over and above 1 slave and 1 apprentice.

[19] A widowed person does not by himself make a secondary nucleus on this system: see Henry, *Manuel de démographie historique* (1967): 44. Biraben, above, Chapter 8, p. 242; Blayo,

At Florence 92.25 % of all households had only one nucleus, 90.8 % in the city of Arezzo, and 80.4 % in the surrounding countryside. There remained then not more than 7.7 % of households at Florence, and 9.2 % at Arezzo, that can be described as multiple, and which included at least one secondary nucleus, that is to say a second conjugal family. But the proportion of nearly 20 % in the Arezzo country district is by no means negligible, and suggests that the extended household had a part to play in rural life in Tuscany.

In urban surroundings, at least in Florence, the proportion of multiple households increases markedly with wealth. The four lower categories of assets which contain some 45 % of all households, have an overwhelming proportion (about 95%) of simple households. The four categories above these, extending over the middle range between 100 and 800 florins, have about average numbers (92–93 % of simple households). But in the three uppermost categories of assets in Florence, comprising about one-fifth of all the returns, the proportion of multiple households increases rapidly, climbing from 10 % to 23 %. These figures bring out the relative importance of 'extended' families at these social levels, families in which several nuclear units live together.

In the 472 richest families in the city, the household composition can be broken down as follows:

Table 10.8　*Composition of the wealthiest Florentine households*

2 nuclear family units	15.7% (Mean of all households	6.5%)
3 nuclear family units	5.3% (Mean of all households	1.1%)
4 nuclear family units	1.7% (Mean of all households	0.1%)
5 or more family units	0.2% (Mean of all households	0.02%)

Overall, while the mean number of nuclear family units per household in Florence was 1.09, it reaches 1.32 in the most affluent group. It will be remembered that the mean size of household in Florence also rises regularly with wealth, so it appears that there is a correlation between dimension of household and number of nuclear family units. But this relationship seems to be much closer in the countryside than in the town. In the city of Arezzo among the 16 % of larger households containing 6 persons or more, 42 % were multiple, while in the surrounding countryside multiple households comprise 54 % of the larger households which make up 30 % of all households.

If we look a little more closely into the composition of simple households, we begin to understand how far Tuscan society was stricken by the weight of the widows and celibates left behind because of the contraction of the population.

above, Chapter 9, pp. 256–258; Dupâquier, see below, Chapter 11, pp. 287, 293; and van der Woude, see below, Chapter 12, pp. 310–311, also define nuclear families in the same way. The definition of principal family differs from that suggested by Laslett, above, Chapter 1, pp. 28–33.

No more than 54.4 % of all the households in Arezzo can be described as entirely conjugal (married couple with or without children, widowed person with children). As for the rest, 15.4 % of households were conjugal families including one or more ascendant widowed persons (11.4 %), or solitary affines generally unmarried (2.6 %), or persons belonging to both these categories (1.4 %). In the countryside the proportion of entirely conjugal families falls to 51.2 %, and the other proportions rise to 19.4 % for those containing either ascendants (11.8 %), or affines (3.6 %), or both (4 %). The remaining simple households (21 % in the city, 10.4 % in the country) were comprised of households of widowed persons, celibates, or solitaries of indeterminate status, with a proportion, which was higher in the town than in the countryside, of solitary widowed persons. Moreover, there ought to be deducted no doubt from households of widowers and widows living alone, those who in fact did not constitute genuine households since they declared no residence. In this way the number of households of solitary widowed persons in the country, 2 % of the total, is reduced by no less than half. It is clear that ascendant widowed persons in the great majority of cases were living in the households of their children.

Naturally the vertical principle was most important in the internal kin relationships within simple households in the town. By contrast, the horizontal principle exerted an important influence on the internal structure of multiple households in the countryside. Thus 81.5 % of the larger households (6 persons or more) in the city of Arezzo had vertical kinship relations, while this proportion was only 66 % in the countryside. If multiple households are taken as a whole, the vertical principle of relationship predominated in two-thirds of the cases in the town, but only in 45 % in the country. *Frérèches*, which have to be defined here as married siblings cohabiting after the death or retirement of their elders,[20] form more than half of the multiple households and over 10 % of all households in the Arezzo countryside.[21] It is therefore clear that the relationship between size of household and the extended family was accentuated at the richest levels of urban society on the one hand and amongst the rural classes on the other hand.

Classificatory exercises of this kind are even more interesting when one takes into account the phenomenon of enormous familial associations called *consorterie* or *consorzi*, which demonstrate the cohesive power of the family group during the fourteenth century. In Florence they were called *società della torri* (lit. tower groups), aggressive gangs of the feudal kind; at Genoa they were called

---

[20] On the other hand, unmarried siblings and conjugal families with resident brothers and sisters of the heads do constitute frérèches as defined by Dupâquier, below, Chapter 11, p. 287. See also Laslett, Chapter 1, pp. 30–31.

[21] Dupâquier, below, pp. 292, 294, associates the frérèches with the frequency of orphanage, while Nakane stresses the need for a large labour force as the factor behind the somewhat rare appearance of this form of household in Tokugawa Japan, see below, Chapter 19, pp. 523–524. Such households were also extremely rare in the eighteenth-century Netherlands, see below, van der Woude, Chapter 12, pp. 306–307.

alberghi (lit. groups of dwellers in great houses), and were more like commercial associations.[22]

Even leaving their extremism out of account, these associations seemed to be limited, at least in Florence, to feudal families or to the urban oligarchy which copied the feudal way of life. Historians have shown how they became altered in the fifteenth century with the growth of economic, political and psychological individualism. The evidence of the catasto, when analysed as we have attempted to do here, will enable us to decide whether great families of this kind did in fact exist among the ruling classes and whether they were to be met with in the circles most caught up with business affairs as well as with those families which were tied to the land; among patrimonies which were easily broken up, as well as amongst land-based fortunes of the stable traditionalist kind.

We hope that our research will enable us to discover whether the small-scale proprietors, who were as loath to divide their land as the rich citizens were to contemplate the break-up of their patrimonies, maintained a higher proportion of multiple households; but what happened to the *mezzadri*, who were a new class of sharecroppers taking short leases from the proprietors, very much more mobile than the old-established peasantry? Were they composed predominantly of conjugal families, rootless remnants of former peasant establishments which had been destroyed? In fact our latest work (April 1972) suggests that the families of the mezzadri were both larger and more complicated than those of the small-scale proprietors.

[22] The società della torri were feudal groupings, or groups of urban families usually kin-related which shared a defensive tower between them, or some other work of fortification, and were housed in connected dwellings around this strong point. Cf. Santini (1887); Tabarrini (1904); Niccolai (1940); Fumagalli (1912). Heers has described the alberghi of Genoa in *Gênes au XVe siècle* (1961): 564–76. Compare Hammel's account of the evolution of the zadruga below, Chapter 14, pp. 335–338.

11. Structure of household and family in Corsica, 1769–71

Jacques Dupâquier and Louis Jadin

The French national archives have preserved a splendid collection of documents relating to the demographic and economic life of the island of Corsica after its accession to the territory of France in 1769. There are five series of papers which have survived and it might be useful to briefly describe each series.[1]

1. Papers relating to a Census in 1758, and to a subsequent undated Census.

2. Papers relating to a nominal Census begun in July 1769 in Bastia and finished in 1771 in Ajaccio. The people responsible for this count were the Commissioners of the King for the ' *Départements*' (Ajaccio, Corte and Bastia). Some villages were undoubtedly left out of this Census; at least two of the *pièves* belonging to Aleria and two villages belonging to Bastia. In the final returns the population which the omitted communities had had in 1758 was allotted to them. Fig. 11.1 presents a particularly interesting extract from one of the original returns.

It is this Census which we have chosen to analyse in the present chapter, in spite of these omissions and the fact that particulars as to names are not entirely regular. The results were eventually collated by hand on printed forms and seem to have been submitted to the French sovereign in 1773. The Census is described in detail below.

3. It would be possible to consider the body of summaries and totals made out by these royal officials in respect of the nominal returns as a document distinct from the Census of 1769–71. Totals are generally slightly inaccurate, and everything which was separately noted and put in as an afterthought is omitted from the summaries.

4. Documents belonging to the General Land Survey of Corsica, 1773–96. There are a few fragments with the returns for Bastia and Cap Corse and some blank forms. Along with these documents there are summaries of the hereditary estates in the Bastia area as they existed at that time, as well as numerous surveys with

---

[1] They are contained in two boxes with reference numbers Q1 298[1] to Q1 298[8]. There is a complicated relationship between the census districts used for the successive enumerations referred to in the text and considerable difficulties about the recording of persons in religious orders. These cannot be considered in the present context, but have an important bearing on the general work of analysis to which the present note is an introduction.

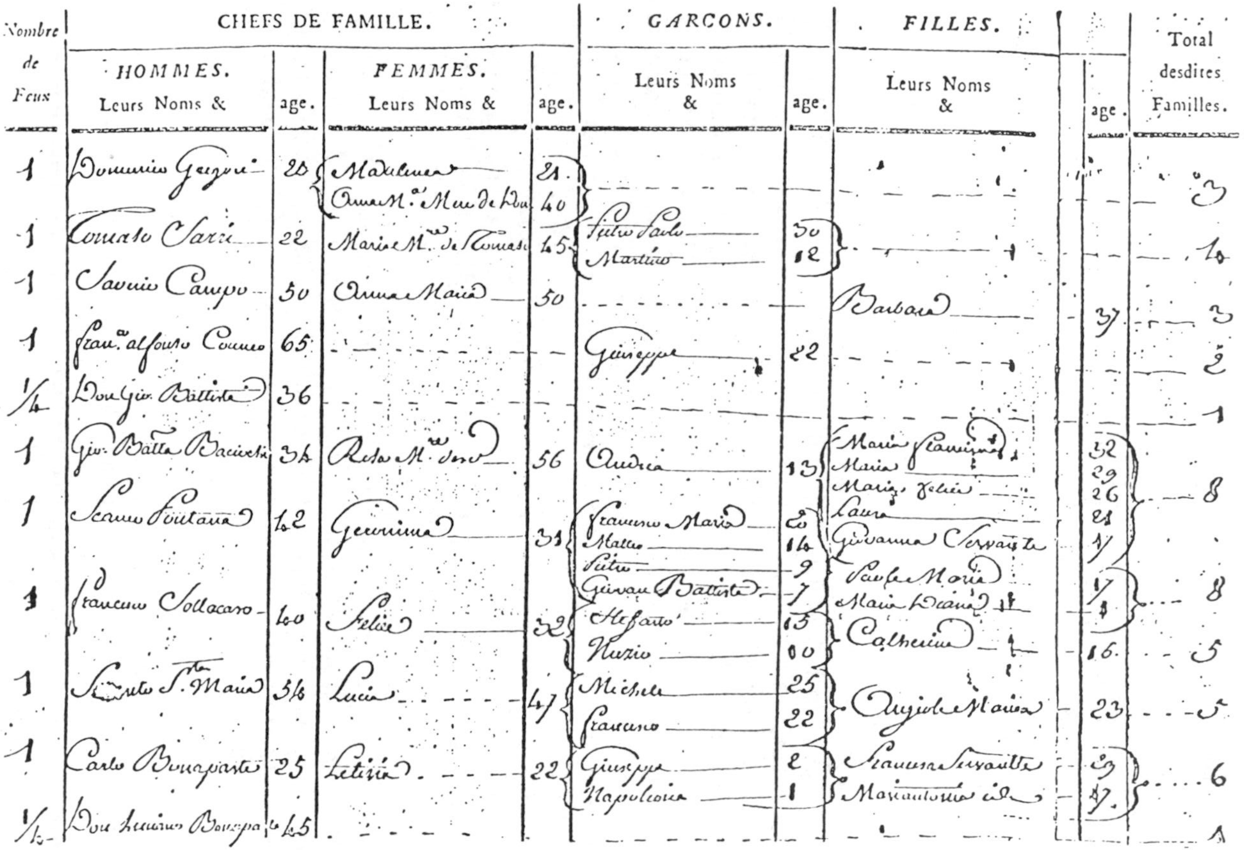

Nombre de Feux	CHEFS DE FAMILLE. HOMMES. Leurs Noms &	age.	FEMMES. Leurs Noms &	age.	GARCONS. Leurs Noms &	age.	FILLES. Leurs Noms &	age.	Total desdites Familles.
1	Domenico Gregori	28	Maddalena Anna M.a Mere de Dom.	21 40					3
1	Corrado Sarri	22	Maria M.a de Tomasi	45	Pietro Paolo Martino	30 12			4
1	Savario Campo	50	Anna Maria	50			Barbara	37	3
1	Fran.co alfonso Cunneo	65			Giuseppe	22			2
1/4	Don Gio. Battista	36							1
1	Gio. Batta Baciochi	34	Rosa M.a serv.	56	Andrea	13	Maria Francesca Maria Maria Felice Laura Giovanna Servante	32 29 26 21 17	8
1	Scenno Fontana	42	Geronima	31	Francesco Maria Matteo Pietro Giovan Battista	20 14 9 7	Paola Maria Maria Diana	17 4	8
1	Francesco Sollacaro	40	Felice	32	Alfonso Nunzio	13 00	Catherina	16	5
1	Simone S. Maria	34	Lucia	47	Michele Francesco	25 22	Angiola Maria	23	5
1	Carlo Bonaparte	25	Letitia	22	Giuseppe Napoleone	2 1	Francesca Servante Mariantonia id.	23 47	6
1/2	Don Luciano Bonaparte	45							1

Fig. 11.1. Facsimile of part of the nominal list for the town of Ajaccio, drawn up in 1770

The tenth family should be noted, that of the Bonapartes. The head is Charles Bonaparte, then aged twenty-five, and he has with him his wife, Letitia, his sons Joseph and Napoleon, and his two servants, Francesca and Maria Antonia. Don Lucian Bonaparte, an uncle in holy orders, lives in the same house, no doubt as part of the household of the young couple.

explanations of the methods on which they were drawn up. A mine of geographical information for the late eighteenth century!

5. Fragments of the Census of 1786 for the jurisdictions of Nebbio, Bonifacio and La Porta. The nominal returns for this Census were drawn up on practically the same basis as those of 1769–71. Under the heading of livestock, numbers of calves and hogs are given, which is the only innovation. The column headed *Observations* is usually left blank. Although they were printed in French, the answers to these questionnaires were filled in in Italian.[2] For the whole of Nebbio the population grew from 5,066 to 5,630 persons, which is a gain of 12 % in seventeen years, though there was a decrease in 3 of the 15 villages.

So much for census documents which have survived for this period for the island of Corsica. Let us now turn to the features of the returns for the years 1769–71 which we have chosen to analyse in detail for the purposes of the study of the size and structure of the household. What follows is a list of the principal features, including the defects of that Census.

a. Kinship connections of individuals within the household are only specified completely, or more or less completely, in the returns from the jurisdictions of Corte, Nebbio, Balagne and in a part of those from Bastia. Elsewhere only a few are mentioned and those erratically.[3]

b. Family names are not always clearly indicated. They happen to be particularly well specified in certain villages in the Niolo area in the jurisdiction of Corte, but not elsewhere. It might be worthwhile quoting an example from the village of Acqualé, where there were 58 households. No less than 44 of them had heads named Aquaviva, and 9 had household heads named Flori. One of the others is dubious because it is not clear whether Simoni is a second forename, or a family name. Nothing at all is known of the four others. Even more typically Corsican, it seems to us, is the apparent division of the village of Bastelica in the piève of Cauro, jurisdiction of Ajaccio, between three names: the Vassellari, the Trocollacci and the Domenicacci.

Kinship connections between different households are sometimes completely specified, particularly in several parishes in the jurisdiction of Corte and Balagne. In these villages a household head may be described as being the eldest son of the previously mentioned household head, or his brother, or his only son, or the only member of a family.

---

[2] The Census of 1758 is in French; the one without a date is in Italian; that of 1769–71 is in French except for one or two pièves which are in Italian: that of 1773–96 is in French; and that of 1786 in Italian. In the 1786 Census there is a great deal of information of sociological and demographic importance. One is told that a son of a particular man has been in America since a particular year, that someone else is studying at Rome, that this family lives in a given place, and so on.

[3] Two sectors can be distinguished. In the first, kinship connections are systematically recorded: it consists of the jurisdictions mentioned above and all the pièves of Bastia with the exception of Cazinca, Orezza and Tavagna. The second in which kinship connections are only rarely indicated, includes the jurisdictions of Cap Corse, Vico, Ajaccio, Sartène, Bonifacio, Aléria, and the pièves of Cazinca, Orezza and Tavagna.

Finally under this heading it should be stated that the distinction between children of the first and a later marriage is only very rarely specified.

c. The presentation of the facts about sex, marital status, etc., is distorted by the exclusive use of categories, 'men, women, boys, girls'. The first two categories are generally reserved for married or widowed persons, but there are exceptions nevertheless, at least for men, though apparently almost never for women. In the jurisdiction of Bastia, for example, married sons living with their fathers are classified amongst 'boys'. In some of the parishes priests are put under the heading 'men' and it often happens that the eldest *unmarried* son of a widow appears amongst the 'men' when 'boys' could logically be expected.

d. Orphans, those that is who had lost either father or mother, are expressly said to be excluded from the Census. But in spite of this fact, several orphans do appear, though only those above the age of twelve years in the case of males, or ten years in the case of females.

e. The very numerous monks on the island, who could sometimes make up 10 % of the male population of a parish above the age of eighteen, are either excluded or counted separately. It is very rare to find them taken into account in totals. When totals of the population were reckoned by the officials of the Crown in the final stage of preparing the Census Report for the King, an allowance was made for each village in respect of monks, priests, clerics (*clercs*) and women in orders, as well as for hedge priests (*ecclésiastiques maquisards*). These officials reckoned the number of feux and of lay inhabitants correctly enough, but completely overlooked the monks who were recorded in the margin of the Census. Using the figures from the margins we have corrected the total of monks and have found it to be particularly high in the jurisdictions of Corte, Nebbio, Balagne and all the pièves of Bastia, with the exception of Cazinca, Orezza and Tavagna. Nuns are only mentioned in the City of Bastia, and Bastia Castle.

f. There is a serious underregistration of young children, under twelve in the case of boys and ten in the case of girls. In many pièves, in Balagne for example, no child of less than a year old is mentioned though they are to be found in the pièves of Niolo and Talcini (Corte), Bigorno and Lota (Bastia).

g. Occupations are only recorded in the City of Bastia and Bastia Castle.

h. The titles of mayor (*podestat*) of a village, and of *pièvan* (incumbent) of a parish occur frequently but are not given in every instance.

i. We have only found one child marriage, and this was in the jurisdiction of Niolo. The husband was twelve and the wife sixteen.

j. The Census records livestock as well as people, specifying the number of animals possessed by each household. Horses, mules, asses, oxen, sheep and goats are everywhere included, and swine in the jurisdictions of Sartène, Vico and a part of that of Ajaccio.

k. There are several columns of observations at the right of each page. The object seems to have been to provide information on the produce and trade of the village, but the columns were very imperfectly filled in. Their contents make up a veritable rag-bag of information of various kinds: notes on the progress of the guerrillas (*maquisards*), on various bandits, and on everyone's liking for a bit of bother, take their place alongside information about persons who were not present to be counted, and those persons who were counted, but who had taken up residence elsewhere. Other topics considered are the existence of religious houses, the idleness of Corsicans, the precocity of boys and girls, the physical types of the inhabitants, church dues, the number of houses and their condition, the presence of noble persons and those exempt from taxation, the existence of ports, the activity of seafaring people, the healthiness of the air, possibilities of colonisation and agricultural development, etc., etc.

The distribution of the population and its age structure has already been studied from the body of documentation so far described, together with a series of comparisons between the situation in 1769–71 and in 1786.[4] In the present chapter we shall, as has been said, confine our attention to the returns for 1769–71 and concern ourselves with the relationships between the following variables:[5]

 a number of nuclear families (conjugal families, widows and widowers) within each household;
 b number of individuals within households with no kinship connection with the household;
 c types of households, set out under the ten following categories:

  1 unmarried solitaries,
  2 entire conjugal families (father, mother, and, where present, unmarried children),
  3 nuclear families headed by widowers,
  4 nuclear families headed by widows,
  5 frérèches: unmarried brothers and sisters living together,[6]
  6 frérèches: conjugal families, which included resident brothers and sisters of the head,[6]
  7 families with married offspring living with the household head,
  8 conjugal families with resident ascendant relatives;
  9 families of a more complex structure, for example families with more distant resident relatives or with ascendant relatives at the same time as brothers and sisters of head,
  10 households where not all members are family connections, especially families with servants;
 d number of surviving children under the age of fourteen;

---

[4] Le Mée, *Un dénombrement des Corses en 1770* (1971.)
[5] The definition of the conjugal or nuclear family differs from that adopted by Laslett, above, Chapter 1, pp. 28–33 but is similar to that used by Biraben, Blayo and Klapisch, above, Chapters 8–10, and by van der Woude, below, Chapter 12.
[6] Compare the definition of frérèches in Laslett, above Chapter 1, pp. 30–31. Klapisch, above, Chapter 10, p. 280, adopts a narrower definition of frérèches: married siblings cohabiting after the death or retirement of their elders.

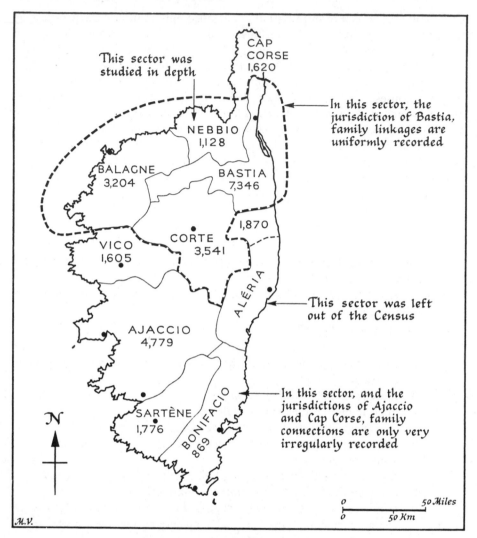

Fig. 11.2.   Distribution of the population of Corsica in 1769–71:
numbers of *feux* and *demi-feux*.

The numbers given here for each sector indicate whole households (*feux*) and denuded households (*demi-feux*), but households of unmarried persons, (*quarts de feux*) were not counted. Moreover, the totals given here are taken from those worked out in the eighteenth century and are slightly inaccurate.

Table 11.1 Structure of households

No. of nuclear units	Sector	Number of individuals outside nuclear unit																		Total	
		0		1		2		3		4		5		6		7		8			
		Gross no.	%	Gross no.	%	Gross no.	%	Gross no.	%	Gross no.	%	Gross no.	%	Gross no.	%	Gross no.	%	Gross no.	%	Gross no.	%
0	Nebbio	—	—	24	2.0	24	2.0	14	1.2	6	0.5	1	0.1	1	0.1	1	0.1	1	0.1	72	6.1
	Bastia	—	—	16	2.4	8	1.2	8	1.2	3	0.4	—	—	—	—	—	—	—	—	35	5.3
	Ajaccio	—	—	14	2.1	4	0.6	3	0.4	3	0.4	—	—	—	—	—	—	—	—	24	3.5
1	Nebbio	807	68.3	69	5.8	22	1.9	4	0.3	1	0.1	—	—	1	0.1	—	—	—	—	904	76.5
	Bastia	439	67.2	47	7.2	10	1.5	2	0.3	3	0.5	2	0.3	—	—	—	—	—	—	503	77.0
	Ajaccio	505	74.9	29	4.3	6	0.9	4	0.6	—	—	—	—	—	—	—	—	—	—	544	80.5
2	Nebbio	174	14.7	15	1.3	—	—	2	0.2	—	—	—	—	—	—	—	—	—	—	191	16.2
	Bastia	97	14.8	5	0.8	2	0.3	—	—	—	—	—	—	—	—	—	—	—	—	104	15.9
	Ajaccio	73	10.8	9	1.3	2	0.3	1	0.1	1	0.1	—	—	—	—	—	—	—	—	86	12.7
3	Nebbio	9	0.8	4	0.3	—	—	—	—	—	—	—	—	—	—	—	—	—	—	13	1.1
	Bastia	10	1.5	1	0.1	—	—	—	—	—	—	—	—	—	—	—	—	—	—	11	1.7
	Ajaccio	18	2.6	1	0.1	—	—	—	—	—	—	—	—	—	—	—	—	—	—	19	2.8
4	Nebbio	—	—	—	—	—	—	—	—	—	—	—	—	—	—	—	—	—	—	—	—
	Bastia	—	—	—	—	—	—	—	—	—	—	—	—	—	—	—	—	—	—	—	—
	Ajaccio	2	0.3	1	—	—	—	—	—	—	—	—	—	—	—	—	—	—	—	3	0.4
5	Nebbio	1	0.1	—	—	—	—	—	—	—	—	—	—	—	—	—	—	—	—	1	0.1
	Bastia	—	—	—	—	—	—	—	—	—	—	—	—	—	—	—	—	—	—	—	—
	Ajaccio	—	—	—	—	—	—	—	—	—	—	—	—	—	—	—	—	—	—	—	—
Total	Nebbio	991	83.8	112	9.4	46	3.9	20	1.7	7	0.6	1	0.1	2	0.2	1	0.1	1	0.1	1,181	100
	Bastia	546	83.5	69	10.5	20	3.0	10	1.5	6	0.9	2	0.3	—	—	—	—	—	—	653	100
	Ajaccio	598	88.6	54	7.9	12	1.8	8	1.1	4	0.5	—	—	—	—	—	—	—	—	676	100

Table 11.2 Distribution of households by size and type

Type of household	Sector	Number of persons per household										Total households of each type		Total persons in these households	Mean no. of persons per household
		1	2	3	4	5	6	7	8	9	10+	Total	%		
1. Unmarried solitaries	Nebbio	24	—	—	—	—	—	—	—	—	—	24	2.0	24	1.0
	Bastia	16	—	—	—	—	—	—	—	—	—	16	2.5	16	1.0
	Ajaccio	14	—	—	—	—	—	—	—	—	—	14	2.1	14	1.0
2. Entire conjugal families	Nebbio	—	61	99	125	100	71	37	14	—	2	511	43.3	2,254	4.4
	Bastia	—	39	67	63	55	34	33	7	5	3	306	46.9	1,383	4.5
	Ajaccio	—	41	77	86	70	47	27	14	1	3	366	54.1	1,631	4.5
3. Nuclear families headed by widows	Nebbio	29	61	68	40	30	14	2	—	—	—	244	20.7	763	3.1
	Bastia	12	16	25	18	12	9	2	—	—	—	94	14.5	319	3.4
	Ajaccio	17	22	26	21	15	3	2	—	—	—	106	15.7	330	3.1
4. Nuclear families headed by widowers	Nebbio	9	6	20	8	6	2	—	1	—	—	52	4.4	163	3.1
	Bastia	11	7	12	7	1	1	—	—	—	—	39	6.0	100	2.5
	Ajaccio	10	3	10	4	4	—	1	1	—	—	33	4.9	97	3.0
5. Frérèches (unmarried brothers and sisters living together)	Nebbio	—	21	13	4	1	1	—	—	—	—	40	3.4	104	2.6
	Bastia	—	9	7	4	—	—	—	—	—	—	20	3.0	55	2.7
	Ajaccio	—	7	4	4	—	—	—	—	—	—	15	2.2	47	3.1
6. Frérèches (conjugal families plus brothers and sisters of head)	Nebbio	—	5	14	20	16	25	2	3	2	1	88	7.5	429	4.9
	Bastia	—	—	7	13	8	12	6	5	2	1	54	8.3	295	5.5
	Ajaccio	—	2	6	6	8	7	5	3	—	1	38	5.6	197	5.2

Table 11.2 *Distribution of households by size and type (continued)*

Type of household	Sector	Number of persons per household										Total households of each type		Total persons in these households	Mean no. of persons per household
		1	2	3	4	5	6	7	8	9	10+	Total	%		
7. Families with resident married children	Nebbio	—	3	10	11	14	14	8	1	6	1	68	5.8	363	5.3
	Bastia	—	1	—	5	4	14	2	5	2	2	35	5.3	208	5.9
	Ajaccio	—	—	1	4	5	4	3	3	—	2	22	3.1	134	6.1
8. Conjugal families with resident ascendant relatives	Nebbio	—	2	21	22	21	15	9	3	—	—	93	7.9	507	5.5
	Bastia	—	1	4	12	11	4	7	8	—	1	48	7.3	266	5.5
	Ajaccio	—	—	9	10	6	7	2	2	—	1	37	5.5	172	4.6
9. Complex families	Nebbio	—	2	10	6	3	9	5	8	3	4	50	4.2	301	6.0
	Bastia	—	1	4	3	7	9	2	1	2	3	32	4.9	186	5.8
	Ajaccio	—	1	1	4	5	4	5	4	3	5	32	4.8	215	6.7
10. Families containing other members and/or servants	Nebbio	—	1	—	1	2	2	1	2	1	1	11	0.9	70	6.3
	Bastia	—	3	1	—	1	1	1	2	—	—	9	1.4	51	5.6
	Ajaccio	—	—	2	1	2	2	2	—	—	4	13	1.9	90	6.9
Total	Nebbio	62	162	255	237	193	153	64	32	14	9	1,181	100	4,978	4.2
	Bastia	39	77	127	125	99	84	53	28	11	10	653	100	2,877	4.4
	Ajaccio	41	76	136	140	115	74	47	27	4	16	676	100	2,927	4.3
Distribution %	Nebbio	5.2	13.7	21.6	20.1	16.3	13.0	5.4	2.7	1.2	0.8	—	—	—	—
	Bastia	6.0	11.8	19.4	19.1	15.2	12.9	8.1	4.3	1.7	1.5	—	—	—	—
	Ajaccio	6.1	11.2	20.1	20.7	17.0	10.9	7.0	4.0	0.6	2.4	—	—	—	—

e   age of head of family;
f   age of head of household;
g   size of household;
h   value of livestock: the list only gives numbers of horses, mules, asses, oxen, cows, pigs, goats and sheep possessed by each family, and the total value has been worked out by the use of the average prices current at the time.

We have calculated the correlations between the above variables three times using a different body of data for each of the three calculations. The first uses data for the jurisdiction of Nebbio, where the material was exhaustively analysed. The second uses the data for the sector of Bastia (jurisdictions of Bastia, Nebbio, Balagne and Corte) where familial possessions jointly owned by individuals in households are expressly mentioned: in this case only one household in twenty was analysed, giving a sample of 653 households. The third uses data for the sector of Ajaccio (jurisdictions of Ajaccio, Vico, Sartène, Bonifacio, and Cap Corse) where family relationships are only very irregularly registered: here again only a twentieth of the households was analysed, giving a sample total of 676 households.

As might be expected, the proportion of households consisting solely of the nuclear family is very high: the 'patriarchal' type of family on the other hand scarcely exists. We may notice in passing that the three results obtained from the three data sets come out very close to each other. This is particularly true of the exhaustive analysis of the Nebbio area and the 1 in 20 sample taken from the Bastia sector (Table 11.1). All this confirms the representativeness of our sample.

The very high proportion of 'nuclear households' makes itself evident again in Table 11.2. But the most striking phenomenon is the existence of *frérèches*, that is to say households of brothers and sisters living together: they vary from 7.8 % in the Ajaccio sector to 10.9 % in the Nebbio sector. These frérèches should not be considered as vestiges of patriarchal families, but rather as living testimonies to the frequency of orphanage. It seems that there were many young children in addition to these, who continued to occupy the family premises after the loss of father and mother no doubt under the supervision of neighbours, but who escaped the attention of the census takers.[7] Nevertheless it should be noted that many of these frérèches which should ordinarily have broken up when their members grew to maturity, persisted because of the ancient custom which required younger sons not to marry and to remain within the household of the eldest brother so that the family holding should not be parcelled out. It is this which explains the relative frequency of 'conjugal families with resident brothers and sisters of head'.[8]

[7] At first sight it seems somewhat unlikely that young children could run their own household without supervision. In England such children would often be taken over by relatives, possibly with some help from the parish: see above, Anderson, Chapter 7, pp. 227–228. It is possible however to find groups of children occupying separate houses in nineteenth-century Serbia: see below, Halpern, Chapter 16, p. 405.
[8] This custom persisted until quite recently in the Nebbio district. A similar custom is to be found in parts of Tokugawa Japan, but for entirely different reasons: see below, Nakane,

Table 11.3   *Numbers of living children by age of head of family.*
Distribution per 1,000 in each age group

Age of head of family		Proportion of families with living children aged fourteen or below									Mean no. of children per family	All France in 1946
		0	1	2	3	4	5	6	7	Total		
Under 25	N[a]	549	333	78	39	—	—	—	—	1,000	0.61	0.65
	B	481	296	185	37	—	—	—	—	1,000	0.78	
	A	610	244	122	24	—	—	—	—	1,000	0.56	
25–34 years	N	273	347	207	120	45	4	4	—	1,000	1.35	1.22
	B	155	368	284	116	52	19	6	—	1,000	1.63	
	A	313	308	227	81	54	16	—	—	1,000	1.30	
35–44 years	N	177	216	299	192	91	18	6	—	1,000	1.89	1.31
	B	195	180	255	235	80	50	5	—	1,000	2.00	
	A	238	157	267	219	76	38	5	—	1,000	1.87	
45–54 years	N	385	222	203	138	37	12	—	3	1,000	1.26	0.45
	B	383	221	221	121	40	—	13	—	1,000	1.27	
	A	368	246	196	110	49	31	—	—	1,000	1.32	
55–64 years	N	762	135	46	42	15	—	—	—	1,000	0.43	0.07
	B	733	137	69	38	15	8	—	—	1,000	0.49	
	A	720	161	93	8	17	—	—	—	1,000	0.44	
65 and above	N	943	49	8	—	—	—	—	—	1,000	0.07	0.07
	B	965	—	35	—	—	—	—	—	1,000	0.07	
	A	706	118	147	29	—	—	—	—	1,000	0.50	
Total	N	444	215	174	113	43	8	2	1	1,000	1.13	
	B	395	211	200	124	44	19	6	—	1,000	1.29	
	A	403	217	201	109	48	21	1	—	1,000	1.25	

[a] N = Nebbio, B = Bastia, A = Ajaccio

The very high proportion of widows in the Nebbio sector should also be noted: this was the region much fought over during the battles of 1768.

The mean number of persons per household varies considerably. This arises in part from demographic causes (fertility, mortality) and in part from social causes (many families containing more than one nucleus).

To press our examination a little further, we have analysed the evidence by age of head of family, using the model laid down by Louis Henry.[9] The figures have been worked out for nuclear families and not for households: total

Chapter 19, pp. 523–524. Klapisch, above, Chapter 10, p. 280, found that in 1427 frérèches formed the majority of multiple households in the economically backward and war-devastated Tuscan countryside. However, it is clear that this type of household was extremely rare in the eighteenth-century Netherlands: see below, van der Woude, Chapter 12, pp. 306–307.

[9] Henry, *Manuel de démographie historique* (1967): 42. This model is also used by Biraben, Blayo and Klapisch, above, Chapters 8–10, and by van der Woude, below, Chapter 12. It differs slightly from that suggested by Laslett, above, Chapter 1.

Table 11.4   *Distribution of households by type and by age of head*

Age of head	Sector	Household types										
		1	2	3	4	5	6	7	8	9	10	Total
Under 30	Nebbio	9.7	26.6	12.1	—	21.0	7.3	—	20.2	3.2	—	100
	Bastia	2.6	42.2	5.2	—	11.9	13.2	—	11.9	3.9	9.2	100
	Ajaccio	9.3	39.8	5.6	—	12.0	9.3	—	15.7	7.4	0.9	100
30–44	Nebbio	1.1	50.0	15.1	3.7	2.4	9.7	1.1	11.6	3.9	0.9	100
	Bastia	0.7	53.0	12.7	3.4	2.7	9.3	0.7	11.3	3.8	1.4	100
	Ajaccio	0.3	64.0	14.9	2.4	0.7	6.6	—	6.9	2.4	1.7	100
45–59	Nebbio	1.0	46.6	25.8	3.7	0.5	7.5	6.3	4.0	3.7	1.0	100
	Bastia	2.3	47.6	17.6	9.1	1.1	5.1	7.4	2.8	6.2	1.1	100
	Ajaccio	—	58.4	19.3	10.0	—	2.9	4.1	—	2.9	2.2	100
60 and above	Nebbio	1.5	32.3	25.6	10.2	0.5	2.6	19.5	—	6.1	1.5	100
	Bastia	0.9	34.2	18.9	11.7	—	6.3	18.0	1.8	7.3	0.9	100
	Ajaccio	—	33.6	24.3	8.4	—	4.2	13.7	—	12.6	3.2	100

of observations this time is 1,328 for the Nebbio sector, 719 for that of Bastia and 750 for that of Ajaccio (Table 11.3).

These figures are only really significant for the age groups from 25 to 54 years, because the numbers in the first group (head of family under 25 years) and of the last group (head of family 65 and above) are trivial. Hence the wide variation from sector to sector.

It is not only the size of the biological family which depends on the age of the head, but also the size of the household, and even its structural type. This is evident from Table 11.4, and there are other points in the figures which should not escape attention. It was to have been expected, for example, that the number of denuded households (*demi-ménages* – types 3 and 4) headed by widowers and widows would rise as the age of the head increased, but it is particularly interesting to see how the number of frérèches (types 5 and 6) declines very quickly in accordance with the same principle. The older the head of the household, the less likely it is to be constituted of brothers and sisters living together, or to have unmarried persons living as part of it. This supports the argument that households of this type are living witnesses to the frequency with which children became orphaned, rather than vestiges of the patriarchal family.

In order to analyse the wealth of families in livestock, we have allotted a value-coefficient to every beast, with the value of the goat equivalent to 1. This gives us 6 for a donkey, 15 for a steer or a cow, and 18 for a horse or a mule. This scale is based on an examination of average prices prevailing at the time, but there are a number of contradictory tendencies and the estimates which we have adopted must be considered very approximate. Moreover it was not possible to take pigs into account, because they were not counted everywhere.

The results of these calculations as to wealth are set out in Table 11.5. The entries in the columns under *Level of wealth in livestock*, refer to the position of the families concerned in relation to the mean, according to what has been called the fan method.[10] Category *A* consists of households whose proportions of wealth lie between the mean and twice the mean, Category *B* those between twice the mean and four times the mean, Category *C* between four times and eight times, and so on to Category *E* ($16\bar{x} - 32\bar{x}$). Category *a* those between the mean and half the mean, Category *b* between half the mean and a quarter of the mean, Category *c* between $\frac{1}{4}$ and $\frac{1}{8}$ and so on to Category *e* ($\frac{1}{16\bar{x}} - \frac{1}{32\bar{x}}$).

A zero category is provided for those with no livestock, and the great advantage of this method is that it allows a graphic representation in a simple and direct way of the distribution of income and particularly of the comparative levels of all sorts of distributions amongst all sorts of populations. In the present instance, nevertheless, it must be confessed that the possession of livestock is a poor indicator of the real distribution of wealth. Townspeople in particular inflate the zero category quite artificially. The family of Bonaparte is found in it, for example, although it had two servants, because it possessed neither horses nor other animals. This is the reason why the wealth in livestock of the Nebbio jurisdiction seems to be greater than those of Bastia and Ajaccio where the higher proportion of urban dwellers brings down the mean.

On the other hand, considerable differences are known to exist within the Bastia and Ajaccio sectors between one village and another, in accordance with differing economic conditions. We thought of correcting these distortions by dividing the villages into classes, but there would have been a risk of freak results. Where communities possessed practically no livestock, the average is so low that anyone who kept a goat or two would be arbitrarily projected amongst the higher categories. All we have been able to do is to allot a particular mean to each of our three sectors and the figures in Table 11.5 must be read with this caution in mind.

A further examination (Fig. 11.3) shows that the types of household least likely to possess livestock were those of unmarried persons, those headed by widows, and frérèches consisting of unmarried siblings. The significant relationship is perhaps the reduced size of these households, as much as their probable poverty. On the other hand households of complex structure, which had taken in an ascendant relative or retained a married child, often possessed livestock.

We have also attempted to find out if this distribution varies appreciably with the age of head of household, but the results are inconclusive. Except in the Bastia sector, random variations blur any tendency for wealth in livestock to increase perceptibly until the onset of old age. It has to be admitted that the size of our sample makes it unsuitable for fine analysis.

To sum up, it can be said that our results are primarily of value in preparing the way for more extensive analysis, which could be undertaken with the help

[10] See Dupâquier, *Problèmes de mesure et de représentation graphique en histoire sociale* (1964).

Table 11.5   *Distribution of households by level of wealth in livestock*

Type of household	Sector	Level of wealth in livestock											% households without livestock
		0	e	d	c	b	a	A	B	C	D	E	
1.	Nebbio	19	—	—	—	1	2	2	—	—	—	—	79.1
	Bastia	7	—	—	—	—	—	—	—	—	—	—	100.0
	Ajaccio	9	—	—	—	—	1	—	—	—	—	—	90.0
2.	Nebbio	174	—	—	12	59	75	110	68	11	1	—	34.8
	Bastia	116	4	9	15	34	40	43	36	11	1	—	37.2
	Ajaccio	139	5	—	20	21	44	48	51	19	4	1	39.5
3.	Nebbio	19	—	1	6	11	3	7	2	2	1	—	36.5
	Bastia	20	1	1	2	2	4	3	4	1	1	—	51.3
	Ajaccio	16	—	1	—	2	6	3	3	1	—	—	50.0
4.	Nebbio	138	—	1	6	18	26	28	16	5	—	1	62.1
	Bastia	58	2	5	2	4	6	8	6	2	—	—	50.0
	Ajaccio	68	—	2	2	5	13	8	7	—	—	—	64.0
5.	Nebbio	22	—	—	1	2	5	6	2	1	1	—	55.0
	Bastia	12	—	—	—	2	—	2	2	—	—	—	66.6
	Ajaccio	8	—	—	—	—	2	5	—	—	—	—	53.3
6.	Nebbio	26	—	—	4	18	10	9	14	4	1	—	31.8
	Bastia	15	—	1	4	1	8	7	7	4	—	—	32.0
	Ajaccio	10	—	1	3	2	3	7	7	5	—	—	28.8
7.	Nebbio	19	—	1	2	6	9	15	9	6	1	—	28.3
	Bastia	6	—	—	—	—	6	7	8	7	—	—	17.6
	Ajaccio	4	—	1	2	1	6	2	2	1	1	—	20.0
8.	Nebbio	18	—	—	4	8	24	19	14	7	—	—	19.1
	Bastia	16	—	1	1	3	6	12	4	3	2	—	33.3
	Ajaccio	15	3	1	2	1	6	6	3	—	—	—	40.6
9.	Nebbio	9	—	—	1	4	3	8	12	11	1	—	18.3
	Bastia	13	—	—	—	1	2	5	5	4	2	—	40.6
	Ajaccio	12	—	1	—	2	7	5	3	1	—	—	38.7
10.	Nebbio	3	—	—	—	2	1	2	2	—	1	—	27.7
	Bastia	8	—	—	—	—	—	—	—	—	1	—	88.8
	Ajaccio	5	—	—	—	—	1	2	2	—	2	1	38.4
Total gross no. of households	Nebbio	449	—	2	34	127	160	203	142	47	7	1	
	Bastia	285	7	17	24	50	75	88	71	32	7	—	
	Ajaccio	283	8	15	29	35	87	87	78	30	12	3	
Total (% by sector)	Nebbio	38.4		1.7	2.9	10.8	13.6	17.6	12.1	4.0	0.5	0.1	
	Bastia	43.5	1.1	2.9	3.7	7.6	11.5	13.4	10.8	4.9	1.1	—	
	Ajaccio	42.5	1.2	2.2	4.3	5.3	13.0	13.0	11.7	4.5	1.8	—	

of a computer. This would enable comparisons to be made between the structure of households in Corsica with that in other populations in the past. Meanwhile it can at least be emphasised that the domestic group in Corsica was comparatively modern in character at the time of the birth of Napoleon Bonaparte.

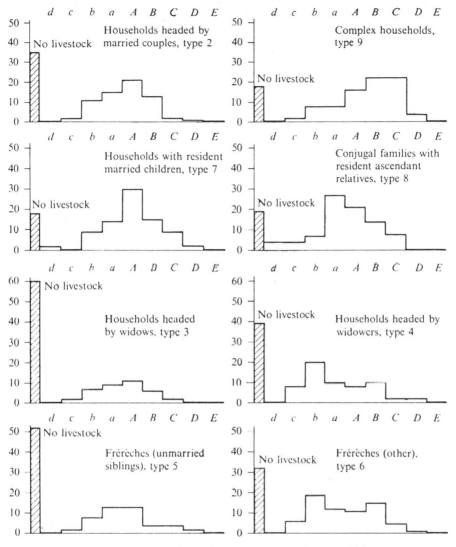

Fig. 11.3   Distribution of wealth in livestock by type of household in percentages
(Nebbio only)

We have sought in vain for something analogous to the zadruga[11] but most of the households consist of conjugal families. The fact that servants are so very uncommon helps to explain why size of household is relatively small, and the frequency with which frérèches are to be found must be viewed as a consequence of the prevalence of orphans, rather than as a survival of patriarchal institutions.

[11] The large and complex households found in the Balkans are described by Hammel, Laslett and Clarke, and Halpern in Chapters 14–16, below.

12. Variations in the size and structure of the household in the United Provinces of the Netherlands in the seventeenth and eighteenth centuries

A. M. van der Woude

My research concerns a district called the Noorderkwartier in the northern area of the province of Holland in the western part of the country, and I have collected data relating to more than 4,000 households between the years 1622 and 1795. Fortunately the eighteenth-century Dutch demographer Nicolas Struyck collected evidence on the size of household in about forty villages in the same part of Holland about the year 1740. His original materials have been lost, but summary totals of inhabitants and households in every village are to be found in his books. What is more, Struyck gives the number of servants (and in some cases lodgers) for most of his villages and even goes so far as to give the sex ratio and the number of children below a certain age.[1] From Struyck's work I have extracted information relating to 8,500 households to add to that for the 4,000 mentioned above.

However, I should like first to discuss the theories developed by Dutch social scientists in the field of the sociology of the family. Historical work gains significance in the light of these sociological theories, and it is appropriate that they be considered before the results of the research referred to above are set out. After the Second World War, interest in the family grew at a much faster rate amongst the Dutch sociologists than amongst the historians. The particular object of attention has been the position of the family in the rapidly changing society of the Netherlands. In considering this issue the sociologists could scarcely avoid putting forward theories on the structure and character of the Dutch family in the past.[2] Only by the juxtaposition of the hypothetical family of the past and the observed family of the present could the real characteristics of the modern family be depicted and the course of future development be explained. Without contrast there could not be full understanding.

A central position in this discussion has been held by the sociologist and

[1] Struyck (1753).
[2] Kruijt (1938) and (1950); Saal (1951); Hofstee (1954); Kooy (1957) and (1967).

demographer, E. W. Hofstee. Shortly after 1950, he formulated his theory of the three reproductive patterns which should have succeeded each other in the Netherlands.³ These three patterns of marriage and reproduction, varying in significance in time and in place, are referred to by the following titles. There is the *agrarian–artisan* pattern, the pattern referred to as the *proletarian–intermediate* stage, and the modern *birth-control* pattern. These conceptions later became part of a much broader theory developed by Hofstee and his collaborators on the genesis of modernisation in the countryside as a whole. It is understandable that the family, as the cornerstone of society, historical and contemporary, should have bulked large in theories of what is called the 'modern dynamic pattern of culture'.⁴

This model of three reproductive patterns succeeding each other in time was explicitly formulated by Hofstee in 1954 with the object of explaining the interesting geographical variation in the birth rate in the Netherlands in the second half of the nineteenth century. It was supposed that this variation was to be explained by fundamental differences between the cultural, social and economic characters of the several regions of the Netherlands. Marital and reproductive habits appeared to take different forms from area to area.

In this model the system of marriage and reproduction on the sandy soils of the eastern and southern parts of the country was directed towards limitation of birth, though without the practice of birth-control within marriage. The object was to keep the population numbers down to the level demanded by the scarce resources characteristic of this area. The system was based on the assumption that marriage only took place when people were certain of a livelihood appropriate to their status. Those who never attained such certainty remained unmarried, and spent the rest of their lives in the parental home. If a farmer had more than one son, and there was only one farmstead to pass on, then typically only one son got married and that at a relatively advanced age. The other sons, and daughters too, remained unmarried on the family farm. In this system the extended family inevitably came into being, and often consisted of brothers and sisters of the married couple, as well as of their children, of one or more of their parents, and even of their uncles and aunts.

That such a system actually existed during the nineteenth century on the sandy soils of the east and the south has not yet been demonstrated by research. But it is true that what look like obvious remnants of extended family households exist even today in some eastern areas. In 1956 a survey of nearly 10,000 farmer households in 23 communities in the eastern provinces revealed that nearly 26 % were extended family households.⁵ There were communities with a proportion as high as 55 % or even 62 %. It was quite reasonable to suppose, moreover, that such

³ Hofstee (1954).
⁴ The best introduction to these theories and concepts is to be found in Op't Land (1966); Droogleever Fortuijn and Kruijer (1966); Hofstee (1966 i–iii); and Petersen, *Fertility trends and population policy* (1966).
⁵ Kooy (1959).

a system was prevalent in the nineteenth century. Such an assumption would explain some of the conspicuous demographic features of the population concerned: a low birth rate, a low percentage of married women between fifteen and forty-five, together with a normal level of age-specific marital fertility.

But Hofstee did not stop there. He assumed that this agrarian–artisan pattern of reproduction which was to be found in the late nineteenth century only on the sandy soils of the east and south, had been the dominant pattern for the entire country in the eighteenth century, indeed had been normal for the whole of Dutch society. In his view it must have been characteristic not only of the farmers but of the farm workers as well. According to him, a servant remained unmarried in the household for as long as a farmer failed to guarantee him a contract for life. He believed that the old, faithful, celibate farm worker, living with the household, was the typical figure of society at that time. He held that this agrarian–artisan reproductive pattern predominated also in the world of small craftsmen and shopkeepers, because there too the father had the same desire to hand on his trade to his son.

Though a historian might have his doubts about a scheme of this kind from the very outset, it is a model peculiarly attractive to the sociologist. It sets our own dynamic society so vividly up against the traditional society which came before it. The cool, impersonal, businesslike social relationships of our own individualistic era are confronted with the strong ties of the individual to all his relatives and with the friendly intercourse of neighbour with neighbour which were so prominent amongst our ancestors. The egoism and individualism of the modern nuclear family are compared with that former sense of responsibility for all relatives. It brings out the willingness to subordinate personal feelings to the common well-being of the family which stood in the place of the modern desire for the greatest possible development of one's own personality. All this assumes a family hierarchy more or less patriarchal in character, with a strong sense of mutual responsibility between the head of an extended family and its members, between the employer and the faithful servant. Against the sexual freedom of our age is placed the sexual restraint and repression which reigned in the society of old. This restraint and repression, this sexual discipline, could only have existed in a society where social control was very firm, where there was no place for a private life, where the doings of each individual were subject to the effective judgement of everyone in his neighbourhood.

These notions became strongly rooted in the Dutch literature on the sociology of the family. They laid it down that the appearance of the nuclear family only began to interrupt the intense communication of the individual with his relatives and his community from about 1900 onwards. Not until after this date did the right of an individual to marry into ranks higher than his own become generally accepted. In addition to the idea of the right to marry, the idea that a person had a right to choose a partner for reasons of personal affection and love also gained ground. Only after 1900, then, did the father lose his patriarchal position within the nuclear family. Wife and children came to have a more equal footing with him, and the patriarchal nuclear family changed into 'a familial democracy'. The emphasis shifted more and more from the economic, procreative and educational functions of the family group, to the sexual and affectionate ones. Not before the twentieth century did family life become a means towards the unfolding of one's own personality. Marriage and the life of the family became less and less a public affair.[6]

TOWN AND COUNTRY IN SEVENTEENTH- AND EIGHTEENTH-CENTURY HOLLAND

In our view historical research and sociological theory ought to march together, and it is the task of the Dutch historian to test this model against the historical reality. It may be true that the situation which it describes can be expected to have existed to a greater or lesser degree in earlier European society. Peter Laslett has given us a penetrating description of the world we have lost, as well as an important corrective to current sociological theory. But it has still to be decided whether the pattern I have sketched was in fact the typical pattern all over the Netherlands before 1900, or even before 1800. The research we are doing at Wageningen in so far as it is concerned with the family cannot be dissociated from these sociological hypotheses and from the very beginning we had reason enough to doubt their general validity for the Netherlands.

The most important parts of the Netherlands in the seventeenth and eighteenth centuries were not peopled by the relatively closed agrarian communities so vividly depicted in the theories just described. The province of Holland was to begin with very heavily urbanised, if not indeed the most heavily urbanised region in Western Europe. As early as 1514, as much as some 46 % of the population of Holland lived in towns, and this proportion rose to 54 % in 1622 and 59 % in 1795.[7] Whilst these towns were still relatively small in the first half of the sixteenth century, the numbers of their inhabitants rose sharply after that, with the result that by the mid-seventeenth century there was one city (Amsterdam) of nearly 200,000 inhabitants, four cities (Haarlem, Leiden, The Hague and Rotterdam) with a population of something between 30,000 and 60,000 inhabitants apiece, six (Alkmaar, Hoorn, Enkhuizen, Delft, Dordrecht and Gouda) each with a population of between 10,000 and 30,000, and at least eight having between 2,500 and 7,000 inhabitants. It is very important to note in this connection that these towns were so regularly distributed over the country that almost no village was at a greater distance than 25 kilometres (15 miles) from one or other, or even several of them. The villages themselves were generally significantly larger than was the rule elsewhere in Europe. Many of them had more than

[6] Demos, in his study of the family and household in colonial America, approaches the problem in the same way but reaches a very different conclusion: see below, Chapter 21, pp. 561–569.
[7] Van der Woude, unpublished research.

2,000 inhabitants, and some even as many as 4,000. Villages having less than 500 inhabitants were exceptional. Population density in the countryside ranged between 40 and 100 inhabitants per square kilometre (100–250 inhabitants per square mile).[8]

Although reliable figures are not yet available it can be assumed that there was extensive migration over the whole territory of the Netherlands. Excess of deaths over births must have been the rule in town populations, which needed a steady influx from the countryside. The story told by Wrigley for London and its agrarian surroundings perhaps holds to an even greater degree for the relationship between the combined Dutch cities and the rural Dutch hinterland.[9] It is known from one parish in Rotterdam that in the second half of the eighteenth century, 29 % of all families on poor relief came from Dutch Brabant, and that 24 % were actually born in Germany.[10] During the seventeenth and eighteenth centuries 50 %–60 % of all bridegrooms in Amsterdam were born outside the city.[11] Many of the immigrants must have stayed in touch with their relatives in the countryside, and a number of them must sooner or later have returned there. Urban ideas and urban ways of life were accordingly not unknown in the villages, and presumably permeated life there to some degree.

In my opinion it is very important that agriculture did not have everywhere that predominance over daily life which is known to have been generally the case elsewhere. Navigation was strongly rooted in the society, and after the sixteenth century it became one of the most important modes of employment. Large parts of the countryside of Holland, Zeeland and Friesland formed a great reservoir of sailors. Thousands and thousands of these country people must yearly have visited harbours between Archangel and Constantinople, and even further afield. This cannot have remained in the long run without its consequences on their way of thinking and so on village life. We can illustrate the difference of the occupational structure from what was usual in the European scene, from the fact that after about the middle of the seventeenth century only 17 % or 18 % of the male working population in these northern parts of Holland can have been earning a living in agriculture.[12]

Since, in studying the family, its economic function is of great importance, we must not fail to emphasise that agriculture in Holland, western Utrecht and south-west Friesland was not of the type most usual elsewhere. Arable farming for corn growing was the normal situation in Western Europe and cattle were primarily kept for manuring the land. The household was to a marked degree self-supporting, and the economy to some extent a natural rather than a monetary one. Only production surpluses went to market. But the province of Holland was primarily a dairy and livestock area. Farmers sold their products, milk, butter, cheese and cattle almost exclusively on the market. Livestock farming in

[8] de Vooys (1953).   [9] Wrigley, *A simple model of London's importance* (1967).
[10] van Voorst van Beest (1955).   [11] Hart (1965).
[12] van der Woude, unpublished research.

fact presupposes a monetary economy and the more or less self-supporting family cannot exist under these circumstances. In Holland, then, farmers had to buy their corn and fuel in exactly the same way as the inhabitants of the towns. In so far as arable farming had a part to play, it was not directed towards the growing of corn but first and foremost to the cultivation of commercial crops: hemp, flax, hops, coleseed, madder and vegetables. Livestock farming was the predominant activity, however, and this undoubtedly had its consequences on the size, structure and life of the family. For livestock farming is labour-extensive; it needs relatively little manpower. As farms were generally small or medium-sized (and what else could be expected in an overcrowded countryside?), there was no place at all for big households with many servants and relatives. Surplus population had to seek a living outside agriculture.

It must be recognised that Dutch livestock farming had a marked, if incidental, effect on the mentality of the people. It favoured not only an attitude which can be called money-directed, but an individualistic attitude too. Common land did not exist in the system and every plot as well as the farms themselves was surrounded by ditches. Although the water was a unifying factor over distances, since it facilitated transport and traffic, it had a divisive effect locally. The most conspicuous common interest was defence against the ever-menacing water itself. But this created rather a spirit of equality, independence and even of democracy, than one of subordination, hierarchy and collectivism. The fact that in parts of Holland repair works on the dykes were not done in common, but on a system whereby they were distributed among landowners in accordance with size of holding, can be taken as an indication of these circumstances.

There can be no doubt whatever that still other variables had a marked effect in creating an outlook of individualism and independence. There was first the fact that the nobility was on the whole of little importance in the western and northern provinces of the Netherlands after the waning of the Middle Ages, and that in some regions it never even came into existence. It may be an exaggeration to say that neither the nobility nor the gentry nor semi-feudal institutions had any part to play after 1600, but one can talk of these things being almost absent when the position in the Netherlands is compared with that elsewhere in Europe under the ancien régime. It was the city, the citizens and urban institutions which had to be reckoned with by village people.

In the second place, in attempting to explain the outlook of that society it is important not to forget that there had been a division along religious lines over the majority of the countryside of Holland ever since the end of the sixteenth century. At a time when religious belief was of crucial importance in every direction, this division made a genuine collective village life virtually impossible. On the one hand it kept Roman Catholics out of office, and on the other hand it compelled everyone, Calvinists, Roman Catholics, Lutherans and Mennonites alike, to consider religious beliefs to be the private affairs of every family. The village community could not have functioned if room had not been found in this

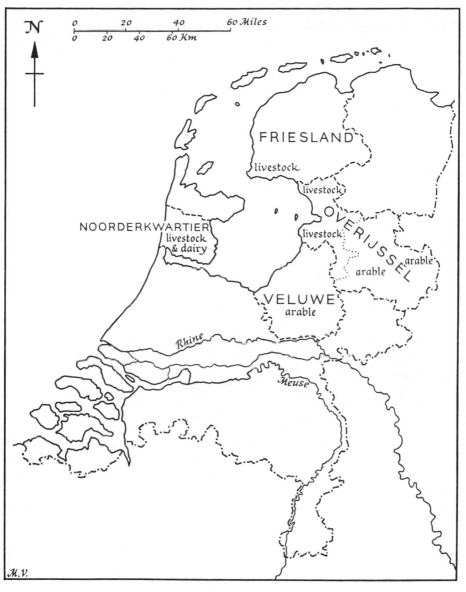

Fig. 12.1   The pattern of farming in certain regions of
the eighteenth-century Netherlands

way for personal convictions and privacy in religious practices. Religion, which was elsewhere the cement of that lost society, here created distance between people living in the same village, the same street, perhaps sometimes under the same roof. It split the community into segments, which coexisted sometimes in enmity, but never in intimacy.

It may be said that it was only in a limited area, that is to say in the province of Holland itself, that these exceptional conditions existed, which favoured a spirit of individualism quite unusual at that time. Holland was indeed restricted in its area, but the fact is that 45 % of the whole population of the Netherlands lived in this province. Moreover some of the circumstances just described, existed in parts of the provinces of Zeeland, Utrecht and Friesland as well.

REGIONAL VARIATIONS IN HOUSEHOLD SIZE AND STRUCTURE

Having considered the infrastructure of Dutch society in the seventeenth and eighteenth centuries, let us now take a look at the results of research into the history of the family in the Netherlands.[13] We may begin with Overijssel. Slicher van Bath[14] found that of the 7,763 households in the province of Overijssel of which the structure could be analysed for the year 1749, no less than 1,596 were extended family households, that is to say 20.5 %. When a distinction is drawn between households situated within the villages themselves and those dispersed over the countryside, the majority of the latter being farmers, then the importance of the extended family household to farming is even more obvious, for in the villages as such the above percentage was 15.3, whilst in the countryside it ran as high as 22.6. The three-generation family was in fact the most usual type of extension, 13.9 % of family households containing three generations.

This means that two-thirds of the extended families were three-generational, consisting to a large extent of fathers and mothers living with their married child on the farmstead. If the data are examined, however, for the variables which are critical for the existence of Hofstee's agrarian–artisan pattern of reproduction, that is for the presence of unmarried brothers and/or uncles residing with the family, it is found that only 278 households can be classified as of this type, that is only 3.6 % of the total.[15]

There was a significant difference in the structure of the household as between the arable farming and livestock-farming areas of the province of Overijssel. In the former, more than 23 % of the households were of the extended family kind,

---

[13] In addition to the works mentioned below, further information on the size and structure of the household can be gathered from Roebroeck (1967): 57–95; Oldewelt (1948–9): 114–17; Coldeweij (1964): 234–45; Roosenschoon (1958). See also Roessingh, *Population change and economic developments in the Netherlands* (1965 ii): 91–2, and Roessingh (1964): 93–4.

[14] Slicher van Bath (1957): esp. 109–16.

[15] Although the classifications are not altogether compatible it is clear that this type of household was more widely represented in both fifteenth-century Tuscany and eighteenth-century Corsica, see above, Klapisch, Chapter 10, p. 280, and Dupâquier, Chapter 11, pp. 290–292.

and in the latter, this percentage fell to 7.7. The same difference holds for the mean size of household, which in the predominantly arable farming areas ran as high as 5.3, but in the typical livestock area in the north-west of the province was only 4.1. This may perhaps be taken as an indication of the importance of the type of agriculture and of the general character of the economy to the problem of the size and structure of the household.

Servants living in formed a greater proportion of the population of Overijssel than resident kin, and were to be found in more households. Information on this point was available for 15,304 households in this province in 1749. It appeared that more than 5,000 households (33 %) had one or more servants living in, that is almost 9,500 in all, forming nearly 12 % of the population.[16] No less than 7.5 % of households had three or more servants living in, though livestock areas had a smaller proportion of such large groups than arable farming areas. Unfortunately information is much more restricted as to age of servants and is available for only two communities. Only six of the 262 servants to be found in these two places were under ten years old, and the highest proportion was in the age group 16–20. Four of the servants living in were older than thirty and none was older than forty. These data alone in my opinion call for extensive revision of the theory of an agrarian–artisan pattern of reproduction. Sooner or later every servant got married and founded his or her own family; in fact nearly all of them did so before the age of thirty.

Another study, by Roessingh,[17] concerns the district of Veluwe, nearer to the centre of the Netherlands than Overijssel (see Fig. 12.1) but also with a very poor sandy soil, where arable farming was the main occupation. He was able to analyse 6,632 households for the year 1749. Since these households made up 44 % of all households in the countryside and 75 % of all those in the towns, his findings must be supposed to be representative.

In Veluwe the proportion of extended family households was much less than in Overijssel, amounting to 7 % in the countryside, as against 20.5 % in Overijssel, and to only 5 % in the towns. The three-generation family was also of less importance than in Overijssel: in Veluwe half of all extended family households contained three generations, whilst in Overijssel the proportion was two in every three. This means to say that almost 14 % of all households in rural Overijssel were composed of three generations but only 4 % in Veluwe, and as little as 2 % in the towns of that district. The classic agrarian–artisan pattern of reproduction – brothers and/or uncles living with the married couple – was in fact confined to 1 % of households overall.

In Veluwe the number of servants living in was also impressive. They were to be found in 32 % of all households, which is the same proportion as in Overijssel,

[16] Compare the almost identical proportion of servants found in pre-industrial English communities, see above, Laslett, Chapter 4, pp. 151–152. See also below, pp. 314–315. Compare the proportion of households with servants in parts of Tokugawa Japan, below, Hayami, Chapter 18, pp. 503–504 and Nakane, Chapter 19, p. 521.
[17] Roessingh (1965 i): 239–49.

and there were 631 servants to every 1,000 heads of household. The proportion of servants living in of the whole population was as high as 14 %, as compared with 12 % in Overijssel, and it was likewise very exceptional to find a servant living in above the age of thirty in Veluwe.

Information on the structure of the household was found by Faber to be very scarce for the province of Friesland.[18] It could only be studied in a single community consisting of 400 households, and that for the year 1744. Only 8 % of these households contained extended families, and only 4 % three-generation families. More however, is known about the mean size of household in the cities and in the villages of Friesland in that year. In the towns the mean size varied between 3.1 and 3.6, and in the countryside between 3.6 and 4.4. Only six of the 30 *grietenijen* (administrative areas) into which the countryside was divided, had a mean household size above 4.0. The only grietenij which could be studied in detail had a mean household size of 4.0, and from these data it can be concluded that the extended family household was of little importance in Friesland, there being very probably considerably fewer than 8 % of all households in this category.

There are data available for Friesland on the number of servants living in for the year 1796, and these show that the number was greater when agriculture was more prominent in the occupational structure. In the grietenijen where 40 % or more of the labour force was engaged in agriculture, the proportion of servants living in almost never fell below 11 % of the total population. But in towns, and in that part of the countryside where shipping and other occupations formed a substantial part of the pattern, the proportion of such servants usually oscillated between 5 % and 10 % of the population.

The proportion of relatives and of servants resident in the household was at least as low in the Noorderkwartier of Holland as it was in Friesland. Households in Holland were composed as a rule of the nuclear family only. This can be inferred simply by comparing mean size of household in the four areas, Overijssel, Friesland, Veluwe and the Noorderkwartier of Holland (Table 12.1). In Overijssel in 1795 mean size of household (N = nearly 28,000) was 4.8, and had been about the same in 1748. In Veluwe it was about 4.1 in the villages in 1749, 4.6 in the countryside outside the villages, and 3.8 in the towns. In the Friesian towns mean size of household was 3.3 and elsewhere 3.8.[19] Struyck's data relating to 8,500 households in the Noorderkwartier of the province of Holland in 1740 point to a mean household size of 3.8. The data which I myself have collected from listings of inhabitants for nearly 4,000 households in the same area indicate a mean size of 3.7. Mean size of household in the Noorderkwartier may be expected to be as low as 3.4 or 3.5 in the towns, that is about the same level as in the Friesian towns. But there are particularly well marked

---

[18] Faber, unpublished research. I am very much obliged to him for his generosity in putting these data at my disposal.

[19] Compare the differences in household size found by Klapisch for fifteenth-century Tuscany, above, Chapter 10, p. 275; by Hélin for eighteenth-century Belgium, below, Chapter 13, pp. 332–333; and by Halpern for nineteenth-century Serbia, below, Chapter 16, pp. 401–402.

Table 12.1   *Mean size of household*

Province/District	Total	Urban	Rural	Farming	Livestock
Overijssel, 1748	±4·8	—	5.2	5.4	±4.1
Overijssel 1795	4.8	4.3	5.1	—	—
Veluwe, 1749	4.3	3.8	4.5	—	—
Friesland, 1744	3.7	3.3	3.8	—	—
Noorderkwartier about 1740 (Struyck data)	—	—	3.8	—	—
Noorderkwartier, 1622– 1795 (own data)	—	—	3.7	—	—

regional differences in the Netherlands when only households outside the towns are compared with each other. Such households had a mean size of 5.2 in Overijssel, 4.5 in Veluwe, 3.8 in Friesland, and 3.7 in the northern parts of Holland (Table 12.1). Besides these marked regional differences, one is particularly struck by the low mean sizes of household in Northern Holland, Friesland and to a certain extent also in the adjoining livestock area of northwest Overijssel. From what we know at present about the mean sizes of household in other parts of Western Europe and in America in historical times, there is enough reason to regard these low figures as quite exceptional. An analysis of the structure of household in the Noorderkwartier of Holland and a comparison with the structure of the household elsewhere can be illuminating. This will be undertaken in the next section. The structure of the English household as laid out by Peter Laslett,[20] is chosen for comparison, firstly because in his pioneering study the most complete analysis is presented and secondly because it is generally considered that Dutch society at this period was more closely paralleled in England than in any other country.

HOUSEHOLD STRUCTURE IN HOLLAND AND ENGLAND

The quality of the data concerning the size and/or structure of households and/or nuclear families is such, that not all the 4,560 'units' (i.e. households or nuclear families) could be used in calculating all variables. The maximum number (N) of usable units has been pooled for each item, and at the end of this section an even more restricted number of households has been brought together for the study of their detailed structure. Thus the size of 4,089 households out of the 4,560 was analysable, and the frequency of the different sizes is given in Table 12.2.[21] The mean size of these Dutch households was 3.72, very much smaller than the English mean household size of 4.75. In Holland households of 1–4 persons formed a much greater proportion (69 %) than in England (52 %): half of the population in Holland (49 %) lived in such small households. In England, on the contrary, less than one in three persons did so (31 %). The

[20] See above, Chapter 4, pp. 125–158.
[21] Compare Laslett, above Chapter 4, pp. 135–136, 142–143.

Table 12.2   *Distribution of the households by size in the Noorderkwartier*
(Mean size = 3.72)

Household size	Household		Persons	
	No.	%	No.	%
1	427	10.4	427	2.8
2	811	19.8	1,622	10.7
3	879	21.5	2,637	17.3
4	698	17.1	2,792	18.3
5	552	13.5	2,760	18.1
6	357	8.7	2,142	14.1
7	197	4.8	1,379	9.1
8	94	2.3	752	4.9
9	44	1.1	396	2.6
10	19	0.5	190	1.2
11	7	0.2	77	0.5
12	3	0.1	36	0.2
13	1	0.0	13	0.1
Total	4,089	100.0	15,223	100.0

Table 12.3   *Households and persons by groups of household size
in the Noorderkwartier and England*

Groups of sizes	Households		Persons	
	Noorderkwartier	England	Noorderkwartier	England
1–4	68.8	52.2	49.1	30.8
5–7	27.0	34.4	41.4	42.0
8–	4.2	13.4	9.5	27.2

differences are most marked between the groups of larger households (i.e. households of eight or more persons). The proportion in England was about three
times higher than in Holland (Table 12.3). In Holland only one in every ten
persons lived in such large households; in England more than one in every four.

By deducting resident kin, servants living in and lodgers[22] from the household,
we get the 'nuclear family' as the remainder. 'Nuclear families' are here defined
as containing married couples with or without children, widowed people with
or without children, or unmarried heads of households.[23] In the Noorderkwartier
it was possible in this way to analyse the structure of 3,740 nuclear families.

[22] Laslett, see above, Chapter 1, pp. 34–39, includes lodgers within the houseful but not within
the household.
[23] It proved impossible to make a sharp distinction between unmarried heads of household
and widowed people living without children. In this study both categories are always taken
together. Widowed people without children do not constitute conjugal family units as
defined by Laslett, above, Chapter 1, pp. 28–33. The distinction corresponds with that
adopted by Biraben, Blayo, Klapisch and Dupâquier, above, Chapters 8–11.

Table 12.4 *Distribution of 'nuclear families' by size in the Noorderkwartier*
(Mean size = 3.01)

Size of nuclear family	Nuclear family		Persons	
	No.	%	No.	%
1	709	19.0	709	5.7
2	793	21.2	1,586	12.8
3	729	19.5	2,187	17.6
4	566	15.2	2,264	18.2
5	417	11.1	2,085	16.8
6	263	7.0	1,578	12.7
7	148	4.0	1,036	8.3
8	70	1.9	560	4.5
9	28	0.7	252	2.0
10	11	0.3	110	0.9
11	4	0.1	44	0.4
12	1	0.0	12	0.1
13	1	0.0	13	0,1
Total	3,740	100.0	12,436	100.0

Their frequency distribution is given in Table 12.4. The most conspicuous facts in this table are:

1. the mean size of these 'nuclear families' was relatively small, on average just above three persons;

2. there was an extremely high proportion of households headed by celibates or widowed persons without children (19 %);

3. large families (6 or more members) are to be found in only 14 % of all cases;

4. most people lived in family units of three, four or five members (52.6 %).

The very high proportion of households in the Noorderkwartier headed by single people can be clearly demonstrated by a comparison with the English data on heads of household.[24] In England 70 % of all households were headed by married couples; in Holland only 57 %. Widowed persons comprised 18 % of all household heads in England; 22 %· in the Noorderkwartier. Only 12 % of English households were headed by single persons; 21 % in the Noorderkwartier. The same difference is obvious in Table 12.5, which shows a somewhat larger proportion of married couples in the English population. A marked difference between England and the Noorderkwartier is the much lower proportion of widowers in England. Was the incentive to marry again so much greater for the English than for the Dutch widower? The most striking difference, however, relates to the proportion of single female heads of household, being three times as high in the Noorderkwartier (see Fig. 12.2 below). Is it to be interpreted as a consequence of a lower nuptiality, an uneven sex ratio or a much greater

[24] Fig. 12.2. See also above, Laslett, Chapter 4, p. 147.

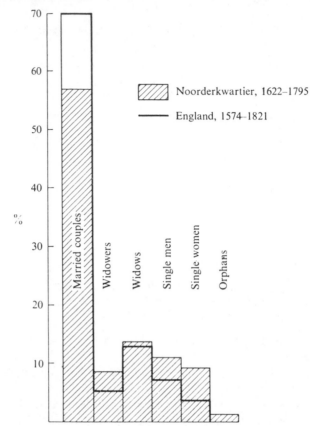

Fig. 12.2   Distribution of households by marital status of heads

inclination in Holland for unmarried daughters to leave the parental home and set up their own household? Or is it a combination of these factors?

As regards children living in the nuclear family, the proportion was greater in the Noorderkwartier than in England (46.3 % against 42.6 %). This is not at variance with a greater proportion of households with children (74.6 % against 66.9 %) and a greater mean size of sibling group (2.72 against 2.52) in England. The fact that the proportion of children living in the nuclear family was lower in England can be explained by the very different structure of the English household, with its relatively large numbers of resident kin and servants, and the correspondingly lower proportion of resident children in the population. Table 12.6 presents the frequency distribution of sibling groups in the households in the Noorderkwartier. More than 16 % of all nuclear families were without children.[25] The highest frequency is of nuclear families with one child.

[25] Nuclear family in this case is defined as containing married couples or one widowed parent plus offspring. See footnote 23.

Table 12.5   *Proportions of population in the Noorderkwartier*
and England by marital status

(N = 3,380)

	Noorderkwartier	England
Married	31.3	33.4
Widowed	6.1	6.2
Unmarried	62.6	60.4

Table 12.6   *Frequency distribution of the size of sibling groups*
in the Noorderkwartier (N = 3,380)

(Mean size = 2.11)

Sibling group	Nuclear families		Children	
	No.	%	No.	%
0	445	16.4	—	—
1	709	26.2	709	12.4
2	595	22.0	1,190	20.9
3	439	16.2	1,317	23.1
4	269	9.9	1,076	18.9
5	148	5.5	740	13.0
6	66	2.4	396	6.9
7	19	0.7	133	2.3
8	10	0.4	80	1.4
9	4	0.1	36	0.6
10	1	0.0	10	0.2
11	1	0.0	11	0.2
Total	2,706	100.0	5,698	100.0

The greater mean size of the English sibling group is to be expected since it is clear that the larger sibling groups were far more common in England than in the Noorderkwartier.[26] No doubt this is one of the reasons for the greater mean size of the English household.

An equally important influence on English mean household size was the number of resident kin, which was a great deal higher than in the Noorderkwartier. It has already been remarked in the preceding section that resident kin in the countryside of Overijssel could be found in 20.5 % of all households, 8 % in the Veluwe and probably less than 8 % in Friesland. In England they were found in 10 % of all households, but in only 3.6 % (N = 3,198) in the Noorderkwartier. In England resident kin comprised 3.4 % of the total population; in

[26] Compare Laslett, above, Chapter 4, p. 148.

Table 12.7   *Composition of servant groups in households* (N = 3,269)

Groups		Households	
Size	Composition	No.	%
1. {	1 male	34	5·9 } 80.9
	1 female	432	75·0 }
2. {	2 males	16	—
	1 male, 1 female	20	15.3
	2 females	52	—
3. {	3 males	3	—
	2 males, 1 female	2	2.6
	1 male, 2 females	3	—
	3 females	7	—
4.+	4 and more	7	1.2
	Total	576	100.0

the Noorderkwartier this proportion was only 1.2 % (148 resident kin in a population of 11,905 persons). Most of these kin were women. The three-generational household of resident brothers and/or uncles was of no significance whatsoever in the Noorderkwartier.

Almost the same difference between the households in England and the Noorderkwartier holds for the number and proportion of servants. In England 13.4 % of the population belonged to this category, i.e. nearly the same proportion as in Overijssel (12 %) and in the Veluwe (14 %). In Friesland this proportion was already lower (9.4 %), and in the Noorderkwartier it only reached 5.9 %. There, servants living in could be found in no more than 17.6 % of all households (N = 3,269). The reliability of this figure is confirmed by Struyck's data, which yield a proportion of 5 % in the total population for resident servants in the Noorderkwartier in about 1740 (1,539 servants in a population of 30,769).[27] This difference was not only caused by the smaller proportion of Dutch households with servants (17.6 % against 28.5 % in England), but also by the lower mean number of servants in the households of the Noorderkwartier. Table 12.7 shows that in most cases (81 %) only one male or female servant was employed. The number of households with three or more servants was less than 4 %. Female servants formed by far the largest number of those living in in the Noorderkwartier. The same holds for the Struyck data. This phenomenon can be explained by the urbanised character of Dutch society, where servants living in were used primarily for domestic work. Their main duties would probably be cheese and butter making, both typical female occupations. Table 12.8 shows that more female servants were attached to households without a housewife than to those with one. The hired male labour force in the Noorderkwartier

[27] Struyck (1753).

Table 12.8   *Maid-servants by presence or absence of housewife*

	Households	With maid-servant	%
With housewife	2,296	349	15.2
Without housewife	613	143	23.3
Total	2,909	492	17.2

came from labourers resident in their own households and even to some extent from seasonal workers, many of them foreigners from German Westphalia.

The greater importance of lodgers in the Noorderkwartier than in England, compensates somewhat for the smaller mean size of the sibling group and the smaller number of resident kin and of servants. Lodgers were to be found in more than 10 % of all households (N = 3,198), and comprised 3.7 % of the total population. Some of these lodgers were almost certainly orphans or children of poor families, lodged with other families by the overseers of the poor. This could be demonstrated for 90 out of a total of 297 lodgers: thus poor and orphaned children probably made up nearly one-third of all lodgers. When these child-lodgers are deducted, the proportion of adult lodgers was probably about 2.5 % of the total population. This is almost in accordance with the number of lodgers given by Struyck in some villages in about 1740, where they made up 2.1 % of the total population. In the English household the lodger was of little importance.[28]

The detailed structure of the household in its component parts (i.e. the nuclear family, resident kin, servants, children, household heads) could be studied in 2,367 households. Of these, 774 households could be selected as well-to-do families and 163 as pauper families receiving outside help. These three groups show significant differences in the size and structure of the household (Table 12.9). The figures confirm once again that mean household size in the Noorderkwartier was 3.7 persons. The nuclear family, with a mean size of 3.3, account for nearly 89 % of these households. The mean size of the well-to-do as well as of the pauper households was a little higher than the general average at about 4.0 persons.

Their structure, however, differed completely. The pauper households were almost totally made up of nuclear families; servants and resident kin being of no significance. Though the mean size of the nuclear family in the well-to-do

[28] See Laslett, *Size and structure of the household in England over three centuries* (1969). This conclusion has now been revised (see above, Laslett, Chapter 4, p. 134). Only 9 listings of inhabitants in pre-industrial England (exclusive of London) record the presence of lodgers but in these settlements the proportion of households with lodgers is as high as 14.7%. In urban areas in nineteenth-century England the proportion of households with lodgers could exceed 20%. See above, Anderson, Chapter 7, p. 220.

Table 12.9   *Mean household size, divided into component parts*

	No. of persons	%	Mean size
All households (N = 2,367)			
Nuclear family	7,845	88.72	3.314
Resident kin	117	1.32	0.049
Servants	578	6.54	0.244
Lodgers	302	3.42	0.128
Total	8,842	100.00	3.736
Wealthier households (N = 774)			
Nuclear family	2,409	77.84	3.112
Resident kin	42	1.36	0.054
Servants	446	14.41	0.576
Lodgers	198	6.40	0.256
Total	3,095	100.00	3.999
Pauper households (N = 163)			
Nuclear family	642	96.98	3.939
Resident kin	3	0.45	0.018
Servants	1	0.15	0.006
Lodgers	16	2.42	0.098
Total	662	100.00	4.061

households was smaller than average, this was more than compensated for by the higher numbers of servants and lodgers. The proportion of resident kin was comparable to that in the total population. There was no difference between households in general and households of the well-to-do as regards household heads (Table 12.10). In the poorer households, however, the extremely high proportion of widows as household heads is very conspicuous (31.3 %), and the very low proportion of single male heads of household receiving poor relief makes a sharp contrast. Those families with large numbers of children stood the greatest chance of receiving relief, especially when the household head was a widow (Tables 12.10 and 12.11).[29] The number and proportion of children in the richer families and in the pauper families is in all instances quite different. This cannot be explained simply as a proof of lower fertility in prosperous families. It has probably more to do with the children of such families leaving the parental household at the period of greatest prosperity.

[29] In pre-industrial England, contemporary observers often saw an association between poverty and families with many children, see above, Wall, Chapter 5, p. 172.

Table 12.10   *Household heads (proportions)*

	All households N = 2,367	Wealthier households N = 774	Pauper households N = 163
Married couple	56.6	55.2	46.0
Widower	9.0	8.1	9.8
Widow	13.3	14.5	31.3
Single male	11.7	12.4	3.1
Single female	8.3	9.4	9.2
Orphan	1.0	0.4	0.6
Total	100.0	100.0	100.0

Table 12.11   *Children*

	All N = 2,367	Wealthier N – 774	Pauper N = 163
Proportion of children in the population	47.0	39.2	59.7
Proportion of households with children	67.4	57.9	83.4
Mean size of groups of children (sibling group ⩾ 1)	2.61	2.48	2.90

CONCLUSION

The facts stated in the preceding sections may lead to the following conclusions.

1. The regional differences that existed in the Netherlands in the nineteenth century can also be found earlier, at least as early as the seventeenth century. It is not unreasonable to presume their existence even before then. The theory put forward by Hofstee, that the agrarian–artisan pattern of reproduction predominated in the Netherlands before 1800, is untenable.

2. There is a chance that the agrarian–artisan pattern of reproduction was in existence on the sandy eastern soils of the Netherlands at least from the eighteenth century on. It is possible that this pattern also existed in the southern sandy soils area, but this has still to be proved. Mean household size in the Veluwe district was so high in the first half of the sixteenth century that the existence of this pattern of reproduction in this area seems possible. However, in the eighteenth century it played no role in that region.

3. Even on the sandy eastern soils the agrarian–artisan pattern of reproduction was mainly found in farming households. Nowhere in the cities, nor in the villages as distinct from the countryside, can this pattern be assumed to have been of any importance. For that reason it is very unlikely that the agrarian–artisan pattern of reproduction was of any importance amongst the artisans, shopkeepers and the lower classes in the towns.

4. In the countryside there seems to have been a correlation between the farming system and the existence of extended family households. Research so far suggests that such domestic groups were only to be found in certain arable farming areas. In grass-growing regions the extended family household was little known.

5. The analysis of the household structure in the different regions of the Netherlands gives us good reason to suppose that the kin ties of the nuclear family were much looser in the western and northern than in the eastern areas.[30] Probably ties with neighbours were also looser in the west and north, since in these regions the practice of sending children into service in other households when about fifteen years old was much less widespread than in the east.

6. The extremely low mean size of household in Holland and Friesland during the seventeenth and eighteenth centuries is not only exceptional when compared with other Dutch regions, but also in comparison with the mean English and American household sizes at that time. Before definitive conclusions about the uniqueness of this Holland–Friesian mean household size can be drawn, however, it is necessary first to study this subject in other regions of Holland, and second to get information on the mean household sizes in other Western European countries at that time.

7. The statement that the nineteenth century economic, social and cultural differences between the various Dutch regions went back far into the past, is not new to the Dutch historian. On the contrary. It is however, very important to emphasize that the study of the history of the Dutch family and household presents a new way of analysing these different cultural patterns and of following their development from historical times to the present. In this sense a new field of socio-historical research awaits exploration.

[30] In this connection compare Kooy, *Urbanisation and nuclear family individualisation* (1963–4): 13–24. This study is based on data compiled by the Dutch Census of 1947 and the General Housing Census of 1956, and Kooy reaches the conclusion that even today regional cultural patterns are the primary factor in the distribution of the degree of family individualisation in the Netherlands. The three large zones of family individualisation, which he could distinguish for the mid-twentieth century, fit perfectly into our historical findings. Kooy writes, 'It would be possible to draw a map which would divide the Netherlands into three large zones of nuclear family individualisation. There would be an almost closed zone where many, or even most, nuclear families live together with relatives. This zone, although penetrating into the heart of the country, no doubt represented relationships which traditionally existed on either side of the Dutch–German boundary. It expresses the existence of a folk culture grown and maintained in isolation from the dynamic development along the North Sea coast. In this folk culture there was little room for the growth of an individualistic conception of life and thus hardly a need for self-expression and privacy as they are expressed in nuclear family individualisation. To prevent any misunderstanding: in technical and economic respects this "dark" zone has been rapidly modernised during the last ninety or one hundred years, but in its basic social relationships it is still "lagging behind" the rest of the Netherlands. In the second place there is a "grey" zone where only an appreciable minority of the nuclear families share their houses with relatives, on the map designated by those agricultural areas with a percentage between 8 and 14. This zone can be defined as marginal, for it falls between the "dark" zone, and the areas where nuclear family individualisation appears to have its focus, viz. the North-Western Netherlands.'

13. Size of households before the Industrial Revolution: the case of Liège in 1801

Étienne Hélin

How many persons to a household? Many demographers have asked themselves this since Guichardin, Vauban, and Quételet: hence a considerable literature devoted to the subject.[1] Historians are perpetually brought back to this issue because north of the Alps the practice of numbering households is more widespread than that of nominal censuses. Thus fiscal returns have been preserved which contain the numbers of hearths liable to tax (*fouages, haertsteden* or *tockages*) for whole provinces, whereas lists called by clergymen *status animarum* or censuses of souls, which provide accounts of every individual, household by household, in a single parish were scarcely ever made up by the parish priests of Western Europe. Who can resist the temptation to calculate the ratio of inhabitants to households in a document of this kind where the evidence is certain, in order to use it as a multiplier elsewhere?

Alas, this expedient which seems to be so simple, is full of pitfalls. There are uncertainties in the boundaries which surrounded communities in earlier times; there are the random fluctuations, which are always extreme in societies subject to famines and epidemics; there are exemptions from taxation, omissions of children, or of those not subject to the jurisdiction of the incumbent of a parish. Father Roger Mols has sifted the published results for scores of European towns, and fifteen years after it was delivered his authoritative critical judgement retains its relevance.[2]

For some while now the attention of demographic historians has been directed elsewhere: they have been calculating intervals between births as a measure of population growth, or fluctuations in mortality. In these fields they are indebted for their results to refinements in the techniques of sampling and of reconstitution of families, and the whole operation rests on registers of baptisms, marriages, and deaths.[3] Although they are a splendid complement to the demographic particulars which can be recovered in this way for earlier times, listings

---

[1] The best previous discussion of this question was by Mols, *Introduction à la démographie historique des villes d'Europe* (1955) II: 100–9.   [2] Mols (1955) II: 110–30.

[3] For up-to-date information and bibliography see Blayo and Henry, *Données démographiques sur la Bretagne et l'Anjou, de 1740 à 1829* (1967). For an overall view see van der Woude (1969).

of inhabitants have not attracted as lively an interest. But their evidence is valuable, particularly in towns, where migratory movements on the one hand and the growth of the tertiary sector on the other, accentuate anomalies which are rarely found in village communities. Without nominal lists, how can we recover distribution by age and matrimonial status, or the proportion of the poor? The analysis of one of these variables only, taken in isolation, is a trivial matter, but when it becomes a question of uncovering the type and frequency of every social and demographic feature in combination, it is imperative that modern methods of handling information be brought in. At Liège we have been given the benefit of these methods thanks to the laboratory for the analysis of ancient languages (L.A.S.L.A.) directed by Professor L. Delatte.[4]

The document which must be studied in the first instance for Liège is the Census of the month Thermidor of the year 9, which is the French Revolutionary expression for July 1801.[5] It covers a city population which was undoubtedly shaken by revolutionary forces, but which still preserved for the most part the demographic characteristics of the *ancien régime*, whose economic basis was not to be altered before the diffusion of technology in the course of the second third of the nineteenth century.

One outstanding trait of this society looks like a foretaste of what was to come with the mutations of our own time, in spite of the fact that the society of Liège was still encased in its archaic framework. This is the small size of household. The 42,173 inhabitants numbered in the community were distributed amongst 11,496 households, which gives a mean of 3.668 individuals to a household. From now on we shall concentrate attention on this particular feature.

CRITICAL REMARKS ON THE SOURCES

The Census of the year 9, 1801, was carried out and checked on 1 Prairial (21 May) and 12 Thermidor (31 July) by five police officials assisted by members of the Welfare Bureau. Comparisons with similar registrations carried out for the years 8 (partial) and 10 (complete) and the cross checking which is occasionally possible with both the records of marriages and deaths and with announcements in the *Gazette de Liège*, speak in favour of the accuracy of our source. The roll of names was drawn up in accordance with conventions which had been traditional since the seventeenth century. The Census takers called at house after house, taking down the surnames, christian names, ages and

---

[4] We take this opportunity to express our grateful thanks to him. We are grateful also to Messieurs E. Evrard and J. Denooz, who wrote the programs for the IBM counter sorter and for the IBM 1620 computer. M. Cl. Desama has given us his active support throughout the work.

[5] The critical examination of this source will be the subject of the first chapter of a book to be written on the population of Liège in 1801. The six original volumes are preserved in the Archives de l'État a Liège, *City of Liège*, reg. 7–12.

callings of the individuals who lived there, always beginning with the head of the household.[6] There were 7,875 occupied houses of which 74.4 % (5,859) contained one household only. The police officials frequently distinguished household from household in cases where there were more households than one to a houseful by drawing a horizontal mark between them. In four districts however, it has been necessary to insert these separations ourselves, making use of the similarities in surnames, mentions of servants, or of kin relationships. The distribution of households artificially arrived at in this way was subject to a χ^2 test which showed that it did not differ significantly from the distribution observed directly in 1801 in the quarters closest to those where household divisions were missing in this way.[7] The one exception was the district of Nord within the walls, where we have followed the distribution into households recorded there in the preceding year for 213 houses occupied by more than one household.

No direction was given to the Census takers explaining what should be considered as a household (*ménage*) and it is to be feared that a word which seemed so neutral scarcely compelled anyone to consult a dictionary or any other work of reference. For lack of an explicit definition we have supposed that we are here faced with an operational unit which as far as we can discover is susceptible of the application of the meaning given to the word by the Belgian National Census of 1947. This definition reads:

'Unit containing one or more persons, consisting either of an individual living alone or of the co-residence of two individuals or more who live habitually together in the same habitation whether or not they have any family connection...'[8]

Apart from the shortcomings of terminology, what other deficiencies are there which might make our results unreliable? First comes the omission of establishments where town officials had no access, prisons which seem to have contained an average of 176 persons on remand or serving sentences,[9] the military hospital, containing 210–40 sick persons, without counting staff, the police barracks, which had 48 adults in 1802; patients in Bavière Hospital, 96 lay persons, men and women; the houses of the commander of the 25th military district (4 adults), of the mayor and of the prefect. Because of the rapid changes to which populations of this sort were subject, living as they did on the margin

---

[6] On the subject of these listings see Mols (1955) I: 14–18 and 64. For Liège, see Hélin, *Les capitations liégeoises* (1962 i): 111–27, 281–94.

[7] Significance level 0.05. The division of Liège into districts and its meaning is examined by Hélin in *La population des paroisses liégeoises* (1959) and *Le paysage urbain de Liège avant la révolution industrielle* (1962 ii).

[8] Institut National de Statistique, *Recensement Général 1947* (1951) Vol. 6: 9. The definition of households and the history of their numeration are discussed by Ockers (1967): 4–9. Definitions of the household current in eighteenth-century England are discussed by Wall, above, Chapter 5, pp. 159–166. See also Blayo, Chapter 9, p. 255 and Laslett, Chapter 1, pp. 23–28, 34–40.

[9] It was decided to transfer convicts after July to Ghent and to Vilvorde, *Gazette de Liège*, 21 July 1801.

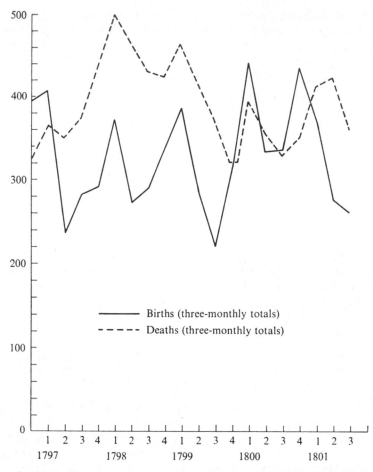

Fig. 13.1   Births and deaths at Liège 1 October 1796–30 September 1801

of civil life, we thought it best not to include them and to keep to the text of the Census of 1801. The following are also outside the scope of our analysis: service men, numbering 253, and immigrants who set up house at Liège after the month of July, that is 313 adults. In all about 1,151 individuals are omitted in this way; if they had been counted, their major effect would have been to swell the number in the class of collective establishments to which hospitals, military and penitentiary institutions belong. The general average household size would have been hardly affected, because it would have stood at 3.74 instead of 3.668.

More serious is the objection which was actually made by the authorities in respect of all the censuses of Liège carried out under the French régime. Convinced that rich families had retired to the countryside, and that young men and servants were hiding from the call-up, central authorities put no faith whatever in municipal censuses. It was officially pronounced that 50,000 persons were to be assigned to the town to inflate its *droits de patente*, a poll tax which was on its highest scale in the big towns. This was easy to do but really deceived nobody: the figures are there to bear witness to a decline up to the year 6 (1798), then a rise starting in the year 7 (1799), (41,863 inhabitants), which was sustained until the year 9 (1801) when we finish up with a total of 42,173. We need place no confidence whatever either in official declarations, or in the totals calculated by town officials district by district,[10] and even less in figures reconstituted afterwards from numbers of households guessed at by comparing levels reached in 1789 and in 1801.

Despite the absence of a precise history of demographic change at the turn of the century, there is good reason to believe that Liège did not differ in any important way from that of many other capital towns of departments. They also had had to suffer their revolutionary troubles, to undergo war, scarcity and the paralysis of commerce which came in the first years of the new régime. After 1800, the situation began to settle down, which is confirmed at Liège by the course of births and deaths; crude birth rate in 1801, 35.6 per 1000, crude death rate 31.6 per 1000 (see Fig. 13.1), and there is no reason to suspect that the composition of households at Liège in 1801 had been affected by any exceptional demographic mishap.

HOUSEHOLDS LARGE AND SMALL

Table 13.1 and Fig. 13.2 show how the distribution by size of the households had a marked lack of symmetry. Besides indices of central tendency (arithmetic mean 3.668: mode 2) it is necessary to consider those of dispersion. The standard deviation of household size is 2.235, skewness shows a value of gamma 1 of 7.23 and kurtosis a value of gamma 2 of 209.66. This last result is a little deceptive since using the 4th moment exaggerates the part played by extreme values. In this case if three households are left out, which each contain more than 50 individuals, gamma 2 scarcely exceeds a value of 6.

The other characteristics of the distribution attract attention first of all to the bottom of the scale of size, that is to say to the households of one or two persons only. We can see at once how untenable it makes the commonly held notion that society in earlier times was composed of large households. More than a third of all domestic groups in Liège consisted of only one or two persons. Reduced to this remnant, even when it consists of a married couple, the family cannot be said to be even complete since it exists without any natural extension forwards or backwards, in time that is, of ascendant relatives or children.

[10] Their errors arose from omissions in the counting of adults. Children (less than twelve years old) were counted folio by folio and inexact totals calculated at the end of the volume. Examples: 8,491 inhabitants instead of 8,406 in the West district; 4,703 instead of 4,664 in the Centre.

Table 13.1 *Distribution of the 11,496 households and their members in 1801*

Persons per household	Households						Persons					
	Numbers			Percentages			Numbers			Percentages		
	City	Suburbs	Liège	City	Suburbs	Liège	City	Suburbs	Liège	City	Suburbs	Liège
1	1,369	583	1,952	18.25	14.59	16.98	1,369	583	1,952	5.10	3.80	4.63
2	1,605	704	2,309	21.40	17.62	20.08	3,210	1,408	4,618	11.97	9.17	10.95
3	1,297	674	1,971	17.29	16.87	17.15	3,891	2,022	5,913	14.51	13.17	14.02
4	1,092	645	1,737	14.56	16.14	15.11	4,368	2,580	6,948	16.28	16.81	16.48
5	777	522	1,299	10.36	13.06	11.30	3,885	2,610	6,495	14.48	17.00	15.40
6	590	413	1,003	7.87	10.33	8.73	3,540	2,478	6,018	13.20	16.14	14.27
7	336	220	556	4.48	5.50	4.84	2,352	1,540	3,892	8.77	10.03	9.23
8	216	121	337	2.88	3.03	2.93	1,728	968	2,696	6.44	6.31	6.39
9	112	63	175	1.49	1.58	1.52	1,008	567	1,575	3.76	3.69	3.73
10	48	25	73	0.64	0.62	0.64	480	250	730	1.79	1.63	1.73
11	22	14	36	0.30	0.35	0.31	242	154	396	0.90	1.00	0.94
12	7	6	13	0.09	0.15	0.11	84	72	156	0.31	0.47	0.37
13 to 100	29	6	35	0.39	0.15	0.30	667	117	784	2.49	0.78	1.86
Total	7,500	3,996	11,496	100	100	100	26,824	15,349	42,173	100	100	100
Percentage	65.24	34.76	100				63.61	36.39	100			

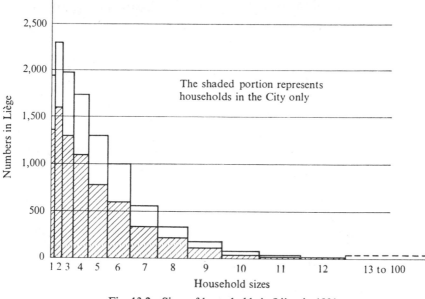

The shaded portion represents households in the City only

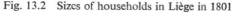

Fig. 13.2   Sizes of households in Liège in 1801

At the other end of the scale households of 8 persons and above are found only exceptionally, only 1 out of every 20. Even rarer, 1 out of 100, are those which contain 10 persons and above. Above that there are practically no family households, only larger units of various kinds; boarding houses are one type, and monastic establishments of the former regular clergy who refused to disband in spite of abolition are another.[11] The most numerous members of establishments of this latter kind were those of the Hospital of Ste. Barbe (51 insane persons and their wardresses), of the Orphanage in the rue Agimont, and of the Home for Incurables in the Isle (a hundred or so old people).

However significant they may be for our purpose, considerations about the number of households are mostly of importance for purposes of statistical comparison alone. Men of the time had neither time nor use for calculations of the sort which are found in Table 13.1. In their era, the household as such was perceived by those who spent their life in it only from an inside point of view. It was the household head who most often thought of the household in this way, because he had to pay the taxes and to balance a budget in which most of the expenditure (food, heating, rent) varied directly with the number of members of the family. Cumulative percentages of persons living in households of various

[11] This was so not only for the Alexiens who cared for the insane, and for the Augustinians at Bavière Hospital, but also for the Capucins. Still numerous at the time of the suppression in 1796, religious communities withered away in the early years of the nineteenth century. Hélin (1959): 392–7.

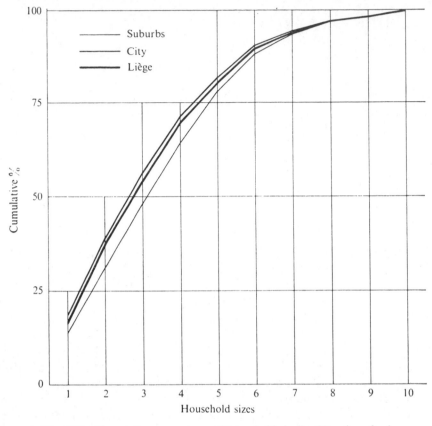

Fig. 13.3 Cumulative percentages of households in the City, the suburbs
and in Liège as a whole

sizes, provide a useful corrective to the percentages contained in Table 13.1.
Only 15.6 % of the population of Liège actually lived in small households (1 and 2
persons); at least three-fifths of the population lived in households containing
up to five persons, and nine-tenths in households of less than nine. The fraction
of the population living in institutional groups is nevertheless underestimated
by Fig. 13.3, because neither prisons nor barracks were within the Census.

ECOLOGICAL FACTORS

The indices presented in Tables 13.2–13.4 have been calculated for each of the
nine districts into which the territory of Liège is divided. Analysis of this kind is
of some interest to today's inhabitants of the place, curious about the origin
of their town. They reveal the deeply embedded layers which a century and

Table 13.2 *Distribution of the population of the City, by households according to rank of lodging*

	House-holds N	Persons		$\bar{x}$	σ	$V = \sigma/\bar{x}$	M_0	As.
		N	%					
1. Households occupying whole houses	3,331	14,757	55.01	4.430	3.234	0.730	2	0.75
2. Households living in 1st lodging in houses occupied by more than 1 household	1,446	5,315	19.31	3.676	2.083	0.567	2	0.80
3. Households living in 2nd lodging in houses occupied by 2 households	835	2,009	7.48	2.406	1.564	0.650	1	0.90
4. Households living in 2nd lodging in houses occupied by more than 2 households	609	1,621	6.04	2.662	1.729	0.650	1	0.96
5. Households living in 3rd lodging in houses occupied by 3 households	303	735	2.74	2.426	1.661	0.685	1	0.85
6. Households living in 3rd lodging in houses occupied by more than 3 households	305	801	2.98	2.626	1.702	0.648	1	0.95
7. Households living in 4th lodging in houses occupied by 4 households	146	313	1.16	2.144	1.385	0.646	1	0.83
8. Households living in 4th lodging in houses occupied by more than 4 households	160	410	1.52	2.563	1.752	0.684	1	0.89
9. Households living in 5th, 6th, 7th lodging in houses occupied respectively by 5, 6, 7 households	148	345	1.28	2.331	1.544	0.662	1	0.85
10. Households living in 5th, 6th, 7th lodging in houses occupied respectively by 5, 6, 7 or more households	217	518	1.93	2.387	1.511	0.633	1	0.92
Totals	7,500	26,824	100	3.577	2.686	0.751	2	0.59

Key: $\bar{x}$ = Arithmetical mean; σ = Standard deviation; V = Coefficient of variation; M_0 = Mode; As. = Skewness.

Table 13.3   *Distribution of the population of the suburbs,*
by households according to rank of lodging[a]

	House-holds N	Persons N	%	$\bar{x}$	σ	$V = \sigma/\bar{x}$	M_0	As.
1	2,528	10,890	70.94	4.308	2.242	0.520	3	0.58
2	586	2,169	14.13	3.701	2.076	0.561	2	0.82
3	411	1,069	6.96	2.601	1.753	0.674	1	0.91
4	174	482	3.14	2.770	1.842	0.665	1	0.96
5	105	253	1.64	2.410	1.896	0.787	1	0.74
6	69	167	1.08	2.420	1.574	0.650	1	0.90
7	38	91	0.59	2.395	1.288	0.538	1	1.08
8	31	74	0.48	2.387	1.287	0.539	2	1.08
9	30	84	0.54	2.800	2.330	0.832	1	0.77
10	24	70	0.45	2.917	1.998	0.685	1	0.96
Total	3,996	15,349	100	3.841	2.235	0.582	2	0.82

[a] See Table 13.2 for titles of rows 1–10.

Table 13.4   *Distribution of the population of Liège as a whole*
by households according to rank of lodging[a]

	House-holds N	Persons N	%	$\bar{x}$	σ	$V = \sigma/\bar{x}$	M_0	As.
1	5,859	25,647	60.81	4.377	2.849	0.651	3	0.48
2	2,032	7,484	17.75	3.683	2.081	0.565	2	0.81
3	1,246	3,078	7.30	2.470	1.631	0.660	1	0.90
4	783	2,103	4.98	2.686	1.755	0.653	1	0.96
5	408	988	2.34	2.422	1.725	0.712	1	0.82
6	374	968	2.29	2.588	1.681	0.650	1	0.94
7	184	404	0.96	2.196	1.369	0.623	1	0.87
8	191	484	1.15	2.534	1.687	0.666	1	0.91
9	178	429	1.02	2.410	1.711	0.710	1	0.82
10	241	588	1.39	2.440	1.574	0.645	1	0.91
Total	11,496	42,173	100	3.668	2.542	0.692	2	0.66

[a] See Table 13.2 for titles of rows 1–10.

a half of evolution has not succeeded in obliterating entirely. For instance the district of Outre-Meuse, which was poverty stricken in 1801 has kept its character, as can be seen from today's tourist guide.

Let us confine ourselves here to those differences which are most clearly marked, and dwell a little on the only ones which are likely to be found elsewhere than at Liège. The most constant of these differences distinguishes the

City (within the walls) sharply from the suburbs.[12] Tables 13.2 and 13.3 make this clear both by the means and measures of dispersion which they contain, and by the proportions of inhabitants distributed between various types of household when households are set out according to rank order of lodging. This order has been established from the sequence in which the occupants of the same building were counted. It is obvious that a household which occupied a house by itself had more space at its disposal than one which was up in the attics in a building divided between four or five tenants. These rank orders then derive from concrete situations and must thus be considered as acting like other ecological factors on the size and structure of the household.

The χ^2 test confirms that the differences in the distribution of households between City and suburbs were not random, and this seems to be true not only for all categories but also for any category taken by itself. There is nothing here to surprise the historian who is quite used to considering any town from the point of view of its growth over time. For this reason he is quicker to notice transitional zones between an old city and the countryside even if such zones are actually inside the town limits.

At Liège every gate in the medieval fortified wall gave rise to the development of a suburban street, which stretched out into a *chaussée*, before branching into hamlets and villages. These chaussées were always industrial in character, because nearby coalmines, ironworks and armament works provided employment for thousands of workers. Habitats of this kind can be thought of as precursors of contemporary urban agglomerations: like them they were what might be called *tentacular* in shape and structure. This tell-tale configuration can thus be traced on the face of the landscape as early as the days of the ancien régime, whilst the suburban population itself exhibited certain demographic traits which marked it off from the inhabitants of the City; for example the enlargement of the base of its age pyramid, and its high level of natality. Size of household is one more indicator of the distinctive character of such suburban industrial communities.

But it is not possible to go so far as to descry any of the family types defined by sociologists in each of the six zones which can be distinguished within an urban concentration. The numerical indications left behind from 1801 are not of a kind to enable us to enter into the mental atmosphere with any confidence, and it is this which is in question when the object is to recover 'semi-patriarchal' families here or 'disintegrated families' there.[13] Still these household statistics do give us some idea of housing conditions.

Table 13.5 merely translates into figures the general tendency to build higher towards an urban centre. Over and above this, the density of households to a house may help us to recover part of the framework of daily life. Perhaps the

[12] The City covered 215 hectares; the built-up part of the suburbs covered only a twentieth of the remaining territory of Liège which was about 1,680 hectares in area. After 1796 three suburbs (Grivegnée et Bressoux, Saint-Nicolas, Glain) were separated arbitrarily from Liège and made into distinct municipalities; they do not figure at all in this chapter.

[13] See Janne and Morsa, *Sociologie et politique sociale* (1962): 34–8.

Table 13.5   *Households per house*

No. of house- holds	City		Suburbs		Liège	
	Buildings	%	Buildings	%	Buildings	%
1	3,331	69.92	2,528	81.23	5,859	74.41
2	835	17.53	411	13.21	1,246	15.82
3	303	6.37	105	3.37	408	5.18
4	146	3.07	38	1.22	184	2.33
5 and over	148	3.11	30	0.97	178	2.26
Totals	4,763	100.00	3,112	100.00	7,875	100.00

distribution of housing space can be used as some sort of measure of the distribution of wealth.[14]

In view of the fact that the household itself is defined in terms of a community physically bounded by a dwelling, it certainly seems possible that the largeness or the smallness of the dwelling itself will have an effect on the number of the members of a household. But in order to investigate this we must first be able to measure the size of houses. Unfortunately houses dating from earlier than 1801 which still exist today do not provide a usable sample, since it is precisely because of their ample size and the quality of their materials that they have escaped demolition. In the absence of information on the number of rooms and the amount of habitable space, all that can be done is to attempt to verify the following hypothesis: that the more households there are under the same roof, the smaller will be the household size. Allowance has to be made for the fact that the last named apartment in a building was likely to be the least considerable: it was a left over, so to speak, and so likely to contain the smallest household.[15]

Some ground plans show numbers of apartment houses divided into two or three sets of dwelling units round a courtyard. It is possible that households in the units on the street were more cramped for room than the others, which had the back area at their disposal and were counted last in the Census. This seems to be true of some shops along the most crowded streets in the centre of the town. But this was by no means the situation everywhere. The mean sizes contained in Tables 13.2, 13.3 and 13.4 (compare row 3 with 4, 5 with 6, 7 with 8, 9 with 10) show that in each rank, the last counted household is the smallest.[16] Of course, households occupying a whole house (row 1) are larger in size than those counted

[14] For the gradation of suburbs by the degree to which they were rural, see Hélin (1962 ii): 14–19 and 26–9, and for housing as an indicator of wealth, see Hélin, *A la recherche d'une mesure des inégalités de fortune* (1966): 155–6.
[15] Compare a statistical analysis of dwellings in 1766 in Roller (1907): 209–16.
[16] There is a significant difference at 0.05 between the distributions, except for households occupying 3rd and 5th lodgings.

first in divided houses (row 2). There is another exception: households occupying the fourth and last dwelling are slightly larger in size than others in the same rank (Table 13.3, rows 7 and 8): this anomaly is confined to a score of large families in one district.

If dimension of household only is considered, differences between households are less marked after the difference between the first named and the rest. Distinctions in size attributable to rank of this kind are not so clear in general when it is a question of intermediate households, that is those neither first nor last named in the list for a building. But when the *composition* of households as distinct from their *dimensions* is considered, the picture is every different. The mean number of children less than twelve years old varies a great deal more than that of adults. It all looks as if households bringing up numbers of children kept away from houses divided into many dwelling units. A considerable number of variables in fact enter into this; marital status of members of the household, age of mother, number and sex of dependent children,[17] not to speak of the occupation of the head of the household, whether or not he owned his house, the period of time he had been in Liège, and so on. Work on the data for 1801 is still in progress and it will only be little by little that the interplay of so many factors can be elucidated.

VALUE OF COMPARATIVE DATA

Counts of persons undertaken in Liège for reasons of subsistence or for poor relief, as well as censuses of souls (*status animarum*) dating from the ancien régime yield counts of the members of the several hundred households which went to make up a parish. When the same community was counted on separate occasions, as for example the parish of Glain in 1728, in 1736 and in 1750, the differences between distributions of households mostly turn out to be insignificant, presumably due to random variation alone.[18]

On the other hand, significance tests show that when the populations come from different districts of the town, the distributions are independent of each other, differing by more than random variation. The value of χ^2 is in nearly all cases significant: for example when sizes of household are compared between St Christophe in 1789 and Glain in 1750, or between Olne in 1789 and Glain in 1750, or between St Thomas in 1789 and St Jean-Baptiste in 1790, or between this last parish in 1790 and District No. 7, which contained it, in 1801. The differences are most often accounted for by households of one person. It should perhaps be pointed out, however, that St Thomas, and St Martin are parishes in the City, Glain and St Christophe are suburbs, and Olne a country village.

[17] Ockers (1967): 35–50, traces the evolution of Belgian households between 1930 and 1961, and goes on to analyse in depth the structure of the family.
[18] Compare the analysis of the changes in the mean household sizes of English settlements in the eighteenth century, see above, Wall, Chapter 5, pp. 191–203.

Nevertheless there are occasions when a distribution of households by size for one community at one date turn out to show no more than random differences from that of another community at another date. An example is the list of households benefiting from a charitable distribution at St Christophe in 1789, and another similar list of benefactors at St Martin in 1790. It will be necessary therefore to make further tests before reaching a conclusion on this important point. Without entering into the question of the variety of criteria which can be held to define a household, it must again be emphasised that the parishes of Liège appear to present more differences than similarities, no doubt because of their small populations, and because of their peculiar mixtures of status and occupation.

Up to now historians have been content for the most part to work out arithmetic means, without paying too much attention to the diversity of situations which can be concealed in an identical figure of this kind. It has been found that in most of the cities of Europe before the last century, as well as in Liège, the mean number of persons to household appears to be remarkably constant: it oscillates between four and five with so much regularity that these values have been adopted as multipliers for all purposes.[19] The average of 3.668 calculated here for Liège in 1801, though it is lower than those of the eighteenth century is in no way out of the ordinary. It is known, to give only a few examples, that the figure of 3.49 can be given for the parish of St Christophe in 1740, 3.04 for Antwerp within the walls in 1755, 3.2 for Brussels at the same date, 3.58 for that city in 1796, 3.8 for Rheims in 1773, 3.7 for Toulouse in 1695, and 3.7 for Geneva in 1797.[20]

Villages on the other hand have household sizes larger than four persons: 5.36 at Gemmenich in 1709; 5.4 at Kanegem in 1713 and 1765; from 5.10 to 7.34 in the lordship of Nevele in 1786 and at Evergem in 1796–8; 4.92 at Erembodegem in 1754, and so on.[21] The same result is apparent from regional studies, at least when care is taken to distinguish population tracts by type. In the district of Veluwe (in Gelderland in the Netherlands) mean size of household was 3.8 in 1749 in the towns, that is to say where less than 7 % of household heads were in agriculture, but in the hamlets where 76 % were in agriculture, the mean rose to 4.6.[22] Data are rarely available in Belgium before the end of the nineteenth

[19] See Hélin, La démographie de Liège (1963): 140–3; Mols (1955) II: 100–9, and Verbeemen, Bruxelles en 1755 (1962). This last article gives the composition of 929 families in the Sablon district, besides numerical particulars of household size, and estimates the influence of wealth of household head on the number of children.

[20] For Brussels see Cosemans (1966): 85–6, and for the other towns see Mols (1955) II: 116–18, 120. After the appearance of Mols' work, several articles have come out amplifying the data contained in Mols (1955) III: 114, fn 7, 200–1 on the subject of the size of households. These include Taute, Recensements à Charleville en 1789 (1957); Ruwet, La population de Saint-Trond en 1635 (1958); Lasch (1965).

[21] References in Hélin (1963): 143. Compare also de Rammelaere, Kanegem (1962): 192, and Cinq études de démographie locale (1966): 76, 127, 218–19.

[22] Roessingh, Population change and economic development in the Netherlands (1965 ii). For further details see above, van der Woude, Chapter 12, pp. 308–309. Households also tended

century, and ever since that time a reduction in mean size of household has been evident in these records, which is confirmed by the last Census.[23]

In brief, the evolution of the household goes forward both in time and in space and can be traced if one proceeds from rural communities buried in the country-side towards urban centres. Precisely because such a multiplicity of variables are at play (availability of premises, degree of industrialisation, relative attractive power of towns, standard of living, tendency towards sharing, functions of the family, etc.) it will be important to use the most complete statistics, and to proceed from the largest possible number of chronological vantage points.

CONCLUSIONS

The examination of households at Liège in 1801 has shown that the arithmetic mean is not the only parameter which should satisfy demographic historians. If he only wishes to estimate a population from the number of *feux*, he must be aware of the error which random variation can bring about. The possibilities of the χ^2 test should persuade him of the importance of publishing the composition of households in full, and not under a number of arbitrarily combined headings. Furthermore the asymmetrical character of the distribution of households by size makes it necessary that expressions of asymmetry should be calculated in order to facilitate comparison.

Arithmetic means, although they varied so little, covered a whole series of dif-ferent situations. These only become apparent at Liège if the City and the suburbs are first separately treated, and then households occupying a whole house are taken separately from those sharing the same premises. It is not sufficient simply to bring into prominence differences of an ecological kind, for these in their turn are sensitive to a variety of influences, either demographic (fertility, mortality) or socio-economic (income level, employment of persons in domestic handi-craft and so on). Future research must be directed towards the composition of households, and establish among other things the frequency of unmarried persons and of children dependent on household heads.

It is established that households of small size, that is less than four persons, were in the majority at Liège well before large scale enterprise established itself and modern machinery won the day. Here we re-echo the conclusions of E. J. Walter, who based them on the figures he recovered for Zurich and Basle in the seventeenth and eighteenth centuries. [24] In the same way as the spread of technical knowledge about the railway, the steam engine, the coking process, preceded the general spread of industrial machinery, it could be that in the cities the multiplication of small households prepared the way for the arrival of a society

to be larger in the countryside in fifteenth-century Tuscany, see above, Klapisch, Chapter 10, p. 275. See also Halpern's study of nineteenth-century Serbia, below, Chapter 16, pp. 401–402.
[23] See Ockers (1967): 14–20 and 130–5, and Wachelder (1964): 146–80.
[24] Walter (1961).

which itself tended towards the atomisation of life. But this preparation took place a long time before the event. Once again it appears that the West was able to spread over several generations the task of adaptation which changes of such a profound kind necessarily implied. It had the good fortune to escape the painful and sudden mutations which now affect so many of the developing countries. It is for the historian to recover the pace and the rhythm of this growth, viewing it in the perspective of the long term evolutionary process, to mark its points of departure, even the occasional retracing of its path. The situation in 1801 has only given us one point of reference on a curve which will be traced out in full only if other censuses are worked upon by the method of cohort analysis, which is a method essentially historical in character.

14. The zadruga as process

E. A. Hammel

I. INTRODUCTION

The large and complex households reported from the Balkans have excited scholarly attention for many years; to intellectuals who were themselves living in an urban–industrial environment and in conjugal units that seldom contained any added relatives other than an unwelcome mother-in-law, households reputed to have up to a hundred members demanded explanation. Such explanations have taken a variety of forms: historical, evolutionist, functional, psychological, economic, legalist. Most of them have had implicit or explicit political or ideological intent, or have at least had such intent attributed to them.[1] They may regard the complex household as a survival of a more primitive state common to many people, or typical of 'retarded' development, or as a retention of alleged Slavic tendencies to peaceful cooperation in contrast to Germanic individuality and aggressiveness. They may suggest social conditions that stimulated its growth: the need for a body of coresident males for defense in frontier situations, the existence of a hearth tax or similar dues that made group living more economical, the advantages to household economy in a finer division of labor – or those that led to its decline: the introduction of private property and of a money economy that stimulated individuality and the division of extended households. Some discussions even attribute variation in the form of the complex household to invidious differences in national character.[2]

[1] Mandić (1950). In this connection compare Klapisch's description of the *società della torri* in medieval Italy, see above, Chapter 10, pp. 280–281.

[2] The literature on the zadruga is extensive. Apart from the individual descriptive monographs in *Srpski Etnografski Zbornik* and similar series, some of the more useful references are: Bogišić (1874); Erlich, *The southern Slav patriarchal family* (1940) and *The family in transition* (1966); Filipović (1945); Halpern, *A Serbian village* (1967); Halpern and Anderson, *The zadruga a century of change* (1970); J. and B. Halpern, *Orašac* (1972); Hammel, *Alternative social structures and ritual relations in the Balkans* (1968): Hammel, *Social mobility, economic change and kinship in Serbia* (1969 i); Hammel, *Structure and sentiment in Serbian cousinship* (1969 ii); Jiriček (1912) and (1952); Jovanović (1896); Karanović (1929); Krauss (1885); Kulišić (1955); Lilek (1900); Mandić (1950); Moseley, *The peasant family* (1940), *Adaptation for survival* (1943) and *The distribution of the zadruga* (1953); Nikolić (1958); Nimac *et al.* (1960); Novaković (1891); Pantelić (1964); Pavković (1961); Sicard, *La zadruga dans la littérature serbe* (1943) and *Problèmes familiaux chez les Slaves du Sud* (1947); Švob and Petrić (1929); Tomasevich, *Peasants, politics and economic change in Yugoslavia* (1955):

With a few notable exceptions,[3] discussions of these households have focused on legal, economic, and political aspects. Only a few authors have examined the data from the standpoint of kinship and of kinship process. Moreover, a good deal of the often acrimonious debate, so tinged with accusations of political orthodoxy or dereliction, is characterized by an abundance of hypotheses in the absence of fact, or by an abundance of fact in the absence of coherent theory. The difficulties are particularly intense in discussion of the decline of the institution of the complex household during the last hundred years; one is never certain whether the baseline of historical comparison is the complex household as it existed or that household as it was envisaged by authors afflicted by the most severe symptoms of romanticism. Thus, while the decline of the institution as a set of behavioral patterns is in part incontestable, it is in part a function of a particular ideology or myth among intellectuals.

For all these reasons, but particularly because of the political connotations associated with 'positions' on the household structure of the Balkans, it is an uncomfortable subject. It is therefore incumbent on any author to make explicit what his analysis is and what it is not about. This chapter is quite definitely not a history of the complex household in the Balkans but at best only a prolegomenon to one. It is not much concerned with its formal legal aspects (and particularly not with the conflicts between Byzantine, medieval, Ottoman, Austrian, and Napoleonic law in respect to it); neither is it much concerned with individual psychology, individualism, the effects of money economy, national character, or explanations by cultural determinism. In failing to give primary weight even to the more useful of these traditional variables (such as legal aspects and economic conditions), it does not omit them but rather views them as general constraints and shifts attention to a set of factors usually ignored. This set concerns kinship and those aspects of social organization related to it. Although analysis from the worm's eye view of kinship is second nature to social anthropologists, its relevance is not always apparent to others, and a few introductory comments on the utility of the anthropological view in analysis of the complex household are in order.

While the existence of complex households on our own doorstep in Europe has

178–89; Tomasić, *Personality and culture in Eastern European politics* (1948). Most of the varying views on the zadruga are covered in these sources. Among the older ones, Bogišić, Novaković, and Sicard provide some of the best data, and Novaković's interpretations are superior to most of those that have followed. Moseley's work is valuable, Halpern and Anderson provide the most sophisticated demographic analysis, and J. and B. Halpern offer additional discussion of change over the last hundred years. A strong Marxist critique of theories is given by Mandić and Tomasevich gives the most extensive, balanced review of the problem in English.

I am indebted to Dr Lorraine Barić for insisting on the individuality of the Croatian zadruga, to Professors Burton Benedict, Maurice Freedman, Peter Laslett, G. William Skinner, Jozo Tomasevich, Arthur Wolf, and Mrs Gail Venti for their comments, and to George Šoć and Virginia Aldrich for assistance in coding and computing. None of them, of course, is responsible for any errors of fact or interpretation that may remain in the analysis.
[3] See below, pp. 362–369.

been a matter for comment and speculation on why Balkan households are so *different*, their presence does not much surprise (as much as it delights) the anthropologist, who is more likely to ask in what ways they are the *same* as the many other manifestations of such household structure with which he is familiar.[4] It is this question – how the Balkan households are similar to other complex households – that concerns us here. An anthropologist would look for typical, underlying, fundamental structural reasons for the similarities – for what my British colleagues are fond of calling 'first principles'. The intent of this chapter is to demonstrate that the combination of some basic principles, such as lineage organization, virifocality, patrilocality, and agnatic bias[5] (which are all of a piece in societies with patrilineal-like organization in the present or in their immediate past), together with certain demographic rates and particular external constraints, will produce the complex households of the Balkans. This chapter will also attempt to show that the historical changes in household organization in the Balkans can be attributed largely to alteration in demographic rates and external constraints, rather than to changes in underlying principles of organization, which have remained remarkably constant.[6]

Studies of the complex household in the Balkans almost always regard those that are actually observed as imperfect examples of a Platonic ideal type, of an archetypical extended household. Some households are observed to be small, others large, but these variations are usually placed on a simple linear scale of achievement of the type. Seldom is any account taken of a variety of conflicting influences or of the possibility that a household can be large at one time and small at another – *in particular that households may have a developmental cycle and that there may also be seasonal variations in their structure.*[7]

These considerations of *cyclical* microvariation in time affect the way in which data from the field or from archival sources are analysed and also the way in which one speaks of macrovariation or *secular* developmental trends in the history of the institution. It is useful, first of all, to differentiate between two major forms of extended household (although in doing this I may appear only to substitute two ideal types for one). One of these was a formally constituted corporation, found principally among Serbs in the Croatian Military Border and codified in Austrian law. This kind of household could grow or diminish in size; one household could divide into several or several could merge into one; persons could be added or dropped. However, changes in its constitution and the acqui-

---

[4] See in particular the study by Goody of dwelling and work groups in Africa and Asia, above, Chapter 3, pp. 103–124.

[5] By virifocality I mean the organization of domestic groups around a core of males, by patrilocality the rule of postmarital residence whereby a wife lives with her husband, who has remained with his own father, and by agnatic bias the tendency for social organization to arrange itself according to groupings of persons related only (in cultural recognition) through males.

[6] See Halpern and Anderson (1970); Hammel (1969 i and 1969 ii).

[7] See Goody, *The developmental cycle in domestic groups* (1958 i). See also above, Goody, Chapter 3, pp. 118, 122.

sition and alienation of property were not casual matters, for it was a formal corporation: important steps had to be agreed to by all adult males and often had to be approved by the local military commandant. This type of household certainly had historical roots in kinship organization, but it was sufficiently formalized, and the possibility of inclusion of nonkin was sufficiently regularized, that it was in its most developed form an institution of rather different surface structure from the ordinary extended household or kinship-based local group found in so many societies and probably common in the proto-Slavic and Indo-European past.[8] I regard it as the *formalized* epitome of a particular form of kinship-based group.[9]

I have thus far avoided using the traditional epithet for these complex households, for use of the word is apt to call only a particular variety of organizational form to mind. The formally corporate household of Croatia, and particularly of the Military Border, was called a zadruga. This paper is not about that kind of zadruga but rather about a second, found principally in Serbia, Montenegro, Hercegovina, and parts of Bosnia, that was precisely of the ordinary, kinship-based type. It is also known in the literature as the zadruga, or more exactly as the *porodična* or *obiteljska* (familial) zadruga. While the formal zadruga has disappeared with the law codes that enshrined it, the familial zadruga still persists in many rural areas. Although nonkin can be included in it, such inclusion is rare, and it shows a clear developmental cycle based in the mechanisms of familial growth. In areas of mixed farming and herding it also exhibits seasonal variation in size and structure. In peasant tradition, the older historical documents, and some of the literature these households were not known as zadrugas at all but simply by the ordinary words for house (*kuća, dom*); zadruga, as a term for them, has come into modern peasant speech from the nationalistic folkloristic literature of the nineteenth and twentieth centuries.[10]

[8] For general parallels in kinship organization among Indo-European peoples see Jiriček (1912) pt. I: 36–9, *passim*, and (1952): 51–2. Olsen, *Farms and fanes of ancient Norway* (1928): 43–6, gives an interesting parallel from Norwegian and Icelandic data, and I am obliged to Harry Todd for bringing it to my attention. Much of the argument for agnatic structure among Indo-European peoples rests on kinship terminology and its possible implications. See particularly Friedrich, *Semantic structure and social structure* (1964) and *The linguistic reflex of social change* (1966); Hammel, *Serbo-Croatian kinship terminology* (1957); Hammel (1968): 26–31; Lounsbury, *A formal account of the Crow- and Omaha-type kinship terminologies* (1964).

[9] The formalized zadruga of the Military Border, in which land ownership was tied to military service, developed with the organization of the Border itself, beginning as early as the sixteenth century. Heritable land was limited almost exclusively to soldiers (in lieu of pay) in 1754 and conditions of ownership were further limited and tied to military service in 1807. Unanimous agreement by all members was required for division until 1850, after which time the majority could decide on division, the severity of other regulations concerning the tie between land ownership and military service was relaxed, and land owned by families in the Border was considered fully heritable and less in the nature of a fief. The Border was demilitarized in 1873. For fuller discussion of the Military Border, see Tomasevich (1955): 74 ff.

[10] Neither the formal–legal zadruga nor the family zadruga are to be confused with the *zemljoradnička* zadruga now found in Yugoslavia; this organization is a farmers' cooperative for the sale of produce and purchase of farm equipment and supplies.

My intention is to show that the familial zadruga is basically a product of patrilocal extension and virifocality, that it seldom remained intact for more than two full generations, and that it existed in the fourteenth and sixteenth centuries in some areas in a form not substantially different in structure or even in size from that found in those areas in the nineteenth century and even today. Although the typical household of modern rural Serbia is not the same as the typical one of the nineteenth century or earlier, the changes have been of degree rather than of kind; the process of change has not been one of dissolution but of reformulation.[11] One cannot accept citation of the number of nonextended conjugal households or of divisions of extended households or mention of other simplistic indicators as *prima facie* evidence for the decay of the institution; indeed, one could have claimed the decline of the zadruga on precisely the same sort of evidence and with equal credibility in the fourteenth or the sixteenth century.[12]

An institution that has been 'decaying' for 600 years is worth looking at again. If the zadruga is an extended household, it can be expected to begin, minimally, with a man and his wife, to add married sons, and then to divide into separate households in the second or later generations. Many of the resulting households will consist of subsets of brothers who have continued their joint endeavors, but others will contain only one man with his wife and children.[13] The existence of minimally extended or nonextended households is not necessarily evidence for the decline of the extended household as an institution but only for the division of particular ones. Even an increase in the number of nonextended households or in that of legal divisions of households cannot be taken as evidence for decline of the institution unless corrections are made for population growth; the number of nuclear households or of divisions of complex ones will increase in a growing population even though their proportion in the set of all households remains the same.

The historical background against which this consistency of kinship is portrayed is anything but constant; indeed, the purpose of the analysis is to point up the rather remarkable conservatism in *underlying* kinship principles *despite* the cultural flux of Balkan history. When the Serbs first came to the Balkans,

---

[11] J. and B. Halpern (1972).   [12] Cf. Bićanić, quoted in Erlich (1964): 337.

[13] In this chapter, I use the English term, 'household', as a gloss for the native terms, *kuća* or *dom*. The terminology used by Laslett and Clarke, Chapter 15, pp. 376–379 (compare Laslett, Chapter 1, pp. 34–40), distinguishes between the *household* as an explicit, coresidential familial unit containing a single conjugal pair or its remnants, with or without miscellaneous added relatives but not including any further conjugal pairs or their remnants who are not related to any member of the primary unit, and *houseful*, as an explicitly coresidential unit consisting of associated *households*. Although that terminology may be useful for English data or for some purposes of comparative analysis, I have not adopted it, for it creates precisely the illusion of sharp difference between the units in the houseful that I wish to avoid and obscures the fundamental *ethnographically valid* developmental continuum in Serbia from the simple conjugal family, through the patrilocal extended family, to the fraternal joint family. A similar problem arises with the Rhode Island Census of 1875, see below, Pryor, Chapter 22, p. 582.

they were probably organized in patrilineages only loosely linked to one another, practicing a combination of simple agriculture and herding. Those that pushed high into the inhospitable limestone mountains, replacing and mixing with the Romanized Illyrians that had preceeded them, came to depend more on herding and manifested a tribal political organisation until the nineteenth century. Those that came under the control of the Serbian medieval state, as it replaced Byzantium, became agricultural serfs. Some serfs fled their bondage to take up herding, some herders came under the control of the medieval state. The political, economic, and ecological histories of the Balkans are inextricably mixed, with populations flowing in enormous migrations from one region, from one ecological niche to another, as conquerors (such as the Turks and Austrians) came and went, as the conditions of life became temporarily better or worse. Much of the variation in family structure and lineage organization can be attributed to shifts from settled agriculture to herding or the reverse, to the appearance and disappearance of opportunities to pioneer new land, to the introduction of economic alternatives such as the opportunity for occasional or permanent employment in provincial mines and industries and the effects of all these factors on traditional patterns of personal interrelationship and authority. Nothing in this analysis should be taken to suggest that *no* change has occurred; rather it is the intent to show that change has indeed taken place, but that it is not simple or unilinear, and that it is the result of the interaction of factors on a fundamental kinship process.[14]

These remarks are intended only to illustrate the theoretical context for and disciplinary bias of the analysis, which is centered on an examination of the earliest explicit household census data for the Balkans now available to me. These data consist of two sixteenth-century Turkish tax rolls (*defter*) translated into Serbo-Croatian by Hazim Šabanović.[15] One of them gives excellent detail on the kinship relationships between coresident adult males in 2,002 households in 156 villages; the other gives the proportion of married to unmarried males in 2,614 households in 146 of the same villages within perhaps two years of the first tax roll, permitting a more accurate interpretation of it. I will first give a brief sketch of Turkish administrative practice and of pertinent historical events (following Šabanović and others) to place these documents in perspective and then go on to a more detailed analysis of the data.

II. THE OTTOMAN CENSUSES

Within a few years of the definitive conquest of the Serbian medieval empire at Kosovo (1389), that is by the reign of Mehmed I (1403–21), the Turks began a series of careful censuses of their changing domain that was to continue for five centuries. Regular census-taking on a large scale in the Balkans seems to have

---

[14] See Hammel (1969 i and 1969 ii) for discussion of the persistence of agnatic ideology.
[15] Šabanović (1964).

Fig. 14.1   Serbia and neighbouring areas

begun with the reign of Mehmed II (The Conqueror, 1451–81), after the fall of Constantinople in 1453. Three known censuses of areas now in Yugoslavia come from this period, but even these were carried out before the classic period of Turkish administration of the Balkans that began with the fall of Smederevo (Semendria) in 1459 and the inclusion of the Serbian Despotism into the Ottoman Empire as the *Sandžak* of Smederevo.

Turkish censuses were generally of two types, with regard to the occasion for their implementation. General censuses of the entire empire were taken on the ascension of a new sultan or at regular intervals thereafter, usually every ten years. Local censuses were taken on the occasion of major changes in the territorial extent of an administrative division of any level, major changes in the organization of governmental administration, or changes in the tax laws. The process of census-taking was thus quite regular and firmly institutionalized. Vassals of the sultan were required to furnish documentary evidence of all sources of income and to bring all their serfs before the census commission. Administrative personnel at all levels, including the headmen of districts or of villages with populations enjoying special status (such as shepherds, see below, p. 345), were directly involved in the process and responsible for the accuracy of their statements and of those of their political subordinates. The preliminary counts made by the census commission were then checked in the field, compared to previous censuses for consistency, and then assembled into the final, detailed, census document (*defter-i müssafal*).

The instructions frequently found in these censuses indicate that officials were required to count, in addition to material resources, all vassals of the sultan, all district and village headmen, and all other persons defined as feudal dependents, including agricultural peasant serfs, shepherds, or other categories of persons from whom feudal dues were demanded. Effectively, the census-takers counted only *mature males capable of work, excluding all women unless they were heads of households and all immature males unless they were living with such female heads of households or were heads of households themselves.* The method of listing persons differed; one roster examined here is apparently organized by households, giving the name of the head and of each coresident adult male, with the kinship linkage of each to the head. Others apparently give only the heads of households, sometimes implying the relationship between heads of households by giving the names of their fathers. A second list examined here gives heads of households and unmarried adult males, without their family connections being explicit in the data or implicit in the ordering of the list. Some censuses give a summary of the tax income due from the village, and some give in addition particular tax rates for individuals in special social categories, such as widows, cripples, or Moslems.

I have given this detail on administrative practice because it bears on the accuracy and interpretation of the data. Šabanović's assessment of the quality of the data is high; he cites the administrative checks and balances designed to reduce error and evasion, including severe fines and other punishment; he also points to the skill and local knowledge of the scribes, who must have been of native origin because of the accuracy of their transcription of Albanian and Serbo-Croatian words into Arabo-Turkish consonantal script. Šabanović does, however, caution the reader not to assume that the census sample constitutes the entire population; even though the entire tributary population was supposed to be counted and although there were severe punishments for evasion, some fraction may have slipped through the net, and some portions of the population were not dependent. The sample thus may not be perfectly representative, not to mention exhaustive. One check on accuracy lies in the consistency of successive censuses of the same area – a check apparently used by the Turks themselves. A brief exercise in the examination of consistency is instructive. I have compared the Censuses of 1528, 1530, 1536 and 1560 for four villages; to do more is not directly germane to this paper but rather to the subject of general population growth and settlement pattern, and the data from just these four will illustrate the problem.

One village (Srednja Ostružnica) had eight households and seventeen adult males in 1528. In 1530 it had twelve households and fourteen adult males, having lost three (or four) households with a total of six males and gained eight new males. By 1536 it had twenty households but had lost nine of those given in 1530 and had added seventeen new males apparently unrelated to anyone in the earlier lists. By 1560 there were only ten households, and only two of these seem related to any of those in the earlier accounts.

The second village (Brusnik or Poresnik) had eleven households with sixteen adult males in 1528. In 1530 it had fourteen households with seventeen adult males but had lost seven of the households present in 1528. In 1536 it had ten households with fourteen males, but only two of the households and four of the men had been present in 1528, and one more household, with one man, had been present in 1530. In 1560 it had eleven households and fifteen adult males, but only one household with one man had been in any previous census (1528). The third village (Marijovac or Markovac) shows much better correspondence. In 1528 there were ten households with twenty-seven males; in 1530 there were twenty-two households with twenty-three males, all but two of whom seem related to the males of 1528. In 1536 there were fourteen households with seventeen males, twelve of whom seem related to males in the Census of 1530. By 1560 there were only three households, with three men, two of whom seem related to males in the Census of 1536. The fourth village (Donji Doljani) had eight households in 1528 with sixteen men. In 1530 it had eight households with ten men, all apparently related to the earlier ones. In 1536 it had ten households with fifteen men, of whom nine seem related to those of 1530, and by 1560 it had eleven households with thirteen men, only three of whom seem related to those of 1536.[16]

---

[16] Compare the durability of households in Tokugawa Japan, below, Smith, Chapter 17, pp. 438–440, 470–471, Hayami, Chapter 18, pp. 513–515, and in nineteenth-century France, above, Blayo, Chapter 9, pp. 261–264.

Judgment of kinship relationship in these lists depends on rather skimpy data; we have only the first names of the males and of their fathers, sometimes with varyingly transparent substitution of nicknames or changes in spelling. Nevertheless, it is clear either that there was a high turnover of population or that the census takers were extraordinarily inefficient. Šabanović's praise of intended administrative efficiency is impressive, and one can hardly imagine that an experienced extractive administration like the Ottoman one would have been excessively lax in counting people for tax purposes.

There are other indications that the variation stems primarily from population movement; this conclusion will prove valuable in subsequent interpretation. For example, in the Census of 1530 there are a number of localities termed *mezra*. A mezra was an abandoned village, the lands of which were worked by inhabitants of a neighboring village, the latter being responsible for the taxes on it. In that Census there was about one mezra for every seven occupied villages, so that an eighth of the villages were abandoned. Additionally, ten of the villages in the Census of 1528 do not even appear as *mezre* (pl.) in the Census of 1530, suggesting that they may have been abandoned but that their lands had not been taken over by neighboring peasants. Thus, almost a fifth of the villages of 1528 may have lost their resident populations by 1530.

III.   THE VLACHS AND THE SERHAT (FRONTIER)
IN THE SIXTEENTH CENTURY

Further evidence, also important for interpretation in comparison with earlier and later statements on household size and structure, lies in the title of the 1528 Census: *Defter-i bazi eflâkân-i livâ-i Semendire*, in Šabanović's Serbo-Croatian translation, *Popis nekih Vlaha Smederevskog Sandžaka (Census of certain Vlachs of the Sandžak of Smederevo)*. The word, 'Vlach,' in this title does not refer to any of the latinic-speaking shepherd groups now known from the Carpathians or the Istrian peninsula but is a generic term for shepherd; Šabanović occasionally gives the parenthetical gloss, *stočar*, stockman.[17] The Vlachs played

---

[17] Vlach is a word of Germanic origin, with the essential meaning 'foreign,' applied to the Celts or to the Romans. In Britain it meant the non-Anglo-Saxon population, that is, the Britons or Romanized Britons and survives in *Welsh, Wales,* Cornwall, and the surname Wallace. OE forms are *Welisc, Waelisc,* etc., from OHG *wal(a)hisc,* corresponding to G. *welsch,* with the meanings 'Roman,' 'Italian,' 'French.' The Dutch form *waalsch* survives as *Walloon.* The Germanic root, *walxaz,* was taken over into Latin – cf. L. *Volcae,* a Celtic tribe. Subsequently, the word was taken over by the Slavs. Miklosich (1963): 68, s.v. *vlah'* notes, 'vocabulum, uti videtur, celticum, quod a celtis ad germanos et ab his ad slavos migravit.' The Slavs used the word to designate the Romanized Illyrians they displaced and also the inhabitants of some cities on the Adriatic. With the passage of time it took on the general meaning of stockman or shepherd and was used in administrative documents of the medieval Serbian state and of the Ottoman Empire in that sense. Janković (1961): 33 esp. note 35, citing Daničić (1962): 131–3, s.v. *vlah,* says (my translation): 'Roman, a man of the ancient Roman settlements (and) the neighboring regions, and occasionally also a man from Dubrovnik, but by the principal occupation of the first of these and all who work with

a special social role both in the medieval Serbian empire and also in the Ottoman.

The social organization of Vlachs in medieval Serbia was distinct from that of agricultural peasants, as was their relation to the state. They lived in relatively independent villages under their own headmen, in contrast to the agricultural serfs, who were known as Serbians (or *meropi*).[18] Vlach villages were called by a special general term, *katun*, rather than the more common *selo*, and were usually only winter villages, the pastoralists spending the summers on high meadows. Generally, stockmen's villages were given particular names different from those applied to agricultural settlements; they were called by lineage names or patronymics. The internal organization of stockmen's villages was probably a lineage organization; it seems likely that a village might have been a local branch of a major lineage (*bratstvo*, fraternity). The head of a village was probably a lineage elder, variously called *knez, primićur*, or *čelnik* (prince, first-inscribed, head). The Vlachs were part of the political and economic structure of the medieval state, as were the meropi, but their life was freer, and their obligations were lighter than those of the agricultural serfs.[19] The two segments of the population were sharply distinguished from each other in law and forbidden to mingle.[20]

As the Serbian state crumbled before the Turks, many agricultural serfs fled into the uplands to take up herding and assumed the status of Vlachs. After the fall of the Serbian Despotism (1459), many peasants escaped across the Sava River into Hungarian territory or to the Serbian interior uplands, and the process of depopulation was accelerated by the depradations of the Hungarian army under Mathias Corvinus. *There was then a massive repopulation of the area by Vlachs, just as there was by peasant-pastoralists in the wake of the Turkish retreat four centuries later.* Djurdjev gives the number of Vlach houses in the Sandžak of Smederevo in 1476 as 7,600 but says that by 1516 the number had climbed to about 12,000. Most of the Vlachs came from the area now known as Stari Vlah (Old Vlah) in extreme western Serbia, from the middle reaches of the

cattle, *pecuarius*; this last meaning occurs most frequently and foremost.' See also Miklosich (1963): 68, Daničić (1962): 131–3, and Onions, ed., *The Oxford Dictionary of English Etymology* (1966): 999, s.v. *Welsh*.

[18] Jiriček (1912) pt. I: 69 suggests that the origin of the word *Serb* lies in an old root meaning 'sharecropper.' citing Russian, Lithuanian, and Greek cognates.

[19] Janković (1961): 33–4; Jiriček (1912) pt. I: 69–70. For a general description of social organisation among agricultural peasants and shepherds, see Jiriček (1912) pt. I: 24–42.

[20] Article 82 of the Code of the Emperor Stefan Dušan, promulgated in the middle of the fourteenth century, reads: 'If a Vlach or Albanian settles down in a village, others should not settle there or follow after him. If he stays by force, he must pay damages and for what his stock have pastured.' (*Gde prestoi Vlah ili Arbanasin na sele, na tom-zi sele da ne prestoi drugi grede za nimi. Ako li po sile stane, da plati potku i što je ispasal* [Janković (1961): 137; Radojčić (1960): 58, 112].) Similarly, intermarriage was discouraged. One of the Dečanska chrysobulls (1330–6) reads: 'A Serb (*viz.* an agricultural serf) must not marry among the Vlachs; if he does, he must bring her into the meropi.' (*Srbin da se ne ženi u vlaseh; ako il se oženi, da ju vede u merophe.*) See Janković (1961): 103.

Drina, from Hercegovina, or from the Montenegrin Brda, classic areas of pastoralism and of lineage organization. They were attracted by open land and by the extraordinary privileges held out to them by Turkish administrators who wished to have the land resettled to increase tax income and to provide better defense against the Hungarians. The Vlachs continued to have their own village headmen and developed a feudal-like structure in which district headmen often assumed the position of *spahis* (military vassals) under the sultan. Their mobility was honored, the Turkish judges did not intrude on them, and it was for a time even forbidden to question them about conditions in enemy territory they might have visited in their pastoral wanderings. Their economic position was also superior to that in medieval Serbia, since their feudal dues and work obligations were less. If they settled on Turkish feudal land, they paid only half the tithe normally charged to ordinary peasants. They were permitted to pay some of their dues in money, were completely free of any corvée obligations, and paid a house tax rather than an individual tax. Even the agricultural peasants were relatively less burdened in the Sandžak of Smederevo than in other areas, as an enticement to remain. By 1536, however, the Turks had secured southern Hungary (the Banat) and firmed their general position for the later advance on Vienna. They had no need of generous enticements, and the differences in administrative treatment of Vlachs and agriculturalists were eliminated.[21]

The Census of 1528 thus falls in a period of forced-draft migration and rapid social change. Many Vlachs were probably still moving into the area, but the Turkish attitude toward them had probably already begun to change, perhaps as early as the Ottoman conquest of Belgrade in 1521 or the success in the battle of Mohacs in 1526. Some Vlachs may have been moving into villages deserted by others, and all of them would have experienced some changes in social organization, probably having adopted a household and village organization that still retained internal aspects of the patrilocal and virifocal local groups of the mountain homeland but that had acculturated in part to the external demands of the Turkish bureaucracy and feudal economy. When we add to this general ferment and movement the fact that even settled Vlachs shifted their position naturally with the seasons and perhaps over a cycle of several years, it is small wonder that successive censuses of the same area were not in perfect accord.

IV.   THE CENSUSES OF BELGRADE COUNTY,
1528 AND 1530

Two of the censuses that were printed by Šabanović in his collection of historical materials[22] are of particular interest for the study of domestic groups in Serbia. Both are tax rolls for villages in the county (*nahija*) of Belgrade. The first is from the *Tahrir defteri* No. 144 in the archives at Istanbul and lacks a date; however,

---

[21] The above account is based on Djurdjev in Babić *et al.* (1960): 76–86.
[22] Šabanović (1964).

it is similar to and has the same instructional introduction as another document from the same archive, the *Tahrir defteri* No. 1011, which covers a different set of villages in the same sandžak. This further document was dated in the first ten days of Ramadan, 934, that is, from 20 to 29 May, 1528. On the basis of internal evidence, Šabanović judges No. 144 to be a second portion of No. 1011 and slightly later in time, but still in the same year (1528). That means that No. 144 was probably finally compiled and sent to Istanbul in the summer or fall of 1528; thus, it was very likely to have been assembled in the field in the preceding winter, and perhaps verified in the spring. The precise date of its assembly may be important in its interpretation.

The second census published by Šabanović in 1964 consists of parts of the *Tapu-defteri* No. 978, also from the Istanbul archive. Although it lacks a date, it is attributed to the period after 1527 because it contains the name of an official, referred to as deceased, who is known to have died in that year. Further, it refers to the Vlachs of the city of Smederevo as 'former' or 'derogated' Vlachs, while the *Tahrir defteri* No.144 described above, refers to them simply as Vlachs. Since withdrawal of privileges from the Vlachs of the region was probably just beginning, and since No. 144 cannot be earlier than 1528, No. 978 must be later than 1528. The next dated census of the sandžak was taken in 1536, by which time the removal of privileges from the Vlachs was an accomplished fact. Šabanović attributes No. 978 to the period 1528–32, certainly before 1536, and probably in 1528–30. To avoid confusion, I refer throughout to the second census as the Census of 1530.

The two Censuses, of 1528 and 1530, differ markedly in their internal construction and apparent purpose. Because the format of the 1528 Census is critical to its interpretation and analysis, I have transcribed Šabanović's listing for a single small village (Tatarin) in 1528 and further to illustrate the differences have translated that listing and its equivalent for the Census of 1530.[23] The Serbo-Croatian text on Tatarin for 1528 is as follows:

Jovan sin Božidara i s njim: Vuk, njegov sin: Petar, njegov sin; Dragoje, njegov sin.
Božidar sin Vukmana i s njim: Dobrica, njegov brat; Petar, njegov sin; Radul, njegov sin; Cvetko, njegov bratcučed.
Radavac sin Vukmana.
Radovan sin Vukašina i s njim: Vuk, njegov brat.
Bora sin Milašina i s njim: Vuk, njegov sin.
Radosav sin Radošina i s njim: Radošin, njegov otac.
Radoje sin Rajčića.
Vuk sin Dragobrata i s njim Radosav, njegov brat.[24]

DOMOVA 8, TABIJA 11.

The English translation of this list for Tatarin and, in parallel, of the list for Tatarin in 1530 are as follows:

[23] See Šabanović (1964): 47–8, 132.
[24] See below, p. 360 fn. 32.

(1528)

Jovan the son of Božidar and with him: Vuk, his son; Petar, his son; Dragoje, his son.

Božidar the son of Vukman and with him: Dobrica, his brother; Petar, his son; Radul, his son; Cvetko, his fraternal nephew.

Radavac the son of Vukman.

Radovan the son of Vukašin and with him: Vuk, his brother.

Bora the son of Milašin and with him: Vuk, his son.

Radosav the son of Radošin and with him: Radošin, his father.

Radoje the son of Rajčić.

Vuk the son of Dragobrat and with him Radosav, his brother.

HOUSES 8
CORESIDENT MALES 11[25]

(1530)

Jovan the son of Božidar
Radivoj the son of Jovan
Petar the son of Jovan
Cvetko the son of Dobrica
Radovan the son of Vukašin
Boža the son of Milašin
Vuk the son of Djura, unknown
Jakša the son of Radoje
Božidar the son of Vukman
Radul the son of Božidar
Dobrica the son of Vukman
Radul the son of Božidar
Dobrica the son of Vukman
Mihail the son of Vučko
Milić the son of Radonja
Vukodrag the son of Janko
Vuk the son of Dragobrat
Radosav the son of Dragobrat

HOUSES 13
UNMARRIED 4
(Subsequent data on taxes omitted here.)

The evidence for population turnover is again clear in comparison of the lists for 1528 and 1530. By 1530, two men had disappeared from the first family in the 1528 list, one had disappeared from the second, and one from the fifth. The third, sixth, and seventh families had disappeared entirely; only the fourth and eighth were intact. Six men not listed in 1528 were given in 1530; only two of them could possibly have been related to anyone in the list of 1528, on the basis of the evidence given: Radivoj, who might have been the son of Jovan in the first family, and Jakša, who might have been the son of Radoje in the seventh.

Some assumptions have to be made in characterizing the groups in the 1528 list as 'families.' Each group is clearly distinguished from the others in several ways. For example, each group is physically separate from the others in the list; they are not run together. The first person named in any group is almost always a man, whose father is named by way of identification of his son. Of course, the father need not have been present at the time and was frequently, no doubt, already dead. Sometimes the name of the father is found at the head of another

---

[25] 'Coresident males' is my rendering of the word *tabija*. Šabanović gives the etymological source as Arabic *tābi'* or *tawābi'* (one who follows, one who belongs) and defines it for these documents as all grown males in a household. It is clear from the lists themselves and numbers of 'houses' and of 'coresident males' given at the foot of the lists that the word refers only to those grown males who were not themselves heads of households.

group, and on rare occasions it is found within the same group at the head of which his son's name is given. It sometimes happens that the person named at the beginning of a group listing is a woman, but she is always noted as a widow, and the name of her dead husband is often given by way of identification; he, of course, is not found elsewhere in the list. The names of persons at the beginning of a group listing are always given in the nominative case; the names of identifiers (such as fathers or husbands) are always given in the genitive case in Serbian. The names of persons following the name of the first person in any group are also given in the nominative case and are accompanied by some specification of kinship linkage to the person named first.

Now, it is difficult to imagine any reason for such grouping other than familial relationship and coresidence, in view of all we know about the traditional structure of Serbian households. These groups cannot be sets of men listed together simply because they were related, because some men with the same father are *not* listed together (cf. Božidar and Radavac, both sons of Vukman; it is not likely that there were two dead or absent fathers named Vukman in the immediate genealogy of this tiny village). Further, this method of listing coresident adult males (and widows if they were heads of households) seems to have been traditional at least from medieval times until the present (see below), and such groups have always been interpreted as coresident by Yugoslav scholars.

It is true that the original documents themselves do not specify the groups as coresident in any explicit way, but[26] using Occam's razor, it seems unnecessary to invent far-fetched reasons for their grouping other than coresidence. I have therefore interpreted each of the groups in the 1528 Census as a set of coresident adult males (with some widows, as noted, sometimes with immature sons, as described below), each male related in a specific way to the person first-named, who is taken as the head of the group. Since it cannot be supposed that these men lived together without women, and since women other than household heads are not named in the source, I propose to call these blocks of males (with occasional female heads) *work groups*. The purpose of what now follows is to convert these work groups into *households* where each first-named person becomes a household head.

Before we proceed to this work of conversion it may be noted that the listing of 1530, although in many ways less useful than that of 1528, contains evidence which gives crucial assistance to the undertaking. The document of 1530 differs from that of 1528 in that all males are named separately with the names of their fathers given; it does not even place brothers in adjacent position on the list. Nevertheless, it gives some information absent in the 1528 list – data on taxes and on the total number of unmarried males. The reasons for these differences are obscure. It is conceivable that, if the 1528 Census had been taken in the fall or winter, the Vlachs would have been gathered in their winter houses in the

---

[26] Cf. the households analysed by Laslett and Clarke, see below, Chapter 15, p. 376, where the specification *is* explicit in the use of the word *dom*.

katun, under one roof or clustered in adjacent sleeping sheds, just as they are today in upland areas in which a seasonal transhumance still prevails. Census-takers going to the winter villages would probably have listed the men according to the households in which they were then living. On the other hand, if the 1530 Census had been taken in the spring or summer, the Vlachs might have been scattered across the upland pastures or at least in separate cabins of a farmyard or upland hamlet, each nuclear family having its own summer hearth. The purposes of the two censuses may also have been different. The second one clearly demanded a personal tax from each individual male (*ispendža*), for it is possible to recompute the total tax for a village from the standard rates and arrive at the total given in the lists. The first census could well have been a house tax or hearth census, with coresident males other than the head listed for other pur-poses, perhaps for a population census, a corvée, or a military levy.

V.   ANALYSIS OF THE 1528 CENSUS

The groups of coresident adult males which I have called *work groups*, must be regarded as the core sets of agnatically related men, important in production and consumption, and the base on which patrilocal extended and fraternal joint households were formed. The structure of such work groups, however, cannot be assumed to be identical with that of complex households formed by combina-tion of conjugal families, since some undetermined number of men in the work groups of the listing of 1528 were probably not married. If they *were* all married, the frequencies of occurrence of various types of work groups would be an adequate representation of the frequencies of occurrence of various types of households, but merely to assume that they were all married would exaggerate the degree of extension of households. Since the Census of 1530, unlike that of 1528, gives some direct evidence on the proportions of married and unmarried adult males, we may use those data to derive a more conservative picture of the constitution of households, in which each male is taken to be married and the head of a coresident conjugal family.

The summary data in 1530 on the 146 villages present in both the 1528 and 1530 returns show that about 13 % of the *adult* males in 1530 were unmarried. (Immature males were not included in the computation.) If 13 % of the *adult* males were also unmarried in 1528, there would have been 567 of them in all the villages given in that Census. Now, some households may have been headed by unmarried males; this could have happened when a lone unmarried son had left his father, or when unmarried adult brothers lived alone, or with a widowed mother who was not the head of the household, or with unmarried sisters, as might happen if both parents had been killed, leaving a sibling set to fend for itself. Nevertheless, I have assumed for purposes of reconstruction that all heads of households in 1528 were married (or widowed). Thus, the 567 unmarried males would have been found only among the 2,636 coresident *adult* males who were not household heads, namely among the *tabije*. Under this assumption, 22 % of the tabije would have been unmarried. In all of this, it should be noted that the proportion of unmarried males is assumed to have been the same in 1528 as in 1530, and that the computations are restricted to households headed by males and to males who are not indicated as immature (*maloletan*) in the returns themselves.

The upshot of all this is that we may take the figure of 22 % as the probability that a tabija (a male who was not a household head) was unmarried. More precisely, we would say that the probability that a tabija was unmarried was 0.22. For convenience in computation, that probability will be taken as 0.25, or 1 in 4; the use of 0.25 rather than 0.22 as the probability of being unmarried simply gives a more conservative estimate of the extended character of households. If this probability is applied to the data on work groups in the conversion of such groups to extended households in which all the listed men are assumed to be married, the number of men who are not heads diminishes by one-fourth. However, determination of the frequency of occurrence of extended households of particular structural types depends not on the simple, wholesale application of this one-in-four probability but on some slight refinements, in which there must be computed the probability that one tabija, two tabije, three tabije, etc. are all unmarried.

The method of reconstructing zadrugas from the distribution of work groups can be illustrated as follows. Suppose, for example, that in some hypothetical Serbian population there occurred but four structural types of work groups or of zadrugas, namely:

(1) A lone man, in the frequency of 100.
(2) A man and one brother, in the frequency of 200.
(3) A man and two brothers, in the frequency of 100.
(4) A man and three brothers, in the frequency of 50.

If these structural types were work groups, it would be irrelevant whether the men in them were married or not. However, if these structural types were zadrugas, we would understand that all the men listed in them were married.

Now, in this hypothetical population the true number of zadrugas corresponding to the first structural type could not be less than the number of work groups corresponding to that type, since, by definition, all heads of households are (or have been) married. The probability of being unmarried cannot be applied to work groups with only one adult male, so that in this hypothetical population, the number of zadrugas of type 1 must be at least 100.

In work groups of the second type, the head of the household must be married, but the 0.25 probability of being unmarried can be applied to the 'extra' brother. Since there are 200 work groups of this type, we should find that on the average one-fourth, or 50, of them would consist of one married brother (the head) and one unmarried brother, so that these 50 would in fact correspond to the structural type given as no. 1, above, in so far as zadrugas were concerned. The remaining 150 would have two married brothers and would thus qualify for inclusion under type 2. Thus, at this point in the reconstruction, the number of zadrugas of type 1 would consist of the 100 work groups of type 1 plus the 50 work groups of type 2 that had been reduced to type 1 by this procedure, a total of 150. By the same token, the 200 work groups of type 2 would have been reduced to only 150.

Passing to work groups of type 3, the probability that two of the brothers who are not head will be unmarried is $(0.25)^2$ or 0.0625, that one will be married and the other unmarried is $(2)(0.25)(0.75)$ or 0.3750, and that both will be married is $(0.75)^2$ or 0.5625. Since there were 100 work groups of type 3 to begin with, the potential distribution of these is (theoretically) 6.25 to type 1, 37.50 to type 2, while 56.25 continue to qualify for inclusion in type 3. In the fourth type of work group, using the same reasoning, the probability that all three 'extra' brothers will be unmarried is 0.0156, that one will be married and two unmarried is 0.1406, that two will be married and one unmarried 0.4219, and that all three will be married also 0.4219. The original 50 work groups of type four must be then distributed 0.78 to the first type of reconstructed zadruga, 7.03 to the second, 21.10 to the third, while 21.10 remain as zadrugas of the fourth type. The final result of the redistribution in this example can be summarized by comparing the original distribution of work group types to the computed distribution of reconstructed zadrugas (data in percents):

	Type			
	1	2	3	4
Work groups	22.2	44.4	22.2	11.1
Zadrugas	34.9	43.2	17.2	4.7

This process of reconstruction was carried out for each of the 70 types of work groups originally inferred from the census list (see ideographs in Fig. 14.2 opposite).

The procedure for reconstruction is, of course, only a crude one. While all household heads with a coresident son were almost certainly married, some lone males in the list of work groups might have been single; nevertheless, the probability of being unmarried was applied only to nonheads and nonfathers. Further, no attempt was made to specify differential probabilities of being unmarried. There are no direct data on such differences in any of the censuses and no age-specific counts of married or unmarried males. Nevertheless, it is intuitively obvious that a coresident son of the head is more likely to be unmarried than a coresident brother of the head, and that younger brothers are more likely to be unmarried than older brothers. It would be possible to refine the analysis by guessing at these differential probabilities, but the actual differences between the distribution of work group types and types of reconstructed zadrugas are

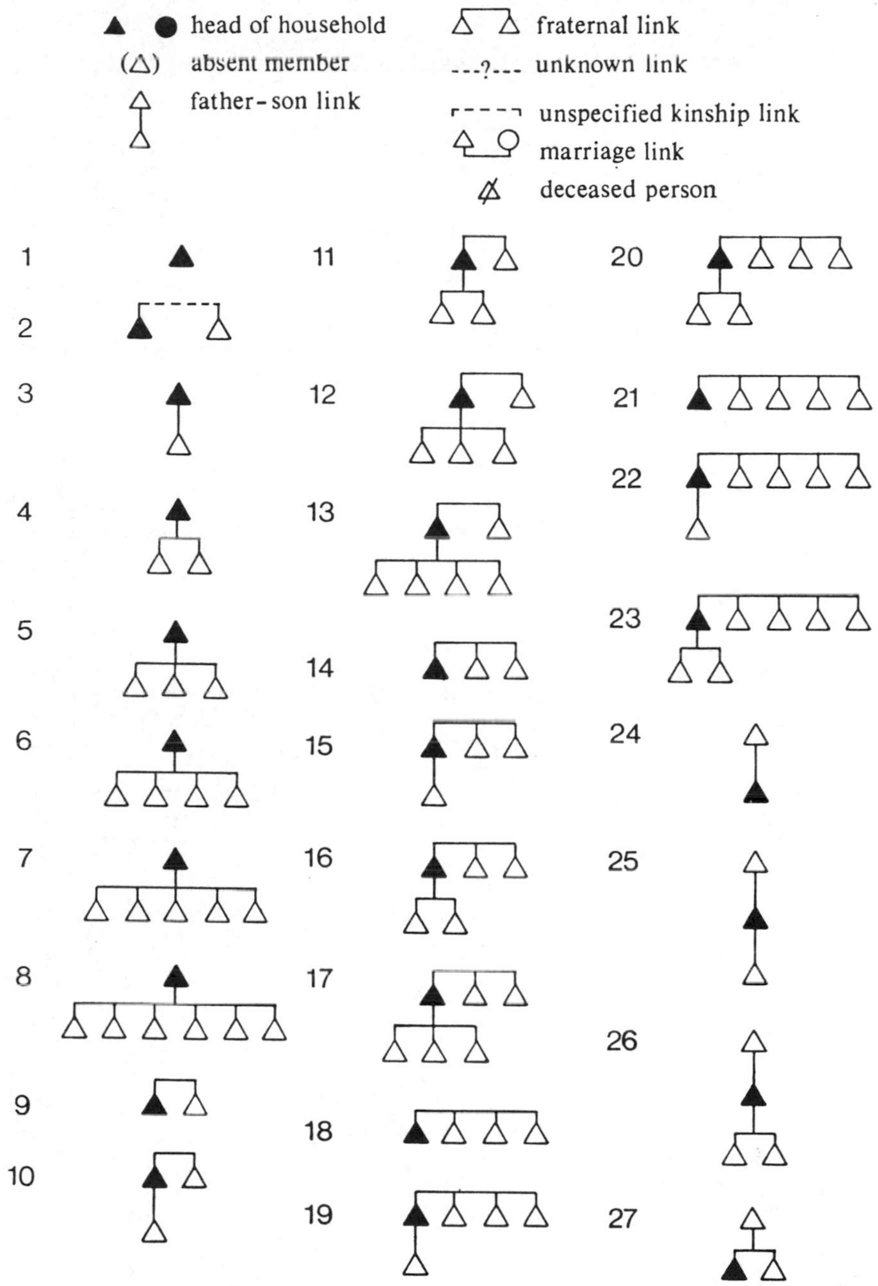
head of household
(△) absent member
father-son link
fraternal link
---?--- unknown link
unspecified kinship link
marriage link
deceased person
1
2
3
4
5
6
7
8
9
10
11
12
13
14
15
16
17
18
19
20
21
22
23
24
25
26
27

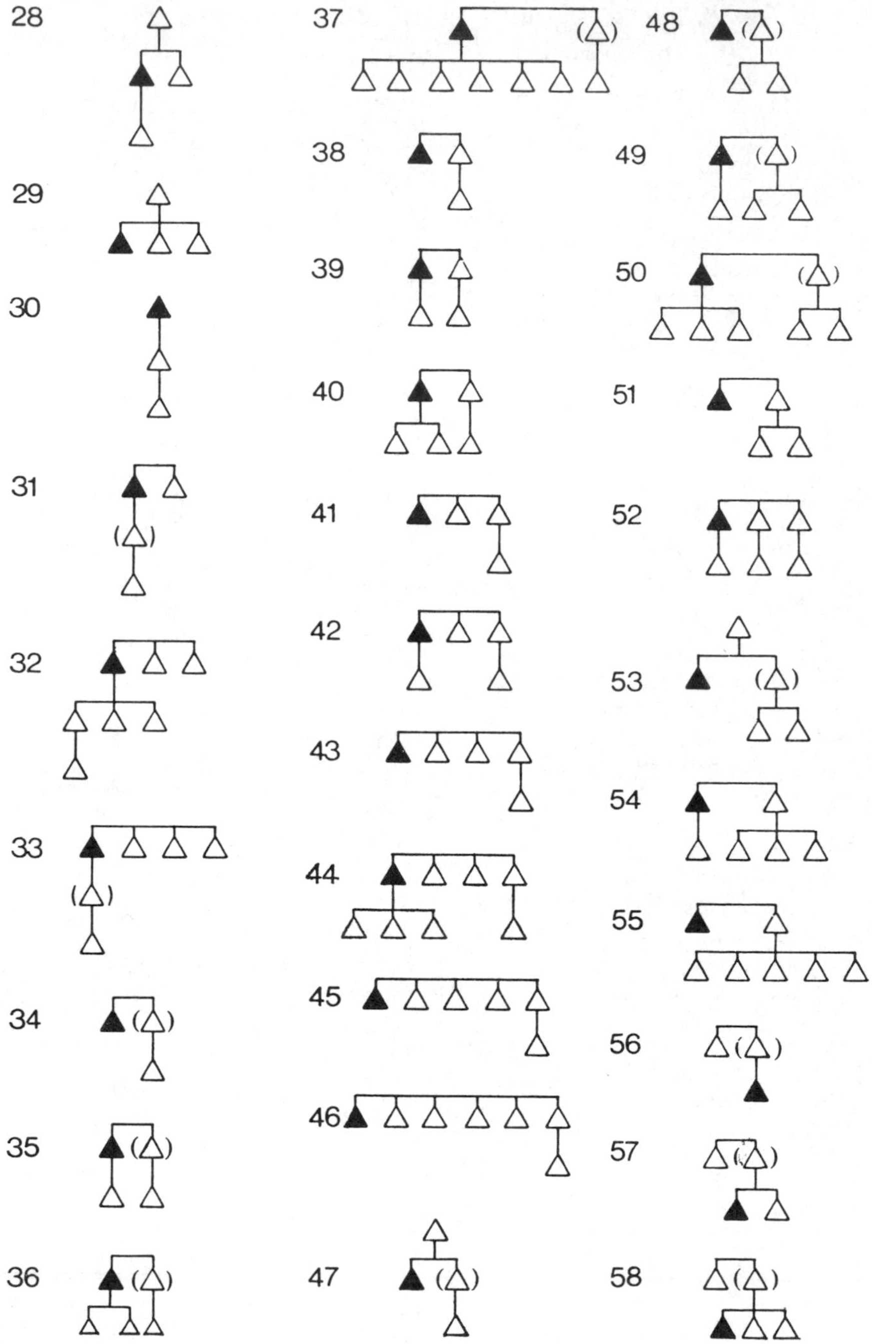
28
29
30
31
32
33
34
35
36
37
38
39
40
41
42
43
44
45
46
47
48
49
50
51
52
53
54
55
56
57
58

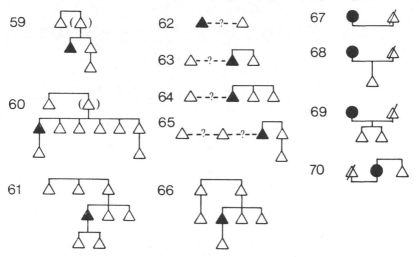

Fig. 14.2   Types of work groups and reconstructed zadrugas in 1528

slight, so that it is unlikely that further minor refinements would lead to important revisions. Fig. 14.2 and Table 14.1 present the immediate results of the analysis in sufficient detail to permit the reader to utilize other systems of classification and reconstruction.[27]

The first column of Table 14.1 gives the identifying numbers of the types of work groups and of zadrugas depicted in Fig. 14.2. The second column gives the frequency of each type of work group and the third column the percentage each type constitutes of the total. The fourth column gives the percentage of each type of reconstructed zadruga out of the total of these, and the fifth presents an approximate distribution of expected frequencies of each type of reconstructed zadruga.[28] This table, like Tables 14.3 and 14.4, refers only to the Orthodox households in the census. There were 49 households identified as Moslem; the distribution of Moslem work group types is given briefly in Table 14.2, but no attempt was made at reconstruction of zadrugas because the Moslem sample is so small.

Tables 14.3 and 14.4 present summary data on the work groups and reconstructed zadrugas, concerning the sex of household head, mean number of males per work group or zadruga, frequency of inclusion of various kin types, genera-

[27] The reliability of these reconstructions is high because of the specificity of the Census; only a few types are ambiguous. In Nos. 48 to 55 I have assumed that all fraternal nephews are brothers *inter se* if there is only one brother of the head in the group or if there is no brother of the head living in the household. If more than one brother and more than one nephew are present, I have divided the nephews as evenly as possible among the brothers. Since there are only 14 such ambiguous cases in 2,002, any distortions introduced are small.

[28] In computing the expected frequencies, all values less than one are given as one, so that the total number is inflated to 2,064, but for illustrative purposes the difference is not important.

Table 14.1   *Distribution of work groups and reconstructed extended household types in 1528   (Orthodox only)*

No.[a]	No. of work groups	Percentage of work groups	Percentage of reconstructed households	Expected frequency of reconstructed households
1	551	27.5	37.8	757
2	6	0.2	0.2	4
3	263	13.1	14.1	282
4	135	6.7	5.5	110
5	58	2.9	1.8	36
6	18	0.8	0.4	8
7	3	0.1	0.1	2
8	1	< 0.1	< 0.1	1
9	365	18.2	19.0	380
10	71	3.5	2.9	58
11	23	1.1	0.8	16
12	9	0.4	0.2	4
13	2	0.1	0.1	2
14	170	8.5	6.2	124
15	21	1.0	0.6	12
16	4	0.2	0.1	2
17	1	< 0.1	0.1	2
18	50	2.5	1.4	28
19	5	0.2	0.2	4
20	1	< 0.1	< 0.1	1
21	9	˙0.4	0.2	4
22	4	0.2	0.1	2
23	1	< 0.1	< 0.1	1
24	9	0.4	0.6	12
25	2	0.1	0.1	2
26	1	< 0.1	< 0.1	1
27	5	0.2	0.2	4
28	1	< 0.1	< 0.1	1
29	2	0.1	0.1	2
30	1	< 0.1	< 0.1	1
31	1	< 0.1	< 0.1	1
32	1	< 0.1	< 0.1	1
33	1	< 0.1	< 0.1	1
34	17	0.8	0.8	16
35	6	0.3	0 3	6
36	6	0.3	0.3	6
37	1	< 0.1	< 0.1	1
38	18	0.8	0.8	16
39	6	0.3	0.3	6
40	3	0.1	0.1	2
41	4	0.2	0.2	4
42	3	0.1	0.1	2
43	1	< 0.1	< 0.1	1
44	1	< 0.1	< 0.1	1
45	2	0.1	0.1	2
46	1	< 0.1	< 0.1	1

Table 14.1 (*contd*)

No.	No. of work groups	Percentage of work groups	Percentage of reconstructed households	Expected frequency of reconstructed households
47	1	< 0.1	< 0.1	1
48	4	0.2	0.2	4
49	3	0.1	0.1	2
50	1	< 0.1	< 0.1	1
51	1	< 0.1	< 0.1	1
52	1	< 0.1	< 0.1	1
53	1	< 0.1	< 0.1	1
54	2	0.1	0.1	2
55	1	< 0.1	< 0.1	1
56	2	0.1	0.1	2
57	1	< 0.1	< 0.1	1
58	2	0.1	0.1	2
59	1	< 0.1	< 0.1	1
60	1	< 0.1	< 0.1	1
61	1	< 0.1	< 0.1	1
62	5	0.2	0.2	4
63	1	< 0.1	< 0.1	1
64	3	0.1	0.1	2
65	1	< 0.1	< 0.1	1
66	1	< 0.1	< 0.1	1
67	40 (71)[b]	2.0 (3.5)	3.8	79
68	61 (32)	3.0 (1.6)	1.2	24
69	2 (0)	0.1 (0.0)	0.0	0
70	1	< 0.1	0.0	0
	2,002	100.0	100.0	2,064

[a] See Fig. 14.2.
[b] Frequencies and percentages of work groups 67, 68 and 69 *not* in parentheses treat those sons of female heads listed as 'young' (*maloletan*) in the census as though they were old enough to work but too young to be married. Frequencies and percentages of those work groups *in* parentheses treat these same sons as immature and listed in the census only because the household head was a female. The corresponding figures for reconstructed zadrugas are not differentiated because, even under the most liberal interpretation, these sons would not have been married. Subsequent interpretation in Tables 14.3 and 14.4 and in the text employs the more conservative estimates represented here in parentheses.

tional depth, and the distribution of nuclear, lineally extended, laterally extended, and both lineally and laterally extended work groups and reconstructed zadrugas.

Regardless of whether one focuses on the work groups or on the reconstructed zadrugas, several important features of social organization are immediately apparent. First, there are very few inclusions that are not based on some explicit kinship linkage. There are no servants listed in the Census, even in the households of district and village headmen.[29] Second, the virifocal and agnatic bias of social

[29] Contrast this with Laslett and Clarke's analysis of Belgrade households in 1733, see below, Chapter 15, pp. 379, 387. The 1528 Census shows only 11 coresident males of unspecified relation to the head.

Table 14.2   *Distribution of types of work groups in 1528*
(Moslems only)

No.[a]	Frequency	Percent
1	19	38.7
3	4	8.2
9	15	30.6
10	1	2.0
14	4	8.2
15	1	2.0
34	1	2.0
38	1	2.0
41	1	2.0
67	1	2.0
68	1	2.0
Total	49	99.7

[a] See Fig. 14.2.

Table 14.3   *Summary data on work groups and extended households in 1528 (Orthodox only)*

Kin or other category[a]	Work groups				Extended households[c]			
	Frequency	Percent of all males	Percent of added males[b]	Per group	Frequency	Percent of all males	Percent of added males[b]	Per household
Brother	1,192	26	45	0.60	964	24	46	0.47
Son	1,094	24	41	0.55	887	22	42	0.43
Brother's son	106	2	4	0.05	98	2	5	0.05
Father	23	< 1	1	0.01	25	< 1	1	0.01
Other kin, misc.	253	6	10	0.13	137	3	6	0.07
Total added males	2,668	58	100	1.33	2,111	52	100	1.02
Male household heads	1,898	42	—	0.95	1,961	48	—	0.92
Total males	4,566	100	—	2.28	4,072	100	—	1.97
Households	2,002	—	—	—	2,064	—	—	—

[a] Kinship categories include only brothers, sons, brother's sons, fathers, father's brothers, father's fathers, son's sons, more distant agnates, and unclassifiable persons. Women are not listed unless given as household heads; thus, while dependent fathers are listed, dependent mothers are not, even if widowed. The absence of matri, sorori- or uxorilateral extensions of any kind in the data accounts for the absence of in-marrying sons-in-law, of sororal nephews, and similar kin types (with one exception, no. 70).

[b] Added males include all adult males (in work groups) and all married males (in extended households) other than the household head. Thus, the sum of added males and of male household heads is the total number of males, and this sum plus the number of female household heads yields the number of households.

[c] Figures for extended households refer to the reconstructed zadrugas in Table 14.1.

Table 14.4 *Principles of work group and extended household organization in 1528*

Generation depth[b]	Work groups		Extended households[a]	
	Frequency	Percent	Frequency	Percent
1	1,232	62	1,383	67
2	756	38	667	32
3	14	1	14	1
Total	2,002	101	2,064	100
Household type, head-centered[c]				
Nonextended	622	31	836	41
Lineally extended	523	26	479	16
Laterally extended	665	33	599	27
Lineally and laterally extended	192	10	150	17
Total	2,002	100	2,064	101
Household type, not head-centered[c]				
Nonextended	622	31	836	41
Lineally extended	307	15	321	16
Laterally extended	610	30	547	27
Lineally and laterally extended	463	23	360	17
Total	2,002	99	2,064	101

[a] Figures for extended households refer to the reconstructed zadrugas in Table 14.1.
[b] Generation depth refers only to adults listed in the census; thus some of the groups of households in each category would be in the next higher category if unlisted children were included.
[c] In classifying head-centered household types, extensions were related strictly to the head. In classifying the same households as non-head-centered, account was taken of the presence of lineal and lateral links to any member of the group or household. Thus, a head plus brother plus brother's son is only laterally extended in a head-centered sense but both lineally and laterally extended in a non-head-centered sense. Note that as in other presentations of the 1528 data no account can be taken of the presence of women who are not household heads, since they are not listed. Many aged mothers, for example, whose presence would make for lineally extended households, are here omitted of necessity.

organization is demonstrated at every point. Women are never heads of households unless they are explicitly listed as widows, and only five percent of the households are of this type; indeed, women are not listed at all unless they are widows. There is only one sororilateral inclusion (No. 70), almost surely an unmarried younger brother living with a widowed sister. All nephews are fraternal. Serbo-Croatian kinship terminology clearly distinguishes fraternal nephews (*bratučed* or *bratić* or *bratanac*) from sororal nephews (*sestrić*), and Šabanović uses only bratučed.[30] There are, surprisingly, no instances at all of uxorilocal sons-in-law; such inclusions are firmly institutionalized (although

[30] Šabanović (1964). It is, of course, possible that the Turkish documents gave the kinship relationship in some form that did not distinguish between fraternal and sororal nephews but that Šabanović used the Serbian *bratučed* as an unmarked lexeme including both fraternal and sororal nephew. There is no simple way to check this possibility, but it is unlikely, since bratučed is never used in that way in Serbian, and since there is a perfectly good term, *nećak*, which refers to any nephew but which Šabanović did not use at all.

empirically not common) in modern Serbian peasant life and kinship terminology.[31] That some kind of extended family organization was the norm is clear from the average number of adult males in work groups or zadrugas, just over two for the former and just under two for the latter.

Table 14.3 shows that the adult males in a work group or zadruga were most often brothers; just under half of all the males other than the head were coresident brothers.[32] The sons of household heads account for slightly more than 40 % of the coresident males. There are few relatives of other types included. Fraternal nephews comprise only about five percent of the additional males apart from the household heads, dependent fathers for only about one percent. Finally, all the other types listed in the census (father's father, father's brother, son's son, miscellaneous agnates, and the very rare unclassifiable and perhaps unrelated persons) amount to ten percent of additional males, while in reconstructed zadrugas they amount to only six percent of additional males. Most groups or households, then, must have consisted of a father and his sons, or of his sons after his death, or of some sons gone off together. *The sons did not remain together long enough to accumulate a large number of sons of their own, for the number of adult sons of brothers is very small.*

Other data, in Tables 14.1 and 14.4, confirm the view that the developmental cycle was of relatively shallow depth. Sixty-two percent of the work groups and two-thirds of the zadrugas were only one adult generation deep. Almost all the rest of the groups are but two generations deep. Of course, one would not expect very many households with three adult generations because the eldest persons would very likely die before their grandchildren reached maturity.

[31] Common terms are *domazet* (house son-in-law), *uljez* (intruder), *miraščija* (one who comes by marriage into a land dowry). The total absence of in-marrying sons-in-law is not easy to explain. All the census data are 'head-centered,' that is, the kinship relationships are given with respect to the head. An in-marrying son-in-law would be listed as such only if a father had had only daughters and one of them had taken in a husband, and if the father had retained the headship. If a daughter in such circumstances had taken in a husband who had himself assumed the headship, the father would have been listed as *tast* (wife's father), but there are no such entries. It would have been most unusual for a daughter to take in a husband if she had any brothers, but if that had occurred, her husband would have been listed as *zet* (sister's husband); alternatively, if her husband had assumed the headship, any brothers would have been listed as *šurak* (wife's brother). None of these terms occur in the census. An in-marrying son-in-law would have appeared as a lone household head, however, if his wife's father had died without male issue, even if the widow were still alive; thus, there may be some in-marrying males hidden in the census.

[32] A further caution on the interpretation of kinship terms concerns the use of the word *brat*. This term can refer both to 'brother' and to 'male first cousin'. Thus, some of the 'brothers' in the census may be cousins, so that the kinship span of the households may be wider than that suggested here. It does not seem likely, however, that *brat* could mean 'cousin' in these data with any frequency. Given the usual patterns of household division, one would expect most cousins to occur in houses still containing their fathers, so that mention of uncles would also be common; nevertheless, there are almost no uncles cited in the data. Most 'brothers' in two-generational households occur where there is only one male of a senior generation, so that they are most likely the sons of one man. This assumption is frequently confirmed in comparison of the village lists from 1528 with those of 1530, in which males listed as 'brothers' in 1528 are seen to have the same father in 1530.

Some 31 % of the work groups and 41 % of the zadrugas were not extended at all, having only a single male; some of these may even have been without wives, for the census did not list wives, a few may have been caring for unmarried sisters or widowed mothers, but most of them probably were married.[33] Lateral extensions from the head of the group or of the zadruga were more important than lineal extensions. Since sons seldom would have succeeded to the headship of an extended household while their father lived (note the small number of dependent fathers), and since their own sons would not have been listed in the census until perhaps eighteen years after their own adulthood, there is another implication that the developmental cycle was shallow, brothers leaving their parental home as their own sons approached maturity, or that fathers died relatively young, or both. The importance of lateral extensions is even clearer when extensions are viewed with respect to the unit as a whole, rather than just with respect to the head. Many of the 'lineal' extensions with respect to the head are both lineal and lateral, from the standpoint of the entire household, because such lineal extensions were often to more than one son, who were themselves laterally linked. It must be stressed that the particular conformation of these households is very much a function of demographic factors, particularly of age structure and life expectancy. Halpern's work[34] points out very clearly that recent lineal extensions of the household depend on increased life expectancy. Age at marriage must also have been crucial because of its effect on fertility; a lower age at marriage for women would increase the rapidity with which constituent nuclear families had children and probably the rapidity with which disputes forced them to divide from one another. Even patterns of nursing, in their effect on the spacing of children, would have been important in the rapidity with which any family built up a sibling core and in the rapidity with which that core dissolved. Unfortunately, no age-specific data on such matters are available to assist in the analysis, so that these effects must remain speculative.

The size of these joint households, in a presumably classic period of Serbian social organization, is also of interest. They were not very large, and only about a quarter of them showed a complexity greater than that of a father with his sons or of two brothers. Later comments will show that the zadruga of 1528 was almost identical in this respect with that of the fourteenth century. Unfortunately, the census data do not give direct information on the total size of households, but average size can be estimated from the data, given a few assumptions. A conservative estimate of sibling net size can be obtained from the 1528 Census by assuming that all brothers remained together permanently, so that a lone household head or a lone son is assumed to have been an only child, a household

---

[33] Division of an extended household could be delayed for many years if the moral authority of a widowed mother remained strong, or if there were enough younger siblings to require that the full complement of older brothers stayed together on the same farm.

[34] Halpern and Anderson (1970).

head living with one brother, or two sons of one man are assumed to have come from a sibling set of only two brothers, and so on. On this basis, the smallest possible average number of brothers surviving to adulthood is about 1.5. A more generous estimate can be reached by counting only those males who are clearly members of a sibling set of at least two – all the men with at least one coresident brother. This estimate is about 2.5. Both estimates ignore any males who died before reaching adulthood, or who might have moved away, or who were still immature, so that the truest estimate is probably closer to the second figure. If the average number of sons per father was 1.5, mean household size would have been around nine; an average of between nine and eleven persons[35] per household would fit well with the structural data, households consisting generally of a father and one married son or two married brothers, or perhaps of a father and two sons or three married brothers. Although our knowledge of demographic conditions does not suffice to make precise comparisons, rough estimates based on vital rates in the 1930s and on ethnographic sources of the late nineteenth century all suggest adult fraternal sets of about 1.5–2.0 and mean household sizes of about 9–11. Thus the data from 1528 do not appear exceptional.

VI. COMPARATIVE DATA

Comparative information from the fourteenth, nineteenth, and twentieth centuries throws further light on the problem of interpretation. One of the most perceptive students of traditional Serbian social organization, Novaković,[36] has provided a summary of data from the medieval period and the nineteenth century. Information on the last century is also supplemented by the work of Bogišić[37] who undertook extensive surveys in the course of his studies of customary law. Information for the twentieth century is scattered and of uneven quality, but there are some good sources, particularly a detailed analysis of change in the zadruga from 1863 to the present in a single village, by Halpern and Anderson.[38]

FOURTEENTH CENTURY

Novaković relies principally on the Dečanska chrysobull of 1330, the Arhandjelska of 1348–53, that of Sveti Stefan in 1313–18, and the Hilandarska of the reign of King Milutin. In general, of the 2,000 houses listed in the Dečanska chrysobull, the majority of *large* extended households fell in the range of 7 to 11

---

[35] Halpern, see below, Chapter 16, p. 406, found a ratio of 1.5 sons (of all ages) per household head for five Serbian villages in the nineteenth century. Mean household size was only 6.7. See also below, pp. 365–368. For a discussion of the wider issues involved in such estimates, see above, Goody, Chapter 3, p. 111 and Burch, Chapter 2 p. 102.

[36] Novaković (1891).   [37] Bogišić (1874).

[38] Halpern and Anderson (1970).

adult males, a few having 13 to 16, and only one reaching 20. One household of 13 adult males is shown to consist of about 30 persons in all.[39] If this ratio of 2.3 coresidents per adult male $(30 \div 13 = 2.3)$ is a fair average, the size range of the typical *large* zadruga would have been 16 to 25 persons. (However, Mijatović's[40] estimate would yield a higher figure.) Vlach houses are said to be smaller than those of agricultural peasants, and the zadruga in general is described as stronger than in modern times (i.e. late nineteenth century) but still modest in size, with great size occasioned more by exceptional fertility than by structural extension, the structure lying within narrow bounds of kinship. Novaković goes on to furnish a sample of household descriptions from chryso-bulls and to give a statistical summary in which he lists the total number of houses and the number of these that were 'strong'.[41] A 'strong' house is defined here (and by implication elsewhere in his work) as one that contained more than two brothers. All others were judged 'weak,' that is, those having only two brothers or one married man with or without children, adult or not. Clearly, Novaković omits a large number of joint families with only two brothers and a large number of patrilocal extended families in which a father and several grown sons (at least two of which might be married under this imprecise defini-tion) would live and work together (cf. the data from 1528). One can compute from his data the following results: agricultural serfs in the Dečanska chrysobull had 16 % strong houses, in the Arhandjelska 26 %, and overall 17 %. Vlachs, who are claimed to have had a weaker tradition of the zadruga, surprisingly had 30 % strong houses in the Dečanska chrysobull, 47 % in the Arhandjelska, 12 % in that of Sveti Stefan, and overall 28 %. (By way of comparison, the Vlachs of Smederevo in 1528 had 24 % strong houses.) There is evidence for great vari-ability in family structure, and the interpretations are inconsistent.[42]

Janković,[43] noting Novaković's assertion that the zadruga must have been very weak among the Vlachs, but not having checked it against the data, goes on to conclude in general that, 'This process of dissolution, the division of large houses, which Novaković has confirmed, was surely fundamentally occasioned by the strengthening of private property and of money economy, especially in the fourteenth century.'[44] Janković ignores Novaković's own major argument, namely, that the process of individualization cannot have been an important

---

[39] Novaković (1891): 230 ff.
[40] Mijatović (1948): 64–5, 66–9.   [41] Novaković (1891): 235 ff.
[42] It would be a mistake, however, to assume territorial homogeneity in the fourteenth century. In particular, the areas bordering on present-day Bulgaria and Greece can be expected to have been different. My own analysis of the chrysobull of Hilandar, to be published separ-ately, shows that nuclear (that is, nonextended and nonjoint) families constituted 80 % of the total. 'Zadruga' organization was quite rare. The villages in this chrysobull were in the Strumica region of extreme southeastern Yugoslavia, only 25 km. from the modern Greek border, and their inhabitants may well have been Greek. See Stojanović (1890): 40–5 and Hammel, *Household structure in fourteenth-century Macedonia* (typescript).
[43] Janković (1961).
[44] Janković (1961): 101–2. Jiriček (1952): 52, interprets Novaković more cautiously and suggests war, skirmishes, pillage, famine and plague as reasons for lower population levels.

factor in the fourteenth century but that the constraints on household organization must be sought in taxation practices and other aspects of the power relationships between feudal lords and their serfs.[45] Novaković, and indeed, Janković
following him, provide some insights into these relationships.

Beginning with citation of Roman and Byzantine practice in levying a household tax (applied also in Bosnia to exactions by the Church and by the Turks
and later called *dimina, dimnica,* from *dim,* smoke), Novaković goes on to
demonstrate by extensive citation from proclamations and legal codes that some
labor obligations were assessed *per capita* (such as haying, reaping), while others
were assessed by household (such as plowing in many cases, or the transport of
salt by Vlachs). It was clearly to the advantage of a family of serfs to live as long
as possible under one roof to minimize the impact of household assessments, for
several adult men in one household could take their turn at fulfilling the obligation, while a lone man would have to meet each such obligation. By remaining
together, a set of coresident brothers could force household obligations to fall
on other sets of brothers. A variety of proclamations attest to the interest of
the state in forcing division of households in order to increase the available labor
pool for household assessments and to the subterfuges employed by the serfs to
appear undivided when they had in fact split.[46]

Although precise data are not available without intensive re-analysis of the
medieval documents, it seems likely that household size was 'artificially' inflated
in the fourteenth century. Novaković's judgment is that medieval times were not
favorable to the zadruga, because of all the state regulations demanding division.[47]

[45] See Novaković (1891): 213–14.
[46] Article 70 of the Code of Stefan Dušan reads: 'And whoever is located in a single house,
whether brothers (first cousins) or father and sons, or others, divided in bread and property,
even if they have one hearth, but it is divided, let them work as other minor [unincorporated]
people' (*I kto se obrete u jednoj kući, ili bratenci, ili otac ot sinov, ili in kto odelan hlebom
i imanijem, i ako bude na jednom ognjištu, a tem-zi odelen, da rabota[ju] i ako ini mali ljudije*),
Radojčić (1960): 56, 109; Janković (1961): 102. Further, a directive of King Vladislav in the
chrysobull of Bistrica (1234–43) reads: 'A married son may live with his father three years;
at the end of three years let him leave and go into (his own) personal service to the church'
(*I sin s ocem da sedi, oženiv se, tri godišta; kon treh godišt da postupa u osobnu rabotu crkvi...*),
Janković (1961): 102. The state used carrot as well as stick, the chrysobull of Sveti Stefan
reading: 'Those who have no sons or brothers or workers, single men, let two of them re-
inforce each other if they have various work in the field, but for other work such as plowing
and the vineyard, let them go separately. The same holds for estate servants and any artisans'
(*I koji ne imaju sina ili brata ili rabotnika, jedinaci, dva da se stišteta, ako i raznu rabotu u
zemlju imata, nj na ine rabote, a oranije i vinograd razno. Takožde i sokalnici i koji ljubo
majstorije*), Novaković (1891): 226. That the Turks continued these practices, as heirs to the
heirs of Byzantium, can be seen in a *ferman* of 1766: 'If some of the Christians wish to live in
cooperation, themselves electing a person for head of their whole family or zadruga, whether
that is at the time of tax assessment or prior to it, there is no need to interfere with their wish,
provided only that the taxes they pay are not thereby diminished' (*Ako neki od hrišćana
požele živeti u zadruzi, izabravši sebi jedno lice za starešinu svekolike porodice ili zadruge
njihove, pa bilo to u vreme zbora mirije ili pre toga, ne treba smetati njihovoj želji samo ako se
time ne smanjavaju prihodi koje oni plaćaju*), Novaković (1891): 215.
[47] Similarly, Tomasevich (1955): 188 suggests that the nineteenth century was also unfavorable
to the zadruga, because of the shift to predominantly crop-type agriculture and the influences

However, my faith lies more with peasant ability to dissemble, and it seems equally reasonable to assume that the pressure of tax demands forced the peasants to remain in larger establishments, against which the various proclamations were only partially effective. That Vlach houses appear somewhat larger (or at least that 'strong' houses appear more frequently among them) may result from the fact that they, too, had labor obligations on a per-household basis (such as salt transport or special military duties) but were more scattered and less subject to state control. Household size among the serfs would have been a compromise between the advantages of continued joint residence, state pressure to divide, and the ordinary pressures for fission from within a household. Household size among the Vlachs would have been a similar compromise, complicated by further pressures for and ease of division inherent in pastoralism, but also by more recent cultural traditions of patrilineal organization that might have led to larger households when the Vlachs moved from herding on barren karstic uplands down to more fertile bottom lands to engage in mixed farming. Similar conditions probably prevailed for Vlach households around 1500 in the Sandžak of Smederevo, with inflation of household size increased by the advantages of the hearth tax and the possibility of concealing their domestic arrangements from the Turks, whose judges were initially forbidden to go among them.

NINETEENTH CENTURY

Perhaps the most interesting aspect of data on the zadruga in the nineteenth century is the degree of apparent conflict in the reports. Novaković found complaints that the largest zadrugas were usually composed of only two or three brothers, and that brothers usually divided when one of them married.[48] Ivanović in 1853 in the Krajina had observed Serbian households of only five or six persons and Vlach houses of only four or five from which Novaković again concluded that the Vlachs more easily divided their zadrugas.[49] He notes a report of the Archimandrate Dučić that there were no 'zadrugas' at all in Montenegro where brothers rarely stayed together after the death of their father.[50] From his summary of Mišković's research in the Rudnik area in 1875, it is possible to compute that in 17 settlements there were 1,103 houses with 1,453 adult males, or 1.3 adult males per household.[51] Comparing and summarizing the work of A. S. Jovanović and of K. Jovanović in the 1870s, Novaković provides data from which one may calculate that in four counties of the Valjevo area there were 12,788 taxable persons, of whom 306 lived in 70 zadrugas. Thus, the 'zadrugas'

---

of out-migration and money. However, the nineteenth-century agricultural zadrugas must have been larger than the contemporary pastoral ones of the karst, and I know of no firm evidence on agricultural zadrugas in Serbia of the late eighteenth century with which to compare those of the nineteenth.

[48] Novaković (1891): 205–6, citing Milišević.
[49] Ibid.: 207. [50] Ibid.: 208.
[51] Ibid.: 208–9.

(presumably 'strong' houses only) would have had 4.4 adult males each, but only 2.4 % of the taxable persons would have been living in such zadrugas.[52] Obradović, on the other hand, had observed many houses with six or seven married men, totalling 50 or 60 persons, sometimes fathers with nine to twelve sons, mostly married, in the Užice area in 1858.[53] Jovanović had given information on the Podrinje, citing a zadruga with 80 members, and another case on the upper Morava in which a large zadruga had divided itself into 20 separate houses to constitute a whole hamlet of 80 persons. In still another instance, one zadruga was reported to have divided into 13 separate houses, and in a fourth case, in Kopaonik, six brothers were reported to live in a single household sheltering 45 persons, using 128 kilograms of wheat every three days, and in winter requiring three fires and three dining tables.[54] Novaković also cites an Austrian complaint of 1718 that a father and two or three sons, sometimes married, often lived together and reported as though they were a single tax unit.[55] Bogišić's detailed reports[56] give maxima of about 20 to 40 persons, with some houses as large as 60, but with most houses having about 6 to 10 persons in all, in Hercegovina, Montenegro, and western and southern Serbia.

The nineteenth-century data indicate that there was a great variation in household composition and size. Although the data do not lend themselves to precise statistical interpretation, it seems clear that zadrugas of this period, like those of earlier years, were not enormous but usually of modest size, the larger usually falling in the range of 9 to 15 persons in all, with rare exceptions. Seldom did the zadrugas include males other than fathers and sons, or brothers, or occasionally nephews and uncles.

TWENTIETH CENTURY

From the structural point of view taken above, there are surprisingly few differences between the patterns common in the fourteenth, sixteenth, and nineteenth centuries and those more recently observed. The most spectacular examples of joint households in this century have been noted among Albanian speakers (Šiptari) in the region of Kosovo and Metohija. According to Krasnići,[57] zadrugas of 20 to 30 members were not uncommon, and households of as many as 80 persons were occasionally found. Nikolić[58] also observes that Serbian zadrugas of 20 to 30 members were found in that area in the 1930s. However, the more recent work of Radovanović[59] in the area of Prizrenski Podgor (Metohija) shows that even with the occurrence of many large households of the kind just referred to, average household size is still relatively modest. In 1953, 47 % of the agricultural population and 41 % of the total population of Prizrenski Podgor

[52] Ibid.: 210.
[54] Ibid.: 207.
[56] Bogišić (1874).
[58] Nikolić (1958).

[53] Ibid.: 206.
[55] Ibid.: 208.
[57] Krasnići (1959–60).
[59] Radovanović (1964).

lived in 'zadrugas' that averaged 12.6 members each. Of the zadrugas 17 % had more than 25 members, but the larger ones were usually Šiptar. Since these census materials make the usual categorical distinction between zadrugas and conjugal or even patrilocal extended households, ignoring their developmental possibilities, the average of 12.6 members per zadruga gives a false picture of household size. Less than half the population of Prizrenski Podgor lived in zadrugas, and average household size for the entire population, in this area remarkable for its extended households, was only 7.2 members.

In less spectacular areas studied by Filipović and Pantelić[60] (Bosnia and Western Serbia), Serbian zadrugas had an average of 8 or 10 members, but these figures again refer only to extended households. Pantelić's data show that the average size for all households in Jadar (Podrinje) was 6.7 in 1895, 6.7 for village households and 6.4 overall in 1900, 5.4 overall in 1948, and 4.3 overall in 1961. Some of the decrease in mean household size is attributable to rapid urbanization; Pantelić notes that upland villages have preserved the zadruga tradition better than those in the bottom lands and closer to large towns, and that some quite large zadrugas persisted into the 1950s. My own research in that area[61] shows that some zadrugas still persist in concealed form; peasants may divide their households officially to allow each segment to acquire the maximum of land permitted by law but still farm jointly. The 1961 Census[62] for the area of Loznica (Podrinje), with the two major towns eliminated, shows a mean household size of 4.7, slightly higher than Pantelić's uncorrected calculation. In those same villages, using a definition of 'strong' household most likely to coincide with Novaković's, namely, more than 6 members, we find that 20 % of households are 'strong.' In the adjacent area of Mali Zvornik, eliminating the town, 32 % of households are 'strong', and in a culturally similar area, Arilje (near Užice), 21 % of village households are 'strong.' These proportions of large households differ scarcely at all from those found in Novaković's analyses of the fourteenth-century materials, or from the data of the sixteenth and nineteenth centuries. Other data support this view of consistency of averages over time, combined with great range: a survey of peasant properties[63] across the entire country shows an average size of 6.1 persons per agricultural household, even though the small-family areas of Slovenia and Croatia are included, as well as the exceptional ones of Kosovo and Metohija. Average household size for the country as a whole is only 4.0, but means as high as 9.5 are reported for some parts of Kosovo and Metohija.

The most detailed examination of household size and constitution is that by Halpern and Anderson.[64] Direct comparison between their data and those of the 1528 Census is difficult because of the different data formats and because the level of aggregation in their analysis is too high to permit recasting. Nevertheless,

[60] Filipović (1945); Pantelić (1964).
[61] Hammel (1968).
[62] Yugoslavia (1965).
[63] Yugoslavia (1964) Table 5.1.
[64] Halpern and Anderson (1970)

some useful comparisons can be attempted. Their data show that mean household size in the village of Orašac (Šumadija) was 8.3 in 1844 and 1863, fell to 6.9 in 1895 (cf. 6.7 in Jadar, above), and to 4.5 in 1961 (cf. 4.7 in the villages around Loznica, above). Computation from their data of the proportion of 'strong' households (i.e. with more than six members) yields a very high 66 % in 1863, 27 % in 1928, and 14 % in 1961. The percentage of large households in Orašac is thus now lower than in the areas of Loznica, Mali Zvornik, and Arilje cited earlier, perhaps because these areas are in the conservative uplands of western Serbia, while Orašac is closer to the heart of Serbia.

Halpern and Anderson point out, however, that measures of household size and shifts in them obscure manifold structural changes. Indeed, readily available and simple statistical or classificatory criteria (such as mean household size or rigid distinctions between extended and nonextended families) often demonstrate a marked disutility for careful comparison between areas or over time. Dependence on them results in serious disagreement, as illustrated in the innumerable disputes over residence and kinship classifications[65] or marked loss of information in analysis.[66] One of Halpern and Anderson's major points is that a marked shift from lateral to lineal extension occurred between 1863 and the present, because of lowered mortality and an ageing population, a lower birth rate that provided fewer siblings per family, and the abandonment of rural life by many sons. In other words, the reduction in mean household size was underlain by a shift from the classic zadruga form of patrilocal and fraternal extension toward the stem family pattern in which only a single son usually remains on the land. It is important to note that the causal factors in this change involve no major shift in the basic ideology of kinship but only the response of behavioral patterns to demographic and ecological alterations.[67]

Some further structural comparisons can be made between Orašac and the Vlachs of Smederevo. Halpern and Anderson's categories of single-person households, married couples without children, widowed persons without lineal or lateral extension, and nuclear families would have fallen into that set of the 1528 data labelled 'nonextended.' Orašac had 36 % of its families in this category in 1863 and 42 % in 1961. The comparable category among the Vlachs in 1528 contained 41 %, squarely within the Orašac range. The differences between Orašac and the Vlachs of 1528 lie in the *kinds* of extensions. Halpern and Anderson provide data on the numbers of brothers and sons in Orašac households, and their table of age distributions permits one to compute the number of coresident brothers and sons over the age of nineteen. If we assume that these men would be equivalent to those defined as adult coresident males in the Ottoman Census of 1528, Orašac had 0.34 brothers and 0.45 sons per household in 1863 and 0.02 brothers and 0.45 sons per household in 1961. Because unmarried

[65] Goodenough, *Residence Rules* (1956); Fischer, *The classification of residence in censuses* (1958); Lounsbury (1964).

[66] Hammel, *Occupational prestige in Belgrade* (1970).   [67] Hammel (1969 i) and (1969 ii).

men are included in these data, the comparable figures from 1528 are those for work groups: 0.60 brothers and 0.55 sons. Although Orašac had a mean household size in 1863 close to that estimated for the 1528 Census, it had many fewer adult brothers per household. The large size of its houses must have been a consequence of very high fertility (probably at or above 40 per 1,000), resulting in households with relatively few coresident adult married brothers, some married sons, and many small children.[68] These differences between Orašac of 1863 and Belgrade County in 1528 would be diminished if there were age-specific data available in the 1528 Census or if Halpern and Anderson's tables permitted the identification of males aged 16 to 18. If males aged 16 to 18, doubtless considered adult in 1528, were added to the coresident adult males in these recomputations of the Orašac data, the number of brothers and sons would increase. If males aged less than nineteen could be removed from the 1528 data, the number of coresident brothers and sons would decrease; in either case, the gap between Orašac and the Vlachs of 1528 would be narrowed.

SUMMARY OF COMPARATIVE DATA

Several points are of interest: (1) variation between areas is very great and is at least equal to that over time; (2) average household size has changed less than one might expect from the funereal remarks made about the zadruga, and it is not a very instructive indicator unless complemented by structural data and information on demographic rates; (3) the basic structural principles of household organization have changed very little over time. Even unusual households, such as one described by Radovanović,[69] are structured along well-defined agnatic lines: the household of Bajram Bujari contained 60 persons in 1958 but all (except of course the wives) were descended from Bajram's own grandfather. The most distantly related adult males were second cousins. The smaller households described by Halpern and Anderson demonstrate the same structural principles under different constraints, of longer life span but truncated developmental cycle, yielding patrilocal and virifocal households of narrower and longer kinship span, with fraternal ties giving way to minimal filial ones.

---

[68] The population of Serbia tripled between 1840 and 1900, largely as a result of migration and territorial expansion, although the birth rate was probably at least 40 per 1,000 in the earlier years of the century. The pressure of the population on the land must have been enormous; indeed, it was the beginning of the process that led to serious overpopulation in the twentieth century. Much of the increase was made possible by the introduction of new crops and a shift to grain cultivation, and particularly by the adoption of maize, which will support more people per hectare than wheat or barley. Maize was not introduced to most areas of Serbia until well into the eighteenth century and did not reach some until the nineteenth. See Tomasevich (1955): 151 ff., on population, and Lutovac (1936) and Tomasevich (1955): 163–4 on the introduction of maize. It is quite possible that the high levels of mean household size in some parts of Serbia in the eighteenth and nineteenth centuries were a direct result of the introduction of maize and adoption of intensive methods of cultivation requiring a large labor force in a small area.

[69] Radovanović (1964): 368.

VII.   CONCLUSIONS

What is most evident from all of these data is that the zadruga is not a thing but a process.[70] Separation of a process into snapshots of its behavior leads only to misinterpretation and the computation of misleading indices, such as simple means of household size, frequency of division of households, or the size of only the largest units, as in the repeated citation of answers to the query, 'How big were the biggest households?' The zadruga, as a process, is a set of rules operating within certain constraints that influence the rates at which persons are added to residential groups and that control the maximum size of these groups by introducing pressures for continued accretion or for division. The intensity of accretion is determined largely by demographic rates under a rule of patrilocal residence. That rule can be taken as a constant for traditional Serbian social organization (unless a man has no sons), and the correspondence between the frequency of large houses and high birth rates among Albanian speakers in Kosovo and Metohija, or among Serbs in the nineteenth century can be no accident. A father who has had four sons live to adulthood and marriage, each of whom has four small children, could easily find himself master of a household of 26 persons: a wife, four sons, four daughters-in-law, and 16 grandchildren. If he had married as early as the age of twenty and had had his first son a year later, and then a child every second year, and if his sons had married equally early, this patriarch of almost Biblical proportions would have been but fifty-seven years old on the birth of his sixteenth grandchild. Families of ten living children are not unknown in these regions, and a bias in the sex ratio could create a house of enormous size in only two adult generations, while the father's authority was still strong enough to keep the sons together.

The pressures for continued accretion and the constraints on it are various. Pastoralism, soil that is poor but abundant, warfare and feud that encourage mobility for flight, and effective state pressure for division will lower household size. The smaller size of Montenegrin families in earlier years and even today is a consequence of their poverty, pastoralism, poor soil, and frequent fission because of feud and flight. Limitation in recent years of the amount of land that may be owned by one household has certainly stimulated the division of modern Serbian farm households. On the other hand, the limited availability of land or other economic opportunity, combined with natural increase, will increase the size of households, for the children have nowhere else to go. The adoption of

[70] Jiriček's view through the mists of romanticism was refreshingly clear. In commenting on the small families characteristic of barren Montenegro, he wrote (my translation): 'That small family could always enlarge under favorable circumstances. Too much attention has been paid to the elaboration of statistics of larger houses in the study of the zadruga. The piling up of large numbers of people in several generations on one peasant or pastoral property is only a hypertrophy of an original, simple aspect, called forth by economic circumstances. The zadruga, in general, is nothing more than a fraternity, a unit tied together by common genetic origin, that has preferred not to divide but to manage its property cooperatively.' See Jiriček (1952): 50–1.

more efficient food-producing techniques, such as the pasturing of hogs in oak forests, the acquisition of some capability for growing grain rather than depending exclusively on sheep herding, and the adoption of more efficient crops (such as maize in the eighteenth and nineteenth centuries) would enlarge the subsistence base and permit larger households, while economics of scale in the division of labor would encourage their growth. Much of the history of the zadruga is a series of responses to changing ecological conditions and to the pressures of taxation, but it is not a simple history, for the external constraints have not always been consistent.

The process itself, within these varying constraints, exhibits great regularity.[71] The household begins with a man and his wife and grows through time until it consists of himself, his wife, and maturing children. As some of the sons marry, they may leave to find new households consisting of only an adult male and his family. They are more likely to remain in the parental household for a time, even if their father dies; certainly the presence of a widowed mother or of immature siblings, particularly sisters, would keep at least some sons on the old homestead. Division of the household seems to be encouraged more by the growth of sons' families than by any other factor, and brothers whose own sons are approaching maturity tend to hive off.[72] Many of the 551 men without coresident adult males in the 1528 census probably had sons approaching maturity; many of those with one or two adult sons had probably been in a fraternal joint family within the last few years. Only rarely does a household remain together long enough to exhibit any great complexity of kinship ties; fraternal nephews in 1528 were most frequently included when their own father was absent, so that their structural position approximated that of adopted sons.

The structural situation is not much different in modern times, although the constraints have shifted.[73] Birth rates are lower, but infant mortality has dropped, so that basic pressures for accretion may not have altered much. Mortality among older persons has lowered, making lineal extension more frequent. Taxation is no longer a matter of feudal dues on a per-household basis; however, government restrictions on the amount of land that can be owned induce formal division but camouflaged cooperation in the same way that medieval law codes induced formal coresidence but clandestine division to avoid labor dues. The increase in personal property has heightened the advantage of early household division, particularly for an energetic man with a small family;

---

[71] Compare Halpern, below, Chapter 16, pp. 404–405.

[72] Confirming evidence on the limited kinship span and generational depth of joint households comes from Radjenović, who observed in Bosanska Krajina in 1933–4 that brothers lived together until their sons began to marry. Radjenović (1948): 463.

[73] See also Novaković's insightful comment (1891): 234 on just these points. Jiriček (1952): 52, in evaluating the medieval sources, says (my translation): 'If one adds to the men the appropriate number of women and children that are not mentioned, then there is not a great difference in number with respect to modern times.' It is important to note that the range of variation from the fourteenth to the twentieth century is no greater than the range over areas in the present decade.

if he leaves his brothers, taking an equal share, his greater productivity will be divided among fewer consumers. However, there is little difference between this situation and that which obtained when land was free for the taking during the period of the great migrations as the Turkish tide ebbed and flowed. A money economy, it is said, spells disaster for the extended household, but any ethnographer of the Balkans or of other peasant areas can point to the way in which cash income for sons living at home but working in provincial industries has played a critical role in preserving the extended family. It is also claimed that urbanization and the advent of capitalism (or industrial socialism, if I may make that substitution) sound the death-knell of kinship, but Laslett and Clarke's analysis of the Census of Belgrade in 1733 shows large households with many kin, as well as servants, and Benedict[74] had demonstrated the importance of family connections in the development of commercial networks. Just a casual acquaintance with the world of petty traders will show that it is difficult to find a Lebanese rug merchant who is not working for a cousin.[75]

This is not to say that there have been no changes in the zadruga or that it is now as strong as it ever was, but it is clear that the evidence cited for its decline is often seriously defective or superficial. Arguments that the zadruga was in the process of unilinear dissolution in the fourteenth century because only 12 % to 46 % of the houses had more than about six members cannot be sustained. That 41 % of the Vlach households of 1528 were nonextended is no better evidence, for any family cycle requires some proportion of smaller units that can become larger ones; even in Metohija today, noted for its unusually large households, 74 % of the units are nonextended.[76] Evidence for the decline of the zadruga as an institution can be found in the increasing *proportion* of nonextended households.[77] The reasons for that increased proportion are not simple, but if there is a principal factor it is that economic changes now make it relatively easy for a lone male with his wife to make a living in the rural zone or to desert it entirely, while the requirements of frontier life and of mixed farming in earlier times gave a decided advantage to small groups of men living jointly. *The cycle of the zadruga has now shortened* (even though the *people* live longer); sons more frequently leave on or before marriage, or they leave sooner after marriage, but the basic cycle persists, grounded in a continuing agnatic ideology of kinship, although modified by changing external constraints, just as it has always been modified by such shifting external constraints.[78]

If one insists that the historical process be simple, so that different social

---

[74] Benedict, *Family firms and economic development* (1968).
[75] I am indebted to Maurice Freedman for stressing that the effects of industrialization and urbanization (or other similar processes) on *household structure* and on *kinship linkages* and on the functions of either of these, must be kept separate (personal communication). My point here is that industrialization and urbanization do not necessarily weaken either the extended household or the extended family (as a nonresidential group) but may strengthen both.   [76] Radovanović (1964).   [77] See Halpern and Anderson (1970).
[78] See particularly Hammel (1969 i) and (1969 ii) for discussion of the retention of agnatic ideology in Serbian kinship and the effects of ecological change on family and lineage structure.

forms, reified and enshrined, appear as beads on a string according to some single and fundamental orientation, this discussion can only have complicated the issue. If, on the other hand, one insists that the fundamental *principles* of social organization be simple, the discussion has at least illuminated its goal. Cyclical and secular process must not be confused, just as maintenance function and origin must be kept separate; the reasons for the division of individual households may not be the reasons for the decline of the extended household as an institution. The surface structures of social forms are the results of an interplay of conflicting forces on fundamental processes; a social institution is not its end products but rather the procedural rules or principles that generate those products under varying constraints. The purpose of this analysis has been to suggest that, although a multitude of such constraints may operate to alter the decision-making patterns in family life, ranging from changes in ecological relationships through factors of economics and of the political system, to changes in the age at marriage and the authority relationships between spouses, siblings, and children, these constraints operate on a fundamental process of kinship that shows great similarity across time and space.[79]

[79] Compare Goody, above, Chapter 3, pp. 103–124. Goody stresses the similarities between domestic groups in Asia, Africa and Europe.

15. Houseful and household in an eighteenth-century Balkan city. A tabular analysis of the listing of the Serbian sector of Belgrade in 1733–4

Peter Laslett and Marilyn Clarke

We present in the following pages a series of tables analysing the list of inhabitants of the Serbian, that is the Orthodox Christian, sector of the city of Belgrade, drawn up evidently, by the responsible clergy, in the year 1733–4.[1] Not being specialists in the subject of Balkan history or society we do not attempt in this brief introduction to study the Serbian household in any detail, either within the settlement from which this evidence comes or in Serbian society as a whole at that time. What we have tried to do is set the pattern of domestic groups recorded in the listing against the pre-industrial English pattern described in Chapters 1 and 4, and relate it to the results of Hammel's and Halpern's work in Chapters 14 and 16.[2]

The year 1733 came in a time of relative peace for Belgrade. The depredations of the warring Turks and Austrians had ravaged the country for long periods and Belgrade had been a major point of resistance before the city fell to the Austrian and Serbian allies in 1717. The Treaty of Pozarevac in 1718 secured peace under Austrian domination and the shattered city was subsequently largely rebuilt under Prince Eugen. Peace probably lasted throughout the duration of Austrian supremacy in North Serbia, that is between 1718 and 1739.

This listing of 1733–4[3] appears to have had as its object the registration of the pastoral condition of the Christian people living in the Sava Suburb. In this it resembles the *liber status animarum*, or *état des âmes*, the drawing up of which was, or should have been, an established feature of the parochial life of the

[1] The exact months in which the list was made out cannot be decided from its evidence alone. There is a brief analysis of this listing by Stoianovich in *Model and mirror of the pre-modern Balkan city* (1970): 103–5. His figures differ from ours in detail though his overall results are much the same.

[2] We wish to gratefully acknowledge the help given by J. M. Halpern who first introduced us to the document, and to E. A. Hammel for his extensive advice on Balkan history and custom.

[3] It is printed in Cyrillic with a commentary by Popović in *Spomenik* (The Proceedings of the Royal Serbian Academy), LXXVIII (1935): 59–76. Our work was made possible by a transliteration and translation undertaken by Mrs Stojana Burton, of Girton College, Cambridge.

Roman West, and to which frequent references are made elsewhere in this volume. The last year during which confession and communion were taken in Belgrade is stated for each mature person, and there is also an appended list (not used in this analysis) of donors to the church. The listing is defective in that the first 34 blocks of names appear to be missing, and also some from the end. In the extant portion a number of pages are damaged, making a few blocks incomplete, but the consequent loss of information does not detract seriously from the exceptional usefulness of this document for the analysis of domestic group structure.

It is evident that an attempt was made to record the name, sex, age, some indication of position in the family or household (filial situation, whether a servant, a lodger, a 'stranger' etc.) of each individual for whom the priests were responsible, which was what the Roman regular clergy were expected to do in the *état des âmes*. The important and interesting difference between the two types of document, however, is that the blocks of names appearing in the Belgrade listing are grouped under the heading of the *Dom*, meaning 'house'. House is perhaps intended in both the senses in which the word is used in English and discussed in Chapter 1 (see pp. 20, 28 and refs.) but it seems that most of the emphasis here is on the house as a set of premises, containing a dwelling, or more than one, a shop, or a workshop. The Belgrade listing, therefore, appears to be drawn up in housefuls, rather than families (conjugal family units) or households.[4]

The Belgrade record, then, appears to be of a kind rather different from those analysed elsewhere in this collection of studies, and the first task of the analyst would seem to be to decide how many dwellings and so how many households each Dom comprised, and which individuals belonged to which. Only thus, as was shown in Chapter 1, would any approach to exact comparability be possible on many of the variables, especially distribution of households by size and structure. A number of tables based on such a series of subdivisions of the blocks of names were submitted to the conference of 1969, and Tables 1.8, 1.13, 1.14 and 1.15 of the series appended to Chapter 1 are also based on a set of decisions as to how each Dom was constituted with reference to households, but made on a different occasion and with slightly different results. It has become clear, in fact, that no division process could be entirely reliable, certainly not to the point of ensuring that another researcher would arrive at the same units. For the other tables of Chapter 1, therefore, blocks of names were simply divided between inmates and the rest, and inmates, whether individuals or groups, left out of the analysis. In the present series, however, the block of persons is treated as a whole,

---

[4] Not enough *libri status animarum* have been examined at Cambridge to enable us to say whether they ever exhibited this feature. Documents approximating to them in England (see Laslett and Harrison (1963)) were either communion lists or lists of inhabitants by household, but they are very rare. On the use of the term 'houseful' see above, Laslett, Chapter, 1, pp. 34–39, Hammel, Chapter 14, p. 339 fn. 13.

as a houseful, in fact as the crew of a building or Dom, except where inmates and groups of inmates themselves are in question as distinct from other persons in the houseful.

Comparison between the present series and those of Chapter 1 referring to Belgrade makes it possible therefore to observe the effect of using the houseful as the basis of analysis rather than one of the expressions for the household.[5] Some of the differences shown up in this way are certainly startling, as for example the mean size of the domestic group itself which is 5.45 for the household thus defined, but 7.14 for the houseful. But most of them show much slighter contrast than might be expected. We have not gone so far as to repeat all the tables of the Chapter 1 series here, and have tried to avoid covering the same ground twice. In treating the blocks of names for the purpose of structural analysis we have had to make a number of detailed presumptions and definitions which are adapted from those used for English materials. These are set out in our appendix. Otherwise presumptions and definitions are the same as in Chapter 1.

Some justification may be thought to be required for the decision to exclude persons called lodgers (*ukućani*) and strangers (*strani*) from the domestic group in Belgrade for the purposes of analysing the familial structure of households, as was done in chapter 1. Each block of names, on this view, should have been regarded as indivisible, and the possibility contemplated that the extra persons described by these titles were in fact connected by kinship in some way with the other members of the houseful. It will be seen that these persons comprise no less than 27 % of the whole population and so are by no means negligible. It is their presence which accounts for such a marked difference between household and houseful size, and they distinguish Belgrade very sharply from the other communities analysed in this volume, as is evident from the comparisons in Chapter 1. Certainly the little we knew about Serbian domestic and social structure did nothing to prepare us for the discovery of such a large class of inmates in Belgrade. We had expected on the contrary that all the extra members of the domestic groups in this area of the traditional multiple household, or *zadruga*, would be likely to be kinsfolk.

Lodging, therefore, did not seem to be at all an expected feature of the society organised on these lines, even in its capital city, an entrepôt centre liable perhaps to harbour transients. But though the expert advice we have since been given has done little to modify our original impression of surprise, it has confirmed that these two categories of individual bear descriptions which certainly were intended by the writers of the list to mark them off as not being within the household, not in any way related to the conjugal family unit – indeed as sharing premises only with the other residents in just the same way that members of a houseful are assumed to do in Chapter 1. It is impossible to be confident however, that this particular section of Belgrade contained the proportion of inmates

---

[5] Household as defined for ratio 5 in Table 4.2 above, exclusive maximal mean size of household.

usual over the whole city. It is likely in fact that inmates might have been much commoner in some of the areas than others, but we have no way of telling whether the Sava Suburb (*Varoš*) was one which had few or many. This circumstance must be borne in mind of course when judging all the results we publish for Belgrade.

The only other pre-industrial communities with as high a level of inmates as this area of Belgrade that have yet come to our notice are some of the central parishes of London in the year 1695, though there all the inmates are called lodgers. Elsewhere in Western Europe inmates were comparatively few in number, though as is shown in Chapter 4, certainly commoner than we thought in 1969, but it is very interesting that lodgers seem to have had a specific role in the familial structure of the settlement of Heidenreichstein in the eighteenth century.[6] It would be difficult to show that their role in Belgrade can have been of the same character as in that rural region where we have accounted the stem family as probably being institutionalised. Nevertheless it will be seen from Chapter 16 that Halpern suspects the unusual number of one-person households present in Arandjelovac in 1863 to be due to boarders in other households being listed separately. He goes on to say, however, that they were clearly either young men at the beginning of their careers or older men temporarily detached from their families. The lodgers of Belgrade differ greatly from this pattern. Far from being the elderly widows or widowers at the end of their lives, or the single young men living away from home to 'make a way in the world', they are frequently young married couples with growing or established families of young children, some with kin coresiding: indeed a few of the lodging groups have servants. Table 15.20 gives some idea of the age distribution of lodgers in comparison with the age distribution of the rest of the population. It is possible that the Turks and/or Austrians had partitioned the city on a 'ghetto principle' compelling all Serbs to live in this one sector, and consequently independent living accommodation would be scarce. Certainly the lodging community looks very like the landlord community in household composition, however unexpected this may be in an area of kin-dominated household structures.

Strangers appear to be unique to Belgrade in the scope of the present volume, and the only possible parallel known to us is in eighteenth-century Iceland.[7] It seems evident that in Iceland these unfortunate people were billetted on the households in which they were found to have been living as a welfare measure. In a society organised so exclusively in households and so little in institutions, this was apparently the only way of keeping people alive under conditions so unfavourable as Iceland was then experiencing. It would be interesting indeed if the 'strangers' of Belgrade could be shown to represent the same response to a similar set of circumstances. Against such an explanation is the fact that there was only one woman amongst the strangers of Belgrade, but it may be significant

[6] See Berkner, *The stem family and the development cycle of the peasant household* (1972).
[7] See Hansen, *Tabulation of the Icelandic Population Census of 1729* (mimeograph).

that all of these men were without families, and were usually living in apparently unrelated groups of anything from two to twelve. In houses where lodgers and/or strangers were living alone, without a resident landlord, there is a strong indication that they were employees of the owner of the Dom. In the nine such cases the absentee landlords are 1 coppersmith, 4 'blanket-makers', 1 tailor, 1 barber and two unspecified (the occupational translations are only approximate).

A reason for the presence of such large numbers of strangers and lodgers may lie therefore in the unsettled state of the Balkan area at that time. The almost solely agricultural economy must have been gravely disrupted by the Austro-Turkish wars and it may be that many of the displaced rural Serbian population had moved into the towns for protection, housing and employment. If occupations had been given for the whole census population they might have made it possible to pronounce on the point. It may be significant that in Iceland when what seems to be a similar 'floating population' of strangers has also been found, it was during a period of major volcanic eruptions and consequently of high if temporary mobility.

Occupations are ordinarily, though inconsistently given for the presumed landlord of each set of premises only. Twenty-four of these landlords do not seem to have actually been resident in the housefuls detailed under their names.

Servants form 10.3 % of the population as shown comparatively in Table 1.12 above. The most common group was of one male servant, though groups do go up to seven in size. There was one group of eight but these were the servants of two separate masters. The two groups of seven appear to have been employed in a business rather than as purely domestic servants – one was in a furrier's house where there were also seven strangers, and the other formed a group living in a house whose non-resident landlord was himself a leather worker. Table 15.19 makes clear the drastic difference in distribution amongst servants in the matter of sex. Serbian servants seem to have been different from those in England and Western Europe, and we cannot pronounce upon their economic and familial roles. But as was insisted in Chapter 1 the point of importance is that they existed at all in a society where it might be thought that the coresidence of suitable kin would provide all the service which the domestic group was in need of.

Table 15.18 seems to reveal a discrepancy in the matter of age. The lack of males under ten is unusual and cannot be explained by the Turkish practice of taking boys between five and seven to be trained as Moslem Janissaries in Turkey, for this practice ceased by the early seventeenth century. Stoianovich puts it down to a higher male death rate. There is also the possibility of under-registration of children generally, for another resemblance to late seventeenth-century London and urban centres generally, is the apparent lack of offspring in the households. Perhaps the most interesting confirmation of this tendency comes from Table 15.9 which, like Table 15.18 compares Belgrade in 1733–4 with Gregory King's contemporary statistical analysis of England in the 1690s. It is known that King believed children to be fewer in London and in urban areas than elsewhere, but that Belgrade had even less than his London total. Part of the explanation may be the early age at marriage for girls, which certainly has a bearing on the great predominance of males among servants. But we do not know enough to go further.

Age gap between spouses is unusually high, often with the husbands ten years or more older than their wives, as was remarked in Chapter 1 (see also p. 75). Though there is heavy bunching at the decennia, which makes any precise calculation based on ages difficult, there is no reason to suppose that the age gap is greatly exaggerated.[8]

Table 15.4 gives a more detailed analysis of the data dealt with in Table 1.10 of the Introduction. The ten 'pauper' children are in fact termed *sirota* in the document, which we have taken loosely to mean dependent. There is one other person termed *sirota*, a woman of fifty.

Resident kin in Belgrade are also analysed in both series of tables, and the very considerable excess over the proportions and types found in Western Europe has been commented upon, though it was pointed out that the level attained at Belgrade was considerably lower than seems to have been usual in Japan. It will be noticed that mothers of heads of households and their brothers and sisters form the largest group, with children's spouses relatively few. The nearest to Belgrade in proportions of kin in European settlements so far analysed in Cambridge seems to be the community of Colorno near Parma in Italy, which appears in Table 1.3 above. In 1782 kin formed 10.8 % of the population there, with grandchildren as the highest category followed by the siblings and then by the parents and nephews and nieces of the household head. Table 15.14, with its figures on familial structure, does not in fact represent the analysis of housefuls as do the rest of the series, for this was found to be impossible. But it goes as far as is practicable in that direction, and its rather problematic values seem to imply that the larger coresident groups in question were not much more complex in structure than the inferred households of Table 1.15.

We must leave it to the reader to decide how far these details bear out what is so often said about the contrast between the kinship system of Southeastern Europe and Northern and Western Europe in historical times. For the rest, we leave our tables to speak for themselves. Perhaps we may be allowed to confess however that our study of the data which allowed us to prepare them leaves us convinced of our own ignorance about the interrelationship between these two extreme wings of European familial culture, if such they are. It is surely paradox enough that two of the few informative comparisons we can yet suggest are with the central districts of London on one hand and the isolated settlements of Iceland on the other – the most prosperous communities of traditional Europe and the most miserable.

[8] Compare the age gap between spouses in fifteenth-century Tuscany, above, Klapisch, Chapter 10, pp. 272–273, and Laslett (1971).

Appendix

Rules for presumption

The following rules were observed in the analysis of the Belgrade listing.

1 PRESUMPTIONS ABOUT MARITAL STATUS
   a Only those who are of opposite sex, and stated to be married, or so indicated by the titles of son-in-law, daughter-in-law, etc. may be presumed to be married.
   b An individual may be presumed widowed who is
      (i) described as either mother or father of the head or other member of the household, a spouse not being present;
      (ii) head of a household containing either or both children with the correct patronymic and a married couple, one of whom has the correct patronymic (only applicable for widowers).
   c An individual may be presumed single who is
      (i) described as a child, son, daughter, nephew, niece, servant, apprentice, bastard, unless there is evidence to the contrary;
      (ii) living in a household in which the only relative is a sibling.
No presumptions have been made about solitaries except where the above rules applied.

2 PRESUMPTIONS ABOUT OFFSPRING
An individual may be presumed offspring who is listed after a married couple, a presumed married couple, a widowed person or a presumed widowed person and has the correct patronymic.

3 PRESUMPTIONS ABOUT KINSHIP
   a An individual may be presumed a grandchild who is described in the list as the offspring of parent(s) whose own/presumed parent(s) head(s) the household.
   b Members of the same household who have the same patronymic may be presumed kin.
No other presumptions about kinship have been made

4 No division of housefuls into households has been made as there is no obvious indication of such separation. Only lodgers' and strangers' groups have been separated from the head of the household's group as they were distinctly labelled and grouped under their respective headings at the end of the main household group.
5 No presumptions about servants have been made. Only those stated to be servants have been counted as such.
6 No presumptions of any kind have been made on an age basis except in the case of *sirota* (pauper children), who have been presumed children by age because of their dependent status.
7 *DEFINITIONS* are the same as given in the introduction except for 4 (ii) and 8 (see pp. 87–88) as no institutions appear to be present in this study.

Table 15.1[a]   *Population by sex and marital status*

	Males		Females		Total	
Marital status	No.	%	No.	%	No.	%
Married	267	44.4	267	47.0	534	45.5
Widowed	7	1.1	57	10.0	64	5.5
Single	328	54.5	246	43.0	574	49.0
Total	602	100	570	100	1,172	100
Unknown	130	—	54	—	184	—

1 of unknown sex and marital status

	No.	%
Males	732	54.0
Females	624	46.0
Total	1,356	100

[a] Tables 15.1–15.20: Belgrade 1733–4 (Sava Suburb); population, 1,357.

Table 15.2 *Distributions of housefuls by size*

	Total population				*All* lodgers and strangers[c] excluded			
	Housefuls		Persons		Housefuls		Persons	
Size	No.	%	No.	%	No.	%	No.	%
1	—	—	—	—	5	2.8	5	0.5
2	6	3.2	12	0.9	11	6.2	22	2.3
3	19	10.0	57	4.2	28	15.6	84	8.6
4	21	11.1	84	6.2	33	18.5	132	13.6
5	22	11.6	110	8.1	26	14.5	130	13.4
6	27	14.3	162	12.0	26	14.5	156	16.1
7	23	12.2	161	11.9	16	9.0	112	11.5
8	18	9.6	144	10.7	12	6.7	96	9.9
9	13	6.9	117	8.7	6	3.3	54	5.5
10	13	6.9	130	9.6	6	3.3	60	6.2
11	7	3.7	77	5.7	3	1.7	33	3.4
12	3	1.6	36	2.6	—	—	—	—
13	5	2.7	65	4.8	2	1.1	26	2.7
14	1	0.5	14	1.3	1	0.6	14	1.5
15	4	2.1	60	4.4		—	—	—
16	4	2.1	64	4.7	3	1.7	48	5.0
17	2	1.0	34	2.5	—	—	—	—
23	1	0.5	23	1.7	—	—	—	—
Total	189	100	1,350[a]	100	178[b]	100	972	100

Mean size of houseful: total population = 7.14; exclusive of lodgers and strangers = 5.45.
Variance: 12.73
Mean experienced houseful size: 8.92.

[a] Excluding 7 people in 3 defective houses.
[b] 9 housefuls consist of lodgers/strangers only and are therefore excluded.
[c] 2 housefuls of servants with no resident landlord are also excluded.

Table 15.3   *Marital status of heads of housefuls
and heads of lodging groups*

Marital status	All housefuls[a]		Lodging groups	
	No.	%	No.	%
1. Married couple	147	82.7	59	90.0
2. Widower	4	2.2	1	1.5
3. Widow	10	5.6	2	3.5
4. Single male	3	1.7	—	—
5. Single female	—	—	—	—
6. Unspecified male	10	5.6	2	3.5
7. Unspecified female	4	2.2	1	1.5
Total	178	100	65	100

[a] Excluding 9 of lodgers with no resident landlord who are included in the lodging groups column, and 2 housefuls of servants with no resident landlord.

Table 15.4   *Children by sex and category and as
a proportion of the population*

| | Children | | | |
Category	Male	Female	Total	%
1. Offspring of houseful head	135	144	279	64.5
2. Grand/great grandchild of head	2	5	7	1.7
3. Offspring of other houseful member:				
(a) Lodgers' children	47	51	98	22.7
(b) Children of other members of houseful unrelated to head	9	15	24	5.6
(c) Strangers' children[a]	1	—	1	0.2
(d) Other offspring of head's *resident* mother (i.e. brothers and sisters)	2	2	4	0.9
(e) Other children	1	—	1	0·2
4. Parish or pauper child[b]	2	8	10	2.3
5. Nephew or niece of head	5	3	8	1.9
Total	204	228	432	100
	Children		432	31.9
	Total population		1,357	100

[a] Doubtful.
[b] For the purposes of analysis those termed *sirota* are classed as paupers, of whom there are 11 in all (10 children, 1 adult). No married children are included.

Table 15.5   *Siblings[a] by groups*

Size	Sibling groups (excluding lodgers)		No. of siblings		Lodgers' sibling groups		No. of lodgers' siblings	
	No.	%	No.	%	No.	%	No.	%
1	55	37.0	55	17.4	23	48.0	23	24.2
2	50	33.6	100	31.8	12	25.0	24	25.3
3	23	15.4	69	21.8	5	10.4	15	15.8
4	15	10.0	60	19.0	7	14.6	28	29.5
5	5	3.3	25	8.0	1	2.0	5	5.2
6	1	0.7	6	2.0	—	—	—	—
7+	—	—	—	—	—	—	—	—
Total	149	100	315	100	48	100	95	100

Mean size of *all* sibling groups = 2.09.
Mean size of lodgers' sibling groups = 2.02.
Mean size of non-lodger sibling groups = 2.11.

[a] Siblings are the offspring present in any conjugal family unit within any houseful.

Table 15.6   *Servants by sex and as a proportion of the population*

	Males		Females	
Category	No.	%	No.	%
Described as servants	118	97.5	19	100
Servants of a specified kind[a]	3	2.5	—	—
Total	121	100	19	100

[a] 2 'in his shop'– a baker's; 1 stranger 'in service'.

	No.	%
Male servants	121	86.5
Female servants	19	13.5
Total servants	140	100

	No.	%
Total servants	140	10.3
Total population	1,357	100

Sex ratio = 637

Table 15.7   *Composition of servant groups by owner of Dom*

Size	Groups Composition	All owners (excluding lodgers) No.	Lodgers only No.	%
1	1 male	18	7	40.5
	1 female	1	—	1.6
2	2 males	11	—	17.7
	1 male, 1 female	6	1	11.3
3	3 males	6	—	9.7
	2 males, 1 female	1	—	1.6
4	4 males	2	—	3.2
	3 males, 1 female	2	—	3.2
5	5 males	1	—	1.6
	4 males, 1 female	1	—	1.6
	2 males, 3 females	1	—	1.6
6	4 males, 2 females	2	—	3.2
7	7 males	2	—	3.2
	Totals	54	8	100 (N = 62)

	No.	%
Housefuls with servants	56	29.6
Total housefuls	189	100

Table 15.8   *Kin other than children and spouses: type and numbers*

Category	Husband	Wife	Widower	Widow	Single or un-specified	Kin of other houseful member (excluding head's and lodger's kin)	Lodger's kin	Total
Father	2	—	—	—	—	—	—	2
Mother	10	10	—	—	5	2	8	35
Brother	13	4	—	—	6	2	9	34
Sister	3	5	1	—	5	2	5	21
Brother's wife	5	1	—	—	1	1	4	12
Sister's husband	2	1	—	—	1	—	—	4
Cousin	1	—	—	—	—	4	—	5
Nephew { brother's child	5	—	—	—	1	—	4	} 13
Nephew { sister's child	2	—	—	—	1	—	—	
Niece { brother's child	3	—	—	—	—.	2	1	} 12
Niece { sister's child	1	—	—	—	4	—	1	
Nephew's wife	1	—	—	—	1	—	—	2
Son-in-law	4		1	2	—	—	—	7
Daughter-in-law	6		1	1	—	—	1	9
Grandchild	1		1	3	—	—	—	5
Other (see below)	1	1	—	—	—	3	—	5
							Total	166

	No.	%
Housefuls with kin	81	43.0
Total housefuls	189	100

Other.   1, Head's wife's, brother's wife's, brother. 2, Cousin's wife. 3, Aunt. 4, Uncle. 5, Uncle's wi[fe]
Proportion resident kin in the population = 12.3 %

Table 15.9 *Proportion of population of various categories
for comparison with figures of Gregory King*[a]

	Persons		Gregory King's percentages		
			London and suburbs	Other cities and great towns	Villages and hamlets
Status	No.	%			
1. Husband and wife	534	39.3	37.0	36.0	34.0
2. Widower	7	0.5	2.0	2.0	1.5
3. Widow	57	4.2	7.0	6.0	4.5
4. Child[b]	432	31.8	33.0	40.0	47.0
5. Servant	140	10.3	13.0	11.0	10.0
6. Sojourner and single person[c]	187	13.9	8.0	5.0	3.0
Total	1,357	100.0	100.0	100.0	100.0

[a] King's figures are taken from his *Natural and Politicall Observations* (1696, 1936): 23.

[b] King's category 4 is assumed to be the same as category 1 in Table 15.4 of this series. The assumption is based on the analysis of King's own listing of the inhabitants of Harefield, Middx. See King, Exercises in political arithmetic (manuscript i).

[c] Category 6 is a residual category, covering all kin other than offspring and widowed parents; lodgers; inmates; etc.

Table 15.10   *Widowed persons by houseful position*

	Widowers				Widows			
Position	Non-lodgers	Lodgers	No.	%	Non-lodgers	Lodgers	No.	%
1. Solitary	—	—	—	—	—	—	—	—
2. Head of houseful or lodging group which includes widowed/ married son[a]	1	—	1	14.0	—	—	—	—
3. Head of houseful or lodging group which includes widowed/ married daughter[a]	1	—	1	14.0	2	—	2	3.0
4. Head of houseful or lodging group which includes unmarried offspring[a]	2	1	3	43.0	7	2	9	16.0
5. Head of houseful or lodging group containing only those not offspring[b]	—	—	—	—	1	—	1	2.0
6. In houseful or lodging group headed by son	—	—	—	—	13	6	19	33.0
7. In houseful or lodging group headed by son-in-law	—	—	—	—	10	1	11	19.0
8. In houseful or lodging group headed by other kin	—	—	—	—	3	2	5	9.0
9. In houseful or lodging group headed by others	2	—	2	29.0	7	3	10	17.0
Totals	6	1	7	100	43	14	57	100

[a] Categories 2 and 3 cover housefuls which contain married and unmarried offspring; category 4 excludes housefuls containing married offspring.
[b] Lodgers.

Table 15.11   *Mean size of houseful by age of head, married heads. Mean size of lodging group by age of lodging head, married heads[a]*

	Mean size		
Age	Houseful including lodgers and strangers	Houseful excluding lodgers and strangers	Lodging groups only
Unknown	6.46	5.40	3.38
20–24	8.00	6.40	5.20
25–29	7.85	7.00	3.71
30–34	7.26	5.30	4.16
35–39	7.06	5.86	6.25
40–44	9.05	5.85	7.50 (4.44)[b]
45–49	6.80	6.20	6.00
50–54	6.80	5.80	7.00
55–59	7.28	7.28	6.00
60–64	7.00	6.25	6.50
65–69	6.66	4.33	3.00
70+	6.00	4.20	3.00
Total	7.23	5.74	4.83

[a] The husband's age is relevant here.
[b] The second figure in brackets is when one group of 23, containing several families, is removed.

Table 15.12   *Lodgers, strangers and landlords – summary table*

Lodgers	No.	%	Strangers	No.	%
Individual lodgers	1	0.07	Individual strangers	8	0.6
Lodgers in lodging groups	303	22.2	Strangers in groups	58	4.3
Male lodgers	148	10.9	Male strangers	65	4.8
Female lodgers	156	11.5	Female strangers	1	0.07
All lodgers	304	22.2	All strangers	66	4.86
Total population	1,357	100	Total population	1,357	100
Lodging groups with offspring	38	58.4	Strangers' groups with offspring[a]	1	0.4
Lodging groups with servants	7	10.8	Strangers' groups with servants[a]	1	0.4
All lodging groups	65[c]	100	All strangers' groups	24	100
Landlords	No.	%	Landlords[b]	No.	%
Landlord housefuls with offspring	38	68.0	Landlord housefuls with offspring	15	62.5
Landlord housefuls with servants	13	23.2	Landlord housefuls with servants	11	46.0
All landlord housefuls	56[c]	100	All landlord housefuls	24	100

[a] Very dubious.
[b] One 'landlord' is a lodger with no proper resident landlord.
[c] There are 9 lodging housefuls with no resident landlord.

	No.	%
All housefuls containing lodgers	65	34.4
Housefuls containing lodgers excluding those with non-resident landlords	56	30.0
Total housefuls	189	100

Table 15.13   *Housefuls by generational depth*

No. of Genera-tions		Description of houseful	Excluding lodgers and strangers		Lodgers only	
			No.	%	No.	%
1	(i)	Containing only members of same generation as head	28	15.5	18	27.7
2	(ii)	Containing offspring of head and/or members of offspring generation	106 ⎫		29 ⎫	
	(iii)	Containing parents of head and/or members of parent generation	9 ⎬ 115	64.0	3 ⎬ 32	49.1
3	(iv)	Containing offspring etc. of head and grandchildren of head and/or members of grandchild generation	5 ⎫		— ⎫	
	(v)	Containing grandchildren of head but without offspring etc. of head	— ⎬ 21	11.6	— ⎬ 2	3.1
	(vi)	Containing offspring etc. of head and parents etc. of head	16		—	
	(vii)	Any other three-generational combination	— ⎭		2 ⎭	
4	(viii)	Containing in addition to contents in (iv) above great grandchildren and/or members of great grandchild generation	— ⎫		— ⎫	
	(ix)	Any other four-generational combination	— ⎬ —	—	— ⎬ —	—
Un-known	(x)	Containing members of unspecified generational relation only[a]	16	8.9	13	20.0
		Total	180	100	65	100

[a] These are mainly housefuls containing more than one nuclear unit with no apparent link between them – especially in the case of lodgers' housefuls.

Table 15.14   *Households by structure*[a]

	With servants	Without servants	No.	%
1. Solitaries				
(a) Widowed	—	1	1	
(b) Singles of unknown marital status	1	4	5	} 3.4
2. No family				
(a) Coresident siblings	—	2	2	
(b) Coresident relatives of other kinds	—	2	2	} 2.8
(c) Persons not evidently related	1	—	1	
3. Simple family households				
(a) Married couples alone	3	10	13	
(b) Married couples with children	19	56	75	} 54.5
(c) Widowers with children	—	1	1	
(d) Widows with children	—	7	7	
4. Extended family households				
(a) Extended upwards	4	9	13	
(b) Extended downwards	1	2	3	} 14.2
(c) Extended laterally	4	5	9	
(d) Combinations of (a)–(c)	—	—	—	
5. Multiple family households				
(a) Secondary units UP	2	6	8	
(b) Secondary units DOWN	5	8	13	
(c) Units all on one level	1	2	3	} 17.6
(d) 'Frérèches'	1	5	6	
(e) Other multiple families	1	—	1	
6. Indeterminate	4	9	13	7.4
	Total		176[b]	100.0

'Stem Families'	5(b)	13
	5(b) & 5(a)	21
	5(b), 5(a) & 4(a)	34 (19.3%)
'Frérèches'	5(d)	8
(alternative	5(d) & 5(c)	11
definitions)	5(d), 5(c) & 4(a)	24
	5(d), 5(c), 4(a) & 2(a)	26 (14.8%)

[a] *Households* as for the definition of ratio 5, see above p. 133.
[b] No servant-only or lodger-only housefuls without resident landlord are included. Also two housefuls where the information is defective and ambiguous are excluded.

Table 15.15   *Mean size of houseful and conjugal family*[a]

Mean size of all housefuls[b]		7.14
Housefuls containing conjugal families		
Mean size of housefuls containing conjugal families[c]		7.21
Mean number of kin	0.58	
Mean number of servants	0.70	
Mean number of others	2.15	lodgers $=$ 1.26 strangers $=$ 0.27 others $=$ 0.61
Mean size of houseful portion not of conjugal family		3.43
Mean number of married and widowed persons	1.89	
Mean number of offspring	1.88	
Mean size of conjugal family		3.77

[a] A conjugal family within any houseful consists of either a married couple with or without the offspring of either of them, or the remaining partner of a broken marriage with offspring and/or step-children. In housefuls containing more than one married couple, the conjugal family is always that of the head of the houseful; in-laws and grandchildren and grandparents are counted as 'kin'.

[b] See Table 15.2 above.

[c] The 8 lodger-only housefuls which contain conjugal units are excluded as being of abnormal structure.

Table 15.16   *Distribution of population by age and sex*

Age	Males		Females		Total	
	No.	%	No.	%	No.	%
Under 1	23	3.7	21	3.6	44 (11)	3.7 (4.1)[a]
1–4	48	7.8	64	10.9	112 (28)	9.3 (10.3)
5–9	65	10.6	82	14.0	147 (35)	12.2 (13.0)
10–14	61	9.9	79	13.5	140 (27)	11.6 (10.0)
15–19	49	8.0	52	8.8	101 (25)	8.3 (9.3)
20–24	82	13.3	63	10.7	145 (34)	12.1 (12.6)
25–29	65	10.6	66	11.3	131 (33)	10.9 (12.2)
30–34	76	12.3	62	10.6	138 (33)	11.5 (12.2)
35–39	35	5.7	23	3.9	58 (9)	4.8 (3.3)
40–44	30	4.9	25	4.2	55 (10)	4.6 (3.7)
45–49	15	2.4	5	0.8	20 (5)	1.7 (1.8)
50–54	28	4.5	20	3.4	48 (7)	4.0 (2.6)
55–59	7	1.1	3	0.5	10 (1)	0.8 (0.4)
60–64	16	2.6	14	2.4	30 (8)	2.5 (3.0)
65–69	5	0.8	1	0.1	6 (1)	0.5 (0.4)
70+	11	1.8	8	1.3	19 (3)	1.5 (1.1)
Total of known age	616	100.0	588	100.0	1,204 (270)	100.0 (100)

Males age unknown	116	8.5
Females age unknown	36	2.6
Total population	1,357	100

Mean age: Males 24.9, Females 21.6, all 23.2
Median age: Males 23.7, Females, 19.6 all 22.8

[a] Figures in parentheses are for lodgers.
Note: 1 of unknown sex – age 24.

Table 15.17 *Marital status by age and sex*

Marital status	Age																											
	0–14		15–19		20–24		25–29		30–34		35–39		40–44		45–49		50–54		55–59		60–64		65–69		70+		Not known	
	No.	%	No.	%	No.	%	No.	%	No.	%	No.	%	No.	%	No.	%	No.	%	No.	%	No.	%	No.	%	No.	%	No.	%
Male																												
Married	—	—	—	—	17	20	32	50	51	67	25	71	26	87	13	87	20	71	7	100	10	62	5	100	7	63	54	47
Widowed	—	—	—	—	—	—	—	—	—	—	—	—	1	3	—	—	1	3	—	—	2	12	—	—	2	18	1	1
Single	183	93	40	82	35	43	15	23	9	12	5	14	1	3	1	7	2	7	—	—	1	6	—	—	1	9	35	30
Unknown	14	7	9	18	30	37	18	27	16	21	5	14	2	7	1	7	5	18	—	—	3	19	—	—	1	9	26	23
Total	197	100	49	100	82	100	65	100	76	100	35	100	30	100	15	100	28	100	7	100	16	100	5	100	11	100	116	100
Female																												
Married	1	—	37	71	56	90	60	90	49	80	16	70	17	69	3	60	5	25	—	—	1	7	—	—	1	12	21	60
Widowed	—	—	—	—	3	5	2	3	5	8	6	26	3	12	2	40	13	65	2	67	10	70	1	100	5	63	5	14
Single	222	90	11	21	2	3	1	2	2	3	1	4	1	4	—	—	—	—	—	—	—	—	—	—	1	12	6	16
Unknown	23	9	4	8	2	3	3	5	6	10	—	—	4	16	—	—	2	10	1	33	3	22	—	—	1	12	4	11
Total[a]	246	100	52	100	63	100	66	100	62	100	23	100	25	100	5	100	20	100	3	100	14	100	1	100	8	100	36	100

[a] Those of unknown sex and marital status amount to 1.

Table 15.18   *Population by age and sex for comparison with figures of Gregory King*[a]

	Males		Females		Total	
Age	King's %	%	King's %	%	King's %	%
Under 1 year	3.3	3.7	2.8	3.6	3.1	3.6
Under 5 years	15.4	11.5	14.5	14.5	14.9	13.0
Under 10 years	28.3	22.0	27.0	28.4	27.6	22.2
Under 16 years	41.5	34.2	39.6	43.1	40.6	38.6
Above 16 years	58.5	65.6	60.4	57.0	59.4	61.3
Above 21 years	48.1	54.6	50.0	44.0	49.0	49.5
Above 25 years	42.5	46.6	44.7	38.6	43.6	42.7
Above 60 years	10.0	5.2	11.8	3.9	10.9	4.5
N =	616	100	588	100	1,204	100

[a] The percentages in this table are derived from King's figures in the table on p. 23 of his *Natural and Politicall Observations* (1696, 1936).

Note: Population used = 1,204. 116 males of unknown age, 36 females of unknown age, 1 of unknown sex.

Table 15.19   *Servants by age and sex*

Age	Male servants		Female servants		Total	
	No.	%	No.	%	No.	%
5–9	—	—	2	10.5	2	1.9
10–14	14	16.2	9	47.5	23	21.7
15–19	23	26.5	3[a]	15.8	26	24.6
20–24	20	23.0	—	—	20	18.9
25–29	11	12.7	1	5.2	12	11.3
30–34	10[b]	11.5	2	10.5	12	11.3
35–39	3	3.4	—	—	3	2.8
40–44	1	1.1	1	5.2	2	1.9
45–49	1	1.1	—	—	1	0.9
50–54	2	2.3	—	—	2	1.9
55–59	—	—	—	—	—	—
60–64	1	1.1	—	—	1	0.9
65–69	—	—	—	—	—	—
70+	1	1.1	1	5.2	2	1.9
Total of known age	87	100	19	99.9	106	100

	No.	%
Male servants age unknown	34	24
Female servants age unknown	—	—
Total servants	140	100

Mean age: males 23.5, females 19.7, all 22.8
Median age: males 21.5, females 14.0, all 20.35.
[a] two married
[b] one married

400

Table 15.20 *Proportions by age and sex in parental households, in service and heading households*

Males

Age	% in parental household		%[a] in service	% Heading household				% in other positions			Total (%)
	Single	Married		Married	Widowed	Single[b]		Lodger	Stranger	Other	
0–9	68	—	—	—	—	—	—	25	1	6	100
10–14	58	—	23	—	—	—	—	13	—	6	100
15–19	22	—	47	—	—	—	—	14	2	14	100
20–24	9	7	25	6	—	3	3	17	19	11	100
25–29	3	1	17	11	—	3	—	25	15	25	100
30–34	—	—	13	34	—	1	—	22	15	15	100
35–39	—	—	9	43	—	3	3	14	11	17	100
40–44	—	—	3	67	3	—	—	23	3	—	100
45+	—	—	6	54	4	4	—	19	8	5	100
Unknown	3	—	29	26	—	1	—	15	11	15	100

Females

Age	% in parental household		% in service	% Heading household				% in other positions			Total (%)
	Single	Married		Married	Widowed	Single[b]		Lodger	Stranger	Other	
0–9	68	—	1	—	—	—	—	24	—	7	100
10–14	47	—	11	—	—	—	—	24	—	18	100
15–19	16	4	6	18	—	—	—	35	—	22	100
20–24	2	5	—	37	—	—	—	31	—	26	100
25–29	—	1	1	56	—	—	—	26	—	15	100
30–34	—	—	3	53	5	—	—	26	—	13	100
35–39	—	—	—	56	9	—	—	17	—	17	100
40–44	—	—	4	58	4	4	—	12	—	17	100
45+	—	—	2	16	8	4	—	18	—	52	100
Unknown	14	—	—	28	—	3	—	28	3	25	100

[a] Married servants or lodgers' servants are counted only in the servants column.
[b] The second column contains those of unknown marital status, but of known age and heading households.

16. Town and countryside in Serbia in the nineteenth-century, social and household structure as reflected in the census of 1863[1]

Joel M. Halpern

Balkan familial and household structure has been the subject of discussion and study for over a century, but not much attention has been paid to the specifics of size and kinship composition. If we give as a brief tentative definition of the *zadruga* an extended household composed of a father and his married sons and their offspring (paternal zadruga), or two or more married brothers and their children (fraternal zadruga), how many people in a given community actually lived in these types of households? What about the size of the households themselves? Much of the literature with respect to the zadruga seems to dwell on the exceptional case which is then described in detail. Such an approach, however, does not help us understand the conditions under which the majority of the people lived. In this chapter an attempt will be made to establish in a preliminary way specific data bearing on household size and composition as it existed in the nineteenth century in certain villages in central Šumadija in Serbia (Orašac, Banja, Bukovik, Kopljare, Stojnik and Topola) and one emergent market town (Arandjelovac).

A glance at Tables 16.1*a*–*h* establishes that with the notable exception of the market town the large majority of households contain six or more people according to the 1863 Census.[2] Arandjelovac has approximately 20 % of its people listed as living alone (see below, Table 16.1*a*), although this may be in part an artifact of the Census since many of these were probably boarders in other

[1] The research on which this paper is based was supported by grants from the National Science Foundation and the National Institute of Mental Health. Appreciation is also acknowledged for assistance provided by the Archives of the Republic of Serbia, permitting access to census records, to personnel at the Serbian Archives who aided in the transcription of data, and to the University of Massachusetts Faculty Research Committee. A related paper, drawing exclusively on Orašac, one of the villages cited here, is Halpern, *The zadruga, a century of change* (1970).
[2] Despite the differences in the structure of households, it is noticeable that in the towns of Western Europe smaller households occurred more frequently than in the surrounding countryside. See above, van der Woude, Chapter 12, pp. 308–309; Hélin, Chapter 13, pp. 332–333. Compare the survey by Klapisch of fifteenth-century Tuscany, see above, Chapter 10, p. 275.

households. Still, it is clear that these merchants and craftsmen were either young men beginning their careers or older men temporarily or permanently detached from their families. From what we know of contemporary rural–urban kin relationships in Serbia it is reasonable to suppose that many of these single people were migrants from surrounding villages, and they probably returned to their home villages fairly regularly. It would seem highly unlikely that they were without important kin ties in the surrounding area. It is also probable that few if any of these single individuals were born in the town. Of course, the whole idea of town or urban center must be used in a very restricted occupational sense, since we are here talking about a settlement of only 566 people.

If we use as our focus of interest the population at large rather than the household structure as such, we can see clearly that again, with the striking exception of Arandjelovac, the majority of the population lived in households size 6 or over, ranging from as high as 89 % in the case of Orašac, to a minimum of 69 % in Bukovik (the settlement adjoining Arandjelovac, and also containing commercial establishments).

If we compare the 1863 data with information available for the same villages for 1890 (Table 16.2) we see that with the exception of the town there have been no dramatic changes. The major change in Arandjelovac is the very sharp decline in households of size 1. This may be in part a characteristic of the way in which the 1863 Census was carried out, or it may be explained by the growth of Arandjelovac as a trading center, so that by 1890 the merchants and craftsmen were more established with families. It is also possible that the decline in single person households in Banja, Bukovik and Stojnik may be explained by the greater accuracy of the later Census. Most important, however, is that the predominance of size 6–10 households continues to include approximately half the number of households and more than half the population in most cases. It also seems significant that, with the exception of Stojnik and Banja and the special case of Arandjelovac, the other villages in this survey show some decline in the relative proportions of households of size 11 and over. This is balanced by some increase in the size 4–5 category in most cases. Broadly viewed when compared to changes which were to occur in the twentieth century, the nineteenth century seems to have been a period of relative stability in household size. If we take all data into account, however, there does seem to have been a steady decline in average household size. In Orašac, for example, there was a decline of 1.4, from a high of 8.3 in 1844 (the first records) to 6.9 in 1890. (In the much shorter period 1910–58, the decline was 2.1, from 6.6 to 4.5.)

However, once we get outside the Serbian culture area a different situation seems to prevail. In considering the case of village areas of the Republic of Dubrovnik for the end of the seventeenth century the differences are dramatic, with only approximately half of the population living in size 6 and larger households (Table 16.3). Interestingly, figures from Dubrovnik are slightly lower than those for the English village of Ealing at the end of the sixteenth century but much closer to the English than the Serbian situation.[3]

This point is further emphasized when compared to other European data. In Belgrade in 1733 80 % of all persons were living in housefuls[4] of 6 and above, but this figure is rivalled by three of the villages in our sample (Banja 79 %, Kopljare 83 % and Orašac 89 %; these are all households, not housefuls), as Tables 16.1a–h show. The mean size for the Serbian villages, taking the household as point of reference, range from 5.5 for Bukovik to 8.3 for Orašac, with the Belgrade data falling within this range. It is too early in this type of research to say that the Serbian data is unique, but from a European point of view it does contrast noticeably with the data from England.[5]

It is possible to set some limits on the frequency of large-size households in nineteenth-century Serbia. The evidence is clear from Tables 16.1a–h that households of size 20 and over were rare. Specifically, they occur in only two of the villages, and there is one case from Belgrade. What do some of these large households look like in terms of kin structure? We can take as an example the 22 member Janko Nedić zadruga of Orašac. Here there is a combination of paternal and fraternal zadruga structure. Unfortunately since all kin are listed in relationship to the head of household we cannot determine the precise pairing of sons with wives and children. Generally, specific daughters-in-law can be linked to sons by age similarities. A further confusion is that although there are Slav words for daughter-in-law (*nevjesta* or *mlada*, for example), the Serbo-Croatian term *snaha* means both daughter-in-law and sister-in-law, thereby combining them in one category, but daughters-in-law are generally listed first, matching the preferential listing given sons over brothers.

Much more common are the households with 10 or more members, i.e. those of approximately half the size of the Nedić household. In Orašac almost half of all households were of size 10 or over (48 %,) and of these the most numerous were those of sizes 10 and 12. Tables 16.1a–h show that there were only one or two households in each category above size 13, representing in most cases no more than one or two percent of the total population in each category. Further, if we consider size 13 and over as a percent of the total population, only 9 % in Bukovik, 17 % in Kopljare and 19 % in Orašac belonged to such households. Although these figures are not insignificant as compared with pre-industrial England for example, where only 1 % of persons lived in such domestic groups, it is clear that most people in these Serbian villages of the 1860s spent at least part of their lives in smaller-size households.

Further examples from Orašac in 1863 of a size 10, a size 8 and a size 6 house-

---

[3] For Ealing see above, Laslett, Chapter 1, Table 1.7, p. 77.

[4] See above Laslett and Clarke, Chapter 15. The authors distinguish between a *household* which is a kinship-family unit and the *houseful* which includes all the inhabitants of a particular house, including lodgers. For an exact definition of these terms see above, Laslett, Chapter 1, pp. 34–40. See also Hammel, Chapter 14, p. 339, footnote 13.

[5] See above, Laslett, Chapter 4, pp. 130–131, 135–143; Wall, Chapter 5, pp. 174–190.

hold give us a better idea of the kinds of family structure within which most people passed their lives. In Orašac approximately 52 % of the population is found in size 6 to 10 households inclusive, and for all settlements the percentage is about 50. The size 10 household of Milosav Nedić may be taken as an illustration: it had two married brothers, aged thirty and twenty-seven, with their wives, one and two years younger respectively. The head of the household had 3 small daughters.Three nieces were also listed, aged fifteen, twelve and seven, though only one of these could have been the child of the younger brother, given the customary age at marriage; they were more likely to have been the orphans of an older deceased brother.[6]

The issue of the adoption of a deceased brother's children and his wife is not without interest in connection with this particular household in Orašac in 1863, since the death of parents in the primary family formation years of twenty-one to forty was much greater in the nineteenth century than it is today. The relative proportion of all deaths in this age group for the period 1881–2 was 15 %, while in 1951–2 it was only 3.8 %.[7] Although scattered death records for Orašac do exist for the 1860s their incompleteness makes comparison with later years unsatisfactory, but it is reasonable to assume that if the comparison were made for the 1860s and the 1960s the contrast would be even greater.

Unlike the size 22 household, which has a maximal combination of married brothers with their children, plus the married sons of the oldest brother and their offspring, the 10-member household of Milosav Nedić was a zadruga of brothers in the process of formation. Obviously at ages thirty and twenty-seven neither brother was likely to have completed the formation of a family in terms of the number of children each young wife might bear.

A size 8 household in Orašac headed by Milan Jovanović, fifty, with a forty-year-old wife and two married sons, aged twenty-five and twenty-three respectively, the two daughters-in-law and two children, gives an example of a paternal zadruga in the process of formation; the daughters-in-law are in an even earlier stage of producing children than are the young couples in the household previously cited. We may finally look at a household of 6 headed by Nikola Pavlović, forty, which included his forty-year-old wife and their 4 children ranging in age from twelve to three. Here the head of the household either had no brother or did not have one he chose to remain with in a zadruga. At the same time, his eldest child had not reached marriageable age.

In households of size 6 and below, the classic nuclear family is most frequent, comprising about a third (31 %) of all households. However, if the nuclear family

---

[6] It is not difficult to imagine the problems eventually faced by this randomly selected household, with six young girls to marry off in the overwhelmingly patriarchal and patrilocal village society of that time. The total holdings of the household were 10 hectares, roughly the same amount as the previously cited zadruga of 22 persons. Therefore it would be reasonable to suppose that this size holding did attract at least one in-marrying male.

[7] Halpern, *Social and cultural change* (1956) Table 13: 121, based on the records of the Orašac Village Council.

is taken as a unit, its formation is not necessarily a simple matter to analyse. For example, in the case of Stevan Lukić, thirty, his wife, twenty-two, his son, two, and daughter, five, judging by the difference in age of husband and wife and by the age of the daughter, there is a possibility that the daughter was borne by a former wife, possibly one who had died in childbirth. We also find a case where a boy of seventeen is listed as the household head living with his brothers aged thirteen, eleven and nine. It is possible that this group occupied a separate house, but received help from neighboring kin.[8] Certainly if there had been fewer brothers, or if they had had more land than the 2.3 hectares due them, they might have been brought up in a paternal uncle's household, if such existed. There were also small nuclear families in Orašac just beginning to make their way, as in the case of Srećko Rajćić, twenty-two, his wife Andjelija twenty-five, and their infant son.

Household size as evidenced by these examples is, of course, something that exists only at one point in time. It is constantly changing, through the birth of new members or the death of the old and also of the young. It is further affected by influences connected with economy of size, by personality conflict and by various other factors such as government or tax regulations, which might cause brothers and their families to split off from each other, or sons to separate from fathers. Although households go through cycles as their members mature, if the sample is large enough, as in a village of a hundred or more households, it is reasonable to find households in various stages of formation as we have seen above.[9]

The obvious economic influence affecting household stability was the size of the land holding. With a large labor force it was possible for the zadruga to save money and purchase land, so that to some extent in the relatively egalitarian peasant economy, a large unit could prosper if well organized, even if it had started out with a small initial holding. In 1863 holdings ranged from a little over one hectare to as much as 14 hectares, but generally there was a fair correlation between the size of the holding and the size of the household. A family of 15 lived on the largest holding in 1863, while the largest household of 22 members had about 11 hectares. Of course, the important variable here was the number of able-bodied males rather than the total number of people in the household.

These statistics seem to me to show that the right combination of several married males together in one household, each with a relatively complete nuclear family, occurred in only a minority of cases.

[8] Compare Dupâquier's statements about households of orphaned children remaining as independent units in Corsica in the 1770s, above, Chapter 11, pp. 292, 294. In England such children would usually be taken in by relatives, possibly with some help from the parish; see above, Anderson, Chapter 7, pp. 227–228.

[9] For an example of the evolution of an individual through eight household formations in the course of seventy years, see Joel and Barbara Halpern, *A Serbian village in historical perspective* (1972). See also above, Hammel, Chapter 14, pp. 370–373.

Tables 16.4*a–f* analyze the distribution of children in Arandjelovac and five of the villages. If children are defined as those eighteen years of age and under, between 60 % and 71 % were children of the head of the household, and 4 % to 15 % were his grandchildren. Offspring of other household members, primarily brothers of the household head, amounted to 20 % to 29 %. This contrasts with Ealing where 89 % of the children were children of the household head.[10] Despite the relatively large number of grandchildren and nieces and nephews, the nuclear family was the basic structural component of the extended family household structure in Serbia.

This is further amplified by Tables 16.5*a–p* where breakdowns are given according to selected kin categories. Characteristic of the most important kin links tying together the Serbian extended family structure in the nineteenth century was the relationship of the head of the household to one or more sons. If we compare Tables 16.5*a* and 16.5*b* and 16.5*e* and 16.5*f*, we see that the number of sons exceeds the number of household heads in every village. The number of daughters also exceeds the number of household heads, though not by such a wide margin. For the five villages we get a ratio of 1.5 sons for every household head,[11] and if daughters are included the ratio rises to 2.6. On this basis, taking households headed by married persons only, including heads' wives but excluding other relatives, we get a mean household size of 4.6. Since the mean size of the household for all villages is 6.7, approximately 70 % of household composition can be attributed to nuclear family relationships. Put another way, using Orašac as an example, in 1863 out of 1,082 inhabitants, 703 were either household head, wife, son or daughter (calculating relationships with respect to the household head). Married coresident sons have been included in the nuclear families of their fathers. (Arandjelovac is excluded from the above calculations and those that follow.)

We can also take as a point of departure the population of children (under eighteen and unmarried). Tables 16.4*a–f* demonstrate that children composed from 52 % to 58 % of the population in the Serbian villages of 1863, whereas in Arandjelovac in that year, Belgrade in 1733[12] and Ealing in 1599[13] children were approximately one-third (31 % to 37 %) of the total population. As we have seen, about two-thirds of the children were the offspring of the head of the household, and between one-fifth and a quarter were the offspring of brothers of the household head, with the remaining numbers (reaching as high as 15 % in Orašac) constituting grandchildren of the household head. It should be noted that there are very few four-generation households. These data reaffirm again the importance of the nuclear family core within the extended family household.

---

[10] Taken from the files of the Cambridge Group. It must be remembered, however, that these figures are for all children (all children present in the households), not simply those under eighteen.

[11] Compare Hammel's analysis of the Serbian Census of 1528, above, Chapter 14, pp. 361–362.

[12] See above, Laslett and Clarke, Chapter 15, pp. 379–380, 385.

[13] Taken from the files of the Cambridge Group.

It may be noticed, however, that the head of the household and his wife were not necessarily a part of this nuclear core. This would seem to be true in about a quarter of the households, when the eldest son had reached an age to found his own family. This occurred generally when the household head and his wife were in their forties (see Tables 16.5a–d).

A good way to follow the cycle of extended household formation, reformulation and division is to focus on nuclear family formation within the extended kin unit. As a son married and produced children, so the date of death of the parents approached. In the circumstances of 1863 in Serbia, the major factor affecting change was the death of the father, although division occasionally occurred before his death. Viewed from another perspective, if there were two married brothers together in a zadruga, they were most likely to divide as their children matured. We can see this by contrasting the age of brothers (Table 16.5j) and of household heads (Table 16.5b); about a quarter of the household heads were over forty but only some 5 % of the brothers were in this category.

If we take households of size 10 and above, we can see that the son ratio rises to 2.5, and the overall ratio of siblings to the household head rises to 4.3. It can simply be stated that households were large in part because of the number of children of the household head. However, these figures and those cited in the preceding paragraphs take no account of the matter of married sons. The relatively larger proportion of mature sons in households of size 10 and above is reflected in the fact that most daughters-in-law are in the larger households (from one-third to three-quarters; see Tables 16.5o and 16.5p). If the small sample of six in Bukovik is disregarded because of the small percentage of sons in the over-twenty age group, then we see that the lowest percentage is 52 %.[14]

Viewed in terms of one specific village, Orašac, 32 % of the households are in the 10-plus category (Table 16.1e), but these households contain 40 % of the sons (Table 16.5e), 60 % of the daughters-in-law (Table 16.5o), 37 % of the daughters (Table 16.5g), 59 % of the brothers (Table 16.5i), 93 % of the nephews (Table 16.5m), and 80 % of the grandsons (Table 16.5k). However, in terms of total population households of over 10 persons contain only 49 % of the population.

If what might be called the key non-nuclear family kin are taken into account, that is daughters-in-law and grandsons, we can see that for Topola and Banja, where 30 % and 37 % of the population are in households of size 10 and above, 52 % and 73 % of the daughters-in-law and 63 % and 54 % of the grandsons are in this category. In these same villages 46 % of the Topola population lives in size 1–7 households and 44 % in Banja. Households of these sizes include, respectively, 47 % and 42 % of the sons, 22 % and 10 % of the daughters-in-law, and 8 % and 15 % of the grandsons. In the case of nephews the percentages for these categories are 13 % and 15 %.

---

[14] Bukovik seems to share a number of characteristics with Arandjelovac, including small average household size and younger age of household head (see Table 16.5b).

This preliminary analysis does not attempt any comprehensive survey of the social structure of households in nineteenth-century rural Serbia. What it seeks to emphasize is that the complex kin relationships which characterized the zadruga were ordinarily participated in at any one time by less than half of the population.

This statement applies not only to non-nuclear kin relationships, such as grandparent–grandchild, father-in-law–daughter-in-law and uncle–nephew, but partly also to those occasioned by multiple siblings, e.g. older brother–younger brother, older sister–younger brother. Much has been written elsewhere about the relationship between a daughter-in-law and a mother-in-law and between daughters-in-law in the same household. Obviously these are the people experiencing the full pattern of kin relationships occurring when the family cycle follows the classic pattern. But what of those families where there was only one son or where parents or siblings died young? What of the household whose limited land holding could support only a restricted number of members? Are these cases not as important as the 'ideal' ones, which can have been experienced by only a minority?

The fraternal and paternal zadrugas or combinations of these have attracted the interest of scholars. Investigations indicate that villagers of high status tended to come from larger, more complex households, which were in a better position to enlarge their holding precisely because of their superior manpower. During the nineteenth century, as the land began to fill up in central Serbia, economic and social competition intensified in the villages, since there was no large-scale outlet through emigration to towns. The ideal of several married sons joining together with their father or, after his death, several brothers and their families continuing to live in a joint household, persisted in a remarkable way. But we may well ask whether the significant proportion of people who lived in nuclear households (one-third) and households of size 5 and under (approximately a half) were in a generally deprived state? The question can be asked with respect to their standard of living, and with regard to their experiencing an emotional environment similar to that of the larger households. Given the realities of the family cycle, many individuals in the course of their lifetimes probably lived in both nuclear and extended family environments.

Scholars concerned with social structure have tended to concentrate on the fully complex, ideal patterns and neglected the smaller nuclear and fragmented households. We will not achieve a full picture of social life in the nineteenth-century Serbian household unless we look at the smaller households as intensively as we have looked at the larger ones.

Appendix[a]

Two measures each for *mean* and *median* size of household, are used. The first (A) states that on the average the household has X people according to the formula

$$\epsilon \frac{si \times hsi}{\text{no. of households}}$$

that is, the size of the household(s) times the number of households in that size category (i), indicating all the different categories taken sequentially, and ϵ representing their sum total, e.g. for Arandjelovac (see Table 16.1a)

$$\frac{1 \times 94 + 2 \times 27 + 3 \times 39 \ldots}{221}$$

The second measure (B) indicates that on the average an individual lives in a household with X people according to the formula

$$\epsilon \frac{si \times psi}{\text{no. of people in village}}$$

e.g. the sum total of the size of the household times the number of people in that size category: for Arandjelovac this would be represented by

$$\frac{1 \times 94 + 2 \times 54 + 3 \times 117.}{566}$$

The second measure is higher because it takes the individual rather than the household as the point of departure, and this is reflected in the mean as well.

Table 16.1a *Arandjelovac*

	Households		Persons	
Size	No.	%	No.	%
1	94	42.53	94	16.60
2	27	12.21	54	9.54
3	39	17.64	117	20.67
4	29	13.12	116	20.49
5	20	9.04	100	17.66
6	6	2.71	36	6.36
7	3	1.35	21	3.71
8	1	0.45	8	1.41
9	—	—	—	—
10	2	0.90	20	3.53
Total	221	100	566	100

Mean size of household	Median no. of persons
A = 2.6	A = 2
B = 3.8	B = 4

[a] The structure of Tables 16.1 to 16.4 follows that established by the Cambridge Group for the History of Population and Social Structure.
[b] Arandjelovac, Banja, Bukovik, Kopljare, Orašac, Stojnik, and Topola (plus comparative data from Dubrovnik, 1673–4).

Table 16.1*b*   *Banja*

Size	Households No.	Households %	Persons No.	Persons %
1	24	12.79	24	2.07
2	11	5.94	22	1.89
3	19	10.27	57	4.91
4	11	5.94	44	3.79
5	17	9.18	85	7.33
6	20	10.81	120	10.35
7	22	11.89	154	13.28
8	15	8.10	120	10.35
9	12	6.49	108	9.31
10	12	6.49	120	10.35
11	4	2.16	44	3.79
12	6	3.24	72	6.21
13	3	1.62	39	3.36
14	2	1.08	28	2.41
15	1	0.54	15	1.29
16	—	—	—	—
17	3	1.62	51	4.40
18	1	0.54	18	1.55
19	2	1.08	38	3.27
Total	185	100	1,159	100

Mean size of household
A = 6.3
B = 8.8

Median no. of persons
A = 6
B = 8

Table 16.1c   *Bukovik*

	Households		Persons	
Size	No.	%	No.	%
1	11	10.28	12	2.03
2	8	7.47	16	2.71
3	10	9.34	30	5.09
4	13	12.14	52	8.82
5	14	13.08	70	11.88
6	21	19.62	126	21.39
7	10	9.34	70	11.88
8	3	2.80	24	4.07
9	3	2.80	27	4.58
10	4	3.73	40	6.79
11	5	4.67	55	9.33
12	1	0.93	12	2.03
13	2	1.89	26	4.41
14	1	0.93	14	2.37
15	1	0.93	15	2.54
Total	107	100	589	100

Mean size of household
    A = 5.5
    B = 7.4

Median no. of persons
    A = 5
    B = 6

Table 16.1d   *Kopljare*

Size	Households		Persons	
	No.	%	No.	%
1	3	3.33	3	0.45
2	3	3.33	6	0.90
3	3	3.33	9	1.35
4	10	11.11	40	6.00
5	10	11.11	50	7.50
6	9	10.00	54	8.10
7	12	13.33	84	12.60
8	13	14.44	104	15.60
9	4	4.44	36	5.40
10	6	6.66	60	9.00
11	3	3.33	33	4.32
12	6	6.66	72	10.80
13	3	3.33	39	5.80
14	2	2.22	28	4.16
15	—	—	—	—
16	1	1.11	16	2.38
17	—	—	—	—
18	1	1.11	18	2.67
19	—	—	—	—
20	1	1.11	20	2.97
Total	90	100	672	100

Mean size of household	Median no. of persons
A = 7.5	A = 7
B = 9.3	B = 8

Table 16.1e *Orašac*

Size	Households		Persons	
	No.	%	No.	%
1	1	0.76	1	0.09
2	2	1.52	4	0.36
3	5	3.81	15	1.38
4	10	7.63	40	3.69
5	12	9.16	60	5.54
6	15	11.45	90	8.31
7	18	13.74	126	11.64
8	17	12.97	136	12.56
9	9	6.87	81	7.48
10	13	9.92	130	12.01
11	3	2.29	33	3.04
12	13	9.92	156	14.41
13	4	3.04	52	4.86
14	2	1.52	28	2.58
15	2	1.52	30	2.77
16	—	—	—	—
17	—	—	—	—
18	2	1.52	36	3.32
19	1	0.76	19	1.75
20	—	—	—	—
21	—	—	—	—
22	1	0.76	22	2.03
23	1	0.76	23	2.12
Total	131	100	1,082	100

Mean size of household   Median no. of persons
$$A = 8.3 \qquad\qquad A = 8$$
$$B = 10.0 \qquad\qquad B = 9$$

Table 16.1*f*   *Stojnik*

Size	Households		Persons	
	No.	%	No.	%
1	14	8.38	14	1.39
2	11	6.59	22	2.18
3	11	6.59	33	3.28
4	20	11.98	80	7.96
5	25	14.97	125	12.43
6	28	16.77	168	16.71
7	15	8.98	105	10.44
8	12	7.19	96	9.55
9	8	4.79	72	7.16
10	5	2.99	50	4.97
11	6	3.59	66	6.56
12	3	1.80	36	3.58
13	2	1.20	26	2.58
14	2	1.20	28	2.78
15	—	—	—	—
16	2	1.20	32	3.18
17	2	1.20	34	3.83
18	1	0.60	18	1.79
Total	167	100	1,005	100

Mean size of household Median no. of persons
A = 6.0 A = 6
B = 8.0 B = 7

Table 16.1g   *Topola*

Size	Households		Persons	
	No.	%	No.	%
1	11	4.40	11	0.68
2	21	8.40	42	2.61
3	13	5.20	39	2.42
4	28	11.20	112	6.96
5	29	11.60	145	9.01
6	32	12.80	193	11.99
7	29	11.60	203	12.61
8	28	11.20	224	13.92
9	18	7.20	162	10.06
10	15	6.00	148	9.19
11	8	3.20	88	5.46
12	6	2.40	72	4.47
13	7	2.80	91	5.73
14	1	0.40	14	0.87
15	2	0.80	30	1.86
16	—	—	—	—
17	1	0.40	17	1.05
18	1	0.40	18	1.11
Total	250	100	1,609	100

Mean size of household	Median no. of persons
A = 6.4	A = 6
B = 8.0	B = 8

Table 16.1*h* *Detailed size of households, all settlements*

	Households		Persons	
Size	No.	%	No.	%
1	158	13.78	158	2.37
2	83	7.24	166	2.49
3	100	8.72	300	4.51
4	121	10.55	484	7.27
5	127	11.08	635	9.54
6	131	11.43	786	11.81
7	109	9.51	763	11.47
8	89	7.76	712	10.70
9	54	4.71	486	7.30
10	57	4.97	570	8.57
11	29	2.53	319	4.79
12	35	3.05	420	6.31
13	21	1.83	273	4.10
14	10	0.87	140	2.10
15	6	0.52	90	1.35
16	1	0.08	16	0.24
17	6	0.52	102	1.56
18	6	0.52	108	1.62
19	3	0.26	57	0.85
20	1	0.08	20	0.30
21	—	—	—	—
22	1	0.08	22	0.33
23	1	0.08	23	0.34
Total	1,149	100	6,650	100

Mean size of household	Median no. of persons
A = 5.8	A = 5
B = 8.3	B = 8

Table 16.2 *Household size in all settlements, by percentages in each category, 1863 and 1890, compared*[a]

				Size			No. of house- holds
Settlement	1	2–3	4–5	6–10	11–15	16+	
Arandjelovac 1863	42.5	29.9	22.2	5.4	—	—	221
1890	8.3	27.7	34.5	26.6	2.6	0.3	383
Banja 1863	12.8	16.2	15.1	43.8	8.6	3.2	185
1890	1.1	6.5	22.9	52.7	13.7	2.7	262
Bukovik 1863	10.3	16.8	25.2	38.3	9.3	—	107
1890	3.1	16.2	33.0	43.0	2.6	2.1	191
Kopljare 1863	3.3	6.7	22.2	48.9	15.5	3.3	90
1890	3.2	14.1	23.7	48.1	7.7	3.2	156
Orašac 1863	0.8	5.3	16.8	55.0	18.3	3.8	131
1890	0.5	13.1	24.8	47.6	12.6	1.4	214
Stojnik 1863	8.4	13.2	27.0	40.7	7.8	3.0	167
1890	1.1	11.3	26.7	47.4	10.1	3.4	266
Topola 1863	4.4	13.6	22.8	48.8	9.6	0.8	250
1890	2.5	17.9	27.6	45.8	5.5	0.5	435

[a] Based on *Population Census of the Kingdom of Serbia 1890* (1892) I: 246, quoted in Halpern (1956) Table 47: 285.

Table 16.3 *Republic of Dubrovnik, 1673–4*[a]

	Households		Persons	
Size	No.	%	No.	%
1	151	3.8	151	0.8
2	462	11.7	924	4.8
3	671	16.9	2,013	10.5
4	758	19.1	3,032	15.7
5	753	19.0	3,765	19.5
6	468	11.8	2,808	14.6
7	299	7.5	2,093	10.9
8	181	4.6	1,448	7.5
9	85	2.1	765	4.0
10	75	1.9	750	3.9
Over 10	62	1.6	1,523	7.9
Total	3,965	100	19,272	100

Mean household size = 5.0.
[a] Sundrica (1959).

Mean size of household	Median no. of persons
A ——	A = 4
B ——	B = 5

Tables 16.4a–f   *Children by kin relationship, sex, and as a*
proportion of the population, 1863, by settlements

Table 16.4a   *Arandjelovac*

| | Children[a] | | | |
Kin relationship	Male	Female	Total	%
Child of head	97	92	189	91.3
Grandchild of head	3	0	3	1.44
Child of other household member[b]	7	8	15	7.24
Total	107	100	207	100

	No.	%
Children	207	37.0
Total population	566	100

[a] Children are defined here as eighteen years or younger and unmarried.
[b] Primarily children of brother of household head.

Table 16.4b   *Banja*

| | Children | | | |
Kin relationship	Male	Female	Total	%
Child of head	179	184	363	60.09
Grandchild of head	41	38	79	13.07
Child of other household member	85	77	162	26.82
Total	305	299	604	100

	No.	%
Children	604	52
Total population	1,159	100

Table 16.4c   *Bukovik*

| | Children | | | |
Kin relationship	Male	Female	Total	%
Child of head	113	108	221	66.96
Grandchild of head	7	6	13	3.93
Child of other household member	55	41	96	29.09
Total	175	155	330	100

	No.	%
Children	339	56
Total population	589	100

Table 16.4*d* *Kopljare*

| | Children | | | |
Kin relationship	Male	Female	Total	%
Child of head	134	124	258	67.01
Grandchild of head	13	9	22	5.71
Child of other household member	49	56	105	27.27
Total	196	189	385	100

	No.	%
Children	385	56
Total population	683	100

Table 16.4*e* *Orašac*

| | Children | | | |
Kin relationship	Male	Female	Total	%
Child of head	196	199	395	63.40
Grandchild of head	56	39	95	15.24
Child of other household member	63	70	133	21.34
Total	315	308	623	100

	No.	%
Children	623	58
Total population	1,082	100

Table 16.4*f* *Topola*

| | Children | | | |
Kin relationship	Male	Female	Total	%
Child of head	329	304	633	71.2
Grandchild of head	38	38	76	8.54
Child of other household member	100	80	180	20.24
Total	467	422	889	100

	No.	%
Children	889	55
Total population	1,609	100

Tables 16.5*a–p*   *Structure of households, by selected kin
categories, 1863, by settlements*[a]

A = Arandjelovac; T = Topola; Ba = Banja; Bu = Bukovik; O = Orašac; K = Kopljare.

Table 16.5*a*   *Percentage of heads of households, by household size*

Household size	A n = 221	T n = 250	Ba n = 185	Bu n = 107	O n = 131	K n = 90
1	42.5	4.4	13.0	10.3	0.8	3.3
2	12.2	8.4	5.9	7.5	1.5	3.3
3	17.6	5.2	10.3	9.3	3.8	3.3
4	13.1	11.2	5.9	12.1	7.6	11.1
5	9.0	11.6	9.2	13.1	9.2	11.1
6	2.7	12.8	10.8	19.6	11.5	10.0
7	1.4	11.6	11.9	9.3	13.7	13.3
8	0.5	11.2	8.1	2.8	13.0	14.4
9	—	7.2	6.5	2.8	6.9	4.4
10 & +	0.9	16.4	18.4	13.1	32.1	25.6
Total	100	100	100	100	100	100

[a] This series is arranged in the order of kin categories used in the 1863 Serbian Census.

Table 16.5*b*   *Percentage of heads of households, by age groups*

Age	A n = 221	T n = 250	Ba n = 185	Bu n = 107	O n = 131	K n = 90
10–19	12.3	4.4	8.1	12.1	3.8	8.9
20–29	36.1	22.4	25.9	29.9	13.7	24.4
30–39	26.5	30.4	23.8	38.3	24.4	25.6
40–49	18.3	23.2	20.5	12.1	28.2	27.8
50–59	5.5	14.0	13.0	2.8	19.1	7.8
60–69	1.4	4.0	7.0	2.8	9.2	4.4
70–79	—	1.6	1.6	—	1.5	1.0
Unknown	—	—	—	1.9	—	1.1
Total	100	100	100	100	100	100

Table 16.5c   *Percentage of wives, by household size*

Household size	T n = 201	Ba n = 130	Bu n = 75	O n = 112	K n = 76
1	—	—	—	—	—
2	5.0	2.3	2.7	1.8	2.6
3	4.0	11.5	10.7	3.6	3.9
4	10.4	5.4	12.0	5.4	10.5
5	12.4	9.2	16.0	7.1	11.8
6	15.4	13.1	22.7	12.5	10.5
7	12.4	14.6	12.0	14.3	14.5
8	13.4	11.5	4.0	14.3	13.2
9	8.5	8.5	4.0	8.0	5.3
10 & +	18.4	23.8	16.0	33.0	27.6
Total	100	100	100	100	100

Table 16.5d   *Percentage of wives, by age groups*

Age	T n = 201	Ba n = 130	Bu n = 75	O n = 112	K n = 76
0–9	—	—	—	—	—
10–19	2.0	0.8	5.3	—	2.6
20–29	31.8	37.7	44.0	25.9	40.8
30–39	34.3	32.3	37.3	35.7	34.2
40–49	19.4	19.2	9.3	20.5	15.8
50–59	9.5	9.2	2.7	17.9	6.6
60–69	2.5	0.8	1.3	—	—
70–79	0.5	—	—	—	—
Total	100	100	100	100	100

Table 16.5e   *Percentage of sons, by household size*

Household size	T $n = 390$	Ba $n = 227$	Bu $n = 119$	O $n = 257$	K $n = 153$
1	—	—	—	—	—
2	0.5	1.3	—	—	0.7
3	2.1	3.1	3.4	0.4	—
4	6.9	3.1	8.4	2.7	6.5
5	10.3	6.2	8.4	6.2	7.2
6	13.8	11.9	26.1	10.1	12.4
7	13.6	16.7	14.3	15.6	13.1
8	13.3	11.0	7.6	19.5	16.3
9	12.6	6.6	5.9	5.8	4.6
10 & +	26.9	40.1	26.1	39.7	39.2
Total	100	100	100	100	100

Table 16.5f   *Percentage of sons, by age groups*

Age	T $n = 390$	Ba $n = 227$	Bu $n = 119$	O $n = 257$	K $n = 153$
0–9	52.1	50.2	61.3	46.3	51.6
10–19	33.8	30.4	34.5	30.7	36.6
20–29	11.8	13.2	4.2	17.5	10.5
30–39	2.3	5.7	—	4.7	1.3
40–49	—	0.4	—	0.8	—
50–59	—	—	—	—	—
Total	100	100	100	100	100

Table 16.5g *Percentage of daughters, by household size*

Household size	T $n = 312$	Ba $n = 195$	Bu $n = 109$	O $n = 203$	K $n = 131$
1	—	—	—	—	—
2	0.6	1.0	1.8	—	—
3	1.0	3.6	2.8	2.0	2.3
4	8.0	5.1	6.3	2.5	4.6
5	10.6	10.8	19.3	4.9	6.9
6	14.1	10.8	22.0	12.3	9.9
7	12.8	16.9	22.9	15.8	14.5
8	15.7	10.8	2.8	17.7	14.5
9	12.8	8.7	5.5	7.9	9.2
10 & +	24.4	32.3	16.5	36.9	38.2
Total	100	100	100	100	100

Table 16.5h *Percentage of daughters, by age groups*

Age	T $n = 312$	Ba $n = 195$	Bu $n = 109$	O $n = 203$	K $n = 131$
0–9	58.7	57.9	71.6	62.6	64.9
10–19	40.1	37.9	28.4	36.0	33.6
20–29	1.3	3.6	—	1.5	1.5
30–39	—	0.5	—	—	—
40–49	—	—	—	—	—
Total	100	100	100	100	100

Table 16.5*i*   *Percentage of brothers, by household size*

Household Size	T $n = 91$	Ba $n = 92$	Bu $n = 41$	O $n = 68$	K $n = 50$
1	—	—	—	—	—
2	4.4	1.1	4.9	—	—
3	4.4	4.3	4.9	1.5	—
4	2.2	2.2	17.1	7.4	8.0
5	6.6	4.3	7.3	4.4	4.0
6	11.0	13.0	17.1	5.9	2.0
7	18.7	17.4	2.4	7.4	14.0
8	16.5	8.7	2.4	5.9	24.0
9	4.4	17.4	7.3	8.8	—
10 & +	31.9	31.5	36.6	58.8	48.0
Total	100	100	100	100	100

Tabel 16.5*j*   *Percentage of brothers, by age groups*

Age	T $n = 91$	Ba $n = 92$	Bu $n = 41$	O $n = 68$	K $n = 50$
0–9	7.7	12.0	29.3	8.8	24.0
10–19	38.5	41.3	24.4	26.5	32.0
20–29	36.3	29.3	34.1	33.8	26.0
30–39	9.9	12.0	7.3	26.5	18.0
40–49	5.5	4.3	4.9	2.9	—
50–59	1.1	1.1	—	—	—
60–69	1.1	—	—	—	—
70–79	—	—	—	1.5	—
Total	100	100	100	100	100

Table 16.5k   *Percentage of grandsons, by household size*

Household size	T n = 38	Ba n = 41	Bu n = 9	O n = 39	K n = 15
1	—	—	—	—	—
2	2.6	—	—	—	—
3	—	—	—	—	—
4	—	2.4	—	—	—
5	—	2.4	—	—	—
6	—	7.3	22.2	—	—
7	5.3	2.4	—	7.7	—
8	15.8	26.8	11.1	—	—
9	13.2	4.9	11.1	12.8	6.7
10 & +	63.2	53.7	55.6	79.5	93.3
Total	100	100	100	100	100

Table 16.5l   *Percentage of grandsons, by age groups*

Age	T n = 38	Ba n = 41	Bu n = 9	O n = 56	K n = 15
0–9	92.1	85.4	77.8	85.7	66.7
10–19	7.9	14.6	11.1	14.3	20.0
20–29	—	—	11.1	—	13.3
30–39	—	—	—	—	—
Total	100	100	100	100	100

Table 16.5m   *Percentage of nephews (brothers' sons), by household size*

Household size	T $n = 62$	Ba $n = 41$	Bu $n = 34$	O $n = 43$	K $n = 25$
1	—	—	—	—	—
2	—	—	—	—	—
3	—	—	—	—	—
4	—	—	2.9	—	—
5	3.2	—	5.9	—	—
6	4.8	4.9	11.8	—	—
7	4.8	9.8	8.8	2.3	4.0
8	14.5	—	5.9	2.3	4.0
9	9.7	2.4	—	2.3	8.0
10 & +	62.9	82.9	64.7	93.0	84.0
Total	100	100	100	100	100

Table 16.5n   *Percentage of nephews, by age groups*

Age	T $n = 62$	Ba $n = 41$	Bu $n = 34$	O $n = 43$	K $n = 25$
0–9	62.7	68.3	67.6	83.7	64.0
10–19	35.5	26.8	23.5	7.0	20.0
20–29	1.6	4.9	8.8	9.3	4.0
30–39	—	—	—	—	8.0
40–49	—	—	—	—	4.0
Total	100	100	100	100	100

Table 16.5o *Percentage of daughters-in-law, by household size*

Household size	T n = 50	Ba n = 40	Bu n = 6	O n = 50	K n = 14
1	—	—	—	—	—
2	—	—	—	—	—
3	—	—	—	—	—
4	2.0	—	—	2.0	—
5	6.0	2.5	—	2.0	—
6	6.0	5.0	16.7	2.0	—
7	8.0	2.5	—	12.0	—
8	14.0	12.5	16.7	10.0	14.3
9	12.0	5.0	33.3	8.0	21.4
10 & +	52.0	72.5	33.3	64.0	64.3
Total	100	100	100	100	100

Table 16.5p *Percentage of daughters-in-law, by age groups*

Age	T n = 50	Ba n = 40	Bu n = 6	O n = 50	K n = 14
0–9	—	—	—	—	—
10–19	10.0	2.5	16.7	4.0	7.1
20–29	82.0	77.5	83.3	80.0	71.4
30–39	8.0	17.5	—	10.0	21.4
40–49	—	2.5	—	4.0	—
50–59	—	—	—	2.0	—
Total	100	100	100	100	100

17. Small families, small households, and residential instability: town and city in 'pre-modern' Japan[1]

Robert J. Smith

INTRODUCTION

The history of urbanism in Japan begins with the building of the capital city of Nara in the early eighth century A.D. Both Nara and its successor Kyoto, built late in the same century, are examples of a phenomenon currently imagined to be peculiar to highly developed technological systems like our own – the 'instant city.' They were architectural expressions of the centralization of political and economic power and were created by fiat on the plan of the capital of T'ang China.

By the Tokugawa Period (1615–1868) with which we are here concerned, there were hundreds of castle towns, post towns, shrine and temple towns, marketing centers, and port towns, many of them scattered along the great highways which served to connect the geographical and political fragments making up

[1] As others who have worked in the documentary sources of the closing period of the Tokugawa can testify, the foreign scholar inevitably incurs debts among his Japanese colleagues which can be acknowledged but not repaid. I should like to express my deepest gratitude to Professor Nakano Takashi of the Tōkyō Kyōiku University, who unwittingly led me into the investigation and subsequently provided characteristically sensible advice. For invaluable assistance in locating and securing the materials on Tennōji, I should like to thank Mr Enju Reiichirō, Mr Tokoro Mitsuo, and Miss Asai Junko, all of the Reference Library of the Ministry of Education, Mr Kanai Madoka of the University of Tokyo's Historiographical Institute, and Professor Hirai Naofusa of the Department of Shinto, Kokugakuin University, Tokyo. For equally essential assistance with the Nishinomiya materials, I must express my debt to Professor Yagi Akihiro of Kōbe University, the members of the staff of the Nishinomiya City Office responsible for the compiling and writing of the history of that city, and Mr Matsuoka Takashi, an *amateur* of local history. (All names are given in the Japanese order, surname first.)

This paper was read originally at a conference sponsored by the Wenner–Gren Foundation in the summer of 1964. For financial assistance, I am indebted to the Wenner–Gren Foundation for Anthropological Research, the Faculty Research Grants Committee of Cornell University, the Comparative Studies of Cultural Change, Department of Anthropology, Cornell University (Contract AID/csd–296 with the Agency for International Development), and the United States Educational Commission in Japan. I alone am responsible for the interpretations made of the materials.

the country. There were in this period three great cities as well: Edo, capital of the *shōgun* with a population of about one million; Kyoto, capital of the Emperors with a population ranging up to one-half million; and Osaka, commercial and trade center, 'kitchen of the world,' with a population between three and four hundred thousand.

Assuming the term 'preindustrial city' to have some utility, I suggest it to be a convenient designation for any urban concentration of a preindustrial society, for I find it difficult to believe that there really are any substantial number of ways in which 'preindustrial cities' are a homogeneous phenomenon. In any event, it is now possible to put into the record some scattered demographic information on Tokugawa Japan. These data have direct bearing upon a variety of questions of some importance.

What was the size of the family and the household in the townsmen's (*chōnin*) quarters of these towns and cities? Were they the large households so often imagined in today's 'invented history' of the period or were they rather more like the 'modern' family and household in respect to size? What was the structure of the residence-unit and how does it compare with that of contemporary Japan? The issue of invented history is an interesting one which cannot detain us here. By it I mean simply that current explanations of any contemporary phenomenon often are made in terms of an imagined past condition from which change is believed to have occurred. That this procedure often falsifies the past in an effort to render the present more readily comprehensible cannot be denied.[2]

How stable was the population of the wards of town and city in Tokugawa Japan?[3] If population turnover proves to be high, how shall we interpret the common view that the wards were village-like in quality as well as structure? Dore is quite right when he writes:[4]

In the Tokugawa period, the towns had something of the same system of formal neighborhood relations as the country. The small wards into which Tokyo is still divided had their origin in the Edo of Tokugawa times. They exercised a certain measure of self-government albeit under the distant supervision of samurai magistrates, and as such their organization resembled that of the villages.

Bellah, drawing a parallel between the ward organization of Tokugawa cities and the barrio system in Latin America, writes in a similar vein:[5]

Even in the cities a strong particularistic nexus of relationships was maintained for purposes of social control. The city only to a limited extent represented a new form of

---

[2] See the engaging paper by Benet, *The ideology of the rural–urban continuum* (1963), on the fallacious nature of the standard presentation of the historical relations of urban centers and rural regions in the United States. See also Wade, *The urban frontier* (1959).

[3] See above, Hammel, Chapter 14, pp. 343–348, for a brief account of the significance of population turnover in sixteenth-century Serbia.

[4] Dore, *City life in Japan* (1958): 255.

[5] Bellah, *Tokugawa religion* (1957): 43.

social organization, that connected with the market and a differentiated economy. For many purposes it was merely a congeries of 'villages' in close geographical contiguity.

I shall try to deal with an issue raised by neither of the two authors cited because it is not central to their argument, and shall offer the following proposition: The structuring of the urban ward of Tokugawa times along the lines of village organization was not, as is so often mistakenly assumed, simply the natural outgrowth of the village-like quality of the units making up an urban agglomeration, but an administrative response to an incredibly high rate of population turnover. I shall also suggest that the relative stability of the *total* population figures for the wards produces the illusion of stability of residence within the wards, an assumption at great variance with the facts.[6]

THE SHŪMON ARATAME CHŌ

Since the Tokugawa government was dedicated to the proposition that the good society was the stable society, its agents at the local level directed the most intense scrutiny at the residents of the unit for which they held administrative responsibility. One of the means by which periodic checks on the population were made was the *ninbetsu aratame* (population inquiry), which provided the model for the later *shūmon aratame chō* and *shūmon ninbetsu chō*. In as much as our data are drawn from these documents, it is necessary to say something about their intent and their quality.[7]

The shūmon aratame chō ('Registers of the Investigation of Religious Sects') and the shūmon ninbetsu chō ('Census Registers by Religious Sect') are simply variants of a form of registration originally instituted in 1616 in connection with the suppression of Christianity and revised in 1626.[8] Two appointed officials were required to conduct an investigation of the religious affiliations of all persons living in a village or ward, whose head (*shōya*) endorsed the report as an accurate accounting of the residents of his unit. This accounting required that every household list its Buddhist temple affiliation, a development which greatly affected the fortunes of that religion in Japan. Prior to the instituting of these registers, the poor farmer, the small merchant, and the servant seem not to have had any regular temple affiliation. Now every man was to demonstrate that he was not a Christian but a good Buddhist. With the new requirement many joined the great popular sect of Shin Buddhism whose regulations were simple and whose fees were modest. Furthermore, early registers show that while in the early seventeenth century the members of one family often did not

[6] Compare Robert J. Smith, *Aspects of mobility in pre-industrial Japanese cities* (1963); Taeuber, *Urbanization and population change in the development of modern Japan* (1960).

[7] Here I draw heavily on the paper by Naganuma (1929).

[8] Hayami has argued that the latter were *originally* concerned with the labor services of the agricultural population: see Hayami, *The population at the beginning of the Tokugawa period* (1967).

belong to the same temple, later in the century all members of a given family listed the same temple affiliation. What was at first established as an administrative system later becomes the custom of the land.

Around 1638 the persecutions of the Christians became increasingly severe and the Tokugawa government undertook to ferret out the concealed Christians in an effort to extirpate the religion. With the formal adoption of the national seclusion policy (*sakoku*) in 1639, a variety of other steps was taken with a view to uncovering Christian converts and forcing them to recant. In 1640 a board of inquiry, the *shūmon aratame* (Investigation of Sects) was established in Edo and in 1664 all feudal lords (*daimyō*), whose income was estimated by the central government to be in excess of 10,000 *koku* of rice, were ordered to institute analogous offices in their fiefs.[9]

Among the various measures undertaken against the Christians we are here concerned only with the registers (shūmon aratame chō) themselves. What had been devised as a means of checking on the religious affiliation of the population soon became a census register of commoners. The registers also were aimed at identifying a variety of people with irregular status: renegade *samurai* (the *rōnin*, members of the warrior class with neither fixed fealty nor residence), criminals, and floaters without passports for travel or certificates permitting change of residence.

In one of the volumes, dated 1760, which we have used in our analysis of Tennōji (see Appendix), the following series of introductory notices appears. They are (1) the decree of 1664 establishing the registers in this form, (2) the admonition appended by the 'mayor' (*nanushi*) of the ward to heed the decree, (3) report of action taken by the nanushi, the 'head' (shōya) and two 'elders' (*toshiyori*), and (4) a notice of compliance signed by all the Buddhist priests of those temples whose parishioners' names appear in the register:

Notice

25th day, 11th month, 1664

Although Christianity is prohibited there appear to be people who have continued its propagation, so that it is not yet extinct. From this time on it is required that officers be appointed to inquire into dubious individuals and to be ever watchful lest there be suspicious activities among households in this region. You will be held responsible for negligence if someone outside your territory discovers that Christianity still exists in it.

The *nanushi* ('mayors') and *gonin-gumi* (five-man groups) should be informed that Christianity was once practiced here, as has earlier been announced in a warning on the public notice-boards. If anyone is opposed to this edict and is discovered by others, or if you know of their opposition and fail to report it, you will be punished, as has often been previously announced. Examine everyone carefully.

Of late there has been much loose talk about how to detect those who believe in Christianity, with the result that instead of giving it up the believers conceal themselves more thoroughly. Therefore, investigate them with no pity and capture them.

Addendum: Those who detect Christians will be rewarded, as has been announced previously.

[9] See Sansom, *History of Japan* (1963) 3: 42.

Third month, 1760

You must resolutely obey what has been proclaimed above. Farmers, tenants, all kinds of servants, mountain priests, strolling flute players, itinerant priests, and acolytes must be investigated with regard to their religious beliefs and all registered. Report immediately priests whose schools are dubious and anyone whose behavior is suspicious. Remember that you will be severely punished if you hide them, should they later be discovered by someone else. Those who make false report of others will also be punished. The *shūmon ninbetsu chō* should be presented at the end of the third month of every year. So far as servants are concerned, you must keep their guardian's certificates (*uke-jō*) as well as the certificates of the temples to which they belong, no matter where they may come from.

Naitō Jūemon

Third month, 1760

We respectfully accept this proclamation. We have examined all the farmers large and small, temples, shrines, and their disciples, and registered them. We submit the register to you with the seals of the main temples (*danna-dera*) affixed. In my superintendence there is no one who has converted to Christianity. If mistakes in the registers are found or if there are any omissions from the registers, we admit the fault and will accept any kind of punishment. As proof and guarantee we hereby affix our signature and seal.

Naitō Jūemon
Settsu, Tojo-gun, Tennōji-mura
Shōya Gorobei
Toshiyori Jinzaemon
Toshiyori Kanbei

Postscript: We hereby affirm that these people have been members of our temples for generations and we submit herewith newly sealed registers. If there is anyone here who believes in the proscribed religion, we will present ourselves anywhere to take responsibility for them. As proof and guarantee we hereby affix our signature and seal. [There are appended the seals of a number of priests, each as guarantor for his own temple.]

It would appear that the registry system was generally more stringently enforced in urban than in rural areas, probably because of the mobility of the population of the towns and cities. As the system became better organized, the central government realized its possibilities and a 1726 edict established a national census of commoners to be conducted every six years. Until 1776 the registers in many districts were taken on an annual basis, and a report of totals by category of residents of ward or village submitted to the authorities every sixth year. After 1776, in the wards with which we are dealing, the volumes of the census are kept by ward, subdivided by Buddhist sect, so that what was earlier simply one catalog of all households of a ward later becomes groupings of the households by their sect of affiliation. This latter style of register persisted until the opening of the Meiji period in 1868, when the modern system of household registers (*koseki-chō*) was introduced.

I have dwelt on the origins and development of the shūmon aratame chō in some detail as it is vital to establish the accuracy of this major source of information on household size. While there is some local variation in enumeration, manner of recording entries, and categories of persons not reported, there is sufficient uniformity to permit comparison of registers from all parts of the country throughout the Tokugawa period.[10] Certainly it was the intent of the government to have available a head-count of people actually resident in a given place. Unlike the modern koseki-chō, which do not enumerate the actual residents of a place, the shūmon aratame chō offer what was intended to be a population census. The enumerations found in them, therefore, more nearly reflect the facts of population composition and movement than do the post-Meiji registers.

Kaempfer, whose descriptions of the highways and cities of Japan in the seventeenth century are well known, was interested in the organization of the wards of Nagasaki. In discussing the duties of the officials of these 'streets' as he called them, he makes several references to the population registers which they were required to maintain:

The otona...keeps books and registers, wherein he enters, what persons are born in the street, how many die, or marry, or go a-travelling, or leave the street, as also what new inhabitants come in, along with their names, birth, religion, trade, and so on.[11]

The 'secretary' is said to be responsible for maintaining all manner of records...

such as, the list of all the houses in the street, and of their Inhabitants, along with their names, age, trade, religion, and so on, a book, wherein are enter'd the names of all the persons that die in the street...a register book containing what passports have been issued out of his office, with the names of the persons to whom they were granted, the business which call'd them abroad, the time of their departure, and their return...[12]

He closes with the observation that in the last month of every year, the 'Street's-messenger' performs the 'hito-aratame':

...that is, he takes down in writing the names of all the inhabitants of every house, old and young, with the time and place of their birth, and the...religion of the land-lords. Women are only counted in this inquisition, and 'tis added to the list how many there are.[13]

Nagasaki was, to be sure, something of a special case, for the coming and going of foreign vessels, as well as the continuing presence of foreigners, put local authorities on the strictest guard against unauthorized intercourse between them and the Japanese, such an anathema was Christianity. Kaempfer also has an account of the street-by-street check of residents upon the occasion of the departure of a Dutch or a Chinese ship, noting how the names of the inhabitants of each dwelling are read out. Clearly these population registers were kept current with a view to continuous use, at least in Nagasaki. At another place in his journals,[14] he comments on the strictness with which the registers of Kyoto were kept. The composition of the registers is simple, direct and informative. The residents of a given house are grouped, each identified by name, age, and in terms of the following list of categories:

[10] See below, Hayami, Chapter 18, pp. 474–475, for a detailed discussion of the weaknesses in the registers.   [11] Kaempfer, *The history of Japan* (1727) I: 279.
[12] Kaempfer (1727) I: 281.   [13] Kaempfer (1727) I: 287.
[14] Kaempfer (1727): I 486 ff.

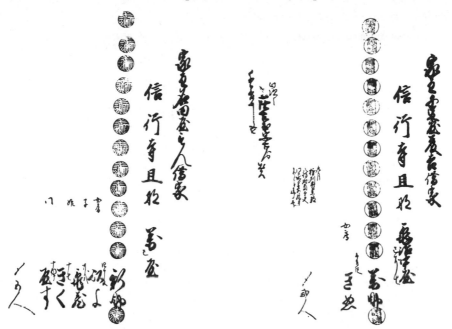

Fig. 17.1   Nishinomiya, Hama-kubo-chō: two pages from the register of 1821

Left page	Right page
Tenant of the Landlord *Nadaya Mon*	Tenant of the Landlord *Senzokuyō Tokichi*
Parishioners of *Shingyō* Temple	Parishioners of *Shingyō* Temple
Yorozuya [House-name]	*Kameji-no-nakaya* [House-name]
[head] *Shinsuke* (born in the year of the serpent, 48 years old)	[head] *Hansuke* (born in the year of the serpent, 1785)
wife *Iyo*. 49	wife *Kinu* (born in the year of the horse, 1786)
son *Kamezo*. 28	In September, married in as a bride from
daughter *Kiku*. 17	Banshū, —————— County, Village of
daughter *Yasu*. 10	Yawata, —————— .
Total: 5 persons	Total: 2 persons

1	Relationship to house-head	Expressed as a kin-term
2	*genin*	Servant sometimes given as *genan*, male servant, and *gejō* female servant
3	*dōke*	Co-resident, an ambiguous category which is discussed below
4	*inkyo*	A retired family member, i.e. a family member who has withdrawn from active participation in household affairs, usually at the age of sixty
5	*dōshinsha* or *deshi*	Acolyte or disciple (Buddhist)
6	*ama*	Nun (Buddhist)

Two sample household listings follow:

Sawaraya (house-name)		
Chōbei	35	Head of house
Tone	27	Wife
Ishimatsu	3	Son
Kane	newborn	Daughter
Tami	62	Mother
Jirōbei	16	*genan* (male servant)
Kō	22	*gejō* (female servant)
Sumiyoshiya (house-name)		
Jihei	50	Head of house
Sato	19	Daughter
Chōjirō	33	*dōke* (co-resident)
Kin	26	Chōjirō's wife
Awa	14	*gejō* (female servant)

These are our data. For each household we have the name, age, and relation to house-head of every resident. In scattered registers annotations appear concerning births, deaths, and migration, but for the most part the fact of movement must be deduced by a matching of registers for consecutive years. I shall present below an analysis of the scale of movement suggested by matching by name all households of a given ward for a run of years over a period of time, yielding a running tally of residential continuity and turnover.

THE DATA

The registers are from two wards in each of two urban communities and are of two kinds – those of the house-owners (*iemochi*) and those of the renters/tenants (*shakuya*). The scope of the data may be shown in a summary chart:

Name of community	Name of ward	Category of register	No. of registers	Span of years
Nishinomiya	Hama-kubo-chō	House-owners	12	1771–1866
Nishinomiya	Hama-kubo-chō	Renters/tenants	10	1771–1868
Nishinomiya	Hama-issai-chō[15]	House-owners and Renters/tenants combined	6	1713–1774
Nishinomiya	Hama-issai-chō	House-owners	7	1784–1861
Nishinomiya	Hama-issai-chō	Renters/tenants	5	1787–1861
Tennōji	Kubo-machi	House-owners	36	1757–1858
Tennōji	Kubo-machi	Renters/tenants	36	1757–1858
Tennōji	Horikoshi-machi	House-owners	36	1757–1858
Tennōji	Horikoshi-machi	Renters/tenants	36	1757–1858

This represents 164 annual registers from four wards for a period of 156 years (1713–1868) with a complete enumeration of the residents of 9,973 households.

[15] One of this series of listings is printed in full, see below, Nakane, Chapter 19, pp. 534–543 and analysed in detail by Laslett, above, Chapter 1, pp. 52–62, 74–85.

ANALYSIS OF REGISTERS

Two of the wards are located in what is now Nishinomiya-shi (city),[16] lying on the northern coast of the Inland Sea, midway between Osaka to the east and Kobe to the west on the island of Honshu. In the earliest of the registers it is called Nishinomiya-mura (village), although it was already a town. Not until the middle of the Tokugawa period does it officially become Nishinomiya-chō (town). This detail of the community's history is of some importance because it is my contention that for the entire period of the registers Nishinomiya was indeed a town. Why, then, was it called a village? In the time of Hideyoshi, at the establishment of the four-class system of Tokugawa Japan (warrior, farmer, artisan and merchant, in descending order, with the nobility and the outcastes at either extreme), there appears to have been some effort made to classify as much as possible of the population of the country as either warriors (the small ruling group) or farmers (the largest class, viewed as the only productive class of the governed). There was little place in the system for either artisans or merchants, and throughout the period the latter were defined as a purely parasitic class. The logic of the classification of the registers was unassailable: since farmers live in villages, the simplest means of achieving the division of society into two major groups was to classify virtually all towns (*chō*) as villages (*mura*). This meant that there were, by administrative fiat, few people classified as townsmen (*chōnin*) and thus the agricultural village (*nōson*) population is proportionally exaggerated in the records.

Historical materials relating to the second community, Tennōji, are extremely scarce.[17] Like Nishinomiya it was designated a village (mura) in early Tokugawa, but appears to have been much more than that, for it lies only two miles to the south of the Osaka castle, well within the boundaries of that great city. Sansom[18] remarks that the castle towns of this region were less important than the:

...expanded village in the environs of Osaka. These ancient rural settlements were spread over a large area in the provinces of Settsu, Kawachi, and Izumi, and, being separated by only short distances from one another, they tended to coalesce and form an urban conglomeration...country towns, such as Hirano, Tennōji, Sumiyoshi, and Sakai, developed close relations and towards the end of the [seventeenth] century had coalesced to form the great national market of which Osaka was the axis.

In the following pages are given tables which show complete information on the size of families and households in the four wards. The data are ungrouped, i.e. figures are given for each of the 164 registers over the 156 years covered in the study. Some comments on a few of the terms used are in order here: 'quasi-family members' in Tables 17.1 and 17.3 to 17.9 include all individuals listed in the censuses for whom a kin-relationship to the house-head is not indicated

---

[16] For a detailed history of Nishinomiya, see Uozumi (1960).
[17] One notable exception is the study by Sasaki (1967).
[18] Sansom (1963) 3: 112.

(servants, co-residents, and other non-kin); 'status unknown' in these same tables includes those individuals for whom no identifying term is given at all; 'family members' in all the tables which follow include only those individuals for whom a kin-relationship with the house-head is indicated.[19]

Table 17.1 presents a breakdown of the registers by ward and by category (whether house-owner, renter/tenant, or combined), showing the average family and household sizes. Although there is no doubt an under-reporting of young children, the totals reveal residential units of very small average size. The smallest figure is that of 2.9 persons per family of renters/tenants in the Nishinomiya ward of Hama-issai-chō in the period 1787–1861; the largest is the household size (4.5) of the combined registers of that same community in the period 1713–1774. In no case is the size of the average household unit markedly greater than that of the average family unit of the same community. (Detailed data are presented in Tables 17.3 to 17.9.) The average size of the 9,973 households in these registers is 3.9.[20]

In Table 17.2 is shown the total number of family and household units having a given number of residents. Of the 9,973 residence units in our registers, the largest household (and there is only one of these) had sixteen members. Grouping of the data presented in this table, and in Tables 17.10 to 17.21, will be found in Table 17.22. The contention expressed in the title of this chapter is clearly borne out in respect to size of residential units. For the entire period of 156 years and for the 9,973 units appearing in the registers, 96.6 % of the families had seven members or less. Neither was the large household a feature of these town and city wards, for 93.6 % of the households had seven or fewer residents. Single-person households account for an astonishing 16.5 % of the total appearing in all the registers.

Comparison of these figures with more recent data on number of persons per household is also possible. Toda,[21] citing the 1920 Census, reports that 95.4 % of all households in Japan had seven members or less. For Tokyo and Osaka in the same year, households with seven members or less accounted for 88.1 % and 90.6 %, respectively. In a study done in 1956 and 1957, Koyama[22] reports that 97.2 % of non-farm households in the former village of Komae, engulfed by the spreading Tokyo metropolis, had seven members or less, while 98.8 % of the households in a large Tokyo apartment complex had fewer than seven members.

Let us now turn to the question of residential stability. I have made an annual

---

[19] Elsewhere in this volume the practice has been to make a distinction between the conjugal family unit and other co-residents. In particular kin are not considered as part of the conjugal family. This means that as far as the 'family' is concerned, detailed comparison with these figures cannot be undertaken. In particular, see above, Laslett, Chapter 1, pp. 28–33.

[20] These figures should be compared with data from twentieth-century Japan: see below, Nakane, Chapter 19, pp. 531–532.

[21] Toda (1937): 217.

[22] Koyama (1960): 57.

tally of the rate of turnover of households (*not* individuals) for the registers of the Tennōji wards, Horikoshi-machi and Kubo-machi, for the years 1757 to 1858. The duration of households is analyzed separately for house-owners and for renter/tenants in Tables 17.23 and 17.24.[23] The nature of the registers is such that it is possible to trace succession; therefore, households of long duration may have had several heads as son succeeded father, widow took over upon the death of husband, etc. It is not possible, however, in the case of single-person households to determine whether the individual moved away or died. A word of explanation is in order concerning the somewhat cumbersome double entries under each category in Table 17.23. We do not have complete consecutive runs of registers for these wards, but the registers for only 36 of the 102 years between 1757 and 1858. In each tabulation in the odd-numbered columns (labeled 'Minimum'), I have shown the number of households of a given number of years' duration as actually found in the scattered registers available. In the even-numbered columns (labeled 'Maximum') I have shown the number of households of a given number of years' duration, calculating the maximum number of years in which they theoretically could have appeared if there were a register available for every one of the 102 years.

For example, we do have the registers for 1757 and 1760, but not for the two intervening years. For any given household appearing in the 1757 register, but not in the 1760 register, the 'Minimum' duration would be one year. The 'Maximum' possible duration, however, would be calculated at three years, since it is theoretically possible that this household would have appeared also in the registers for 1758 and 1759, only to drop out in 1760. The truth probably lies somewhere between the two, and I would guess that the former underestimates actual duration, while the latter overestimates it.

The evidence for a very high degree of turnover in these Tennōji wards accords nicely with the findings of Yokoyama[24] for a ward in Kyoto for the period 1786–1867. Yokoyama found that of the 343 households listed in the registers of the ward Koromo-no-tana-chō during this 82-year period, 70 % appeared for five years or less and 87 % for ten years or less, while five households (1.5 %) persisted throughout the entire period. In Tennōji's two wards, 1,095 households appear in the 102-year period. Taking our 'Maximum' figures, 44.7 % appeared for five years or less; 60.1 % for ten years or less; twelve households (1.1 %) persisted throughout the entire period.

The figures given in Tables 17.23 and 17.24 show that the duration of house-owner households is very much greater than that of the renters/tenants. Using the 'Maximum' figures for Horikoshi-machi, we see that whereas no renter/

[23] For further information on the durability of households in Tokugawa Japan, see below, Hayami, Chapter 18, pp. 513–515. Compare Blayo's analysis of the development of 184 conjugal households in the French village of Grisy-Suisnes, above, Chapter 9, pp. 261–264. See also Hammel's analysis of population turnover in sixteenth-century Serbia, above, Chapter 14, pp. 343–344, 348.

[24] For further details see Yokoyama (1949) and Robert J. Smith (1963): 419–20.

tenant household has a span greater than fifty years, nine house-owner house-holds (9.2 % of the total) persist throughout the entire 102 years. In Kubo-machi the story is much the same; only one renter/tenant household has a span of more than fifty years, while only three house-owner households (1.6 % of the total) persist throughout the entire 102 years. I have not tabulated the Nishinomiya wards, but careful inspection of the registers suggests that the situation was essentially like that of Tennōji and Kyoto.

IMPLICATIONS

The outcome is clear. These wards were far from stable communities. When one is reminded that it is *household*, not *individual* mobility which is under considera-tion, the implications can be seen even more clearly. The people who lived in these communities and the officials responsible for their administration were all exposed to a social environment of constantly shifting composition. Although the continuity of the house-owners is more marked than that of the renters, even they move as households with great frequency. The 'Maximum' median span of households of house-owners in Horikoshi-machi was only seven years; in Kubo-machi it was only seventeen years. The renter/tenant households in both wards for this same period had a span of three and four years respectively. The average 'Maximum' duration was in every case higher than the median case, but was only 27.2 years at the longest (for the house-owners of Kubo-machi). The median 'Maximum' duration was only seven years for households of all types.

Faced with such rates of in- and out-migration, it is hardly surprising that the administrative structure of the urban wards was based on the village prototype. Only through incessant checking on residents and frequent enumeration could the Tokugawa government retain a degree of control over the population of the cities. That the administrators were faced not merely with a declining or rising population is evident. If we take the overall population figures for the four wards under consideration we find that even the variation in these figures does not reveal with any clarity the fluidity of the actual composition of the wards. When it is further stressed that the individuals enumerated in one annual census of a ward may be almost entirely replaced within the decade, the scale of the problem faced by the Tokugawa government can be better appreciated.

CONCLUSIONS

I do not know that the size of the family and household was equally small in urban communities in the pre-industrial periods of other societies, nor am I cer-tain that their rates of turnover were so extraordinarily high. For the Japanese case, however, it is possible to offer some generalisations.

The situation which I have outlined here had, I think, become typical of the wards of city-dwelling commoners in Japan's towns and cities by the early eighteenth century. At least three features of the system strongly predisposed the Japanese to swift and easy urbanization on the 'early industrial' model. First, commercial and small manufacturing endeavors were, well before the 1870s and 1880s, already in the hands of small households with small-family nuclei made possible by the general practice of single-heir inheritance. Whether expressed through primogeniture, ultimogeniture, or 'adopted husband' marriage (so that the daughter of a house is used to guarantee continuity of the line through adoption of a husband for her who takes her family name and assumes the status of legitimate heir), it was the custom to select only one child as successor to the name and property, and custodian of the ancestral tablets of the house. The first Meiji civil code simply regularized this custom by giving preference before the law to first-son succession.

Second, the small size of the residential unit appears to have facilitated mobility, or at least not to have inhibited it. Our data, as well as Yokoyama's,[25] show quite clearly that urban mobility was not limited to single individuals, and that families moved in and out of cities as units well before the 'modern period'.[26] Further analysis may reveal whether they were simply circulating about the city or back and forth between the city and the countryside. Wherever their residents came from and whatever their destination, the fluidity of the composition of the wards cannot be denied.[27]

[25] Yokoyama (1949).
[26] In this connection, the discussion by Dickinson, *The West European city* (1962): 171–83, of one instance of a high rate of turnover of population as a feature of modern urbanism is instructive. Writing of Rotterdam, which had a population of over 600,000 in 1939, he says of two new districts of that city: 'These new districts are occupied by people of low income, who find the rent of their former dwelling too high...The residents in these new outer districts are not 'settled in.' On the contrary, a high proportion shift quickly and there are many removals after a short period of those who seek cheaper and better houses in a more desirable neighbourhood. Thus, the new district of Bergpolder at the end of 1934, scarcely one and a half years after the construction of the first houses, had already changed many of the tenants. Of 2,552 dwellings, in October 1934 no less than 380 had second, and 37 third, tenants, and there had been no less than 464 removals! Of the removed families, only one-third remained in the district, a sixth left Rotterdam (for a neighbouring sub-urban district)...In Rotterdam on the average there were 50,000 removals annually. Without exaggeration, we can say that a third of the total population is involved in this 'nomadic' movement. This mobility, however, in the outer districts is greatest in the tenement districts where there is attachment neither to dwelling nor to neighbourhood' (1961: 176). 'The movement of population indicates that there is a lack of attachment to home or neighborhood. A habit of moving from one house to another develops. This psychological feature is especially marked in the new and monotonous, characterless multi-storeyed apartment blocks. That type of dwelling does not foster any attraction for hearth, home or neighborhood...This aspect of our present urban society, in effect a sort of 'modern nomadism,' is one that deserves very thorough attention from social psychologists; it is tied up with many of the problems of neurosis and the family...' (1961: 183).
[27] Taeuber, *The population of Japan* (1958): 27 makes the interesting observation that: 'The urbanization of the population increased in the modern period, but the great city was not a product of that period. And movements of surplus youth from the rural areas to the cities were adjustments of population to resources and employment opportunities that ante-dated

Third, I would maintain that the nature of Japanese kinship terminology also has important bearing on the ease with which transition to the urban–industrial style was made. Japanese terminology, as first recorded in the tenth century A.D., was and remains bilateral.[28] 'Yankee' in type, it differs from contemporary American usage in only one important particular; there is an age distinction in sibling terms. Members of these small families, then, identified an extremely limited range of kin by specific terms and 'cousin' usages appear to have been as ambiguous in eighteenth-century Japan as they are in contemporary Britain and the United States. In the registers with which we have dealt, the number of kin terms which appears is extremely small and all terms used are of the modern Japanese bilateral system.

The Japanese were early possessed of what some writers have claimed is a kin terminology closely associated with modern urbanized industrial societies with highly developed commerce, attenuation of kin ties, high rates of mobility, and increasingly universalistic relationships. The terminology itself is far older than the development of such a state of affairs in Japan, suggesting that caution must be exercised in proposing an inevitable connection between the two. Nevertheless, its prior existence would, I feel, have greatly facilitated the adjustment of the family to the changes required at the start of Japan's emergence as a modern state. Our data show that many of the features of that country's emergence, so often ascribed to the Meiji period (1868–1912), were in fact well developed by the early part of the eighteenth century.

modern industrialization by some centuries.' A very useful discussion of a local situation in the Tokugawa period is by Hanley, *Population trends and economic development in Tokugawa Japan* (1968).

[28] For further details see Robert J. Smith, *Japanese kinship terminology* (1962 i) and *Stability in Japanese terminology* (1962 ii).

Appendix

Table 17.1 *Registers of all categories in all wards, 1713–1868: size and composition of family and households*

Ward	No. of house-holds	Family members				Quasi-family members				Status unknown			All household residents			
		Male	Female	Total	No. per house	Male	Female	Total	No. per house	Male	Female	Total	Male	Female	Total	No. per house
Combined[a]																
Nishinomiya, Hama-issai-chō (1713–1774)	841	1,793	1,814	3,607	4.282	112	30	142	0.169	20	22	42	1,925	1,866	3,791	4.508
House-owners																
Nishinomiya, Hama-kubo-chō (1771–1868)	1,176	2,128	2,252	4,380	3.675	199	261	460	0.391	31	43	74	2,358	2,556	4,914	4.178
Nishinomiya, Hama-issai-chō (1784–1861)	707	1,204	1,364	2,568	3.632	78	99	177	0.250	13	13	26	1,295	1,476	2,771	3.919
Tennōji, Kubo-machi (1757–1858)	1,729	3,244	2,883	6,127	3.543	648	400	1,048	0.606	2	1	3	3,894	3,284	7,178	4.151
Tennōji, Horikoshi-machi (1757–1858)	805	1,610	1,548	3,158	3.922	534	294	828	1.028	3	1	4	2,147	1,843	3,990	4.956
Totals	4,417	8,186	8,047	16,233	3.675	1,459	1,054	2,513	0.568	49	58	107	9,694	9,159	18,853	4.268
Renters/tenants																
Nishinomiya, Hama-kubo-chō (1771–1868)	1,615	2,325	2,544	4,869	3.015	165	191	356	0.220	47	56	103	2,537	2,791	5,328	3.299
Nishinomiya, Hama-issai-chō (1787–1861)	503	647	807	1,454	2.890	30	49	79	0.157	6	12	18	683	868	1,551	3.083
Tennōji, Kubo-machi (1757–1858)	1,119	1,862	1,780	3,642	3.254	54	52	106	0.094	1	1	2	1,917	1,833	3,750	3.351
Tennōji, Horikoshi-machi (1757–1858)	1,478	2,569	2,348	4,917	3.326	143	104	247	0.167	—	2	2	2,712	2,454	5,166	3.494
Totals	4,715	7,403	7,479	14,882	3.156	392	396	788	0.167	54	71	125	7,849	7,946	15,795	3.349
Grand totals	9,973	17,382	17,340	34,722	3.481	1,963	1,480	3,443	0.345	123	151	274	19,468	18,971	38,439	3.855

[a] No distinction is drawn in these registers between 'House-owners' (*iemochi*) and 'renters/tenants' (*shakuya*).

Table 17.2 Registers of all categories in all wards, 1713–1868: number of family members compared with number of residents per household

Ward		1	2	3	4	5	6	7	8	9	10	11	12	13	14	15	16	Total	%
											Number of persons								
Combined[a]																			
Nishinomiya, Hama-issai-chō (1713–1744)	Family (no.)	67	100	140	170	144	105	62	32	15	3	1	2	—	—	—	—	841	
	Household (no.)	59	82	141	163	150	107	70	38	15	9	3	3	1	—	—	—	841	
	Family (%)	8.0	11.9	16.6	20.2	17.1	12.5	7.4	3.8	1.8	0.4	0.1	0.2	—	—	—	—		100
	Household (%)	7.0	9.8	16.8	19.4	17.8	12.7	8.3	4.5	1.8	1.0	0.4	0.4	0.1	—	—	—		100
House-owners																			
Nishinomiya, Hama-kubo-chō (1771–1866)	Family (no.)	179	172	218	212	182	110	65	21	9	6	2	—	—	—	—	—	1,176	
	Household (no.)	140	156	206	198	177	128	90	41	16	12	7	2	3	—	—	—	1,176	
Hama-issai-chō (1784–1861)	Family (no.)	99	129	145	118	104	49	34	15	9	4	1	—	—	—	—	—	707	
	Household (no.)	80	125	131	119	102	67	45	15	11	7	5	1	—	—	—	—	707	
Tennōji, Kubo-machi (1757–1858)	Family (no.)	436	195	254	300	217	170	62	61	20	9	8	4	—	—	—	—	1,729	
	Household (no.)	343	148	217	289	255	192	107	80	59	25	8	6	—	—	—	—	1,729	
Horikoshi-machi (1757–1858)	Family (no.)	164	64	94	145	161	87	55	22	13	—	—	—	—	—	—	—	805	
	Household (no.)	163	31	51	106	113	102	98	55	37	23	13	4	5	1	2	1	805	
Totals	Family (no.)	878	560	711	775	664	416	216	119	51	19	4	4	—	—	—	—	4,417	
	Household (no.)	726	460	605	712	647	489	340	191	123	67	33	12	8	1	2	1	4,417	
	Family (%)	19.9	12.7	16.1	17.5	15.0	9.4	4.9	2.7	1.2	0.4	0.1	0.1	—	—	—	—		100
	Household (%)	16.5	10.4	13.7	16.1	14.6	11.1	7.7	4.3	2.8	1.54	0.73	0.27	0.18	0.02	0.04	0.02		100
Renters/tenants																			
Nishinomiya, Hama-kubo-chō (1771–1868)	Family (no.)	419	292	314	263	162	86	38	29	8	4	—	—	—	—	—	—	1,615	
	Household (no.)	352	291	303	273	165	107	55	34	23	7	2	3	—	—	—	—	1,615	
Hama-issai-chō (1787–1861)	Family (no.)	132	112	96	78	44	22	10	6	2	1	—	—	—	—	—	—	503	
	Household (no.)	120	104	89	88	50	27	14	6	4	1	—	—	—	—	—	—	503	
Tennōji, Kubo-machi (1757–1858)	Family (no.)	213	221	215	180	158	105	18	7	2	—	—	—	—	—	—	—	1,119	
	Household (no.)	191	224	216	174	163	113	28	7	2	1	—	—	—	—	—	—	1,119	
Horikoshi-machi (1757–1858)	Family (no.)	232	300	324	297	161	82	52	19	7	3	1	—	—	—	—	—	1,478	
	Household (no.)	194	284	316	312	182	89	64	23	9	4	1	—	—	—	—	—	1,478	
Totals	Family (no.)	996	925	949	818	525	295	118	61	19	8	1	—	—	—	—	—	4,715	
	Household (no.)	857	903	924	847	560	336	161	70	38	13	3	3	—	—	—	—	4,715	
	Family (%)	21.1	19.6	20.1	17.4	11.1	6.3	2.5	1.3	0.4	0.18	0.06	—	—	—	—	—		100
	Household (%)	18.2	19.1	19.6	18.0	11.9	7.1	3.4	1.5	0.80	0.28	0.06	0.06	—	—	—	—		100
Grand totals	Family (no.)	1,941	1,585	1,800	1,763	1,333	816	396	212	85	30	6	6	—	—	—	—	9,973	
	Household (no.)	1,642	1,445	1,670	1,722	1,357	932	571	299	176	89	39	18	9	1	2	1	9,973	
	Family (%)	19.5	15.9	18.0	17.7	13.4	8.2	3.9	2.08	0.9	0.3	0.06	0.06	—	—	—	—		100
	Household (%)	16.5	14.5	16.7	17.3	13.6	9.3	5.7	3.0	1.8	0.9	0.4	0.17	0.09	0.01	0.02	0.01		100

[a] No distinction is drawn in these registers between 'house-owner' (iemochi) and 'renter/tenants' (shakuya).

Table 17.3 *Nishinomiya, Hama-kubo-chō. Registers of the iemochi (house-owners), 1771–1866 : size and composition of family and household*

Year	No. of households	Family members				Quasi-family members				Status unknown			All household residents			
		Male	Female	Total	No. per house	Male	Female	Total	No. per house	Male	Female	Total	Male	Female	Total	No. per house
1771	113	257	225	482	4.265	33	33	66	0.584	5	7	12	295	265	560	4.955
1782	112	231	243	474	4.232	23	32	55	0.491	2	4	6	256	279	535	4.775
1786	106	208	203	411	3.877	23	27	50	0.471	7	5	12	238	235	473	4.462
1795	99	210	193	403	4.070	25	24	49	0.494	—	—	—	235	217	452	4.565
1806	100	176	188	364	3.640	13	13	26	0.260	1	4	5	190	205	395	3.950
1810	106	172	183	355	3.349	15	16	31	0.292	4	9	13	191	208	399	3.764
1816	101	164	193	357	3.534	9	23	32	0.316	4	3	7	177	219	396	3.920
1818	103	170	200	370	3.592	14	25	39	0.378	2	3	5	186	228	414	4.019
1822/3	97	162	188	350	3.575	11	21	32	0.322	—	1	1	173	210	383	3.910
1843/4	86	145	156	301	3.525	14	24	38	0.441	5	5	10	164	185	349	4.066
1865	74	112	137	249	3.364	10	10	20	0.270	1	2	3	123	149	272	3.675
1866	79	121	143	264	3.341	9	13	22	0.278	—	—	—	130	156	286	3.620
Totals	1,176	2,128	2,252	4,380	3.724	199	261	460	0.391	31	43	74	2,358	2,556	4,914	4.179

Table 17.4 *Nishinomiya, Hama-kubo-chō. Registers of the shakuya (renters/tenants), 1771–1868: size and composition of family and household*

Year	No. of households	Family members				Quasi-family members				Status unknown			All household residents			
		Male	Female	Total	No. per house	Male	Female	Total	No. per house	Male	Female	Total	Male	Female	Total	No. per house
1771	113	203	165	368	3.256	9	4	13	0.115	20	13	33	232	182	414	3.664
1781	135	222	221	443	3.281	9	9	18	0.133	3	4	7	234	234	468	3.466
1806	174	262	280	542	3.114	10	15	25	0.143	6	18	24	278	313	591	3.396
1810	165	252	255	507	3.072	17	18	35	0.212	5	6	11	274	279	553	3.351
1816	173	246	275	521	3.011	29	26	55	0.317	3	1	4	278	302	580	3.355
1819	172	238	277	515	2.994	20	21	41	0.238	1	—	1	259	298	557	3.238
1822/3	172	241	291	532	3.093	17	16	33	0.190	2	2	4	260	309	569	3.308
1843/4	209	271	316	587	2.805	31	32	63	0.283	2	2	4	304	350	654	3.108
1865	154	186	232	418	2.714	14	27	41	0.266	2	9	11	202	268	470	3.051
1868	148	204	232	436	2.945	9	23	32	0.216	3	1	4	216	256	472	3.189
Totals	1,615	2,325	2,544	4,869	3.015	165	191	356	0.220	47	56	103	2,537	2,791	5,328	3.299

Table 17.5 *Nishinomiya, Hama-issai-chō. Registers of all categories, 1713–1861: size and composition of family and household*

Year	No. of households	Family members				Quasi-family members				Status unknown			All household residents			
		Male	Female	Total	No. per house	Male	Female	Total	No. per house	Male	Female	Total	Male	Female	Total	No. per house
						Combined[a]										
1713	131[b]	291	296	587	4.480	62	9	71	0.537	5	4	9	358	309	667[b]	5.091
1733	136	297	300	597	4.389	7	3	10	0.073	6	5	11	310	308	618	4.544
1737	157	318	321	639	4.070	9	3	12	0.076	1	4	5	328	328	656	4.178
1744	138	315	298	613	4.442	4	2	6	0.043	—	2	2	319	302	621	4.500
1757	175	366	381	747	4.268	9	5	14	0.080	2	4	6	377	390	767	4.382
1774	104	206	218	424	4.076	21	8	29	0.278	6	3	9	233	229	462	4.442
Totals	841	1,793	1,814	3,607	4.289	112	30	142	0.169	20	22	42	1,925	1,866	3,791	4.508
						House-owners										
1784	108	200	211	411	3.805	13	5	18	0.166	2	5	7	215	221	436	4.037
1788	112	193	218	411	3.669	20	25	45	0.401	—	—	—	213	243	456	4.071
1792	109	195	217	412	3.779	9	16	25	0.229	—	—	—	204	233	437	4.009
1800	105	185	218	403	3.838	15	20	35	0.333	4	2	6	204	240	444	4.229
1820	97	138	180	318	3.278	7	12	19	0.195	2	—	2	147	192	339	3.495
1847	94	158	166	324	3.446	10	8	18	0.191	5	6	11	173	180	353	3.755
1861	82	135	154	289	3.524	4	13	17	0.207	—	—	—	139	167	306	3.731
Totals	707	1,204	1,364	2,568	3.632	78	99	177	0.250	13	13	26	1,295	1,476	2,771	3.919
						Renters/tenants										
1787	98	118	171	289	2.948	8	14	22	0.224	3	1	4	129	186	315	3.214
1792	109	140	177	317	2.908	4	10	14	0.128	1	—	1	145	187	332	3.045
1820	101	136	154	290	2.871	8	10	18	0.178	—	—	—	144	164	308	3.049
1847	103	139	160	299	2.902	5	4	9	0.087	2	9	11	146	173	319	3.097
1861	92	114	145	259	2.815	5	11	16	0.173	—	2	2	119	158	277	3.010
Totals	503	647	807	1,454	2.890	30	49	79	0.157	6	12	18	683	868	1,551	3.083

[a] No distinction is drawn in these registers between 'house-owners' (*iemochi*) and 'renters/tenants' (*shakuya*).
[b] This listing has also been used by Nakane, see below, Chapter 19, pp. 519, 521, 534–543 and by Laslett, above, Chapter 1, pp. 52–62, 74–85. The totals differ slightly.

Table 17.6 *Tennōji, Kubo-machi. Registers of the iemochi (house-owners), 1757–1858: size and composition of family and household*

Year	No. of house-holds	Family members				Quasi-family members				Status unknown			All household residents			
		Male	Female	Total	No. per house	Male	Female	Total	No. per house	Male	Female	Total	Male	Female	Total	No. per house
1757	55	92	79	171	3.109	18	16	34	0.618	—	1	1	110	96	206	3.745
1760	58	101	91	192	3.310	26	17	43	0.741	—	—	—	127	108	235	4.051
1761	58	108	89	197	3.396	28	18	46	0.793	—	—	—	136	107	243	4.189
1762	59	110	86	196	3.322	25	17	42	0.711	—	—	—	135	103	238	4.033
1763	58	110	87	197	3.396	23	17	40	0.689	—	—	—	133	104	237	4.086
1765	57	111	90	201	3.526	21	13	34	0.596	—	—	—	132	103	235	4.122
1766	57	110	91	201	3.526	24	16	40	0.701	—	—	—	134	107	241	4.228
1767	58	109	89	198	3.413	28	17	45	0.775	—	—	—	137	106	243	4.189
1784	51	95	87	182	3.568	35	19	54	1.058	—	—	—	130	106	236	4.627
1785	51	101	94	195	3.823	33	19	52	1.019	—	—	—	134	113	247	4.843
1788	51	93	85	178	3.490	35	24	59	1.180	—	—	—	128	109	237	4.647
1795	51	95	92	187	3.666	29	23	52	1.019	1	—	1	125	115	240	4.705
1797	54	104	92	196	3.629	32	17	49	0.907	—	—	—	136	109	245	4.537
1798	50	93	93	186	3.720	34	20	54	1.080	—	—	—	127	113	240	4.800
1802	50	95	92	187	3.740	32	23	55	1.100	—	—	—	127	115	242	4.840
1805	49	98	96	194	3.959	34	17	51	1.040	—	—	—	132	113	245	5.000
1806	51	96	96	192	3.764	29	22	51	1.000	1	—	1	126	118	244	4.784
1816	47	89	90	179	3.808	25	17	42	0.893	—	—	—	114	107	221	4.702

1817	47	93	91	184	3.914	22	16	38	0.808	—	—	—	115	107	222	4.723
1831	46	96	85	181	3.934	20	10	30	0.652	—	—	—	116	95	211	4.586
1834	48	104	94	198	4.125	15	8	23	0.479	—	—	—	119	102	221	4.604
1837	45	95	81	176	3.911	12	6	18	0.400	—	—	—	107	87	194	4.311
1838	46	93	77	170	3.695	8	6	14	0.304	—	—	—	101	83	184	4.000
1840	44	88	82	170	3.863	7	3	10	0.227	—	—	—	95	85	180	4.090
1843	43	80	72	152	3.534	5	3	8	0.186	—	—	—	85	75	160	3.720
1844	42	78	73	151	3.595	6	2	8	0.190	—	—	—	84	75	159	3.785
1847	42	75	59	134	3.190	4	3	7	0.166	—	—	—	79	62	141	3.357
1848	42	71	61	132	3.142	4	3	7	0.166	—	—	—	75	64	139	3.309
1849	39	70	61	131	3.358	4	1	5	0.128	—	—	—	74	62	136	3.487
1850	41	75	62	137	3.341	4	1	5	0.121	—	—	—	79	63	142	3.463
1851	39	75	59	134	3.435	5	1	6	0.153	—	—	—	80	60	140	3.589
1852	40	75	64	139	3.475	5	1	6	0.150	—	—	—	80	65	145	3.625
1854	42	72	70	142	3.380	4	1	5	0.119	—	—	—	76	71	147	3.500
1855	38	62	60	122	3.210	4	1	5	0.131	—	—	—	66	61	127	3.342
1856	40	65	58	123	3.075	4	1	5	0.125	—	—	—	69	59	128	3.200
1858	40	67	55	122	3.050	4	1	5	0.125	1	—	—	71	56	127	3.175
Totals	1,729	3,244	2,883	6,127	3.543	648	400	1,048	0.606	2	1	3	3,894	3,284	7,178	4.151

Table 17.7 *Tennōji, Kubo-machi. Registers of the shakuya (renters/tenants), 1757–1858: size and composition of family and household*

Year	No. of house-holds	Family members				Quasi-family members				Status unknown			All household residents			
		Male	Female	Total	No. per house	Male	Female	Total	No. per house	Male	Female	Total	Male	Female	Total	No. per house
1757	32	30	31	61	1.906	—	—	—	—	—	—	—	30	31	61	1.906
1760	33	40	39	79	2.393	—	—	—	—	—	—	—	40	39	79	2.393
1761	30	48	44	92	3.066	—	—	—	—	—	—	—	48	44	92	3.066
1762	31	47	50	97	3.129	—	—	—	—	—	—	—	47	50	97	3.129
1763	37	53	53	106	2.864	—	—	—	—	—	—	—	53	53	106	2.863
1765	35	45	48	93	2.657	—	—	—	—	—	—	—	45	48	93	2.657
1766	31	43	47	90	2.903	—	—	—	—	—	—	—	43	47	90	2.903
1767	28	37	48	85	3.035	1	—	1	0.035	—	1	1	38	49	87	3.107
1784	43	72	66	138	3.209	3	5	8	0.186	—	—	—	75	71	146	3.395
1785	39	67	59	126	3.230	1	3	4	0.102	—	—	—	68	62	130	3.333
1788	35	59	54	113	3.228	3	1	4	0.114	—	—	—	62	55	117	3.342
1795	42	66	57	123	2.928	6	4	10	0.238	—	—	—	72	61	133	3.166
1797	41	65	52	117	2.853	4	1	5	0.121	—	—	—	69	53	122	2.975
1798	44	72	50	122	2.772	1	2	3	0.068	—	—	—	73	52	125	2.840
1802	42	65	59	124	2.952	1	—	1	0.023	—	—	—	66	59	125	2.976
1805	51	78	84	162	3.176	2	3	5	0.098	1	—	1	81	87	168	3.294
1806	53	85	92	177	3.339	2	4	6	0.113	—	—	—	87	96	183	3.452
1816	27	55	44	99	3.666	6	5	11	0.407	—	—	—	61	49	110	4.074

1817	24	50	38	38	3.666	3	1	4	0.142	—	—	—	53	39	92	3.833
1831	20	27	25	52	2.600	3	3	6	0.300	—	—	—	30	28	58	2.900
1834	26	41	41	82	3.153	3	6	9	0.346	—	—	—	44	47	91	3.500
1837	18	36	36	72	4.000	1	1	2	0.111	—	—	—	37	37	74	4.111
1838	16	28	32	60	3.750	2	—	2	0.125	—	—	—	30	32	62	3.875
1840	23	45	40	85	3.695	1	—	1	—	—	—	—	45	40	85	3.695
1843	22	35	36	71	3.227	—	1	1	0.043	—	—	—	36	36	72	3.272
1844	26	45	49	94	3.615	2	2	4	0.038	—	—	—	45	50	95	3.653
1847	26	52	51	103	3.961	2	1	3	0.153	—	—	—	54	53	107	4.115
1848	30	57	59	116	3.866	1	—	1	0.100	—	—	—	59	60	119	3.966
1849	27	52	59	111	4.111	1	1	2	0.037	—	—	—	53	59	112	4.148
1850	28	53	54	107	3.821	1	1	2	0.071	—	—	—	54	55	109	3.892
1851	29	53	54	107	3.689	—	1	1	0.074	—	—	—	54	55	109	3.448
1852	24	48	47	95	3.958	1	—	1	0.041	1	—	—	48	48	96	4.000
1854	23	46	36	82	3.565	—	—	—	0.043	—	1	—	47	36	83	3.608
1855	22	44	45	89	4.045	—	—	—	—	—	—	—	44	45	89	4.045
1856	29	63	54	117	4.034	1	3	4	0.137	—	—	—	64	57	121	4.172
1858	32	60	47	107	3.343	2	3	5	0.156	—	—	2	62	50	112	3.500
Totals	1,119	1,862	1,780	3,642	3.254	54	52	106	0.094	1	1	2	1,917	1,833	3,750	3.351

Table 17.8 Tennōji, Horikoshi-machi. Registers of the iemochi (house-owners), 1757–1858: size and composition of family and household

Year	No. of households	Family members				Quasi-family members				Status unknown			All household residents			
		Male	Female	Total	No. per house	Male	Female	Total	No. per house	Male	Female	Total	Male	Female	Total	No. per house
1757	28	45	44	89	3.178	20	10	30	1.034	—	—	—	65	54	119	4.250
1760	24	44	36	80	3.333	16	11	27	1.080	—	—	—	60	47	107	4.458
1761	25	47	43	90	3.600	17	11	28	1.120	1	—	1	65	54	119	4.760
1762	25	46	41	87	3.480	15	6	21	0.840	—	—	—	61	47	108	4.320
1763	23	42	43	85	3.695	15	8	23	1.000	—	—	—	57	51	108	4.695
1765	22	46	38	84	3.818	19	11	30	1.363	—	—	—	65	49	114	5.181
1766	22	47	43	90	4.090	20	7	27	1.227	—	—	—	67	50	117	5.318
1767	22	48	44	92	4.181	18	10	28	1.272	1	1	2	67	55	122	5.545
1784	24	41	45	86	3.583	30	15	45	1.875	1	—	—	71	60	131	5.458
1785	25	40	43	83	3.320	25	17	42	1.680	1	—	1	66	60	126	5.040
1788	27	43	47	90	3.333	24	17	41	1.518	—	—	—	67	64	131	4.851
1795	21	37	45	82	3.904	33	17	50	2.380	—	—	—	70	62	132	6.285
1797	19	34	36	70	3.684	31	16	47	2.473	—	—	—	65	52	117	6.157
1798	19	33	38	71	3.736	33	18	51	2.684	—	—	—	66	56	122	6.421
1802	17	33	34	67	3.529	29	21	50	2.941	—	—	—	62	55	117	6.882
1805	18	36	35	71	3.789	28	19	47	2.611	—	—	—	64	54	118	6.555
1806	19	38	40	78	4.105	28	14	42	2.210	—	—	—	66	54	120	6.315

Year															
1816	19	33	39	72	3.789	27	17	44	2.315	—	—	—	60	56	116	6.105
1817	20	36	44	80	4.000	28	17	45	2.250	—	—	—	64	61	125	6.250
1831	22	42	42	84	3.819	27	14	41	1.863	—	—	—	69	56	125	5.681
1834	23	49	50	99	4.304	9	3	12	0.521	—	—	—	58	53	111	4.826
1837	24	50	48	98	4.083	8	4	12	0.500	—	—	—	58	52	110	5.583
1838	25	51	46	97	3.880	7	3	10	0.400	—	—	—	58	49	107	4.280
1840	26	52	52	104	4.000	7	3	10	0.384	—	—	—	59	55	114	4.384
1843	25	53	50	103	4.120	2	1	3	0.120	—	—	—	55	51	106	4.240
1844	23	50	50	100	4.347	7	3	10	0.434	—	—	—	57	53	110	4.782
1847	23	48	49	97	4.217	7	1	8	0.347	—	—	—	55	50	105	4.565
1848	21	46	48	94	4.476	1	—	1	0.047	—	—	—	47	48	95	4.523
1849	22	47	44	91	4.136	1	—	1	0.045	—	—	—	48	44	92	4.181
1850	20	48	40	88	4.400	1	—	1	0.050	—	—	—	49	40	89	4.450
1851	21	47	39	86	4.095	—	—	—	—	—	—	—	47	39	86	4.095
1852	22	49	39	88	4.000	—	—	—	—	—	—	—	49	39	88	4.000
1854	21	49	42	91	4.333	1	—	1	0.047	—	—	—	50	42	92	4.380
1855	22	52	42	94	4.272	—	—	—	—	—	—	—	52	42	94	4.272
1856	21	53	41	94	4.476	—	—	—	—	—	—	—	53	41	94	4.476
1858	25	55	48	103	4.120	—	—	—	—	—	—	—	55	48	103	4.120
Totals	805	1,610	1,548	3,158	3.922	534	294	828	1.028	3	1	4	2,147	1,843	3,990	4.956

Table 17.9 Tennōji, Horikoshi-machi. Registers of the shakuya (renters/tenants), 1757–1858: size and composition of family and household

Year	No. of households	Family members				Quasi-family members				Status unknown			All household residents			
		Male	Female	Total	No. per house	Male	Female	Total	No. per house	Male	Female	Total	Male	Female	Total	No. per house
1757	24	33	26	59	2.458	—	—	—	—	—	—	—	33	26	59	2.458
1760	48	72	66	138	2.875	1	1	2	0.041	—	—	—	73	67	140	2.916
1761	51	76	75	151	2.960	2	5	7	0.137	—	—	—	78	80	158	3.098
1762	46	72	66	138	3.000	2	1	3	0.065	—	—	—	74	67	141	3.065
1763	52	82	74	156	3.000	1	1	2	0.036	—	—	—	83	75	158	3.038
1765	40	73	46	119	2.975	1	1	2	0.050	—	1	1	74	48	122	3.050
1766	42	68	46	114	2.714	3	—	3	0.071	—	—	—	71	46	117	2.758
1767	43	73	51	124	2.883	1	2	3	0.069	—	1	1	74	54	128	2.976
1784	36	61	58	119	3.305	1	1	2	0.055	—	—	—	62	59	121	3.361
1785	39	62	71	133	3.410	1	1	2	0.051	—	—	—	63	72	135	3.461
1788	37	62	73	135	3.648	3	2	5	0.135	—	—	—	65	75	140	3.783
1795	38	72	69	141	3.710	7	1	8	0.210	—	—	—	79	70	149	3.921
1797	41	84	86	170	4.146	5	2	7	0.170	—	—	—	89	88	177	4.317
1798	43	87	85	172	4.000	7	2	9	0.209	—	—	—	94	87	181	4.209
1802	45	90	80	170	3.777	6	2	8	0.177	—	—	—	96	82	178	3.955
1805	56	112	98	210	3.750	6	2	8	0.142	—	—	—	118	100	218	3.892
1806	51	103	94	197	3.862	6	3	9	0.176	—	—	—	109	97	206	4.039

1816	49	107	78	185	3.775	4	4	8	0.163	—	—	—	111	82	193	3.938
1817	47	100	68	168	3.574	4	3	7	0.148	—	—	—	104	71	175	3.723
1831	43	62	67	129	3.000	10	3	13	0.302	—	—	—	72	70	142	3.302
1834	49	78	69	147	3.000	11	3	14	0.285	—	—	—	89	72	161	3.285
1837	40	69	69	138	3.450	7	5	12	0.300	—	—	—	76	74	150	3.750
1838	39	63	56	119	3.051	2	3	5	0.123	—	—	—	65	59	124	3.179
1840	41	71	61	132	3.219	2	4	6	0.146	—	—	—	73	65	138	3.365
1843	30	54	52	106	3.500	4	5	9	0.300	—	—	—	58	57	115	3.833
1844	36	57	64	121	3.361	6	9	15	0.416	—	—	—	63	73	136	3.777
1847	34	62	61	123	3.617	3	5	8	0.235	—	—	—	65	66	131	3.852
1848	34	65	68	133	3.911	5	6	11	0.323	—	—	—	70	74	144	4.235
1849	35	58	60	118	3.371	2	4	6	0.171	—	—	—	60	64	124	3.542
1850	37	66	58	124	3.351	5	4	9	0.243	—	—	—	71	62	133	3.594
1851	40	68	67	135	3.375	5	3	8	0.200	—	—	—	73	70	143	3.575
1852	43	71	65	136	3.162	6	4	10	0.232	—	—	—	77	69	146	3.395
1854	42	67	60	127	3.023	4	6	10	0.238	—	—	—	71	66	137	3.261
1855	38	62	58	120	3.157	4	2	6	0.157	—	—	—	66	60	126	3.315
1856	36	55	52	107	2.972	4	2	6	0.166	—	—	—	59	54	113	3.138
1858	33	52	51	103	3.121	2	2	4	0.121	—	—	—	54	53	107	3.242
Totals	1,478	2,569	2,348	4,917	3.326	143	104	247	0.167	—	2	2	2,712	2,454	5,166	3.494

Table 17.10   *Nishinomiya, Hama-kubo-chō. Registers of the* iemochi *(house-owners), 1771–1866: numbers of houses with given number of family members*

Year	Number of family members											Total no. of houses
	1	2	3	4	5	6	7	8	9	10	11	
1771	6	14	19	28	23	9	7	4	1	2	—	113
1782	12	13	20	21	14	15	8	6	2	1	—	112
1786	10	15	30	13	18	9	6	2	2	1	—	106
1795	10	8	22	17	24	10	5	1	1	—	1	99
1806	17	16	15	20	15	10	4	1	1	1	—	100
1810	24	19	12	22	14	7	7	1	—	—	—	106
1816	18	18	16	19	13	10	4	2	—	1	—	101
1818	16	21	16	18	14	9	7	1	—	—	1	103
1822/3	17	10	19	19	18	9	4	1	—	—	—	97
1843/4	18	9	19	16	10	6	6	2	—	—	—	86
1865	15	15	13	9	9	9	3	—	1	—	—	74
1866	16	14	17	10	10	7	4	—	1	—	—	79
Total	179	172	218	212	182	110	65	21	9	6	2	1,176
%	15.2	14.6	18.5	18.0	15.5	9.4	5.5	1.8	0.8	0.5	0.2	100

Registers of the shakuya *(renters/tenants), 1771–1868: numbers of houses with given number of family members*

1771	19	26	26	18	10	6	4	3	1	—	—	113
1781	23	32	22	29	13	7	5	4	—	—	—	135
1806	47	30	37	22	14	14	2	6	2	—	—	174
1810	38	39	35	22	16	3	4	3	2	3	—	165
1816	51	23	39	27	14	10	5	3	—	1	—	173
1819	49	27	30	34	19	4	5	4	—	—	—	172
1822/3	46	28	34	28	22	6	4	3	1	—	—	172
1843/4	67	36	36	30	26	10	2	2	—	—	—	209
1865	38	23	27	32	11	18	4	—	1	—	—	154
1868	41	28	28	21	17	8	3	1	1	—	—	148
Total	419	291	314	263	162	86	38	29	8	4	—	1,615
%	26.0	18.1	19.5	16.3	10.0	5.3	2.4	1.8	0.4	0.2	—	100

Table 17.11   *Nishinomiya, Hama-kubo-chō. Registers of the* iemochi (*house-owners*), *1771–1866: number of households with given number of residents*

Year	Number of residents													Total no. of houses
	1	2	3	4	5	6	7	8	9	10	11	12	13	
1771	4	12	18	27	23	8	6	6	2	2	3	1	1	113
1782	9	11	16	19	17	17	10	7	2	1	1	1	1	112
1786	8	16	26	11	13	10	13	2	3	3	1	—	—	106
1795	8	7	22	13	20	11	8	6	2	—	1	—	1	99
1806	13	14	15	21	14	13	7	1	—	2	—	—	—	100
1810	20	15	14	21	13	10	8	4	—	1	—	—	—	106
1816	15	17	15	15	15	11	7	3	2	1	—	—	—	101
1818	13	19	15	17	13	12	7	3	1	2	1	—	—	103
1822/3	14	9	16	21	15	13	7	1	1	—	—	—	—	97
1843/4	8	11	18	19	11	7	6	5	1	—	—	—	—	86
1865	13	14	13	7	11	8	5	2	1	—	—	—	—	74
1866	15	11	18	7	12	8	6	1	1	—	—	—	—	79
Total	140	156	206	198	177	128	90	41	16	12	7	2	3	1,176
%	11.9	13.3	17.4	16.8	15.1	10.9	7.6	3.5	1.4	1.0	0.6	0.2	0.3	100

Registers of the shakuya (*renters/tenants*), *1771–1868: number of households with given number of residents*

1771	16	25	25	17	8	7	6	5	2	—	1	1	—	113
1781	17	31	25	32	11	9	5	4	1	—	—	—	—	135
1806	37	31	36	27	14	12	8	5	4	—	—	—	—	174
1810	31	41	32	23	17	6	3	3	6	2	1	—	—	165
1816	45	20	39	27	16	10	6	4	4	2	—	—	—	173
1819	41	26	34	32	21	5	8	3	2	—			—	172
1822/3	41	30	28	31	20	11	2	5	1	2	—	1	—	172
1843/4	59	37	32	30	25	13	8	4	—	1	—	—	—	209
1865	30	22	26	29	17	21	6	—	2	—	—	1	—	154
1868	35	28	26	25	16	13	3	1	1	—	—	—	—	148
Total	352	291	303	273	165	107	55	34	23	7	2	3	—	1,615
%	21.8	18.0	18.8	16.9	10.2	6.6	3.4	2.1	1.4	0.5	0.1	0.2	—	100

Table 17.12   *Nishinomiya, Hama-issai-chō. Registers of all categories, 1713–1861: number of houses with given number of family members*

Year	Number of family members												Total no. of houses
	1	2	3	4	5	6	7	8	9	10	11	12	
Combined[a]													
1713[b]	9	21	16	24	23	16	10	4	5	1	—	2	131
1733	11	13	21	28	28	16	10	5	2	1	1	—	136
1737	15	17	29	33	27	21	11	3	1	—	—	—	157
1744	14	9	22	28	25	18	11	7	3	1	—	—	138
1757	10	20	32	41	32	16	14	7	3	—	—	—	175
1774	8	20	20	16	9	18	6	6	1	—	—	—	104
Total	67	100	140	170	144	105	62	32	15	3	1	2	841
%	8.0	11.9	16.6	20.2	17.1	12.5	7.4	3.8	1.8	0.4	0.1	0.2	100
House-owners													
1784	11	21	20	17	22	6	7	2	1	1	—	—	108
1788	13	21	22	21	15	13	4	2	1	—	—	—	112
1792	14	20	24	14	16	7	7	4	3	—	—	—	109
1800	13	22	13	22	17	4	6	5	2	1	—	—	105
1820	17	16	22	22	11	4	4	1	—	—	—	—	97
1847	14	18	26	9	16	5	3	—	1	2	—	—	94
1861	17	11	18	13	7	10	3	1	1	—	1	—	82
Total	99	129	145	118	104	49	34	15	9	4	1	—	707
%	14.0	18.2	20.5	16.7	14.7	6.9	4.8	2.1	1.3	0.6	0.2	—	100
Renters/tenants													
1787	25	20	18	19	9	2	4	—	1	—	—	—	98
1792	31	24	18	17	7	8	1	2	—	1	—	—	109
1820	23	22	26	12	14	2	1	1	—	—	—	—	101
1847	26	28	14	17	9	4	2	3	—	—	—	—	103
1861	27	18	20	13	5	6	2	—	1	—	—	—	92
Total	132	112	96	78	44	22	10	6	2	1	—	—	503
%	26.2	22.3	19.1	15.5	8.7	4.4	2.0	1.2	0.4	0.2	—	—	100
Grand totals													
	298	341	381	366	292	176	106	53	26	8	2	2	2,051
%	14.5	16.6	18.6	17.8	14.2	8.6	5.2	2.6	1.3	0.4	0.1	0.1	100

[a] No distinction is drawn in these registers between 'House-owners' (*iemochi*) and 'Renters/tenants' (*shakuya*).

[b] This listing has also been used by Nakane, see below, Chapter 19, pp. 519, 521, 534–543 and by Laslett, above, Chapter 1, pp. 52–62, 74–85.

Table 17.13   *Nishinomiya, Hama-issai-chō. Registers of all categories,*
1713–1861: number of houses with given number of residents

Year	Number of residents													Total no. of houses
	1	2	3	4	5	6	7	8	9	10	11	12	13	
Combined[a]														
1713[b]	8	12	18	16	26	17	14	7	5	4	2	2	—	131
1733	9	11	21	28	30	16	11	6	—	3	1	—	—	136
1737	14	18	25	32	31	20	10	5	2	—	—	—	—	157
1744	14	8	22	29	23	20	10	7	4	—	—	1	—	138
1757	9	19	32	41	31	17	15	6	3	1	—	—	1	175
1774	5	14	23	17	9	17	10	7	1	1	—	—	—	104
Total	59	82	141	163	150	107	70	38	15	9	3	3	1	841
%	7.0	9.8	16.8	19.4	17.8	12.7	8.3	4.5	1.8	1.0	0.4	0.4	0.1	100
House-owners														
1784	9	19	20	18	17	11	10	1	2	1	—	—	—	108
1788	11	23	17	19	13	13	8	3	2	2	1	—	—	112
1792	13	16	24	11	19	11	8	4	3	—	—	—	—	109
1800	9	20	14	20	20	6	6	4	1	2	3	—	—	105
1820	14	17	18	25	9	8	4	2	—	—	—			97
1847	9	19	22	13	16	7	4	—	2	2	—	—	—	94
1861	15	11	16	13	8	11	5	1	1	—	1	—	—	82
Total	80	125	131	119	102	67	45	15	11	7	5	—	—	707
%	11.3	17.7	18.7	16.8	14.4	9.4	6.4	2.1	1.6	0.9	0.7	—	—	100
Renters/tenants														
1787	24	16	16	21	10	4	5	—	2	—	—	—	—	98
1792	30	22	19	16	8	8	2	2	1	1	—	—	—	109
1820	20	22	22	16	16	2	2	1	—	—	—	—	—	101
1847	22	28	12	20	9	7	2	3	—	—	—	—	—	103
1861	24	16	20	15	7	6	3	—	1	—	—	—	—	92
Total	120	104	89	88	50	27	14	6	4	1	—	—	—	503
%	23.9	20.6	17.7	17.5	9.9	5.4	2.8	1.2	0.8	0.2	—	—	—	100
Grand totals														
	259	311	361	370	302	201	127	59	30	17	8	3	1	2,051
%	12.6	15.2	17.6	18.1	14.7	9.8	6.2	2.9	1.5	0.8	0.4	0.15	0.05	100

[a] No distinction is drawn in these registers between 'House-owners' (*iemochi*) and 'Renters/
tenants' (*shakuya*).
[b] This listing has also been used by Nakane, see below, Chapter 19, pp. 519, 521, 534–543
and by Laslett, above, Chapter 1, pp. 52–62, 74–85.

Table 17.14   *Tennōji, Kubo-machi. Registers of the* iemochi (*house-owners*), *1757–1858: number of houses with given number of family members*

Year	Number of family members												Total no. of houses
	1	2	3	4	5	6	7	8	9	10	11	12	
1757	9	8	17	12	7	2	—	—	—	—	—	—	55
1760	14	4	14	11	11	1	2	—	1	—	—	—	58
1761	13	6	14	9	8	5	1	1	1	—	—	—	58
1762	14	6	13	12	7	3	2	2	—	—	—	—	59
1763	12	5	14	12	9	4	—	2	—	—	—	—	58
1765	12	4	11	11	13	5	—	1	—	—	—	—	57
1766	10	6	12	13	8	6	1	1	—	—	—	—	57
1767	9	7	13	15	11	1	1	1	—	—	—	—	58
1784	8	12	3	12	8	5	1	2	—	—	—	—	51
1785	7	12	3	11	6	5	5	2	—	—	—	—	51
1788	10	10	5	11	7	4	2	2	—	—	—	—	51
1795	12	6	8	7	6	9	1	1	—	—	—	1	51
1797	14	10	4	5	8	7	4	1	—	—	—	1	54
1798	12	8	8	3	5	7	5	1	—	—	—	1	50
1802	10	3	11	10	7	3	3	3	—	—	—	—	50
1805	10	4	8	7	8	5	3	3	1	—	—	—	49
1806	13	4	7	8	8	4	3	3	1	—	—	—	51
1816	12	6	5	6	8	4	1	3	1	—	—	1	47
1817	11	5	7	8	5	1	4	4	1	1	—	—	47
1831	11	6	6	4	5	6	3	3	2	—	—	—	46
1834	11	7	5	5	5	6	1	4	2	2	—	—	48
1837	12	6	3	7	5	4	2	2	4	—	—	—	45
1838	12	6	6	7	4	3	3	4	1	—	—	—	46
1840	14	2	5	3	7	8	1	2	1	1	—	—	44
1843	15	1	4	10	2	6	4	—	1	—	—	—	43
1844	14	2	4	7	6	4	3	—	2	—	—	—	42
1847	17	2	3	8	5	4	1	2	—	—	—	—	42
1848	17	3	4	7	3	4	2	2	—	—	—	—	42
1849	13	2	5	7	5	5	—	2	—	—	—	—	39
1850	14	3	7	5	4	5	—	2	—	1	—	—	41
1851	13	3	4	7	2	7	1	2	—	—	—	—	39
1852	12	4	4	7	3	8	—	2	—	—	—	—	40
1854	13	5	4	9	2	5	2	1	1	—	—	—	42
1855	11	6	4	9	2	5	—	—	—	—	1	—	38
1856	13	6	4	9	2	5	—	—	—	1	—	—	40
1858	12	5	5	6	5	4	—	—	—	3	—	—	40
Total	436	195	254	300	217	170	62	61	20	9	1	4	1,729
%	25.2	11.3	14.7	17.4	12.6	9.8	3.5	3.5	1.2	0.5	0.1	0.2	100

Table 17.15   *Tennōji, Kubo-machi. Registers of the* iemochi (*house-owners*),
1757–1858: number of houses with given number of residents

Year	Number of residents												Total no. of houses
	1	2	3	4	5	6	7	8	9	10	11	12	
1757	9	5	15	8	7	5	4	1	1	—	—	—	55
1760	13	3	6	12	10	6	1	6	1	—	—	—	58
1761	11	5	7	9	11	6	4	2	3	—	—	—	58
1762	10	5	12	9	7	7	4	4	1	—	—	—	59
1763	8	5	12	9	11	5	2	6	—	—	—	—	58
1765	7	7	6	13	14	3	2	3	2	—	—	—	57
1766	6	8	7	10	12	7	2	3	2	—	—	—	57
1767	3	10	8	14	10	6	3	3	1	—	—	—	58
1784	5	9	4	8	8	7	3	—	4	3	—	—	51
1785	2	8	8	6	9	3	8	3	2	2	—	—	51
1788	8	4	3	7	12	8	5	1	—	2	1	—	51
1795	9	1	2	11	11	8	4	2	1	—	1	1	51
1797	12	3	3	9	7	11	2	4	1	—	1	1	54
1798	9	2	5	7	7	7	8	1	1	1	—	2	50
1802	7	1	4	10	9	6	8	3	—	1	1	—	50
1805	7	2	5	7	11	2	5	5	3	1	—	1	49
1806	9	1	6	10	7	3	6	3	5	—	1	—	51
1816	10	4	2	8	7	2	4	4	4	1	—	1	47
1817	9	3	4	8	7	3	3	4	3	3	—	—	47
1831	8	5	4	6	7	5	4	2	2	3	—	—	46
1834	7	6	7	6	5	5	3	4	2	2	1	—	48
1837	8	3	9	7	3	6	2	3	4	—	—	—	45
1838	9	4	9	5	3	4	5	5	2	—	—	—	46
1840	11	1	7	5	7	7	2	1	2	1	—	—	44
1843	13	2	4	10	2	7	2	2	1	—	—	—	43
1844	11	3	5	7	7	4	3	—	1	1	—	—	42
1847	14	4	3	8	6	4	1	1	1	—	—	—	42
1848	14	5	4	7	4	4	2	1	1	—	—	—	42
1849	12	2	5	7	6	5	—	1	1	—	—	—	39
1850	13	3	7	5	5	5	—	1	1	1	—	—	41
1851	12	3	4	7	3	7	1	—	2	—	—	—	39
1852	11	4	5	5	5	8	—	—	2	—	—	—	40
1854	13	3	6	8	3	5	1	1	2	—	—	—	42
1855	10	5	6	8	3	4	1	—	—	—	1	—	38
1856	12	5	6	8	3	4	1	—	—	—	1	—	40
1858	11	4	7	5	6	3	1	—	—	3	—	—	40
Total	343	148	217	289	255	192	107	80	59	25	8	6	1,729
%	19.8	8.6	12.6	16.7	14.8	11.1	6.2	4.6	3.4	1.4	0.5	0.3	100

Table 17.16   *Tennōji, Kubo-machi. Registers of the* shakuya *(renters/tenants),*
1757–1858: number of houses with given number of family members

Year	Number of family members									Total no. of houses
	1	2	3	4	5	6	7	8	9	
1757	15	8	6	3	—	—	—	—	—	32
1760	10	10	7	3	2	1	—	—	—	33
1761	6	8	5	4	4	2	1	—	—	30
1762	8	4	7	5	2	5	—	—	—	31
1763	8	9	9	5	3	3	—	—	—	37
1765	10	9	6	4	5	1	—	—	—	35
1766	6	7	8	5	4	1	—	—	—	31
1767	6	4	8	6	1	3	—	—	—	28
1784	6	12	9	5	8	2	—	—	1	43
1785	6	11	7	6	4	3	1	1	—	39
1788	3	7	11	9	4	—	1	—	—	35
1795	9	12	5	9	4	2	1	—	—	42
1797	10	14	5	2	5	4	1	—	—	41
1798	12	9	12	2	6	3	—	—	—	44
1802	9	9	8	8	7	1	—	—	—	42
1805	10	12	7	10	8	2	1	1	—	51
1806	12	8	7	12	7	5	1	1	—	53
1816	5	2	4	7	3	6	—	—	—	27
1817	6	1	2	6	4	5	—	---	—	24
1831	8	2	3	5	2	—	—	—	—	20
1834	5	4	7	4	4	2	—	—	—	26
1837	3	1	3	2	5	3	1	—	—	18
1838	2	3	2	2	4	3	—	—	—	16
1840	2	5	4	4	4	3	1	—	—	23
1843	3	7	3	1	7	1	—	—	—	22
1844	3	5	5	4	6	1	2	—	—	26
1847	2	4	4	5	5	6	—	—	—	26
1848	1	5	8	5	6	4	1	—	—	30
1849	—	4	6	5	8	4	—	—	—	27
1850	2	4	7	5	5	4	—	1	—	28
1851	2	6	6	5	7	2	1	—	—	29
1852	1	4	7	3	3	5	1	—	—	24
1854	5	4	4	2	3	3	1	—	1	23
1855	3	2	4	5	2	3	2	1	—	22
1856	5	2	3	7	3	8	—	1	—	29
1858	9	3	6	5	3	4	1	1	—	32
Total	213	221	215	180	158	105	18	7	2	1,119
%	19.0	19.8	19.2	16.1	14.1	9.4	1.6	0.6	0.2	100

Table 17.17 *Tennōji, Kubo-machi. Registers of the* shakuya *(renters/ tenants), 1757–1858: number of houses with given number of residents*

	Number of residents										Total no. of houses
Year	1	2	3	4	5	6	7	8	9	10	
1757	15	8	6	3	—	—	—	—	—	—	32
1760	10	10	7	3	2	1	—	—	—	—	33
1761	6	8	5	4	4	2	1	—	—	—	30
1762	8	4	7	5	2	5	—	—	—	—	31
1763	8	9	9	4	4	3	—	—	—	—	37
1765	10	9	6	4	5	1	—	—	—	—	35
1766	6	7	8	5	4	1	—	—	—	—	31
1767	5	5	8	6	1	3	—	—	—	—	28
1784	5	8	13	5	9	2	—	—	1	—	43
1785	4	11	9	6	4	3	1	1	—	—	39
1788	3	6	12	8	3	2	1	—	—	—	35
1795	6	12	7	8	6	2	1	—	—	—	42
1797	8	15	6	1	4	6	1	—	—	—	41
1798	10	11	11	2	6	3	1	—	—	—	44
1802	9	9	8	8	6	2	—	—	—	—	42
1805	9	13	7	9	7	3	2	1	—	—	51
1806	10	9	7	14	7	3	3	1	—	—	53
1816	4	3	2	6	3	7	—	—	1	—	27
1817	5	1	2	6	5	5	—	—	—	—	24
1831	7	3	2	4	3	1	—	—	—	—	20
1834	4	3	7	4	4	4	—	—	—	—	26
1837	3	1	3	1	5	4	1	—	—	—	18
1838	2	3	2	1	4	4	—	—	—	—	16
1840	2	5	4	4	4	3	1	—	—	—	23
1843	3	6	3	1	6	2	1	—	—	—	22
1844	2	6	5	4	6	1	2	—	—	—	26
1847	1	5	4	4	5	6	1	—	—	—	26
1848	1	5	7	4	8	4	1	—	—	—	30
1849	—	4	6	4	9	2	2	—	—	—	27
1850	2	4	5	7	6	3	—	1	—	—	28
1851	2	6	4	7	5	4	1	—	—	—	29
1852	1	4	7	4	2	3	3	—	—	—	24
1854	5	4	4	2	3	3	1	—	—	1	23
1855	3	2	4	5	2	3	2	1	—	—	22
1856	4	2	3	7	4	8	—	1	—	—	29
1858	8	3	6	4	5	4	1	1	—	—	32
Total	191	224	216	174	163	113	28	7	2	1	1,119
%	17.1	20.0	19.3	15.5	14.6	10.1	2.5	0.6	0.2	0.1	100

Table 17.18   *Tennōji, Horikoshi-machi. Registers of the* iemochi (*house-owners*), *1757–1858: number of houses with given number of family members*

Year	Number of family members									Total no. of houses
	1	2	3	4	5	6	7	8	9	
1757	6	4	7	5	3	2	1	—	—	28
1760	5	3	5	5	3	2	1	—	—	24
1761	6	3	4	3	3	3	3	—	—	25
1762	6	3	3	4	5	3	1	—	—	25
1763	3	5	1	6	5	2	—	1	—	23
1765	4	3	3	3	5	2	—	2	—	22
1766	4	3	3	1	6	2	1	—	2	22
1767	3	3	4	—	6	4	—	1	1	22
1784	5	5	1	3	8	—	1	—	1	24
1785	7	4	1	4	7	1	—	1	—	25
1788	10	1	4	2	5	2	3	—	—	27
1795	2	2	4	4	6	3	—	—	—	21
1797	2	2	4	5	4	2	—	—	—	19
1798	2	1	6	4	4	1	1	—	—	19
1802	1	3	4	2	4	2	—	1	—	17
1805	2	1	4	5	3	1	2	—	—	18
1806	3	—	4	4	3	3	2	—	—	19
1816	4	1	5	1	2	5	1	—	—	19
1817	3	4	1	2	4	4	2	—	—	20
1831	5	1	4	3	5	1	2	1	—	22
1834	5	—	2	4	6	2	2	2	—	23
1837	6	—	2	5	6	2	1	1	1	24
1838	7	—	2	6	5	3	—	1	1	25
1840	6	1	2	6	4	4	1	2	—	26
1843	6	1	1	4	8	1	3	—	1	25
1844	4	1	2	4	6	2	3	—	1	23
1847	5	1	2	4	4	3	2	2	—	23
1848	3	1	1	7	3	2	2	1	1	21
1849	4	1	—	9	3	3	1	—	1	22
1850	3	1	—	7	4	2	2	—	1	20
1851	5	—	1	6	4	2	2	1	—	21
1852	5	1	1	6	4	2	2	1	—	22
1854	5	1	—	4	4	3	2	2	—	21
1855	6	1	1	3	2	4	4	—	1	22
1856	5	1	2	2	2	3	4	1	1	21
1858	6	1	3	2	5	4	3	1	—	25
Total	164	64	94	145	161	87	55	22	13	805
%	20.4	8.0	11.7	18.0	20.0	10.8	6.8	2.7	1.6	100

Table 17.19 *Tennōji, Horikoshi-machi. Registers of the iemochi (house-owners), 1757–1858: number of houses with given number of residents*

Year	Number of residents																Total no. of houses
	1	2	3	4	5	6	7	8	9	10	11	12	13	14	15	16	
1757	6	3	3	5	3	4	1	1	—	—	1	—	1	—	—	—	28
1760	5	1	1	7	1	5	3	—	—	—	—	—	1	—	—	—	24
1761	6	1	1	3	3	5	3	1	1	—	—	—	1	—	—	—	25
1762	6	2	1	2	7	1	4	1	—	1	—	—	—	—	—	—	25
1763	3	3	—	4	5	6	—	1	—	—	—	—	—	1	—	—	23
1765	4	1	1	3	4	2	3	3	—	—	—	—	—	—	—	1	22
1766	4	1	1	1	6	2	3	1	2	—	—	—	—	—	1	—	22
1767	4	1	1	1	3	4	4	2	1	—	—	—	—	—	1	—	22
1784	5	2	2	—	3	4	1	—	2	3	2	—	—	—	—	—	24
1785	7	3	1	1	1	2	2	3	—	4	1	—	—	—	—	—	25
1788	10	1	2	—	—	2	5	2	1	3	1	—	—	—	—	—	27
1795	2	—	2	1	3	1	5	2	3	1	1	—	—	—	—	—	21
1797	2	1	—	2	1	4	3	3	2	—	—	—	1	—	—	—	19
1798	2	—	2	—	—	6	1	4	2	1	1	—	—	—	—	—	19
1802	1	—	3	—	—	3	4	2	—	1	1	2	—	—	—	—	17
1805	2	—	2	1	1	1	4	2	2	2	—	1	—	—	—	—	18
1806	2	1	1	1	2	2	2	4	1	2	—	1	—	—	—	—	19
1816	4	—	1	1	1	2	2	1	5	1	1	—	—	—	—	—	19
1817	3	1	1	2	—	—	4	4	3	—	2	—	—	—	—	—	20

Table 17.19 *continued*

Year	Number of residents																Total no. of houses
	1	2	3	4	5	6	7	8	9	10	11	12	13	14	15	16	
1831	5	—	1	1	2	4	4	2	1	1	1	—	—	—	—	—	22
1834	4	1	2	3	5	2	2	2	1	—	—	—	1	—	—	—	23
1837	6	—	1	5	5	2	1	2	1	—	1	—	—	—	—	—	24
1838	7	—	2	4	5	2	2	1	1	1	—	—	—	—	—	—	25
1840	6	1	2	4	4	3	3	2	—	1	—	—	—	—	—	—	26
1843	6	1	1	3	7	3	3	—	1	—	—	—	—	—	—	—	25
1844	4	—	3	2	6	2	4	3	1	—	—	—	—	—	—	—	23
1847	5	—	2	3	4	4	2	1	1	—	—	—	—	—	—	—	23
1848	3	—	2	7	3	2	2	—	1	—	—	—	—	—	—	—	21
1849	4	—	1	9	3	3	1	—	1	—	—	—	—	—	—	—	22
1850	3	1	—	7	4	1	3	—	1	—	—	—	—	—	—	—	20
1851	5	—	1	6	4	2	2	1	—	—	—	—	—	—	—	—	21
1852	5	1	1	6	4	2	2	1	—	—	—	—	—	—	—	—	22
1854	5	1	—	4	4	3	2	1	1	—	—	—	—	—	—	—	21
1855	6	1	1	3	2	4	4	—	1	—	—	—	—	—	—	—	22
1856	5	1	2	2	2	3	4	1	1	—	—	—	—	—	2	—	21
1858	6	1	3	2	5	4	3	1	—	—	—	—	5	1	—	1	25
Total	163	31	51	106	113	102	98	55	37	23	13	4	5	1	2	1	805
%	20.2	3.9	6.3	13.2	14.1	12.7	12.2	6.8	4.6	2.9	1.6	0.5	0.6	0.1	0.2	0.1	100

Table 17.20　*Tennōji, Horikoshi-machi. Registers of the* shakuya *(renters/tenants), 1757–1858: number of houses with given number of family members*

Year	Number of family members											Total no. of houses
	1	2	3	4	5	6	7	8	9	10	11	
1757	6	5	9	4	—	—	—	—	—	—	—	24
1760	7	15	10	10	6	—	—	—	—	—	—	48
1761	9	17	7	8	5	5	—	—	—	—	—	51
1762	10	12	5	10	5	4	—	—	—	—	—	46
1763	10	13	10	9	6	4	—	—	—	—	—	52
1765	9	6	12	5	7	1	—	—	—	—	—	40
1766	14	5	8	9	6	—	—	—	—	—	—	42
1767	11	5	13	9	3	2	—	—	—	—	—	43
1784	4	8	7	10	5	2	—	—	—	—	—	36
1785	4	5	12	10	7	—	—	1	—	—	—	39
1788	2	8	7	11	5	2	1	1	—	—	—	37
1795	—	11	7	7	8	5	—	—	—	—	—	38
1797	1	6	8	12	6	2	5	1	—	—	—	41
1798	2	5	9	13	8	2	3	1	—	—	—	43
1802	5	5	16	6	5	—	6	2	—	—	—	45
1805	9	10	10	9	7	3	4	3	1	—	—	56
1806	10	8	5	10	8	2	4	3	1	—	—	51
1816	4	7	15	10	4	2	6	1	—	—	—	49
1817	9	5	11	11	3	3	3	1	—	1	—	47
1831	7	15	6	8	3	2	1	1	—	—	—	43
1834	12	12	9	7	3	2	3	1	—	—	—	49
1837	7	10	5	4	8	3	2	1	—	—	—	40
1838	8	12	5	3	8	2	—	1	—	—	—	39
1840	7	8	13	4	3	4	1	1	—	—	—	41
1843	5	2	9	8	3	1	1	—	—	1	—	30
1844	7	5	8	10	1	3	1	—	—	1	—	36
1847	5	3	11	5	5	3	1	—	1	—	—	34
1848	2	4	13	5	5	2	1	—	1	—	1	34
1849	4	6	11	8	2	3	—	—	1	—	—	35
1850	7	6	8	8	3	3	1	—	1	—	—	37
1851	5	9	8	10	4	2	1	—	1	—	—	40
1852	6	11	11	6	4	4	1	—	—	—	—	43
1854	7	13	7	9	1	3	2	—	—	—	—	42
1855	6	10	7	10	—	2	3	—	—	—	—	38
1856	5	11	7	9	1	3	—	—	—	—	—	36
1858	6	7	5	10	3	1	1	—	—	—	—	33
Total	232	300	324	297	161	82	52	19	7	3	1	1,478
%	15.7	20.3	21.9	20.1	10.9	5.5	3.5	1.3	0.5	0.2	0.1	100

Table 17.21   *Tennōji, Horikoshi-machi. Registers of the* shakuya *(renters/ tenants), 1757–1858: number of houses with given number of residents*

Year	Number of residents											Total no. of houses
	1	2	3	4	5	6	7	8	9	10	11	
1757	6	5	9	4	—	—	—	—	—	—	—	24
1760	7	14	9	12	6	—	—	—	—	—	—	48
1761	8	15	8	9	6	5	—	—	—	—	—	51
1762	9	13	4	11	4	5	—	—	—	—	—	46
1763	9	14	9	10	6	4	—	—	—	—	—	52
1765	7	7	13	4	8	1	—	—	—	—	—	40
1766	13	6	8	8	6	1	—	—	—	—	—	42
1767	11	5	11	8	6	2	—	—	—	—	—	43
1784	4	6	7	7	10	2	—	—	—	—	—	36
1785	4	5	12	9	7	1	—	1	—	—	—	39
1788	2	7	6	12	5	3	1	1	—	—	—	37
1795	—	10	5	9	8	5	—	1	—	—	—	38
1797	1	6	8	10	5	4	4	2	—	—	—	41
1798	2	5	9	12	6	5	4	—	1	—	—	43
1802	5	5	15	6	3	2	6	3	—	—	—	45
1805	7	11	9	10	6	4	5	3	1	—	—	56
1806	6	10	6	7	10	3	4	4	1	—	—	51
1816	3	7	14	9	6	2	7	1	—	—	—	49
1817	9	5	11	8	4	3	5	1	—	1	—	47
1831	7	10	7	11	3	2	2	—	1	—	—	43
1834	8	14	8	7	5	2	3	2	—	—	—	49
1837	4	10	6	5	8	3	2	2	—	—	—	40
1838	7	11	5	5	8	2	—	1	—	—	—	39
1840	6	6	14	6	3	4	1	1	—	—	—	41
1843	4	2	6	10	5	1	1	—	—	1	—	30
1844	5	5	6	12	3	3	1	—	—	1	—	36
1847	3	5	7	8	6	2	2	—	1	—	—	34
1848	1	5	10	7	5	1	2	—	1	1	1	34
1849	3	5	12	8	3	2	1	—	1	—	—	35
1850	4	7	8	9	4	2	2	—	1	—	—	37
1851	3	8	10	10	4	3	1	—	1	—	—	40
1852	4	9	13	8	4	2	3	—	—	—	—	43
1854	6	8	11	11	1	2	3	—	—	—	—	42
1855	6	8	6	12	1	2	3	—	—	—	—	38
1856	5	8	9	8	3	3	—	—	—	—	—	36
1858	5	7	5	10	4	1	1	—	—	—	—	33
Total	194	284	316	312	182	89	64	23	9	4	1	1,478
%	13.1	19.2	21.4	21.1	12.3	6.0	4.3	1.6	0.6	0.3	0.1	100

Table 17.22   *Percentage of houses with given number of persons per family and household: 1713–1868, all wards and all categories of register (n = 9,973 households)*

	No. of persons						
	1	2–3	4–5	6–7	8–12	13–16	%
Registers combining house-owners and renters/tenants							
Family	8.0	28.5	37.3	19.9	6.3	—	100
Household	7.0	26.6	37.2	21.0	8.1	0.1	100
Registers of the house-owners							
Family	19.9	28.8	32.5	14.3	4.5	—	100
Household	16.5	24.1	30.7	18.8	9.64	0.26	100
Registers of the renters/tenants							
Family	21.1	39.7	28.5	8.8	1.9	—	100
Household	18.2	38.7	29.9	10.5	2.7	—	100
Registers of all categories:							
Totals { Family	19.5	33.9	31.1	12.1	3.4	—	100
Household	16.5	31.2	30.9	15.0	6.27	0.13	100

Table 17.23 Tennōji, Horikoshi-machi and Kubo-machi. Duration of households, 1757–1858

Number of years duration	Horikoshi-machi House-owner Col. 1 Minimum No.	%	Col. 2 Maximum No.	%	Renter/tenant Col. 3 Minimum No.	%	Col. 4 Maximum No.	%	Kubo-machi House-owner Col. 5 Minimum No.	%	Col. 6 Maximum No.	%	Renter/tenant Col. 7 Minimum No.	%	Col. 8 Maximum No.	%
1	38	38.8	8	8.2	159	36.9	62	14.4	37	19.5	11	5.8	155	41.2	54	14.3
2	3	3.1	5	5.1	64	14.9	40	9.3	20	10.5	8	4.2	57	15.2	19	5.1
3	–	–	14	14.4	23	5.3	61	14.2	6	3.2	19	10.0	21	5.6	70	18.6
4	7	7.1	7	7.1	24	5.6	26	6.0	9	4.7	7	3.7	30	8.0	41	10.9
5	2	2.0	2	2.0	28	6.5	17	3.9	6	3.2	8	4.2	23	6.1	10	2.6
1–5	50	51.0	36	36.8	298	69.2	206	47.8	78	41.1	53	27.9	286	76.1	194	51.5
6–10	14	14.3	24	24.6	48	11.1	61	14.2	16	8.4	22	11.6	32	8.5	62	16.5
11–20	4	4.1	5	5.1	53	12.3	99	22.9	28	14.8	26	13.7	41	10.9	75	20.0
21–30	11	11.2	10	10.2	22	5.1	45	10.4	15	7.9	32	16.8	10	2.6	36	9.5
31–40	3	3.1	7	7.1	7	1.6	15	3.5	11	5.7	12	6.3	4	1.1	4	1.1
41–50	2	2.0	2	2.0	3	0.7	5	1.2	12	6.3	10	5.3	2	0.5	4	1.1
51–60	–	–	–	–	–	–	–	–	3	1.6	8	4.2	1	0.3	1	0.3
61–70	3	3.1	2	2.0	–	–	–	–	8	4.2	7	3.7	–	–	–	–
71–80	–	–	1	1.0	–	–	–	–	3	1.6	4	2.1	–	–	–	–
81–90	1	1.0	–	–	–	–	–	–	5	2.6	5	2.6	–	–	–	–
91–100	1	1.0	1	1.0	–	–	–	–	8	4.2	8	4.2	–	–	–	–
101	–	–	1	1.0	–	–	–	–	–	–	–	–	–	–	–	–
102	9	9.2	9	9.2	–	–	–	–	3	1.6	3	1.6	–	–	–	–
Totals	98	100	98	100	431	100	431	100	190	100	190	100	376	100	376	100
Average duration in years	20.5		23.2		6.1		9.9		23.0		27.2		5.1		8.8	
Median duration in years	5		7		2		3		11		17		2		4	

Table 17.24 *Tennōji, Horikoshi-machi and Kubo-machi, 1757–1858: Duration of house-owner and renter/tenant households, compared with duration of all households*

Number of years duration	All house-owners				All renters/tenants				All households			
	Col. 1 Minimum		Col. 2 Maximum		Col. 3 Minimum		Col. 4 Maximum		Col. 5 Minimum		Col. 6 Maximum	
	No.	%	No.	%	No.	%	No.	%	No.	%	No.	%
1	75	26.0	19	6.6	314	38.9	116	14.4	389	35.5	135	12.3
2	23	7.9	13	4.5	121	15.0	59	7.3	144	13.2	72	6.6
3	6	2.1	33	11.4	44	5.5	131	16.2	50	4.6	164	15.0
4	16	5.6	14	4.9	54	6.7	67	8.3	70	6.4	81	7.4
5	8	2.8	10	3.5	51	6.3	27	3.3	59	5.4	37	3.4
1–5	128	44.4	89	30.9	584	72.4	400	49.5	712	65.1	489	44.7
6–10	30	10.4	46	16.0	80	9.9	123	15.2	110	10.0	169	15.4
11–20	32	11.1	31	10.8	94	11.7	174	21.6	126	11.5	205	18.7
21–30	26	9.1	42	14.6	32	4.0	81	10.1	58	5.3	123	11.2
31–40	14	4.9	19	6.6	11	1.3	19	2.4	25	2.3	38	3.5
41–50	14	4.9	12	4.2	5	0.6	9	1.1	19	1.7	21	1.9
51–60	3	1.0	8	2.8	1	0.1	1	0.1	4	0.4	9	0.8
61–70	11	3.8	9	3.1	—	—	—	—	11	1.0	9	0.8
71–80	3	1.0	5	1.7	—	—	—	—	3	0.3	5	0.5
81–90	6	2.1	5	1.7	—	—	—	—	6	0.5	5	0.5
91–100	9	3.1	9	3.1	—	—	—	—	9	0.8	9	0.8
101	—	—	1	0.3	—	—	—	—	—	—	1	0.1
102	12	4.2	12	4.2	—	—	—	—	12	1.1	12	1.1
Totals	288	100	288	100	807	100	807	100	1,095	100	1,095	100
Average duration in years	22.2		25.8		5.7		9.4		10.0		13.9	
Median duration in years	8		14		2		5		3		7	

18. Size of household in a Japanese county throughout the Tokugawa era

Akira Hayami and Nobuko Uchida

INTRODUCTORY

We have three main purposes in this chapter. First, to examine the structure and size of households in pre-industrial Japan. Second, to present the results of the historical demographic research which is being carried out by the study group at Keio University on the demographic history of changes in household size during the Tokugawa era (1603–1868). Finally, to present material which can be used in international cross comparison with the results presented by Peter Laslett for England.[1]

Fortunately the myth that the evolution of the small family was a product of industrialisation does not exist in Japan. The most common explanation given today is that small families or households consisting of one married couple and several children became common throughout the nation between the sixteenth and eighteenth centuries, and took the place of the larger households of earlier periods, many or most of which had more than one married couple apiece. There are household registers of a much earlier period in the eighth and ninth centuries and the fragments which survive indicate a very large household size, perhaps as big as 20 to 30 persons per household on average. After a long break in the records, suitable material for comparison becomes available again in the seventeenth century. Notwithstanding considerable variation from region to region, the great majority of Japanese households consisted of from 5 to 10 members during that period. Although families of from 20 to 30 are not rare in the seventeenth-century records, the average household size was almost certainly less than 10 in the areas near cities, where market economy and transportation facilities were well-developed. A persistent and uninterrupted decline in average household size continued throughout the Tokugawa era, so that by the middle of the eighteenth century, the usual family size reached that common today, 4 or 5 members.

There has been little research until recently on the decline in the size of households during the pre-industrial stage of Japanese history. The study group at

[1] See above, Chapter 4, pp. 125–158.

Keio University is engaged in the systematic analysis of the *shūmon-aratame-chō* as one listing source, and has adopted the method known as family reconstitution to test a number of indicators useful in demographic studies.

SOURCES: THE SHŪMON-ARATAME-CHŌ[2]

The first question to be raised with regard to the shūmon-aratame-chō concerns their reliability. At first glance, one is taken aback by the number of inaccuracies. For example, the births which occurred after the registration had been taken in one year should appear in the following year's register, but some children were not entered until they were three or four years old. If birth rates are calculated without regard for these omissions, they are 'so low as to be improbable'.[3] This is true of death rates also.

Another important issue in determining the reliability of the shūmon-aratame-chō is deciding who among the registered family members was actually resident. The rule was that every resident recorded should be one who was indeed situated in a family group in the village at the time. In many cases however, it is not clear whether 'family member' refers to a person actually living in the family, or merely a registered member who was in fact living elsewhere. In actual practice absent members were often registered, and persons who were in fact situated in the family group were omitted from the register.

With the coming of the nineteenth century and greater mobility in the population, the reliability of the registers certainly declined. In general, the number of omissions increased in cities, where the demand for workers had grown as a result of commercial and manufacturing development. On the other hand in agricultural villages, the actual number of residents was often less than the number recorded in the shūmon-aratame-chō.

There are also problems throughout the Tokugawa era arising from the unit upon which the shūmon-aratame-chō were based. The village was the basic unit used, but some villages were under the control of more than one *daimyō*, and there exist examples of the register for one village being divided into a number of parts, each under the jurisdiction of a different daimyō. In large villages shūmon-aratame-chō were often made up separately for each of the religious sects to which the villagers respectively belonged. Therefore it was possible for members of the same family to be listed in different registers, since there were no restrictions against marriage between different religious sects. Thus the demographic information obtained from various registers often turns out to be of little value unless all of the various parts of the register can be located.

Another problem in using the shūmon-aratame-chō as a source for demographic data has to do with the calculation of age. It was the custom in Japan

---

[2] See above, Smith, Chapter 17, pp. 431–436, for an account of the origin and content of these registers. See also, Hayami, *Population at the beginning of the Tokugawa period* (1967).

[3] Taeuber, *Population of Japan* (1958): 29.

to count a person as being one year old at birth, and to add one year at the beginning of every new calendar year. Thus it is necessary to subtract approximately one year from every age mentioned in order to obtain the age according to the Western method of calculation. Also babies born in a specific year who died before registration was undertaken were not recorded. It is therefore very difficult to estimate the birth rate using shūmon-aratame-chō.

Nevertheless there can be no doubt of the demographic value of the shūmon-aratame-chō in spite of these defects, especially in the case of communities which have preserved successive registration recordings over long periods of time without break.

HANDLING AND ANALYSIS OF DATA

In total there are 800 volumes of the shūmon-aratame-chō available for 120 communities in Suwa County. The 38 communities where data were most ample were selected and their records analysed. Data items for each household were copied on to a basic data card, recording age and position within the family for each household member. The data for one particular village – the village of Yokouchi – where documents survive for no less than 140 years between 1671 and 1871, had already been worked on in an earlier study,[4] and we drew upon those workings as necessary. The map in Fig. 18.1 shows the position of the county, the lake and the village.

There are three distinguishable classes of settlement among the 38 communities chosen. First come the *machi* or *shuku*, which may be translated as 'towns', since they displayed some of the urban characteristics typical of the Tokugawa era. Secondly there were the villages which had existed before the coming of the Tokugawa regime, and finally the *shinden*, or newly settled villages, which were founded under the Tokugawa themselves.

It will be noted that there are only two towns (machi) included in this study, namely Tomono-machi and Kanazawa. Furthermore neither of these two was a castle town, but rather a post town (shuku) along a highway, or perhaps a local centre. Since these two towns mostly shared the characteristics of agricultural villages, we have not set them apart in this study.

We have divided the 38 communities analysed into four geographical districts which are also to be seen in Fig. 18.1. These are: (1) District W, west of Lake Suwa, and (2) District E on the east bank of the lake. Both the W and E Districts are located on the flat land area near Lake Suwa and developed early. Castle towns were located there, highways were built and a market economy developed to a high degree. It should be particularly borne in mind that the silk industry was introduced into the W District after 1830. (3) In general District C consists of villages located in the valleys of a mountainous area and a road going to Edo by way of Kōfu runs through this district. (4) The fourth district, desig-

[4] Hayami, *Aspects démographiques d'un village japonais* (1969).

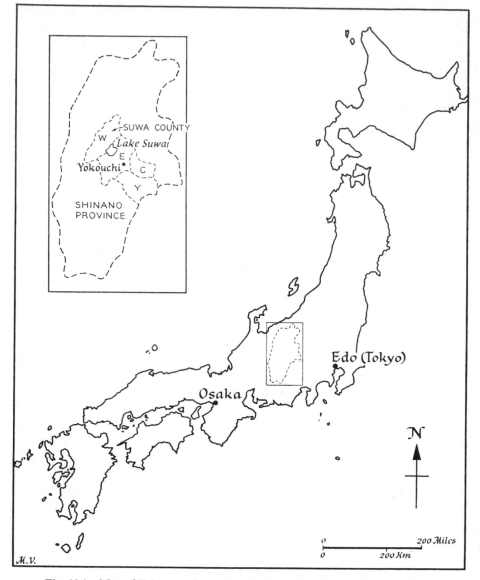

Fig. 18.1   Map of Tokugawa Japan showing Suwa County and district divisions

nated as District Y, lies on the west side of Mt Yatsugatake and is a gently sloping area. This district was developed and settled in the seventeenth century and was well advanced after that time. Shinden, that is 'newly settled villages', were numerous in this region, and the eight villages which we have analysed were all founded after 1600.

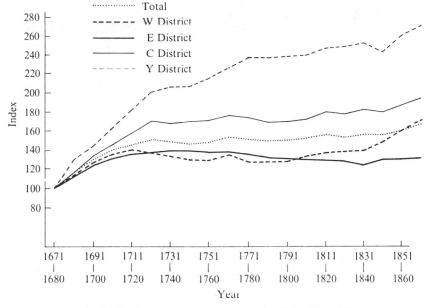

Fig. 18.2   Population trends, by district (1671–80 = 100)

Fig. 18.2 traces the course of indices of population for each district in the County. These were obtained in previous studies of this region.[5] There are area differences in the indices, but in general the population grew during the problematic early period, was stagnant during the middle period, and then tended to grow again in the last part of the Tokugawa era.

Unfortunately the shumon-aratame-chō of these 38 communities have not in every case been kept in a manner which is most convenient to our analysis. In order to average these out and still take advantage of the largest possible number of cases, the following procedure was adopted. First the 200-year period from 1671 to 1871 has been divided into twenty sub-periods of ten years each, omitting 1871. Then from among the body of data for each community, figures have been chosen from as near to the midpoint of each ten-year sub-period as possible for the purpose of analysis. For example in the case of a community where figures for the sub-period 1671 to 1680 are available for 1673, 1679 and 1680, we have chosen those for 1673, i.e. the year closest to the middle of the sub-period. In this way we have avoided the error of choosing data in such a manner that observations would be concentrated around a particular year. The list of communities whose figures have been used is given in Table 18.1. This table also presents the population, number of households and mean size of household (hereafter referred to as MHS) for each community. Thus for the 38 communities we have a total of 382 cases available for analysis.

[5] Hayami (1968 ii).

Table 18.1   *38 Communities in Suwa County, Shinano Province, Japan, 1671–1871 in date order, giving population, households and mean size of household*

No.	Community	Date	Population	Households	MHS
W-11	Ayuzawa	1673	84	12	7.00
		1684	83	12	6.92
		1699	103	13	7.92
		1703	107	12	8.92
		1717	94	14	6.71
		1724	113	16	7.06
		1736	105	18	5.83
		1741	100	19	5.26
		1757	115	17	5.53
		1766	134	28	4.79
		1777	134	25	5.36
		1788	132	28	4.71
		1795	132	27	4.89
		1821	134	29	4.62
W-12	Misawa	1688	246	19	12.95
		1699	293·	22	13.32
		1710	239	35	6.83
		1717	280	35	8.00
		1724	298	35	8.51
		1739	295	54	5.46
		1757	290	55	5.27
		1766	280	56	5.00
		1788	243	50	4.86
		1796	239	55	4.35
		1810	260	56	4.64
		1840	290	64	4.53
		1860	351	86	4.08
W-13	Hashihara	1684	143	18	7.94
		1703	149	17	8.77
		1730	150	26	5.77
		1736	159	24	6.63
		1741	150	23	6.52
		1766	170	33	5.15
		1777	163	35	4.66
		1788	172	38	4.53
		1796	162	37	4.38
		1819	165	33	5.00
		1866	201	51	3.94
W-14	Koguchi	1678	194	31	6.26
		1690	207	35	5.91
		1701	243	39	6.23
		1750	255	53	4.81
		1767	245	49	5.00
		1782	209	51	4.10
		1796	212	53	4.00
		1807	220	56	3.93
		1823	221	57	3.88
		1840	199	59	3.37
		1866	268	62	4.32

Table 18.1 *continued*

No.	Community	Date	Population	Households	MHS
W-15	Imai	1757	442	80	5.53
		1766	451	79	5.71
		1799	413	108	3.82
W-16	Takei	1693	95	22	4.32
		1717	134	30	4.47
		1750	114	32	3.56
		1756	103	31	3.32
		1767	104	33	3.15
		1795	79	20	3.95
		1822	69	18	3.83
		1856	99	25	3.96
		1862	100	23	4.34
W-10	Tomo-no-Machi	1794	380	94	4.04
		1814	418	102	4.10
		1830	481	116	4.26
W-21	Hagikura-Shinden	1714	42	10	4.20
		1729	58	10	5.80
		1747	69	13	5.31
		1765	91	12	7.58
		1828	168	34	4.94
		1844	134	30	4.47
		1855	165	28	5.89
E-31	Kosaka	1689	242	37	6.54
		1703	292	42	6.95
		1719	364	62	5.87
		1728	382	80	4.78
		1766	395	96	4.11
		1787	406	97	4.19
		1799	395	95	4.16
		1839	481	114	4.22
		1866	617	137	4.50
E-32	Aruga	1684	801	124	6.46
		1700	848	143	5.93
		1716	825	161	5.12
		1724	829	180	4.61
		1742	760	184	4.13
		1751	743	187	3.97
		1788	591	146	4.05
		1795	627	154	4.07
		1849	697	161	4.33
E-41	Ueno-Shinden	1684	26	5	5.20
		1700	51	7	7.29
		1716	71	13	5.46
		1724	59	12	4.92
		1742	69	15	4.60
		1751	75	16	4.69
		1788	109	22	4.95
		1795	119	22	5.41
		1849	140	26	5.38

Table 18.1 *continued*

No.	Community	Date	Population	Households	MHS
E-42	Ushiroyama-Shinden	1687	53	9	5.89
		1695	74	10	7.40
		1703	86	12	7.17
		1716	100	13	7.69
		1726	97	13	7.46
		1749	135	23	5.87
		1755	131	23	5.70
		1766	136	28	4.86
		1782	148	25	5.92
		1799	128	25	5.12
		1811	113	29	3.90
		1858	128	30	4.27
E-33	Okuma	1687	353	65	5.43
		1695	429	69	6.22
		1707	425	85	5.00
		1719	430	98	4.39
		1725	399	95	4.20
		1739	406	100	4.06
		1750	459	109	4.12
		1759	405	111	3.65
		1766	415	114	3.64
		1783	347	92	3.77
		1796	290	90	3.22
		1809	305	89	3.43
		1854	308	81	3.80
E-34	Shimokaneko	1673	438	63	6.95
		1688	409	64	6.39
		1718	449	57	7.88
		1760	389	82	4.74
		1771	371	81	4.58
		1782	337	72	4.68
		1796	337	74	4.55
		1811	387	82	4.72
		1854	364	90	4.04
		1866	359	89	4.03
E-35	Fukushima	1689	251	53	4.74
		1696	254	53	4.79
		1705	230	45	5.11
		1717	182	38	4.79
		1757	248	57	4.35
		1767	271	65	4.17
		1775	274	70	3.91
		1782	291	74	3.93
		1796	306	74	4.14
		1821	337	75	4.49
		1855	359	79	4.54
		1866	347	83	4.18
E-36	Ijima	1672	256	44	5.82
		1684	285	43	6.63
		1700	315	50	6.30

Table 18.1 *continued*

No.	Community	Date	Population	Households	MHS
		1705	322	48	6.71
		1716	272	53	5.13
		1725	307	61	5·03
		1750	294	62	4.74
		1754	280	65	4.31
		1767	292	72	4.06
		1774	279	73	3.82
		1788	280	64	4.38
		1795	279	62	4.50
		1802	303	70	4.33
		1852	294	67	4.39
		1861	296	68	4.35
E-37	Arai	1673	197	24	8.21
		1686	198	22	9.00
		1695	185	25	7.40
		1705	173	30	5.77
		1716	176	29	6.07
		1726	169	38	4.45
		1745	163	36	4.53
		1753	173	41	4.22
		1766	177	40	4.43
		1776	182	43	4.23
		1788	169	44	3.84
		1800	185	46	4.02
		1815	214	50	4.28
		1821	221	55	4.02
		1839	233	60	3.88
		1858	245	54	4.54
		1869	290	60	4.83
E-38	Uehara	1680	673	104	6.47
		1684	707	99	7.14
		1694	814	107	7.61
		1707	770	104	7.40
		1711	768	112	6.86
		1724	738	123	6.00
		1738	700	124	5.65
		1742	681	123	5.54
		1754	615	118	5.21
		1773	579	118	4.91
		1795	538	127	4.24
		1811	569	135	4.21
		1838	515	141	3.65
		1851	544	147	3.70
		1865	559	145	3.86
E-39	Yokouchi	1675	201	29	6.93
		1685	224	30	7.47
		1695	263	41	6.41
		1705	283	44	6.43
		1715	320	50	6.40
		1725	356	50	7.12
		1734	388	72	5.39

Table 18.1 *continued*

No.	Community	Date	Population	Households	MHS
		1745	430	77	5.58
		1755	462	77	6.00
		1765	483	89	5.43
		1775	511	102	5.01
		1786	470	99	4.75
		1796	479	98	4.89
		1805	462	100	4.62
		1815	500	96	5.21
		1825	498	97	5.13
		1836	477	104	4.59
		1846	471	107	4.40
		1855	443	114	3.89
		1866	496	112	4.43
E-51	Chino	1674	325	51	6.37
		1681	372	54	6.89
		1706	592	85	6.96
		1724	581	102	5.70
		1769	571	127	4.50
		1783	544	124	4.39
		1791	480	117	4.10
		1814	490	122	4.02
		1841	537	131	4.10
		1852	583	136	4.29
		1864	613	146	4.20
E-52	Nakagawara	1676	77	12	6.42
		1682	72	10	7.20
		1694	84	11	7.64
		1720	136	22	6.18
		1754	153	33	4.64
		1766	174	38	4.58
		1776	163	40	4.08
		1783	152	39	3.90
		1795	145	38	3.82
		1805	185	42	4.40
E-43	Sakamuro-Shinden	1674	68	10	6.80
		1681	60	12	5.00
		1706	54	8	6.75
		1724	85	10	8.50
		1769	133	26	5.12
		1783	157	28	5.61
		1791	152	33	4.61
		1814	165	33	5.00
		1841	159	45	3.53
		1852	177	43	4.12
		1864	194	45	4.31
C-61	Kifune-Shinden	1725	148	21	7.05
		1747	134	34	3.94
		1756	153	37	4.14
		1775	166	35	4.74
		1796	179	38	4.71
		1815	200	40	5.00

Table 18.1 *continued*

No.	Community	Date	Population	Households	MHS
C-70	Kanazawa-Machi	1725	637	99	6.43
		1747	588	106	5.54
		1756	610	124	4.92
		1775	630	132	4.77
		1796	582	124	4.69
		1815	597	133	4.49
C-71	Sezawa	1689	302	27	11.19
		1697	347	29	11.97
		1707	337	29	11.62
		1724	405	37	10.95
		1744	367	37	9.92
		1834	309	82	3.77
		1858	294	78	3.77
		1864	301	78	3.86
C-72	Tsukue	1684	148	18	8.22
		1699	155	17	9.12
		1729	255	27	9.44
		1736	233	29	8.03
		1788	249	30	8.30
		1802	254	30	8.47
		1857	280	64	4.38
C-73	Shimotsutagi	1678	134	20	6.70
		1684	126	21	6.00
		1724	160	32	5.00
		1756	153	36	4.25
		1765	143	39	3.67
		1788	110	31	3.55
		1792	107	34	3.15
		1809	122	31	3.94
		1837	150	34	4.41
		1864	164	38	4.32
C-74	Tabata	1688	92	12	7.67
		1724	126	20	6.30
		1746	130	26	5.00
		1756	138	26	5.31
		1768	139	29	4.79
		1775	139	29	4.79
		1788	133	30	4.43
		1795	150	30	5.00
		1839	123	33	3.73
		1855	142	37	3.84
		1864	160	40	4.00
C-75	Kuzukubo	1687	205	23	8.91
		1766	263	33	7.97
		1796	300	42	7.14
		1843	335	81	4.14
		1857	362	85	4.26
		1864	419	96	4.36
C-76	Okkoto	1747	769	103	7.47
		1768	885	125	7.08
		1812	960	217	4.42

Table 18.1 *continued*

No.	Community	Date	Population	Households	MHS
		1823	947	218	4.34
		1833	985	218	4.52
		1843	958	218	4.39
		1864	1,019	234	4.35
C-62	Sezawa-Shinden	1671	209	31	6.74
		1703	400	29	13.79
		1719	474	49	9.67
		1750	500	74	6.76
		1815	413	91	4.54
Y-81	Aragami-Shinden	1717	195	21	9.29
		1725	212	24	8.83
		1748	181	30	6.03
		1755	207	30	6.90
		1766	202	34	5.94
		1773	214	40	5.35
		1788	227	44	5.16
		1799	245	53	4.62
		1846	212	58	3.65
Y-82	Kamisugasawa-Shinden	1673	45	8	5.63
		1688	54	10	5.40
		1694	60	10	6.00
		1724	101	11	9.18
		1737	101	11	9.18
		1747	115	12	9.58
		1754	121	13	9.31
		1766	127	16	7.94
		1795	116	26	4.46
		1816	125	27	4.63
Y-83	Kikuzawa-Shinden	1675	88	15	5.87
		1685	114	16	7.13
		1699	135	15	9.00
		1855	306	69	4.43
Y-84	Anayama-Shinden	1688	197	22	8.95
		1706	272	22	12.36
		1718	310	23	13.48
		1724	326	33	9.88
		1747	339	37	9.16
		1755	370	38	9.74
		1766	412	46	8.96
		1782	434	51	8.51
		1795	476	53	8.98
		1807	477	59	8.08
		1815	465	77	6.04
		1848	458	95	4.82
		1855	501	98	5.11
		1865	514	104	4.94
Y-85	Yamada-Shinden	1686	218	21	10.38
		1695	258	23	11.22
		1703	279	29	9.62
		1712	277	45	6.16

Table 18.1 *continued*

No.	Community	Date	Population	Households	MHS
		1724	280	39	7.18
		1789	337	76	4.43
		1800	360	79	4.56
		1810	345	82	4.21
		1834	327	86	3.80
		1867	283	73	3.88
Y-86	Tsukinoki-Shinden	1688	184	21	8.76
		1695	224	22	10.18
		1707	255	22	11.59
		1716	295	24	12.29
		1725	322	25	12.88
		1735	383	36	10.64
		1776	540	81	6.67
		1789	526	97	5.42
		1795	517	97	5.33
		1803	469	96	4.89
		1838	573	134	4.28
		1857	637	157	4.06
		1870	704	156	4.51
Y-87	Nakamichi-Shinden	1680	117	18	6.50
		1688	117	14	8.35
		1695	156	15	10.40
		1706	190	17	11.18
		1718	229	17	13.47
		1724	244	18	13.56
		1755	333	23	14.48
		1768	375	29	12.93
		1789	430	43	10.00
		1795	438	41	10.68
		1815	496	112	4.43
		1834	523	119	4.39

In the analysis itself, we have occasionally divided the whole period of 200 years into five other sub-periods, as follows:

Period	Years
1	1671–1700
2	1701–1750
3	1751–1800
4	1801–1850
5	1851–1870

As Laslett has stated, the words 'family' or 'household' are difficult to define. It is clearly inappropriate to look for evidence to satisfy our preconceptions, especially in historical documents. In this study the following rule is observed. A unit which is treated as a group within the context of the shūmon-aratame-chō is regarded as a household for the purpose of analysis.

There is some difference of opinion about the nature of the unit used in the religious registrations. There are undoubtedly a few cases of households which appear unlikely to have existed in fact, for example, a household consisting of one child only two years of age. Moreover it must always be borne in mind that some of the household units may not have been economically or socially independent, and that this may not be apparent from the data appearing in the document.[6] Nevertheless in this chapter we have decided to confine our attention to those points which are apparent from the data in their original form, ignoring the vagueness and shortcomings mentioned above.

The reason why the word 'household' has been used in this chapter rather than 'family' is simply because 'household' appears to be the more general term.

DISTRIBUTION OF THE MEAN SIZE OF HOUSEHOLD

In general, household size in Suwa County from 1671 to 1870 showed a tendency to decline. The figures for totals in the final section of Table 18.2 show that during the sub-period 1671 to 1700 MHS over all areas was 7.04; during the next three fifty-year periods the ratio declined as follows, 6.34, 4.90, 4.42. By 1851–1870 the average size was 4.25, only 60 % of the size at the beginning.

This decrease was by no means uniform. If we examine changes which went on in districts during the rough time divisions of Table 18.2, it is clear that there were differences in the rate of decline. The trend in MHS for each region is shown in Fig. 18.3 in ten-year sub-periods, and here the differences are even more apparent. In the plain area near Lake Suwa, decline in household size is already well advanced by the end of the seventeenth century, and by the end of the eighteenth century the ratio falls as low as 4.5 to 4.0. Over the next 100 years it appears that household size was almost completely stable.

In Districts C and Y, on the other hand, reduction in household size occurs more slowly, especially in District Y where stabilisation in the 4.5 to 4.0 region does not take place until 1830. Furthermore MHS was higher at the beginning of the eighteenth century as compared to other regions, the highest figures of all being 12.7 for District C and 11.2 for District Y. When undertaking MHS analysis under these conditions, it is impossible to proceed directly to the use of correlation coefficients as Laslett has done, using the mean of the MHS over all regions as the dependent variable. This is because the MHS is not here homogeneous. In order to examine the widely differing causes and conditions for the composition of MHS we have been obliged first to examine its distribution and then to use analysis by correlation coefficient. The variables selected were those believed to have a strong relationship with MHS.

When using the figures of Table 18.2, it must not be forgotten that sample sizes differ from district to district and period to period. Nevertheless this table makes it quite evident that variation in household size grew decidedly less

[6] On this point see Nomura, *Cultural conditions affecting population trends* (1953).

Table 18.2 *Preliminary figures and ratios in each district, by period*

Periods	1671–1700	1701–1750	1751–1800	1801–1850	1851–1870	Totals
(1) W District						
Communities	9	20	24	12	6	71
Population	1,448	3,164	5,095	2,759	1,184	13,650
Households	184	515	1,094	654	275	2,722
MHS (overall)	7.87	6.14	4.66	4.22	4.31	5.01
MHS (mean of means)	8.06	6.28	4.79	4.29	4.42	5.51
MHS (median)	7.00	6.03	4.75	4.31	4.20	6.26
Minimum size of households	4.32	3.56	3.15	3.37	3.94	3.15
Maximum size of households	13.32	8.92	7.58	5.00	5.89	13.32
Variance	8.43	1.98	0.94	0.22	0.46	3.54
Standard deviation	2.90	1.41	0.97	0.47	0.68	1.88
(2) E District						
Communities	32	44	55	23	19	173
Population	9,605	15,807	17,542	8,459	7,216	58,629
Households	1,480	2,901	4,013	1,964	1,726	12,084
MHS (overall)	6.49	5.45	4.37	4.31	4.18	4.85
MHS (mean of means)	6.59	5.76	4.47	4.32	4.22	5.14
MHS (median)	6.53	5.61	4.35	4.28	4.27	4.74
Minimum size of households	4.74	4.06	3.22	3.43	3.70	3.22
Maximum size of households	9.00	8.50	6.00	5.38	4.83	9.00
Variance	0.89	1.29	0.34	0.25	0.08	1.45
Standard deviation	0.95	1.13	0.59	0.50	0.28	1.21
(3) C District						
Communities	9	16	19	13	9	66
Population	1,718	5,663	5,229	6,353	3,141	22,104
Households	198	752	1,004	1,426	750	4,130
MHS (overall)	8.68	7.53	5.21	4.46	4.19	5.35
MHS (mean of means)	8.50	7.93	5.13	4.63	4.13	6.03
MHS (median)	8.22	7.21	4.77	4.53	4.26	4.86
Minimum size of households	6.00	3.94	3.15	3.73	3.77	3.15
Maximum size of households	11.97	13.79	8.30	8.47	4.38	13.79
Variance	3.68	7.03	1.99	1.34	0.06	5.87
Standard deviation	1.92	2.65	1.41	1.16	0.24	2.42
(4) Y District						
Communities	14	20	21	11	6	72
Population	1,967	4,926	7,007	4,470	2,945	21,915
Households	230	496	1,007	945	657	3,338
MHS (overall)	8.55	9.93	6.94	4.73	4.48	6.39
MHS (mean of means)	8.13	10.31	7.64	4.84	4.49	7.78
MHS (median)	8.56	9.75	6.90	4.43	4.47	7.56
Minimum size of households	5.40	6.24	4.43	3.66	3.88	3.66
Maximum size of households	11.22	13.56	14.48	8.08	5.11	14.48
Variance	3.78	4.81	7.91	1.42	0.19	8.64
Standard deviation	1.94	2.19	2.81	1.19	0.44	2.96

Table 18.2 *continued*

Periods	1671–1700	1701–1750	1751–1800	1801–1850	1851–1870	Totals
			All Districts			
Communities	64	100	110	59	40	382
Population	14,738	29,560	34,873	22,041	14,486	115,698
Households	2,092	4,664	7,121	4,989	3,408	22,274
MHS (overall)	7.04	6.34	4.90	4.42	4.25	5.19
MHS (mean of means)	7.40	7.12	5.20	4.48	4.27	5.86
MHS (median)	8.22	8.64	5.35	4.62	4.41	5.00
Minimum size of households	4.32	3.56	3.15	3.37	3.70	3.15
Maximum size of households	13.32	13.79	14.48	8.47	5.89	14.48
Variance	3.65	6.15	3.39	0.75	0.17	4.92
Standard deviation	1.91	2.48	1.84	0.87	0.41	2.22

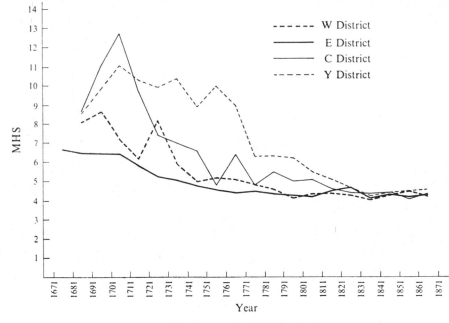

Fig. 18.3   Trends in MHS, by district

everywhere as the years went by. Variance and standard deviation of household size, the usual statistical measures of dispersion, can be seen to be higher at the beginning than at the end, and the range between maximum and minimum size goes down as well. All this holds good both for districts and for individual communities as well as for the whole collection.

If the values of the various indicators are drawn graphically, the tendency towards convergence in the variance of household size which accompanied the general decline in size itself is seen to be very marked indeed. But space is not available to display the full effect and all that we can do is to lay strong emphasis on the following point. By the end of the Tokugawa era differences in the distribution of households by size which are referable to locality, to the various districts into which we have divided the material, vanish entirely. The distribution of households by size is identical in every region by the 1870s. We regard this as a conclusion of considerable importance for the study of the size and structure of the household, in Japan and everywhere else.

Figures 18.4 and 18.5 have been prepared with international comparison in mind. The first contrasts distribution of households by size in Districts E, W and C (where the pattern of distribution stabilises early) for the years 1751 to 1800, with the distribution worked out by Laslett for 91 communities in the 1564–1821 period for England. The Japanese percentage figures for MHS refer to 98 communities, consisting of 6,111 households with a total population of 27,866, and a general MHS equal to 4.56. In the case of Japan the distribution of households by size is concentrated in the range from 3 to 5, which appears to be somewhat higher than that in England. In Japan indeed 55.8 % of households consist of 3 to 5 members, as against 47.1 % in England. Households with 1 to 2 members and those with more than 7 members were commoner in England than Japan.

Figure 18.5 shows the distribution of communities by mean household size with a unit interval of 0.5 persons. It will be seen that in the period 1701 to 1750 MHS is highly dispersed. The largest group, that containing 5 to 5.5 persons, occupies only 12 % of the total area of the distribution. However by 1801 to 1850 the interval from 3.5 to 5.0 persons occupies 80 % of the distribution area, whilst in England 80 % of households are concentrated in the 4 to 5.5 member area. The resemblance of the shape of the English graph to that of Japan in the final stage of household development there suggests to us the possibility that this distribution may be characteristic of societies where the process of reduction in household size and of variation in size between households is well advanced.

It is a notable fact in comparing Japan with England that the values of MHS and variance of MHS in the final years of the Tokugawa era were actually lower than those found in England between the sixteenth and the nineteenth centuries. When the rate of shrinkage in household size is looked at geographically some sort of pattern emerges. It is in the flat area around Lake Suwa that MHS converges most rapidly and distinctly. In the Y and C Districts, especially in the Y region, which is in a more remote mountain area, MHS remains quite high until late in the Tokugawa era. All this suggests to us that the trend in household size can be thought of as one accompanying the spread of a monetary economy. In the final period the MHS of all communities converges in the 3.0 to 5.0 region.

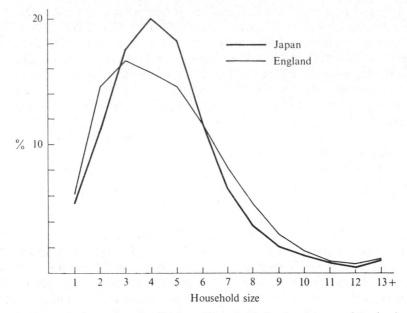

Fig. 18.4   Percentage distribution of households by size, Japan and England
Japan: 98 communities, 1751–1800 (MHS 4.56) England: 91 communities, 1564–1821 (MHS 4.72)

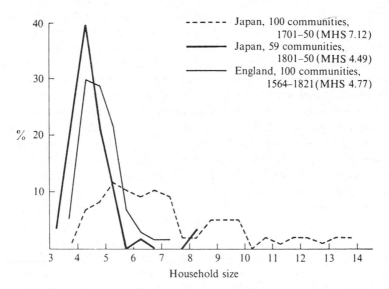

Fig. 18.5   Percentage distribution of communities by mean household size,
Japan and England

CORRELATION COEFFICIENCY ANALYSIS OF THE MHS

What variables were important in determining the MHS? If we suppose that size of household reflects all types of economic and social forces affecting human life, the number of such variables increases without limit. Our present object is to examine the correlation of MHS with a number of the variables which can be recovered from historical data, and then use these correlations as a guide to the understanding of the composition of the Japanese household in Tokugawa times. The variables we have chosen are more demographic in nature than those used in the studies of England.[7] This is due to the limitations of the data, since it is not possible to determine occupation or social position from the shūmon-aratame-chō.

The following fifteen possible explanatory variables for the MHS have been selected, all of which are measurable.

(1) The ratio of the number of households with two or more married couples to the number of households with at least one couple. It has been said that during the Tokugawa period the fragmentation of large agricultural households into small households was very common, as was the dissolution of multiple family groups. To confirm this statistically we must examine the correlation between this variable and MHS.

(2) The average number of married couples per household, where the average is taken only over households with at least one such couple.

(3) The ratio of households with a married head to the total number of households.

(4) The ratio of the number of households with three or more generations to the total number of households.

(5) The ratio of households without resident kin to the total number of households. If variable (5) is correlated with MHS, the sign of the coefficient should be negative. If we define resident kin more precisely, they are the members of the household which are left after exclusion of the head of the household, his wife, his lineal ascendants and descendants, and his servants. It is impossible to determine from the data itself whether resident kin are relatives of the husband or of the wife.

(6) The ratio of the number of households with one or more of several types of servants to the total number of households.

(7) The average number of servants in households with one or more servants.

(8) The number of servants in the total population. Since decline in household size may have been due to the dissolution of agricultural units dependent upon servant labour, explanatory variables (6), (7) and (8) serve to test this theory.

(9) The number of unmarried children of the head of the household.

(10) Fertility. Since fertility cannot be measured in a direct way from the data, we have used the ratio of the number of children under ten to the number

[7] See above, Laslett, Chapter 4, p. 155.

Table 18.3   *Variables correlated with mean household size (382 communities)*

Coefficient when household size is correlated with:

(1) Proportion of households with two or more couples in the households with at least one married couple	0.835
(2) Mean of the number of couples in households with at least one married couple	0.899
(3) Proportion of households headed by married couples	0.600
(4) Proportion of households with three or more generations	0.529
(5) Proportion of households without resident kin	−0.684
(6) Proportion of households with servants	0.444
(7) Mean number of servants in households with servants	0.248
(8) Mean number of servants over all households	0.402
(9) Mean number of unmarried sons and daughters of household heads	0.529
(10) Fertility[a]	0.319
(11) Proportion, males married, age 16–60	0.032
(12) Proportion, females married, age 21–40	−0.167
(13) Mean age at marriage, females[b]	−0.045
(14) Sex ratio	0.021
(15) Proportion of those working temporarily away from home	0.086

[a] See pp. 499, 508–511.   [b] See pp. 499, 507–508.

of wives between sixteen and fifty as a function of fertility, and as a substitute variable. Whether this is a valid measure of fertility or not can be confirmed from Yokouchi, where fertility can be measured more directly.

(11) The proportion married of males between sixteen and sixty.

(12) The proportion married of females between twenty-one and forty, the age range of highest fertility.

(13) Age at marriage for women. Since this cannot be computed directly from the data, we have taken the age when the proportion married exceeds 50 % and used it as a function of the age at marriage. This proportion has been arrived at graphically, by joining together the levels showing proportion married in successive five-year female age groups and observing the point at which this line crosses the 50 % level. For example, if in one age group in one village the proportion married for females in the age group sixteen to twenty is 40 %, while that for twenty-one to twenty-five-year-olds is 60 %, drawing a straight line between these two levels and locating the point where the line crosses the 50 % level gives an estimate of the average marital age, in this case 20.5 years. As in the case of variable (10), we can compare the results of this approximation with the age at marriage computed for Yokouchi, where data permit age at marriage to be exactly calculated from family reconstitution.

(14) The sex ratio.

(15) The ratio to the total population of persons leaving the household temporarily for outside work.

The above fifteen variables were employed in correlation coefficiency analysis, where MHS was taken as the dependent variable. The correlation coefficients (r) using all 382 cases are given in Table 18.3. The correlation of variables numbers (11: proportion of males married), (13: female age at marriage), (14: sex ratio) and (15: absent workers) with the MHS is low, and may be regarded as insignificant. For the remaining variables the coefficients are all significant at the 1 % level. (For 400 degrees of freedom at the 1 % significance level the value of r must be 0.128 or higher.)

The correlations obtained for variables numbers (1), (2), (3), (4), (5), and (9) are particularly high.[8] Variables (1) and (2) relate to the number of married couples per household and variable (4) measures the number of generations per household which is virtually the same as the number of married couples per household. It is clear that the size of the household is strongly affected by the number of married couples which it contains. The high negative value for variable (5) implies that the number of resident kin has likewise a marked influence on the size of households. Variable (9) is the number of unmarried children of the head of the household, and, like variable (10), may be regarded as an indication of fertility. No comment appears to be necessary on variable (3).

The set of variables with the next highest correlation coefficients are nos (6), (7), (8), (10) and (12) covering servants, fertility and proportion married. Variable (8) indicates the number of servants in the total population. It will be seen that the earlier the period, the larger the number of servants per household and we shall discuss this relationship below. As for variable (10) – children per married woman – it may be remarked that a marked fluctuation in the death rate amongst children, which is certainly possible at that time, would have given rise to a higher correlation of this variable with mean household size than is found in our results. Variable (12) – proportion of women married – yields a negative correlation with MHS, but a high proportion married has both a positive and a negative effect on the size of households. The positive effect occurs because the birth rate increases, and the negative effect because marriages give rise to independent households of smaller size.

The above analysis relates to all regions and all time periods. It has been emphasized that MHS itself varies widely from region to region, and the same can be said about variables (1) to (15). For this reason, it is necessary to calculate correlation coefficients for regions and by time period; and the results of this are given in Table 18.4.

The variable most closely correlated with the MHS over the whole period is the number of married couples per household. As we shall emphasise later in the discussion, it is interesting to notice how other factors become more important after this variable stabilises. For example in District E, the correlation coefficient for married couples gradually declines, and other variables, such as the number of generations per household, or the number of children per household rise to

---

[8] These differ sharply from the variables having a significant effect on mean household size in pre-industrial England, see above, Laslett, Chapter 4, pp. 155–156.

Table 18.4   *Variables correlated with mean household size, by district*

(1) W District

Variable	1671–1700 (n = 9)	1701–1750 (n = 20)	1751–1800 (n = 24)	1801–1850 (n = 12)	1851–1870 (n = 6)	Total (n = 71)
			Correlation coefficients			
1	0.606	0.834**	0.873**	0.540	0.913*	0.785**
2	0.474	0.763**	0.891**	0.502	0.941**	0.715**
3	0.437	0.505*	0.492*	0.685*	0.240	0.627**
4	0.705*	0.260	0.704**	0.684*	0.693	0.511**
5	−0.926**	−0.626**	−0.852**	−0.418	−0.832*	−0.696**
6	−0.059	0.385	0.491*	—	—	0.467**
7	−0.025	0.810**	−0.002	—	—	0.010
8	−0.083	0.448*	0.426*	—	—	0.410**
9	0.899**	0.723**	0.690**	0.936**	0.884*	0.874**
10	0.059	0.500*	0.038	0.209	−0.088	0.361**
11	−0.617	−0.200	0.210	0.528	0.082	−0.036
12	0.047	−0.289	0.506*	0.501	0.581	−0.192
13	0.950**	−0.719**	0.486*	0.499	—	0.171
14	−0.027	−0.199	0.454*	0.004	0.688	−0.042
15	−0.102	0.204	−0.542**	0.473	−0.556	0.365**

(2) E District

Variable	1671–1700 (n = 32)	1701–1750 (n = 44)	1751–1800 (n = 55)	1801–1850 (n = 23)	1851–1870 (n = 19)	Total (n = 173)
			Correlation coefficients			
1	0.620**	0.864**	0.728**	0.478*	−0.013	0.734**
2	0.652**	0.869**	0.733**	0.581**	0.094	0.792**
3	0.429*	0.596**	0.581**	0.589**	0.509	0.703**
4	0.179	0.643**	0.641**	0.734**	0.558*	0.279**
5	−0.378*	−0.610**	−0.597**	−0.234	−0.401	−0.472**
6	0.473**	0.240	0.391**	—	—	0.640**
7	0.436*	−0.100	−0.015	—	—	0.287**
8	0.607**	0.210	0.235	—	—	0.632**
9	0.307	0.349*	0.157	0.194	0.575**	0.647**
10	0.121	0.049	0.125	0.120	0.272	0.328**
11	−0.438*	0.365*	0.145	0.182	0.048	−0.034
12	−0.340	0.315*	−0.074	0.279	0.030	−0.205**
13	−0.146	−0.119	−0.088	0.170	−0.008	−0.034
14	0.294	−0.056	0.024	0.254	0.047	0.087
15	0.096	−0.065	−0.156	0.040	−0.362	0.306**

(3) C District

Variable	1671–1700 (n = 9)	1701–1750 (n = 16)	1751–1800 (n = 19)	1801–1850 (n = 13)	1851–1870 (n = 9)	Total (n = 66)
			Correlation coefficients			
1	0.918**	0.789**	0.922**	0.833**	−0.041	0.877**
2	0.974**	0.906**	0.942**	0.943**	−0.044	0.929**
3	0.003	0.581*	−0.166	0.196	−0.167	0.528**
4	0.840**	0.814**	0.678**	0.256	0.500	0.635**
5	−0.460	−0.694**	0.868**	−0.687**	−0.766*	−0.678**

Table 18.4 *continued*

(3) C District					
1671–1700	1701–1750	1751–1800	1801–1850	1851–1870	Total
(n = 9)	(n = 16)	(n = 19)	(n = 13)	(n = 9)	(n 66)

Variable		Correlation coefficients			
6	0.210	0.708**	0.059	−0.067	—	0.705**
7	0.181	0.746**	0.287	—	—	0.573**
8	0.300	0.837**	0.117	−0.067	—	0.707**
9	0.146	0.692**	0.283	0.305	0.564	0.690**
10	0.011	0.750**	0.240	0.229	0.345	0.585**
11	−0.180	−0.356	−0.299	−0.207	−0.641	−0.260*
12	0.415	−0.460	0.156	0.040	−0.550	−0.381**
13	0.438	0.379	−0.359	−0.623*	−0.518	0.171
14	0.438	−0.333	0.214	0.340	−0.455	−0.028
15	−0.598	0.347	0.108	0.115	0.335	0.159

(4) Y District					
1671–1700	1701–1750	1751–1800	1801–1850	1851–1870	Total
(n = 14)	(n = 20)	(n = 21)	(n = 11)	(n = 6)	(n = 72)

Variable		Correlation coefficients			
1	0.717**	0.842**	0.874**	0.748**	0.162	0.811**
2	0.846**	0.960**	0.980**	0.977**	0.333	0.946**
3	0.483	0.248	0.523*	0.564	0.215	0.593**
4	0.570*	0.622**	0.403	0.653*	0.869*	0.499**
5	−0.285	−0.368	−0.828**	−0.880**	−0.767	−0.654**
6	0.578*	−0.238	—	—	—	0.273
7	0.456	0.539*	—	—	—	0.511**
8	0.473	−0.033	—	—	—	0.258
9	0.539	−0.125	0.568**	0.233	0.477	0.422**
10	0.183	0.016	0.347	0.178	0.476	0.299*
11	0.163	0.457*	−0.273	0.138	−0.152	0.018
12	−0.003	0.355	0.021	0.165	−0.038	−0.195
13	0.572*	−0.258	−0.433*	−0.598	−0.094	−0.081
14	−0.082	−0.318	0.486*	−0.183	−0.789	0.010
15	0.044	−0.215	0.007	0.205	—	0.236

* Significant at 0.05.   ** Significant at 0.01.

prominence. In Districts C and Y we find that MHS remained high until late in the Tokugawa period and that the number of resident kin was significant to MHS over the whole period studied.

Servants do not seem to have had a uniform effect on MHS. The correlation coefficient in District E is high from 1671 to 1700, but for District W it is negative and very low. District C shows high values for 1701 to 1750, but after 1801 the relationship disappears, because of the absolute drop in the number of servants.

The most interesting result apparent from Table 18.4 is that there are several coefficients which are high in the Total column even though they are low for each sub-period. For example in District E, variable (10) – children per married woman – is low in every period, never significant even at the 5 % level. However, in total the value of r is 0.328, which is above the critical value required at the 1 % level. When trying to decide on determinants of MHS, therefore, it is necessary to distinguish between those having an influence in the long run and those having an influence in the short run.

Variable (10), which indicates fertility, is always significantly related to MHS over the whole period of analysis, that is in the Total column, at the 5 % level or better, but in the sub-periods the relationship barely reaches the level required for 5 % significance. Other variables which perform very differently in the long and short run are nos (3), (6), (7), (8) and (9). Variables nos (1), (2), (4) and (5), on the other hand, appear to be effective in both the short and long run.

CHANGES IN THE VARIABLES

As was mentioned in the previous section, some of the variables which influence the MHS underwent substantial change during the period studied. In this section we shall consider changes in the major variables.

NUMBER OF MARRIED COUPLES PER HOUSEHOLD

In each region and in every period except the last, the strongest relationship is that between MHS and the number of married couples. The trends in the average number of married couples per household over time for each region are given in Fig. 18.6. Values for Districts E and W, east and west of Lake Suwa, are very similar and they decline together slowly over the years. For District Y – the new village area – before the 1810s, and especially up to the 1760s, the figures remain at a very high level. District C – the mountains – is in between the two mentioned above, so far as these figures are concerned. Data on the ratio of the number of households with only one married couple, to all households, for the four regions over time are shown in Figure 18.7. If we adopt the principle that the small family is dominant when this ratio reaches 50 %, the period of dominance arrives in 1730 in District W, in 1720 in District E, in 1800 in District C and in 1810 in District Y. The time lag between regions is relatively small. In Districts W and E, this ratio stabilises after 1780 at about 65 % to 70 %, except for a short period. In 1830 District C joins Districts W and E in this range. When this ratio stabilises, its correlation with MHS goes down. A high correlation between the number of couples per household and MHS is characteristic of periods when shrinkage in the household size is not taking place. Table 18.5 shows the average value by region and period for variable (1), that is to say the ratio of households with two or more couples to all households with at least one married couple. Table 18.6 shows the mean of means for variable (2) i.e. the average number of couples in households with at least one couple.

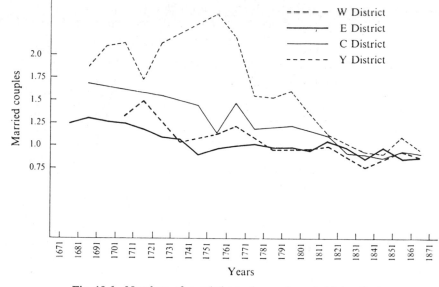

Fig. 18.6 Numbers of married couples per household, by district

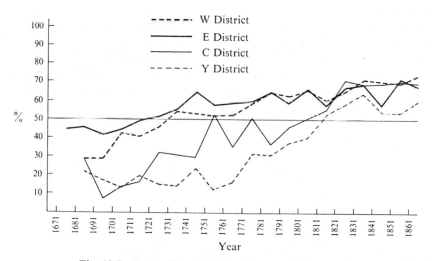

Fig. 18.7 Ratio of households with one couple to total number
of households, by district

Table 18.5   *Variable 1: Ratio of households with two or more couples to all households with at least one married couple, by district*

	W	E	C	Y	Total
1671–1700	0.527	0.342	0.505	0.481	0.421
1701–1750	0.333	0.303	0.511	0.658	0.413
1751–1800	0.262	0.225	0.316	0.533	0.302
1801–1850	0.244	0.215	0.259	0.369	0.259
1851–1870	0.188	0.188	0.161	0.278	0.195
Total	0.306	0.261	0.357	0.511	0.333

Table 18.6   *Variable 2: Mean number of couples in households with at least one married couple, by district*

	W	E	C	Y	Total
1671–1700	1.97	1.45	1.85	1.83	1.66
1701–1750	1.41	1.40	1.79	2.34	1.65
1751–1800	1.32	1.25	1.43	2.05	1.43
1801–1850	1.25	1.24	1.29	1.37	1.28
1851–1870	1.20	1.18	1.16	1.30	1.20
Total	1.41	1.31	1.51	1.92	1.48

RESIDENT KIN PER HOUSEHOLD

Shrinkage in household size was also a function of the drop in the number of resident kin per household, and it will be seen that the number of resident kin was large in areas like Districts Y and C where the MHS was also large. Figure 18.8 shows the trend in the average number of resident kin per household. Up to the year 1820 we find once more a trend which is unique to District Y, the new villages, but after this point the average converges to 0.5 for all regions.

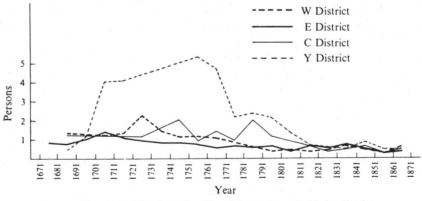

Fig. 18.8   Number of resident kin per household, by district

BIRTH RATE AND FERTILITY

Both birth rate and fertility might be considered as determinants of the size of households, but in the data we have used in this study and with the methods we have employed, it is impossible to observe these two variables directly. As has already been stated, all that could be done was to compute a fertility index from the ratio of children to wives. There are two ways of reckoning this index. The first is by age groups, and the second is by relationship to the head of household. In the first case the ratio of children under ten in the community to the number of married women between twenty-one and forty is computed, and in the second the number of resident unmarried children of the head of the household.

There are several points which must be borne in mind when these figures are used as functions of the birth rate or of the degree of fertility. The first is the death rate among children. If there are large changes in this rate, then it will be impossible to assume that there is a stable relationship between the substitute ratio series and the actual birth and fertility rates. This point can be examined and explained once again from the detailed study of the village of Yokouchi, where we have undertaken family reconstitution.

The next issue is that of mobility, which will create problems if it affects children under ten years of age. Geographic movement of children in that age group independent of their parents is difficult to imagine, but it must be kept in mind that the practice of adopting both male and female children was very common in Japan during this period. In some cases it is possible to distinguish adopted children from other children, but not in every case. The data for Yokouchi provides a check here as well. The third question about the use of the substitute series for fertility concerns the extent to which information on the birth and fertility rates is consistent with information on the population married and on age at marriage. If we suppose that the proportion married and the age at marriage vary widely, then these substitute variables will not be good indications of the birth rate, which makes it essential that the proportion married and age at marriage be closely examined where possible. There is yet a further consideration which arises because the number of unmarried children depends on the average age at marriage. If the age at marriage falls, the number of unmarried children declines, but because the birth rate rises the figures for MHS will move in the opposite direction. In actual fact, however, it is hard to imagine that age at marriage would vary sufficiently over a short period to affect the birth rate.

Taking all these things into consideration, it seems perfectly possible that the correlation of our substitute fertility figures with MHS could be low over short periods. We find that the correlation results, with the exception of those for District W, are in fact low and unstable for sub-periods, but higher in the long term. Table 18.7 shows the trend in the number of unmarried children per

Table 18.7   *Variable 9: Mean number of unmarried children of household head, by district*

	W	E	C	Y	Total
1671–1700	2.80	2.53	2.61	2.49	2.57
1701–1750	1.91	1.95	1.84	1.97	1.93
1751–1800	1.36	1.45	1.23	1.37	1.38
1801–1850	1.43	1.34	1.19	1.25	1.31
1851–1870	1.47	1.45	1.29	1.35	1.40
Total	1.72	1.76	1.57	1.73	1.72

Table 18.8   *Variable 10: Fertility:[a] ratio of children aged 10 or under to wives aged 16–50, by district*

	W	E	C	Y	Total
1671–1700	2.25	2.24	2.33	2.35	2.28
1701–1750	2.04	1.82	1.90	1.99	1.91
1751–1800	1.73	1.62	1.48	1.49	1.59
1801–1850	1.84	1.65	1.59	1.56	1.66
1851–1870	1.64	1.87	1.58	1.63	1.73
Total	1.89	1.82	1.74	1.82	1.81

[a] See pp. 508–511.

household, and Table 18.8 shows the ratio of children under ten to the total number of wives between 16 and 50 for each community. As we can see from Table 18.8, differences in the ratio from district to district are not large for simultaneous periods, and changes over time seem to be larger than the variation across communities for any given interval. In all districts the figures are highest for 1671 to 1700, lowest for 1751 to 1800 (except only in District W), and rise slightly thereafter. The figures given in Table 18.8 show virtually the same trends as those in Table 18.7. We can state quite confidently that the birth rate and degree of fertility in all districts of Suwa County showed a virtually identical pattern over time.

PROPORTION MARRIED

The marriage rate for males aged sixteen to sixty is given in Table 18.9, although it is not directly related to fertility. Except for the fact that District Y – the area of new settlements – appears to be slightly higher than the rest, there seem to be no meaningful trends in the series, and as we have seen, correlation with MHS was found to be low. The proportion of married females aged twenty-one to

Table 18.9   *Variable 11: Proportion of married males, age 16–60, by district*

	W	E	C	Y	Total
1671–1700	0.614	0.553	0.577	0.663	0.589
1701–1750	0.552	0.549	0.558	0.567	0.555
1751–1800	0.579	0.561	0.602	0.639	0.585
1801–1850	0.557	0 592	0.616	0.584	0.588
1851–1870	0.638	0.556	0.578	0.581	0.577
Total	0.577	0.560	0.587	0.611	0.577

Table 18.10   *Variable 12: Proportion of married females,*
age 21–40, by district

	W	E	C	Y	Total
1671–1700	0.699	0.749	0.652	0.801	0.739
1701–1750	0.672	0.740	0.725	0.731	0 722
1751–1800	0.812	0.811	0.812	0.838	0.816
1801–1850	0.768	0.824	0.817	0.825	0.811
1851–1870	0.804	0.808	0.794	0.826	0.807
Total	0.750	0.783	0.768	0.798	0.777

forty is a different matter and is given in Table 18.10. In every district it is apparent that between the two sub-periods 1671 to 1700 and 1701 to 1750, and the rest of the period of analysis, there is a considerable difference in the value of this index. The rate is ten per cent higher after 1750 than before, and it is also clear that the rate is slightly higher in District Y than elsewhere.

AGE AT MARRIAGE

Since the average age at marriage cannot be measured directly from the data, we have used, as has been said, a substitute series. Table 18.11 gives the trend for females for all our villages over all sub-periods, and the figures vary little across districts, but do change significantly over time. The highest marriage ages occur in 1701–50 in every district, while the periods when the average age at marriage is lowest are 1751–1800 and 1801–50. This result appears to contradict the data in Tables 18.7 and 18.8, and an explanation is required.

First it is clear that the rate of child mortality fell over the whole period, and that this must have led to a lengthening of the average life span. The proportion of children who lived at least to the age of ten in Yokouchi was 62 % in 1671–1700 for a sample of 227 births, 60 % in 1701–25 for 302 births, but 70 % in 1726–50 for 278 births and 79 % in 1751–75 for 309 births. Thus the survival rate for the

1–10 age group increased over the years, and an average life expectancy at two years of age based on estimates of the age of death, went as follows; in 1671–1700 it was 24.8 years for males, 29.8 years for females; during the period 1751–75 it increased to 35.9 for males and 38.3 for females.

This increase in expectation of life is also clear from the ratio of births to the number of married females able to bear children, and from the ratio of the number of children under ten to the number of females able to bear children. The first ratio represents degree of fertility, and the second ratio represents fertility in combination with the child mortality rate. If both rates are converted to index form and compared, we find that in the first period the two indices gradually approach each other, while in the later period the index representing both fertility and the effects of changes in the child mortality rate becomes higher. Since this index is inversely related to the child mortality rate this gives us strong grounds for supposing that the change can be explained solely in terms of the decrease in the child mortality rate.

If this is in fact the case, and if there were no large changes in the proportion of females married or in the age at marriage, the average number of children per household should have increased. However as Tables 18.7 and 18.8 show, the number of children per household in fact decreased. How can this be explained? In the analysis of Yokouchi, the relationship between the movements in the average age at marriage of females and the number of births was carefully examined and it was found that in the latter half of the period the consistent relationship between the two sets of figures disappeared. From this we drew the tentative conclusion that some kind of artificial constraint was operating on the number of births. Family reconstitution carried out for this village led us to the same conclusion.

The fact that child mortality was declining over the whole period means that the imposition of birth control which we have assumed must have kept down the number of births to a very low level. It is this we believe which explains why the number of children per household was lower during the second half of the period.

Table 18.11   *Variable 13: Mean age at time of marriage,*
females,[a] by district

	W	E	C	Y	Total
1671–1700	20.0	20.3	19.9	18.5	19.9
1701–1750	22.0	21.2	21.6	21.1	21.3
1751–1800	19.9	20.6	19.5	18.3	19.9
1801–1850	19.7	20.2	20.0	20.0	20.0
1851–1870	21.2	20.7	21.3	20.3	20.7
Total	20.4	20.6	20.6	19.7	20.4

[a] See pp. 507–508.

SERVANTS[9]

The number of servants per household varies widely. The category 'servants' includes (i) so-called 'subordinate servants', who were engaged in agricultural labour and who remained with the household on a hereditary basis, and (ii) domestic servants. It would seem that the work-system of the agricultural household changed over the period of analysis, finally coming to depend primarily on family labour. The number of servants in category (i) accordingly decreased. Servants of the second type persisted longer in some agricultural households, but eventually their numbers also declined. There were cases, as we have seen, where the number of servants dropped to zero and it was impossible to compute a correlation coefficient.

The trend in the variable representing the number of servants per household, variable (8), is given in Fig. 18.9. It is clear from the graphs that District C – the mountainous area – had a larger number of servants than elsewhere. In other districts the average number of servants per household had already fallen to 0.1 as early as 1730. The figure for District C finally fell below 0.1 in 1770. The correlation between MHS and mean number of servants per household for the whole period studied can therefore only be measured for District C and for the first two periods at most in the case of the remaining districts. In Tables 18.12 and 18.13 will be found the time series for variable (6), the ratio of the number of households with servants to the total number of households, and for variable (7) the average number of servants per household. At the peak, in the series for

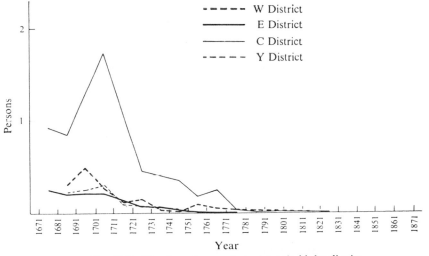

Fig. 18.9 Number of servants by household, by district

[9] See also below, Nakane, Chapter 19, pp. 519–523. Compare the proportion of households with servants in pre-industrial England, above, Laslett, Chapter 4, pp. 151–152, and eighteenth-century Netherlands, above, van der Woude, Chapter 12, pp. 307–308, 314–315.

Table 18.12   *Variable 6: Proportion of households*
with servants, by district

	W	E	C	Y	Total
1671–1700	0.212	0.132	0.361	0.091	0.167
1701–1750	0.060	0.042	0.166	0.063	0.070
1751–1800	0.012	0.005	0.043	—	0.011
1801–1850	—	—	0.002	—	0.000
1851–1870	—	—	—	—	—
Total	0.048	0.037	0.102	0.035	0.050

Table 18.13   *Variable 7: Mean of the number of servants*
in households with servants, by district

	W	E	C	Y	Total
1671–1700	2.63	2.16	3.01	1.20	2.24
1701–1750	2.57	1.82	3.24	1.65	2.17
1751–1800	3.58	1.00	2.19	—	2.03
1801–1850	—	—	2.00	—	2.00
1851–1870	—	—	—	—	—
Total	2.88	1.83	2.76	1.48	2.17

Table 18.14   *Proportion of households with*
three or more generations, by district

	W	E	C	Y	Total
1671–1700	0.375	0.267	0.330	0.331	0.305
1701–1750	0.266	0.226	0.313	0.447	0.292
1751–1800	0.270	0.230	0.221	0.303	0.250
1801–1850	0.290	0.296	0.307	0.336	0.304
1851–1870	0.283	0.297	0.270	0.391	0.303
Total	0.287	0.252	0.281	0.361	0.284

District C, 36.1 % of the households had one or more servants. The number of servants did not simply decline progressively, as perhaps might be expected, for households having servants suddenly ceased to employ them.

EFFECT OF EXPLANATORY VARIABLES IN COMBINATION

Let us now turn to the examination of the combined effects of various explanatory factors which we have been discussing. Figure 18.10 traces the course of what might be called residual mean household size after resident kin and servants

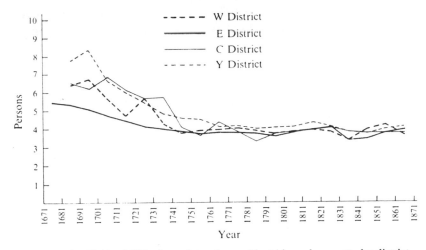

Fig. 18.10   MHS after subtracting resident kin and servants, by district

have been subtracted, and this residual is taken to be what is called elsewhere in this volume the primary, elementary or nuclear family of the household head, his wife and children. It will be noticed that the large differences in MHS across various districts fall markedly when resident kin and servants are excluded in this way. It appears, therefore, that the reason for the higher MHS in Districts Y and C was chiefly the larger number of resident kin per household. It is clear from the data in this figure that convergence to a smaller household size had already begun in 1740.

TEMPORAL AND SPATIAL FACTORS

Two types of variable can be distinguished amongst those which we have been analyzing: (*a*) those that vary over time but not across districts and (*b*) those that vary across districts. The variables presented in Tables 18.4, 18.7, 18.8, 18.10 and 18.11 show variation over time but not across districts; and those presented in Tables 18.5, 18.6, 18.12, 18.13 and 18.14 show variation across districts but not over time. The variables showing variation over time include the number of married couples per household, the number of servants and the generational depth of households, whilst those showing variation across districts comprise the proportion married, the age at marriage and the number of children. We shall call the variables of type (*a*) temporal factors and those of type (*b*) spatial factors. When variables exhibiting spatial or temporal variation are used in correlation analysis with MHS, it will be expected that there should be differences in the types of correlation obtained. In the case of temporal factors, the correlation with MHS is strong, in whatever area or in whatever period it is examined. The same may be said of the Total column for each of these temporal variables. But in the case of the spatial variables, the relationship is weak, especially in the analysis by sub-period for each district. Nonetheless in the Total column correlation values for a few of the spatial variables are fairly high.

POPULATION CHANGE AND MHS

Finally we would like to examine the changes in the population and in MHS and the relationship between the two. In a study of another area, the province of Bungo, in the 1620s, published in 1968,[10] the author concluded that the large size of the households there was due to some kind of constraint upon the increase in population. Conditions were such that the number of agricultural serfs living in the household went up, but so few of them married that the birth rate was held down. Thus a balance seemed to be maintained between births and deaths.

If this conclusion was in fact correct, decline in MHS due to a decline in the number of resident kin and servants meant that one of the factors keeping the growth of population in check was very gradually being eroded in Suwa County during the Tokugawa era. For this reason it would be natural to expect some increase in the population. Figure 18.2 shows that there was an upward trend which was especially strong in District Y, and it should be noted that the rise in the population coincides with the change in the MHS.[11] In almost all cases decrease in MHS was accompanied by increase in the population, except for the 1671 to 1720 period in District Y, where although the population was increasing very rapidly, MHS was in fact increasing.[12] We undertook the following exercise in order to test this observation.

The amount of increase in population in one district in one ten-year interval was correlated with the amount of decrease in MHS in the same district during

---

[10] For example the following statistics are available for Hayami County for the year 1622.

	Married	Unmarried	Proportion married
Blood relatives	991	31	97.0%
Servants	34	358	8.7%
	See Hayami (1968 i): 92.		

[11] In England in the late eighteenth century the tendency was for MHS and population to increase together, see above, Wall, Chapter 5, pp. 199–203. Greven, see below, Chapter 20, p. 555, also equates a rise in MHS with a rapid growth of population in two counties in Massachusetts.

[12] This exception can be explained in the following way. The increase in the MHS for District Y during this period is not due to the appearance of a large household system having a large number of servants with a low marriage rate. For some reason the branching off of households after the marriage of the offspring of the head of the household was restricted. Thus the number of direct relatives of the head of the household and resident kin increased above what it would have been with the normal amount of branching. For the high marriage rate in District Y, see Tables 18.11 and 18.12.

the same sub-period. Only about half the possible cases could be analysed in this way and the results were somewhat complicated for presentation here, and rather variable in quality. It can be stated, however, that there was a significant inverse relationship between household size and population growth in all districts except District C, the mountain area. There were exceptions in some periods and regions and in District E, east of the lake, correlation was low in the earlier period. Nevertheless, it appears that we can conclude from the above analysis that the decrease in MHS or the transition to the small family was generally accompanied by an increase in the population.

Moreover, it can usually be said that the faster the fall in the size of household, the faster the rate of population growth. In Suwa County it seems that the increase of population which accompanied evolution towards the small family rose to a peak in the earlier period of the Tokugawa era. After the middle of the eighteenth century when, except in District Y, the nuclear family stabilised in size, population restrictions were introduced. The large household system, which acted as a restraint on the growth of population, gradually relaxed its influence and population began to rise rapidly, making new restraints necessary. The method chosen to restrain the growth of population was not a return to the large household system, but cruder artificial restraints on population growth.

ANALYSIS OF THE VILLAGE OF YOKOUCHI

So far we have analysed 38 communities in Suwa County, divided into four districts. One village of the 38, Yokouchi, in District E on the plain east of Lake Suwa (see map in Figure 18.1), has the most continuous collection of the shūmon-aratame-chō for the 201 years from 1671 to 1871. No less than 144 individual years are covered by the listings which have survived. The object of this final section is to make use of this quite exceptional source of information in order to try to resolve some of the problems left outstanding in our analysis so far. We have two general purposes in mind. The first is to test one or two of the hypotheses which have been suggested in the foregoing discussion of the 38 communities in the Suwa area. The second is to exploit some special features of the data for Yokouchi, in order to attempt a more thorough analysis of the major issues posed in the earlier portion of this chapter.

The first problem is to decide how reliably age at marriage can be measured indirectly by the method described above, that is by making use of the trend revealed by the changing proportion of married persons in successive age groups. The results of this exercise can be checked at Yokouchi since both age at marriage and proportion married at various ages can be measured directly from the data over practically the whole Tokugawa era. Figure 18.11 presents the outcome of this test. It is clear that the indirect measure adopted is a good one. Indirect computation using the proportion married as described above should, therefore, usually give a close approximation to the average age at marriage.

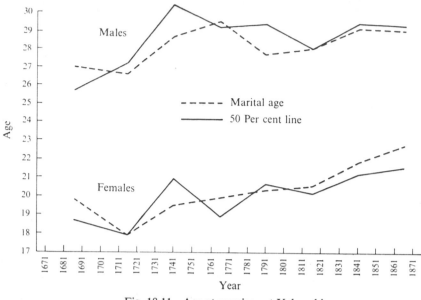

Fig. 18.11   Age at marriage at Yokouchi

The next problem is to pronounce on the efficiency of our indirect measures of fertility. Fertility is calculated as the number of births to every woman of marriageable age, so the problem of measuring it will be solved if we can compute the ratio of children born to the number of wives present at a given point in time. The age of all persons and the number of births is available for Yokouchi, so that it is possible to compose the two following ratios: first the ratio of all births to the number of wives in the most fertile age group, 21 to 40, and second the ratio of the number of children under ten to the number of wives in the age group 16 to 50. This comparison is given in Figure 18.12, and its noteworthy features are as follows: (i) Both the actual and the substitute series have roughly the same trend. (ii) There is a time lag between the two series: if we examine the peaks we find that the second lags behind the first by about seven years. (iii) There is change over time. In the early period the first ratio is higher than the second; in the middle period the two ratios are approximately equal, but in the later period the first ratio is lower than the second. (iv) Both ratios reach a low point in the period 1770–90. (v) Both series have a cycle of almost twenty years. This set of results raises some detailed interpretative issues, but we must pass them over on this occasion.

There are one or two other questions which can be referred to research results from Yokouchi. The first is the extent of the adoption of children under ten years of age. Adoption played an important role in Japanese life since it was an expedient against the extinction of family lines, and the practice was fairly

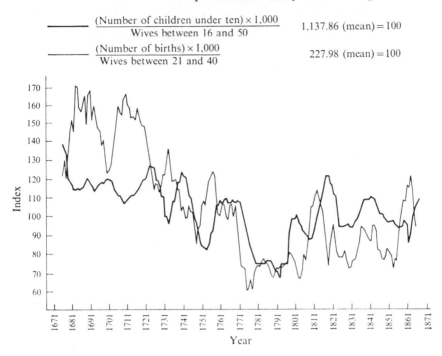

$$\frac{(\text{Number of children under ten}) \times 1,000}{\text{Wives between 16 and 50}} \qquad 1,137.86 \ (\text{mean}) = 100$$

$$\frac{(\text{Number of births}) \times 1,000}{\text{Wives between 21 and 40}} \qquad 227.98 \ (\text{mean}) = 100$$

Fig. 18.12   Fertility measures for Yokouchi (nine-year moving averages)

common. This raises the possibility of error in using figures for the number of children under age ten as a measure of fertility. Table 18.15 shows the prevalence of the practice at Yokouchi, where only ten per cent of the total number of the children in question were adopted under the age of ten. This is not large enough to bias any computation. As for child mortality, Table 18.16 has been drawn up from previous research results so as to provide finer detail. It shows that the death rate of children decreased substantially over the Tokugawa era. Those living to age eleven or more rose from 62 % early in the period to 79 % at the end.

Finally the results for age specific fertility obtained from the analysis of family reconstitution forms may be mentioned. These are given in Figure 18.13 and reveal clear differences in level at different periods. We believe that this was due to some restraint on population increase, rather than to a decrease in fecundity. The distribution of the number of births by age at marriage is set out in Figure 18.14 as evidence for this hypothesis. During the earlier period, when we believe there were no restrictions on population there was an obvious relationship between the number of births and the age at marriage, and it is in our view a highly significant fact that this relationship becomes less marked during the later part of the period.

The main feature of the sources for the village of Yokouchi is that enough has

Table 18.15   *Total adopted children and adopted children under ten at Yokouchi*

Periods	Recorded as adopted	
	Total	Under age ten
1671–1700	11	1
1701–1750	13	0
1751–1800	38	0
1801–1850	35	2
1851–1870	32	4
Total	129	7 (5.4%)

Table 18.16   *Child mortality and survival rate at Yokouchi*

Year of birth		1671–1700	1701–1725	1726–1750	1751–1775	Total
Number of births		227	302	278	309	1,116
Number of deaths at age:	1	—	2	—	1	3
	2	32	37	19	14	102
	3	10	31	16	19	14
	4	24	26	12	9	71
	5	9	14	12	8	43
Sub-total		75	110	59	51	295
	6	3	4	11	8	26
	7	3	5	5	1	14
	8	2	1	4	2	9
	9	1	1	1	2	5
	10	2	—	2	2	6
Sub-total		11	11	23	15	60
Grand total		86	121	82	66	355
Number of survivals to age over 11		141	181	196	243	761
Rate of deaths age 1 to 5		0.33	0.36	0.21	0.17	0.26
Rate of deaths age 1 to 10		0.38	0.40	0.30	0.21	0.31
Survival rate at age 11		0.62	0.60	0.70	0.79	0.69

been preserved to allow us to follow for no less than 200 years the demographic activity of each individual in each household. This provides the opportunity for analysis by family reconstitution, the results of which have already been reported,[13] and we should like to record here some of its implications for the problems raised above. Figure 18.15 shows trends in population, in number of households and

[13] Hayami (1969).

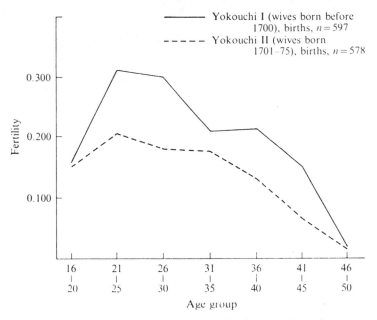

Fig. 18.13   Age-specific fertility at Yokouchi

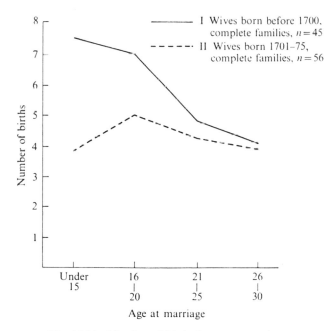

Fig. 18.14   Number of births by age at marriage
(wives in complete families only) at Yokouchi

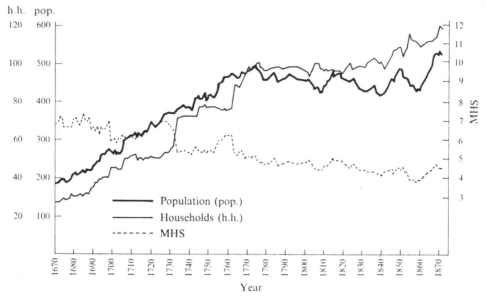

Fig. 18.15   Trends in population, number of households and
mean size of household at Yokouchi

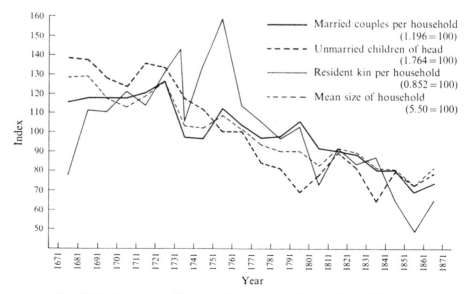

Fig. 18.16   Mean size of household: married couples, resident children and
resident kin per household at Yokouchi

in MHS over the 200-year period of analysis. Comparison with Figures 18.2 and 18.3 suggests that the shape of these curves for Yokouchi is virtually the same as those exhibited by District E, the area east of Lake Suwa in which Yokouchi itself is located. Population growth does not quite conform, since the population of Yokouchi went on growing until the 1770s.

Figure 18.16 sets MHS alongside the following: number of married couples per household; number of resident kin, and the number of unmarried children of the head of the household. The values of MHS and the trend in the MHS time series are virtually the same as those for District E as a whole.

The feature of this evidence which best illustrates the decline of MHS is the change from households containing several married couples to households with one only. Where decline in MHS was accompanied by an increase in population it seems likely that this was usually the result of the break-up of households. In analysing this phenomenon we will ignore the sociological factors making for the preservation of the household line and concentrate on the demographic aspects of the fragmentation process. Table 18.17 shows the rate of household fission over approximate twenty-five year intervals. Each household usually divided into two, but there were also cases where one household broke up into three or four others. If the number of households which were split up in this way is divided by the total number of households, we find that the ratio is highest in the years around 1700. In general during the earlier half of the period the ratio is high, low from 1776 to 1850, and that there is a slight increase after 1851. The behaviour of this ratio corresponds well with the movement of the indices in Figure 18.15.

The evidence from Yokouchi allows us to trace the fission process for a single household over the full 200 years. It is possible to work out from the successive listings the lineage of the households which had their origin in household number 12 of the first year, 1671. This household was originally composed of three couples and a total of eleven members. Table 18.18 has been prepared from

Table 18.17 *Division of households at Yokouchi, by period*

Periods	Dividing to				Mean no. dividing per year	Ratio of divided to whole households
	2	3	4	Total		
1671–1700	25	1	—	26	0.86	2.57
1701–1725	10	1	—	11	0.44	0.90
1726–1750	21	6	—	27	1.08	1.53
1751–1775	16	4	1	21	0.84	0.96
1776–1800	7	2	—	9	0.36	0.37
1801–1825	14	—	—	14	0.56	0.56
1826–1850	14	—	—	14	0.56	0.53
1851–1871	17	3	—	20	0.95	0.84
Total	124	17	1	142	0.71	0.93

Table 18.18   *A Yokouchi household of 1676 and its successor households: households, household members and married couples*

(For years when division actually took place)

Years	Households	Members	Married couples
1676	1	12	3
1678	3	13	3
1689	4	18	5
1699	5	26	7
1706	6	32	7
1732	7	39	11
1734	9	47	13
1746	10	62	13
1763	12	62	16
1767	14	68	18
1769	16	70	19
1801	14	55	13
1802	14	49	12
1832	13	64	14
1836	14	72	15
1840	15	75	14
1844	16	82	16
1854	19	84	18
1859	19	77	18
1863	19	78	15
1870	19	77	19

this evidence, giving for each sub-period the number of members and the number of couples in each household for the whole complex which originated in household number 12 of 1671.

From this table it is clear that the tempo of change in MHS is about the same as that of the rest of the village and even of District E itself. The original household eventually gave rise to twenty-seven further households during the course of the 200-year period of analysis, that is there was on average a division once every 7.4 years. Nine households died out, so that by 1871 the total number of households in the lineage was nineteen. The total number of members in all the related households at the end of the period was 6.4 times the number at the beginning, and the number of couples multiplied by 6.3. This increase in households and in married couples was only one-third of the increase in the number of households in the village over the period. There is no reason to believe that household number 12 of 1671 was an exception in the history of Yokouchi.[14]

---

[14] Smith, see above, Chapter 17, pp. 438–440, 470–471, also assesses the durability of households in Tokugawa Japan. Compare Blayo's analysis of the development of 184 conjugal households in the French village of Grisy-Suisnes, above, Chapter 9, pp. 261–264. See also Hammel's account of population turnover in sixteenth-century Serbia, above, Chapter 14, pp. 343–344, 348.

Table 18.19 *Number of households in each lineage at Yokouchi*

No. of house-holds	1671	1700	1725	1751	1775	1801	1825	1850	1871
1	1	3	3	5	6	5	6	6	7
2	1	3	1	1	1	—	—	—	—
3	1	1	1	2	3	2	—	—	—
4	1	—	—	—	—	—	—	—	—
5	1	1	1	2	3	3	3	3	3
6	1	2	2	1	2	2	—	—	—
7	1	1	2	2	2	3	3	4	4
8	1	—	—	—	—	—	—	—	—
9	1	1	2	3	3	3	4	4	5
10	1	2	2	2	2	2	2	1	—
11	1	2	3	5	4	5	6	5	3
12	1	5	6	10	16	13	12	16	19
13	1	4	4	8	9	9	9	11	8
14	1	1	—	—	—	—	—	—	—
15	1	—	—	—	—	—	—	—	—
16	1	1	2	2	2	3	3	4	4
17	1	1	2	4	5	4	4	4	6
18	1	2	2	4	5	3	2	2	2
19	1	2	2	3	5	4	4	5	3
20	1	4	4	7	11	11	12	16	25
21	1	2	1	1	2	1	—	—	—
22	1	1	1	1	1	1	1	1	1
23	1	1	1	3	5	5	3	2	2
24	1	2	2	2	3	5	4	4	4
25	1	1	2	2	2	—	—	—	—
26	1	—	—	—	—	—	—	—	—
27	1	2	3	6	8	9	11	11	11
Others[a]	—	1	1	1	1	2	8	10	13
Total	27	46	50	77	101	95	97	109	120

[a] Including households which moved from elsewhere and households whose origin is unclear.

Table 18.19 gives the change in the number of households for each lineage by twenty-five-year intervals. Original household number 20 gave rise to the largest number of successor households: twenty-five separate households arose from it over the 200 years. Household number 22, on the other hand, did not divide once over the entire period. Eleven of the original twenty-seven households died out completely, thus giving a rate of attrition of about 40 %. On average the number of households increased 6.7 times in 200 years, when the number which actually survived is taken as the divisor. When the original number of households is taken as the divisor, the number of households increased four times.

19. An interpretation of the size and structure of the household in Japan over three centuries

Chie Nakane

In Peter Laslett's contribution, on the English household, to this volume It Is stated that the transformation of English society by the process of industrialisation does not appear to have been accompanied by any decrease in the size of the average household.[1] This is of great interest to me as being directly applicable to the results of my analysis of the Japanese data. In the Tokugawa censuses for various regions of Japan that I have studied so far, I have found a mean household size of 5 or a little under, which corresponds to that of the modern national censuses of 1920–55. It is true that Tokugawa censuses are imperfect in some ways, and processing them is a complicated business. Nevertheless, abundant records are available bearing on the issue, and it may well be that Japan possesses one of the richest archives of such materials. The analysis and interpretation of these data make it possible to infer the standard size and structure of households in Tokugawa Japan.

Detailed investigation of the data on village communities in the Tokugawa era shows that household structure at that time was identical with that of the modern period succeeding it. The standard pattern consisted of the household head, his wife and their unmarried sons and daughters. The system which governed the structure of the Japanese household 家 (Ie)[2] was based on a rule named 'one-son succession', a rule which is discussed at length in my recent book.[3] If the household had not been founded by its current head, but by a predecessor, then the head's parents, or one of them, might be present. If the designated successor to the household head was already married at the time the listing was made out, then his wife and children were included in the domestic

---

[1] See above, Laslett, Chapter 4, p. 126.

[2] *Ie* is pronounced as two syllables: *e* in the Japanese romanisation is always pronounced as é in French. Traditionally the term *ie* is used for either household or family without a conceptual distinction. In the modern census, *setai* is used for household and *kazoku* for family.

[3] Nakane, *Kinship and economic organization in rural Japan* (1967): esp. 1–7.

group. But otherwise the standard form was that of the elementary family living by itself, as has been stated.

Because of this one-son succession rule, a household including more than one married couple of the same generation was uncommon in Japan. The maximum number of couples in one household would be three, though, as one would expect, this happened only very rarely. Indeed, it was always considered so unusual that the three couples comprising such a household used to be asked to be the first to step on to a new bridge as a 'lucky' symbol on an auspicious occasion. Even the presence of two couples of successive generations was unlikely to continue for long, and such a period would have been shorter in earlier times, when life expectancy was generally lower than it is today. An elementary family with a widowed mother or mother-in-law of the head must have been more common as a household composition. It should always be borne in mind that there were a considerable number of households established by non-successors, and these naturally consisted simply of the elementary family alone. Considering the traditional structure of the Japanese household, the basis of which is the elementary family, mean household size in pre-industrial Japan could not have been very large, and was in fact 5 or a little under.

In Japan, the extended or joint household in which married brothers or sisters lived together was a rarity in all periods covered by known numerical records. Although some instances of large households so composed can be found, the structural principle remains the same as that of ordinary households, with the simple addition of extra members, as I shall explain presently. By a large household is meant here an average of six persons to the domestic group over an area of some size, including several villages. Table 19.1 presents the best illustrative examples of mean household size in different regions in pre-industrial Japan for the period 1644–1879.

In this table, each community or set of communities for which mean household size is known is classified according to its surroundings. Class I stands for the vicinity of a commercial centre; Class II means typically rural, mainly agricultural; Class III means a remote area. Instances of places or regions with exceptionally large mean household size have been deliberately included, and it will be seen that Takayama, number 10, has the highest mean household size at 9.46. But at the end of the list of households, which includes the names and ages of each individual member, it is stated that this community consisted of 48 if houses are counted, but 133 counting the number of hearths.[4]

Takayama was in fact one of the largest towns in the hilly central area of Japan and had developed round the castle of a feudal lord. It seems to have been a customary arrangement in such a town, where the residential area was necessarily restricted, that a newly married couple not in the line of succession lived in an annexe attached to the natal house of one of the spouses. Alternatively part of a large house was often rented to a small family. Tokugawa registration

4 *Gifu-ken* (1968): 448–67.

Table 19.1 *Mean household size, Japan 1644–1879*
Fourteen samples in date order

	Date	Locality	Population	House-holds	MHS	Classi-fication
1	1644	Wakae (Osaka Prefecture)	1,306	230	5.68	I
2	1649	Wakayama Prefecture (7 communities)	3,230	730	4.42	II
3	1654	Ikeda district (gun) (Gifu Prefecture)	93	19	4.90	II
4	1669	Fief of Ueda (Nagano Prefecture)	30,844	7,150	4.31	II
5	1698	Okazaki Renjaku-chō (Aichi Prefecture)	780	121	6.45[a]	I
6	1713	Nishinomiya Hama-issai-chō[b] (Hyogo Prefecture)	653	132	4.95	I
7	1713	Gorohei-shinden (Nagano Prefecture)	467	122	3.83	II
8	1734	(Tokugawa model village)	120	24	5.00	—
9	1800	Gorohei-shinden (Nagano Prefecture)	791	175	4.52	II
10	1843	Takayama (Gifu Prefecture)	454	48 (133)	9.46[a] (3.41)	I
11	1864	Futagawa (Shizuoka Prefecture)	1,468	322	4.56	I
12	1867	Hida Shirakawa-mura (Gifu Prefecture)	2,314	252	9.18[a]	III
13	1870	(National total)	32,794,897	7,058,961	4.65	—
14	1879	Aomori Prefecture (3 communities)	459	63	7.29[a]	III

[a] Exceptionally large: explanation in text.
[b] For original document and its analysis see Appendix I. This listing is also used by Smith, above, Chapter 17, pp. 447, 458–459 and Laslett, above, Chapter 1, pp. 52–62, 74–85. The totals differ slightly.

forms usually divide the population up into blocks of persons which are ordinarily understood to correspond to households. In Appendix I the listing for community number 6, Nishinomiya Hama-issai-chō, is printed at length, in ideographic form and it will be seen that the blocks of persons do appear to be households.[5] Some returns, unfortunately, list inhabitants simply by house or by compound, and that for Takayama in 1843 is exceptional in distinguishing numbers of hearths from numbers of houses.

The general arrangement of the Japanese house is such that within one compound only one house is found with store house and cowshed, etc. occasionally attached, and the house is occupied by the members of one household. But

[5] For further information on household structure in this ward see above, Smith, Chapter 17, pp. 447, 458–459 and Laslett, above, Chapter 1, pp. 52–62, 74–85. See also the reproduction of two pages from the registers of a neighbouring ward, Hama-kubo-chō, above, p. 435.

Table 19.2   *Mean size of household, Ueda Fief: 1663 with summary data for 1959*[a]

Town				Countryside			
Street names	Population	Households	MHS	Villages[b]	Population	Households	MHS
Shiromawari	—	245	—	Shiojiri (12)	3,396	693	4.9
Unno-chō	657	77	8.5	Kokubunji (13)	2,111	431	4.9
Kaji-chō	282	42	6.7	Arauma (10)	4,553	918	4.9
Yoko-chō	353	65	5.4	Tanaka (19)	3,659	779	4.7
Hara-chō	790	99	8.0	Koizumi (11)	3,925	862	4.5
Yanagi-chō	136	31	4.4	Urano (15)	4,166	972	4.3
Konya-chō	234	26	9.0	Shiota (22)	5,273	1,617	3.3
Tamachi	158	23	6.9	Takeishi (1)	1,151	270	4.3
Total	2,610	608	7.2	103 villages	28,234	6,542	4.2

Totals: 1663 Town and Countryside: Population 30,844: Households 7,150; MHS 4.5
Totals: 1959
   Town of Ueda: Population 66,600; households 14,722; MHS 4.5
   Rural Area: Population 58,906; households 12,061; MHS 4.9
   Total: Population 125,506; households 26,783; MHS 4.7

[a] Figures rearranged from *Ueda Chisagata-shi*, Historical Section no. 2, a reference supplied by Dr S. Oishi.
[b] Each name indicates a district (*gun*), and the number of villages in the *gun* is given in brackets.

merchant houses in town are somewhat different: part of a large house or an annexed guest house may sometimes be offered to a household of relatives, or rented to other people. In the Tokugawa listing, therefore, one house may include a small attached household besides the household of the owner. Moreover, merchant households normally included servants who were treated like family members, so that in general it would appear that mean household size was larger in towns than in the countryside. In Table 19.2 two sets of relevant figures are given for a particular Japanese fief (as it would be called in medieval Europe, the area under a feudal lord), that of Ueda, part of the present Nagano Prefecture. The first set relates to the year 1663 and the second set to the year 1959 in the same geographical area: it will be seen what an interesting contrast there is between household size in rural and urban areas at the two dates.

There is a remarkable similarity in mean household size in 1663 and in 1959, but whereas the urban household was much larger in 1663 than the rural household, in 1959 the rural household was a little larger than the urban. In the Tokugawa countryside, moreover, mean size of household seems to have been very much the same as it is today over the whole country, as can be seen from Table 19.6 on page 531 below. This only holds, of course, if the unit is the same in each case, that is if the block of persons between divisions in the Tokugawa listing corresponds to the *setai*, or commensal group, which defines the household in the contemporary Japanese census. The Takayama example seems to me to confirm that this correspondence does hold, and that the hearth or household in that listing must be taken as having a mean size of 3.41, the figure 9.46 being reserved for the houseful.

We know quite a lot about another of the urban communities listed in Table 19.1. This is number 5, Okazaki Renjaku-chō, that is the street called Renjaku in the town of Okazaki in 1698. Okazaki was the birth place of Ieyasu, the first Tokugawa Shogun. The Renjaku was a street specialising in dealings in cloth used for *kimono*, and the census[6] states that out of a population of 780, 362 were servants, of whom 185 were male and 177 female. Only 64 of these came from Okazaki itself, the remaining 298 (80 %) coming from adjacent areas including villages in the hinterland, as was customary not only in this but in many other regions. In the Renjaku-chō in Okazaki in 1698, 68 out of 121 households had servants who were distributed as follows: one household had more than 20 servants; 10 households had more than 10; 28 households had more than 5; and 28 households had less than 5. The total population excluding servants was 418, which means that the mean size of the immediate family was 3.47 as compared with a mean household size of 6.45.[7]

Among the villages listed in Table 19.1 there is a large variation in mean household size ranging from 3.83 (number 7) to 5.68 (number 1). Such differences can be shown to be related to the economic situation. The more favourable the environment, such as a village on fertile land situated close to a commercial centre, the larger the mean household size. This is illustrated by comparing two villages in the same year, 1713: Nishinomiya Hama-issai-chō with a household size of 4.95 and Gorohei-shinden with a household size of 3.83. The distribution of households by size in the two villages is shown in Fig. 19.1. As its classification in Table 19.1 indicates, Nishinomiya Hama-issai-chō was a fairly prosperous fishing village. It was situated near Kobe, one of the largest ports in Japan, while Gorohei-shinden was a typical agricultural village in central Japan having little contact with commercial activities. The listing for Nishinomiya Hama-issai-chō and its analysis in Appendix I must be taken to represent the composition of a commercially active Tokugawa rural community; Gorohei-shinden would present a very different picture. Village number 1 in Table 19.1, Wakae, was one of the comparatively advanced communities situated in the vicinity of Osaka, the largest commercial centre of feudal Japan. In this village 42 % of the total households employed servants, the remaining 58 % being small households without servants.[8]

The high proportion of households with servants in the towns and prosperous

---

[6] Sekiyama (1958): 222; Nagao (1938).

[7] The districts analysed by Akira Hayami, see above, Chapter 18, pp. 503–504, contained on average far fewer servants. Compare the proportion of households with servants in pre-industrial England, above, Laslett, Chapter 4, pp. 151–152 and eighteenth-century Netherlands, above, van der Woude, Chapter 12, pp. 307–308, 314–315.

[8] Takao (1958): 33.

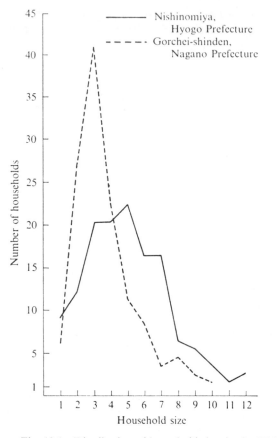

Fig. 19.1   Distribution of households by size in 1713

rural communities of the Tokugawa era implies an exchange of persons with other areas. For the servants did not come from the communities where they served, but for the most part from the less prosperous and less developed adjacent areas. It can be inferred that the mean household size of the villages which used to supply servants must have been smaller than that of the towns and villages where servants were employed.

Households which had lost some of their members because they had gone into service usually continued to exist, but only as small domestic groups. There were even cases where a whole family went into service in different households and therefore ceased to form a household of its own. But instances of an entire family taking up employment as servants as a complete unit seldom occurred in Japan. Occurrences of these two kinds would of course have reduced the number of households, but on the whole, so far as the various local records show, such things were rare, and servants' natal households were mostly still to be found in their original villages. Mean household size should, therefore, have remained under 5 over an entire region, including a commercial centre, and a tract of countryside, and the fief of Ueda is a fair example. The total population of the entire region under the Lord of Ueda was 30,844 in 1663, including the urban and rural areas, and the mean household size was 4.5. The largest mean household size was 9.0 for Konya-chō in Ueda town, and the smallest was 3.3 for Shiota *gun* (a set of 22 villages in the hinterland). As I have already pointed out the figure of 4.5 for 1663 is remarkably close to that of 4.7 in 1959 for the same geographical area, and even closer to the figure of 4.65 of national average household size in 1870 (Table 19.1, no. 13).

From the analysis of the census data so far mentioned, it would seem that the average size of Tokugawa households must have been 5 at the most, and perhaps rather less than this. It should also be noted that the standard village taken as a model in 1734 by the Tokugawa government for administrative (revenue collecting) purposes,[9] also had a mean household size of 5.[10] The actual size of the ordinary household at the time must surely have been reflected in this figure. Since this household size corresponds so closely to that of modern Japan, at least up to 1955, it can be justifiably assumed that mean household size has not changed during the process of rapid industrialisation.

Numbers 12 and 14 in Table 19.1 are special cases and need some explanation. They are exceptional because they contain households which include married collaterals, a very unusual arrangement indeed for Japan. An example of such a household is to be seen in Fig. 19.2 taken from a household in Shimokita, Aomori Prefecture,[11] and another in Fig. 19.3 taken from Hida Shirakawa-mura, Gifu Prefecture.[12]

These two communities were of a very similar economic type, though the actual basis of the economy was entirely different. Shirakawa-mura has become so notorious for the huge size of its households that we shall have to devote the next section to discussing it. It may be noticed that in both villages arable land was very limited and soil poor so that employment other than agricultural had to be found for subsistence. The people of Shimokita took to fishing, for abalones and tangles in particular, and the people of Hida Shirakawa-mura to silk cultivation. These are both types of household industry which require a large labour force; the larger the size of household therefore, the larger the income.[13]

The remote and isolated situation of both communities was undoubtedly related to the mixed economy which characterised them. Shimokita was situated on the narrow northern coastal strip of Honshū, the main island of Japan,

[9] See Nakane (1967): 42.
[10] See above, Table 19.1, no. 8.
[11] Takeuchi (1968): 203–301, esp. 294, Figure.
[12] See below, p. 530.
[13] Somewhat different explanations are offered for the formation of frérèches in eighteenth-century Corsica, see above, Dupâquier, Chapter 11, pp. 292, 294 and fifteenth-century Tuscany, see above, Klapisch, Chapter 10, p. 280.

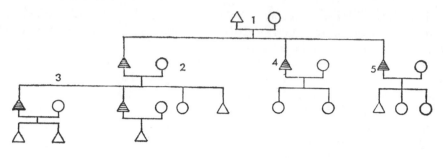

☠ Members of the fishing crew

Fig. 19.2   Composition of a household at Skimokita in 1927

between the mountains and the sea, and Hida was in the heart of the central mountain range. It may be that the kin network was practically the only source of labour. In Shimokita, each household formed the crew of a fishing boat; and it was the traditional custom of the village that allocation of rights in resources derived from fishing and other similar economic activities were held by the household unit. Fig. 19.2 is taken from one of the most successful households, in which five of the men in the household worked as a fishing crew, and their wives cultivated the small landholding. Such household industries have survived in Japan for more than half a century after the national transformation to an industrial economy.

Apart from these exceptional cases where the large family formed an economic unit, many wealthy households in other areas were engaged in various kinds of local industry, and formed large domestic groups along with their employees, who were called *hōkōnin* (servants). Such household economies seem to have been most prevalent and prosperous between the later half of the nineteenth century and the early part of the twentieth century. These large establishments and those of Shimokita and Hida, seem to me to have existed for economic reasons alone: they were not a reflection of the family ideology of traditional Japan. The composition and status grouping of such large households certainly strongly suggest that this was so, as well as the process of their disintegration, which is discussed in the next section. Although such large households existed at a certain period in specific localities, their effect on the average size of the total number of households in Japan seems to have been negligible.

SHIRAKAWA-MURA: A MISLEADING EXAMPLE OF EXTENDED HOUSEHOLDS

The large families of Hida Shirakawa-mura in Gifu Prefecture and its adjacent areas have been fairly well known in Japan for some time. Some of the houses once lived in by these large families were recently taken over by the government for the nation and have proved a strong tourist attraction. For many years, scholars believed that these large families were a remnant of an ancient large family system or of a matrilineal tradition. However, as further work has been done, it has now become clear that these families like those at Shimokita, were a product of the specific economic situation of the remote hill area where they lived, where resources were exceptionally limited.[14]

Shirakawa-mura, a district consisting of the twenty-three villages (*buraku*) set out in Table 19.4, is situated in a narrow valley in the heart of hilly country adjoining the Japanese Alps. Although the area is sited along an old trade route traversing the hill regions between centres in the northern and southern delta plains, communications between the villagers and the outside world were poor until the early twentieth century. Owing to the limited space and poor soil, wet rice cultivation was difficult, and agricultural production was very low. The villagers depended mostly on land cleared from the forest slopes and used for dry field farming: deccan-grass and millet were the crops. It is said that their main meals consisted of these deccan-grasses eked out with horse-chestnuts collected from the forest.

Acute shortage of arable land seems to have begun during the later period of the Tokugawa era (that is by the first half of the nineteenth century), when the number of households permitted in a village became fixed. Thus it became very difficult for families to establish new branch households for second and third sons. According to the local records, before that time a new branch household was occasionally set up by a group of persons (i.e. an elementary family, with or without additional members) dividing off from the original household. This was the normal procedure followed in many other villages in Japan, although the time of separation came later than usual in this particular area. The split did not occur immediately after the marriage of second and third sons, but when several children had been born and their families had become fairly large.

The branching off of households in this way seems to have been stopped by the middle of the nineteenth century, as is shown by the genealogical evidence for several households. Table 19.3 is an illustration of this from the household of the Tōyama family line.

The seventeen members of the Tōyama household in 1853 included two families of brothers of the head, beside that of his successor, who was the husband of his eldest daughter, an adopted son-in-law. The problems of subsistence created by such large households were solved by the cultivation of silk, which required a large labour force and yielded a cash return for the payment of taxes and the purchase of staple foods, cotton clothes and other basic household needs. It is said that silk provided about 60 % of the income of a prosperous household at that time.

Thus by the middle of the nineteenth century, the unique custom had de-

---

[14] For details see Ema (1942) and (1943); Fukushima (1954); Honjō (1920); Koyama (1936); Kodama (1953); Okamura (1929); Tamaki (1959).

Table 19.3   *Numbers of persons in the household of the*
Tōyama family line, Shirakawa-mura, 1818–1955[a]

1818	9	1880	36	1930	20
1853	17	1909	40	1940	16 (8)[b]
1867	26	1915	36	1945	14
1877	31	1920	31	1955	5

[a] Data from Tamaki (1959): 288–91.
[b] Actual number of resident members: smaller than official registration figure, see Fig. 19.3.

veloped whereby second and third sons were kept in their natal house with their wives and children. This custom developed even further, so that daughters and sons remained at home without a formal marriage, as members of the family labour force, the men visiting their women at night. Though a form of visiting marriage had prevailed in this area and elsewhere in Japan, it was practised only during the early stage of the union, usually before a couple had children. In Shirakawa this custom had become a life-pattern. Children were kept and fed in their mother's natal house, and the husband worked for *his* natal house, not for his wife and children, although he occasionally supplied his children with food and clothes.

Only the son who was the successor to the household had a formal marriage ceremony, and could take his wife and children to his home. The members not in the succession line, were called *oji* (for men) and *oba* (for women) connoting lower status as extra household members, although the terms literally mean 'uncle' and 'aunt'. These sons and daughters had to remain in their natal households, since no alternative means of subsistence was open to them. It was almost impossible to set up a household without permission from the household head and even if they could build a small hut, it would have been out of the question to find work or a piece of land to live on. The area was covered with thick snow during the long winter, and it was essential to have a properly built house. Communications were very poor and towns a long way away; in any case a move to the town would not always mean certain employment. Thus internal and external conditions combined in this area in producing these unique large families. It was essential to the continued existence of the natal household that kin should stay at home, because of the great difficulty in getting labour from outside. In some less remote regions adjacent to this particular area, it was possible to hire outside labour so that the practice of sericulture was not a necessary correlate of a large family even under these conditions.

During the period between the middle nineteenth century and the early twentieth century, this area had the largest household size in Japan. Table 19.4 shows that mean size of household was 9.5 in 1853 and 9.2 in 1867 throughout the twenty-three villages (*buraku*). The largest sizes were found in Kitani village,

Table 19.4   *Households, population and mean household size,*
Shirakawa-mura, nineteenth century[a]

	1853			1867		
	House-holds	Popula-tion	MHS	House-holds	Popula-tion	MHS
Ogami	6	63	10.5	7	73	10.4
Fukushima	2	17	8.5	2	26	10.5
Maki	2	32	16.0	2	32	16.0
Mihoro	4	78	19.5	4	80	20.0
Nagase	13	227	17.5	13	201	15.4
Hirase	7	117	16.7	7	118	16.8
Kitani	7	147	21.0	7	140	20.0
Total	41	681	16.6	42	670	16.0
Hokiwaki	6	64	10.7	6	40	6.6
Noya	3	27	9.0	3	23	7.6
Omaki	12	106	8.8	13	95	7.3
Okubo	2	26	13.0	2	23	11.5
Mogari	8	65	8.1	8	75	9.4
Total	31	287	9.3	32	256	8.0
Hagi-machi	80	600	7.5	63	410	6.5
Shima	6	78	13.0	7	60	8.6
Ushikubi	5	46	9.2	6	48	8.0
Hatoya	18	107	5.9	18	103	5.7
Iijima	49	359	7.3	53	399	7.5
Total	157	1,190	7.6	147	1,020	6.9
Uchigae	3	32	10.7	3	39	13.0
Kasura	6	65	10.8	6	79	13.1
Tsubakihara	5	48	9.6	5	53	10.6
Arigahara	3	50	16.7	3	60	20.0
Ashikura	5	65	13.0	5	71	14.2
Koshirakawa	9	66	7.3	9	70	7.8
Total	31	326	10.5	31	372	12.0
Grand total	261	2,478	9.5	252	2,314	9.2

[a] Data from Tamaki (1959): 158–9. He also gives overall figures for 1797 and 1821: MHS was 9.4 in both years.

at 21.0 in 1853 and 20.0 in 1867. The smallest were for Hatoya village, at 5.9 in 1853 and 5.7 in 1867. The change in the mean size of household at Hirase, where many numerical records are available between 1853 and 1942 can be seen in Table 19.5. The figures reach a peak at the beginning of the twentieth century, and then gradually decrease, indicating clearly the effect of industrialisation.

Molybdenum mining began to expand at the end of the nineteenth century and in 1908 the Shokawa Timber Company was established. This was a time of great

Table 19.5   *Mean size of household at Hirase, 1853–1949*[a]

	Households	Persons	MHS
1853	7	117	16.7
1867	7	118	16.8
1876	7	128	18.3
1887	7	152	21.7
1902	7	163	23.3
1907	9	149	16.5
1913	10	133	13.3
1916	14	165	11.8
1917	19	164	8.6
1920	21	166	7.9
1925	32	168	5.3
1937	61	276	4.5
1942	92	486	5.3

[a] Data from Tamaki (1959): 158, 170, 311.

prosperity associated with the Russo-Japanese War when much industry was springing up in Japan. These economic changes seem to have also affected the remote mountain villages in Hida Shirawaka-mura, and resulted in many members of the old households becoming wage earners. In fact the local records show that from 1907 second and third sons began to leave their native villages, most of them going to Takayama,[15] one of the towns which developed during the feudal age in Gifu Prefecture situated about 64 km. from Shirakawa-mura. The appearance of the term 'runaway' in Tokugawa records suggests that even at that time there were some who left their native villages. Up to 1891–7 these numbers gradually increased, but this migration was very small as compared with that experienced in 1907 and after. This exodus was a major factor in the dissolution of the large household, though the final and main cause of its decline was the construction of a hydro-electric power station in Hirase Buraku in 1923–5.

Detailed study of the process of disintegration in these large households reveals that such a unique institution was not a reflection of a traditional family system, nor of the sociological ideology of the Japanese people, but the outcome of the specific problems of this remote area which necessitated such a way of life for reasons of subsistence. Many members of these households were dissatisfied with their situation, and when it became easier to obtain jobs outside the village almost all second and third sons left with their wives and children. They established independent households of their own without having to wait for gifts of land or property from their native household, the *Ie*.

The wealthier households, which were also larger than the average for this area, were somewhat slower in splitting up. For example of this we may turn

[15] No. 10 of Table 19.1, see above p. 519.

back to the Tōyama family the figures for which are given in Table 19.3. It was the analysis of the lineal descendants of the man who founded the house which showed that in 1818 there were only 9 persons, forming an elementary family. Since second and third sons remained in the household after marriage, membership increased to 26 by 1867, and the peak came in 1909 when there were 40 members, including 23 unmarried children. But nearly everyone left the household during the following thirty years; all the men and women not in line of succession departed, except for one or two of the older ones. The linkages between persons and approximate dates of departure can be seen in Fig. 19.3. It can be said of this example and by extension of the whole society of Hida Shirakawa-mura, that the unusually large family institution lasted for only half a century.

The principle of one-son-succession, which was common to all Japan, is well illustrated by the analysis of the Tōyama family. Members other than son-successors (normally the eldest son) were simply accommodated in the house as labourers, rather than as family members of equal status, and therefore these large families were not, strictly speaking, exceptional in terms of Japanese family structure. But though the frequent portrayal of the disintegration of the large family during the process of industrialisation does seem to be true in this particular case, the large family as such was not the traditional basis of the Japanese family institution. Since these large households were the product of a specific economic situation in the late feudal age, such a disintegration would presumably have been brought about by any change for the better, economically speaking, and not necessarily by the advent of industrialism. Furthermore, if the village had been in an area of good arable land and near an outlet both for the sale of produce and for the migration of surplus population, large families would never have existed at all.

There are large Hindu families in India, where the process of disintegration was somewhat different from that of the Hida families of Japan. Though the larger household group did split into smaller units, they continued to maintain strong ties between former members. These ties included their descendants, and the result was the formation of a kinship network, bound together partly by religion, and partly by economics. I have even come across cases where industrialisation, and the consequent increase in income per head, has actually created large joint families. This is understandable if it is remembered that among the Hindus, the large joint family was the traditional ideal, and only an unfavourable environment would stop this from being achieved. In Japan on the other hand, a small family (not including more than one married collateral) was the ideal, and the peculiar environment in this case was the cause of the growth of unusually large families. These two types of large households are entirely different in concept (and structure) and cannot be equated, though when industrialisation occurs they both present the phenomenon of a large family unit disintegrating into scattered, independent small family groups.

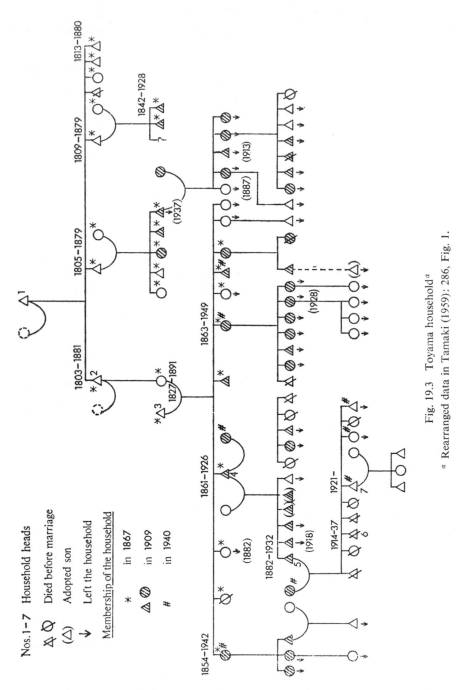

Fig. 19.3 Toyama household[a]

[a] Rearranged data in Tamaki (1959): 286, Fig. 1.

Table 19.6   *Mean household size, fertility and mortality rates,*
Japan, 1920–65

| | Mean household size | | | | |
	Whole country	Rural	Urban	Birth rate	Death rate
1920	4.89	4.99	4.47	35.0	23.0
1925	4.88	5.01	4.43	34.0	19.8
1930	4.98	5.11	4.61	31.8	18.1
1935	5.03	5.18	4.74	31.6	16.8
1940	5.00	5.25	4.62	29.4	16.5
1950	4.97	5.34	4.45	28.1	10.9
1955	4.97	5.31	4.73	19.4	7.8
1960	4.54	4.95	4.36	17.2	7.6
1965	4.05	4.48	3.86	18.6	7.1

MEAN HOUSEHOLD SIZE IN JAPAN AND IN ENGLAND

I am convinced that mean household size in Japan changed little from the early seventeenth century at least until 1955 and must have been fairly constant at about 4.9 persons per household during this period. Table 19.6 gives the census figures and demographic rates for the years 1920 to 1965.

We have no entirely reliable figures before the first date in this table, but it seems very unlikely to me that the Japanese household size before 1920 was any larger than it was found to be in the first two official censuses. In Table 19.1 a national figure of 4.65 is given for the year 1870: this 'census' was based on the statistical data assembled and reported upon by the office of every former feudal lord on the winding up of its feudal administration.

Transition to an industrial economy seems to have had little immediate influence on mean household size, unless in fact it caused it to increase somewhat in the early stages of the transformation. The rise between 1925 and 1930, and again to 1935, appears to have been the result of a general improvement in the standard of living and to the fact that fertility decreased rather more slowly than mortality. This effect may have its analogue in England, but Laslett's figures for that country show that it was much less obvious there, and its greater prominence in Japan is due no doubt to the fact that industrialisation started so much later and was so much more rapid. It is my view that the estimate of 4.9 for Japanese mean household size applies to the period 1920–65 but it must have been smaller before that time.

Table 19.7 presents a comparison between mean household size in Japan and in England over what I think are comparable periods of time, i.e. stages in the process of industrialisation. This table demonstrates that decline in household size began in both countries during what might be thought of as a second stage in industrial development, when it has begun to penetrate every part of the

Table 19.7   *Decline in mean household size, England and Japan*

	England		Japan
1901	4.49	1950	4.97
1911	4.36	1955	4.97
1921	3.99	1960	4.54
1931	3.72	1965	4.05

national society. Two points stand out: that the decrease in size was much faster in Japan than in England, and that the reduction in Japan took place at a time when the proportion of the population engaged in agriculture was rapidly decreasing. As for the first point, English household size fell by 17 % in thirty years between 1901 and 1931, and Japanese household size by 18.5 % between 1955 and 1965: it could be said that the fall in our country went on at no less than three times the pace.

As for the shrinkage in agriculture, the proportion of the Japanese labour force engaged in various agricultural occupations between 1955 and 1965 was as follows: 38.5 % in 1955, 23.0 % in 1960, and 19.3 % in 1965. Japanese rural society was rapidly changing in structure in this period, and was much affected by migration to urban areas as well as by the expansion of industrial establishments into the countryside.

It will be seen that the average size of the Japanese household has been consistently larger by 0.3 to 0.4 than that of England for comparable periods, and this I believe can be attributed to differences in family (household) system between the two societies. In Japan, as has already been mentioned, it was the tradition that one son (usually the eldest), would succeed to his father's household, so that he, his wife and his children used to live with his parents. Households which had no son to succeed in this way adopted sons-in-law to marry their daughters and finally to succeed as household heads. In the absence of either a daughter or a son, a young couple would be adopted as successors to the household, living with the household head and his wife.

The effect of the rules of succession and adoption was, therefore, that the Japanese household almost always included members of successive generations. Sons who were not successors to their fathers' households, tried to find a household without a son where they could be adopted as sons-in-law. Alternatively their parents might give them a small house and land to live on, or they might move to the cities to find work and settle.

Considering the dissimilarity in family system, the difference of 0.3 or 0.4 between Japanese and English mean household size seems reasonable. It is logical to presume that the size of Japanese households would be a little larger in comparison with English households in a similar situation. This presumption is borne out by the fact that Japanese mean household size in cities during the period in question was smaller than that in the countryside, and closer to the figures for the average English household. It is true that many of the young couples who were not able to succeed to established households would set themselves up in urban areas in domestic groups with a composition similar to that of the English household, that is without the presence of an older generation. Nevertheless, even then, as the second generation grew up, the elder son and his family would probably remain in his parents' household, so that average household size in urban Japan would still be larger than in England.

However, the traditional family system in terms of the *Ie*, that is the house in the dynastic institutional sense, is quickly dying out, and Japanese mean household size will continue to decrease. Particularly in urban areas young couples are now refusing to live with parents, especially the parents of the husband, and much prefer a house of their own where they can produce a small family and enjoy a higher standard of autonomous modern living. The institution of the *Ie* was abolished in the New Civil Code of 1947, and the traditional system of adopting a son-in-law also became invalid in that year. However, the change in social custom which could be expected to accompany the decline in the concept of the *Ie* has been very slow, and only in the last ten years or so has such a change become obvious. This has certainly been encouraged by the different economic pattern of family life where the succession of the household has no functional meaning any more. It is interesting to notice that the proportion of elementary families living with the wife's parents has increased at the expense of the traditional arrangement where the married couple resided with the husband's parents. This may appear to be a new trend, but in fact it is closely linked with the age-old domestic pattern of the household with an adopted son-in-law. Considering these circumstances, I think that Japanese mean household size will continue to be slightly larger than the English mean size, although rapidly approaching this figure.

Appendix I

Japan Nishinomiya Hama-issai-chō, 1713

Diagrams of Households [A = by adoption]

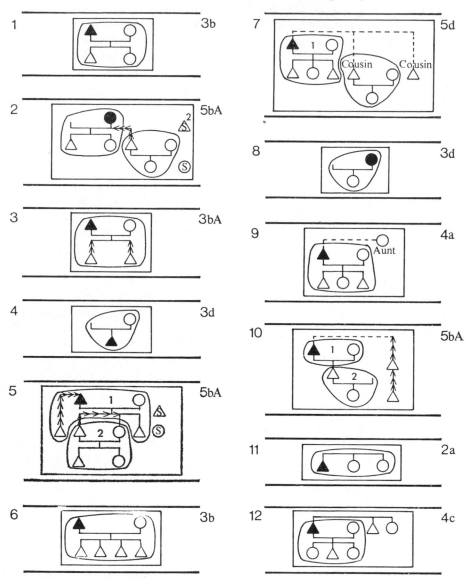

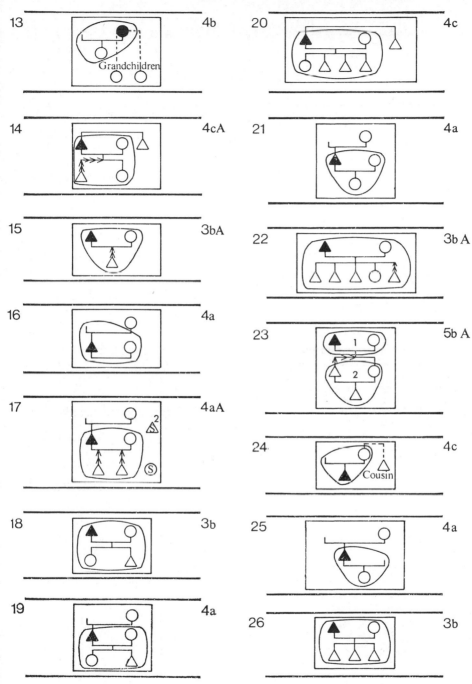

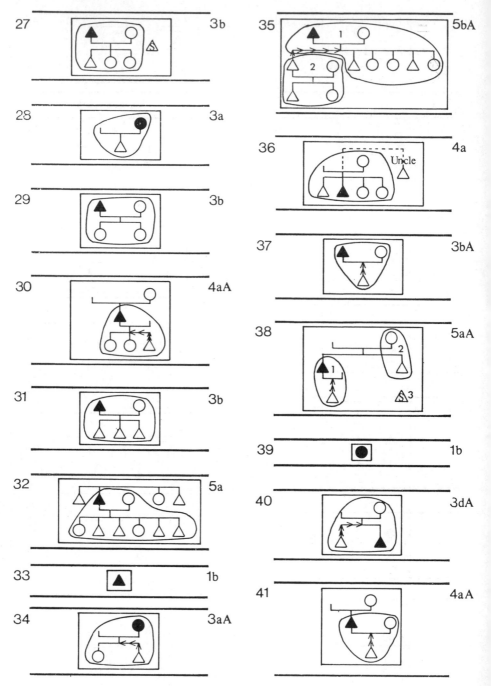

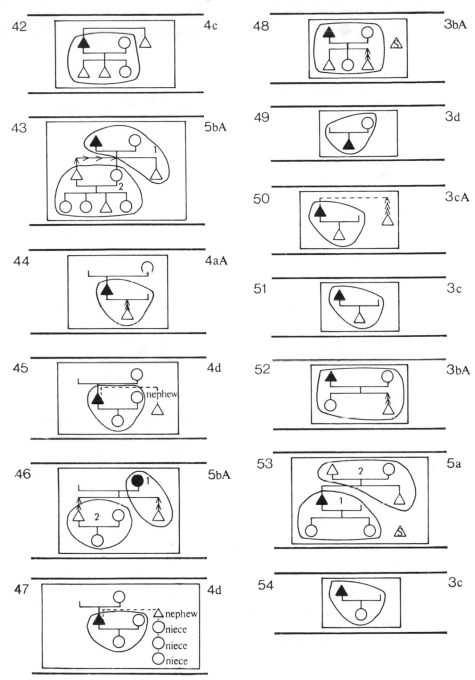

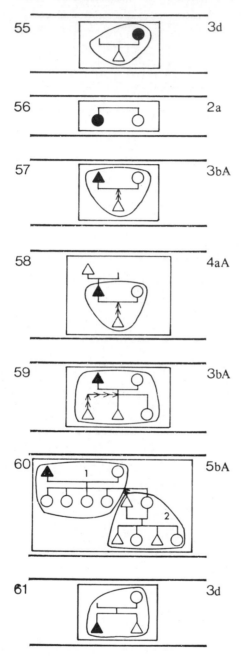

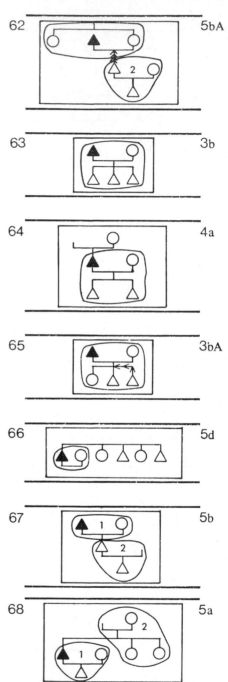

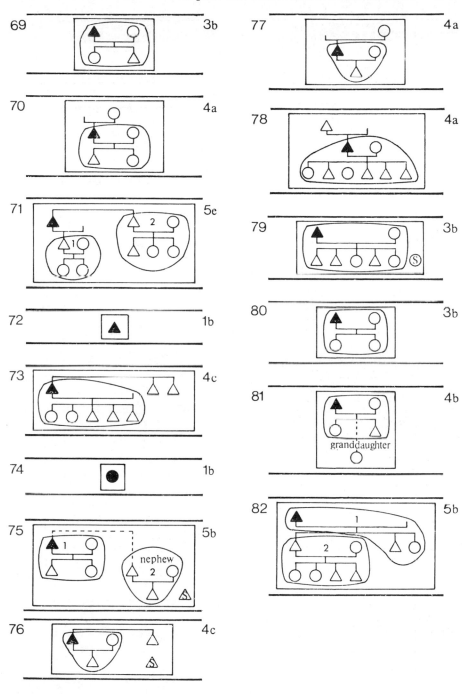

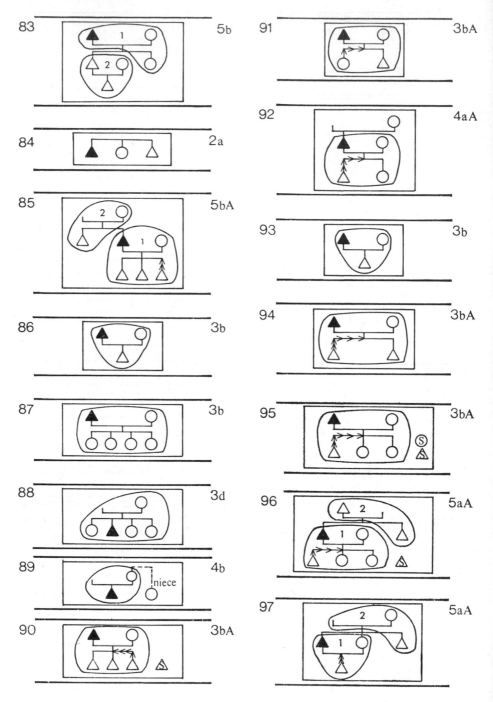

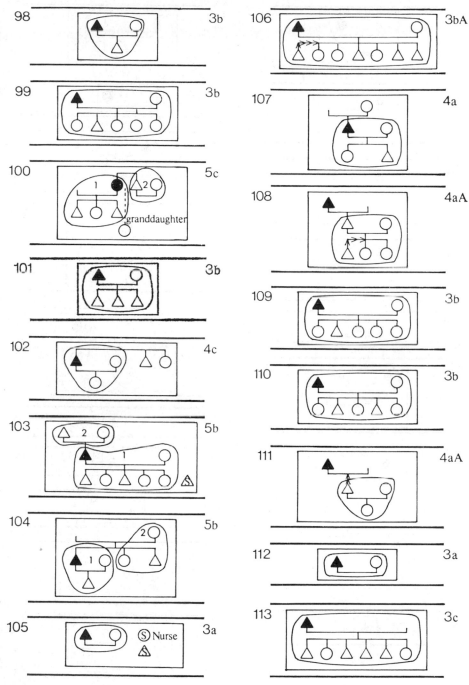

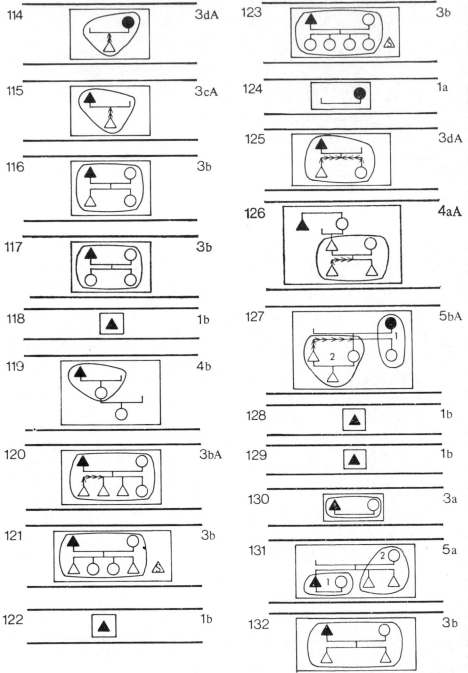

EDITORIAL NOTE

The details of the listing of Nishinomiya Hama-issai-chō 1713, were originally supplied by Professor Nakane in translated words and digits. It was decided editorially to convert these words and digits into ideographs in order to illustrate the use of the ideographic system described in Chapter 1, and the results were checked against a printed copy of the original Japanese characters. Ages were omitted in the ideographic translation.

Miss Nakane made it clear that in adopting this arrangement she did not necessarily accept all the implications of the ideographic system as applied to her material. She insisted in particular that the practice of adoption was more complex than might seem to be indicated by the arrowed lines appearing in the relevant cameos. She hoped however that these first attempts at ideographic representation would lead in time to a more efficient set of conventions for the non-linguistic representation of domestic group structures.

20. The average size of families and households in the Province of Massachusetts in 1764 and in the United States in 1790: an overview

Philip J. Greven, Jr

Although historians have referred occasionally to the large sizes of families in eighteenth-century America, few attempts have yet been made to establish reliable or even suggestive data about family and household size in the British colonies or the new United States. Local records could provide data for individual families, of course, and the abundant genealogical evidence which has been collected for American families could be used in determining the sizes of families in many different periods and places. More general data, however, covering larger numbers of families, more places, and different periods of time are more difficult to gather in most of the colonies and states prior to 1790. The most useful sources for such data are censuses, particularly those which include data on the number of families,[1] houses, and total population in given places. Unfortunately, though, such censuses appear to be exceedingly rare, judging by the printed versions which are presently available. In fact, only thirteen separate censuses for colonies or for states appear to exist for the eighteenth century which contain information about families or housefuls:[2] one taken in 1764 of towns in fourteen counties in the Province of Massachusetts (including three counties now in the present state of Maine);[3] one taken in 1774 of twenty-

---

[1] By family is meant persons living together and provided for by a common head. Compare Pryor, below, Chapter 22, pp. 572–574. The term was also used in this sense in English censuses of the nineteenth century, see above, Wall, Chapter 5, p. 160. See also above, Laslett, Chapter 1, pp. 23–28, 34–36.

[2] For an explanation of this term, see above, Laslett, Chapter 1, pp. 36–39.

[3] The Massachusetts Census of 1764 has been reprinted several times. Benton published one version from the Crane manuscript in *Early census making in Massachusetts* (1905). The censuses which I have used are printed in two different versions: the one which I have used as the basis for most of my calculations of average sizes of families and of housefuls in 1764 is found in Greene and Harrington, *American population before the federal census of 1790* (1932): 21–30, which is a collation of both manuscript versions of the census; the other version of the 1764 Census, printed in the United States Bureau of the Census, *A century of population growth 1790–1900* (1909) Table 81: 158–61, is a corrected version taken from Benton (1905). The figures in these different versions of the Census vary, and each contains

nine towns in the Province of Rhode Island;[4] and the extraordinarily detailed listings of heads of families in towns, counties, and districts of eleven states taken in 1790.[5] Together, they constitute invaluable sources for the history of the family in eighteenth-century America.

This chapter presents only an overview of data on the average sizes of families and housefuls derived from the Massachusetts Census of 1764 and the Censuses of 1790. From the 1764 Census, I have calculated the average sizes of families and of housefuls in individual towns and counties, using the data from Greene and Harrington. The 1790 Censuses provide listings with precise details about particular heads of families, with their names and the number of persons in their families, thus presenting a truly remarkable amount of information about families in 1790. An analysis of these data, however, would require a tremendous amount of time and effort in order to establish the exact composition of specific families in specific localities, with the ranges of family sizes from town to town, and from county to county. Since I have not been able to undertake such an analysis myself, I have relied upon the summaries of data for towns, counties, or districts which precede the actual census listings for each of the eleven states. These summaries provide the basis for the calculations of overall average sizes of families which I have done for the counties and districts in each of these states. My purpose in this chapter, therefore, is not to provide an exhaustive study of family size either in 1764 or in 1790 but simply to present a general picture which will serve to reveal the larger variations in average family size from county to county, and from state to state. My hope is that this preliminary inquiry will encourage others to undertake more detailed and refined studies of families in particular localities.

In order to evaluate the data on the sizes of families and of housefuls derived from these censuses, it is important to determine how men in the eighteenth century defined a family and whom the census takers included when listing the members of families in particular towns or counties. Since the Massachusetts Census of 1764 and the Summary of the population of towns and counties in

some obvious errors which I have corrected in my own calculations. But since I cannot tell which of the versions corresponds more closely to the manuscript, I chose to use Greene and Harrington's version. In terms of the average sizes of families, the two versions provide almost identical data for all of the counties except for Plymouth (the Greene and Harrington data yields an average of 6.05 persons per family and the Census Bureau yields an average of 5.95 per family) and for Berkshire (Greene and Harrington data yield an average of 6.17 and the Census Bureau data yield an average of 6.62 per family). Overall, both versions yield an average for Massachusetts counties (excluding three now in Maine) of 5.94 persons per family.

[4] The Rhode Island Census of 1774 is published in United States Bureau of Census (1909) Table 84: 162–3.

[5] The eleven censuses which have survived in manuscript have been printed in their entireties in the United States Bureau of the Census, *Heads of families at the first census of 1790* (1907–8). The data which I have used for my calculations for average sizes of families in 1790 are derived from the summaries of population by counties and towns in 1790 which are printed on pp. 9–10 in each of the volumes for the eleven states. Unless otherwise noted, the data for these states are derived entirely from these summaries.

Massachusetts in 1790 contain data on the number of houses as well as of families, it appears that some distinction between a houseful and a family must have been made even in the eighteenth century. The 1764 Census lists whites under sixteen years, whites over sixteen years, Negroes and Mulattoes (but does not distinguish between free and slave), Indians, and French neutrals (refugees from Acadia, presumably white), and the total population. Unfortunately, what cannot be determined from this listing is who actually were considered members of a family. My presumption, however, is that the composition of families in 1764 did not differ significantly from families in 1790.

The precise details of the listings of heads of families in 1790 help to clarify the complex question of the composition of families somewhat, since they permit us to see who actually comprised a given 'family.' The census listings provide information about the actual name of the head of a 'family,' followed by the numbers (in vertical columns) of free white males of sixteen years and upward, including heads of families, of free white males under sixteen years, of free white females of all ages, including heads of families, of all other free persons (meaning blacks), and of slaves. From these numerical listings, it is evident that families varied considerably in terms of their actual composition. Some families consisted only of whites, some only of free blacks, but some white families also contained members who were free blacks or slaves. Although it is impossible to tell for certain from the listings, some whites in families probably were not kindred but were either servants or hired hands living with the family head.[6] Resident servants, white or black, free or slave, thus appear to have been considered to be members of families as well as immediate kin.[7] The average sizes of families will thus reflect, in varying degrees, the presence of persons not related by kinship to the heads of families as well as of persons related by kinship. But, since there are many identical surnames listed in sequence (which suggests residential proximity) I suspect that in most instances the families which were registered consisted only of two generations – parents and their own children – with grandparents (even if resident in the same household) being listed separately. Except in those instances where servants might have been

---

[6] This assumption cannot be confirmed directly from the census data, but the presence of families such as that of the Honourable Samuel Phillips, Esquire, of Andover, Massachusetts, who was the leading merchant and magistrate in the town in 1790, makes such an assumption necessary. His 'family' consisted of 15 white males of sixteen years or more, 5 white males of less than sixteen years, 12 white females and 1 free black, totalling 33 persons. Since the second largest family in Andover consisted only of 14 persons in all, the extraordinary size of Phillips' family surely must be accounted for by the inclusion of adult white servants or hired hands in the listing of family members. See United States Bureau of Census (1907–8): 63.

My guess, however, is that in New England, at least, we can assume that the averages established for 'families' from census data will not be greatly inflated by the inclusion of servants or non-kindred, since the overwhelming majority of the white population probably did not have resident servants. Only further studies of servitude and labor in the eighteenth century will enable us to be certain, though.

[7] This is standard European procedure, see above, Chapters 4–13.

included, a 'family' in 1790 thus appears to have been considered to be what we now call a nuclear family.

A houseful in 1790, however, was not necessarily identical with a nuclear family which consisted only of parents and children. The presence of servants (free blacks are often listed as members of families headed by whites) and of slaves (also listed as members of white families) indicates the fact that a houseful sometimes contained non-kindred. But what cannot be determined satisfactorily from these listings is the frequency with which housefuls contained two or more 'families.' More specifically, it is impossible to tell whether or not grandparents or other kindred might also be living in a family with parents and children, thus forming families consisting of three or more generations. I am convinced, however, that such extended families (families with three generations of kindred living together in a single dwelling) existed in 1790 and before. In Massachusetts, at least, both in 1764 and in 1790, it is demonstrable that a 'family' and a 'houseful' could not have been identical for the simple reason that in both of these years there were more families or more heads of families listed in the censuses than there were houses in which they might have lived.[8] Some houses thus must have contained more than one family.[9]

In 1764, the eleven counties in Massachusetts contained a total of 31,129 houses with a total of 37,827 families, according to the figures from Greene and Harrington, thus averaging 7.21 persons per house but only 5.94 persons per family; according to corrected totals from another version, printed by the Bureau of the Census, the total number of houses in 1764 was 30,952 with a total of 37,688 families, with an average of 7.23 persons per house compared with an average of 5.94 persons per family. In 1790, a total of 46,781 houses provided dwellings for 56,287 families in seven counties, with an average of 6.9 persons per house and an average of 5.84 persons per family. Although no data are given for three counties and the data for the fourth (Barnstable) appear to be

[8] Unfortunately, none of the summaries for the censuses of other states in 1790 contain information on the number of houses in addition to the number of heads of families. Nevertheless, I see no reason to assume that similar disparities between the number of houses and the number of families might not also have been found in the other states as well.

[9] This assumption has been challenged by John Demos, who has argued against it consistently in his studies of families and households in seventeenth-century Plymouth Colony and in Bristol, Rhode Island, during the seventeenth and the eighteenth centuries. See Demos, *Notes on life in Plymouth Colony* (1965): esp. 279–80 and *Families in colonial Bristol, Rhode Island* (1968): esp. 44–5. I am convinced, however, that Demos errs when he asserts (1965): 279, that 'In colonial Plymouth, there were no extended families at all, in the sense of "under one roof".' The Census of 1764 (in Greene and Harrington (1932): 28) indicates that there were 3,071 houses in Plymouth County for a total of 3,693 families, so that 622 families must not have had houses of their own. Some of these 622 families surely must have lived with other relatives in houses which had to contain more than one family, and probably more than two generations. In the town of Plymouth itself, for instance, there were 256 houses for 373 families, with a total population in the town of 2,246 persons, thus making the average house contain 8.8 persons, whereas the average family had only 6.02 members, and leaving 117 families without houses of their own. If this was the case in 1764, it probably was the case earlier as well, although perhaps to a lesser extent, during the period discussed by Demos.

erroneous, the overall average number of persons per house in the state must have been at least 7. Accordingly, both in 1764 and in 1790, the average houseful in Massachusetts was larger by more than one person than the average family. Although the great majority of houses contained only one family, multi-family dwellings were to be found throughout the state, in small rural communities and in larger urban communities. Some housefuls consisted of families related by kinship, thus forming extended families residing together in a single dwelling.[10] Other housefuls consisted of families which were unrelated by kinship, sharing a house as tenants or as boarders. Undoubtedly many variations in houseful composition occurred.

HOUSEFUL SIZE IN MASSACHUSETTS

In eighteenth-century Massachusetts, the size of the average houseful varied considerably from county to county. From the number of persons dwelling in single houses, it is apparent that houses in some counties were more crowded than in others, as Table 20.1 indicates.

In both 1764 and 1790, the least crowded housing in Massachusetts was to be found in the inland counties of Hampshire and Worcester, where the average number of persons per house was only 6.7 in 1764 and even less in 1790. In Worcester, the number of houses grew by a total of 4,050 between 1764 and 1790, an increase of nearly 90 %, while in Hampshire County, which was growing with tremendous rapidity, becoming the most populous county in the state by 1790, the number of houses rose from 2,586 in 1764 to 9,181 in 1790, an increase of 255 %. Despite the growth in population, housing increased with sufficient rapidity to provide housing which was even less crowded in 1790 than before, with a remarkably low 4.5 % of the families lacking houses of their own (see Table 20.2). In Berkshire County, the most distant from the coast and still mostly unsettled in 1764, housing was less crowded in 1790 than it had been earlier, reflecting the immense increase in the number of houses. By 1790, these inland counties, containing many towns of recent origin, provided the most abundant housing for their populations. The great majority of families evidently had houses of their own.

Many of the families living in the more densely populated older counties along the Massachusetts coast were less fortunate in terms of their residences. Housing in these counties was much more crowded than in the inland counties. Although the most crowded housing in 1764 was to be found on the offshore island of Nantucket, the most populous of the counties in 1764, Essex, which also had the second largest population in 1790, was the most crowded of the mainland counties in terms of the percentage of families without houses, and one of the most crowded in terms of the average number of persons per house. By

---

[10] For further discussion, see Greven, *Four generations: Population, land and family in colonial Andover, Massachusetts* (1970).

Table 20.1   *The average number of persons per house in Massachusetts counties in 1764 and in 1790*

County	Established	1764[a]		1790	
		Total population	Average no. per house	Total population	Average no. per house
Hampshire	1662	17,298	6.7	59,681	6.5
Worcester	1731	30,464	6.7	56,807	6.6
Bristol	1685	18,070	6.9	31,709	7.0
Middlesex	1643	33,804	7.0	42,737	7.1
Barnstable	1685	12,472	7.1	17,354	—
Plymouth	1685	22,356	7.3	29,535	—
Berkshire	1760	3,029	7.5	30,291	6.8
Essex	1643	43,231	7.6	57,913	7.6
Suffolk	1643	36,420	7.9	44,875	7.1
Dukes	1695	2,719	8.3	3,265	—
Nantucket	1695	3,526	8.5	4,620	—
Average			7.2		6.9

[a] Figures for 1764 based upon Greene and Harrington version.

Table 20.2   *Houses and families in Massachusetts counties in 1764 and 1790*

County	1764[a]			1790		
	Houses	Families	% Families sharing houses	Houses	Families	% Families sharing houses
Hampshire	2,586	2,867	9.8	9,181	9,617	4.5
Worcester	4,563	5,070	10.0	8,613	9,729	11.5
Bristol	2,611	3,115	16.2	4,514	5,541	18.5
Middlesex	4,860	5,810	16.4	5,998	7,580	20.9
Barnstable	1,765	2,106	16.2	1,343[b]	2,889	—
Plymouth	3,071	3,693	16.8	—	5,173	—
Berkshire	403	491	17.9	4,476	4,899	8.6
Essex	5,759	7,971	27.8	7,644	10,883	29.8
Suffolk	4,593	5,549	17.2	6,355	8,038	20.9
Dukes	328	364	9.9	—	558	—
Nantucket	413	602	31.4	—	872	—

[a] Figures based upon Greene and Harrington.
[b] Number of houses is obviously underrecorded.

1790, housing along the coast was becoming even more crowded than it had been earlier. In part, at least, this probably reflected the relatively low increases in the number of new houses constructed in these counties between 1764 and 1790, since the number of houses in Middlesex County increased by only 23.4 %, while in Essex and Suffolk Counties, they increased by 32.6 % and by 38.4 % respectively. Housefuls in the densely populated coastal counties thus tended to be larger than in the inland counties, with proportionately more families sharing houses. In some of the towns, houses were very crowded indeed, particularly in the port communities such as Boston (with an average of 9.3 persons per house in 1764 but only 7.6 per house in 1790), or Marblehead (with an average of 9.6 per house in 1764 and 9.2 per house in 1790). These towns were exceptional, however, although some of the rural inland towns also had very high averages as well.

THE SIZE OF FAMILIES

The traditional assumption that families in eighteenth-century America were very large is borne out by data from the summaries for the Federal Censuses of Heads of Families in eleven states taken in 1790. The overall average number of free persons per family was 5.80, while the overall average per family, including slaves, was 6.61 persons. By the middle of the nineteenth century, the average number of free persons per household[11] had declined, reaching 5.55 per household in 1850 and 5.28 per household in 1860. By 1880, the average number of persons per household had fallen to 5.04, then dropping to 4.93 in 1890 and to 4.76 in 1900. Thereafter the average size of American households continued to decline decade by decade, reaching 3.77 in 1940 and a low of 3.52 in 1950.[12] Since 1950, however, the average size of the household has begun to increase slightly again, to 3.67 in 1960 and to 3.70 in 1967.[13] The average family in 1790 thus was larger by 2.1 persons than the average household in 1967. The average American family in 1790 was also larger by about one person than the average household in England between the late sixteenth and the early nineteenth centuries,[14] and presumably the average houseful in America in 1790 would have been even larger in relation to English housefuls.[15] The average family in eleven of the united states in 1790 was thus larger than the average household in pre-industrial England for more than two centuries, or than in the modern industrial United States since 1850.

[11] It is assumed here that the units described as families in the eighteenth and as households in the nineteenth and twentieth centuries are comparable. See above, footnote 1, p. 545.
[12] United States Bureau of the Census, *Historical statistics of the United States* (1960) Series A 255–63: 16.
[13] United States Bureau of the Census, *Statistical abstract of the United States: 1968* (1968) Table 40: 35.
[14] See above, Laslett, Chapter 4, p. 138.
[15] The overall mean size of households in 100 parishes in England between 1474 and 1821 was 4.768. See above, Laslett, Chapter 4, ratio 3 in Table 4.2, p. 133.

Table 20.3   *The average sizes of families with freemen only and of families with slaves in the Eleven States in 1790*[a]

State	Loca-tion	No. of family heads	Total free popula-tion	Average no. per free family	Average of county averages (free)	Total popula-tion	Average no. per family with slaves
South Carolina	S	26,185	141,979	5.42	5.15	249,073	9.51
North Carolina	S	57,827	323,993	5.60	5.53	427,250	7.39
Maine	N	17,098	96,769	5.66	5.49	96,769	5.66
Vermont	N	14,983	85,341	5.70	5.67	85,341	5.70
Connecticut	N	40,878	235,370	5.76	5.83	238,127	5.83
New York	M	54,884	318,882	5.81	5.65	340,211	6.20
Massachusetts	N	64,907	378,787	5.84	5.75	378,787	5.84
New Hampshire	N	24,080	141,739	5.89	5.84	141,896	5.89
Rhode Island	N	11,306	67,877	6.00	5.94	68,825	6.09
Pennsylvania	M	62,951	378,251	6.01	6.02	381,385	6.09
Maryland[b]	S	32,965	199,254	6.04	5.76	290,657	9.09
Totals and averages		408,064	2,368,242	5.80	5.69	2,698,321	6.61
Medians		—	—	5.73	5.59	—	7.59

[a] Based upon the summaries of population by counties and towns for the states in U.S. Bureau of the Census, *Heads of Families*.
[b] Figures incomplete for heads of families in three counties. These data are for counties with complete information only.

The average size of families ranged from a low of 5.42 for freemen in families in South Carolina in 1790 to a high of 6.04 for freemen in all but three counties of Maryland (see Table 20.3). Of the four states with the lowest averages of freemen per family, two were southern (South Carolina and North Carolina) and two were northern (Maine and Vermont). Three of these states were relatively new in terms of the residency of their populations, and much of the land in at least two of these states was still mostly wilderness, as their low populations indicate. This suggests that in terms of the overall average size of families of freemen, those states which were older or settled longer had larger families overall than did the more recently settled or frontier states. In states like New Hampshire, which were still sparsely settled in terms of space but in which many of the settlements had been undertaken earlier in the eighteenth century, the average size of families tended to be larger. The three states with the largest average sizes of families represented the three major sections of the country, although one (Rhode Island) was the smallest in size with the least number of people, and another (Pennsylvania) was one of the largest with the second highest number of people.

The presence of slaves could have a profound effect upon the size of the family, since slaves were often listed as members of white families in those states which permitted it in 1790, but the extent of slavery varied widely from state to state. In New Hampshire, for instance, the relatively few slaves made virtually no difference to the average size of a family, whereas in a middle state like New York the average size of a family was increased from 5.81 to 6.20 by the inclusion of slaves. In the northern and middle states, however, the presence of slaves in free families made relatively little difference in terms of the average sizes of families. The most striking disparities between the sizes of families of freemen and of families with slaves included were to be found in the southern states. South Carolina, which had the lowest average size of families of freemen, had an average of 4.09 slaves per family, and Maryland, with the largest free families, had an average of 3.05 slaves per family. The presence of slaves must have made a great difference to families both in terms of size and in terms of the character of housefuls.

The size of the family was more variable in 1790 than the overall averages for the states might suggest. For example, the evidence from the three northern New England states of Vermont, New Hampshire and Maine suggests the general conclusion that the overall average size of families in the newest, most recently settled frontier areas was appreciably smaller than the sizes of families in the more established areas of these states. Contrary to popular myth, frontier families in these states apparently were not especially large. Perhaps the relatively small sizes of these frontier families reflects the demographic circumstances characteristic of such new communities, in which many of the inhabitants presumably would be young, male and unmarried, or young and newly married, with relatively few of their children being born as yet, and with relatively few of their families being completed as yet. In the older communities, families would probably be represented by a more diverse range of ages and sizes, with more of the inhabitants having already completed their families, thus increasing their sizes. Perhaps other factors, particularly those relating to fecundity and mortality played a discernible role as well. But whatever the explanations, it seems evident from this data that in New England, at least, families on the frontiers were likely to be smaller than were families in the post-frontier communities.

Massachusetts

Massachusetts, as one of only two states for which a comparison is possible between the sizes of families in towns and counties at different periods of the eighteenth century, is worth studying in greater detail. In 1764, the earliest year for which calculations about family size in the state or colony as a whole is possible, the average size of families in eleven counties (excluding the three northern counties which were then part of the state but which now form part of Maine) was 5.94 overall, ranging from a low of 5.42 in Essex County to a high of 7.47 in Dukes County (Martha's Vineyard). By 1790, the overall average number of people per family had dropped to 5.84, ranging from a low of 5.30

Table 20.4   *Average family size by county:*
Massachusetts in 1764 and in 1790[a]

Date established	County	Location	1764 Average family	1790 Average family
1695	Nantucket	E island	5.86	5.30
1643	Essex	E coast	5.42	5.32
1643	Suffolk	E coast	6.56	5.58
1643	Middlesex	E coast	5.82	5.64
1685	Plymouth	E coast	6.05	5.71
1685	Bristol	E coast	5.80	5.72
1731	Worcester	M inland	6.01	5.84
1695	Dukes	E island	7.47	5.85
1685	Barnstable	E coast	5.92	5.89
1760	Berkshire	W inland	6.17	6.18
1662	Hampshire	W inland	6.04	6.21
	Average number of persons per family, 1764		5.94	
	Average number of persons per family, 1790		5.84	
	Average of county averages, 1764		6.10	
	Average of county averages, 1790		5.75	

[a] The Census of 1764 does not distinguish between blacks who were free and those who were enslaved; by 1790, all blacks in the state were free. These figures include both whites and blacks in both years.

for families on Nantucket to 6.21 for families in Hampshire County. Although the difference between the overall averages for the two censuses is relatively small, it does suggest that there was probably some change in the size of families in Massachusetts between 1764 and 1790, momentous years which witnessed both the Revolution and the establishment of the independent nation of the United States. A more detailed comparison of family sizes in various counties during these two years reveals some of the changes even more clearly than this overall change might suggest. (See Table 20.4.)

In 1764, according to data from Greene and Harrington, five counties in Massachusetts had averages for families ranging between 5.42 and 5.92, with another five counties having averages for families ranging between 6.01 and 6.56. By 1790, however, nine of the eleven counties had averages of fewer than six persons per family (ranging between 5.20 and 5.89) and only two counties had averages of more than 6.0.

The average overall size of families decreased in all but two of the counties between 1764 and 1790. The decreases in family size in Essex, Middlesex, Bristol, Worcester, and Barnstable counties were relatively small, however, which suggests that the average sizes of families in these counties were fairly stable during this period. On the two offshore islands of Nantucket and Martha's

Vineyard, family size changed more, although the small populations of the islands may account for the magnitude of these changes. Apart from these islands, the most striking decrease in the overall average size of families occurred in Suffolk County, from 6.56 to 5.58, and probably reflects the even more striking decrease in average family size in the town of Boston, which fell from the remarkably high average of 7.50 persons per family in 1764 to 5.40 per family in 1790. By 1790, it was evident that the three oldest counties – Essex, Middlesex, and Suffolk – and all of the coastal counties except for Barnstable (Cape Cod) had lower averages for family sizes than the three inland counties. The two counties which were most distant from Boston – Hampshire and Berkshire – had the largest overall averages for family size of any of the counties in 1790. Hampshire was the only county in which an appreciable increase in family size occurred. This may reflect not only the tremendous growth in its population during the second half of the eighteenth century[16] but also the fact that many of its towns were relatively well established by 1790, with only 12 of the towns being incorporated after 1780 and with 37 towns being incorporated prior to 1770. Berkshire County, which also grew rapidly during this period, was relatively well settled by 1790, with 12 towns incorporated before 1770, 9 during the 1770s, and only 4 during the 1780s. Neither of these western counties could be considered to be frontier areas in 1790; both, with their large overall average family sizes were mostly post-frontier areas, very similar to Hillsborough County, New Hampshire, or to Bennington County, Vermont. Indeed in the northern states, as in Massachusetts, post-frontier counties appear to have been the ones with the largest families, while those counties which were among the oldest in the State had the smallest families.

In towns throughout Massachusetts in 1790, families ranged in size from an average of 4.23 to 7.57.[17] Both in 1764 and in 1790, the overwhelming majority of the towns in the state had families consisting of at least five but fewer than seven persons on the average (see Table 20.5), with most varying within the range of five or six persons per family. Between 1764 and 1790, however, it is evident that an increasing proportion of towns had smaller families. During this period, there was an increase of 9.19 % in the proportion of towns with families averaging between 5.0 and 5.9 persons, and a decrease of 7.56 % in the proportion of towns with families averaging between 6.0 and 6.9 persons. None of the towns either in 1764 or in 1790 had fewer than 4 persons per family on the average, and almost none had 8 persons per family or more. The general trend between 1764 and 1790 thus appears to be in the direction of somewhat smaller family sizes in a number of towns in the state. Whether this is a continuation of a longer trend or not cannot be determined, unfortunately, owing

---

[16] Compare Hayami, above, Chapter 18, pp. 506–507; Wall, above, Chapter 5, pp. 199–203.

[17] I have excluded Mashpee Plantation in Barnstable County, which had an average of 12.32 persons per family in 1790, since it was populated mostly by Indians who may not have lived in families comparable to those of whites in the plantation.

Table 20.5   *Average number of persons per family*
in Massachusetts towns in 1764 and in 1790

Average no. per family	1764		1790	
	No. of towns	%	No. of towns	%
3.0–3.9	0	—	0	—
4.0–4.4	1	0.50	1	0.36
4.5–4.9	3	1.51	3	1.08
5.0–5.4	26	13.13	49	17.75
5.5–5.9	67	33.83	106	38.40
6.0–6.4	67	33.83	82	29.71
6.5–6.9	24	12.12	24	8.68
7.0–7.4	5	2.52	6	2.17
7.5–7.9	4	2.02	4	1.44
8.0–8.4	1	0.50	0	—
8.5–8.9	0	—	0	—
9.0+	0	—	1	0.36
Total	198	99.96	276	99.95

to the lack of data for the period prior to 1764. My guess, however, would be that families in many Massachusetts towns during the seventeenth century would have been larger than they were in the mid-eighteenth century, especially in the coastal counties.[18] If further studies of particular towns confirm this supposition, then the decreases in family size between 1764 and 1790 which are evident in most of the counties and many of the towns will reflect a long term tendency towards smaller family size. In part, such a tendency probably would reflect

[18] In Andover, Essex County, Massachusetts, the average size of completed families varied from generation to generation. First generation families, which produced children during the middle decades of the seventeenth century, had an average of 8.3 children born of whom an average of 7.2 lived to age 21. Second generation families, whose children were born during the later seventeenth and early eighteenth centuries, had an average of 8.7 children born with an average of 7.2 living to age 21. Third generation families, however, whose children were born during the middle decades of the eighteenth century had only an average of 7.6 children born and only an average of 5.5 surviving to age 21. For further details, see Greven (1970).

The study of Quaker families in America undertaken by Robert V. Wells, of Union College, Schenectedy, N.Y., also indicates substantive changes in the sizes of families over time. As Mr Wells kindly informed me, in a personal letter, July 6, 1969, his study is based upon family reconstitutions for '276 Quaker families in which the wife was born not later than 1785' in the Middle colonies. His general conclusion is that 'The average number of children born to a husband and wife was 5.69. When the families under study were divided into three groups defined by the date of birth of the wife in such a way that the last child would have been born by 1775, 1800, and 1830 respectively, the following change in the size of the family was observed: from an average of 6.68 per couple in the first group, the number of children fell to 5.67 and 5.02 in the last two groups.' Mr Wells' study undoubtedly will be a major contribution to the demographic and familial history of early America.

increased rates of mortality and decreasing fertility as well as changes in ages of marriage, particularly in the counties which had been settled longest and which were the most crowded.[19]

South Carolina

Another state worth examining in detail is that of South Carolina since it was distinctive among the states in 1790 in terms both of the size of families of free-men and of the size of families with slaves included. In terms of all the states covered by the 1790 Censuses, the lowest overall average size for free families in any county or district was to be found in the Charleston District of South Carolina, which included not only the port and town of Charleston but also some of the large rice and indigo plantations characteristic of the coastal lowlands. Indeed, it is striking that the three coastal districts had both the smallest sizes of free families and the largest numbers of slaves per family of any of the districts in the state. The largest average sizes of free families were to be found in the most distant western districts, which also had the smallest numbers of slaves per family. As a whole, South Carolina had both the smallest average family size in the United States in 1790 and the largest average number of slaves per family. The variety of sizes and the probable variety in the actual composition of families and of households in this state make it one of the most fascinating, in demographic and familial terms, of any of the states at the end of the eighteenth century.

A more detailed examination of family size in the coastal district of Charleston in 1790 provides some of the most extraordinary figures respecting the family to be found anywhere in the United States at that time. In terms of freemen only, it is evident that nine out of twelve parishes in the District had families which

Table 20.6   *Average family size by district: South Carolina in 1790*

Date established	District	Location	Average no. per family (free only)	Average no. per family (with slaves)
1785	Charleston	E (M) coast	4.23	17.32
1785	Georgetown	E (N) coast	4.62	11.36
1785	Beaufort	E (S) coast	4.66	19.35
1785	Orangeburgh	M (S)	5.27	7.76
1785	Cheraw	M (NE)	5.56	7.97
1785	Camden	M (NW)	5.78	7.52
1785	Ninety-six	W	5.92	6.97
	Average number of free persons per family		5.42	
	Average number with slaves per family		9.51	
	Average of district averages (free only)		5.15	

[19] For an examination of each of these factors as they affected pre-industrial Japan, see above, Hayami, Chapter 18, pp. 491–496, 499–502, 507–511.

Table 20.7   *Average family size in parishes in the*
Charleston District of South Carolina in 1790

Parish	Average no. per family (free only)	Average no. per family (with slaves)
St Pauls	3.04	45.17
St Johns (Colleton Co.)	3.10	27.10
St Thomas	3.50	31.19
St Andrews	3.56	25.85
St James Santee	3.70	31.12
Christ Church	3.82	19.56
St James Goose Creek	3.85	23.62
St Johns (Berkley Co.)	3.86	30.37
St Stephens	3.98	47.95
St Bartholomews	4.20	23.34
St Phillips & St Michaels	4.49	8.46
St Georges (Dorchester Co.)	5.26	17.69

averaged fewer than four persons, ranging from 3.04 to 3.98 per family, and that only one parish had an average of more than five persons per family, yet this was below the overall average of 5.80 persons per family in the eleven states together. (See Table 20.7.)

The parish which included the town of Charleston, with a population of 8,675 freemen and 7,684 slaves, had an average of only 4.49 free persons per family, the lowest average for families in any town with more than 5,000 population in 1790 in any of these eleven states.

A combination of several factors may account for these unusually low averages for free white family size. The coastal districts of South Carolina were notoriously unhealthy, and might very well have been among the least healthful areas in which to live anywhere in the United States in 1790. It seems highly probable, therefore, that these low figures for family size reflect very high rates of mortality along the coast.[20] But it is also likely that they reflect the peculiar character of families in the counties and districts which were dominated by the large plantations characteristic of the coastal lowlands where the overwhelming majorities of the populations were black slaves. In the Charleston District, for example, there were 50,633 slaves in a total population of 66,985; in Beaufort District, there were 14,236 slaves out of a total population of 18,753. Most of these slaves, of course, did not live in households with white or free families but in large groups on plantations with relatively few whites, a circumstance which would account for the extraordinarily high proportion of slaves per family in many of

[20] For comparison, see Dunn, *The Barbados census of 1680* (1969): esp. 22–5. He found that the 'mean number of persons per family' was 7.38, of whom 3.74 were white and 3.64 were slaves and that the mortality rate was 'appallingly high'.

the parishes in Charleston District, for instance. The white families which were living in these parishes were almost certain to be very different from families living either in the town of Charleston or in some of the interior districts. In the town of Charleston the number of slaves per family was strikingly lower than in other parishes in the district while the average size of the family of freemen was appreciably larger. This suggests not only that the composition of free families differed in the town and the surrounding countryside but also that many of the slaves living in the town may very well have been a part of free households, thus adding significantly to the average number of people who might constitute a functioning household. Given the relatively small numbers of freemen per family and the relatively large numbers of slaves per household in Charleston, and in other southern localities as well, it is evident that there must have been some profound differences in the nature of the family in South Carolina, compared with families in the middle and northern states.

CONCLUSIONS

The most general conclusion to be drawn from the data presented in this chapter confirms what several generations of historians have taken for granted without seeking to confirm their impressions with quantitative evidence: namely, that the average family in eighteenth-century America was very large in comparison with families in modern America. This conclusion is established firmly by the data drawn from the Massachusetts Census of 1764 and from the Federal Censuses of 1790.[21] In comparison with households in England, too, during the eighteenth century and earlier, it is clear that, overall, American families were larger.[22] Thus, in terms of the history of the family, it now seems fair to assume that families, in all of the states or colonies for which censuses exist and which provide relevant information for the second half of the eighteenth century, were generally larger than they have been subsequently in the United States or than they were in England from about 1600 to the present. For once, at least, it is comforting to know that the intuitive judgments of historians have been confirmed by quantitative evidence.

The most important general conclusion to be drawn from this collection of data on the average sizes of families in eleven states in 1790, however, is not simply that families were large, but rather that the averages of family sizes were so remarkably variable from town to town, from county to county, and, to a lesser degree, from state to state. Although these variations in average size occurred within what may seem to be a very small range, mostly from five to seven persons per family in the United States in 1790, they undoubtedly reflect great differences

---

[21] What these data do not confirm, however, is the common assumption among historians that families in early America often contained between 15 and 25 children. I am confident the further analysis of the 1790 Censuses will demonstrate that families of this size are most unusual and the result of successive marriages.

[22] See above, Chapters 4–5, pp. 125–203.

in the experiences of families in different localities. The sizes of families must have been influenced profoundly by the innumerable variations in environment, circumstance, population, health, marriage ages, and even attitudes towards family size itself, found throughout the United States. From the few local studies which have been done so far, it is already clear that the sizes of families and of housefuls were sensitive to numerous circumstances which varied over time even within the same localities, and which certainly must have varied even more noticeably from one locality to another. If, as I expect, the size of the family proves to be a sensitive register of differences and of similarities in the human condition throughout the American states in 1790, and perhaps even earlier, we will have discovered an immensely useful guide to the complexities of experience which shaped the character of the family and of American society in the pre-industrial era.

21. Demography and psychology in the historical study of family-life: a personal report

John Demos

In the whole, gathering effort to promote the historical study of family-life, one approach – an essentially 'quantitative' or 'demographic' approach – seems to have largely predominated. Perhaps this is fitting, since some of the most immediate and elementary questions about the family do indeed present a quantitative aspect. In this chapter, I propose now to examine the relation between the demographic or quantitative approach and what I would call a psychological one.[1] What I have to offer is quite fragmentary – no more than a tentative and incomplete sampling of some work currently in progress. Hence my rather informal style of presentation, and the purposely cautious subtitle, 'A Personal Report.'

When I first came to the study of family-life, and more specifically family-life in colonial America, the question of houschold size and membership was an open one. The notion that maybe there were quite a few 'extended' households around still seemed to have some life in it, particularly with reference to the seventeenth century, the period of settlement as such and immediately thereafter. My work on Plymouth Colony was initially directed right to this point; and I might add that Professor Greven was doing very much the same thing with his materials on Andover in the Massachusetts Bay Colony. Our findings, it seems to me, were really very similar – though we have managed to keep arguing about their meaning ever since. What I concluded for Plymouth can be summarized as follows: the average household size, throughout the period in question, was just under six persons.[2] Typically, this meant a man and his wife, perhaps three children, and in some cases a servant or two. Occasionally, moreover, a household included a parent – and very rarely, two parents – of either spouse. These last would be elderly persons; and the prospect of death imposed definite limits on the length of their residence in such households.

---

[1] Compare Anderson's stress on the influence of economic motives on coresidence in industrial England, see above, Chapter 7, pp. 226–227.

[2] See Demos, *Notes on life in Plymouth colony* (1965) and *Families in colonial Bristol, Rhode Island* (1968). The mean size of households in Bristol in 1689 was 5.85 persons, and the median was 5.72. A recently discovered census of three Connecticut towns in 1670 yields a slightly lower set of figures. The mean size of households in Wethersfield was 5.64, in Windsor 5.63, and in Hartford 5.39.

Now even where you do find in these households servants and/or aged parents (perhaps it would be clearer to call them grandparents), their basically 'nuclear' character seems clear. By contrast, a true 'extended-family' household would in my view contain two or more conjugal units (related as siblings or cousins) and their respective children.[3] They might well span three full generations, but not necessarily so. This, I take it, is roughly what anthropologists have in mind when they talk of 'extended family' systems. Yet if one thing is evident from countless wills, deeds of gift, and marriage settlements written in early American communities, it is the fact that married siblings *never* resided in the same household.[4]

But why do I insist on making *this* – the question of married siblings – the decisive and literally definitive factor? Here I must bring forward the essentially psychological bias of my inquiry. An 'extended-family' household, as I have chosen to define it, creates above all a radically different set of *emotional* arrangements. For example, it offers the strong likelihood of some type of 'multiple mothering' (with broad consequences for child-rearing), and a considerably diluted relationship between spouses. These possibilities now seem to have been largely ruled out by my findings for Plymouth, and also, I submit, by Professor Greven's work on Andover. Children were raised by one set of parents at a time,[5] and the relation of husband and wife sustained an overpowering emotional and practical significance. These are conclusions of the first importance, in my view. Indeed they are the reason, or a large part of the reason, why we wish to learn about household size and membership in the first place.

And now a further point about these same findings. I have stated that the average household size in Plymouth Colony seems to have been roughly six persons. But it is also well to recognize that some households were very much larger than this – in fact, that nearly *all* households were, *for some period*, much larger. Married couples produced, over the entire span of the wife's child-bearing years, an average of eight children apiece. Like all families (at least 'nuclear' ones) these at Plymouth started small, expanded steadily so as to reach a maximum size as the parents approached middle age, and then contracted again when the children grew up and moved out in order to 'be for themselves' (the period phrase). But for some considerable number of years, they were large indeed – reaching in many cases a total of a dozen or more persons.

These patterns gain added significance when viewed against the physical setting of family-life in early America. New England houses of that period seem astonishingly small when measured against the standards of our own time, or even of seventeenth-century England. The great majority were built on a simple, single-bay, story-and-a-half plan, with ground-floor measurements of some-

---

[3] See above, Laslett, Chapter 1, pp. 28–33, for a detailed examination of this problem.
[4] See Demos, *Family life in Plymouth colony* (1970 i): 62–4.
[5] Admittedly some children were raised by *foster* parents or guardians. But they remained in any case the responsibility of one particular couple – and this, for my purposes, is the central point. On the practice of 'putting out' children into families other than their own, see Morgan, *The Puritan family* (1966): 38, and Demos (1970 i): 71–5, 120–2.

thing like 15×20 feet. Most of this space belonged to the so-called 'hall.' Make-shift interior partitions created some further complexity, but rooms apart from the hall served chiefly for sleeping or storage.[6] The main point is this: virtually all important daytime activities were sustained *in one room*, by groups comprising six, eight, ten, and even a dozen persons.

Now if we accept, with most of modern psychology, that all men harbor very basic impulses of both a loving *and* hostile kind, what of the latter under these conditions? How, in brief, did these cramped little households avoid an atmo-sphere of constant bickering and conflict? One cannot be certain that they *did* avoid such an atmosphere, but neither court records nor personal documents contain much evidence of intra-family conflict. What the records *do* quite strongly indicate is an extraordinary degree of contentiousness among neighbors. The men and women of these communities went to court again and again, to do battle over land titles, property losses, wayward cattle, rundown fences, unringed pigs – not to mention slander, and witchcraft, and assault and battery. Particular testimonies given in such cases often suggest a deep strain of personal bitterness.

If these various facts are brought together – the large families, the small houses, the apparent absence of intra-family conflict, and the chronic enmity among neighbors – there emerges the germ of an hypothesis which is worth, I hope, an explicit statement. For the issue involved is a telling one: namely the way people learn to handle their own feelings of anger and aggression. It remains only to emphasize the importance of the family as *the primary unit* in virtually all phases of seventeenth-century life. In short, the family had to maintain a smooth kind of operational equilibrium; basic disruptions and discontinuities must be avoided at all costs. What this probably meant in practice was a strong unconscious restraint on the expression of hostile impulses against the members of one's own household.

To call this restraint 'unconscious' is not to imply that it was easy to main-tain, or that family-life under these conditions reflected some natural tendency towards inner harmony. Formal restraints could, of course, also be applied when necessary and appropriate – particularly with the very young. Firm discipline was a touchstone of household organization in this culture, though after childhood it was a process largely internal (that is, *self*-discipline). In either case it imposed a cost in terms of energy and effort. Domestic peace, in short, was achieved only with an element of real struggle.

But it seems that *occasions* for abrasive contact must have been there aplenty, and the anger that resulted had to find some outlet in behavior. This is the point at which the field of neighborly relations derives a real, if somewhat sinister, significance. Chronic hostility among neighbors obviously created problems in its own right; but all things considered, this was preferable to the same con-ditions within the sphere of the family. The process is one that psychologists

[6] On these questions of domestic architecture, see Demos (1970 i), Ch. 1 and 2. On English houses in the same period, see Barley, *The English farmhouse and cottage* (1961).

know by the clinical term 'displacement.' but there is nothing very extraordinary about it. It appears indeed in the life of virtually every individual and every society. We are all occasionally confronted with impulses which, while rooted deep within us, are not acceptable in some given context. Displacement represents a rather simple way of resolving such conflicts. At its worst, it can generate the most vicious kind of scapegoating. But in other instances it may serve a purpose which is largely constructive in the long run. And such, perhaps, was the typical case in these earliest American communities – when a man cursed his neighbor in order to keep smiling at his parent, spouse, or child.

Let me turn now to another area in the study of family-life, in which 'quantitative' information can serve to enliven issues of a more psychological character. I am thinking of the 'life cycle,' the whole process of individual growth and change – infancy, childhood, adolescence, and beyond. There is room, of course, for argument about the definition of these various stages, their boundaries in time and their internal character, but the bare fact of development is quite beyond dispute. Unfortunately, obvious as all this seems, historians have mostly missed its significance. Consider, as a general point, the study of children and their role in society at large. The relatively few historical works on this subject have applied rather static and undifferentiated models of childhood.[7] They have missed what I see as the essential task – the need to discover the dynamic interconnections between experience at an earlier and a later stage, to appreciate that a child is always *developing*, according to influences that proceed from within as well as from the wider environment. It makes, in short, a very real difference that a particular event occurs earlier or later, that love or fright or encouragement or restriction enters the child's world at one time rather than another. His experience of 'outside' pressures locks together with his own *internal* developmental necessities at any given moment, and the outcome may be of lasting consequence for his future.

The specific concerns in my own work with early American families may be introduced here by way of illustration, and in order to give the discussion a sharper focus. Take, first, the matter of adolescence. All the evidence we have suggests that adolescence as we know it – a turbulent period of inner stress – barely existed before the twentieth century.[8] Here, it seems, is a developmental crisis largely created, or at least sharply intensified, by the progress of modern

[7] See, for example, Fleming, *Children and puritanism* (1933), and Earle, *Child life in colonial days* (1927). The same sort of defect can, in my opinion, be attributed to more recent and more sophisticated studies – even to the seminal work of Ariès, *Centuries of childhood* (1962). For a significant exception to this comment see Hunt, *Parents and children in history* (1970). Hunt applies a 'life cycle' perspective to materials from seventeenth-century France – with fascinating results.

[8] On this point, see J. and V. Demos, *Adolescence in historical perspective* (1969) and Demos, (1970 i): 145–50. Various aspects of the psychological and sociological theory of adolescence can be found, for example, in Keniston, *Social change and youth in America* (1962); Erikson, *Youth: fidelity and diversity* (1962); and R. Benedict, *Continuities and discontinuities in cultural conditioning* (1967).

history. Now the reasons for this are many and complex, and cannot be fully unravelled at present. But *one* factor of real importance relates in a direct way to the demographic materials mentioned previously. Since births were usually spaced at intervals of two years or more, and since the whole period of child-bearing for a given couple might encompass as much as twenty years, the children of each family formed a community of persons of quite different ages and radically different stages of development. For example, the household of a man forty-five years old might well contain a full-grown son about to marry and begin his own farm, and an infant still at the breast – not to mention all of the children in-between. This is, of course, much in contrast to the situation that commonly prevails today, when parents not only have many fewer children all told but also try to have them within a certain limited space of time. (The age at which the average American mother now has her last child is twenty-six.) The modern pattern tends to highlight the distance between the generations, and to make of childhood a quite tangible, or at least visible, condition. But in Plymouth Colony, and indeed in any society where the same sort of family predominates, these differences were considerably blurred. The way to maturity appeared not as a cliff to be mounted in a series of sudden and precarious leaps, but as a gradual ascent the stages of which were quite literally embodied in the many siblings variously situated along the way.

Consider, too, the period of infancy as experienced in these seventeenth-century communities. 'Quantitative' analysis supplies us with certain preliminary facts of considerable value. In the average family, as we have already noted, children were spaced roughly two years apart (or a bit longer near the end of the wife's child-bearing span). This pattern is consistent with a practice of breast feeding each infant for about twelve months, since lactation normally presents a biological impediment to a new conception. The exceptional cases can nearly always be explained in the same terms. When one finds an interval of only twelve or fifteen months between two particular deliveries, one also finds that the older baby died at or soon after birth. (Here there would be no period of breast feeding, to speak of, and hence nothing to delay the start of another pregnancy.)[9]

But these data must be viewed in a wider context. If we try to pull together the various bits of evidence bearing on infancy in Plymouth Colony, we are left with the impression – no stronger word could be justified – that for his first year or so a baby had a relatively tranquil and comfortable time. The ebb and flow of

[9] There is one alternative explanation for these data which must at least be considered. It is just possible that the culture supported a taboo against sexual relations between husband and wife whenever the latter was nursing a child. A custom of this type has been noted among many preindustrial peoples in the world today. (Copious documentation on this point can be obtained by consulting the appropriate category, number 853, in the Human Relations Area File.) I know of no evidence for such a practice in any European or American community of the seventeenth century; but this is not the kind of thing that would likely show up, either in written comment from the period, or in secondary works by modern historians.

domestic life must have been constantly around him: large families in small houses created an inevitable sense of intimacy. Often he must have been set close to the fireside for warmth. His clothing was light and not especially restrictive, yet the covers laid over him heightened his sense of protection. And most important, he had regular access to his mother's breast[10] – with all that this implies in the way of emotional reassurance, quite apart from the matter of sound physical nourishment. Illness was, of course, a real danger; the death rate for infants under one year seems to have been substantially higher than for any later age.[11] But this fact may well have encouraged an attitude of particular concern and tenderness towards infants.

All such statements are somewhat conjectural, and so too is any impression we may try to form of the subsequent phases of a child's life. Still, with this strong word of caution, it seems worth proceeding somewhat further. Consider for a moment a passage in the writings of the 'Pilgrim pastor,' John Robinson, on the requirements of the child by way of discipline:

And surely there is in all children...a stubborness, and stoutness of mind arising from natural pride, which must, in the first place, be broken and beaten down; that so the foundation of their education being laid in humility and tractableness, other virtues may, in their time, be built thereon...For the beating and keeping down of this stubborness parents must provide carefully...that the children's wills and wilfulness be restrained and repressed, and that, in time; lest sooner than they imagine, the tender sprigs grow to that stiffness, that they will rather break than bow. Children should not know, if it could be kept from them, that they have a will in their own, but in their parents' keeping; neither should these words be heard from them, save by way of consent, 'I will' or 'I will not.'[12]

This comment by Robinson may be regarded, I think, as being broadly representative of 'Puritan' attitudes toward child-rearing. And translated into the language of modern psychology it amounts to a blanket indictment of the child's strivings for self-assertion, and particularly of any impulses of direct aggression. The terms 'break' and 'beat down' ('destroy' is also used further on) seem to admit of no qualification. Robinson urged, moreover, that this sort of discipline be started very early. It had to be accorded 'the first place' in a whole sequence of socialization, because until the child's inherent 'stubborness' was thoroughly restrained training in the more positive virtues would not really take hold.

[10] Admittedly, to put it this way skirts one very important question: what *sort* of feeding schedule the infant experiences. It makes considerable difference, of course, both for his immediate comfort and for his later development whether (1) he can obtain the breast simply by crying out for it, or (2) his mother adheres to a firm timetable of feedings at fixed intervals, regardless of his own demands. But there is simply no way of ascertaining what was the usual practice in early American families.

[11] This, of course, is always the case – and the critical question is the *extent* of the difference between the rates of mortality in infancy and at subsequent ages. Unfortunately, there are as yet no solid data on this question (with regard to colonial America). Clearly, however, the rate of death in the first year of life was more than 10%, and perhaps as high as 20%. And it was less than half as great for all subsequent years.

[12] Robinson, *Works* (1851) I: 246–7.

Precisely what age Robinson had in mind here is not clear; but we may suspect that it was somewhere between one and two years. This, at any rate, is the period when *every* child develops the ability to assert his own will far more directly and effectively than was possible earlier. His perceptions of himself as apart from other people grow progressively sharper; his world is for the first time explicitly organized in terms of 'I' and 'you', 'mine' and 'yours.' He makes rapid progress with muscular control and coordination, and thus gains new power to express all his impulses. Even today, with our much more permissive style of child-rearing, the second year is a time for establishing limits, and often for the direct clash of wills between parent and child.[13] In all likelihood these first raw strivings of the infant self seemed to sincere Puritans a clear manifestation of original sin – the 'fruit of natural corruption and root of actual rebellion against God and man,' as Robinson himself put it. Such being the case, the only appropriate response from parents was a repressive one.

And there was more still. The second year of life was for many children bounded at either end by experiences of profound loss. Somewhere near its beginning, we have surmised, the child was likely to be weaned; and near its end the arrival of a new baby might be expected. All this would serve to heighten the crisis imposed by the crushing of the child's assertive and aggressive drives.

The pattern is striking in itself; but it gains added significance when set alongside an important theme in the *adult* life of the colonists – namely the whole atmosphere of contention, of chronic and sometimes bitter enmity, to which we have already alluded. This point merits the strongest possible emphasis, because it serves to call in question some extremely venerable and widespread notions about Puritanism. It has long been assumed that the people of this time and culture were peculiarly concerned – were effectively 'neurotic,' if you will – about all aspects of their sexuality. But there is now a growing body of evidence to the contrary; and it might even be argued that the Puritans took sex more nearly in their stride than most later generations of Americans.[14] Perhaps, though, there was a *different* bugbear in their lives – and psyches – namely, a tight cluster of anxieties about aggression. To read the records of Plymouth, and also those of the other New England settlements, is to sense a very special sort of preoccupation with any overt acts of this character. Here, it seems, was the one area of emotional and interpersonal life about which the Puritans were most concerned, confused, conflicted.[15]

John Robinson's thoughts are pertinent once again, right at this point. His

[13] These few sentences represent the briefest summary of a huge psychological literature. For a useful introduction to this literature, see Mussen, Conger, and Kagan, *Child development and personality* (1963), Ch. 7. The same overall viewpoint is apparent in a number of popular books as well – most notably, perhaps, in Spock's *Baby and child care* (1945).

[14] The most useful study of this matter is Morgan, *The Puritans and sex* (1942).

[15] This conclusion is, in my opinion, vividly confirmed through a reading of other types of material from the period. See, for example, Demos, *Underlying themes in the witchcraft of seventeenth century New England* (1970 ii). Compare the ideas of family history formulated by Dutch sociologists and summarized by van der Woude, above, Chapter 12, pp. 301–302.

Works contain a number of essays dealing successively with each of the most basic human instincts and emotions; and the one entitled 'Of Anger' stands out in a very special way. Robinson could find nothing at all to say in favor of anger – no circumstance that could ever truly justify its expression, no perspective from which its appearance was less than totally repellent. The imagery which he summoned to describe it is intensely vivid. Anger, he wrote, 'God so brands, as he scarce doth any created affection:' for it 'hath always evil in it.' The 'wrathful man' is like a 'hideous monster,' with 'his eyes burning, his lips fumbling, his face pale, his teeth gnashing, his mouth foaming, and other parts of his body trembling and shaking.'[16]

But anger, of course, is not easily avoided; efforts to suppress it can succeed only partially and at a very considerable cost. This leads us back to the opening stages in the life of a Puritan child. If his experience was, first, a year or so of general indulgence, and then a radical turn towards severe discipline – if, in particular, his earliest efforts at self-assertion were met with a crushing counter-force – it should not be surprising that aggression was a theme of special potency in the culture at large. Patterns of this kind are usually mediated. to a great extent, by fundamental practices and commitments in the area of child-rearing.[17] The latter create what psychologists call a 'fixation'. Some essential part of the child's personality becomes charged with strong feelings of guilt, anxiety, fear – and fascination. And later experiences cannot completely erase these trends.

The developmental theory of Erik Erikson (in my view the most useful of all such theories) helps to fill out this picture: it suggests quite powerfully certain additional lines of connection between infant experience and basic Puritan character structure. The time between one and two years forms the second stage in Erikson's larger developmental sequence, and he joins its characteristic behaviors under the general theme of 'autonomy'. 'This stage', he writes, 'becomes decisive for the ratio between love and hate, for that between freedom of self-expression and its suppression.' Further: while the goal of this stage is autonomy, its negative side – its specific vulnerability – is the possibility of lasting 'shame and doubt'. It is absolutely vital that the child receive support in 'his wish to "stand on his own feet" lest he be overcome by that sense of having exposed himself prematurely and foolishly which we call shame, or that secondary mistrust, that "double-take," which we call doubt'. If a child does not get this type of support – if, indeed, his efforts to assert himself are firmly 'beaten down' – then a considerable preoccupation with shame can be expected in later life as well.

At just this point the evidence on the Puritans makes a striking fit; for considerations of shame (and of 'face-saving' – its other side) loom very large in

---

[16] Robinson (1851) I: 226.
[17] There is an enormous literature in anthropology, tending to bear out this point of view. And among anthropologists it is particularly associated with the work of the so-called 'culture and personality' school. See, for example, Kardiner, *The psychological frontiers of society* (1945).

a number of areas of their culture. Such considerations are manifest, for example, throughout the legion of court cases that had to do with personal disputes and rivalries. Many of these cases involved suits for slander or defamation – where the issue of public exposure, the risk of shame, was absolutely central. Moreover, when a conviction was obtained, the defendant was normally required to withdraw his slanderous statements, and to apologize for them, *in public*. Note, too, that a common punishment, for many different types of offense, was a sentence to 'sit in the stocks'. Presumably the bite here was the threat of general ridicule.

A second point, more briefly: Erikson contends that each of man's early stages can be fundamentally related to a particular institutional principle. And for the stage we are now discussing he cites 'the principle of *law and order*, which in daily life as well as in the high courts of law apportions to each his privileges and his limitations, his obligations and his rights.' Surely few people have shown as much concern for 'law and order' as the Puritans.[18]

We have strayed rather far afield with these last speculations, but the general point should be clear. In studying children – and, for that matter, older persons as well – it is often important to be aware of 'life cycle' issues. To achieve this kind of perspective we, as historians, must always ask not only how society has treated its constituent members but also how it has distinguished between different stages and periods of growth. In the process 'quantitative' information assumes a real and particular significance. It provides us – if all goes well – with certain concrete bench-marks: age of weaning, age of marriage, rate of mortality, and so forth. And in a broader sense it helps to sensitize us to all of the continuing possibilities of developmental change.

Here, then, I return to my overall theme: the hope of fruitful interchange between 'demographic' and 'psychological' research on the history of the family. I truly feel that the two approaches are, or should be, mutually complementary. Psychological theory cries out for solid evidence on the timing of certain crucial 'life-happenings'. Demographic results, on the other hand, are arid – and sometimes quite meaningless – without a leavening of 'qualitative' insight.

[18] The material contained in these three paragraphs is drawn particularly from Erikson, *Identity and the life cycle* (1959), 65–74. Re 'shame' in Puritan child-rearing, note the following attributed to John Ward in Mather, *Magnalia Christi Americana* (1853) i: 522, 'Of young persons he would himself give this advice: "Whatever you do, be sure to maintain shame in them; for if that be once gone, there is no hope that they'll ever come to good".'

22. Rhode Island family structure: 1875 and 1960[1]

Edward T. Pryor, Jr

INTRODUCTION

A neglected area of family sociology is that of historical research concerning the development of the American family. In his recent commentaries on the family,[2] one of Goode's principal themes has been the lack of historical research by sociologists that would provide sound empirical tests of the common theories of change in family organization. He writes:

> The study of family change is especially plagued by the prevalence of myths about the past. Most discussions of the U.S. family contain such a myth, which typically depicts a harmonious life down on grandmother's self-sufficient farm. Whether this myth corresponds to reality, we do not know, since very little historical research has attempted to test it. Not a single history of the U.S. family would meet modern standards of historical research.[3]

This chapter is a partial report of an effort to reconstruct the demographic history and to measure specific structural and compositional changes in organization between 1875 and 1960 within the Rhode Island family. Simply, how has the family changed? More explicitly, what observable demographic changes in the Rhode Island family can be found for 1875 in comparison with the present?[4]

DATA USED

Family and household data were collected from the original, handwritten, 1875 Rhode Island State Census listings. Using a five percent sample of families from this 1875 Census, family and household characteristics were reconstructed as closely as possible in conformity to the 1960 United States Census family and household definitions. The 1875 Rhode Island State Census is an important document in that it is one of the earliest state-wide census sources in the United States which provides information on 'relationship to family head' of each member of the family. In addition, data are provided in this Census concerning

[1] Revision of a paper read at the annual meeting of the Population Association of America, April 1967. The material for this chapter is taken from Pryor, *Family structure and change* (1966). I am indebted to John F. Kantner for his careful reading and many suggestions regarding this revision.
[2] Goode, *The family* (1964) and *World revolution and family patterns* (1963).
[3] Goode (1964): 105.   [4] The discussion in this chapter pertains only to 'white' families.

the age, sex, place of birth, place of birth of parents, and occupation of each person. The occupational information is generally susceptible to classification according to current United States Census occupational categories in that: (1) the occupation descriptions are specific and (2) the relative stability of occupations in Rhode Island over time, especially in the cotton and wool mill industries, make classification by current standards plausible.

The classifications of the 1875 sample data were in accord, whenever possible, with the 1960 Bureau of the Census family and household concepts. The purpose was to extract comparable 1875 and 1960 information relevant to such family and household characteristics as generational composition, presence of extended kin, frequency of subfamilies,[5] and presence of nonrelatives in the household. These variables incorporate the basic dimensions in structural terms around which postulates of family change have been constructed.[6]

METHODOLOGICAL ISSUES[7]

In general, the format of the 1875 Rhode Island State Census materials permitted its codification in conformity with 1960 Census definitions. However, since the concept of 'primary individual' was not used in 1875 no doubt this category of household type is underestimated for 1875. Primary individuals in 1875 can only be so classified in 1875 for those households which contain no relatives of the head.[8] Undoubtedly, a considerable number of persons enumerated as 'boarders' or 'roomers' in 1875 would be classified as 'primary individuals' under 1960 definitions. Although no controls can be exercised for this definitional change, Table 22.11 illustrates the change in the proportion of primary individual households between 1875 and 1960.

In 1875 there was also the problem that some 'families' at that time would be

---

[5] See below p. 582.

[6] For 1875–1960 comparisons, 'presence of own children of head' was not used as a measure of familism. Although there is argument for its use, problems of interpretation negate the few advantages. The enumeration of children, especially those eighteen years of age and over, lacks comparability from 1875 to 1960. The *de facto* enumeration of college students, those in the armed forces, etc. in 1960 removes specific populations from families in a fashion that was not prevalent in 1875. This fact reduces the validity of any comparisons of those children of the head eighteen years of age and older, because, in terms of using the presence of children of the head as an index of familism, this is the very population which counts the most.

[7] See Pryor (1966), Ch. 3 for a fuller description of the data and methods used for this research.

[8] In 1875, a family was defined as follows: 'By the term "family" is meant either one person living separately in a house, or part of a house, and providing for himself or several persons living together. Thus a family may be one person living alone, or any number of persons living together and provided for by a common head. The resident inmates and regular boarders of each hotel are to be all reckoned together as one family, and the inmates of each jail, poor-house, boarding school, or other institution, are to be reckoned together, including the keeper and officers, as one family.' From Snow, *Report upon the Census of Rhode Island, 1875* (1877): 144. Similar definitions seem to have been adopted in earlier censuses, see above Greven, Chapter 20, p. 545 and in English censuses of the eighteenth and nineteenth centuries, see above, Wall, Chapter 5, pp. 160–166. See also Laslett, Chapter 1, pp. 23–28.

categorized as 'group quarters' in 1960. Conformity to the 1960 definitions was generally achieved by removing such cases from the household classification.

The possibility that 'subfamilies' may have been underenumerated in 1875 must also be recognized. However, there is no evidence of a greater tendency in 1875 than in 1960 to classify subfamilies as separate families.

In general, the problems of comparability are considered minor, since, in 1875, the relationship of each family member to the head was explicit, thereby making classification according to 1960 Census standards generally straight-forward. What problems there are as we have seen involve only a small percentage of the total 1875 sample.

Cross-sectional comparisons at two points in time, especially on a long-term basis as in this study, invite speculation about the nature of the trend linking the two. Nothing conclusive can be said on this score although general knowledge of the processes of social change would not lead one to expect abrupt alterations in family structure.

The apparent solution of this problem would be the inclusion of similar data for intervening periods between 1875 and 1960. Curiously, the data of the best quality are at each end of the period under question, namely, 1875 and 1960. In fact, the family data available in 1875 are equal, or better in organization to those contained in subsequent state censuses.[9] At the opposite end of the period, the 1960 Census is the first federal census to collect information in terms of family kinship structure as such.[10] In consideration of the availability and condition of longitudinal family data, the direct comparison here is considered a feasible and defensible strategy.

The 1875 data allowed considerable flexibility in controls and cross-tabulations; however, the available 1960 data are limited in terms of controls by household and family type with households variously distinguished or subclassified as:

1. All households (total)
2. Primary individuals and primary families
3. Primary individuals, head-wife families and other families
4. Primary individuals, head-wife families, other families with male head and other families with female head.

Not all of these classifications are available for all cross-tabulations with the result that information on family type available for 1875 sometimes had to be collapsed. However, the general rule has been to maximize the refinement of 1875–1960 comparisons to the extent allowed by the data.[11]

[9] The 1905 Rhode Island State Census is the last state census of Rhode Island to provide comprehensive information on family characteristics.
[10] Previous tabulations, as in the 1940 and 1950 United States Censuses, of 'relationship to the head' are *by person* and not 'by family.'
[11] For 1960, cross-tabulations of family and household characteristics by occupation, ethnicity, income, etc. are limited. The primary deficiency for purposes here is the lack of tabulations of 'generations within the family' by 'occupation of the head'. See United States Bureau of the Census, *United States Census of Population: 1960* (1961): xxiv.

THE RHODE ISLAND FAMILY: 1875 AND 1960

A basic thesis of structural change in the American family centers around the nuclear-extended character of the family. Corollary hypotheses focus on the prevalence of the 'normal,' two generation, nuclear family in contrast to the 'abnormal,' one or three generation family. The presence of nonrelatives in a *household* may be a type of covert 'extended' *family*. This paper is addressed to these possible types of change, in general, by social class, ethnicity and residence. Separate sections are devoted to:

1. Variations in family composition as indexed by presence of extended kin of head, number of generations present, and the presence of subfamilies:

2. Variations in household composition as measured by the presence in the household of nonrelatives of the head.

FAMILY COMPOSITION

A fundamental desideratum in the classification of family types is the marital status of the head. Table 22.1 shows that the proportion of families with spouse of head present is practically the same for 1875 (84 %) and 1960 (85 %). This constancy of basic family type is somewhat surprising given the change in mortality over the period. It suggests the operation of compensating factors (e.g. change in nuptiality).

Presence of extended kin of head

One of the fundamental questions concerning changes in the American family involves the prevalence of extended families. Preliminary evidence[12] suggests that, in Rhode Island, the extended and/or multigenerational household was not pervasive in the later nineteenth century but probably more common then than in 1960. From Table 22.2 it is evident that change in extended family living has been two-directional. In the case of head-wife families, there was a slightly smaller proportion in 1960 of families with extended kin of both types. In the instances of head-only families, the reverse is the case with the proportions of families with parents and/or grandchildren of the head (16 %) remaining the same while the proportion of families with 'other kin' actually increased by 9 % from 1875 to 1960. The basic fluctuation between 1875 and 1960 has been in the presence of extended kin *other than* parents or grandchildren of the family head. Table 22.3, which is a detailed comparison of 1875 and 1960 family types, provides specific evidence that the changing distribution of family types is far from unidirectional, especially in the contrast of head-wife and head-only families in regard to the presence of extended kin. In total, the change in nuclear

---

[12] See Pryor (1966), Ch. 3. For similar evidence regarding Massachusetts in the latter part of the nineteenth century, see Beresford and Rivlin, *Privacy, Poverty, and Old Age* (1966): 248–51.

Table 22.1   *Families^a by type, white, for Rhode Island:*
1875 and 1960^b

(1875, 5 percent sample: 1960, based on 5 percent sample)

Year	Total %	Head-wife families %	Other families (head only) %
1875 (N: 2,563)	100	84	16
1960 (N: 216,021)	100	85	15

^{a} The definition of 'family' used in this analysis is that of the 1960 United States Census: 'A family consists of two or more persons in the same household who are related to each other by blood, marriage, or adoption; all persons living together in one household who are related to each other are regarded as one family.' United States Bureau of the Census (1961): xi.
^{b} United States Bureau of the Census (1961). Unpublished data, Table 61.

Table 22.2   *Families by type and presence of relatives of head,*
white, for Rhode Island: 1875 and 1960^a

(1875, 5 percent sample: 1960, based on 5 percent sample)

Family type and year	Total (%)	With or without own children of head		
		No other members (nuclear families) (%)	Parents and/or grand-children of head (%)	With extended kin other than parents or grandchildren of head (%)
Head-wife families				
1875 (N: 2,161)	101	85	9	7
1960 (N: 184,533)	100	90	7	3
Head-only families				
1875 (N: 402)	100	67	16	17
1960 (N: 31,488)	100	58	16	26
Total				
1875 (N: 2,563)	100	82	10	8
1960 (N: 216,021)	100	85	8	7

^{a} United States Bureau of the Census (1961). Unpublished data, Table 60.

families has not been remarkable with only a 3 % increase in the proportion of nuclear families from 1875 to 1960. The hypothesis of change from an extended to a nuclear type of family organization receives little support for the period under review. The evidence here illustrates rather that extended family living was relatively uncommon at either point in time with only a slight decrease between 1875 and 1960. The concentration of extended families within 'other' or head-

Table 22.3 Generations within the family and presence and type of subfamilies, white, for Rhode Island: distribution for 1875 and 1960 and percent difference from 1875 to 1960[a]

(1875, 5 percent sample: 1960, based on 5 percent sample)

Family type and year	All families (%)	With own children of any age						With no own children of any age					
		No other members	With other members by relationship to head					No other members	With other members by relationship to head				
			Neither pts nor grdchln		Pts but no grdchln	Grdchln but no pts	Pts and grdchln		Neither pts nor grdchln		Pts but no grdchln	Grdchln but no pts	Pts and grdchln
			No bro or sistr	With bro or sistr					No bro or sistr	With bro or sistr			
Head-wife families:													
1875 (N: 2,161):													
No subfamily	96.1	65.3	1.1	3.0	3.6	0.6	—	19.2	0.6	1.0	1.3	0.4	—
One subfamily	3.6	0.9	0.1	0.1	0.4	1.8	0.2	—	—	—	—	0.1	—
Two or more subfamilies	0.3	0.1	—	—	—	0.2	—	—	—	—	—	—	—
Total	100.0	66.3	1.2	3.1	4.0	2.6	0.2	19.2	0.6	1.0	1.3	0.5	—
1960 (N: 184,533):													
No subfamily	98.2	60.9	1.0	0.8	3.4	0.1	—	29.3	0.5	0.8	1.2	0.2	—
One subfamily	1.8	0.2	—	—	0.4	1.0	—	—	—	0.1	0.1	—	—
Two or more subfamilies	—	—	—	—	—	—	—	—	—	—	—	—	—
Total	100.0	61.1	1.0	0.8	3.8	1.1	—	29.3	0.5	0.9	1.3	0.2	—
Per cent difference, 1875–1960:													
Total		−5.2	−0.2	−2.3	−0.2	−1.5	−0.2	+10.1	−0.1	−0.1	0.0	−0.3	—
Head-only families:													
1875 (N: 402):													
No subfamily	87.8	67.2	1.0	2.2	2.5	1.2	0.3	—	0.5	10.0	2.2	1.0	—
One subfamily	11.4	2.7	0.3	0.5	0.2	6.5	0.2	—	—	—	0.8	0.2	—
Two or more subfamilies	0.8	—	—	—	—	0.5	—	—	—	—	—	—	—
Total	100.0	69.9	1.3	2.7	2.7	8.2	0.5	—	0.5	10.0	3.0	1.2	—
1960 (N: 31,488):													
No subfamily	94.1	58.0	1.0	1.3	2.4	0.7	0.1	0.4	3.6	17.5	8.5	0.6	—
One subfamily	5.9	0.8	0.1	0.3	0.2	3.0	—	—	0.1	0.9	0.4	0.1	—
Two or more subfamilies	—	—	—	—	—	—	—	—	—	—	—	—	—
Total	100.0	58.8	1.1	1.6	2.6	3.7	0.1	0.4	3.7	18.4	8.9	0.7	—
Per cent difference, 1875–1960:													
Total		−11.1	−0.2	−1.1	−0.1	−4.5	−0.4	+0.4	+3.2	+8.4	+5.9	−0.5	—

[a] United States Bureau of the Census (1961). Unpublished data, Table 60.

only families suggests that extended family living may be a culturally approved substitute for 'normal,' head-spouse family arrangements. In this sense, extended family living may be more closely related to differentials in male and female mortality than to any change in the attitude toward familism (as measured by living arrangements).

Social class and presence of extended kin of head

Comparable occupational or income measures of social class for nuclear-extended structures are not available for both 1875 and 1960. In the absence of such comparative data, occupational groups[13] are used for 1875 (see Table 22.4). For 1960, 'family income in 1959' is available in relation to nuclear-extended characteristics (see Table 22.5). Obviously these two measures give different dimensions of social class and thus comparisons are tenuous. Moreover family income in 1959 may reflect contributions of 'extended or multigenerational' members.[14] Nevertheless, if it is granted that both 'nonmanual' and higher income (especially $10,000 and over) represent the upper levels of the class structure, it would appear that a shift has occurred since 1875 in the direction of

Table 22.4   *Families by type, occupation of head, extended structure and presence of multigenerational families, white, for Rhode Island: 1875[a]*

(5 percent sample)

Family type and occupation of head	Percent of all families containing:	
	Extended kin	Three or more generations
Head-wife families		
Nonmanual (N: 425)	17	7
Manual (N: 1,381)	14	6
Farm (N: 286)	21	12
Total (N: 2,092)	15	7
Head-only families		
Nonmanual (N: 21)	43	24
Manual (N: 88)	48	12
Farm (N: 20)	60	25
Total (N: 129)	49	16

[a] Comparable data by occupation are not available for 1960.

13 Based on the coding of occupations in 1875, the following reclassification was used: *Nonmanual* (professional, technical, and kindred workers: managers, officials and proprietors, except farm; clerical and kindred workers; sales workers): *Manual* (craftsmen, foremen, and kindred workers: operatives and kindred workers: private household workers: service workers, except private household: farm laborers and foremen; laborers, except farm and mine): and *Farm* (farmers and farm managers).

14 I would like to thank John C. Beresford for pointing this out to me.

Table 22.5   *Families by type, family income in 1959, extended structure[a] and presence of multigenerational families, white, for Rhode Island: 1960[b]*

(Based on 5 percent sample)

Family type and income	Percent of all families containing:	
	Extended kin	Three or more generations[c]
Head-wife families		
$10,000 and over (N: 23,327)	19	10
$6,000–$9,999 (N: 64,039)	12	7
$4,000–$5,999 (N: 55,306)	6	3
Under $4,000 (N: 41,861)	4	1
Total (N: 184,533)	10	5
Head-only families		
$10,000 and over (N: 2,753)	55	10
$6,000–$9,999 (N: 5,840)	49	12
$4,000–$5,999 (N: 6,542)	50	7
Under $4,000 (N: 16,353)	32	4
Total (N: 31,488)	41	6

[a] There is a minor qualification within this table in the separation of nuclear-extended families because, from the data available, a small number of families containing extended kin could not be distinguished from nuclear families.

[b] United States Bureau of the Census (1961). Unpublished data, Table 61.

[c] In the following tables measuring generational composition there is a slight variation between the 1960 data and the 1875 figures used in this chapter in that 1875 data were coded according to the actual count of generations present. There is a slight loss in accuracy of generations present for 1960 in that a few 'other relatives' in the 1960 Census cannot be classified by generation in relation to the head. However, for 1875, if the 1960 classification were used, it was found that the variation was less than one percent (0.6%).

greater extendedness among upper class families. With industrialization then, it is the upper class family which seemingly can afford the 'luxury' of extended family living arrangements, even though in some cases the 'luxury' may be generated by 'necessity'.[15] An alternative interpretation postulates that with social mobility dependent on individualistic standards of achievement, lower class families have the least investment in extended family patterns as a means of social advancement. Despite this problem of causation, the data here do suggest that with the development through the later stages of full industrialization a pattern of class differences in structural nuclearity does emerge even though there is no marked change overall in the extent of extended family arrangements.

[15] A characteristic which it shares with many more primitive societies. See above Goody Chapter 3, pp. 122–123; and the detailed studies of pre-industrial England, Laslett, Chapter 4, pp. 153–154; rural Lancashire, Anderson, Chapter 7, pp. 220–221; and Tuscany, Klapisch, Chapter 10, pp. 275–277.

Table 22.6 *Families by major foreign stock head,[a] extended structure and presence of multigenerational families, white, for Rhode Island: 1875 and 1960[b]*

(1875, 5 percent sample: 1960, based on 5 percent sample)

	Percent of all families containing	
Year and foreign stock of head	Extended kin	Three or more generations
1875		
English (N: 254)	13	7
Irish (N: 668)	15	7
French Canadian (N: 98)	14	6
1960		
Irish (N: 10,181)	21	3
Polish (N: 5,949)	14	4
Russian (N: 5,722)	12	4
Italian (N: 32,250)	15	7

[a] For 1875, the groups presented here encompass 90% of all families with head of foreign stock: for 1960, the comparable figure is 95%, excluding, among others, families with 'other foreign stock' head which were not tabulated for all primary families in 1960.
[b] United States Bureau of the Census (1961). Unpublished data, Table 60.

Foreign stock and presence of extended kin of head

Comparative data on family composition according to ethnic group are scarce mainly because the principal foreign stock groups shifted from 1875 to 1960 (see Table 22.6). Irish foreign stock is the only ethnic group delineated in 1960 that was also relatively large in 1875. In this specific case, there is a small increase from 1875 to 1960 in extended families. Although the data are not available by age for both years, the Irish is an upwardly mobile and probably an 'older' population in 1960 and thus more likely to be composed of extended families. While the evidence is scanty, being confined to comparison for a single ethnic group, there is no evidence of great change in the extent of extended family living. The change that is observable among the Irish can possibly be ascribed to aging or upward mobility.

Residence and presence of extended kin of head

Although the rural–urban trichotomies used for 1875 and 1960 are not strictly comparable[16] (see Table 22.7) definite rural and urban patterns are obvious in the case of head-only families. For both years, among such families rural families tend to be the most extended. Significantly, the major decline from 1875 to

[16] For the classification by residence used in 1875, see Pryor (1966): 150–1. For United States Census definitions of residence used in 1960, see United States Bureau of the Census (1961): xiv. The relatively few rural families for both years should be kept in mind throughout the analysis presented here.

Table 22.7   *Families by type, urban–rural residence, extended structure, presence of multigenerational families, and presence of subfamilies, white, for Rhode Island: 1875 and 1960[a]*

(1875, 5 percent sample: 1960, based on 5 percent sample)

Family type, year and residence	Percent of all families containing		
	Extended kin	Three or more generations	One or more subfamilies[b]
Head-wife families			
1875			
Urban (N: 1,644)	16	7	4
Urban–rural (N: 350)	13	6	3
Rural (N:167)	16	10	5
Total (N: 2,161)	15	7	4
1960			
Urban (N: 159,135)	10	5	2
Rural non-farm (N: 24,664)	8	4	2
Rural (N: 734)	8	3	3
Total (N: 184,533)	10	5	2
Head-only families			
1875			
Urban (N: 314)	33	13	12
Urban–rural (N: 60)	23	8	10
Rural (N: 28)	46	18	21
Total (N: 402)	33	13	12
1960			
Urban (N: 27,984)	43	6	6
Rural non-farm (N: 3,419)	33	5	5
Rural (N: 85)	49	0	0
Total (N: 31,488)	42	6	6
All families			
1875			
Total (N: 2,563)	18	8	5
1960			
Total (N: 216,021)	15	5	2

[a] United States Bureau of the Census (1961). Unpublished data, Table 60.
[b] The percentage of families containing two or more subfamilies was very small in both 1875 (0.4%) and 1960 (0.04%).

1960 in nuclearity (increase in extendedness) among head-only families occurs among non-rural families: in the case of head-wife families, on the other hand, nuclearity increases and does so uniformly in relation to residence.

Multigenerational families

One of the basic questions concerning families in the United States is the extent of, and change in, multigenerational (three or more generations) family living. Table 22.7 indicates that overall there was a small decline (3%) in multigenerational families; however, even in 1875, the proportion of such families (8 %) was quite small. Distinguished by family type, there was a slight difference in the percentage decline but for both head-wife (2 %) and head-only families (7 %) the direction was the same. The result is that in 1960 the small proportion of multigenerational families (5 %) was about equally distributed regardless of family type. Table 22.3 provides the additional evidence that in either year no particular type of multigenerational family was prevalent.

Social class and multigenerational families

Again, using occupation and family income as measures of social class for 1875 and 1960 respectively, a pattern of change is revealed somewhat similar to that found with respect to change in extended family structure. In 1875, higher class (nonmanual) families are not the most multigenerational in structure (see Table 22.4), whereas, in 1960, they are (see Table 22.5).[17]

Foreign stock and multigenerational families

The evidence in Table 22.6 supports the conclusion that in both 1875 and 1960 families of ethnic background are very similar to native families in terms of generational character. In fact, for both years, no ethnic group with the family head of foreign stock contained more than 7 % multigenerational families. Controls for ethnicity have failed, generally, to produce serious structural differentials in multigenerational living. This evidence suggests that ethnic contrasts in familism have not been expressed in terms of family living arrangements. Although ethnic histories document the importance of family solidarity and propinquity, the evidence here suggests the structural adaptation of the ethnic family to the American residential pattern.

Residence and multigenerational families

For 1875, rural families contained the highest proportion of multigenerational families (see Table 22.7). In 1960, although again the differences are not dramatic, the pattern is reversed with the relatively small number of rural families, regardless of type, containing the smallest proportion of multigenerational families (see Table 22.7). Since, even in 1875, Rhode Island was basically an urbanized state, the multigenerational rural family (if it ever had existed) had disappeared. By 1960, residence, in these terms, obviously fails to elicit, especially among head-wife families, important differentials in multigenerational composition.

[17] The one exception is in the case of head-only families with income of $10,000 or more (see Table 22.5). Again, these data must be interpreted with reservations since family income may be partly a function of the generational character of the family. Also, more refined information in terms of age (and social class) of the family head in relation to generations present would allow us to differentiate the extent to which generational structure is related to these variables.

Subfamilies

An additional index of familism used throughout this research is the presence of subfamilies within the family.[18] For 1875, subfamilies were found to be relatively infrequent with a larger proportion found among head-only families (12 %). In the comparison of 1875 and 1960, a trend is found similar to that uncovered with the other measures of familism (see Table 22.7).[19] Although proportionately few families contained subfamilies in 1875 (5 %), even fewer do so in 1960 (2 %). Again the larger decline is in the case of head-only families with a reduction of 6 % in families with subfamilies present. Subfamily living, as expressing a *stem* or *joint* family system, was not common in Rhode Island even in 1875. By 1960, subfamily structures are an exceptional family pattern.

Table 22.8   *Primary families, occupation of head and presence of subfamilies, white, for Rhode Island: 1875 and 1960*[a]

(1875, 5 percent sample: 1960, based on 5 percent sample)

Year and occupation of head	Total (%)	No sub-families present (%)	One or more subfamilies present (%)
1875			
Nonmanual (N: 446)	100	95	5
Manual (N: 1,469)	100	96	4
Farm (N: 306)	100	91	9
Total (N: 2,221)	100	95	5
1960			
Nonmanual (N: 58,642)	100	98	2
Manual (N: 99,098)	100	98	2
Farm (N: 1,419)	100	97	3
Total (N: 159,159)	100	98	2

[a] United States Bureau of the Census (1961). Unpublished data, Table 23.

[18] In 1875, probably more subfamilies were 'lost' in that they may have been enumerated as separate families, i.e. present in the same dwelling unit but enumerated as having own family head. The only partial check available was the presence of two or more families with the same family name residing in the same dwelling unit. Although a preliminary check of the data revealed few such instances no record was kept for the entire sample of 'dwelling units containing more than one family with the same surname'. Even then, evidence concerning multifamily dwellings in terms of living arrangements does not justify the assumption that related families in the same dwelling were not separate families. Serbian census material can give rise to similar problems. See Laslett & Clarke, Chapter 15, pp. 376–379, Hammel, Chapter 14, p. 339. See also Laslett, Chapter 1, pp. 23–28, 34–39, Anderson, Chapter 7, p. 218.

[19] Table 22.3 supplies for both years the membership of subfamilies in terms of relationship to head.

Table 22.9   *Primary families, family income in 1959 and presence of*
subfamilies, white, for Rhode Island: 1960[a]

(Based on 5 percent sample)

Income	Total (%)	No sub-families present (%)	One or more subfamilies present (%)
$10,000 and over (N: 26,101)	100	93	7
$6,000–$9,999 (N: 69,918)	100	97	3
$4,000–$5,999 (N: 61,880)	100	99	1
Under $4,000 (N: 59,122)	100	99	1
Total (N: 216,021)	100	98	2

[a] United States Bureau of the Census (1961). Unpublished data, Table 23.

Social class and presence of subfamilies

In the case of subfamilies it was possible to construct comparable data for *primary*
families in terms of occupation (see Table 22.8). In consideration of the in-
frequency of subfamilies in general, the lack of variation by occupation is not
unexpected. For both years the distribution by occupation is quite even with
only farm families in 1875 showing a noticeably higher proportion (9 %) of
subfamilies. Interestingly, using income as an index, upper class families in 1960
again demonstrated a slightly greater tendency toward familism (see Table 22.9).
The trend here parallels that found in the examination of extended families and
generational composition in 1960, i.e. higher class strata (measured by family
income) illustrate more frequent signs of familistic living. The contrast in 1960
between using occupation and family income does suggest that 'family income'
and such measures of familism (generations present, presence of extended kin
or subfamilies) are not independent.

Foreign stock and presence of subfamilies

If anything, families with the head of foreign stock tend to have fewer subfamilies than families of native background (see Table 22.10). However, the
differences are minimal. The only group comparable by year, the Irish, is an
interesting example. Among Irish families, subfamilies were highly unusual in
1875 or 1960 (only 1 %). The evidence is convincing, at least for Rhode Island,
that the Irish rural stem family tradition was not an imported structural type.

Residence and presence of subfamilies

In terms of rural–urban residence the pattern of change is consistent (see
Table 22.7). For both family types, the proportion of families with subfamilies
decreased from 1875 to 1960 within each residential category. The most im-

Table 22.10   *Husband–wife families by major foreign stock head[a] and presence of subfamilies, white, for Rhode Island: 1875 and 1960[b]*

(1875, 5 percent sample: 1960, based on 5 percent sample)

Year and foreign stock of head	Total (%)	No sub-families present (%)	One or more subfamilies present (%)
1875			
English (N: 223)	100	96	4
Irish (N: 524)	100	99	1
French Canadian (N: 89)	100	93	7
1960			
Irish (N: 7,626)	100	99	1
Polish (N: 2,218)	100	98	2
Russian (N: 5,198)	100	99	1
Italian (N: 28,499)	100	97	3

[a] See Table 22.6.
[b] United States Bureau of the Census (1961). Unpublished data, Table 59.

portant decline was within head-only families where, for both urban and rural families, the trends involved a considerable drop in the proportion with sub-families present.

The result of change is that by 1960 rural–urban differences in subfamilies are negligible among head-wife families. Probably expressing the disappearance of a rural 'way of life' in Rhode Island, among head-only families, the trend is reversed from 1875 to 1960 with rural families containing the largest proportion (21 %) with subfamilies in 1875 and the least (0 %) in 1960.

HOUSEHOLD COMPOSITION

Table 22.11 is a general table illustrating both changes in the distribution of household types (primary individuals and primary families), and changes in the size of primary families by persons present in the family. Looking first at house-hold types, the proportion of 'other' (head-only) households composed of primary individuals more than doubled from 1875 to 1960. This pattern is true for both male and female head 'other' households. This rather significant in-crease is probably explained by both the increase in one-person households (see Table 22.12) and changes in the identification and enumeration of persons classified as 'primary individuals'.[20]

Turning to primary family size, the obvious change is in the direction of smaller families in 1960 regardless of household type (Table 22.11). Whereas in

[20] For a discussion of this point see above p. 572.

Table 22.11   *Households, by type and size, white,*
for Rhode Island: 1875 and 1960[a]

(1875, 5 percent sample: 1960, based on 5 percent sample)

Household type and size	Husband–wife households		Other male head households		Female head households	
	1875 (N: 2,161) (%)	1960 (N: 184,533) (%)	1875 (N: 143) (%)	1960 (N: 19,692) (%)	1875 (N: 385) (%)	1960 (N: 48,215) (%)
Primary individuals	—	—	30	60	22	51
Primary family heads						
2 persons in family	15	29	10	22	18	25
3 persons in family	20	23	20	11	16	13
4 persons in family	18	22	12	4	17	6
5 persons in family	15	14	6	2	10	3
6 persons in family	12	6	13	1	8	1
7 persons in family	8	3	4	—[b]	5	—[b]
8 persons in family	5	1	1	—[b]	1	—[b]
9 or more persons in family	7	1	3	—[b]	3	—[b]
All households (Total)	100	99	99	100	100	99

[a] United States Bureau of the Census (1961). Unpublished data, Table 2.
[b] Less than 0.5%.

1875 husband–wife primary families containing six or more persons comprised about a third of such families, by 1960, the modal family contains only two persons with large (six or more persons) families making up only about ten percent of all primary families. Among head-only primary families in 1960, the great majority was composed of only two or three persons. These changes in family size reflect both the reduction in fertility taking place between 1875 and 1960 and the decline in the number of persons unrelated to the head living in households.

Presence of nonrelatives in households

The reduction in the proportion of households containing nonrelatives of the head is probably the most significant change in the structural character of the Rhode Island family between 1875 and 1960 (see Table 22.12). For both primary individuals and primary families the change was such that in 1960 only a small proportion of households contained nonrelatives.

The sizeable reduction (30 %) in the presence of nonrelatives in households headed by primary individuals probably overstates the change. As pointed out several times previously, an undeterminable number of one-person households enumerated in 1960 would not have been counted as 'separate families' (i.e.

Table 22.12   *Households by type and presence of nonrelatives of the head,*
white, for Rhode Island: 1875 and 1960[a]

(1875, 5 percent sample: 1960, based on 5 percent sample)

Household type and year	Total (%)	With no nonrelatives (%)	With one or more nonrelatives (%)
Primary individuals			
1875 (N: 126)	100	63	37
1960 (N: 36,419)	100	93	7
Primary families			
1875 (N: 2,563)	100	77	23
1960 (N: 216,021)	100	99	1
Total			
1875 (N: 2,689)	100	76	24
1960 (N: 252,440)	100	98	2

[a] United States Bureau of the Census (1961). Unpublished Data, Table 24.

'households' by 1960 standards) in the 1875 state census. However, even allowing for this qualification, the evidence is convincing that there has been a *real* increase in one-person households as an alternative living pattern in place of either living with nonrelatives or within extended family arrangements.[21]

In the case of primary families, the decline (22 %) in the proportion of families containing nonrelatives has been almost as significant. Basically, this reduction is explained by: (1) the changes in definition described above where persons enumerated in 1875 as nonrelatives in households would be primary individuals in 1960; (2) the decline in persons living in households as boarders and roomers; and (3) the virtual disappearance of a 'living-in' servant class.[22] The result is that where in 1875 almost a quarter (23 %) of all families contained nonrelatives, by 1960 such arrangements had literally passed from the scene. In 1960, in terms of persons involved in families, family and household were practically synonymous.

In total, the 1875 to 1960 change in the Rhode Island household is apparent. In 1875, about one-fourth (24 %) of all households contained a nonrelative of the head. In 1960, the presence of such persons in the household (2 %) was a very uncommon occurrence. This revision of the household toward greater homo-

[21] The evidence here adds limited, but clear, historical confirmation to the conclusion of Beresford and Rivlin (1966): 250, that privacy in living arrangements is a relatively recent and increasing occurrence in American family patterns. They say: '...it seems reasonable to conclude that the increase in privacy which occurred in the country as a whole after World War II was a new phenomenon, not a continuation of a long trend.'

[22] For an interesting article in this regard, see A. C. Anderson and M. J. Bowman, *The vanishing servant and the contemporary status system of the American South* (1953): 215–30. The authors conclude: 'The waning of the servant, a key feature of traditional southern life, manifests the shift from familistic toward impersonal and equaliterian culture traits' (1953): 215. For the parallel development in England, see Laslett, Chapter 1, pp. 156–157

Table 22.13   *Households by occupation of head and presence of nonrelatives*
of head, white, for Rhode Island, 1875 and 1960[a]

(1875, 5 percent sample: 1960, based on 5 percent sample)

Year and occupation	Total (%)	With no nonrelatives (%)	With one or more nonrelatives (%)
1875			
Nonmanual (N: 463)	100	63	37
Manual (N: 1,508)	100	81	19
Farm (N: 317)	100	77	23
Total (N: 2,288)	100	77	23
1960			
Nonmanual (N: 65,523)	100	98	2
Manual (N: 105,829)	100	99	1
Farm (N: 1,539)	100	97	3
Total (N: 172,891)	100	98	2

[a] United States Bureau of the Census (1961). Unpublished data, Table 24.

geneity reflects increasing cultural individualism and equalitarianism at the
expense of earlier familistic patterns. More clearly, the structural change of the
household does demonstrate a changing economic organization which has made
the presence of nonrelatives in the household economically infeasible and/or
unnecessary.

Social class and the household

Class changes in the presence of nonrelatives of the head in households can be
examined by means of comparable occupation data for 1875 and 1960 (see
Table 22.13). As shown in this table, within each occupational group there has
been a significant decline in the presence of nonrelatives. The greatest decrease
(35 %) from 1875 to 1960 is within nonmanual occupations. This decline no
doubt substantiates the disappearance of servants as a feature of household
organization. In fact, the general decline in nonrelatives of all types – servants,
boarders, roomers, and farm hands – documents the removal from the household of all categories of nonrelatives. The picture in 1960 is one where nonrelatives are seldom found with practically no social class differences in the
distribution. In other words, by 1960, social class differentials in household
formation virtually have vanished.

Residence and the household

Not surprisingly, a similar pattern emerges in terms of rural–urban residence
(see Table 22.14). Regardless of residence, there has been a significant decline
in the presence of nonrelatives in households. The continued greater utility of

Table 22.14   *Households by urban–rural residence and presence of nonrelatives of head, white, for Rhode Island: 1875 and 1960*[a]

(1875, 5 percent sample: 1960, based on 5 percent sample)

Year and residence	Total (%)	With no nonrelatives (%)	With one or more nonrelatives (%)
1875			
Urban (N: 2,050)	100	76	24
Urban–rural (N: 424)	100	76	24
Rural (N: 215)	100	80	20
Total (N: 2,689)	100	76	24
1960			
Urban (N: 220,267)	100	98	2
Rural non-farm (N: 31,224)	100	98	2
Rural (N: 949)	100	93	7
Total (N: 252,440)	100	98	2

[a] United States Bureau of the Census (1961). Unpublished data, Table 24.

nonrelatives in rural households may partially account for the fact that among rural households the decline has been the least severe. Leaving aside rural households, the evidence clearly shows the almost complete irrelevance of nonrelatives in the urban and non-farm households by 1960.

CONCLUSION

This analysis has attempted to review change (1875–1960) in the Rhode Island family through a set of basic structural characteristics. In terms of the frequency of extended families, multigenerational families, and the presence of subfamilies, the evidence shows that change in family structure has been minor but remarkably consistent. In the examination of each of these structural variables, the general conclusion is that there was a slight decline (3 % for each) in the proportion of extended families, multigenerational families, and families containing subfamilies. Of greater significance is the finding that *even in 1875* multigenerational or extended family arrangements were not pervasive forms of family life. Even in 1875 only 8 % of all families were multigenerational and only 5 % contained subfamilies. If it is argued that in 1875 for 18 % of all families to be extended in structure is unexpected in the light of images of the large, extended family of the nineteenth century, then the slight decline of 3 % in such families by 1960 is even more unexpected.

Unless the decline in nonrelatives is viewed as an indicator of reduced familism the evidence concerning *family* structure *per se* emphasizes the considerable stability in family patterns in Rhode Island using 1875 and 1960 as points of comparison.

The evidence from Rhode Island indicates that the American 'small family' tradition was exactly that – at least, from 1875 onward. Family organization and 'rules of residence' have precluded generally the extended family or heterogeneous (in membership) household. If this be true then the American family tradition in this respect was well suited to the powerful sweep of industrialization.[23] As the evidence here suggests, the more observable change in the American family has been the revision in household organization brought on both by changing loci of production (industrialism) and by changes in class structure. The demise of the live-in servant and boarder–roomer points to the lack of clients to occupy such positions and the decreasing economic justification for recruiting such persons. Perhaps the passing of a household tradition has been too easily viewed as inferring ramifications concerning the family itself.

A current quest in the sociology of the family concerns the development of evidence documenting the changing meaning of family relations and interaction. The problems of increased life expectancy ('aging') and the dilution of ethnic and religious differences in family living have generated an interest in exactly what functions the contemporary family does play especially in relation to aged parents and other relatives.[24] The prevalence of nuclear families and the scarcity of multigenerational families have been considered convincing evidence that the modern family is unique in its problems of kinship interaction and mutual aid. Litwak, among others, takes the position that the present family is not as nucleated and individualistic as such living arrangements may imply:

The modified extended family concept would suggest that the nuclear family be housed independently but remain active in situations where extended family aid as well as institutional aid can be given. In fact this is what the author feels actually does happen in our society.[25]

The evidence gathered in this research into the Rhode Island family would suggest that the pattern described by Litwak is not something new and unique only for contemporary American family life *vis à vis* the extended, diffuse family of the immediate or distant past. In the light of developing historical demographic evidence, the 'modified extended family concept' may well be appropriate to describe the American family system which has prevailed for a good part of our history.

[23] Smelser has provided a classic study of the relationship of the family and the British cotton industry which could be the model for similar historical research in the United States. See Smelser, *Social change in the industrial revolution* (1959).
[24] For example, see Burgess, *Family structure and relationships* (1960): 276–87. The central foci of the volume edited by Shanas and Streib, *Social structure and the family* (1965) are the problems of family relations and intergenerational interaction.
[25] Litwak, *Extended kin relations in an industrial democratic society* (1965): 291.

Bibliography

Books published in London unless otherwise stated

Adams, R. N., 1960 'An inquiry into the nature of the family'. In: Dole, G. E. and Carneiro, R. L., eds., *Essays in the science of culture*. New York

Aikin, J., 1795 *A description of the country from thirty to forty miles round Manchester*

Aldous, Joan, 1967 *International bibliography of research in marriage and the family 1900–1964*. With Hill, Reuben. Minneapolis

Allan, W., 1967 *The African husbandman*. Edinburgh

Allison, K. J., 1963 'An Elizabethan village census'. *Bulletin of the Institute of Historical Research*, XXXVI: 91–103

Anderson, Arnold C., 1953 'The vanishing servant and the contemporary status system of the American South'. With Bowman, Mary Jean. *American Journal of Sociology*, LIX: 215–30

Anderson, David, 1970 *See* Halpern, Joel, 1970

Anderson, M., 1971 *Family structure in nineteenth century Lancashire*. Cambridge
1972 (i) 'Sources and techniques for the study of family structure in nineteenth century Britain'. In: Wrigley, E. A., ed., *The study of nineteenth century society*
1972 (ii) 'Standard tabulation procedures for houses, households, and other groups of residents, in the enumeration books of the censuses of 1851 to 1891'. In: Wrigley, E. A., ed., *The study of nineteenth century society*

Anderson, Robert, T., 1971 *Traditional Europe. A Study in anthropology and history*. Belmont, Cal.

Anthony, K. R. M.,1968 *Field study of agricultural change: Northern Katsina, Nigeria*. With Johnston, B. F. Food Research Institute Preliminary Report No. 6. Stanford

Arensberg, C. M., 1937 *The Irish countryman, An anthropological study*
1940 (1961) *Family and community in Ireland*. With Kimball, S. T. Cambridge, Mass.

Ariès, Philippe, 1960 (1962) *L'enfant et la vie famille sous l'Ancien Régime*. Paris. Translated by Baldick, Robert, as *Centuries of Childhood*.

Armstrong, W. A., 1966 'Social structure from early census returns'. In: Wrigley, E. A., ed., *An introduction to English historical demography*
1967 'The social structure of York, 1841–51'. Unpublished Ph.D. thesis, Birmingham
1968 'The interpretation of census enumerators' books for Victorian towns'. In: Dyos, H. J., ed., *The study of urban history*
1972 'The use of information about occupation'. In: Wrigley, E. A., ed., *The study of nineteenth century society*

Aronson, H., 1912 'Liberalism in the village'. *Nation*, 18 May 1912

Atkyns, Robert, 1712 *The ancient and present state of Gloucestershire*

Babić, Vladimir *et al.*, eds., 1960 *Istorija naroda Jugoslavie, Knjiga II: Od početka XVI do kraja XVIII veka*. Belgrade

Bailyn, B., 1960 *Education in the forming of American society*. Williamsburg, Va.

Baldwin, K. D. S., 1956 *See* Galletti, R., 1956

Banfield, E. C., 1958 *The moral basis of a backward society*. New York
Barclay, G. W., 1958 *Techniques of population analysis*. New York
Barić, Lorraine (née Lancaster), 1958 'Kinship in Anglo-Saxon Society'. *British Journal of Sociology*, 9: 230–50, 359–77
    1961 'Some conceptual problems in the study of family and kin ties in the British Isles'. *British Journal of Sociology*, 12: 317–31
    1967 'Levels of change in Yugoslav kinship'. In Freedman, Maurice, ed., *Social Organization: Essays presented to Raymond Firth*
Barley, M. W., 1961 *The English farmhouse and cottage*
Barnett, G. E., 1936 *Two tracts by Gregory King*. Baltimore
Bartholomew, John, 1943 (1966) *Gazetteer of the British Isles*
Belgium Census *See* Institut National de Statistique, 1951
Bell, N. W., 1960 *A modern introduction to the family*. With Vogel, E. F., Glencoe, Ill.
Bellah, Robert N., 1957 *Tokugawa religion*. Glencoe, Ill.
Bender, Donald, R., 1967 'A refinement of the concept of household: Families, co-residence and domestic functions'. *The American Anthropologist*, 69, 5: 493–504
Benedict, Burton, 1968 'Family firms and economic development'. *Southwestern Journal of Anthropology*, 24: 1–19
Benedict, Ruth, 1967 'Continuities and discontinuities in cultural conditioning'. *Psychiatry and Social Sciences Review* I: 161–7
Benet, Francisco, 1963 'Sociology uncertain: The ideology of the rural–urban continuum'. *Comparative Studies in Society and History*, 6, 1:1–23.
Benton, Josiah H., 1905 *Early Census making in Massachusetts*. Boston
Beresford, John C., 1966 'Privacy, poverty and old age'. With Rivlin, Alice M. *Demography*, III
Berkner, L. K., 1972 'The stem family and the developmental cycle of the peasant household: an eighteenth century Austrian example'. *American Historical Review*, 77
Bernier, A., ed., 1835 *Journal des États Généraux de France tenus à Tours en 1484*. Paris
Besta, E., 1933 *La famiglia nella storia del diritto italiano*. Padua.
Biraben, J. N., 1963 'Inventaire des listes nominatives de recensement en France'. *Population*, 18: 305–28
Blayo, Yves, 1967 *See* Henry, Louis, 1967 (ii)
    1970 'La mobilité dans un village de la Brie vers le milieu du XIXe siècle'. *Population*, 25: 573–605.
Bloch, M., 1931 *Les caractères originaux de l'histoire rurale française*. Instituttet for sammenlignende kulturforskning. Oslo
Block, Alexander, 1946 *Estimating housing needs*
Blomefield, Francis, 1739–75 (1805–10) *Topographical history of…Norfolk*. With Parkin, C.
Bogišić, Baltazar, 1874 *Zbornik sadašnjih pravnih običaja u južnih Slavena*. Zagreb
Bogue, D. J., 1969 *Principles of demography*. New York
Bohannan, P., 1954 *Tiv farm and settlement*. Colonial Research Studies, no. 15. H.M.S.O.
Booth, C., ed., 1892 *Life and labour of the people in London*, vol. 3
Booth, C., 1894 *The aged poor in England and Wales*
Bowman, Mary Jean, 1953 *See* Anderson, Arnold C., 1953
Boys, William, 1792 *Collections for an history of Sandwich in Kent*. Canterbury
Bray, William, 1804–14 *See* Manning, Owen, 1804–14
Bridges, John, 1791 *History and antiquities of Northamptonshire*

Brooke, M. Z., 1970   *Le Play: engineer and social scientist*
Brown, R., 1799   *General view of the agriculture of the West Riding of Yorkshire.*
    With Rennie, G. Edinburgh
Brown, S. P., 1951   'Analysis of a hypothetical stationary population by family units –
    a note on some experimental calculations'. *Population Studies*, 4: 380–94
Brown, T., 1794   *General view of the agriculture of Derby*
Burch, Thomas K., 1967   'The size and structure of families, a comparative analysis
    of census data'. *American Sociological Review*, 32, 3: 347–63
    1970   'Some demographic determinants of average household size: an analytic
    approach'. *Demography*, 7
Burgess, E. W., 1945 (1953)   *The family*. With Locke, H. J. New York
    1960   'Family structure and relationships'. In: Burgess, Ernest W., ed., *Aging in
    Western societies*. Chicago
Burguière, André, 1969   'Le colloque de démographie historique de Cambridge. La
    famille 'réduite': une réalité ancienne et planétaire'. *Annales E.S.C.*, 24:
    1423–6
Calhoun, Arthur W., 1917–19 (1960)   *A social history of the American family*. Cleve-
    land, Baltimore, 1960
Call, J., 1800   'An abstract of baptisms and burials, in four parishes of fifty counties
    in England, collected by Sir John Call, Bart. and communicated to the Board of
    Agriculture, with an Address, dated 2nd February 1800'. In: Board of Agriculture,
    *Communications to the Board of Agriculture on subjects relative to the husbandry
    and internal improvement of the country* (1800) II: 479–92
Carrasco, P., 1959   *Land and polity in Tibet*. Seattle.
Casini, B., 1964   *Il catasto di Pisa del 1428–29*. Pisa
    1965   *Aspetti della vita economica e sociale di Pisa dal catasto del 1427–28*. Pisa
Castillo, G. T., 1968   'The concept of the nuclear and extended family'. With Weisblat,
    A. M. and Villareal, F. R. *International Journal of Comparative Sociology*, 9: 1–40
Census   1. National – *See under* respective countries
    2. Local – Not separately listed. For details, including location, see text
Chalmers, G., 1782 (1802)   *An estimate of the comparative strength of Great
    Britain*
Chambers, J. D., 1957   'The Vale of Trent'. *Economic History Review*, Suppl. 3
Chang, Chih-i, 1948   *See* Fei, Hsiao-Tung, 1948
Chayanov, A. V., 1925 (1966)   *The theory of the peasant economy*. Eds., Thorner, D.,
    Kerblay, B. and Smith, R. E. F. Homewood, Ill., 1966
Church, R. A., 1966   *Economic and social change in a Midland town: Victorian
    Nottingham, 1815–1900*
Clamagéran, J. J., 1857–76   *Histoire de l'impôt de France*. Paris
Clapham, J. H., 1950   *Economic history of modern Britain*. Cambridge
Clark, Christopher, 1811 *Historical and descriptive account of the town of Lancaster.*
    Lancaster
Coale, A. J., 1965   'Estimates of average size of household'. In: Coale, A. J. *et al.*,
    Aspects of the analysis of family structure. Princeton
    1966   *Regional model life tables and stable populations*. With Demeny, P., Princeton
Coldeweij, J. A., 1964   'De papiermakerij op de Veluwe: hoofd-of bijzaak?' In:
    Bijlage , C., ed. *Bijdragen en mededelingen Gelre*, LXI. Arnhem
Collinson, John, 1791   *History and antiquities of the county of Somerset*. Bath
Collver, A., 1963   'The family cycle in India and the United States'. *American Socio-
    logical Review*, 28: 86–96.
Conger, John J., 1956 (1963)   *See* Mussen, Paul H. 1956 (1963)

Conti, E., 1966 'I catasti agrari della republica fiorentina'. In: *La formazione della struttura agraria moderna nel contado fiorentino*. vol. III, pt. I, sez. 1. Rome

Corsica   *See under* France

Cosemans, A., 1966   *Bijdrage tot de demographische en sociale geschiedenis van de stad*. Brussels

Cregeen, Eric, R., 1963   *Inhabitants of the Argyll Estate, 1779*. Scottish Record Society. Edinburgh

Crozier, D., 1965   'Kinship and occupational succession'. *Sociological Review*. New Series, XIII, 1: 15–43

Cruikshank, G., 1851   *Comic Almanack and Diary*

Cudworth, William, 1896   *Manningham, Heaton and Allerton, townships of Bradford, treated historically and topographically*. Bradford

Daničić, Djuro, 1863–4 (1962)   *Rječnik iz književnih starina srpskih*, I–III. Graz, Austria. Reproduced, Belgrade, 1962

Davenport, W., ed., 1961   *See* Mintz, S. W. 1961

Davies, D., 1795   *The case of labourers in husbandry stated and considered*

Deane, P., 1962   *See* Mitchell, B. R., 1962

Demeny, P., 1966   *See* Coale, A. J., 1966

Demolins, Edmond, 1894   'Préface'. In: Butel, Fernand. *Une vallée Pyrenéene: la vallée d'Ossau*. Pau

Demos, John, 1965   'Notes on life in Plymouth Colony'. *William and Mary Quarterly*. Third Series, XXII: 264–86

  1968   'Families in colonial Bristol, Rhode Island: An exercise in historical demography'. *William and Mary Quarterly*, Third Series, XXV: 41–57

  1969   'Adolescence in historical perspective'. With Demos, Virginia. *Journal of Marriage and the Family*, XXXI: 632–8

  1970 (i)   *A little commonwealth: family life in Plymouth Colony*. New York

  1970 (ii)   'Underlying themes in the witchcraft of seventeenth century New England'. *American Historical Review*, LXXV: 1311–26

Demos, Virginia, 1969   *See* Demos, John, 1969.

De Rammelaere, C. 1962   'Kanegem...' In: *De Leiegouw*, IV. Courtrai

  1966   *Cinq études de démographie locale*. Brussels

De Vooys, A. C., 1953   'De bevolkingsspreiding op het Hollandse platteland in 1622 em 1795'. *Tijdschrift Nederlands Aardrijkskundig Genootschap*, 70: 316–30

Dickinson, Robert E., 1951 (1962)   *The West European city*. 2nd ed. (1962).

Dina, I. O., 1956   *See* Galletti, R., 1956

Dore, Ronald P., 1958   *City life in Japan*. Berkeley and Los Angeles

Droogleever Fortuijn, A. B., 1966   *See* Kruijer, G. J., 1966

Duckham, B. F., 1956   'The economic development of York, 1830–1914'. Unpublished M.A. thesis, Manchester

Dunn, Richard S., 1969   'The Barbados census of 1680; profile of the richest colony in English America'. *William and Mary Quarterly*, Third Series, XXVI: 3–30

Dupâquier, J., 1964   *Problèmes de mesure et de représentation graphique en histoire sociale*. Actes du 89° Congrès de Sociétés Savantes, Lyon

Earle, Alice Morse, 1927   *Child life in colonial days*. New York

Eden, F. M., 1797   *The state of the poor*

  1800   *An estimate of the number of inhabitants in Great Britain and Ireland*

Ema, Mieko, 1942   *Hida no onnatachi (Women of Hida)*

  1943   *Shirakawa-mura no daikazoku (Large families in Shirakawa-mura)*

Enfield, W., 1774   *Essay towards the history of Liverpool*

Engels, F., 1884 (1940)   *Der Ursprung der Familie, des Privateigenthums und des Staats. Im Anschluss an L. H. Morgan's Forschungen.* Zurich. Translated as *The origin of the family, private property and the state.* London, 1940
England   *See* United Kingdom
Epstein, T. S., 1962   *Economic development and social change in South India.* Manchester
Erikson, Eric, 1959   *Identity and the life cycle.* New York
    1962   'Youth: fidelity and diversity'. *Daedalus*, 91: 5–27.
Erlich, Vera Stein, 1940   'The southern Slav patriarchal family'. *Sociological Review.* 32: 224–41
    1964 (1966)   *Porodica u transformaciji.* Zagreb. Translated and published as *The family in transition, a study of 300 Yugoslav villages.* Princeton, 1966
Esmonin, E., 1913   *La taille en Normandie au temps de Colbert.* Paris
Faber, J. A., 1965   *See* Roessingh, H. K., 1965 (ii)
Fallers, L. A., 1965   'The range of variation in actual family size; a critique of Marion J. Levy Jr.'s argument'. In: Coale, A. J. *et al., Aspects of the analysis of family structure.* Princeton
Fei, Hsiao-Tung, 1948   *Earthbound China. A study of rural economy in Yunnan.* With Chang, Chih-i
Festy, O., 1953   'Les essais de statistiques économiques'. *Annales historiques de la Révolution Française*, xxv: 161–76
    1955   'Les mouvements de la population française'. *Annales historiques de la Révolution Française*, xxvii: 27–49
Filipović, Milenko S., 1945   *Nesrodnička i predvojena zadruga.* Belgrade
    1961   'Poslednji dani ustanove kućne zadruga u Bosni'. *Sociologija*, 3: 70–82.
Firth, R., 1964   'Family and kinship in industrial society'. In: Halmos, P., ed., *The development of industrial societies. Sociological Review Monograph*, no. 8, Keele
Fischer, Jack, 1958   'The classification of residence in censuses'. *American Anthropologist*, 60: 508–17
Fiumi, E., 1957   'L'imposta diretta nei comuni medioevali della Toscana'. In: *Studi in onore di A. Sapori*: 327–53. Milan
Fleming, Sandford, 1933   *Children and Puritanism.* New Haven, Conn.
Fleury, Michel, 1956   *Des registres paroissiaux à l'histoire de la population; manuel de dépouillement et de l'exploitation de l'état civil ancien.* With Henry, Louis, Paris
Flinn, M. W., 1965   'Introduction'. In Chadwick, Edwin, *Report on the sanitary condition of the labouring population of Great Britain.* Ed. Flinn, M. W. Edinburgh
Fortes, M., 1949 (i)   *Web of kinship among the Tallensi: the second part of an analysis of the social structure of a Trans-Volta tribe*
    1949 (ii)   'Time and social structure'. In: *Social structure: studies presented to A. R. Radcliffe-Brown.* Oxford
    1950   'Kinship and marriage among the Ashanti'. In Radcliffe-Brown, A. R. and Forde, D., eds., *African systems of kinship and marriage*
    1958   'Introduction'. In: Goody, J. R., ed., *The developmental cycle in domestic groups.* Cambridge
Fosbroke, T. D., 1807   *Abstracts of records and manuscripts respecting the county of Gloucester; formed into a history, correcting the very erroneous accounts, and supplying numerous deficiencies in Sir R. Atkins and subsequent writers.* Gloucester
Foster, J. O., 1967   'Capitalism and class consciousness in earlier nineteenth-century Oldham'. Unpublished Ph.D. dissertation. Cambridge
Frampton, M. F., 1936   *See* Zimmerman, C. C., 1936

France Corsica
    1. Censuses: 1758, 1769–71, 1786 (French National Archives. Ref. Q¹298¹⁻⁸)
    2. Other: General land survey, 1773–96 (French National Archives, 3.)
        Le Mée, R., 1971 'Un dénombrement des Corses en 1770'. *Annales Historiques de la Révolution Française*, 203: 23–44
Franklin, S. H., 1969 *The European peasantry: the final phase*
Friedrich, Paul, 1964 'Semantic structure and social structure: an instance from Russia'. In: Goodenough, W. H., ed., *Explorations in cultural anthropology*. New York
    1966 'The linguistic reflex of social change from Tsarist to Soviet Russian kinship'. *Sociological Inquiry*, 36: 159–85
Fukushima, Masao, 1954 'Sanson no *ie* to shihonshugi (*Ie* of a hill village, and capitalism)'. *Tōyobunka-kenkyūjo-kiyō*, 6: 1–97
Fumagalli, C., 1912 *Il diritto di fraterna nella giurisprudenza da Accursio alla codificazione*. Turin
Furney, Manuscript 'A history of Gloucester and its suburbs 1749' (Bodleian Library, Oxford. Ref. MS Top Glouc. C 4)
Furstenberg, Frank, F., 1966 'Industrialization and the American family: a look backward'. *American Sociological Review*, 31: 326–37
Galletti, R., 1956 *Nigerian cocoa farmers. An economic survey of Yoruba farming families*. With Baldwin, K. D. S. and Dina, I.O.
Gaudemet, Jean, 1963 *Les communautés familiales*. Paris
Geddes, W. R., 1954 *The land dyaks of Sarawak*. Colonial Research Studies, no. 14. H.M.S.O.
General Register Office, 1968 *Sample Census, 1966. Household composition tables.* H.M.S.O.
George, Mary Dorothy, 1925 (1965) *London life in the Eighteenth Century*
Gifu-ken, 1968 *Gifu-ken shi* (*History of Gifu Prefecture*). Gifu
Gilbert, B. B., 1966 *The evolution of National Insurance in Great Britain*
Gill, H., 1910 *The Rector's Book of Clayworth, Notts.* With Guilford, E. L. Nottingham
Glass, D. V., 1965 (i) 'Gregory King and the population of England and Wales at the end of the seventeenth century'. In: Glass, D. V. and Eversley, D. E. C., eds., *Population in history*
    1965 (ii) 'Gregory King's estimate of the population of England and Wales 1695'. In: Glass, D. V. and Eversley, D. E. C., eds., *Population in history*
    1966 'London inhabitants within the walls'. *The London Record Society*, II
Gluckman, M. 1950 'Kinship and marriage among the Lozi of Northern Rhodesia and the Zulu of Natal'. In: Radcliffe-Brown, A. R. and Forde, D., eds., *African systems of kinship and marriage*
Goldfield, E. D., 1968 'Preservation of confidential records'. *Historical Methods Newsletter*, II 1: 3–6
Goldthwaite, R. A., 1968 *Private wealth in Renaissance Florence. A study of four families*. Princeton
Goode, W. J., 1961 'Illegitimacy, anomie and cultural penetration'. *American Sociological Review*, 26: 910–25
    1963 *World revolution and family patterns*. New York
    1964 *The family*. Englewood Cliffs, N.J.
    1966 'Note on problems in theory and method; the New World'. *The American Anthropologist*, 68: 486–92
    1968 'The theory and measurement of family change'. In: Sheldon, E. H. and Moore, W. E., eds., *Indicators of social change* New York

Goodenough, Ward, 1956   'Residence rules'. *Southwestern Journal of Anthropology*, 12:22–37
    1961   'Kindred and hamlet in Lalakai'. *Ethnology*, 1: 5–12
Goodsell, W., 1934   *A history of marriage and the family*. New York
Goody, J. R., 1966   *The social organisation of the Lowiili*
Goody, J. R., ed. 1958 (i) (1966)   *The developmental cycle in domestic groups*. Cambridge
Goody, J. R., 1958 (ii)   'The fission of domestic groups among the LoDagaba'. In: Goody, J. R., ed., *The developmental cycle in domestic groups*. Cambridge
    1970   'Sideways or downwards'. *Man*, New series, 5: 627–38
    1972   'Inheritance and women's labour in Africa'. *Africa*
Goubert, Pierre, 1969   'La Famille Française au XVIIIe siècle'. In: Bachi, L., ed., *Sossi di demografi storica*. University of Florence, Statistical Department, Serie Ricerche Empiriche, no. 2, Florence
Graunt, J., 1662   *Natural and political observations upon the Bills of Mortality*
Great Britain   *See* United Kingdom
Greenberger, M., 1961   *See* Orcutt, G. H., 1961
Greene, Evarts B., 1932 (1966)   *American population before the Federal census of 1790*. With Harrington, Virginia D. Gloucester, Mass.
Greenfield, S. M., 1961   'Industrialization and the family in sociological theory'. *American Journal of Sociology*, 67: 312–22
Greven, Philip J., 1970   *Four generations: Population, land and family in colonial Andover, Massachusetts*. Ithica, N.Y.
Guilford, E. L., 1910   *See* Gill, H., 1910
Hajnal, J., 1965   'European marriage patterns in perspective'. In: Glass, D. V. and Eversley, D. E. C., eds., *Population in history*
Hallam, H. E., 1957   'Some thirteenth century censuses'. *Economic History Review*, x: 352–61
    1961   'Population density in medieval Fenland'. *Economic History Review*, 14: 71–81
    1963   'Further observations on the Spalding serf lists'. *Economic History Review*, 16: 338–50
Halpern, Barbara, 1972   *See* Halpern, Joel, 1972
Halpern, Joel, 1956   *Social and cultural change in a Serbian village*. Human Relations Area Files. New Haven
    1967   *A Serbian village*. New York
    1969   'Yugoslavia: Modernization in an ethnically diverse state'. In: Vucinich, W., ed., *Yugoslavia*. Berkeley
    1970   'The zadruga, a century of change'. With Anderson, David. *Anthropologica*, xii, 1: 83–97
    1972   *A Serbian village in historical perspective*. With Halpern, Barbara. New York
Hammel, E. A., 1957   'Serbo-Croatian kinship terminology'. *Papers of the Kroeber Anthropological Society*, 16: 45–75. Berkeley
    1968   *Alternative social structures and ritual relations in the Balkans*. Englewood Cliffs, N.J.
    1969 (i)   'Social mobility, economic change, and kinship in Serbia'. *Southwestern Journal of Anthropology*, 25: 188–97
    1969 (ii)   'Structure and sentiment in Serbian cousinship'. *The American Anthropologist*, 71: 285–93
    1970   'The ethnographer's dilemma: alternative models of occupational prestige in Belgrade'. *Man*, New Series, 5: 652–70

(Typescript) *Household structure in 14th century Macedonia*
Forthcoming   *See* Laslett, P., Forthcoming
Hanley, Susan B., 1968 'Population trends and economic development in Tokugawa Japan: the case of Bizen province in Okayama'. *Daedalus*, 97, 2: 622–35
Hansen, H. O. (Mimeograph)   *Design of a CPR-Register for tabulation of population Census registration. An example, the Icelandic population Census of 1729.* Institute of Statistics, University of Copenhagen
Harrington, Virginia D., 1932 (1966)   *See* Greene, Evarts B., 1932 (1966)
Harris, C. C., 1965   *See* Rosser, C., 1965
Harrison, John, 1963   *See* Laslett, Peter, 1963
Hart, S., 1965   *Bronnen voor de historische demografie van Amsterdam in de 17e en 18e eeuw.* A mimeotyped paper for the meeting of the Dutch Historical Demography Society
Hatton, E., 1708   *A new view of London*
Hattori, Korefusa, ed., 1956   *See* Nishioka, Toranosuke, 1956
Hayami, Akira, 1967 'The population at the beginning of the Tokugawa period – an introduction to the historical demography of pre-industrial Japan'. *Keio Economic Studies*, 4
   1968 (i)   *Nihon keizaishi e no shikaku*
   1968 (ii)   'Kinsei shinshu Suwa chihō no jinkō sūsei (Population trends in Suwa county)'. *Mitagakkai Zasshi*, 61, 2
   1969 'Aspects démographiques d'un village japonais 1671–1871'. *Annales E.S.C.*, 24: 617–39
Heers, J., 1961   *Gênes au XVe siècle: activité économique et problèmes sociaux.* Paris
Hélin, E., 1959   *La population des paroisses liégeoises.* Liège
   1962 (i)   *Les capitations liégeoises.* Louvain
   1962 (ii)   *Le paysage urbain de Liège avant la révolution industrielle.* Liège
   1963   *La démographie de Liège aux XVIIe et XVIIIe siècles.* Brussels
   1966 'À la recherche d'une mesure des inégalités de fortune: l'apport des rôles fiscaux liégeois'. In: *L'impôt dans le cadre de la ville et de l'État.* Brussels
Henry, Louis, 1956   See Fleury, Michel, 1956
   1960   *Anciennes familles Genévoises.* Paris
   1967 (i)   *Manuel de démographie.* Geneva and Paris
   1967 (ii) 'Données démographiques sur la Bretagne et l'Anjou de 1740 à 1829. With Blayo, Yves. *Annales de Démographie Historique*, 91–171
Herlihy, D., 1969 'Viellir à Florence au Quattrocento'. *Annales E.S.C.*, XXIV: 1338–52
Hilaire, Jean, 1957 'La régime des biens entre époux dans la région de Montpellier du début du XIII siècle à la fin du XVI siècle: contribution aux études d'histoire du droit'. Thèse, Faculté de Droit, Université de Montpellier
Hill, Christopher, 1964   *Society and puritanism in pre-revolutionary England*
Hill, Reuben, 1967   *See* Aldous, Joan, 1967
Hofstee, E. W., 1954 'Regionale verscheidenheid in de ontwikkeling van het aantal geboorten in Nederland in de tweede helft van de 19e eeuw'. *Akademiedagen*: 59–100. Amsterdam
   1956 'Traditional household and neighbourhood group: survivals of the genealogical–territorial societal pattern in eastern parts of the Netherlands'. With Kooy, G. *Transactions of the Third World Congress of Sociology*, IV: 75–9
   1966 (i) 'Over het modern-dynamisch cultuurpatroon'. *Sociologische Gids*, 13: 139–54

Hofstee, E. W. continued
　1966 (ii)　'Weereens, de geboortecijfers in Nederland'. *Sociologische Gids*, 13: 173–5
　1966 (iii)　'Commentaar op commentaar'. *Sociologische Gids*, 13: 187–9
Hollingsworth, T. H., 1964　'Demography of the British Peerage'. *Population Studies*, Supplement, November.
　1969　*Historical Demography*. Ithaca, N.Y.
Homans, G. C., 1941 (1970)　*English villagers of the thirteenth century*. Cambridge, Mass.
Honjō, Eijīrō, 1920　'Hida shirakawa no daikazoku-sei. (Large family institution in Hida Shirakawa)'. *Keizaishi-kenkyū* Kyoto
Howlett, John, 1781　*An examination of Dr Price's essay on the population of England and Wales*. Maidstone
Hsu, Francis L. K., 1943　'The myth of Chinese family size'. *American Journal of Sociology*, 48: 555–62
Hunt, David, 1970　*Parents and children in history*. New York
Hunter, Joseph, 1819 (1869)　*Hallamshire. The history and topography of the parish of Sheffield...with historical and descriptive notices of the parishes of Ecclesfield, Hansworth, Treeton and Whiston, and of the chapelry of Bradfield*. Ed., Gatty, A. Sheffield, 1869
Hutchins, J., 1774 (1796–1815, 1861–73)　*The history and antiquities of the county of Dorset*. 1796–1815 eds., Gough, R. and Nichols, J.; 1861–73 eds., Shipp, W. and Hodson, J. W.
Hutchinson, William, 1785–94　*The history and antiquities of the county palatine of Durham*. Newcastle
　1794　*A history of the county of Cumberland and some places adjacent*. Carlisle
Iceland, 1703 (1960)　*Manntarid 1703* (Population census 1703). Statistics Bureau of Iceland, Statistics of Iceland, II, 21. Reykjavik
India, 1967　*Indian agriculture in brief*, 8th ed. Ministry of Food, New Delhi
Institut National de Statistique, 1951　*Recensement général 1947*. Brussels
Italy: Tuscany,
　1. Census, 1427 (Archives of Florence and Pisa)
Janković, Dragoslav, 1961　*Istorija države i prava feudalne Srbije (XII–XV vek)*, 3rd ed. Belgrade
Janne, H., 1962　*Sociologie et politique sociale*. With Morsa, J. Brussels
Jiriček, Constantin, 1912　'Staat und Gesellschaft im mittelalterlichen Serbien. Studien zur Kulturgeschichte des 13–15 Jahrhunderts'. *Denkschriften der Kaiserlichen Akademie der Wissenschaften, Philosophisch-Historische Klasse*, Band LVI, II. Vienna
　1911, 1918 (1952)　'Geschichte der Serben'. In: the first section [*Geschichte der europäischen Staaten*] of the general series, *Allgemeine Staatengeschichte*, 2 vols. Gotha. 2nd ed., tr. Radonić, J., published as *Istorija Srba: Knjiga II, kulturna istorija*. Belgrade, 1952
Johnson, Alvin, 1930–5　*See* Seligman, E. R. A., 1930–5
Johnston, B. F., 1968　*See* Anthony, K. R. M., 1968
Jones, G. P., 1959　'Some population problems relating to Cumberland and Westmorland in the eighteenth century'. *Transactions of the Cumberland and Westmorland Archaeological Society*, 58: 123–39
Jovanović, Aleksa S., 1896　*Istorijski razvitak srpske zadruge*. Belgrade
Kaempfer, Englebert, 1727　*The history of Japan* (2 vols, tr. Scheuchzer, J. G., 1727)
Kagan, Jerome, 1956 (1963)　*See* Mussen, Paul H., 1956 (1963)
Karadžić, Vuk Stefan, 1898　*Srpski rječnik istumačen njemačkijem i latinskijem riječima (Lexicon serbico-germanico-latinum)*, 3rd (state) edn, revised and enlarged. Belgrade

Karanović, M., 1929 'Nekolike velike porodične zadruge u Bosni i Hercegovini'. *Glasnik Zemaljskog Muzeja Bosne i Hercegovine*, 41, 2: 63–80 (Series title varies.) Sarajevo

Kardiner, Abram, 1945 *The psychological frontiers of society.* New York

Karmin, O., 1960 *La legge del catasto fiorentino del 1427.* Florence

Keniston, Kenneth, 1962 'Social change and youth in America'. *Daedalus*, 91, 1: 145–71

Kimball, S. T., 1940 (1961) *See* Arensberg, C. M., 1940 (1961)

King, Gregory, 1696 (1936) *Natural and politicall observations and conclusions upon the state and condition of England.* Printed by Barnett, G. E. Baltimore, 1936

(Manuscript i) Burns Journal. Manuscript notebook (Greater London Council, Members Library, John Burns Collection.)

(Manuscript ii) Exercises in political arithmetic and various miscellaneous papers (Public Record Office. Ref. P.R.O. T.64/302)

(Manuscript iii) 'Computation of the numbers of people in England 1695'. In: Exercises in political arithmetic and various miscellaneous papers (Public Record Office. Ref. P.R.O. T.64/302)

(Manuscript iv) Miscellaneous papers (British Museum, Department of Manuscripts. Ref. Harleian 6832)

Kirkpatrick, Clifford, 1955 (1963) *The family as process and institution.* New York

Klapisch, C., 1969 'Fiscalité et démographie en Toscane 1427–1430'. *Annales E.S.C.*, XXIV: 1313–37

Kodama, Kōta, 1953 'Hida shirakawa-mura no daikazoku-scido to sono keizai-teki kiso (Large family institution in Hida Shirakawa-mura and its economic basis)'. *Kinsei-nōson-shakai no kenkyū*

Kono, Shigemi (Typescript) *The determinants and consequences of population trends.* United Nations Population Division

(Mimeograph) *Analyses and projections of households and families.* United Nations Population Division

Kooy, G., 1956 *See* Hofstee, E., 1956

Kooy, G. A., 1957 *Het veranderend gezin in Nederland.* Assen

1959 *De oude samenwoning op het nieuwe platteland.* Assen

1963–4 'Urbanisation and nuclear family individualization; a causal connection?' *Current Sociology*, XII

1967 *Het modern-Westers gezin.* Hilversum-Antwerpen

Korbel, J., 1961 *See* Orcutt, G. H., 1961

Koyama, Takashi, 1936 'Sankan-shūraku to kazoku-kōsei (Hill communities and family composition)'. *Nenpō-shakaigaku*, 4

Koyama, Takashi, ed., 1960 *Gendai Kazoku no kenkyū (A study of the modern family).* Tokyo

Krasnići, M., 1959–60 'Šiptarska porodična zadruga u kosovsko-metohiskoj oblasti'. *Glasnik Muzeja Kosova i Metohije*, 4–5: 137–71. Priština

Krause, J. T., 1956 'The medieval household: large or small?' *Economic History Review*, IX: 420–32

1967 'Some aspects of population change, 1690–1790'. In: Jones, E. L. and Mingay, G. E., eds., *Land, labour and population in the industrial revolution, Essays presented to J. D. Chambers*

Krauss, F. S., 1885 *Sitte und Brauch der Südslaven.* Vienna

Kruijer, G. J., 1966 'Daling en niveau van de geboortecijfers in Nederland: bijdragen tot een discussie'. With Droogleever Fortuijn, A. B. *Sociologische Gids*, 13: 154–71

Kruijt, J. P., 1938   'Het gezinsleven in de verschillende delen van ons land'. *Theologie en praktijk*: 333–44
1950   'Het gezin sedert de middeleeuwen'. *Sociologisch Bulletin:* 79–94
Kulišić, Špiro, 1955   *O postanku slovenske zadruge*. Bilten Instituta za Proučavanje Folklora. Sarajevo
Land, C. Op't., 1966   'Het cultuurpatroon als analytisch instrument bij de studie van veranderingsprocessen'. *Sociologische Gids*, 13: 130–8
Lang, O., 1946   *Chinese family and society*. New Haven
Lasch, M., 1965   'Die Kasseler Einwohnerverzeichnisse der Jahre 1731 und 1751'. *Zeitschrift des Vereins für hessische Geschichte*, LXXV. Kassel
Laslett, Peter, ed., 1949   *Patriarcha and other works of Sir Robert Filmer*. Oxford
Laslett, Peter, 1963   'Clayworth and Cogenhoe'. With Harrison, John. In: Bell, H. E. and Ollard, R. L., eds., *Historical essays presented to David Ogg*
1964   'Market society and political theory'. Review of Macpherson, C. B., *Political theory of possessive individualism. Historical Journal*, VII: 150–4
1965 (i) (1969, 1971)   *The World we have lost*. 1969 Translated Campos, C., as *Un Monde que nous avons perdu*. Paris. 2nd English edn (revised and extended) 1971
1965 (ii)   *Remarks on the multiplier*. Unpublished paper contributed to the Third International Conference on Economic History, Munich
1966 (i) 'Social structure from listings of inhabitants'. In: Wrigley, E. A., ed., *An introduction to English historical demography*
1966 (ii)   'New light on the history of the English family'. *The Listener*, 17 February
1968   'Le brassage de la population en France et en Angleterre au XVIIᵉ et au XVIIIᵉ siècles'. *Annales de Démographie Historique:* 99–109
1969   'Size and structure of the household in England over three centuries'. *Population Studies*, XXIII: 199–223
1970 (i) 'The decline of the size of .the domestic group in England'. *Population Studies*, XXIV: 449–54
1970 (ii)   'The comparative history of the household and family'. *Journal of Social History*, 4; 75–87
1971   'Age at menarche in Europe since the early 18th century. Evidence from Belgrade in 1733/4'. *Journal of Interdisciplinary History*
Forthcoming   'Comparing household structure over time and between cultures'. With Hammel, E. A.
Law, C. M., 1969   'Local censuses in the 18th century'. *Population Studies*, XXIII: 87–100
Leach, E. R., 1961   *Pul Eliya, a village in Ceylon: a study of land tenure and kinship*. Cambridge
Le Play, P. G. F., 1855 (1877–9, 1936)   *Les ouvriers Européens*. Paris. Tours, 1877–9. 1936. (Part translated in: Zimmerman, C. C. and Frampton, M. F., eds., *Family and society*: 361–595)
1862   *Instruction sur la méthode d'observation dite des monographies de familles propre à l'ouvrage intitulé Les Ouvriers Européens*. Paris
1864 (1901)   *La réforme sociale*. Paris. 3rd edn 1901. Vol. I, book III
1871 (1875, 1884)   *L'organisation de la famille selon le vrai modèle signalé par l'histoire de toutes les races et de tous les temps*. Paris. Tours, 1875 and 1884
Lerner, Daniel, 1958   *The passing of traditional society: modernizing the Middle East*. With Pevsner, L. W. Glencoe, Ill.
Le Roy Ladurie, E., 1966   *Les paysans de Languedoc*. Paris
1967   'Van Waterloo tot Colyton'. *Spiegel Historiael*, II, 6: 347–55. Bussum
Levy, Marion J., 1949   *The family revolution in modern China*

1965 'Aspects of the analysis of family structure'. In: Coale, A. J. *et al.*, eds., *Aspects of the analysis of family structure*. Princeton

Lewis, O., 1958 *Village life in Northern India. Studies in a Delhi village*. New York

Lilek, Emilijan, 1900 'Beleške o zadružnim i gospodarstvenim prilikama u Bosni i Hercegovini'. *Glasnik Zemaljskog Muzeja Bosne i Hercegovine*, 12 (Series title varies). Sarajevo

Linton, Ralph, 1936 *The study of man*. New York

Lipscomb, G. 1799 *A journey into Cornwall*. Warwick

Litchfield, R. B., 1969 'Demographic characteristics of Florentine patrician families, 16th to the 19th centuries'. *Journal of Economic History*, xxix, 2: 191–205

Litwak, Eugene, 1965 'Extended kin relations in an industrial democratic society'. In: Shanas, Ethel, and Streib, Gordon F., eds., *Social structure and the family: generational relations*. Englewood Cliffs, N.J.

Locke, H. J., 1945 (1953) *See* Burgess, E. W., 1945 (1953)

Lonsdale, Henry, ed., 1870 *The life of J. Heysham and his correspondence with Mr J. Milne relative to the Carlisle Bills of Mortality*. London and Edinburgh

Lounsbury, Floyd, 1964 'A formal account of the Crow- and Omaha-type kinship terminologies'. In: Goodenough, W., ed., *Explorations in cultural anthropology*. New York

Low, M. F. H., 1961 *Mutala survey of Buchanga Bunyoro District*. Bunyoro agricultural services (mimeo). Hoima

Lowe, R., 1798 *General view of the agriculture of Nottingham*

Lowie, R. H., 1920 *Primitive society*. New York

Lugli, V., 1909 *I trattatisti della famiglia nel Quattrocento*. Bologna

Lutovac, Milisav, 1936 'Geografsko rasprostiranje kulture kukuruza u Jugoslaviji'. *Glasnik Geografskog Društva*, 22: 59–67. Belgrade

Malinowski, B., 1930 'Kinship'. *Man*, 30: 19–29

Mandić, Oleg, 1950 'Klasni karakter buržoaskih teorija o postanku zadruge'. *Istorisko-Pravni Zbornik*, 3–4: 131–55. Sarajevo

Manerio, I. B., 1697 *Tractatus de numeratione personarum*. Naples

Manning, Owen, 1804–14 *History and antiquities of the county of Surrey*. With Bray, William

Marshall, L. M., 1934 *The rural population of Bedfordshire*. Aspley Guise

Mather, Cotton, 1853 *Magnalia Christi Americana*. Hartford

Middleton, J., 1798 (1807) *General view of the agriculture of Middlesex*

Middleton, R., 1960 *See* Nimkoff, M. F., 1960

Mijatović, Stanoje, 1948 'Belica'. *Srpski Etnografski Zbornik*, 56: 3–213. Belgrade

Miklosich, Franz von, 1862–5 (1963) *Lexikon palaeoslavonico-graeco-latinum, emendatum auctum*. Vienna. Reproduced, Aalen, 1963

Mintz, S. W., ed., 1961 'Working papers in Caribbean social organization'. With Davenport, W. A special number of *Social and Economic Studies*, 10, 4

Mitchell, B. R., 1962 *Abstract of British historical statistics*. With Deane, P. Cambridge

Mogey, J. M., 1956 *Family and neighbourhood: two studies in Oxford*

Mols, P. R., 1955 *Introduction à la démographie historique des villes d'Europe*. Louvain

Montanari, P., 1966 'Documenti su la populazione di Bologna alla fine del Trecento'. *Fonti per lo studio di Bologna*, ɪ

Morgan, Edmund S., 1942 'The puritans and sex'. *New England Quarterly*, xv: 591–607

1944 (1966) *The puritan family, religion and domestic relations in 17th century New England*. Boston. New York, 1966

Morsa, J., 1962 *See* Janne, H., 1962

Moseley, P. E., 1940 'The peasant family: the zadruga or communal joint-family

in the Balkans and its recent evolution'. In: Ware, Caroline F., ed., *The cultural approach to history*. New York
1943   'Adaptation for survival: the Varžić zadruga'. *Slavonic East and European Review*, 21, 56: 147–73
1953   'The distribution of the zadruga within southeastern Europe'. The Joshua Starr Memorial Volume. *Jewish Social Studies*, 5: 219–30
Mumtaz, K. K., 1965   *See* Wakeley, P. I., 1965
Murdock, G. P., 1949   *Social Structure*. New York
1957   'World ethnographic sample'. *The American Anthropologist*, 59: 664–87
Mussen, Paul H., 1956 (1963)   *Child development and personality*. With Conger, John J. and Kagan, Jerome. 2nd edn, New York, 1963
Naganuma, Kenkai, 1929   'Shūshi nimbetsu aratame no hattatsu (Development of the investigation of religious sects)'. *Shigaku-zasshi (The Journal of History)*, 40, 11: 13–62
Nagao, Shoken, 1938   'Okazaki-jokamachi no rekishi-chiriteki-kenkyū'. *Rekishigaka-kenkyū*, 7–8
Nakane, Chie, 1967   *Kinship and economic organization in rural Japan*
1970   *Japanese Society*. Berkeley
Nash, T. R., 1781–99   *Collections for the history and antiquities of Worcestershire*
Niccolai, F., 1940   'I consorzi nobiliari ed il Comune nell' alta e media Italia'. *Rivista di storia del diritto italiano*, XIII
Nichols, J., 1795–1815   *History and antiquities of the county of Leicester*
1780–1800   *Bibliotheca Topographica Britannica*
Nikolić, Vidosava, 1958   'Srpska porodična zadruga u metohijskim selima'. *Glasnik Etnografskog Instituta*, 7: 109–21. Belgrade
Nimac, Franjo *et al.*, 1960   'Seljačke obiteljske zadruge'. *Publikacije Etnološkog Zavoda*, 3. Zagreb
Nimkoff, M. F., 1940 (1960)   *See* Ogburń, W. F., 1940 (1960)
1955   *See* Ogburn, W. F., 1955
1960   'Types of family and types of economy'. With Middleton, R. *American Journal of Sociology*, 66: 215–25
Nimkoff, M. F., ed., 1965   *Comparative family systems*. Boston
Nishioka, Toranosuke, ed., 1956   *Nihon rekishi chizu (Historical maps of Japan)*. With Hattori, Korefusa. Tokyo
Nixon, J. W., 1970   'Size and structure of the household in England over three centuries: a comment'. *Population Studies*, XXIV: 445–7
Noël, R., 1967   'La population de la paroisse de Laguiole d'après un recensement de 1691'. *Annales de Démographie Historique*, 3: 197–223
Nomura, Kanetarō, 1953   *On cultural conditions affecting population trends in Japan.* Science Council of Japan, Division of Economics and Commerce, Economic Series no. 2. Tokyo
Novaković, Stojan, 1891   'Selo: iz dela "Narod i zemlja u staroj srpskoj državi"'. *Srpska Kraljevska Akademija*, Glas XXIV. Belgrade
Ockers, J., 1967   'De gezinnen in Belgie'. *Population et Famille*, 11. Brussels
Ogburn, W. F., 1940 (1960)   *Sociology*. With Nimkoff, M. F. Boston. English edn. *A handbook of sociology*. London, 1960
1955   *Technology and the changing family*. With Nimkoff, M. F. Boston
Okamura, Seiji, 1929   *Hida-shirakawa-mura no daikazoku-sei (Large family institution in Hida-shirakawa-mura)*
Oldewelt, W. F. A., 1948–9   'De bevolking van s-Gravenhage omstreeks 1674'. *Die Haghe*

Olsen, Magnus, 1928 *Farms and fanes of ancient Norway*. Oslo
Onions, C. T., ed., 1966 *The Oxford Dictionary of English Etymology*
Orcutt, G. H., 1961 *Microanalysis of socioeconomic systems, a simulation study*. With Greenberger, M., Korbel, J. and Rivlin, A. M. New York
Origo, I., 1955 'The domestic enemy: eastern slaves in Tuscany in the 14th and 15th centuries'. *Speculum*, xxx: 321–66
Otterbein, K. F., 1965 'Caribbean family organization: a comparative analysis'. *The American Anthropologist*, 67: 66–79
Palli, H. (Typescript) *Size of household in the Parish of Karuse, Esthonia*
Pantelić, Nikola, 1964 'Srodstvo i zadruga. Jadar – Vukov zavičaj'. *Glasnik Etnografskog Muzeja u Beogradu*, 27: 369–400
Parkin, C., 1739–75 (1805–10) *See* Blomefield, Francis, 1739–75 (1805–10)
Parliamentary Papers *See under* United Kingdom
Parsons, T., 1954 'The incest taboo in relation to social structure and the socialization of the child'. *British Journal of Sociology*, 5: 101–17
Parten, M., 1937 'Size and composition of American families'. With Reeves, R. J. *American Sociological Review*, 2: 638–49
Pavković, Nikola, 1961 'Selo i zadruga'. *Glasnik Zemaljskog Muzeja Bosne i Hercegovine*, 15–16: 187–202 (Series title varies). Sarajevo
Peacock, W., ed., 1903 (1922), *Selected English essays*
Percival, Thomas, 1807 Collected edition, 1807: *The works, literary, moral and medical of Thomas Percival – To which are prefixed, memoirs of his life and writings and a selection from his literary correspondence*
Petersen, K. K., 1968 'Demographic conditions and extended family households: Egyptian data'. *Social Forces*, 46: 531–7
Petersen, W., 1966 'Fertility trends and population policy: some comments on the Van Heck–Hofstee debate', *Sociologische Gids*, 13: 176–87
Petrić, Franko, 1929 *See* Švob, Držislav, 1929
Petty, William, 1899 *Economic writings of Sir William Petty*. Ed. Hull, C. H.
Pevsner, L. W., 1958 *See* Lerner, Daniel, 1958
Plymley, J., 1803 *General view of the agriculture of Shropshire*
Polwhele, Richard, 1797 *A history of Devonshire*. Exeter
Popović, Dušan J., 1935 'Belgrade in 1733–4'. *Spomenik* (Proceedings of the Royal Serbian Academy), LXXVIII: 59–76. Belgrade
Price, Richard, 1779 (1780, 1792, 1803, 1816) 1779: 'An account of progress from the Revolution and the present state of population'. In: Morgan, W. *The doctrine of annuities and assurances on lives and survivorships*
  1780, first separate edn: *An essay on the population of England from the Revolution to the present time*
  1792 (1803, 1816) Collected editions, 1792 (1803): *Observations on reversionary payments, and on schemes for providing annuities for widows, and for persons in old age and on the method of calculating the value of assurances on lives, and on the National Debt, also essays on different subjects in the doctrine of Life Annuities and Political Arithmetic. A collection of new tables and a postscript on the population of the kingdom.*
  1816: *The works of Richard Price with memoirs of his life by W. Morgan*
Proctor, W., 1966 'Poor Law administration in Preston Union, 1838–48'. *Transactions of the historical society of Lancashire and Cheshire*, CXVII: 145–66
Pryor, Edward T., 1966 'Family structure and change: Rhode Island 1875 and 1960'. Unpublished Ph.D. thesis. Brown University
Radjenović, Petar, 1948 'Unac'. *Srpski Etnografski Zbornik*, 56: 445–640. Belgrade

Radojčić, Nikola, 1960 'Zakonik Cara Stefana Dušana 1349 i 1354'. *Srpska Akademija Nauka i Umetnosti.* Belgrade

Radovanović, Milovan V., 1964 'Stanovništo Prizrenskog Podgora'. *Glasnik Muzeja Kosova i Metohije,* 9: 253–415. Priština

Reeves, R. J., 1937 *See* Parten, M., 1937

Rennie, G., 1799 *See* Brown, R., 1799

Riehl, W. H., 1854 *Die Naturgeschichte des Volkes als Grundlage einer deutschen Social–Politik. Band 3: Die Familie...Neunte mit vielen Zusätzen vermehrte Auflage.* Stuttgart and Tübingen

Rivlin, Alice M., 1961 *See* Orcutt, G. H., 1961

1966 *See* Beresford, John C., 1966

Robbins (ed.), 1799–1801 *The annual Hampshire repository.* Winchester

Robertson, A. F., 1967 'An analysis of the social change processes resulting from the migration of diverse tribal groups to Bugerere County, Buganda'. Ph.D. thesis. Edinburgh

Robinson, John 1851 *The works of John Robinson.* Ed. Ashton, Robert. Boston, 1851

Roebroeck, E., 1967 *Het land van Muntfort.* Assen

Roessingh, H. K., 1964 'Het Veluwse inwonertal 1526–1947'. *A.A.G. Bijdragen,* 11: 79–150

1965 (i) 'Beroep en bedrijf op de Veluwe in het midden van de 18e eeuw'. *A.A.G. Bijdragen,* 13: 181–274

1965 (ii) 'Population changes and economic developments in the Netherlands'. With Faber, J. A., Slicher van Bath, B. H., van der Woude, A. M. and van Xanten, H. J. *A.A.G. Bijdragen,* 12: 47–113

Roller, O. K., 1907 *Die Einwohnerschaft der Stadt Durlach.* Karlsruhe

Roosenschoon, C. W., 1958 'De samenstelling van de boerenhuishouding in Borne en Tubbergen in 1748 en 1859'. Unpublished study in the library, Afdeling Agrarische Geschiedenis, University of Wageningen

Rosser, C., 1965 *The family and social change.* With Harris, C. C.

Rudder, S., 1779 *A new history of Gloucestershire.* Cirencester

Russell, J. C., 1948 *British medieval population.* Albuquerque

1958 *Late ancient and medieval population.* Philadelphia

1962 'Demographic limitations of the Spalding serf lists'. *Economic History Review,* 15: 138–44

1965 'Recent advances in medieval demography'. *Speculum,* XL: 84–101

Ruwet, J., 1958 'La population de Saint-Trond en 1635'. *Bulletin de la Société d'Art et d'Histoire du diocèse de Liège,* XL. Liège

Saal, C. D., 1951 'Het gezinsleven in Nederland, met name ten plattelande'. *Sociologisch Jaarboek:* 29–64

Šabanović, Hazim, 1964 *Katastarski popisi Beograda i okoline 1476–1566. Turski izvori za istoriju Beograda,* Knjiga I, Sveska I, Gradja za istoriju Beograda. Belgrade

Sahlins, M. D., 1965 'On the sociology of primitive exchange'. In: Benton, M., ed., *The relevance of models for social anthropology:* 139–236

Salvioni, G. B., 1898 'Zur Statistik der Haushaltungen'. *Allgemeine Statistiske Archiv,* VI

Sansom, George, B, 1963 *History of Japan,* 3. Stanford

Santini, P., 1887 'Società della torri in Firenze'. *Archivio Storico Italiano,* ser. IV, V, XXL: 25–8, 178–204

Sasaki, Yōichirō, 1967 'Tokugawa jidai kōki toshi jinkō no kenkyū – Settsu no kuni, Tennōji mura (An urban population in the later Tokugawa period – Tennōji, Nishinari County, Province of Settsu)'. *Shikai,* 14

Schneider, D. M., 1965 'Kinship and biology'. In: Coale, A. J. *et al.*, eds., *Aspects of the analysis of family structure*. Princeton
Schofield, Roger, 1970 'Age specific mobility in an eighteenth century English parish'. *Annales de Démographie Historique*: 261–74
Schücking, Levin Ludwig 1929 (1969) *Die Familie im puritanismus*. Leipzig. Translated as *The Puritan family; a social study from literary sources*. New York, 1969
Sekiyama, Naotarō, 1958 *Kinsei nihon no jinkō kōzō* (*Demographic structure of early modern Japan*). Tokyo
Seligman, E. R. A., ed., 1930–5 *Encyclopaedia of the social sciences*. With Johnson, Alvin. New York
Sennett, Richard, 1970 *Families against the city: middle class homes of industrial Chicago, 1872–1890*, Cambridge, Mass.
Serbia *See also under* Yugoslavia
Serbia, 1892 *Population census of the Kingdom of Serbia 1890*. Belgrade
Shah, A. M., 1968 'Changes in the Indian family'. *Economic and Political Weekly* Annual number, January
Shanas, Ethel, ed., 1965 *Social structure and the family: generational relations*. With Streib, Gordon F. Englewood Cliffs, N.J.
Shaw, S., 1798–1801 *History and antiquities of Staffordshire*
Shifini d'Andrea, S., 1971 'Exploitation des listes nominatives de population à Fiesole'. *Population*, 26: 573–80
Short, T., 1767 *A comparative history of the increase and decrease of mankind...*
Sicard, Emile, 1943 *La zadruga dans la littérature Serbe* (*1850–1912*). Paris
    1947 *Problèmes familiaux chez les Slaves du Sud*. Paris
Siegel, Sidney, 1956 *Non-parametric statistics for the behavioral sciences*. New York
Sigsworth, E. M., 1961 'Modern York'. In: Tillott, P. M., ed., *Victoria County History: a history of Yorkshire: city of York*: 254 310
Sills, David L., ed., 1968 *International encyclopaedia of the social sciences*. New York
Sinclair, J., 1791–1799 *The statistical account of Scotland*
Slicher van Bath, B. H., 1957 *Een samenleving onder spanning. Geschiedenis van het platteland van Ovarijssel*. Assen
    1965 *See* Roessingh, H. K., 1965 (ii)
Smelser, Neil, 1959 *Social change in the industrial revolution*. Chicago
Smith, M. G., 1955 *The economy of Hausa communities of Zaria*. Colonial Research Studies, no. 16. H.M.S.O.
    1962 *West Indian family structure*. Seattle.
Smith, R. J., 1968 'Social structure of Nottingham and adjacent districts in the mid 19th century'. Unpublished Ph.D. thesis. Nottingham
Smith, Raymond T., 1956 *The negro family in British Guiana*
    1963 'Culture and social structure in the Caribbean; some recent work on family and kinship studies'. *Comparative Studies in Society and History*, 6: 24–46
    1968 'The Family: comparative structures'. In Sills, David, L., ed., 1968
Smith, Robert J., 1962 (i) 'Japanese kinship terminology: the history of a nomenclature'. *Ethnology*, 1, 3: 349–59
    1962 (ii) 'Stability in Japanese kinship terminology: the historical evidence'. In: Smith, Robert J. and Beardsley, Richard K., eds., *Japanese culture: its development and characteristics*. Viking Fund Publications in Anthropology, 34: 25–33
    1963 'Aspects of mobility in pre-industrial Japanese cities'. *Comparative Studies in Society and History*, 5, 4: 416–23
Snow, Edwin H., 1877 *Report upon the census of Rhode Island 1875*. Providence R.I.

Solien, N. L., 1960 'Household and family in the Caribbean'. *Social and Economic Studies*, 9: 101–6

Sorbi, U., 1962 *Aspetti della struttura e principali modalità di stima dei catastt senese e fiorentino del XIV e XV secc.* Florence

Spearman, Diana, 1966 *The Novel and Society*

Spens, M. T., 1970 'Family structure in a Dominican village'. Ph.D. thesis, Cambridge

Spock, Benjamin, 1945 *Baby and child care.* New York

Srpski Etnografski Zbornik Monographs are listed under respective authors

Stanford Food Research Institute, Field Study of agricultural research, *Reports.* Preliminary Report no. 2, Jan. 1969 Uchendy, Victor C. and Anthony, K. R. M., *Economic., cultural and technical determinants of agricultural change in tropical Africa.* Kisii District, Kenya; Preliminary Report no. 3, Feb. 1969. Teso District, Uganda; Preliminary Report no. 4, Feb. 1969. Geita District, Tanzania; Preliminary Report no. 5, Dec. 1968. Mazabuka District, Uganda; Preliminary Report no. 6, Dec. 1968. Anthony, K. R. M. and Johnston, B. F., Northern Katsina, Nigeria; Preliminary Report no. 7, March 1969. Bawku District, Ghana; Preliminary Report no. 8, June 1969. Uchendu, Victor C. *The cocoa farmers of Akim Abuakwa.* Eastern region, Ghana

Stehouwer, J., 1965 'Relations between generations and the three generation household in Denmark'. In Shanas, E. and Streib, G. F., eds., *Social structure and the family: generational relations:* 142–62. New Jersey

Stenning, D. J., 1959 *Savannah nomads. A study of the Wodaabe pastoral Fulani of Western Bornu Province, Northern Region, Nigeria*

Stoianovich, Traian, 1970 'Model and Mirror of the pre-modern Balkan city'. *Studia Balcanica*, III, *La Ville Balkanique XVe–XIXe SS:* 103–5. Sofia

Stojanović, Ljubomir, 1890 'Stari srpski hrisobulji, akti, biografije, letopisi, tipici, pomenici, zapisi i dr'. *Spomenik*, III, Belgrade

Streib, G. F., ed., 1965 *See* Shanas, Ethel, 1965

Struyck, N., 1753 *Vervolg van de beschrijuing van de staartsterren en nadere ontdekkingen omtrent den staat van het menschelyk geslagt.* Amsterdam

Sundrica, Zdravko, 1959 'Popis stanovištva Dubrovačke Republike iz 1673/74'. In: *Archivskom Vjesnik*, 2, Pt II: 419–56. Zagreb

Švob, Držislav, 1929 'Zadruga Domladovac'. With Petrić, Franko. *Zbornik za Narodni Život i Običaje Južnih Slavena*, 27: 92–110

Tabarrini, M., 1904 'Le consorterie nella storia fiorentina del medio evo'. In: *La vita italiana nel Trecento:* 98–128. Milan

Taeuber, Irene B., 1958 *The population of Japan.* Princeton
    1960 'Urbanization and population change in the development of modern Japan'. *Economic Development and Cultural Change*, 9, 1, pt 2: 1–28

Takao, Kazuhiko, 1958 *Kinsei no nōson seikatsu (Life in rural villages in the Tokugawa era)*

Takeuchi, Toshimi, ed., 1968 *Shimokita no sonraku-shakai (Village society in Shimokita).* Tokyo

Tamaki, Hajime, 1959 *Nihon ni okeru daikazoku-sei no kenkyū (A study of the large family institution in Japan: a socio-economic analysis of large families in Shirakawamura, Gifu Prefecture)*

Tamassia, N., 1910 *La famiglia italiana nei seccXV° e XVI°.* Milan

Taute, Stéphane, 1957 'Recensements à Charleville en 1789'. In: *Études ardennaises*, 11: 55–60. Mezières

Templeman, T., 1729 *A new survey of the globe, or an accurate mensuration of all the empires, kingdoms,. . .and islands in the world. . .with notes explanatory and political, wherein the number of people in all ye principall countries and cities of Europe are severally calculated*

Tetteh, P. A., 1967 'Marriage, family and household'. In: Birmingham, Neustadt, I. and Omaboe, E. N., *A study of contemporary Ghana*, vol. 2, ¦*Some aspects of social structure*

Throsby, John, 1791 *History and antiquities of the ancient town of Leicester.* Leicester

Tillott, P. M., 1972 'Inaccuracies of census statistics resulting from the method of collection in 1851 and 1861'. In: Wrigley, E. A., ed., *The study of nineteenth century society*

Titow, J. Z., 1961 'Some evidence of the 13th century population increase'. *Economic History Review*, XIV: 218–23

Toda, Teizō, 1937 *Kazoku kōsei (Structure of the family)*. Tokyo

Tomasevich, Jozo, 1955 *Peasants, politics and economic change in Yugoslavia.* Stanford

Tomasić, Dinko, 1948 *Personality and culture in Eastern European politics.* New York

Tomkins, S. S., 1965 'The biopsychosociality of the family'. In Coale, A. J. *et al.*, eds., *Aspects of the analysis of family structure.* Princeton

Toulmin, Joshua, 1791 *History of the town of Taunton.* Taunton

Tranter, N. L., 1967 'Population and social structure in a Bedfordshire parish: The Cardington listing of inhabitants 1782'. *Population Studies*, 21, 3: 261–82

Tuscany *See under* Italy

United Kingdom Parliamentary Papers.

1. Censuses. *See also under* General Register Office

1801–2: VI *Abstract of answers and returns pursuant to Act 41 George 3, for taking account of the population of Great Britain*

1833: XXXVI *Abstract of the population returns of Great Britain, 1831*

1852–3: LXXXV *Census of Great Britain 1851. Population Tables. Part I. Numbers of inhabitants in the years 1801, 1811, 1821, 1831, 1841 and 1851*

1852–3: LXXXVIII *Census of Great Britain 1851. Population Tables. Part II. Ages, civil condition, occupations etc.*

2. Other

1833: XX First report of the...Commissioners...(on)...the employment of children in factories...with minutes of evidence...

1834: XXVII Report from His Majesty's Commissioners for inquiring into the administration and practical operation of the poor laws

1836: XXXIV Poor inquiry, Ireland, Appendix G. Report on the state of the Irish poor in Great Britain

1837–8: XIX Report by the Select Committee of the House of Lords...(on)... several cases...(arising from)...the operation of the Poor Laws Amendment Act...with minutes of evidence...

1842: XXXV Evidence taken, and report made, by the Assistant Poor Law Commissioner sent to inquire into the state of the population of Stockport

1859: Session 2. VII Minutes of evidence taken before the Select Committee on irremovable poor

United Nations Statistical Office, Department of Economic and Social Affairs 1967 *Statistical Year Book 1966.* New York

United States Census *See also* Benton, Josiah H., 1905; Greene, Evarts B. and Harrington, Virginia D., 1932 (1966)

United States Bureau of the Census 1907–8 *Heads of families at the first census of* 12 vols. Washington, D.C.

1909   *A century of population growth from the first census of the United States to the twelfth 1790–1900.* Washington, D.C.

1960   *Historical statistics of the United States, colonial times to 1957.* Washington, D.C.

1961   *United States census of population: 1960. Subject Report: Families.* Final Report PC (2)–4A. Washington, D.C.

1968 *Statistical abstract of the United States: 1968.* 89th edn. Washington, D.C.

Uozumi, Sōgorō, ed., 1960   *Nishinomiya-shi-shi (History of Nishinomiya City).* 8 vols. Nishinomiya

Upton, M., 1966   'Agriculture in Uboma'. In: Oluwasanmi, H. A., Dema, I. S. *et al.*, *Uboma, a socio-economic and nutritional survey of a rural community in Eastern Nigeria.* Geographical publications Ltd., The World Land Use Survey, Occasional Paper No. 6. Bude

Van der Woude *see* Woude

Vauban, Sebastian, 'Le Prestre de' 1707 (1933)   *Projet d'une dixme royale.* Ed., Coornaert, E., Paris, 1933

Verbeemen, J., 1962   'Bruxelles en 1755'. *Bijdragen tot de Geschiedenis*, 3e série, XIV. Brussels

Villareal, F. R., 1968   *See* Castillo, G. T., 1968

Vogel, E. F., 1960   *See* Bell, N. W., 1960

Van Voorst van Beest, C. W., 1955   *De katholieke armenzorg in Rotterdam in de 17e en 18e eeuw*

Wachelder, J., 1964   'De gemiddelde grote van het gezin en het houden in Limburg vanaf 1829 tot 1960'. In: *Studies over de sociaal-economische geschiedenis van Limburg*, IX. Maastricht

Wade, Richard, C., 1959   *The urban frontier.* Cambridge, Mass.

Wakely, P. I., 1965   *Bui Resettlement Survey, 1965.* With Mumtaz, K. K. Faculty of Architecture, Kumasi University, Ghana (mimeo)

Wales, William, 1781   *An enquiry into the present state of population in England and Wales*

Walter, Emil J., 1961   'Kritik einiger familier soziologischer Begriffe im Lichte der politischen Arithmetik des 18 Jahrhunderts'. In: *Schweizerische Zeitschrift für Volkswirtschaft und Statistik.* Berne

Watson, John (manuscript)   Collections for Cheshire (Bodleian Library, Oxford. Ref. MS. Top. Cheshire b. 1)

Waugh, E., 1867 (1881)   'Home life of the Lancashire factory folk during the cotton famine'. In: *Works*, vol. 2. Manchester, 1881

Weber, Max, 1923 (1961)   *Wirtschaftsgeschichte.* München. Translated as *General Economic History.* London, 1961

Weber, R. E. J., 1967   'De trekschuit'. *Spiegel Historiael*, 2: 301–5

Weisblat, A. M., 1968   *See* Castillo, G. T., 1968

White, Gilbert, 1789 (1947)   *The natural history and antiquities of Selborne in the county of Southampton.* Ed. Fisher, James, 1947

Williams, W. M., 1963   *A West Country village: family kinship and land*

Willis, B., 1755   *History and antiquities of the town hundred and deanery of Buckingham*

Willmott, P., 1957   *Family and kinship in East London.* With Young, M.

1960   *Family and class in a London suburb.* With Young, M.

Wirth, Louis, 1938   'Urbanism as a way of life'. *American Journal of Sociology*, XLIV: 1–24

Woude, A. M. van der, 1965   *See* Roessingh, H. K., 1965 (ii)

1969   'De historische demografie, in de ontwikkeling van de geschiedwetenschap'. *Tijdschrift voor Geschiedenis*, 82: 183–205. Groningen

Wrigley, E. A., ed. 1966 (i) *An introduction to English historical demography*
  1966 (ii) 'Family limitation in pre-industrial England'. *Economic History Review,*
    19: 82–109
  1967 'A simple model of London's importance in changing English society and
    economy'. *Past and Present,* 37: 44–70
  1968 'Mortality in pre-industrial England: The example of Colyton, Devon, over
    three centuries'. *Daedalus,* 97, 2: 546–80
  1969 *Population and history*
Wrigley, E. A., ed., 1972 *The study of nineteenth century society*
Xanten, H. J., van, 1965 *See* Roessingh, H. K., 1965 (ii)
Yokoyama, Sadao, 1949 'Kinsei toshi shūraku no dōtaisei to shūdansei (Movement
    and groupings in the urban community of the early modern period)'. In: *Gendai
    shakaigaku no shomondai (Problems of modern sociology)*: 523–46. Kōbundō
Young, Arthur, 1770 *A six months tour through the north of England*
  1774 *Political arithmetic*
  1784–1815 *Annals of agriculture*
  1804 *General view of the agriculture of Norfolk*
  1813 *General view of the agriculture of Suffolk*
Young, M., 1957 *See* Willmott, P., 1957
  1960 *See* Willmott, P., 1960
Yugoslavia *See also under* Serbia
Yugoslavia, 1960 *Popis stanovništva 1953.* Knjiga x, Fertilitet. Belgrade
  1964 *Akneta o seljačkim gazdinstvima 1962.* Statistički Bilten 295. Belgrade
  1965 *Popis stanovništva 1961.* Knjiga xvi, Veličina i izvori prihoda domaćinstava,
    rezultati za naselja. Belgrade
Zimmerman, C. C., 1936 *Family and society.* With Frampton, M. F.

Index